TABLE 2.5 Average Wages and Earnings of Production Workers in Manufacturing, 1914–1983

Year	Weekly Earnings (current dollars)	Average Weekly Hours Paid For	Average Hourly Wage (current dollars)	Consumer Price Index (1914 = 100)[a]	Index of Real Weekly Earnings (1914 = 100)	Index of Real Hourly Wages (1914 = 100)
1914	10.92	49.4	0.22	100	100	100
1920	26.02	47.4	0.55	199	120	126
1925	24.11	44.5	0.54	174	127	141
1930	23.00	42.1	0.55	166	127	151
1935	19.91	36.6	0.54	137	133	179
1940	24.96	38.1	0.66	140	163	214
1945	44.20	43.5	1.02	179	226	259
1950	58.32	40.5	1.44	240	223	273
1955	75.70	40.7	1.86	266	261	318
1960	89.72	39.7	2.26	295	278	348
1965	107.53	41.2	2.61	314	314	378
1970	133.73	39.8	3.36	386	317	396
1975	189.51	39.4	4.81	536	324	408
1980	288.62	39.7	7.27	820	322	403
1983	354.48	40.1	8.84	995	322	404

[a]The figures in this column should be interpreted with some caution. They are generated by pricing out a fixed "market basket" of consumer goods each year. Over time, however, new goods have become available and old ones improved in quality, so that comparability of the "baskets" used in making the index diminishes over time.

SOURCES: U.S. Bureau of the Census, *Historical Statistics of the United States, Colonial Times to 1970* (Washington, D.C.: U.S. Government Printing Office), 1975.

U.S. Department of Labor, Bureau of Labor Statistics, *Handbook of Labor Statistics 1977*, Bulletin 1966 (Washington, D.C.: U.S. Government Printing Office), 1977.

U.S. President, *Economic Report of the President* (Washington, D.C.: U.S. Government Printing Office, February 1984).

2nd Edition

Modern Labor Economics

Ronald G. Ehrenberg
Robert S. Smith
Cornell University

Scott, Foresman and Company
Glenview, Illinois   London, England

For Our Families, With Love

Library of Congress Cataloging in Publication Data

Ehrenberg, Ronald G.
  Modern labor economics.

  Includes index.
  1. Labor economics.   I. Smith, Robert Stewart.
II. Title.
HD4901.E34   1985   331   84-23541

ISBN 0-673-18105-7

Preface

Modern Labor Economics: Theory and Public Policy has grown out of our experiences over the last fifteen years in teaching labor market economics and in conducting research that was meant to influence public policy. Our text develops the modern theory of labor market behavior, summarizes empirical evidence that supports or contradicts each hypothesis, and illustrates in detail the usefulness of the theory for public policy analysis. We believe that showing students the social implications of concepts enhances the motivation to learn them and that using the concepts of each chapter in an analytic setting allows students to see the concepts in action. The extensive use of detailed policy applications constitutes a major innovation in this text.

Modern Labor Economics is designed for one-semester or one-quarter courses in labor economics at the undergraduate or graduate level for students who may not have extensive backgrounds in economics. Since 1974 we have taught such courses at the New York State School of Industrial and Labor Relations at Cornell University. The undergraduate course requires only principles of economics as a prerequisite, and the graduate course (for students in a professional program akin to an MBA program) has no prerequisites. We have found that it is not necessary to be highly technical in one's presentation in order to convey important concepts and that students with limited backgrounds in economics *can* comprehend a great deal of material in a single course. However, for students who have had intermediate microeconomics, we have included appendices to several chapters that discuss more advanced material or develop technical concepts in much greater detail than the text discussion permits.

Chapter 2 presents a quick overview of demand and supply in labor markets so that students will see from the outset the interrelationship of the major forces at work shaping labor market behavior. This chapter can be skipped or skimmed by students with strong backgrounds in economics or by students in one-quarter courses. Chapters 3 to 5 are concerned primarily with the demand for labor, while Chapters 6 to 10 focus on labor supply issues. Compensation, unionism, public sector labor markets, and discrimination are treated in Chapters 11–14. The final two chapters treat the macroeconomic issues of unemployment and inflation.

In addition to the use of public policy examples and the inclusion of technical appendices, the text has a number of unique pedagogical features. First, each chapter contains boxed examples that illustrate an application of that chapter's theory in nontraditional, historical, business, or cross-cultural settings. Second, each chapter contains a number of discussion or review questions that allow students to apply what they have learned to specific policy questions. Third, lists of selected readings at the ends of chapters refer students to more advanced sources of study.

Our goal in writing *Modern Labor Economics: Theory and Public Policy* was to provide a comprehensive survey of the field of labor economics written in a style that is interesting and accessible to students of varying backgrounds. We believe this second edition furthers these goals in four important ways.

First, chapters have been revised to make pedagogical improvements (most notably Chapters 5, 7, 13, and 16) or to present new applications or theoretical/ empirical developments. To the latter end, we have incorporated discussions of implicit contracting and asymmetric information (Chapters 11 and 15), selectivity bias in rates of return to education (Chapter 9), sex differences in the choice of college majors (Chapter 9), firm size and gender effects on quit rates (Chapter 10), the effects of unions on profitability (Chapter 12), and determinants of retirement age (Chapter 7). Moreover, in the chapter on discrimination (Chapter 14) we have expanded our discussion of ethnicity and included discussions of "crowding" and comparable worth. In addition, we have incorporated extensive analyses of state fair employment practice laws and Title VII of the Civil Rights Act that were written by Robert J. Flanagan for our jointly authored text *Labor Economics and Labor Relations*. Throughout all chapters, of course, descriptive data and references have been updated.

Second, we have sought to enrich the basic textual material by expanding our footnoted references to recent work in each area and by adding appendices for more advanced students. To the original appendices, for Chapters 3, 4, 9, and 15, we have added ones on compensating wage differentials for both certain and uncertain layoff probabilities (Chapter 8); an analysis of the efficiency properties of union contracts that specify only a wage rate (Chapter 12); the effects of arbitration, arbitral uncertainty, and risk aversion on the incentive to bargain (Chapter 13); and a brief introduction to regression analysis in the context of how "comparable worth" gaps are measured in practice (Chapter 14). The new appendix to Chapter 16, on the long-run Phillips curve, covers material formerly treated in the text of the chapter.

Third, we have attempted to heighten student interest with several new boxed examples. Many represent applications of interest to business students: recruiting strategies (5.1), employment strategies in the face of product demand fluctuations (5.3), absenteeism (6.1), the relationship between mental health and skill level (9.1), job satisfaction (10.1), job rotation (10.2), concession bargaining (12.2), and "comparable worth" (14.2). Other additions are a discussion of compensating wage differentials in 19th-century Great Britain (8.2) and an examination of differences between "economic" and "political" immigrants (10.4).

Finally, we have prepared an Instructor's Manual to accompany the second edition. It contains overviews of each chapter, a listing of the major concepts or factual understandings presented, answers to the review questions at the end of each chapter, and suggested essay and objective questions.

Acknowledgments

Several colleagues have contributed, through their thoughtful evaluations of the first edition, to the development of the second. While we have not always taken their advice, we appreciate the suggestions and criticisms of the following people:

John Abowd, University of Chicago
Dennis Ahlburg, University of Minnesota
Richard Butler, Brigham Young University
Carmel U. Chiswick, University of Illinois at Chicago
Donald A. Coffin, Illinois State University
Joe Davis, Trinity University, San Antonio
Eugene B. Gendel, Lafayette College
John C. Haltiwanger, UCLA
Hannah Hiles, Wesleyan University
Kevin J. Murphy, University of Tennessee, Knoxville
Solomon Polachek, State University of New York, Binghamton
Cynthia Rence, Michigan State University
Greg Saltzman, Brandeis University
Ronald Warren, University of Virginia

Special thanks go to Professor Robert J. Flanagan at Stanford, who, as noted above, wrote some of the material in Chapter 14 in connection with our other textbook. He also reviewed several chapters and made many helpful suggestions in the course of writing that text, and his work on that text has strengthened this one.

The above list is only a partial indicator of the extensive developmental editing of *Modern Labor Economics* and the concern of our editor, George Lobell, that we produce a book that accurately reflects the current state of labor economics and is comprehensible to students of varying backgrounds. Indeed, to ensure the book's accessibility, we circulated widely drafts of *Modern Labor Economics* while writing the first edition. Only space constraints prevent us from acknowledging again the 27 economists who provided invaluable help in our writing of the first edition. We also acknowledge the able copyediting of Diane Culhane, whose expertise has enhanced the readability of the text.

Enormous debts are also owed to three other groups of people. First are those instrumental in teaching us the concepts and social relevance of labor economics when we were students: Frank Brechling, George Delehanty, Dale Mortensen, John Pencavel, Orme Phelps, and Mel Reder. Second are the generations of undergraduate and graduate students we have taught who have forced us to clarify our thinking and who sat through the lectures that preceded *Modern Labor Economics*. Third are the secretaries who typed the many drafts of the manuscript: Jean Brown, Patricia Kauppinen, and Jean Morano.

Ronald G. Ehrenberg
Robert S. Smith

Contents

1

Introduction

Economic theory provides powerful, and often surprising, insights into individual and social behavior. At a purely scientific level, these insights are interesting because they help us understand important aspects of our lives. Beyond this, however, government, industry, labor, and other groups have increasingly come to understand the usefulness of the concepts and thought processes of economists in formulating social policy. This theory of behavior is simple yet compelling, and provides a systematic approach to the analysis of economic problems.

This book presents a comprehensive and understandable application of economic analysis to the behavior of, and relationship between, employers and employees. The aggregate compensation received by employees from their employers was $1,856 billion in 1982, while all *other* forms of personal income that year—from investments, self-employment, pensions, and various government welfare programs—amounted to $714 billion. The *employment* relationship, then, is one of the most fundamental relationships in our lives, and as such it attracts a good deal of legislative attention. A mastery of the fundamentals of labor economics is thus essential to an understanding of a huge array of social problems and programs.

As economists who have been actively involved in the analysis and evaluation of labor-related programs adopted or considered by the government, we obviously believe labor economics is useful in understanding the effects of these policies. Perhaps more important, we also believe policy analysis can be useful in teaching the fundamentals of labor economics. We have therefore incorporated such analyses into each chapter with two pedagogical reasons in mind. First, we believe that seeing the relevance and social implications of concepts studied enhances the student's motivation to learn. Second, using the concepts of each chapter in an analytical setting serves to reinforce understanding by permitting the student to see them ''in action.''

THE LABOR MARKET

There is a rumor that one recent Secretary of Labor attempted to abolish the term "labor market" from departmental publications. He believed it demeaned workers to think of labor as being bought and sold like so much grain, oil, or bonds. True, labor is somewhat unique. Labor services can only be rented; workers themselves cannot be bought and sold. Further, because labor services cannot be separated from workers, the conditions under which such services are rented are often as important as the price. Put differently, *nonpecuniary factors*—such as work environment, risk of injury, personalities of managers and flexibility of work hours—loom larger in employment transactions than they do in markets for commodities. Finally, a host of institutions and pieces of legislation that influence the employment relationship do not exist in other markets.

Nevertheless, the circumstances under which employers and employees rent labor services clearly constitute a market for several reasons. First, institutions have been developed to facilitate contact between buyers and sellers of labor services. This contact may come about through want ads, union hiring halls, employment agencies, placement offices, or plant personnel offices.

Second, once contact is arranged, information about price and quality is exchanged. Employment applications, interviews, and even "word-of-mouth" information from friends illustrate this kind of exchange in the market for labor.

Third, when agreement is reached, some kind of *contract* is executed covering compensation, conditions of work, job security, and even duration of the job. At times the contract is formal, such as with collective bargaining (union–management) agreements. At other times the agreement is unwritten and informal, with only an implied understanding between the parties based on past practices and experience. Nonetheless, it is often useful to think of the employment relationship as governed by a contract.

Labor contracts typically call for employers to compensate employees for their *time* and not for what they produce. Only 14 percent of U.S. workers receive piece-rate wages or commissions, in which compensation is computed directly on the basis of output. The vast majority are paid by the hour, week, or month. They are paid, in short, to show up for work and (within limits) to follow orders. This form of compensation requires that employers give careful attention to worker motivation and dependability in the selection and employment process.

The end result of employer–employee transactions in the labor market is, of course, the placement of people in jobs at certain rates of pay. This allocation of labor serves not only the personal needs of individuals, but the needs of the larger society as well. Through the labor market, our most important national resource—labor—is allocated to firms, industries, occupations, and regions.

LABOR ECONOMICS: SOME BASIC CONCEPTS

Labor economics is the study of the workings and outcomes of the market for labor. More specifically, labor economics is primarily concerned with the behavior of employers and employees in response to the general incentives of wages, prices, profits, and nonpecuniary aspects of the employment relationship (such as working conditions). These incentives serve both to motivate and to limit individual choice. The focus in economics is on inducements for behavior that are impersonal and apply to wide groups of people.

In this book we shall examine, for example, the relationship between wages and employment opportunities, the interaction between wages, income, and the decision to work, the way general market incentives affect occupational choice, the relationship between wages and undesirable job characteristics, the incentives for and effects of educational and training investments, and the effects of unions on wages, productivity, and turnover. In the process, we shall analyze the employment and wage effects of such social policies as the minimum wage, overtime legislation, pension reform regulations, the Occupational Safety and Health Act, welfare reform, payroll taxes, unemployment insurance, immigration policies, the rise in the mandatory retirement age, and antidiscrimination laws.

Our study of labor economics will be conducted on two levels. Most of the time we shall use economic theory to analyze "what is"; that is, we shall explain people's behavior using a mode of analysis called *positive economics*. Less commonly, we shall use *normative* economic analysis to judge "what should be."

Positive Economics

Positive economics is a theory of behavior in which people are typically assumed to respond favorably to benefits and negatively to costs. In this regard, positive economics closely resembles Skinnerian psychology, which views behavior as shaped by rewards and punishments. The rewards in economic theory are pecuniary and nonpecuniary gains (benefits), while the punishments are forgone opportunities (costs). For example, a person motivated to become a surgeon because of the earnings and status surgeons command must give up the opportunity to be a lawyer and be available for emergency work around the clock. Both the benefits and costs must be considered in making this career choice. Likewise, a firm deciding whether to hire an additional worker must weigh the wage and salary costs against the added revenues or cost savings made possible by expanding its work force.

Scarcity.   The most all-pervasive assumption underlying economic theory is that of resource *scarcity*. According to this assumption, individuals and society alike do not have the resources to meet all their wants. Hence, any resource devoted to satisfying one set of desires could have been used to satisfy other wants, which means that there is a cost to any decision or action. The real cost of using labor hired by a government contractor to build a road, for example, is the production lost by not devoting this labor to the building of an airport or some other good. Thus, in popular terms, "there is no such thing as a free lunch," and we must always make choices and live with the rewards and costs these choices bring us. Moreover, we are always constrained in our choices by the resources available to us.

Rationality.   The second basic assumption of positive economics is that people are *rational* in the sense that they have an objective and pursue it in a reasonably consistent fashion. When considering *persons*, economists assume that the objective being pursued is *utility maximization*; that is, people are assumed to strive toward the goal of making themselves as happy as they can (given their limited resources). Utility, of course, encompasses both pecuniary and nonpecuniary dimensions. When considering the behavior of *firms*, which are inherently nonpersonal entities, economists assume the goal of behavior to be that of *profit maximization*. Profit maximization is really just a special case of utility maximization in which pecuniary gain is emphasized and nonpecuniary factors are ignored.

The assumption of rationality implies a *consistency* of response to general economic incentives and an *adaptability* of behavior when those incentives change. These two characteristics of behavior underlie predictions about how workers and firms will respond to various incentives. Rationality cannot be directly proven, however, and even totally habit-bound or unthinkingly impulsive people might be forced to alter their behavior in predictable ways if the resources at their command changed.[1] Thus, while we shall maintain the assumption of rationality throughout this text, this assumption is not absolutely necessary to the derivation of at least *some* of the behavioral predictions contained herein.

The Models and Predictions of Positive Economics

Behavioral predictions in economics flow more or less directly from the two fundamental assumptions of rationality and scarcity. Workers must continually make choices, such as whether to look for other jobs, accept overtime, seek promotions, move to another area, or acquire more education. Employers must also make choices concerning, for example, the level of output and the mix of machines and labor to use in production. Economists usually assume that, when making these choices, employees and employers are guided by their desires to maximize utility or profit, as the case may be, and that they weigh the costs and benefits of various decisions in a reasonably careful way.

One may object that these assumptions are unrealistic and that people are not nearly as calculating, as well-informed about alternatives, or as well-endowed with choices as economists assume. Economists are likely to reply that if people are not calculating, are totally uninformed, or do not have any choices, then most predictions suggested by economic theory will not be supported by real-world evidence. They thus argue that the theory underlying positive economics should be judged on the basis of its *predictions* and that there may be *enough* information, calculation, and available options to make the theory useful in explaining or predicting a wide range of behavior.

The reason we need to make assumptions and create a relatively simple theory of behavior is that the actual workings of the labor market are almost impossibly complex. Millions of workers and employers interact daily—all with their own sets

---

[1]Gary Becker, "Irrational Behavior and Economic Theory," *Journal of Political Economy* 70, 1 (February 1962), pp. 1–13.

of motivations, preferences, information, and perceptions of self-interest. A detailed description of the individual outcomes and the processes that determine them would clearly be of limited feasibility and usefulness. What we need to discover are general principles that provide useful insights into the labor market. These principles could not be expected to predict or explain behavior with the same accuracy as the laws of physics predict the movement of an object through space, because we are dealing with human beings capable of making choices. Nevertheless, we hope to show that a few forces are so basic to labor market behavior that they alone can predict or explain many of the outcomes and behaviors we observe in the labor market.

Any time we attempt to explain a complex set of behaviors and outcomes using a few fundamental influences, we have created a *model*. Models are not intended to capture every complexity of behavior; instead, they are created to strip away random and idiosyncratic factors so we can focus on general principles. An analogy from the physical sciences might make the nature of models and their relationship to actual behavior more clear.

Using calculations of velocity and gravitational pull, physicists can predict where a ball would land if it were kicked with a certain force at a given angle to the ground. The actual point of landing might vary from the predicted point due to wind currents and any spin the ball might have—factors that were ignored in the calculations. If 100 balls were kicked, none might ever land exactly on the predicted spot, although they would tend to cluster around it. The accuracy of the model, while not perfect, might be good enough for a football coach to make a decision about whether to attempt a field goal or not. The point is that we usually just need to know the *average tendencies* of outcomes for policy purposes. To estimate these tendencies we need to know the important forces at work, but must confine ourselves to few enough influences so that calculating estimates remains feasible.

To really grasp the assumptions and predictions of economic models, it is necessary to consider a concrete example. Suppose we begin by asserting that, being subject to resource scarcity, workers will prefer high-wage jobs to low-paying ones *if* all other job characteristics are the same in each job. Thus, in pursuit of their own well-being, they will quit low-paying jobs to take better-paying ones for which they qualify if they believe sufficient improvement is likely. This principle does not imply that workers care only about wages or that all are equally likely to quit. Workers obviously care about a number of employment characteristics, and improvement in any of these characteristics makes turnover less likely. Likewise, some workers are more receptive to change than others. Nevertheless, if we hold these other factors constant and increase only wages, we should clearly observe that the probability of quitting will fall.

On the employer side of the market, we can consider a similar prediction. Firms need to make a profit to survive. If they have high turnover, their costs will be higher than otherwise because of the need to hire and train replacements. With high turnover they could not, therefore, afford to pay high wages. However, if they could reduce turnover enough by paying higher wages, it might well be worth incurring the high wage costs. Thus, both the utility-maximizing behavior of employees and the profit-maximizing behavior of firms lead us to expect low turnover to be associated with high wages and high turnover with low wages, other things equal.[2]

It is important to note several things about the above predictions:

1. The predictions emerge directly from the twin assumptions of rationality and scarcity. Employees and employers, both mindful of their scarce resources, are assumed to be on the lookout for chances to improve their well-being. The predictions are also based on the assumptions that employees are aware of, or can learn about, alternative jobs and that these alternatives are open to them. If any of these assumptions are invalid or inappropriate, the predictions would not be consistently borne out by observed behavior.

2. The prediction of a negative relationship between wages and voluntary turnover is made holding other things equal. The theory does not deny that job characteristics other than wages matter to employees or that employers can lower turnover by varying policies other than the wage rate. However, holding these other factors constant, we should observe the predicted negative relationship if the basic assumptions are valid.

3. The *assumptions* of the theory concern *individual* behavior of employers and employees, but the *predictions* are about an *aggregate* relationship between wages and turnover. The prediction is *not* that all employees will remain in their jobs if they experience an increase in wages, but that *enough* will for turnover to be cut by raising wages. The test of the prediction thus lies in finding out if the predicted relationship between wages and turnover exists as one looks at aggregate data from firms or industries.

In fact, there is abundant evidence that these predictions about turnover are accurate. Two of the more convincing studies estimate that if an industry increased its wage rate by 10 percent relative to other industries, holding all other job characteristics constant, it would reduce its voluntary turnover by 3 to 20 percent.[3]

Normative Economics

Any normative statement—a statement about what *ought* to exist—is based on some underlying value. The value premise upon which normative economics rests is that of *mutual benefit*. A mutually beneficial transaction is one in which there are no losers and, therefore, one that everyone in society could support. A transaction can be unanimously supported when

a. all parties affected by the transaction gain,
b. some gain and no one else loses, or
c. some gain and some lose from the transaction, but the gainers fully compensate the losers.

---

[2]In this example the expected relationship between wages and worker/firm behavior is clear-cut. While this is often the case, the expected relationship is not always that clear. We shall see examples of this later on—especially in Chapter 6.

[3]John Pencavel, *An Analysis of the Quit Rate in Manufacturing Industry* (Princeton: Industrial Relations Section, Princeton University, 1970); Farrell Block, "Labor Turnover in U.S. Manufacturing Industries," *Journal of Human Resources* 14, 2 (Spring 1979), pp. 236–46.

When the compensation in *c* takes place, case *c* is converted to case *b*. In practice, economists often judge a transaction by whether the gains of the beneficiaries exceed the costs borne by the losers, thus making it *possible* that there would be no losers. If the losers sustain losses that the gainers could not possibly compensate, then the transaction could never be mutually beneficial to all and the wisdom of the transaction must be questioned.

To illustrate a mutually beneficial transaction, suppose that people who formerly owned and operated small subsistence farms in West Virginia—earning the equivalent of $4,000 per year—take jobs in the growing coal mining industry at $15,000 a year. Assuming the switch in jobs is voluntary, these workers are clearly better off. The income gain of $11,000 per year might be offset to some extent by the disagreeableness of working in a mine, but the fact that the people voluntarily choose to move into mining tells us that they believe their utility will be enhanced. Mine owners likewise enter into the transaction voluntarily, implying that they obtain at least $15,000 in output from these new workers. Such a transaction benefits the parties it affects, and as a result it benefits society as a whole. There has been an increase in social output from $4,000 to $15,000 per worker, but, more important, there has been an increase in the overall utility of workers (the miners are better off and no one else is worse off).

To illustrate a transaction that is not mutually beneficial, suppose that society sought to increase the income of these same subsistence farmers by giving them a cash allowance raised by taxing others. This program would simply transfer money from the pockets of some people to the pockets of others, with no increase in output. There would be no possibility for the gainers (farmers) to compensate the losers (those taxed), so unanimous consent about the transaction could not be secured. While economists would not say that this transaction was bad or unwarranted, it could not be justified on the grounds of mutual benefit. Some other ethical principle—not based on unanimous consent—would have to be invoked to justify it. (One such principle is that the rich should share their wealth with the poor.)

Normative economics, then, is the analysis of actual and potential transactions to see if they conform to the standard of being mutually beneficial. Transactions may fail to meet this standard—or transactions that meet the standard may not occur—for one of several reasons.

Ignorance.   First, people may be ignorant of some important facts and thus led to make decisions that are not in their self-interest. For example, a worker who smokes may take a job in an asbestos-processing plant not knowing that the combination of smoking and inhaling asbestos dust substantially raises the risk of disease. Had the worker known this, he or she would probably have stopped smoking or changed jobs, but both transactions were "blocked" by ignorance.

Transactions barriers.   Second, there may be some barrier to the completion of a transaction that could be mutually beneficial. Often these barriers are created by government laws. For example, a firm may be willing to offer overtime to production workers at rates no more than 10 percent above their normal wage. Some workers might be willing to accept overtime at the 10 percent premium. However, this transaction, which is desired by both parties, could not legally be completed in most instances because of a law (the Fair Labor Standards Act) requiring almost all production workers to be paid a 50 percent wage premium for overtime. In this case, overtime would not be worked and both parties would suffer.

Another barrier to mutually beneficial transactions may be the expense of completing the transaction. Unskilled workers facing very limited opportunities in one region might desire to move to take better jobs. Alternatively, they might want to enter job training programs. In either case, they might lacks the funds to finance the desired transaction.

Nonexistence of market.   A third reason why transactions that are mutually beneficial may not occur is that it may be impossible or uncustomary for buyers and sellers of certain resources to transact. As an illustration, assume a woman who does not smoke works temporarily next to a man who does. She would be willing to pay as much as 50 cents per hour to keep her working environment smoke-free, and he could be induced to give up smoking for as little as 25 cents per hour. Thus, the potential exists for her to give him 35 cents per hour and for both to benefit. However, custom or the transience of their relationship might prevent her from offering him money in this situation, in which case the transaction would not occur.

Normative Economics and Government Policy

The solution to problems that impede the completion of mutually beneficial transactions frequently involves government intervention. When law creates the barrier to a transaction, the "intervention" might be to repeal the law. Laws prohibiting women from working overtime, for example, have been repealed in recent years as their adverse effects on women have become recognized.

In other cases, however, the government might be able to undertake activities to reduce transactions barriers that the private market would not undertake. We shall cite three examples, each of which relates to a barrier discussed above.

Public goods.   First let us take the case of the dissemination of information. Suppose that workers in noisy factories are concerned about the effects of noise on their hearing, but that ascertaining these effects would require an expensive research program. Suppose, further, that a union representing sawmill workers considers undertaking such research and financing the project by selling its findings to the many other unions or workers involved. The workers would then have the information they desire—albeit at some cost—which they could use to make more intelligent decisions concerning their jobs.

The hitch in the scheme is that the union doing the research may not have any customers *even though* others find the information it produces valuable. As soon as the union's findings are published to its own members or its first customers, the results can easily become public knowledge—and thus available *for free* from newspapers or by word of mouth. Other unions may be understandably reluctant to pay for information they can get for free, and the union doing the research ends up getting very little, if any, reimbursement for its expenses. Anticipating this problem, the union will probably decide not to undertake the research.

Information in this example is called a *public good*—a good that can be consumed by any number of people at the same time, including those who do not pay for it. Because nonpayers cannot be excluded from consuming the good, no potential customer will have an incentive to pay. The result is that the good never gets produced by a private organization. Because the government, however, can *compel* payment through its tax system, it is natural to look to the government to produce public goods. When information on occupational health hazards is to be produced on a large scale, the government will likely have to be involved.

Capital market imperfections.   An example of a second type of situation in which the government might have to step in to overcome a transaction barrier involves a case in which loans are not available to finance job training or interregional moves, even though such loans might give workers facing a very poor set of choices access to better opportunities. Such loans are not typically provided by the private sector because they are not backed (secured) by anything other than the debtor's promise to pay them back. Banks cannot ordinarily afford to take the risks inherent in making such loans, particularly when the loan recipients are poor, because a number of defaults could put them out of business (or at least lower their profitability). This lack of available loans to finance worthwhile transactions represents a "capital market imperfection."

The government, however, might be willing to make loans in such situations even if it faced the same risk of default, because enabling workers to move to areas of better economic opportunity could improve social welfare and strengthen the economy. In short, because society would reap benefits from encouraging people to enter job training programs or move to areas where their skills could be better utilized, it might be wise for the government to make the loans itself.

Establishing market substitutes.   A third type of situation in which government intervention might be necessary to overcome transaction barriers occurs when a market fails to exist for some reason. In the example above, a smoker and nonsmoker were temporarily working next to each other and their transitory relationship prevented a mutually beneficial transaction from taking place. A solution in this case might be for the government to impose the same result that a market transaction would have generated—and require the employer to designate that area a nonsmoking area.

In each case, when government does intervene, it must make sure that the transactions it undertakes or imposes on society create more gains for the beneficiaries than they impose in costs on others. Since it is costly to produce information, for example, the government should do it only if the gains are more valuable than the resources used in producing it. Likewise, the government would want to make loans for job training or interregional moves only if these activities enhanced social welfare. Finally, imposing nonsmoking areas would be socially desirable only if the gainers gained more than the losers lost. Thus, while normative economics suggests a role for government in helping accomplish mutually beneficial transactions, the role is not an unlimited one.

PLAN OF THE TEXT

With this brief review of economics in mind, we turn now to the specific subject-matter areas of labor economics. The study of labor economics is mainly a study of the interplay between employers and employees—or between demand and supply. Chapter 2 presents a quick overview of demand and supply in the labor market, allowing students to see from the outset the interrelationship of the major forces at work shaping labor market behavior. (This chapter contains many concepts that will be familiar to students who have a background in microeconomics.) Chapters 3–5 are concerned primarily with the demand for labor, while Chapters 6–11 emphasize labor supply issues.

The special topics of unionism and discrimination are treated in Chapters 12–14. The final two chapters deal with the macroeconomic issues of unemployment and inflation.

REVIEW QUESTIONS

1. Using the concepts of normative economics, when would the labor market be judged to be at a point of optimality? What imperfections might prevent the market from achieving this point?
2. Are the following statements "positive" or "normative"? Why?
   a. Society should not prohibit women from working more than 40 hours per week.
   b. If women are prevented from working overtime, they will not be as valuable to employers as their male counterparts of similar skill.
   c. If the military draft is prohibited, military salaries will increase.
   d. The military draft *compels* people to engage in a transaction they would not voluntarily enter into; it should therefore be avoided as a way of recruiting military personnel.

SELECTED READINGS

Amacher, Ryan C., Tollison, Robert D., and Willet, Thomas D., eds. *The Economic Approach to Public Policy*. Ithaca, N.Y.: Cornell University Press, 1976.

Friedman, Milton. *Essays in Positive Economics*. Chicago: University of Chicago Press, 1953.

Lindbeck, Assar. *The Political Economy of the New Left: An Outsider's View*. New York: Harper and Row, 1971.

McCloskey, Donald. "The Rhetoric of Economics," *Journal of Economic Literature* 21(June 1983): 481–517.

2

Overview
of the Labor Market

Every society—regardless of its wealth, its form of government, or the organization of its economy—must make certain basic decisions. It must decide what and how much to produce, how to produce it, and how the output shall be distributed. These decisions require finding out what consumers want, what technologies for production are available, and what the skills and preferences of workers are; deciding where to produce; and coordinating all such decisions so that, for example, the millions of people in New York City and the isolated few in an Alaskan fishing village can each buy the milk, bread, meat, vanilla extract, mosquito repellent, and brown shoe polish they desire at the grocery store. The process of coordination involves creating incentives so the right amount of labor and capital will be employed at the right place at the required time.

These decisions can, of course, be made by administrators employed by a centralized bureaucracy. The amount of information this bureaucracy must obtain and process to make the millions of needed decisions wisely and the amount of incentives it must give out to ensure that these decisions are coordinated are truly mind boggling. It boggles the mind even more to consider the major alternative to centralized decision making—the decentralized marketplace. Millions of producers striving to make a profit observe the prices millions of consumers are willing to pay for products and the wages millions of workers are willing to accept for work. Combining these pieces of information with data on various technologies, they decide where to produce, what to produce, whom to hire, and how much to produce. No one is in charge, and while imperfections impede progress toward achieving the best allocation of resources, millions of people find jobs that enable them to purchase the items they desire each year. The production, employment, and consumption decisions are all made and coordinated by price signals arising through the marketplace.

The market that allocates workers to jobs and coordinates employment decisions is *the labor market*. With over 100 million workers and 5 million employers in the United States, thousands of decisions about career choice, hiring, quitting, compensation, and technology must be made and coordinated every day. This chapter will present an overview of what the market does and how it works. For those students who may have already mastered microeconomic theory, this chapter can provide a review of basic concepts.

THE LABOR MARKET: DEFINITIONS, FACTS, AND TRENDS

Every market has buyers and sellers, and the labor market is no exception: the buyers are employers and the sellers are workers. Because there are so many buyers and sellers of labor at any given time, the decisions that are made in any particular case are influenced by the behavior and decisions of others. A firm, for example, may decide to increase compensation when other employers are doing likewise to remain competitive in its ability to attract and hold workers. Likewise, a current or prospective teacher may choose to go into personnel work if he or she discovers that teachers are having a difficult time finding jobs.

The *labor market* is thus composed of all the buyers and sellers of labor. Some of these participants may not be active at any given moment in the sense of seeking new jobs or new employees, but on any given day thousands of firms and workers will be ''in the market'' trying to transact. If, as in the case of doctors or mechanical engineers, buyers and sellers are searching throughout the entire nation for each other, we would describe the market as a *national labor market*. If buyers and sellers only search locally, as in the case of secretaries or automobile mechanics, the labor market is a *local* one.

Some labor markets, particularly those in which the sellers of labor are represented by a union, operate under a very formal set of rules that partly govern buyer–seller transactions. In the construction and longshoring trades, for example, employers must hire at the union hiring hall from a list of eligible union members. In other unionized markets, the employer has discretion over who gets hired, but is constrained by a union-management agreement in matters like the order in which employees may be laid off, procedures regarding employee complaints, the compensation schedule, the workload or pace of work, and promotions. The markets for government jobs and jobs with large nonunion employers also tend to operate under rules that constrain the authority of management and ensure fair treatment of employees. When a formal set of rules and procedures guide and constrain the employment relationship *within* a firm, an *internal labor market* is said to exist.[1]

In many cases, of course, labor market transactions are not made within the context of written rules or procedures, as is clearly the case in most transactions in which an employee is changing employers or newly entering the market. Written rules or procedures generally do not govern within-firm transactions—such as promotions and layoffs—among smaller, nonunion employers. While jobs in this sector of the labor market can be stable and well paying, many are not. Low-wage,

---

[1]P. Doeringer and M. Piore, *Internal Labor Markets and Manpower Analysis* (Lexington, Mass.: D. C. Heath and Company, 1971).

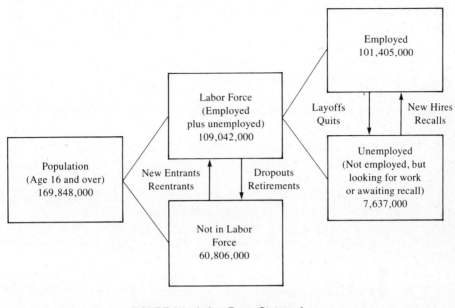

**FIGURE 2.1 Labor Force Status of
the U.S. Adult Population, 1980**

unstable jobs are sometimes considered to be in the *secondary labor market*.[2] We will discuss the concept of secondary labor markets in greater detail in Chapter 14.

When we speak of a particular "labor market"—for taxi drivers, say—we are using the term loosely to refer to the companies trying to hire people to drive their cabs and the people seeking employment as cabdrivers. The efforts of these buyers and sellers of labor to transact and establish an employment relationship constitute the market for cabdrivers. However, neither the employers nor the drivers are confined to this market; both could simultaneously be in other markets as well. An entrepreneur with $100,000 to invest might be thinking of operating either a taxi company or a car wash, depending on the projected revenues and costs of each. A person seeking a cabdriving job might also be trying to find work as an electronics assembler. Thus, all the various labor markets that we can define on the basis of industry, occupation, geography, transaction rules, or job character are interrelated to some degree. We speak of these narrowly defined labor markets for the sake of convenience, and doing so should not suggest that people are necessarily or permanently locked in to markets that are independent of other markets.

The Labor Force and Unemployment

Figure 2.1 highlights some basic definitions concerning labor market status. The term *labor force* refers to all those over 16 years of age who are either employed, actively seeking work, or awaiting recall from a layoff. Those in the labor force

---

[2]Doeringer and Piore, *Internal Labor Markets and Manpower Analysis.*

who are not employed for pay are the *unemployed*.[3] People who are not employed and are neither looking for work nor waiting to be recalled from layoff by their employers are not counted as part of the labor force. The total labor force thus consists of the employed and the unemployed.

The quantities and identities of people in each labor market category are always changing, and as we shall see in Chapter 15, the flows of people from one category to another are sizable. As Figure 2.1 suggests, there are four major flows between labor market states:

1. Employed workers become unemployed by voluntarily *quitting* or *being laid off* (being involuntarily separated from the firm, either temporarily or permanently).
2. Unemployed workers obtain employment by *being newly hired* or *being recalled* to a job from which they were temporarily laid off.
3. Those in the labor force, whether employed or unemployed, can leave the labor force by *retiring* or otherwise deciding against taking or seeking work for pay *(dropping out)*.
4. Those who have never worked or looked for a job expand the labor force by *newly entering* it, while those who had dropped out do so by *reentering* the labor force.

In 1980 there were 109 million people in the labor force, representing 64 percent of the entire population over 16 years of age. An overall *labor force participation rate* (labor force divided by population) of 64 percent is substantially higher than the rates around 60 percent that have prevailed throughout the last 30 years, as is shown by the data in Table 2.1. This table also indicates the most important fact about labor-force trends in this century: *labor force participation rates for men are falling while those for women are increasing dramatically.* These trends and their causes will be discussed in detail in Chapter 6.

The ratio of those unemployed to those in the labor force is the *unemployment rate*. While this rate is crude and has several imperfections, it is the most widely cited measure of labor market conditions. When the unemployment rate is in the 3–4 percent range in the United States, the labor market is considered *tight*—indicating that jobs in general are plentiful and hard for employers to fill and that most of those who are unemployed will find other work quickly.[4] When the unemployment rate is higher—say, 7 percent or above—the labor market is described as *loose*, in the sense that workers are abundant and jobs are relatively easy for employers to fill. To say that the labor market as a whole is loose, however, does not imply that no shortages can be found anywhere; to say it is tight can still mean that in some occupations or places the number of those seeking work exceeds the number of jobs available at the prevailing wage.

---

[3]The official definition of unemployment for purposes of government statistics includes those who have been laid off by their employers, those who have been fired or have quit and are looking for other work, and those who are just entering or reentering the labor force but have not found a job as yet.

[4]Some people are beginning to argue that labor markets are tight when unemployment is around 5 percent or even a bit more. This issue will be discussed in Chapter 15.

TABLE 2.1   Labor Force Participation Rates by Sex,
1900–1980 (in percent)

Year	Total		Men		Women	
	Of Those Over 14	*Of Those Over 16*	*Over 14*	*Over 16*	*Over 14*	*Over 16*
1900	54.8 (100)		87.3 (100)		20.4 (100)	
1910	55.7 (102)		86.3 (99)		22.8 (112)	
1920	55.6 (102)		86.5 (99)		23.3 (114)	
1930	54.6 (100)		84.1 (96)		24.3 (119)	
1940	52.2 (95)		79.0 (91)		25.4 (125)	
1950	53.4 (98)	59.9	79.0 (91)	86.8	28.6 (140)	33.9
1960	55.3 (101)	60.2	77.4 (89)	84.0	35.4 (169)	37.8
1970	55.8 (102)	61.3	73.0 (84)	80.6	39.9 (196)	43.4
1980	—	64.2	—	77.9	—	51.6

Note: Index numbers, with 1900 = 100, are shown in parentheses. From 1900 to 1930, the labor force was defined as those "gainfully employed." Gainful workers were those who, whether they were working at the time or not, reported themselves as having an occupation at which they usually worked. In 1940 the present concept of labor force replaced the concept of gainful worker, with the result that inexperienced people looking for their first job were now counted in the labor force. It is the judgment of Clarence D. Long *(The Labor Force Under Changing Income and Employment*, p. 45) that intercensal comparisons remain meaningful despite this change.

Sources for data on ages 14 and older:

1900–1950; Clarence D. Long, *The Labor Force Under Changing Income and Employment* (Princeton: Princeton University Press, 1958), Table A–2.

1960: U.S. Department of Commerce, Bureau of the Census, *Census of Population, 1960; Employment Status*, Subject Reports, PC(2)–6A, Table 1.

1970: U.S. Department of Commerce, Bureau of the Census, *U.S. Census of Population, 1970; Employment Status and Work Experience*, Subject Reports, PC(2)–6A, Table 1.

Sources for data on ages 16 and older:

U.S. President, *Employment and Training Report of the President* (Washington, D.C.: U.S. Government Printing Office), transmitted to the Congress 1981, Table A–1.

Table 2.2 displays the overall unemployment rate for the first 84 years of this century. The data clearly show the extraordinarily loose labor market during the Great Depression of the 1930s and the exceptionally tight labor market during World War II. However, when we look at long stretches of nonwar years, excluding the years of the Great Depression, two interesting patterns emerge. First, the average unemployment rate has clearly risen: it was 4.4 percent in 1900–14, but in the most recent nonwar periods it was 5.3 percent (1954–65) and 7.2 percent (1973–83). Second, in recent years the unemployment rate has fluctuated less than it did in 1900–14. In the years from 1900 to 1914, the average yearly change in the unemployment rate was 1.9 percentage points; in contrast, from 1954 to 1965 it was .8 percentage points, and from 1973 to 1983 it was .9 percentage points. The labor market, then, would appear to be more stable now than it was at the turn of the century, but it operates with proportionately more unemployment. Chapter 15 will present a more detailed analysis of the determinants of the unemployment rate.

TABLE 2.2   Unemployment Rates for the Civilian
Labor Force over 14 Years Old, 1900–1983

Year	Rate	Year	Rate	Year	Rate (old series)	Rate (new series)	Year	Rate
1900	5.0	1926	1.9	1947	3.6	3.9	1958	6.8
1901	2.4	1927	4.1	1948	3.4	5.9	1959	5.5
1902	2.7	1928	4.4	1949	5.5	5.3	1960	5.6
1903	2.6	1929	3.2	1950	3.0	3.3	1961	6.7
1904	4.8	1930	8.9	1951	2.7	3.1	1962	5.6
1905	3.1	1931	15.9	1952	2.5	2.9	1963	5.7
1906	0.8	1932	23.6	1953	5.0	5.6	1964	5.2
1907	1.8	1933	24.9	1954	4.0	4.4	1965	4.6
1908	8.5	1934*	21.7	1955	3.8	4.2	1966	3.8
1909	5.2	1935*	20.1	1956	4.0	4.3	1967	3.8
1910	5.9	1936*	17.0	1957			1968	3.6
1911	6.2	1937*	14.3				1969	3.5
1912	5.2	1938*	19.0				1970	4.9
1913	4.4	1939*	17.2				1971	5.9
1914	8.0	1940*	14.6				1972	5.6
1915	9.7	1941*	9.9				1973	4.9
1916	4.8	1942	4.7				1974	5.6
1917	4.8	1943	1.9				1975	8.5
1918	1.4	1944	1.2				1976	7.7
1919	2.3	1945	1.9				1977	7.1
1920	4.0	1946	3.9				1978	6.1
1921	11.9						1979	5.8
1922	7.6						1980	7.1
1923	3.2						1981	7.6
1924	5.5						1982	9.7
1925	4.0						1983	9.6

Note: After 1966, unemployment rates for only those 16 and over are published. The differences between the rates for those over 14 and over 16 in the years where both were computed are very small. Therefore, a parallel series in this table was not considered necessary. The rates shown from 1967 on relate to those over 16, and the prior data related to those over 14.

In 1957 the definition of the term *unemployed* was changed to include those who were waiting to be called back to a job from which they had been laid off, were waiting to report to a new wage or salary job scheduled to start within the next 30 days (and were not in school during the survey week), or would have been looking for work except that they were temporarily ill or believed no work was available in their line of work or in the community. Prior to 1957, part of those whose layoffs were for definite periods of less than 30 days were classified as employed, as were all those waiting to report to a new job. This new definition was also applied to unemployment data for the years 1947–57.

In the years indicated by an asterisk, workers in some government job creation programs were counted as unemployed, which raised these published unemployment rates by 4 to 7 percentage points. See Michael R. Darby, "Three-and-a-Half Million U.S. Employees Have Been Mislaid: Or, An Explanation of Unemployment, 1934–1941," *Journal of Political Economy* 84(February 1976):1–16.

SOURCES: 1900–1954 (old series): Stanley Lebergott, "Annual Estimates of Unemployment in the United States, 1900–1950," *The Measurement and Behavior of Unemployment*, NBER Special Committee Conference Series no. 8 (Princeton, 1957), pp. 213–239.

1955–1957 (old series): U.S. Bureau of the Census, *Annual Report on the Labor Force*, Current Population Reports, Series P–50 (1955, 1956, 1957).

1947–1966 (new series): U.S. Bureau of Labor Statistics, *Employment and Earnings*, vol. 13, no. 7 (January 1967), Table A–1.

1967–1983: U.S. President, *Economic Report of the President* (Washington, D.C.: U.S. Government Printing Office, February 1984), p. 259.

Industries and Occupations: Adapting to Change

As we pointed out earlier, the labor market is the mechanism through which workers and jobs are matched. Over the years in this century, the number of some kinds of jobs has expanded and the number of others has contracted. Both workers and employers had to adapt to these changes in response to signals provided by the labor market.

An examination of the industrial distribution of employment from 1900 to 1980 reveals the kinds of changes the labor market has had to facilitate. Table 2.3 discloses a major shift: *agricultural employment has declined drastically while employment in service industries has expanded.* Manufacturing jobs increased proportionately to the increase in total employment in the first seven decades, but manufacturing's share fell sharply from 1970 to 1980. The largest employment increases have been in the service sector. Retail and wholesale trade, which increased from 9.2 percent of employment in 1910 to 21.7 percent in 1980, showed the largest increases in nongovernment services. However, the largest percentage increase has been in government employment—which more than quadrupled its share of total employment over the 80-year period. Some describe this shift in

TABLE 2.3 Employment Distribution by Major Industrial Sector, 1900–1980 (in percent)

Year	Agriculture[a]	Goods-Producing Industries[b]	Nongovernment Services[c]	Government Services[d]
1900	38.1	37.8	20.0	4.1
1910	32.1	40.9	22.3	4.7
1920	27.6	44.8	21.6	6.0
1930	22.7	42.1	28.1	7.1
1940	18.5	41.6	31.1	8.8
1950	12.1	41.3	36.4	10.2
1960	6.6	41.4	38.8	13.2
1970	3.8	39.8	40.5	15.9
1980	3.6	32.8	46.3	17.3

Note: From 1900 to 1930, "employment" refers to "gainful workers." From 1940, "employment" refers to experienced civilian labor force. Where applicable, persons not assigned to an industry were assumed to have the same employment distribution as those who were.

[a]Agriculture includes forestry and fishing.

[b]Included are manufacturing, mining, construction, transportation, communications, and public utilities.

[c]Included are trade; personal, professional, and business services; entertainment; finance; and real estate.

[d]Includes federal, state, and local government workers.

SOURCES: 1900–1940: U.S. Bureau of the Census, *Historical Statistics of the United States, Colonial Times to 1957*, 1960, Table D57–71.

1950: *U.S. Census of Population 1950*, Subject Reports, Vol. IV, Chapter 1D, 1955, Table 15.

1960: *U.S. Census of Population 1960*, Subject Reports, PC (2)–7F, 1967, Table 1.

1970: *U.S. Census of Population 1970*, Subject Reports, PC (2)–7B, 1972, Table 1.

1980: U.S. Bureau of the Census, *Statistical Abstract of the United States*, 103rd edition, 1982, Tables 624 and 629.

TABLE 2.4   Occupational Distribution of Experienced Civilian Labor Force, 1900–1980 (in percent)

	1900	1910	1920	1930	1940	1950	1960	1970	1980
White-collar workers	17.6	21.0	25.0	29.4	31.1	36.6	42.2	47.5	52.2
Professional and technical	4.3	4.6	5.4	6.8	7.5	8.6	11.3	14.6	16.1
Managers	5.9	6.5	6.6	7.4	7.3	8.7	8.5	8.1	11.2
Clerical	3.0	5.2	8.0	8.9	9.6	12.3	14.9	17.8	18.6
Sales	4.5	4.6	4.9	6.3	6.7	7.0	7.5	7.0	6.3
Manual workers	35.8	37.5	40.2	39.6	39.8	41.1	39.7	36.6	31.7
Craft workers	10.6	11.4	13.0	12.8	12.0	14.2	14.3	13.9	12.9
Operatives	12.8	14.4	15.6	15.8	18.4	20.4	19.9	17.9	14.2
Laborers (nonfarm)	12.5	11.8	11.6	11.0	9.4	6.6	5.5	4.7	4.6
Personal-service workers	9.1	9.4	7.9	9.8	11.8	10.5	11.7	12.9	13.3
Domestics	5.4	4.9	3.3	4.1	4.7	2.6	2.8	1.5	1.1
Other[a]	3.6	4.5	4.5	5.7	7.1	7.9	8.9	11.3	12.3
Farm workers	37.5	30.4	27.0	21.2	17.4	11.8	6.3	3.1	2.8
Farmers and farm managers	19.9	16.3	15.3	12.4	10.4	7.4	3.9	1.8	1.5
Farm laborers	17.7	14.2	11.7	8.8	7.0	4.4	2.4	1.3	1.3

Note: From 1900 to 1930, employment data relate to "gainful workers." From 1940 on, data relate to experienced civilian labor force. 1980 data are not strictly comparable because they relate only to the *employed* labor force 16 and over.

[a]Included are attendants, barbers, cooks, guards, janitors, police, practical nurses, ushers, waiters, etc.

SOURCES: 1900–1950: U.S. Bureau of the Census, *Historical Statistics of the United States, Colonial Times to 1957*, (1960), Table D72–122.

1960: U.S. Bureau of the Census, *Census of Population 1960*, Subject Reports, PC(2)–7A, 1967, Table 1.

1970: U.S. Bureau of the Census, *Census of Population 1970*, Subject Reports, PC(2)–7A, 1972, Table 1.

1979: U.S. President, *Employment and Training Report of the President* (Washington, D.C.: U.S. Government Printing Office, 1981), p. 149.

employment from agriculture to services as a shift from the *primary* to the *tertiary* sector (manufacturing being labeled the *secondary* sector). Others describe it as the arrival of the "post-industrial" state. In any case, the shift in employment has been accompanied by large population movements off the farms and to urban areas. These population movements have also been largely coordinated by the labor market, as Chapter 10 will show.

The combination of shifts in the industrial distribution of jobs and shifts in the production technology within each sector has also required that workers acquire new skills and work in new jobs. Table 2.4 shows that a large increase in *white-collar*, or nonmanual, jobs has taken place concurrently with a large decline in agricultural jobs. Manual workers have witnessed a small decline in their share of total employment, while personal-service workers have shown relatively modest increases since 1900. The largest single gain has come about in clerical jobs, although professional and technical jobs (teachers, engineers, lawyers, and so forth) have also increased disproportionately fast.

Labor markets must work very effectively if enormous shifts in the industrial and occupational distribution of employment are to be accomplished without long delays or undue hardship. There is disagreement over how effectively and humanely labor markets operate, but the labor market clearly plays an incredibly large and important role in society.

The Earnings of Labor

The actions of buyers and sellers in the labor market serve both to allocate and to set prices for various kinds of labor. From a social perspective, these prices act as signals or incentives in the allocation process—a process that relies primarily on individual and voluntary decisions. From the worker's point of view, the price of labor is important in determining income—and hence purchasing power.

Nominal and real wages. The *wage rate* is the price of labor per working hour.[5] The *nominal wage* is what workers get paid per hour in current dollars; nominal wages are most useful in comparing the pay of various workers at a given time. *Real wages*, nominal wages divided by some measure of prices, suggest how much can be purchased with workers' nominal wages. For example, if a worker earns $64 a day and a pair of shoes costs $32, one could say the worker earns the equivalent of two pairs of shoes a day (real wage = $64/$32 = 2).

Calculations of real wages are especially useful in comparing the purchasing power of workers' earnings over a period of time when both nominal wages and product prices are changing. Thus, real wages are normally expressed as an *index number*, which compares the purchasing power of an hour of work to some base period (the base is set equal to 100). To understand how index numbers are constructed, refer to the last column in Table 2.5, where the index of real hourly wages in 1983 is listed as 404. This means that hourly real wages were almost exactly four times higher in 1983 than in the base year, which was chosen arbitrarily as 1914.

To arrive at an index of *real* hourly wages requires that we calculate an index of nominal wages *and* an index of prices. An index of nominal wages can be constructed for each year (with 1914 as a base) by dividing the wage in each year by $0.22—the hourly wage in 1914—and multiplying by 100. This fixes the index at 100 in 1914 and yields an index number of 4018 for 1983 [(8.84 ÷ 0.22) × 100]. The Consumer Price Index, which is based on "pricing out" a "market basket" of goods from year to year, is 995 for 1983 if 1914 is the base year. Dividing the price index (995) into the index for nominal wages (4018) and multiplying by 100 gives us the figure of 404 noted in the table.

---

[5]In this book we define the hourly wage in the way most workers would if asked to state their "straight-time" wage. It is the money a worker would lose per hour if he or she had an unauthorized absence. When wages are defined in this way, a paid holiday becomes a "fringe benefit," as we note below, because leisure time is granted while pay continues. Thus, a worker paid $100 for 25 hours—20 of which are working hours and 5 of which are time off—will be said to earn a wage of $4.00 per hour and receive time off worth $20.

An alternative is to define the wage in terms of actual hours worked—or as $5.00 per hour in the above example. We prefer our definition, because if the worker seizes an opportunity to work one less hour in a particular week, his or her earnings would fall by $4.00, not $5.00 (as long as the reduction in hours does not affect the hours of paid holiday or vacation time for which the worker is eligible).

TABLE 2.5   Average Wages and Earnings of Production Workers in Manufacturing, 1914–1983

Year	Weekly Earnings (current dollars)	Average Weekly Hours Paid For	Average Hourly Wage (current dollars)	Consumer Price Index (1914 = 100)[a]	Index of Real Weekly Earnings (1914 = 100)	Index of Real Hourly Wages (1914 = 100)
1914	10.92	49.4	0.22	100	100	100
1920	26.02	47.4	0.55	199	120	126
1925	24.11	44.5	0.54	174	127	141
1930	23.00	42.1	0.55	166	127	151
1935	19.91	36.6	0.54	137	133	179
1940	24.96	38.1	0.66	140	163	214
1945	44.20	43.5	1.02	179	226	259
1950	58.32	40.5	1.44	240	223	273
1955	75.70	40.7	1.86	266	261	318
1960	89.72	39.7	2.26	295	278	348
1965	107.53	41.2	2.61	314	314	378
1970	133.73	39.8	3.36	386	317	396
1975	189.51	39.4	4.81	536	324	408
1980	288.62	39.7	7.27	820	322	403
1983	354.48	40.1	8.84	995	322	404

[a]The figures in this column should be interpreted with some caution. They are generated by pricing out a fixed "market basket" of consumer goods each year. Over time, however, new goods have become available and old ones improved in quality, so that comparability of the "baskets" used in making the index diminishes over time.

SOURCES: U.S. Bureau of the Census, *Historical Statistics of the United States, Colonial Times to 1970* (Washington, D.C.: U.S. Government Printing Office), 1975.

U.S. Department of Labor, Bureau of Labor Statistics, *Handbook of Labor Statistics 1977*, Bulletin 1966 (Washington, D.C.: U.S. Government Printing Office), 1977.

U.S. President, *Economic Report of the President* (Washington, D.C.: U.S. Government Printing Office, February 1984).

Wages, earnings, compensation, and income.   We often apply the term *wages* to payments received by workers who are paid on a salaried (monthly, for example) basis, rather than an hourly basis. The term is used this way merely for convenience and is of no consequence for most purposes. It is important, however, to distinguish among wages, earnings, and income, as we do schematically in Figure 2.2. The term *wages* refers to the payment for a *unit* of time, while *earnings* refers to wages multiplied by the number of time units (typically hours) worked. Thus, earnings depend on both wages and the length of time the employee works. *Income*—the total command over resources of a person or family during some time period (usually a year)—includes both earnings and *unearned income*, which includes dividends or interest received on investments and transfer payments received from the government in the form of food stamps, welfare payments, unemployment compensation, and the like.

Table 2.5 shows the long-run trends in earnings and wages for U.S. manufacturing production workers. While real weekly earnings were over three times higher in 1983 than in 1914, the fall in paid weekly hours from 49 to about 40 represented an additional gain in the general standard of living for workers. Probably the best index of living standards is how much workers receive *per hour*, and Table 2.5

shows that real hourly wages were four times as high in 1983 as in 1914, which implies that an hour of work paid for four times more goods and services in 1983 than in 1914.

The actual increase in living standards attainable by the ordinary worker is perhaps even greater than indicated in Table 2.5. Both wages and earnings are normally defined and measured in terms of direct monetary payments to employees (before taxes for which the employee is liable). *Total compensation*, on the other hand, consists of earnings plus *fringe benefits*—benefits that are either payments in kind or deferred. Examples of *payments in kind* are employer-provided health care and health insurance, where the employee receives a service or an insurance policy rather than money. Paid vacation time is also in this category, since employees are given days off instead of cash. *Deferred* payments can take the form of employer-financed retirement benefits, including social security taxes, in which employers set aside money now that enables their employees to receive pensions later.

In 1976 earnings as conventionally defined constituted only 75 percent of the total compensation of manufacturing production workers. Vacations, pensions, and health care were the largest categories of fringe benefits. Because fringe benefits were virtually nonexistent before 1940, we can assume that total earnings and total compensation were essentially the same in the early 1900s. If earnings in more recent years are adjusted to reflect fringe benefits, we arrive at the conclusion that real compensation per hour in the mid-'70s was more than five times higher than in 1914 for the typical manufacturing worker.

The next section will shift from labor market *outcomes* over time to an analysis of how the market *operates* to generate these outcomes. This analysis of labor market functioning is the central focus of labor economics.

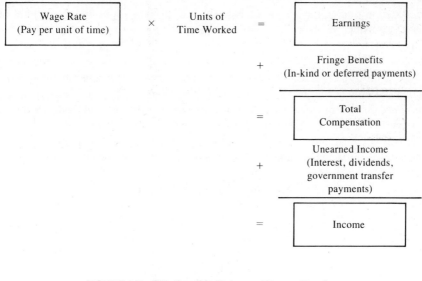

FIGURE 2.2   Relationship Between Wages, Earnings, Compensation and Income

HOW THE MARKET WORKS

The study of the labor market begins and ends with an analysis of the demand for and supply of labor. On the demand side of the labor market, we shall study employer behavior regarding the hiring of labor. On the supply side, the behavior of both workers and potential workers will be explored. The interaction of demand and supply is basically what determines working conditions, employment and compensation levels, and the allocation of labor to various occupations, industries, and employers. One can thus think of any labor market outcome as always affected, to one degree or another, by the forces of demand and supply. To paraphrase economist Alfred Marshall, it takes both demand and supply to determine economic outcomes, just as it takes two blades of a scissors to cut cloth.

In this chapter we present the basic outlines and broadest implications of the simplest economic model of the labor market. In later chapters we shall add some complexities to this basic model and explain assumptions and implications more fully. However, the simple model of demand and supply presented here offers some insights into labor market behavior that can be very useful in the formulation of social policy. Every piece of analysis in this text is an extension or modification of the basic model presented in this chapter.

The Demand for Labor

Firms combine various factors of production—mainly capital and labor—to produce goods or services that are sold in a product market. Their total output and the way in which they combine labor and capital depends on product demand, the amount of labor and capital they can acquire at given prices, and the choice of technologies available to them. When we study the demand for labor, we are interested in finding out how the number of workers employed by a firm or set of firms is affected by changes in one or more of these three forces. To simplify the discussion, we shall study one change at a time and hold all other forces constant.

Wage changes.   Of primary interest for most purposes is the question of how the number of employees (or total labor hours) demanded varies when wages change. Suppose, for example, that we could vary the wages facing a certain industry over a long period of time but keep the technology available, the conditions under which capital is supplied, and the relationship between product price and product demand unchanged. What would happen to the quantity of labor demanded if, say, the wage rate were *increased*?

First, higher wages imply higher costs and, usually, higher product prices. Because consumers respond to higher prices by buying less, employers would tend to reduce their level of output. Lower output levels, of course, imply lower employment levels (other things being equal). This decline in employment is called a *scale effect*—the effect on desired employment of a smaller scale of production.

Second, as wages increase (assuming the price of capital does not change, at least initially), employers have incentives to cut costs by adopting a technology that relies more on capital and less on labor. Thus, if wages were to rise, desired employment would fall because of a shift toward a more ''capital-intensive'' mode

TABLE 2.6 **Labor Demand Schedule for a Hypothetical Industry**

Wage Rate	Desired Employment Level
$3.00	250
4.00	190
5.00	160
6.00	130
7.00	100
8.00	70

Note: Employment levels can be measured in number of employees *or* number of labor hours demanded. We have chosen here to use number of employees.

of production. This second effect might be termed a *substitution effect*, because as wages rise, capital is *substituted* for labor in the production process.

The effects of various wages on employment levels might be summarized in a table showing the labor demanded at each wage level. Table 2.6 illustrates such a *demand schedule*. The relationship between wages and employment tabulated in Table 2.6 could be graphed as a *demand curve*. Figure 2.3 shows the demand curve generated by the data in Table 2.6. Note that the curve has a negative slope, indicating that as wages rise, less labor is demanded.

A demand curve for labor tells us how the desired level of employment, measured in either labor hours or number of employees, varies with changes in the price of labor when the other forces affecting demand are held constant. These other forces, to repeat, are the product demand schedule, the conditions under which capital can be obtained, and the set of technologies available. If wages change and these other factors do not, one can determine the change in labor demanded by moving up or down along the demand curve.

Changes in other forces affecting demand.   What happens when one of the other forces affecting labor demand changes?

FIGURE 2.3   Labor Demand Curve

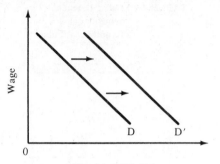

**FIGURE 2.4   Demand for Labor Shifts
Due to an Increase
in Product Demand**

First, suppose that *demand for the product* of a particular industry were to increase, so that at any output price, more of the goods or services in question could be sold. Suppose in this case that technology and the conditions under which capital and labor are made available to the industry do not change. Output levels would clearly rise as firms in the industry sought to maximize profits, and this *scale* (or *output*) *effect* would increase the amount of labor demanded. (As long as the relative prices of capital and labor remain unchanged, there is no *substitution effect*.)

How would this change in the demand for labor be illustrated using a demand curve? Since the technology available and the conditions under which capital and labor are supplied have remained constant, this change in product demand would increase the labor desired at any wage level that might prevail. In other words, the entire labor demand curve *shifts* to the right. This rightward shift, shown as a movement from *D* to *D'* in Figure 2.4, indicates that at every possible wage rate the number of workers demanded has increased.

Second, consider what would happen if the product demand schedule, technology, and labor-supply conditions were to remain unchanged, but *the supply of capital* changed so that capital prices fell to 50 percent of their prior level. How would this change affect the demand for labor?

Our analysis of this situation is exactly the same as our analysis of a wage change. First, when capital prices decline, the costs of producing tend to decline. Reduced costs stimulate increases in production, and these increases tend to raise the level of desired employment at any given wage. The scale effect of a fall in capital prices thus tends to increase the demand for labor at each wage level—which can be represented in Figure 2.5 by a shift to the right of the labor demand curve.

The second effect of a fall in capital prices would be a substitution effect, whereby firms adopt more capital-intensive technologies in response to cheaper capital. Such firms would substitute capital for labor and would use less labor to produce a given amount of output than before. With less labor being desired at each wage rate, the demand-for-labor curve shifts to the left, as shown in Figure 2.6. In some cases this leftward-shifting tendency of the substitution effect would be stronger than the rightward-shifting tendency of the scale effect; in other cases, the scale effect would be stronger.

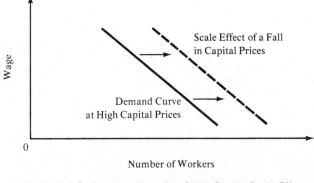

FIGURE 2.5   Demand for Labor Shifts Due to Scale Effect
Resulting from Fall in Capital Prices

The hypothesized changes in product demand and capital supply just discussed have tended to *shift* the demand curve for labor. It is important to distinguish between a *shift* in a demand curve and *movement along* a curve. A labor demand curve graphically shows the *labor desired* as a function of the *wage rate* (the wage is on one axis and the number employed is on the other). When the *wage* changes and other forces are held unchanged, one *moves along* the curve. However, when one of the *other forces* changes, the labor demand curve *shifts*. Unlike wages, these forces are not directly shown when the demand curve for labor is drawn. Thus, when they change, a different relationship between wages and employment prevails, and this shows up as a shift of the demand curve. If more labor is desired at any given wage rate, then the curve has shifted to the right. If less labor is demanded at each wage rate that might prevail, then the demand curve has shifted left.

FIGURE 2.6   Demand for Labor Shifts Due to Substitution
Effect Resulting from Fall in Capital Prices

Market, industry, and firm demand.   The demand for labor can be analyzed on three levels:

1. To analyze the demand for labor *by a particular firm*, we would examine how an increase in the wage of machinists, say, would affect their employment by a particular aircraft manufacturer.
2. To analyze the effects of this wage increase on the employment of machinists *in the entire aircraft industry*, we would utilize an industry demand curve.
3. Finally, to see how the wage increase would affect the *entire labor market* for machinists, in all industries in which they are used, we would use a market demand curve.

We shall see in Chapters 3 and 4 that firm, industry, and market labor demand curves vary in *shape* to some extent because *scale* and *substitution effects* have different strengths at each level. However, it is important to remember that the scale and substitution effects of a wage change work in the same direction at each level, so that firm, industry, and market demand curves *all slope downward*.

Long run vs. short run.   One can also distinguish between *long-run* and *short-run* labor demand curves. Over very short periods of time, employers find it difficult to substitute capital for labor (or vice versa), and customers may not change their product demand very much in response to a price increase. It takes *time* to fully adjust consumption and production behavior. Over longer periods of time, of course, responses to changes in wages or other forces affecting the demand for labor are larger and more complete.

In Chapters 3 and 4 we shall draw some important distinctions between short-run and long-run labor demand curves. At this point we need only point out that while these curves will differ, *they both slope downward*. Thus, an increase in the wage rate will reduce the demand for labor, although perhaps by different amounts, in both the short and long run.

The Supply of Labor

Having looked at a simple model of behavior on the buyer (or demand) side of the labor market, we now turn to the seller (or supply) side of the market. For purposes of this chapter, we shall assume that workers have already decided to work and that the question facing them is what occupation and what employer to choose.

Market supply.   To first consider the supply of labor to the entire market (as opposed to the supply to a particular firm), suppose that the market we are considering is the one for stenographers. How will supply respond to changes in the wages stenographers might receive? In other words, what does the supply schedule of stenographers look like?

If the salaries and wages in *other* occupations are *held constant* and the wages of stenographers rise, we would expect to find more people wanting to become stenographers. For example, suppose that each of 100 people in a high school

**FIGURE 2.7   Supply Curve for
Stenographers**

graduating class has the option of becoming an insurance agent or stenographer. Some of these 100 people will prefer to be insurance agents even if stenographers are better paid because they like the challenge and sociability of selling. Some would want to be stenographers even if the pay were comparatively poor because they hate the pressures of selling. Many, however, could see themselves doing either job; for them the compensation in each occupation would be a major factor in their decision. If stenographers were higher paid than insurance agents, more would want to become stenographers. If the pay of insurance agents were higher, the number of people choosing the insurance occupation would increase and the supply of stenographers would decrease. Of course, at some ridiculously low wage for stenographers, *no one* would want to become one.

Thus, the supply of labor to a particular market is positively related to the wage rate prevailing in that market, holding other wages constant. That is, if the wages of insurance agents are held constant and the stenographer wage rises, more people will want to become stenographers because of the relative improvement in compensation (as shown graphically in Figure 2.7).

As with demand curves, each supply curve is drawn holding other prices and wages constant. If one or more of these other prices or wages were to change, it would cause the supply curve to *shift*. As the salaries of insurance agents *rise*, some people will change their minds about becoming stenographers and choose to become insurance agents. Fewer people would want to be stenographers at each level of stenographic wages as salaries of insurance agents rise. In graphic terms (see Figure 2.8), increases in the salaries of insurance agents would cause the supply curve of stenographers to shift to the left.

Supply to firms.   Having decided to become a stenographer, the individual would then have to decide which offer of employment to accept. If all employers were offering stenographic jobs that were more or less alike, the choice would be based on compensation. Any firm unwise enough to attempt paying a wage below what others paid would find it could not attract any employees (or at least it could not attract any of the caliber it wanted). Conversely, no firm would be foolish enough to pay more than the going wage because it would be paying more than it would have to pay to attract a suitable number and quality of employees. The supply

**FIGURE 2.8 Labor Supply Curve
for Stenographers Shifts
as Salaries of
Insurance Agents Rise**

curve to a firm, then, would be horizontal, as can be seen in Figure 2.9. The horizontal supply curve to a firm indicates that at the going wage, a firm could get all the stenographers it needs. If it paid less, however, supply would shrink to zero.

The difference in slope between the market supply curve and the supply curve to a firm is directly related to the type of choice facing workers. In deciding whether to enter the stenographic labor market or not, workers must weigh both the compensation *and* the job requirements of alternative options (such as being an insurance agent). If wages of stenographers were to fall, fewer people would want to enter the stenographic market. However, not everyone would withdraw from the market, because the jobs of insurance agent and stenographer are not perfect substitutes. Some people would remain stenographers after a wage decline because they disliked the job requirements of insurance agents.

Once the decision to become a stenographer had been made, the choice of which employer to work for would be a choice between alternatives in which the job requirements were nearly the *same.* Thus, the choice would have to be made on the

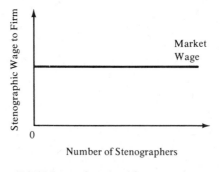

**FIGURE 2.9   Supply of Stenographers
to a Firm**

grounds of compensation alone. If a firm were to lower its wage offers below those of other firms, it would lose all its applicants. The horizontal supply curve is, therefore, a reflection of supply decisions made among alternatives that are perfect substitutes for each other.

We have argued that firms wishing to hire stenographers must pay the going wage or lose all applicants. While this may seem unrealistic, it is not. If a firm offers jobs *comparable* to those offered by other firms but at a lower level of total compensation, it might be able to attract a few applicants of the quality it desires because a few people will be unaware of compensation elsewhere. Over time, however, knowledge of the firm's poor relative pay would become more widespread, and the firm would find it had to rely solely on less qualified people to fill its jobs. It could secure quality employees at below-average pay only if it offered *noncomparable* jobs (more pleasant working conditions, longer paid vacations, and so forth). This factor in labor supply will be discussed in Chapter 8. For now, we will assume that individual firms, like individual workers, are usually *wage takers*; that is, the wages they pay to their workers must be pretty close to the going wage if they face competition in the labor market. Neither individual workers nor firms can set a wage much different from the going wage and still hope to transact. (Exceptions to this general proposition will be noted in later chapters.)

The Determination of the Wage

The wage that prevails in a particular labor market is heavily influenced by the forces of demand and supply, regardless of whether or not the market involves a labor union. However, because unions are labor-market institutions designed to alter the market outcome, we shall first discuss wage determination in nonunionized labor markets.

The equilibrium wage.   Recall that the market demand curve indicates how many workers employers would want at each wage rate, holding capital prices and consumer incomes constant. The market supply curve indicates how many workers would enter the market at each wage level, holding the wages in other occupations constant. These curves can be placed on the same graph to reveal some interesting information, as shown in Figure 2.10.

For example, suppose the market wage were set at W_1. At this low wage, demand is large but supply is small. More importantly, Figure 2.10 indicates that at W_1 demand *exceeds* supply. At this point, employers will be competing for the few workers in the market and a shortage of workers would exist. Firms' desires to attract more employees would lead them to increase their wage offers, thus driving up the overall level of wage offers in the market.

As wages rose, two things would happen. First, more workers would choose to enter the market and look for jobs (a movement along the supply curve); second, increasing wages would induce employers to seek fewer workers (a movement along the demand curve). If wages were to rise to W_2, supply would exceed demand. Employers would desire fewer workers than the number available and not all those

Example 2.1

The Black Death and the Wages of Labor

An example of what happens to wages when the supply of labor suddenly shifts occurred when plague—the Black Death—struck England (among other European countries) in 1348–1351. Estimates vary, but it is generally agreed that plague killed between 17 and 40 percent of the English population in that short period of time. This shocking loss of life had the immediate effect of raising the wages of laborers. As the supply curve shifted to the left, a *shortage* of workers was created at the old wage levels, and competition among employers for the surviving workers drove the wage level dramatically upward.

Reliable figures are hard to come by, but many believe wages rose by 50–100 percent over the three-year period. A thresher, for example, earning two and one-half pence per day in 1348 earned four and one-half pence in 1350, while mowers receiving 5 pence per acre in 1348 were receiving 9 pence in 1350. Whether the overall rise in wages was this large or not, there was clearly a labor shortage and an unprecedented increase in wages. A royal proclamation commanding landlords to share their scarce workers with neighbors and threatening workers with imprisonment if they refused work at the pre-plague wage was issued to deal with this shortage, but it was ignored. The shortage was too severe and market forces were simply too strong for the rise in wages to be thwarted.

The discerning student might wonder at this point about the *demand* curve for labor. Did it not also shift to the left as the population—and the number of consumers—declined? The answer is that it did, but this leftward shift was not as pronounced as the leftward shift in supply. While there were fewer customers for labor's output, the customers who remained consumed greater amounts of goods and services per capita than before. The money, gold and silver, and durable goods that had existed prior to 1348 were divided among many fewer people by 1350, and this rise in per capita wealth was associated with a widespread and dramatic increase in the level of consumption, especially of luxury goods. Thus, the leftward shift in labor demand was dominated by the leftward shift in supply, and the predictable result was a large increase in wages.

SOURCES: Harry A. Miskimin, *The Economy of Early Renaissance Europe 1300–1460* (Englewood Cliffs, N.J.: Prentice-Hall, Inc., 1969); George M. Modlin and Frank T. deVyver, *Development of Economic Society* (Boston: D.C. Heath,1946); Douglass C. North and Robert Paul Thomas, *The Rise of the Western World* (Cambridge: Cambridge University Press, 1973); Philip Ziegler, *The Black Death* (New York: Harper & Row, 1969).

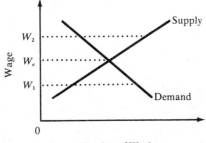

FIGURE 2.10   Market Demand and Supply

desiring employment would be able to find jobs, resulting in a surplus of workers. Employers would have long lines of eager applicants for any opening. These employers would soon reason that they could fill their openings with qualified applicants even if they offered lower wages. Further, if they could pay lower wages, they would want to hire more employees. Some employees would be more than happy to accept the lower wages if they could just find a job. Others would leave the market and look for work elsewhere as wages fell. Thus, demand and supply would become more equal as wages fell from the level of W_2.

The wage rate at which demand equals supply is the *market-clearing* or *equilibrium* wage. At W_e in Figure 2.10, employers can fill the number of openings they have and all employees who want jobs in this market can find them. At W_e there is no surplus and no shortage. All parties are satisfied, and no forces exist that would alter the wage. The market is in equilibrium in the sense that the wage will remain at W_e.

The equilibrium wage is the wage that eventually prevails in a market. Wages below W_e, for example, will not prevail because the shortage of workers leads employers to drive up wage offers. Wages above W_e likewise cannot prevail because the surplus leads to downward pressure on wage rates. The market-clearing wage, W_e, thus becomes the *going wage* that individual employers and employees must face. In other words, wage rates are determined by the market and "announced" to individual market participants. Figure 2.11 graphically depicts market demand and supply in panel a, along with the demand and supply curves for a typical firm in that market in panel b. All firms in the market pay a wage of W_e, and total employment of L equals the sum of employment in each firm.

Disturbing the equilibrium.   What could happen to change the equilibrium (market) wage once it has been reached? Once equilibrium has been achieved, changes could arise from shifts in either the demand or the supply curve. For example, consider what might happen to the wages of stenographers (the majority of whom at present are women) if job opportunities for women in management and other prestigious fields were to improve. The greater availability and improved pay for women in these alternative careers would probably cause some women to leave the stenographer market and seek work in these other fields. Fewer women would

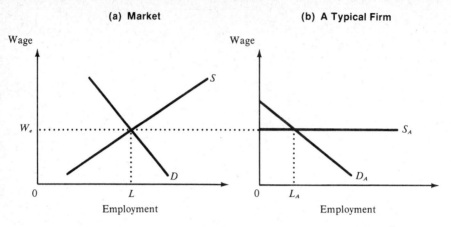

FIGURE 2.11   Demand and Supply at the "Market" and "Firm" Level

want to become stenographers at the going wage. As Figure 2.12 shows, the market supply curve for stenographers would shift to the left.

As can be seen from Figure 2.12, after the supply curve has shifted, W_e is no longer the market-clearing wage. There is now a shortage of stenographers (because demand exceeds supply) at W_e. As employers scramble to fill stenographic jobs, the wage rate is driven up. The new equilibrium wage is W_e' which of course is higher than W_e. Better opportunities for women in management would thus lead to a smaller supply of stenographers, and to fill stenographic jobs the wage rate paid to stenographers would have to rise. The end result of the improved opportunities elsewhere would be to increase the wages of stenographers.

Shifts of the demand curve to the right would also cause wages to rise. Suppose, for example, that the increase in paperwork accompanying greater government regulation of industry causes firms to demand more stenographic help than

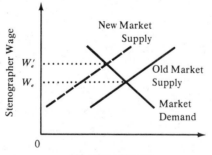

FIGURE 2.12   New Labor Market
Equilibrium after Supply
Shifts Left

FIGURE 2.13 **New Labor Market Equilibrium After Demand Shifts Right**

before. Graphically, as in Figure 2.13, this greater demand would be represented as a rightward shift of the demand curve. This rightward shift would depict a situation in which, for any given wage rate, the number of stenographers desired had risen. The old equilibrium wage (W_e) would no longer equate demand and supply. If W_e were to persist, there would be a labor shortage in the stenographer market (because demand would exceed supply). This shortage would induce employers to improve their wage offers and eventually drive up the stenographic wage to W_e^*.

Both the leftward shift in supply and the rightward shift in demand initially created shortages—shortages that led to increases in the market wage rate. The supply-caused shift, however, led to a fall in employment (as compared to the old equilibrium level of employment). Conversely, the demand-caused shift induced an increase in the equilibrium level of employment.

Equilibrium wages can also fall, of course. Although *money* wages are rarely cut, in a period of rising prices *real* wages can fall quite readily. Between 1976 and 1977, for example, money wages for nonagricultural production workers rose by 8.0 percent (from $203.70 per week to $219.91), but their real wages fell by 3 percent because prices rose by 11 percent.[7] Money wages in an occupation can also fall relative to wages in other occupations. Thus, when we speak of a declining wage rate, it can imply a decline *relative to product prices or to other wages*, as well as a fall in the money wage rate.

A fall in the equilibrium wage rate would occur if there were increased supply or reduced demand. An increase in supply would be represented by a rightward shift of the supply curve, as more people entered the market at each wage (see Figure 2.14). This rightward shift would cause a surplus to exist at the old equilibrium wage (W_e) and lead to behavior that reduced the wage to W_e'' in Figure 2.14. Note that the equilibrium employment level increased. What could cause this rightward shift of the supply curve? For stenographers, the cause of increased supply at each wage could be a greater desire among people to become stenographers, or reduc-

---

[7]U.S. President, *Economic Report of the President* (Washington, D.C.: U.S. Government Printing Office, January 1980), Tables B-36 and B-49.

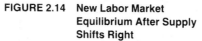

FIGURE 2.14   **New Labor Market Equilibrium After Supply Shifts Right**

tions in the wages of competing occupations (such as insurance agents in our example above).

A decrease (leftward shift) in demand would also cause a decrease in the equilibrium wage, although such a shift would be accompanied by a fall in employment, as we can see in Figure 2.15. The leftward shift of the demand curve would cause a surplus at the original equilibrium wage (W_e). When firms found the ratio of applicants to openings was greater than usual and when workers found that jobs were harder to come by, downward pressure on the wage would exist and the market-clearing wage would fall to W_e^{**}. Money wages might go up, but any increases would be smaller than those received in other occupations. Sadly for the authors, the decline in demand for college professors brought on by a number of financial and demographic pressures offers an excellent example of a surplus market. The result was a 17 percent decline in real, after-tax earnings for college professors over the 1967–78 period.

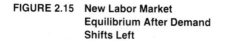

FIGURE 2.15   **New Labor Market Equilibrium After Demand Shifts Left**

FIGURE 2.16 New Labor Market Equilibrium After Supply Shifts Right and Demand Shifts Left

It is possible, of course, for equilibrium to be disturbed by shifts in both demand and supply at the same time. These simultaneous shifts might either reinforce each other or work against each other. An example of a reinforcing shift occurs when a leftward shift in demand is accompanied by a rightward shift in supply, as shown in Figure 2.16. If the demand curve alone shifted, wages would fall from W_{1-1} to W_{2-1}, but when accompanied by a rightward shift in supply, wages fall to W_{2-2}.

Shifts may also tend to work against each other. For example, if the invention and spread of tape-recording devices reduced the demand for people with stenographic skills at the same time that opportunities for women outside the clerical occupations were increasing, it would be difficult to predict the effects on stenographers' wages (see Figure 2.17). The leftward shift of demand would exert downward pressure on wages, while the leftward shift of supply would tend to cause wages to rise. The ultimate effect would depend on which force was greater. In panel a of Figure 2.17, the forces generated by the contraction of demand were dominant, and the equilibrium wage is depicted as falling from W_{1-1} to W_{2-2}. In panel b, however, the contraction of supply was dominant, and wages are shown as rising from W_{1-1} to W_{2-2}.

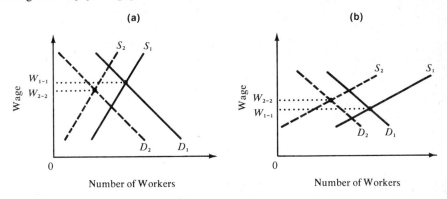

FIGURE 2.17 New Labor Market Equilibria After Supply and Demand Shift Left

APPLICATIONS OF THE THEORY

Although this simple model of how a labor market functions will be refined and elaborated upon in the following chapters, it can explain many important phenomena, including those that follow.

The Allocation of Labor to Inhospitable Climates

The labor market, as we emphasized earlier, performs the task of matching employers and employees. In accomplishing this task, it fulfills the important social role of allocating a scarce resource—labor—among potential users. Moreover, this allocation takes place voluntarily. Our model of the labor market explains how this allocation happens and with what effects.

Any society wanting to allocate its resources by taking into account the wishes of both consumer and worker must invent a mechanism that readily reflects both sets of wishes. The market is just such a mechanism. The wishes of consumers are expressed through the labor demand schedules of employers. The more of a particular output consumers want and the more they are willing to pay for it, the more labor (and capital) will be demanded by producers. For example, Figure 2.18 shows that firm A has a stronger demand for workers than does firm B; therefore, at a wage of W_0, it hires more workers.

The labor market also reflects worker preferences. If all jobs were alike, preferences would not be important. However, jobs vary in difficulty, level of tension, location, working conditions, hours, security, and so forth. Workers are understandably more reluctant to do some kinds of work than other kinds, and the allocation process must take this reluctance into account. The supply curves to various labor markets are a convenient way to represent worker preferences. When the jobs are pleasant, many people are willing to offer their services at each wage level. When jobs are distasteful, fewer are willing to do so.

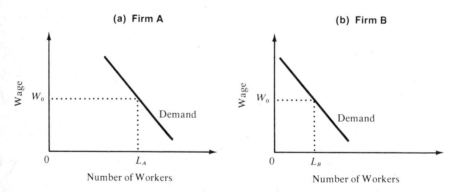

FIGURE 2.18 The Demand for Labor in Two Firms

The effect of worker preferences on the allocation of labor can be understood by comparing labor markets in which the job *duties* are the same but the conditions of work are radically different. Suppose, for example, that one market is offering clerical jobs in the continental United States, while the other market is offering such jobs with companies building a pipeline in a harsh, inhospitable, remote location near the Arctic Circle. If wages were equal in both places, the jobs near the Arctic Circle would not be filled, as workers prefer more hospitable climates. To attract workers to the unappealing location requires that compensation be higher there. The high wages would cause employers to economize on the use of labor in these places—most, in fact, would not even locate there. Some, however, would have such strong incentives for locating there that they would be willing to pay the high wages. The high wages, of course, would serve to compensate workers for the inhospitable location of their jobs.

The building of the trans-Alaska pipeline in the mid-1970s provides an example of how disagreeable working conditions affect wages. The work entailed long hours (84 hours a week), cruel winter weather (frequently 55 degrees below zero), and anything but a normal personal life (dormitory living). Under these conditions, it took hourly wages 50 percent higher than those received by similarly skilled workers in the continental United States, with time and one-half for overtime and double time on Sundays, to recruit and hold the required labor force. However, workers who chose to work there could make $60,000 per year—almost four times what they could make in roughly the same job in the continental United States.

The Accommodation of "Baby Boom" Workers

During the late 1970s, the overall labor market was forced to accommodate a huge influx of new workers searching for jobs. These new entrants were born in the late 1950s—a period of the so-called baby boom. The number of 20-year-olds in the population in 1977 was 44 percent larger than the number in 1962 and equally large compared to the numbers projected for 1992.[8] Thus, there was a bulge in the number of inexperienced workers seeking jobs. What would be the predictable effect as this bulge in supply hit the labor market?

First, new entrants are, by definition, inexperienced workers, and such workers are not very good substitutes for experienced workers. Inexperienced workers tend to be offered *entry-level jobs*, while more complicated or responsible jobs higher up on the career ladder are reserved to some extent for experienced workers. Thus, the experienced and the inexperienced are, to a degree, in different labor markets.

What happens when a big bulge of population enters a labor market? The sheer increase in population shifts the supply curve to the right because more people are offering themselves for work at every wage level. Figure 2.19 illustrates this shift from S_1 to S_2. This shift in supply, if not accompanied by a correspondingly large shift in demand, will reduce wages. (Figure 2.19 shows that the equilibrium wage fell from W_e to W_e'.)

[8]Data for this section were obtained from Finis Welch, "Effects of Cohort Size on Earnings: The Baby Boom Babies' Financial Bust," *Journal of Political Economy* 87, 5 (October 1979): S65–98.

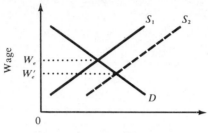

FIGURE 2.19   Labor Market Equilibrium
for Teenagers After
Population Increase

Did the "baby boom" bulge in the late 1970s cause wages of inexperienced workers to fall? To answer this question we must pick a standard against which to measure the fall. Money wages rarely fall, especially when prices are rising. We could, therefore, measure whether *real wages* fell over some time period. However, real wages have tended to rise due to improvements in technology—a force we would like to filter out if possible so that we can focus only on changes produced by the shift in supply.

The best way to measure the fall in the wages of inexperienced workers is to compare their wages to those of adults in their peak earnings years. These adults will be the beneficiaries, along with inexperienced workers, of technological advances, but they are far enough removed from the "baby boomers" in experience that the bulge of new labor force entrants will not affect their wages directly. Measured against this group, earnings of new entrants fell dramatically in the late 1970s.

Table 2.7 tells the story. In every educational category, the proportion of inexperienced workers in the labor force increased during the period from 1967 to

TABLE 2.7   Economic Position of New Entrants in Labor Force
by Level of Schooling

Years of School Completed	Percent of Work Force with Less Than 5 Years of Experience in Each Schooling Category		Weekly Wages of New Entrants Relative to Peak Earners	
	1967–69	*1973–75*	*1967–69*	*1973–75*
8–11 years	8.9	15.4	0.53	0.46
12 years	15.0	20.8	0.63	0.55
1–3 years of college	19.0	25.2	0.59	0.52
4 or more years of college	18.7	22.9	0.63	0.54

SOURCE: Finis Welch, "Effects of Cohort Size on Earnings: The Baby Boom Babies' Financial Bust," *Journal of Political Economy* 87, 5 (October 1979): S65–S98.

Example 2.2

Restricted Labor Supply in the Soviet Union

Examples of the effects of a restricted labor supply to areas where the weather is extraordinarily harsh can be found in socialist, as well as capitalist, countries. In the Soviet Union, where production is centrally planned but labor is recruited voluntarily through the use of incentives, workers in the Far North are paid wages and supplements 60–180 percent higher than in the populated areas in central, southern, and western Russia. Only part of the differential is to compensate workers for the higher costs of living in northern Siberia. Even a society that philosophically prefers wage equality must pay its workers in the Far North a *real wage* much higher than elsewhere if it hopes to voluntarily assemble a work force large enough to produce in that region.

SOURCE: Paul R. Gregory and Robert C. Stuart, *Soviet Economic Structure and Performance*, 2nd ed. (New York: Harper & Row, 1981), pp. 190–92.

1975—a clear indication that the number of young workers was increasing faster than the number of older workers. This abnormally large rise in employment was accompanied by a 12–15 percent decline in the earnings of new workers relative to adults. Thus, as our model of labor-market behavior suggests, the large increase in employment necessary to accommodate the "baby boom" entrants was facilitated by a decline in their wage. The influx of inexperienced workers created a surplus at the former wage level, and as new workers competed for jobs, the wage level was driven down.

Effects of Unions

Although we shall discuss the role and effects of unions on the labor market later in this text, it is important here to briefly establish that the model outlined in this chapter can also apply to unions. This analysis will look only generally at the effects of unions on wages. Later chapters will analyze union effects on wages in more detail and will also examine their effects on productivity, turnover, and wage differentials across race and sex groups.

Unions represent workers and, as such, primarily affect the *supply* curves to labor markets. They do so in two ways. First, most unions operate under labor-management agreements—called *contracts* or *collective-bargaining agreements*—that permit employer discretion in the selection of workers. These contracts cover wages, other forms of compensation, working conditions, procedures for employee complaints, and rules governing promotions and layoffs. The provisions of the contracts are the result of a bargain struck between management and all workers collectively. In effect, workers band together, agree to a bargaining position, and negotiate as a group. All are bound by the final provisions of the contract, which means that all must receive the agreed-upon wage.

**FIGURE 2.20   Effects on Labor Market
Equilibrium of
Industrywide Unions**

Many of the most prominent collective-bargaining agreements, in effect, are industrywide. These agreements, which include those in the auto, steel, rubber, coal, and trucking industries, affect the supply curves in the relevant labor markets by making them horizontal. No one can get paid more or less than the wage agreed upon in the contract (see Figure 2.20).

In Figure 2.20 the supply curve without a union is S and the market-clearing wage is W_e. However, the union raises the wage above W_e to W_u, the wage specified in the contract, by preventing firms and workers from offering or accepting wages below W_u. The result is a wage above equilibrium, employment levels below those that would prevail if the wage were lower, and a "surplus" of labor (at W_u, L_s workers want work in these jobs but only L_u can find work). Because the wage cannot fall, the surplus remains and will manifest itself in long lines of workers applying for job openings with union employers.

The above analysis was based on the assumption that unions raised the wage above market-clearing levels. This is probably a useful assumption, given that unions certainly intend to do this. Not all unions have the power to affect wages much, for reasons we shall discuss in Chapter 4. If these unions agree to wages equal to W_e, the market equilibrium wage, then clearly they do not affect wage or employment outcomes in the labor market.

The second way in which some unions affect the supply to markets is by *directly* limiting supply. Some unions operate under agreements in which employers hire all labor from the union and in which the union controls which and how many members it lets in. The dual power of being able to restrict its membership and to require employers to hire only union members permits the union to set the level of labor supply to the market (see Figure 2.21).

In Figure 2.21, S_u represents the level of supply determined by union policy and W_u the resulting wage. S_u is drawn as a vertical line because wage increases or decreases do not affect supply. Supply is set at L_u by union policy.

The wage and employment levels under the union—W_u and L_u—can be compared to the lower wages (W_e) and higher employment levels (L_e) that would prevail in the absence of a union. The major difference between this case, in which unions control supply, and the more common situation, in which employers choose work-

**FIGURE 2.21   How Unions That Control
Supply of Labor to a
Market Affect Labor
Market Equilibrium**

ers but make contracts with all workers collectively, is that there is no surplus of workers standing at the employer's hiring gate. The long line of disappointed people is at the union's office. Examples of labor unions that control supply are those representing skilled construction workers, longshoring workers, and theater lighting technicians.[9]

The model of labor market behavior presented in this chapter has here been used to explain how unions affect wages. If unions are successful in driving such wages above equilibrium, the model can also be used to analyze the consequences of this wage increase. First, as wages rise above the market-clearing level, employment will be reduced. Second, as union wages rise, the number of people wanting union jobs will increase. However, the limited job opportunities will make it difficult for many of these people to find work, and a surplus of labor will come to exist in the unionized markets. (See Chapters 3 and 12 for an analysis of union effects on wages and employment in nonunion labor markets.)

Who Is Underpaid and Who Is Overpaid?

In casual conversation one often hears a worker say that he or she is "underpaid." Just as often one hears employers claiming workers are "overpaid." Clearly, each is using a different standard for judging wages. People tend to judge the wages paid or received against some notion of what they "need," but there is no universally accepted standard of need. A worker may "need" more income to buy a larger home or finance a recreational vehicle. An employer may "need" greater profits to pay for sending a child to college. In general, almost all of us feel we "need" more income!

---

[9]This is not to say that all unions that *can* control supply are equally prone to do it. Some may fear the presence of a large number of qualified workers outside the union and figure that it is better to take them in, collect their dues, and ration jobs among all members than to face stiff nonunion competition. Restricting entry into the union is *most likely* when employers *must* hire only union workers.

Despite the difficulties of assessing needs, there are still important reasons for defining "overpaid" and "underpaid." For example, the public utilities commissions in every state must consider and approve rate increases requested by the telephone, gas, and electric companies. These companies desire increases partly to keep up with production costs, which the companies obviously want to pass on to consumers. Suppose, however, that a public utilities commission observed that the *level* of wages paid by these companies or the *increases* in such wages were "excessive." In the interests of holding down consumer prices, it might want to consider adopting a policy whereby excessive labor costs could not be passed on to consumers in the form of rate increases. Instead, it might decide that such costs should be borne by the company or its shareholders. Obviously, such a policy would require a definition of what constitutes overpayment.

We pointed out in Chapter 1 that a fundamental value of normative economics is that, as a society, we should strive to complete all those transactions that are mutually beneficial. Another way of stating this value is to say that we must strive to use our scarce resources as effectively as possible, which implies that output should be produced in the least costly manner so that the most can be obtained from such resources. This goal, combined with the labor market model outlined in this chapter, suggests a useful definition of what it means to be overpaid.

We shall define workers as *overpaid* if their wages are higher than the market equilibrium wage for their job. Because a labor surplus exists for jobs that are overpaid, a wage above equilibrium has two implications (see Figure 2.22). First, employers are paying more than they have to in order to produce (they pay W_H instead of W_e). They could cut wages and still find enough qualified workers for their job openings. In fact, if they did cut wages, they could expand output and make their product cheaper and more accessible to consumers. Second, more workers want jobs than can find them (Y workers want jobs, and only V openings are available). If wages were reduced a bit, more of these disappointed workers could find work. A wage above equilibrium thus causes consumer prices to be higher and output to be smaller than is possible, and it creates a situation in which not all workers who want the jobs in question can get them.

With this definition of overpayment, the public utilities commission in question would want to look for evidence that wages were above equilibrium. The commis-

FIGURE 2.22   Effects of an Above-Equilibrium Wage

sion might be able to compare wages paid by utilities to those of comparable workers in the general labor market. Doing so would require measures of worker quality, of course—data that are hard to quantify in some cases. Alternatively, the commission could look to employee behavior for signs of above-market wages. If wages were above those for comparable jobs, current employees would be *very* reluctant to quit because they would know their chances of doing better were small. Likewise, the number of applicants would be unusually large.

An interesting—although perhaps extreme—example of above-equilibrium wage rates could be seen in New York City in 1974–75. New York City fire fighters and police officers during this period were receiving salaries roughly 40 percent greater than skilled mechanics and machinists working in the city and some 50 percent greater than area truck drivers. Perhaps the most convincing evidence of overpayment and the attendant surplus was that there were enormous numbers of qualified applicants who had passed job-related tests and were waiting for openings. For fire fighters there were about 12,000 qualified applicants—compared to a total employment of only 10,000—at a time when the city was not even hiring fire fighters. For police officers there were more than 42,000 qualified applicants on the waiting list, 23,000 current employees, and no hiring to speak of.[10]

An even larger surplus existed for sanitation workers, whose $14,770 yearly salary (in 1974 dollars) was 60 percent higher than the area average for laborers/materials handlers. In that department there were 36,849 on the waiting list of people who had passed a job-related examination—or 3.4 qualified applicants for each current employee! Again, hiring was almost nil during this period. These numbers clearly point to a labor surplus—and thus to overpayment.

To better understand the social losses attendant on overpayment, let us return to the principles of normative economics. Can it be shown that reducing overpayment will create a situation in which the gainers gain more than the losers lose? Suppose in the case of sanitation workers that *only* the wages of *newly hired* sanitation workers were lowered—to $10,000. Current workers thus would not lose, but many laborers working at $9,200 per year (the prevailing wage for them in 1974) would jump at the chance to take a $10,000-a-year job. Taxpayers, knowing that garbage-collection services could now be expanded at lower cost than before, would increase their demand for such services, thus creating jobs for these new workers.[11] Thus, some workers would gain while no one lost—and social well-being would be clearly enhanced.[12]

---

[10]Sharon P. Smith, *Equal Pay in the Public Sector: Fact or Fantasy* (Princeton, N.J.: Industrial Relations Section, Princeton University, Research Report Series No. 122, 1977), p. 20.

[11]These new workers, of course, have wanted sanitation jobs with New York City all along, but the high wage prevented job opportunities in that field from expanding.

It should be noted that if the wages of *current* sanitation workers were lowered, city taxpayers could obtain their current level of service for less money. Their gains (in tax savings) would equal the income losses of sanitation workers, and if we were to arrange the transaction so that no one lost, the gainers would have to compensate the losers by restoring their lost income. For this reason we have assumed that salaries for current sanitation workers are not cut.

[12]If the workers who switched jobs were getting paid approximately what they were worth to their former employers, these employers would lose $9,200 in output but save $9,200 in costs—and their welfare would thus not be affected. The presumption that employees are paid what they are worth to the employer is discussed at length in Chapter 3.

FIGURE 2.23 **Effects of a Below-Equilibrium Wage**

Employees can be defined as *underpaid* if their wage is below equilibrium. At below-equilibrium wages, employers have difficulty finding workers to meet the demands of consumers, and a labor shortage thus exists (firms want more workers than they can find at the prevailing wage). They also have trouble keeping the workers they do find. If wages were increased, output would rise and more workers would be attracted to the market. Thus, an increase would benefit the people in society in *both* their consumer and worker roles. Figure 2.23 shows how a wage increase from W_L to W_e would increase employment to V from X (at the same time wages were rising).

Wages in the U.S. Army illustrate how the market adjusts to below-equilibrium wages. In 1962, for example, when the military draft was in effect, the military paid enlisted personnel salaries and allowances that came to around 80 percent of the earnings of comparable civilian workers. Total compensation was so low for the job that an enormous gap between the quantity demanded and the quantity supplied existed. As a result, a large percentage of all new recruits had to be *drafted* to deal with the shortage. Fifteen years later, when shortages could no longer be met through conscription, cash wages for Army recruits had risen to 95 percent of civilian wages!

How do these definitions of underpayment and overpayment accord with notions of fairness or equity? They square very well with the concept of *horizontal equity*—treating equals equally. If the equilibrium wage were paid to each worker in a particular labor market, no one would be underpaid or overpaid. Equal workers would receive equal pay for essentially the same work.

These definitions, however, are ambiguous in relation to the concept of *vertical equity*—treating different groups differently. How can we justify paying a professor more or less than a sanitation worker? The answer suggested by our definitions is that it is less a matter of justice than it is of getting the job done. We have to pay professors and sanitation workers whatever it takes to get them to provide the level of services we desire. If so few people want to collect garbage that it requires a relatively high wage to attract them, so be it. If we are to have this valuable service performed without resorting to involuntary servitude, there is no choice but to pay the wages necessary to attract the required number and quality of workers.

Labor "Shortages": A Policy Application

The government is frequently urged to undertake programs to cope with perceived labor shortages. Underlying these proposals is usually an assumption that market forces are not working effectively to generate an adequate supply of workers to the occupations in question, but this assumption is often based on faulty reasoning. We can use the insights developed in this chapter to point out two common errors in this assumption and the dangers of not recognizing them.

Wrong definition of shortage. Perhaps the most common error is to define a shortage in terms that are independent of demand. For example, one book on occupational safety and health argued that there was a shortage (in 1973) of 19,700 industrial nurses, even though the same book estimated that the number of jobs available for such nurses exceeded their supply by only 700.[13] In what sense did the author perceive a shortage?

It is clear that the author's definition was inconsistent with the concept as we have defined it. According to our definition a shortage exists if, at the prevailing wage rate for a given occupation, demand exceeds supply. If the figures quoted above for industrial nurses were correct, a minor shortage of 700 could be said to exist. The author, however, ignored what demand *actually* was and based his definition of a shortage on what he felt demand *should be*! He argued that to do an adequate job of protecting workers from the dangers of health hazards on the job, we needed to have 19,700 more nurses than we had. His definition was thus based on a perception of *need* as compared to supply—rather than on *demand* as compared to supply.

The distinction between a need-based definition of a shortage and a demand-based definition is not just semantic. The central problem addressed by economics is that resources are scarce, so our individual or social *needs* for newer cars, larger houses, cleaner air, better schools, and more mass transit will not necessarily get translated into *demand*. That workers would be healthier if we employed 19,700 more industrial nurses no more indicates that these nurses would be hired than the fact that all families would be happier with five-bedroom houses suggests more such homes could be sold! Given limited resources, firms and homeowners alike might not choose to pay the added costs of meeting those needs.

Acceptance of a need-based definition of labor shortage by the government poses two related dangers. Declaring that the "shortage" of industrial nurses amounts to 19,700 might imply to new workers that many more jobs are available than in fact actually exist. Many individuals might enter the field believing the opportunities are better than they really are. The other danger is that the government might uncritically adopt expensive programs to increase supply in an environment in which the added workers would not find jobs available in the field.

In the 1960s, for example, the government initiated a $300 million program to increase the supply of professional nursing graduates by 29 percent in five years.

---

[13]Nicholas Ashford, *Crisis in the Workplace* (Cambridge, Mass.: MIT Press, 1976), p. 455.

The program was adopted after a report by the Surgeon General calculated a huge shortage of nurses based on a needs approach. The report contended that 50 percent of direct patient care should be provided by registered nurses (as opposed to nursing aides), because below this level patient satisfaction is significantly reduced. The problem with trying to increase the supply of nurses to meet this "shortage" was that, at the time, supply did not seem to be falling short of effective demand!

The hallmark of a shortage (as we have defined it) is a wage rate that rises faster than average. If demand exceeds supply at the prevailing wage, firms with unfilled vacancies attempt to attract workers by offering higher wages, and thus wages in the shortage occupation rise relative to those in occupations not experiencing a shortage. (Put differently, shortages exist because the wage rate is below market-clearing levels; the market response is for these wages to rise.) There is no evidence that, as of the mid-1960s, nursing salaries were rising faster than average.[14] The relationship of these salaries to all workers, all female workers, and all female professional workers remained essentially constant from 1950 to 1963, showing no tendency to rise. This fact suggests that the effective demand for nurses did not exceed supply at the prevailing wage,[15] and the essential balance between demand and supply probably explains why the supply of nurses rose by 3 percent, not 29 percent, as a result of the government program.[16] Future employment and salary prospects simply did not seem attractive enough to lure more students to the field.

What the Surgeon General and the government failed to recognize was that the problem they perceived in providing adequate patient care was one of *demand*, not supply. Nurses were in abundant enough supply to fill available jobs; it was the number of *jobs* that was the problem. Ironically, a program shifting the *demand* for nurses was initiated later in the 1960s, when Medicare and Medicaid were adopted, and the labor market responses to this program indicate a properly functioning market. Nursing salaries rose relative to those in other occupations, and the number of nurses employed rose quickly (mainly because the higher wages attracted many who were *already* trained as nurses back into the field). These responses suggest that the government's efforts to cure a "supply" problem in the nursing market using subsidies were unnecessary as well as unproductive.

Wrong conclusion of market failure.   For a prolonged period in the 1950s, firms complained of unfilled vacancies for engineers, despite the fact that wages in this market were rising faster than average. The market signals (a rising wage) seemed to be working, but the shortage did not appear to abate. This situation led some to conclude that the market was not functioning effectively and that government help was required (in the form of engineering educational subsidies).[17]

---

[14]Donald Yett, *An Economic Analysis of the Nursing Shortage* (Lexington, Mass.: Lexington Books, 1975), p. 160.

[15]Many economists believe the nursing labor market is dominated by just a few buyers of labor in each city, as we shall discuss in Chapter 3. While a lack of competition on the employer side of the market does have a bearing on the perception of shortages, it is nevertheless true that if hospitals were trying to hire beyond current levels, they would behave in a way that would drive nursing salaries up.

[16]Yett, *An Economic Analysis of the Nursing Shortage.*

[17]See Kenneth Arrow and William Capron, "Dynamic Shortages and Price Rises: The Engineer-Scientist Case," *Quarterly Journal of Economics* 73, 2 (May 1959): 292–308.

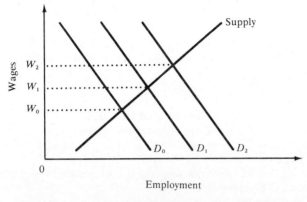

FIGURE 2.24   A Shortage Persists When the Demand Curve
Continues to Shift

The above conclusion was based on the partially *correct* analysis that a rising wage should cure a shortage in two ways. First, as wages rise, more workers will be attracted to the occupation in question. Second, the increased wage dampens demand by firms. What the conclusion *missed*, however, is that a shortage can continue despite rising wages if the demand curve *continues to shift* to the right (or the supply curve continues to shift to the left).

To illustrate this point, suppose that the market for engineers begins in equilibrium, but that a shortage occurs when the demand for engineers shifts to the right for some reason. (As Figure 2.24 shows, the demand curve would shift from D_0 to D_1.) Suppose further that it takes a year or two for firms and workers to adjust to the shortage. (A longer adjustment period can cause other problems, which will be discussed in the Chapter 9 section on "cobweb models.") Workers need time to perceive the salary increases and shift occupational plans. Firms need time to discover that their problem of unfilled vacancies is not a random event and to initiate wage increases as a response. However, if no further changes in demand or supply occur, wages would rise to W_1 in a year or two, and the shortage would be over.

Suppose, though, that in the year or two after the *initial* shift in demand, the demand curve shifts *again* (to D_2, say). Figure 2.24 shows how the rise in wages to the level of W_1 would not alleviate the shortage, because after this second shift W_2 is the market-clearing wage. A shortage would continue to exist, and it would persist as long as the demand curve continued to move out and as long as the adjustment to it by firms and workers was not instantaneous!

Something like this pattern appears to have caused the prolonged shortage of engineers in the 1950s. The shortage was felt most acutely among research and development (R&D) engineers and was the apparent result of an increase in R&D expenditures by the federal government. As these expenditures continued to increase, the market never had time to fully adjust before the next increase was felt.[18] The market was not failing; indeed, engineering salaries and employment levels were rising just as theory predicts! The market was simply being asked to

---

[18]Arrow and Capron, "Dynamic Shortages and Price Rises."

facilitate a *series* of changes in demand, and the adjustment to one change was not completed before the next one was felt.

REVIEW QUESTIONS

1. The Central Intelligence Agency (CIA) finds out that compensation for coal miners in the Soviet Union is rising much faster than compensation in general in that country. It knows that the Soviet labor market is free in the sense that it relies on incentives (not compulsion) in the allocation process.

   What can the CIA infer from this sharp rise in mining wages? Can it infer that coal output is increasing? Explain your answers.
2. Analyze the impact of the following changes on wages and employment in a given occupation:
   a. A fall in the danger of the occupation.
   b. An increase in product demand.
   c. Increased wages in other occupations.
3. What would happen to the wages and employment levels of engineers if government expeditures on research and development programs were to fall? Show the effect graphically.
4. Suppose a particular labor market were in equilibrium. What could happen to cause the equilibrium wage to fall? If all money wages rose each year, how would this market adjust?

SELECTED READINGS

Dunlop, John T., and Galenson, Walter, eds. *Labor in the Twentieth Century*. New York: Academic Press, 1978.

Rottenberg, Simon. "On Choice in Labor Markets." *Industrial and Labor Relations Review* 9,2 (January 1956):183–99. Lampman, Robert J. "On Choice in Labor Markets: Comment." *Industrial and Labor Relations Review* 9,4 (July 1956):629–36. "On Choice in Labor Markets: Reply." *Industrial and Labor Relations Review* 9,4 (July 1956):636–41.

Yett, Donald. *An Economic Analysis of the Nursing Shortage*. Lexington, Mass.: Lexington Books, 1975.

3

The Demand
for Labor

The demand for labor is a derived demand. In most cases, employers hire labor not for the direct satisfaction that such action brings them, but rather for the contribution they believe labor can make towards producing some product for sale. Not surprisingly, then, employers' demand for labor is a function of the characteristics of demand in the product market. It is also a function of the characteristics of the production process—more specifically, the ease with which labor can be substituted for capital and other factors of production. Finally, the demand for labor is a function not only of the price of labor, but also of the prices of other factors of production. This chapter and the next will illustrate how knowledge of characteristics of the demand for labor can be used in various policy applications.

For the purpose of making or evaluating social policy, the demand for labor has two important features. The first is that it can be shown theoretically—and demonstrated empirically—that labor-demand curves slope downward. This chapter discusses the downward-sloping nature of the demand-for-labor curve. The second is that the quantity of labor demanded has varying *degrees of responsiveness* to changes in the wage. While the quantity of labor demanded always declines as the wage increases, this decline is larger in some cases than in others. For most policy issues, the degree of responsiveness is of critical importance. Thus, Chapter 4 will discuss the forces that determine this responsiveness and suggest ways policymakers can make some guesses about the degree of responsiveness when explicit empirical estimates are not available.

When the demand for labor is analyzed, two sets of distinctions are typically made. First, one must specify whether one is concentrating on demand by *firms* or on the demand curves for an entire *market*. As noted in Chapter 2, firm and market labor-demand curves have different properties, although both slope downward. Second, one must specify the *time* period for which the demand curve is drawn: the short run or the long run. The *short run* is defined as a period over which a firm's capital stock is fixed; the only input that is free to be varied is labor. The *long run* is defined as a period over which a firm is free to vary all factors of production, in this case both labor and capital. This distinction between short run and long run is a conceptual one, and the two concepts do not necessarily correspond closely to any actual period of calendar time. For example, an owner of a steel mill may find that it takes several years to construct a new steel plant, in which case anything less than two years might be considered the short run. In contrast, the owner of a small firm that hires people to shovel driveways may find that he can vary his capital stock instantaneously (by buying new shovels). In this case, the firm may never face the short run; it will always be involved in making decisions about both labor and capital! However, in spite of the fact that the short run and long run do not correspond neatly to specified calendar periods of time, the distinction does allow us to be more specific about the different forces that influence the demand for labor.

A SIMPLE MODEL OF LABOR DEMAND

Our analysis of the demand for labor will begin with a simple model that yields very basic, but fundamental, behavioral predictions. To simplify the discussion, this model is derived using the four assumptions noted below. Later on in the chapter, two of the assumptions will be dropped to see what difference they make. A third assumption will be dropped in Chapter 5 and the fourth in Chapter 13.

The Assumptions

Our first assumption is that employers seek to maximize *profit* (the difference between the revenue they take in from the sales of their product and their costs of production). This is a standard assumption of positive economics, but it is not absolutely necessary to derive the fundamental conclusion of the chapter—namely, that the demand curve for labor is a downward sloping function of the wage rate.[1] We shall relax this assumption in Chapter 13 when we consider the demand for labor in the public sector.

Second, we shall initially assume that firms employ two homogeneous factors of production—labor and capital—in their production of goods and services. That is, we assume that there is a two-factor *production function* that indicates how various amounts of labor (L) and capital (K) can be combined to produce output (Q):

$$Q = f(L, K) \tag{3.1}$$

In equation (3.1) f stands for "a function of" and is used to represent a *general* mathematical relationship between Q and the factors of production. The *specific* relationship between Q and the two factors of production depends on the technology utilized. Later in this chapter we shall relax this two-factor assumption, noting that there are many categories of labor. Firms also use other inputs besides *capital* (defined as machinery, equipment, and structures) in their production process,

---

[1]Totally impulsive or random demand patterns are consistent with downward-sloping demand curves if people or firms have limited resources—a point made by Gary Becker in "Irrational Behavior and Economic Theory," *Journal of Political Economy* 70,1(February 1962):1–13.

**TABLE 3.1 The Marginal Product of Labor
in a Hypothetical Car Dealership
(capital held constant)**

Number of Salespersons	Total Cars Sold	Marginal Product of Labor
0	0	
1	10	10
2	21	11
3	26	5

including materials and energy. Chapter 4 will discuss issues relating to energy usage.

Third, we shall assume that the hourly wage cost is the only cost of labor. We shall initially ignore the existence of hiring and training costs, as well as those fringe benefit costs (like holiday pay, vacation pay, and sick leave as well as many forms of social insurance) that do not vary with weekly hours of work. By ignoring these costs here and assuming that the length of the work week is fixed, we gloss over the distinction between the number of employees a firm hires and the total number of person hours[2] of labor it employs. In Chapter 5 we shall drop our simplifying assumption and consider the question of how the firm determines its optimal work week—as well as how hiring, training, and nonvariable fringe-benefit costs affect the demand for labor.

Finally, we shall initially assume that both a firm's labor market and its product market are competitive. If the firm's labor market is competitive, we can treat the wage rate that it must pay its workers as given; if its product market is competitive, we can treat the product price it faces as given. (Both of these assumptions are relaxed later in the chapter.) The following analyses of labor demand by the firm, in both the long and the short run, are primarily verbal. The derivation of demand curves through graphic analysis is presented in the appendix to this chapter.

Short-Run Demand for Labor by Firms

In the short run, when a firm's capital stock (K) and production function are not free to vary, the number of units of output that a firm produces can change only if it changes the number of units of labor that it employs—see equation (3.1). The additional output that can be produced by a firm when it employs one additional unit of labor, with capital held constant, is called the *marginal product of labor* (MP_L). For example, if a car dealership can sell 10 cars a month with one salesperson and 21 cars a month with two, the marginal product of hiring one salesperson is 10 and the marginal product of hiring the second is 11 cars per month. If a third equally persuasive salesperson were hired and sales rose to 26 per month, the marginal product of hiring the third salesperson is 5 cars per month. These hypothetical data are summarized in Table 3.1.

---

[2]Person hours, also called labor hours, are calculated by multiplying the number of employees times the average length of work week per employee.

Table 3.1 shows that adding an extra salesperson increased output (cars sold) in each case. As long as output *increases* as labor is added, labor's marginal product (the change in output brought about by adding another unit of labor) is *positive*. In our example, however, the marginal product of labor increased at first (from 10 to 11), but then fell (to 5). Why?

The initial rise in marginal product is *not* because the second salesperson is better than the first; we ruled out this possibility by our assumption (stated above) that labor is homogeneous. Rather, the rise could be the result of the two generating promotional ideas or helping each other out in some way. Eventually, however, as more salespeople are hired, the marginal product of labor must fall. A fixed building (remember capital is held constant) can contain only so many customers, and thus each additional increment of labor produces progressively smaller increments of output. This law of *diminishing marginal returns* is an empirical proposition that derives from the fact that as employment expands, each additional worker has a progressively smaller share of the capital stock to work with.

For expository convenience, we shall assume that the marginal product of labor is always decreasing.[3] Figure 3.1 shows a marginal product of labor schedule (MP_L) for a representative firm. In this figure the marginal product of labor is tabulated on the vertical axis and the number of units of labor employed on the horizontal axis. The negative slope of the schedule indicates that each additional unit of labor employed produces a progressively smaller (but still positive) increment in output.

The marginal product of labor is measured as units of added output per unit increase of labor. Suppose we denote the money (nominal) wage rate that the firm pays per unit of labor by W and its product price per unit of output by P. These variables have dimensions of dollars per unit of labor and dollars per unit of output, respectively. Thus, the *real wage rate* that the firm pays—its money wage divided by its price level (W/P)—also has the dimension *units of output per unit of labor*.

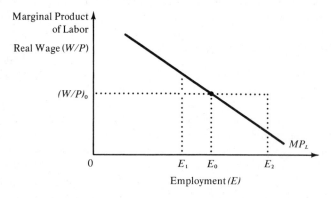

FIGURE 3.1   Demand for Labor in the Short Run

---

[3]We lose nothing by this assumption, because we show later in this section that a firm will never be operated at a point where its marginal product of labor schedule is increasing.

For example, if a woman is paid $10 per hour and the product she makes sells for $2, she gets paid, from the firm's point of view, five units of output per hour (10 ÷ 2). These five units represent her real wage, and because the real wage and the marginal product of labor are both measured in the same dimension, we can plot both on the vertical axis of Figure 3.1.

In the short run, a firm's demand-for-labor curve coincides with the downward-sloping portion of its marginal-product-of-labor schedule. This result arises from the assumption that firms seek to maximize profit. In order to accomplish this objective, a firm should employ labor up until the point that the marginal revenue (or additional revenue) it receives from hiring the last employee is just equal to its marginal (or additional) cost of employing that worker. Since a firm's profit is simply equal to revenues minus costs, if its marginal revenue exceeds its marginal cost, overall profits can be increased by expanding employment. Analogously, if its marginal revenue is less than its marginal cost, a firm is losing money on the last unit of labor hired, and it could increase its profit by reducing employment. As a result, the only employment level that is consistent with profit maximization is that level at which the marginal revenue of hiring the last unit of labor (MR_L) is just equal to its marginal cost (MC_L):

$$MR_L = MC_L. \tag{3.2}$$

Given the assumptions that we have made, the marginal cost of a unit of labor is simply the money wage rate (W) that must be paid. The marginal revenue obtained from hiring an additional unit of labor, or labors' *marginal revenue product* (*MRP*), is equal to the value of the additional output produced. *MRP* equals the marginal product of labor multiplied by the additional revenue that is received per unit of output (*MR*):

$$MR_L = MRP = (MP_L) \cdot (MR). \tag{3.3}$$

Because we assumed that the firm sells its output in a competitive market—and hence that product price does not vary with output—the additional revenue per unit of output is simply the firm's product price (P). Thus, for firms that operate in competitive output markets, the marginal revenue product obtained from an additional unit of labor equals the product price for the firm's output multiplied by its marginal product of labor:

$$MRP = P \cdot (MP_L). \tag{3.4}$$

The marginal revenue of labor is just equal to its marginal cost, and profits are maximized by the competitive firm, at the point at which the marginal revenue product equals the money wage:

$$P \cdot (MP_L) = W. \tag{3.5}$$

Dividing both sides of equation (3.5) by the firm's product price yields an alternative way of stating the profit-maximizing condition, which is that labor should be hired until its marginal product equals the real wage:

$$MP_L = \frac{W}{P}. \tag{3.6}$$

Given any real wage (by the market), the firm should thus employ labor to the point at which the marginal product of labor just equals the real wage. In other words, *the firm's demand for labor in the short run is equivalent to the downward-sloping segment of its marginal-product-of-labor schedule.*[4] To see that this is true, pick any real wage—for example, the real wage denoted by $(W/P)_0$ in Figure 3.1. We have asserted that the firm's demand for labor is equal to its marginal-product-of-labor schedule and consequently that the firm would employ E_0 employees. Now suppose that a firm initially employed E_2 workers as indicated in Figure 3.1, where E_2 is any employment level greater than E_0. At the employment level E_2, the marginal product of labor is less than the real wage rate; the marginal cost of the last unit of labor hired is therefore greater than its marginal revenue product. As a result, profit could be increased by reducing the level of employment. Similarly, suppose instead that a firm initially employed E_1 employees, where E_1 is *any* employment level less than E_0. Given the specified real wage $(W/P)_0$, the marginal product of labor is greater than the real wage rate at E_1—and consequently the marginal revenue that an additional unit of labor produces is greater than its marginal cost. As a result, a firm could increase its profit level by expanding its level of employment.

Hence, to maximize profit, given any real wage rate, a firm should stop employing labor at the point at which any additional labor would cost more than it would produce. This profit-maximization rule implies two things. First, the firm should employ labor up to the point at which its real wage equals the marginal product of labor—but not beyond that point. Second, its profit-maximizing level of employment lies in the range where its marginal product of labor is *declining*. (If $W/P = MP_L$ but MP_L is *increasing*, then adding another unit of labor will create a situation in which marginal product *exceeds* W/P. As long as adding labor causes MP_L to exceed W/P, the profit-maximizing firm will continue to hire labor. It will only stop hiring when an extra unit of labor would reduce MP_L below W/P, which will only happen when MP_L is declining. Thus, the only employment levels that could possibly be consistent with profit maximization are those in the range where MP_L is decreasing.)

The demand curve for labor can therefore be thought of in two equivalent ways. It may be thought of as the *downward-sloping section of the firm's marginal-product-of-labor schedule*—in which case it indicates how many units of labor will be hired at each *real wage*. Alternatively, it can be thought of as the *downward-sloping portion of the firm's marginal revenue product of labor schedule*—which is simply the *marginal product* schedule multiplied by *marginal revenue* (or product price, for a competitive firm). In this second case, the labor demand curve indicates the profit-maximizing level of employment for any given *nominal* or *money* wage. Which version of the demand curve one employs depends solely on analytical convenience because they are equivalent alternatives. In Example 3.1, which reviews some important aspects of the demand for labor in a concrete way, it is more convenient to express the demand curve in terms of marginal revenue product of labor.

---

[4]One should add here, "provided that the firm's revenue exceeds its labor costs." Above some real wage level this may fail to occur, and the firm will go out of business (employment will drop to zero).

Example 3.1

Store Detectives and the Optimal Rate of Shoplifting

At a business conference one day, a department store executive boasted that his store had reduced theft to 1 percent of total sales. A colleague shook her head slowly and said, "I think that's too low. I figure it should be about 2 percent of sales."

How can more shoplifting be better than less? The answer is based on the fact that reducing theft is costly in itself. A profit-maximizing firm will not want to take steps to reduce shoplifting if the added costs it must bear in so doing exceed the value of the savings it generates.

The table below shows a hypothetical marginal revenue product (*MRP*) schedule for department-store detectives. Hiring one detective would, in this example, save $50 worth of thefts per hour. Two detectives could save $90 worth of thefts each hour, or $40 more than hiring just one. The *MRP* of hiring a second detective is thus $40. A third detective would add $20 worth more to thefts prevented, and thus add $20 more to revenues.

Number of Detectives on Duty During Each Hour Store is Open	Total Value of Thefts Prevented per Hour	Marginal Value of Thefts Prevented per Hour (MRP)
0	$ 0	$—
1	50	50
2	90	40
3	110	20
4	115	5
5	117	2

The *MRP* does *not* decline from $40 to $20 because the added detectives are incompetent; in fact, we shall assume that all are equally alert and well trained. *MRP* declines, in part, because surveillance equipment (capital) is fixed; with each added detective, there is less equipment per person. However, the *MRP* also declines because it becomes progressively harder to generate savings. With just a few detectives, the only thieves caught will be the more obvious, less-experienced shoplifters. As more detectives are hired, it becomes possible to prevent theft by the more expert shoplifters, but they are harder to detect and fewer in number. Thus, *MRP* falls because theft prevention becomes more difficult once all those who are easy to catch are apprehended.

To draw the demand curve for labor, we need to determine how many detectives the store will want to employ at a given wage. For example, at a wage of $50 per hour, how many detectives will the store want? Using the *MRP* = *W* criterion, it is easy to see that the answer is "one." At $40 per hour, the store would want to hire two, and at $20 per hour the number demanded would be three. The demand for labor curve that summarizes the store's profit-maximizing employment of detectives is shown in the accompanying graph.

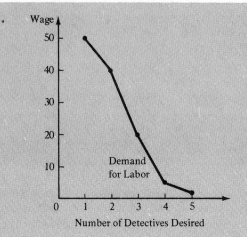

The graph illustrates a fundamental point: the demand for labor curve in the short run slopes downward because it *is* the *MRP* curve—and the *MRP* curve slopes downward because of diminishing marginal productivity. The demand curve and the *MRP* curve coincide, as demonstrated by the fact that if one were to graph the *MRP* schedule in the table, one would arrive at exactly the same curve as in our graph. When one is hired, *MRP* is $50; when two are hired, *MRP* is $40; and so forth. Since *MRP* always equals *W* for a profit maximizer who takes wages as given, the *MRP* and labor demand curves expressed as functions of the money wage must be the same.

Another point to be made in this example is that there is some level of shoplifting that the store finds more profitable to tolerate than to eliminate. At high wages for store detectives, this level will be higher than at lower wages. To say the theft rate is too low thus implies that the marginal costs of crime reduction exceed the marginal savings generated, and the firm is therefore failing to maximize profits.

It is important to emphasize that the marginal product of any individual is *not* a function solely of his or her personal characteristics. Figure 3.1 and Example 3.1 demonstrate that the marginal product of a worker depends upon the number of employees the firm has already hired. Similarly, an individual's marginal product depends upon the size of the firm's capital stock; increases in the firm's capital stock shift the entire marginal-product-of-labor schedule up. It is therefore incorrect to speak of an individual's productivity as an immutable factor that is associated only with his or her characteristics, independent of the characteristics of the other inputs he or she has to work with.

Marginal productivity and the allocation of baseball players. The fact that one's marginal productivity is not independent of other inputs being used helps explain the allocation of certain professional baseball players across the various teams. Before 1975, professional baseball players were bound to the team for which they played. They could choose not to play baseball, of course, but they could not choose the baseball team for which they would play. Being bound to a team naturally limited their options and held down their salaries. Other teams could not bid them away from the teams to which they were bound; a player could change teams only if both owners involved agreed on the terms on which the player would be sold or traded to the new team.

In 1975 a labor-relations ruling was issued (later followed by a collective-bargaining agreement) that allowed certain players to become *free agents*, which meant that they could sell their services to any team. Owners initially objected to the free-agent system. One argument they advanced was that it would harm the competitive balance among the teams by enabling the best and richest teams to grab up all the star players. Our observations about marginal productivity and profit-maximization can be used to evaluate and refute the owners' contention about competitive imbalance.

If team owners are profit maximizers, they will hire a star only if the extra revenue he will generate is greater than his salary. That is, the star's *MRP* must not be lower than his wage. If a team is *already* loaded with stars, an additional good player will not bring in very much in terms of added revenues. However, if a team has no star, or very few, the addition of the *same* good player will quite possibly generate a lot of added revenue. Thus, because the *MRP* of a star will probably be lower, *other things equal*, on the best teams, these teams will tend to be the least willing to put up money for the star free agents. Capital stock is one of the "other things" that must be held equal for this prediction to hold, however. For example, if team quality is held constant, one's *MRP* will be higher on teams that have larger stadiums and larger television markets.

The above considerations suggest that the teams that will bid most aggressively for the free agents will be those that tend to have poorer records or are located in areas with large potential markets. Although there are instances to the contrary, it is interesting to note that 31 of the first 46 "star-quality" free agents (through 1984) signed with teams that had poorer records than the team they were on—and of the remaining 15, 7 signed with teams located in larger markets.[5] Thus, free agency has not had, nor could it be expected to have, harmful effects on the competitive balance of professional baseball teams. If anything, it has helped equalize the distribution of talent across teams.

Objections to the marginal productivity theory of demand.

Two kinds of objections are sometimes raised to the theory of labor demand introduced in this section. The first is that firms do not know what labor's MP_L is, that almost no employer can ever be heard uttering the words "marginal revenue product of labor," and that the theory assumes a degree of sophistication on the part of employers that just is not there. This objection can be answered as follows: Whether employers can verbalize the profit-maximization conditions or not, they must instinctively *know* them to survive in a competitive environment. Competition will "weed out" employers who are not good at generating profits, just as competition

---

[5]The authors are indebted to Theo Smith and his enormous collection of baseball cards for these data.

will weed out pool players who do not understand the intricacies of how speed, angles, and spin affect the motion of bodies through space. Yet one could canvas the pool halls of America and probably not find one player who could verbalize Newton's laws of motion! The point is that firms can *know* rules without being able to verbalize them. Those that are not good at maximizing profits will not last very long in competitive markets. Conversely, those that survive, whether they can verbalize the general rules or not, *do* know how to maximize profits.

The second objection to the marginal productivity theory of demand is that in many cases it seems that adding labor while holding capital constant would not add to output at all. For example, one secretary and one typewriter can produce output, but it might seem that adding a second secretary while holding the number of typewriters constant could produce nothing extra, since that secretary would have no machine on which to work. The answer to this objection is that the second secretary could address envelopes by hand—a slower process, but one that would free the secretary at the typewriter to type more letters per day. The two secretaries could trade off using the typewriter, so that neither became fatigued to the extent that mistakes increased and typing speeds slowed down. The second secretary could also answer the telephone and in other ways expedite work. Thus, even with technologies that seem to require one machine per person, labor will generally have an *MRP* greater than zero (capital held constant).

Example 3.2
Coal Mining

That wage increases have both a *scale effect* and a *factor substitution effect*, both of which tend to reduce employment, is widely known—even by many of those pushing for higher wages. John L. Lewis was president of the United Mine Workers during the 1920s, 1930s, and 1940s, when wages for miners were increased considerably with full knowledge that this would induce the substitution of capital for labor. Lewis explained:

> Primarily the United Mine Workers of America insists upon the maintenance of the wage standards guaranteed by the existing contractual relations in the industry, in the interests of its own membership. . . . But in insisting on the maintenance of an American wage standard in the coal fields the United Mine Workers is also doing its part, probably more than its part, to force a reorganization of the basic industry of the country upon scientific and efficient lines. The maintenance of these rates will accelerate the operation of natural economic laws, which will in time eliminate uneconomic mines, obsolete equipment, and incompetent management. . . .
>
> The policy of the United Mine Workers of America will inevitably bring about the utmost employment of machiney of which coal mining is physically capable. . . . Fair wages and American standards of living are inextricably bound up with the progressive substitution of mechanical for human power. It is no accident that fair wages and machinery will walk hand-in-hand.

SOURCE: John L. Lewis, *The Miners' Fight for American Standards* (Indianapolis: The Bell Publishing Company, 1925), pp. 40, 41, 108.

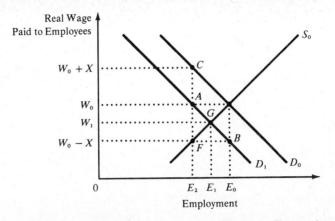

FIGURE 3.2 **Who Bears the Burden of an Employer-Financed Payroll Tax?**

Market Demand Curves

The demand curve (or schedule) for an individual firm indicates how much labor that firm will want to employ at each real wage level. A *market demand curve* (or schedule) is just the *summation* of the labor demanded by all firms in a particular labor market at each level of the real wage.[6] If there are three firms in a certain labor market, and if at $(W/P)_0$ Firm A wants 12 workers, Firm B wants 6, and Firm C wants 20, then the market demand at $(W/P)_0$ is 38 employees. More important, because market demand curves are so closely derived from firm demand curves, they too will *slope downward* as a function of the real wage. When the real wage falls, the number of workers that existing firms want to employ increases. In addition, the lower real wage may make it profitable for new firms to enter the market. Conversely, when the real wage increases, the number of workers that existing firms want to employ decreases, and some firms may be forced to cease operations completely.

Figure 3.2 shows a hypothetical market demand-for-labor curve (D_0) and a labor supply curve (S_0). (Disregard the curve labeled D_1 for the moment.) The supply curve has been drawn as an upward-sloping function of the real wage, since higher real wages induce more individuals to enter this labor market. In this competitive labor market, the equilibrium real wage (W_0) and employment (E_0) levels are determined by the intersection of the labor demand and supply curves. If the real wage were lower than W_0, the number of workers that employers would want to hire would exceed the number of individuals who wanted to work. Employ-

---

[6] If firm demand curves are drawn as a function of the money wage, they represent (as we noted) the downward-sloping portion of the firms' marginal revenue product curves. In a competitive industry, the price of the product is "given" to the firm, and thus at the firm level the marginal revenue product of labor has imbedded in it a given product price. When aggregating labor demand to the *market* level, product price can no longer be taken as given, and the aggregation is no longer a simple summation. However, the market demand curves drawn against money wages, like those drawn as a function of real wages, slope downward—which at this point is all that is important.

ers, facing unfilled positions, would be forced to raise their real wage offers to eliminate the job vacancies. In contrast, if the real wage were above W_0, employers would face an excess supply of applicants. The number of individuals willing to work would exceed the number of employees firms wanted to hire, and employers would eventually realize that they could reduce their real wage offers and still attract the necessary workers.[7]

Policy Application: Who Bears the Burden of the Payroll Tax?

In the United States several social insurance programs are financed by payroll taxes. Employers, and in some cases employees, make mandatory contributions of a fraction of the employees' salaries, up to a maximum level (or taxable wage base), to the social insurance trust funds. For example, the social security retirement, disability, and medicare programs (OASDHI) are financed by a payroll tax paid by both employers and employees, while in most states unemployment insurance and workers' compensation insurance programs are financed solely by payroll-tax payments made by employers. It is not clear just why payroll taxes on *employers* are so heavily used in the social insurance area. There seems to be a prevailing notion that such taxes result in employers' "footing the bill" for the relevant programs, but this is not necessarily the case.

With our simple labor market model, we can show that the party making the social insurance payment is not necessarily the one that bears the burden of the tax. Suppose for expository convenience that only the employer is required to make payments and that the tax is a fixed dollar amount (X) per employee, rather than a percentage of payroll. Now consider the demand curve D_0 in Figure 3.2, which is drawn in such a way that desired employment is plotted against the real wage *employees receive*. Prior to the imposition of the tax, the wage employees receive is the same as the wage employers pay. Thus, if D_0 were the demand curve before the tax was imposed, it would have the conventional interpretation of indicating how much labor a firm would be willing to hire at any given wage. However, *after* imposition of the tax, employer wage costs would be X above what employees received. Thus, if employees received W_0, employers would face costs of $W_0 + X$. They would no longer demand E_0 workers; rather, because their costs were $W_0 + X$, they would demand E_2 workers. Point A would become a point on a *new* demand curve, formed when demand shifted down because of the tax (remember, the wage on the vertical axis of Figure 3.2 is the wage *employees receive*, not the wage employers pay). Only if employee wages fell to $W_0 - X$ would the firm want to continue hiring E_0 workers—for then *employer* costs would be the same as before the tax. Thus, point B would also be on the new, shifted demand curve. Note that, with a tax of X, the new demand curve (D_1) is parallel to the old one and the vertical distance between the two is X.

Now the tax-related shift in the demand curve to D_1 implies that there would be an excess supply of labor at the previous equilibrium real wage of W_0. This surplus

---

[7]The reduction in real wages need not occur through a reduction in money wages. Rather, all that is required during a period when prices are rising is that money wages remain constant or rise less rapidly than product prices.

of labor would create downward pressure on the real wage, and this downward pressure would continue to be exerted until the wage fell to W_1, the point at which the quantity of labor supplied just equaled the quantity demanded. At this point, employment would also have fallen to E_1. Thus, *employees* bear part of the burden of the payroll tax in the form of *lower wage rates and lower employment levels*. The lesson is clear: the party legally liable to make the contribution (the employer) is not necessarily the one that bears the full burden of the actual cost.

Figure 3.2, however, does suggest that employers bear at least *some* of the tax, because the wages received by employees do not fall by the full amount of the tax ($W_0 - W_1$ is smaller than X, which is the vertical distance between the two demand curves). The reason for this is that, with an upward-sloping supply curve, employees withdraw labor as their wages fall, and it becomes more difficult for firms to find workers. If wages fell to $W_0 - X$, the withdrawal of workers would create a labor shortage that would serve to drive wages to some point (W_1 in our example) between W_0 and $W_0 - X$. Only if the labor supply curve were *vertical*—meaning that lower wages have no effect on labor supply—would the *entire amount of the tax* be shifted to workers in the form of a decrease in their wages by the amount of X, as shown in panel a of Figure 3.3.

FIGURE 3.3   Conditions That Affect the Shifting of an Employer Payroll Tax

In general, the extent to which the labor *supply curve* is sensitive to wages determines the proportion of the employer payroll tax that gets shifted to employees' wages. The less responsive labor supply is to changes in wages, the higher the proportion of the tax that gets shifted to workers in the form of a wage decrease. Panel a of Figure 3.3 shows that a payroll tax on the employer will depress employee wages more with supply curve S_0' than with supply curve S_0'' (the wage corresponding to point L is lower than that corresponding to point M). It must also be pointed out, however, that to the degree employee wages do *not* fall, employment levels *will*: employment losses with supply curve S_0'' are larger than with curve S_0'. When employee wages do not fall much in the face of an employer payroll tax increase, employer labor costs are increased—and this increase reduces the quantity of labor they demand.

The other major influence on the extent to which payroll taxes are shifted to employees is the shape of the demand curve. If the demand curve were very sensitive to changes in labor costs, there would be relatively large employment losses and strong downward pressures on employee wages. On the other hand, if employer demand were not very responsive to labor costs, both employment losses and employee wage changes would be small. These two conclusions are illustrated by the two sets of demand curves in panel b of Figure 3.3. The wage and employment levels for each initial demand curve (D_0 and D_0') are assumed to be the same (W_0 and E_0). When an employer payroll tax of X is imposed, it shifts *both demand curves down by the vertical distance of* X, so that the new curves are D_1 and D_1'. Point N, which lies on the demand curve D_1', where employment is relatively insensitive to wages, is a lot closer to W_0 and E_0 than is point R—the intersection between the supply curve and the demand curve D_1, where demand is more sensitive to wages.

A number of empirical studies have sought to ascertain what fraction of employers' payroll tax costs are actually passed on to employees in the form of lower wages or lower wage increases. Although the evidence is by no means unambiguous, two recent studies concluded that less than half of employers' payroll tax contributions are actually shifted onto labor in the form of real wage decreases.[8]

MODIFIED MODELS OF LABOR DEMAND

Monopoly in the Product Market

We have assumed so far that firms take product prices as given. If a firm faced a downward-sloping demand curve for its output—so that as it expanded employment and output, its product price fell—then the marginal revenue (MR) it received from the last unit of output it produced would not be the product price (P). Rather, the marginal revenue would be less than the product price because the lower price

---

[8]Ronald G. Ehrenberg, Robert Hutchens, and Robert S. Smith, *The Distribution of Unemployment Insurance Benefits and Costs*, Technical Analysis Paper No. 58, ASPER, U.S. Department of Labor, October 1978; Daniel Hamermesh, "New Estimates of the Incidence of the Payroll Tax," *Southern Economic Journal* 45 (February 1979): 1208–19.

applied to all units it sold, not just the marginal unit. As a result, equations (3.5) and (3.6) do *not* define the demand for labor in the presence of product market monopoly.

A monopoly trying to maximize profits and facing a competitive *labor* market will hire workers until its marginal revenue product (MRP) equals the wage rate:

$$MRP = (MR)(MP_L) = W. \qquad (3.7)$$

Now one can express the demand for labor in the short run in terms of the real wage by dividing both sides of equation (3.8) by the firm's product price, P, to obtain

$$\frac{MR}{P} \cdot MP_L = \frac{W}{P}. \qquad (3.8)$$

Since marginal revenue is always less than a monopoly's product price, the ratio (MR/P) in equation (3.8) is less than one. As such, the demand-for-labor curve for a firm that has monopoly power in the output market will lie below and to the left of the demand for labor curve for an *otherwise identical* firm that takes product price as given. Put another way, just as output is lower under monopoly than it is under competition, other things equal, so is the level of employment.

The *wage* rates that monopolies pay, however, are not necessarily different from competitive levels even though *employment* levels are. An employer with a product market monopoly may still be a very small part of the market for a particular kind of employee, and thus be a *price taker* in the labor market even though a *price maker* in the product market.[9] For example, a local utility company might have a product market monopoly, but it would have to compete with all other firms to hire secretaries and thus would have to pay the going wage.

There are circumstances, however, in which economists suspect that product market monopolies might pay wages that are *higher* than competitive firms would pay.[10] The monopolies that are legally permitted to exist in the United States are regulated by governmental bodies in an effort to prevent them from exploiting their favored status and earning monopoly profits. This regulation of profits, it can be argued, gives monopolies incentives to pay higher wages than they would otherwise pay for two reasons.

First, regulatory bodies allow monopolies to pass on the costs of doing business to consumers. Thus, while unable to maximize profits, the managers of a monopoly can enhance their *utility* by paying high wages and passing the cost along to consumers in the form of higher prices. The ability to pay high wages makes a manager's life more pleasant by making it possible to hire people who might be more attractive or personable or have other characteristics managers find desirable.

Second, monopolies that are as yet unregulated may not want to attract attention to themselves by earning the very high profits usually associated with monop-

---

[9]A *price taker* is someone who is such a small part of a particular market that he or she cannot influence market price. Thus, to such a person, the market price is a given. A *price maker* is someone with enough monopoly power that he or she can influence prices.

[10]For a full statement of this argument, see Armen Alchian and Reuben Kessel, "Competition, Monopoly, and the Pursuit of Money," H. G. Lewis, ed., *Aspects of Labor Economics* (Princeton, N.J.: Princeton University Press, 1962).

oly. They, too, may therefore be induced to pay high wages in a partial effort to "hide" their profits. The excess profits of monopolies, in other words, may be partly taken in the form of highly preferred workers—paid a relatively high wage rate—rather than in the usual monetary form.

The evidence on monopoly wages, however, is not very clear as yet. Some studies suggest that monopolies *do* pay higher wages than competitive firms for workers with the same education and experience, while others find no such evidence.[11]

Monopsony in the Labor Market

When only one firm is the buyer of labor in a particular labor market, such a firm is called a *monopsonist*. Because the firm is the only demander of labor in this market, it can influence the wage rate. Rather than being a *price (wage) taker* and facing the horizontal labor supply curve that competitive firms are confronted with, monopsonists face an upward-sloping supply curve. The supply curve confronting them, in other words, is the *market* supply curve. To expand its work force, a monopsonist must increase its wage rate. (In contrast, a competitive firm can expand its work force while paying the prevailing market wage as long as that wage is not below market-clearing levels.)

The unusual aspect of a *firm's* being confronted with an upward-sloping labor supply curve is that the *marginal cost of hiring labor exceeds the wage*. If a competitive firm wants to hire 10 workers instead of 9, the hourly cost of the additional worker is equal to the wage rate. If a monopsonist hires 10 instead of 9, it must pay a higher wage to all workers *in addition to* paying the bill for the added worker. For example, suppose that a monopsonist could get 9 workers if it paid $7 per hour but that if it wished to hire 10 workers it would have to pay a wage of $7.50. The labor cost associated with 9 workers would be $63 per hour (9 times $7), but the labor cost associated with 10 workers would be $75 per hour (10 times $7.50). Hiring the additional worker would cost $12 per hour—far more than the $7.50 wage rate![12]

The fact that the marginal cost of hiring labor is above the wage rate affects the labor market behavior of monopsonists. To maximize profits, we know that any firm should hire labor until the point at which marginal revenue product equals marginal cost. Hence, the monopsonist should hire workers up to the point at which labor's marginal revenue product equals the marginal cost of hiring additional workers (MC_L),

$$MRP_L = MC_L. \tag{3.9}$$

[11]James Dalton and E. J. Ford, "Concentration and Labor Earnings in Manufacturing and Utilities," *Industrial and Labor Relations Review* (October 1977), pp. 45–60; Ronald Ehrenberg, *The Regulatory Process and Labor Earnings* (New York: Academic Press, 1979); Leonard W. Weiss, "Concentration and Labor Earnings," *American Economic Review* 56, 1 (March 1966): 96–117.

[12]We assume here that the monopsonist does not know which workers it can hire for $7 per hour and which workers could only be hired at $7.50. All it knows is that if it wants to hire 10 workers it must pay $7.50, while if it wants to hire 9 it can pay only $7.00. Therefore, all workers get paid the same wage.

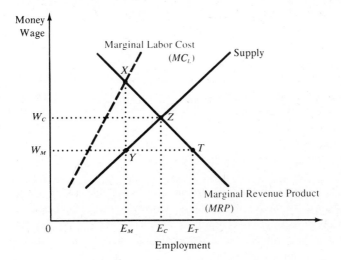

FIGURE 3.4 The Effects of Monopsony

Since the marginal cost of hiring labor for a monopsonist is *above* the wage rate, it will stop hiring labor at some point at which marginal revenue product is above the wage rate. In terms of Figure 3.4, the monopsonist hires E_M workers because at that point marginal revenue product equals marginal labor costs (point X). However, the wage rate necessary to attract E_M workers to the firm—which can be read off the supply curve—is W_M (see point Y). Thus, wages are below marginal revenue product for a monopsonist.

If the market depicted in Figure 3.4 were competitive, each firm in the market would hire labor until marginal revenue product equaled the wage, and the marginal revenue product schedule would be the demand curve for labor.[13] Thus, the wage rate would be W_C and the employment level would be E_C. Note that in a market that is monopsonized, wages and employment levels are *below* W_C and E_C.

Examples of pure monopsony in the labor market are difficult to cite: isolated coal-mining towns or sugar plantations, where the mines or sugar companies are literally the only employers, are increasingly rare. However, some employers may be large relative to the market and may, therefore, find themselves confronted with an upward-sloping supply curve.

Some economists argue that the market for registered nurses—particularly in small towns—is partially monopsonized. Hospitals employ the majority of registered nurses, and in many small towns there is only one hospital. These hospitals, it is argued, behave like monopsonists and pay lower wages than they otherwise would.[14]

---

[13]Since a monopsonist never takes the wage rate as given, a monopsonist does not face a demand curve for labor, just as a monopolist in the product market does not face a supply curve of output.

[14]Richard Hurd, "Equilibrium Vacancies in a Labor Market Dominated by Non-Profit Firms: The 'Shortage' of Nurses," *Review of Economics and Statistics* 55, 2 (May 1973): 234–40: C. R. Link and J. H. Landon, "Monopsony and Union Power in the Market for Nurses," *Southern Economic Journal* 41 (April 1975): 649–59.

If the market for registered nurses is characterized by monopsony, this situation could help explain why the nursing shortage discussed in Chapter 2 was perceived to exist even though nursing salaries were not being bid up. At wage W_M in Figure 3.4, the monopsonized employer (the hospital in this case) will hire only E_M workers because that is where marginal revenue and marginal cost are equal. However, *if* it could do all its additional hiring at W_M, it would *like* to hire E_T. Since at W_M supply falls short of E_T, there might appear to be a shortage. In this case, then, hospitals find themselves in the position of wanting to hire more nurses at wage W_M—and being unable to do so—while at the same time being unwilling to raise wage offers necessary to increase employment beyond E_M! The shortage is thus more apparent than real.

Another market that may be monopsonized is the market for public school teachers outside of metropolitan areas.[15] However, there is not much evidence that private firms in metropolitan areas have monopsony power. Wages that these firms pay appear to be essentially unaffected by the concentration of employment in the hands of a very few employers.[16]

Long-Run Demand for Labor by Firms

In the long run, employers are free to vary their capital stock as well as the number of workers they employ. An increase in the wage rate will affect their desired employment levels for two reasons. First, wages affect employment through a *scale* or *output effect*. A profit-maximizing firm will produce up to the point at which the marginal revenue from the last unit of output produced is just equal to its marginal cost of production. Now an increase in the wage rate tends to increase the marginal cost of production without affecting the marginal revenue. As a result, at the firm's previous equilibrium level of output, marginal cost *exceeds* marginal revenue. The firm is losing money on the last units of output that it produces, and it can increase its profits after the wage increase by cutting back on its production level. Reducing output will generally cause the firm to reduce its usage both of capital and of labor.

The second reason why an increase in the wage rate affects a firm's desired employment level in the long run is that it induces *factor substitution*. To maximize profit, a firm must minimize the cost of producing whatever level of output it produces. This cost minimization is achieved when the last dollar the firm spends employing capital yields the same increment to output as the last dollar the firm spends employing labor. To illustrate this point, assume that a firm has a given level of output, Q, and is considering changing its mix of capital and labor to see if it can reduce cost. Suppose it finds that a dollar's worth of labor adds one unit of output to production, but a dollar's worth of capital adds two units to output. If it decreased its employment of labor by the equivalent of a dollar and increased its employment

---

[15]Ronald Ehrenberg and Gerald Goldstein, "A Model of Public Sector Wage Determination," *Journal of Urban Economics* 2 (April 1975): 223–45.

[16]*See* Robert L. Bunting, *Employer Concentration in Local Labor Markets* (Chapel Hill: University of North Carolina Press, 1962).

of capital by the equivalent of 50 cents, it could produce output level Q at a lower cost. The *current* mix of capital and labor in this example would clearly not be profit-maximizing, and extending this reasoning leads to the conclusion that the firm would reach its optimal mix of inputs only when an added dollar spent on (or taken away from) labor and an added dollar spent on (or taken away from) capital led to equal changes in output.

To better understand factor substitution, let C represent the rental cost per period of a unit of capital equipment. Rental cost depends upon a number of things, including the purchase price of new capital equipment, the interest rate a firm must pay on borrowed funds, and various provisions that affect the income tax treatment of firms' investment expenditures (the specific formula for C need not concern us here). Now, if a firm is to minimize the cost of producing any given level of output, it must employ labor and capital up until the point that the marginal cost of producing the last unit of output is the same regardless of whether capital or labor is employed in generating that last unit. A formal way of stating this requirement is that the wage divided by the marginal product of labor (which is the cost of producing an added unit of output using just labor) must equal the cost of capital (C) divided by the marginal product of capital (MP_K):

$$(W/MP_L) = (C/MP_K). \tag{3.10}$$

We can rewrite equation (3.10) as

$$(W/C) = (MP_L/MP_K). \tag{3.11}$$

Equation (3.11) indicates that, to minimize its cost of production, a firm must employ capital and labor up until the point that their relative marginal costs are just equal to their relative marginal productivities.

Consider what happens when wages increase and capital costs do not. The increase in W/C distorts the equality in equation (3.11), and the left-hand side is now greater than the right-hand. Since the marginal cost of producing a unit of output is now greater when a firm adds new labor than when it adds new capital, the firm has an incentive to substitute capital for labor—to increase its usage of capital and decrease its usage of labor. The increase in usage of capital leads to a decline in the marginal product of capital, while the decrease in usage of labor leads to an increase in the marginal product of labor. Eventually the equality in equation (3.11) is restored, with fewer workers employed.

More Than Two Inputs

Thus far we have assumed that there are only two inputs in the production process: capital and labor. In fact, labor can be subdivided into many categories (for example, labor can be categorized by age, race, sex, educational level, and occupation). Other inputs that are used in the production process include materials and energy. If a firm is seeking to minimize costs, in the long run it should employ all inputs up until the point that the marginal cost of producing a unit of output is the same regardless of which input is used. This generalization of equation (3.10) leads to the somewhat obvious result that the demand for *any* category of labor will be a

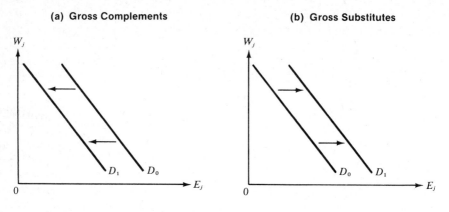

**FIGURE 3.5   Effect of an Increase in the Price of One Input *(k)*
on the Demand for Another Input *(j)***

function not only of its own wage rate, but also of the wage rates of all other
categories of labor and of the prices of capital and other inputs.

The demand curve for each category of labor will be a downward-sloping
function of the wage rate paid to workers in the category, for the reasons discussed
earlier. Changes in the prices of the other categories of labor or in the prices of other
inputs may shift the entire demand curve for a given category of labor to the right or
left. If an increase in the price of one input shifts the demand for another input to the
left, as in panel a of Figure 3.5, the two inputs are *gross complements*; if it shifts the
demand for the other input to the right, as in panel b of Figure 3.5, the two inputs
are *gross substitutes*. Whether two inputs are gross complements or gross substitutes is a function of both the production process and product demand conditions.

Consider our earlier example of a snow-removal firm. Suppose that snow could
be removed using either unskilled workers (with shovels) or skilled workers who
drove snowplows, and let us focus on the demand for skilled workers. Other things
equal, an increase in the wage of skilled workers would cause the employer to
employ fewer of them; their demand curve would be a downward-sloping function
of their wage. If the wage rate of unskilled workers increased, however, the
employer would employ fewer unskilled workers than before and more of the now
relatively cheaper skilled workers to remove any amount of snow. To the extent that
this substitution effect dominated over the scale effect (the higher unskilled wage
leading to reduced output and employment of all inputs), the demand for skilled
workers would shift to the right. In this case, skilled and unskilled workers would
be gross substitutes. In contrast, however, if the reduction in the scale of output
caused employment of skilled workers to be reduced, on balance, even though
skilled workers were being substituted for unskilled workers in the production
process, skilled and unskilled workers would be considered gross complements.[17]

---

[17]This example highlights that *both* the production process and demand conditions determine whether
two inputs are gross substitutes or complements.

Similarly, if the price of snowplows went up, the employer would want to cut back on their usage, which would result in a reduced demand at each wage for the skilled workers who drove the snowplows. This reduction would occur both because snowplows and skilled drivers were complements in production and because the scale effect served to reduce the demand for drivers. Hence, inputs that are complements in production are always gross complements.[18]

To answer many policy questions requires knowledge of the characteristics of demand curves for particular categories of labor. For example, would a subsidy paid to employers who hired teenagers significantly increase teenage employment? The answer depends upon how responsive the demand for teenage labor would be to their wage. How would an *investment tax credit*, an implicit subsidy paid to employers for increasing their capital stock, affect the employment of skilled and unskilled workers? The answer would depend upon the extent to which the cost of capital affected the demand curves for skilled and unskilled workers. To take a final example, how does government legislation that prohibits sex discrimination by requiring equal pay for equal work affect the employment levels of men and women? To answer this, one needs to know how the legislation affects men's and women's wages and then how responsive the demand curve for *each* type of labor is to *both* wage rates.

In each of the above examples, the effect of a policy depends upon the responsiveness of one variable to another. Economists refer to this responsiveness as an *elasticity*, or the percentage change in one variable induced by a given percentage change in another variable. For example, the *own-wage elasticity of demand* for a category of labor is defined as the percentage change in the demand for the category induced by a 1 percent increase in its wage rate. *Cross-wage elasticity of demand*, or the elasticity of demand for factor j with respect to the price of factor k, is defined as the percentage change in the demand for category j induced by a 1 percent change in the price of factor k. Since the magnitudes of various elasticities of labor demand are so important for policy discussions, the next chapter will be devoted to a discussion of the determinants of elasticities of demand and will apply this concept to various policy issues. The following discussion of minimum wage legislation should illustrate the use of the analytical tools developed thus far.

POLICY APPLICATION: MINIMUM WAGE LEGISLATION
History and Description

The *Fair Labor Standards Act of 1938* was the first major piece of protective labor legislation adopted at the national level in the United States. Among its provisions were a minimum wage rate, or floor, below which hourly wages could not be reduced, an overtime pay premium for workers who worked long work-weeks, and restrictions on the use of child labor. The minimum wage provisions were designed to guarantee each worker a reasonable wage for his or her work effort and thus to reduce the incidence of poverty.

---

[18]This statement assumes that all inputs are *noninferior* inputs, that an increase in output does not reduce the usage of any input. We maintain this assumption throughout.

TABLE 3.2 Minimum Wage Legislation in the United States, 1938–1984[b]

Effective Date of Minimum Wage Change	Nominal Minimum Wage	Percent of Nonsupervisory Employees Covered[a]	Minimum Wage Relative to Average Hourly Wage in Manufacturing	
			Before	After
10/24/38	$0.25	43.4	—	0.403
10/24/39	0.30	47.1	0.398	0.478
10/24/45	0.40	55.4	0.295	0.394
1/25/50	0.75	53.4	0.278	0.521
3/1/56	1.00	53.1	0.385	0.512
9/3/61	1.15	62.1	0.431	0.495
9/3/63	1.25	62.1	0.467	0.508
9/3/64	1.25	62.6		
2/1/67	1.40	75.3	0.441	0.494
2/1/68	1.60	72.6	0.465	0.531
2/1/69	1.60	78.2		
2/1/70	1.60	78.5		
2/1/71	1.60	78.4		
5/1/74	2.00	83.7	0.363	0.454
1/1/75	2.10	83.3	0.423	0.445
1/1/76	2.30		0.410	0.449
1/1/78	2.65		0.430	0.480
1/1/79	2.90		0.402	0.440
1/1/80	3.10		0.417	0.445
1/1/81	3.35		0.403	0.435

[a]Excludes executive, administrative, and professional personnel (including teachers in elementary and secondary schools) from the base. Coverage peaked at 87.3 percent of the nonsupervisory work force in September 1977. As of 1978, however, a court decision eliminated most state and local government workers from coverage. As a result, worker coverage fell from 56,100,000 in 1976 to 51,900,000 in 1978.

[b]In 1984, the nominal minimum wage was still pegged at $3.35 an hour.

When initially adopted, the minimum wage was set at $0.25 an hour and covered roughly 43 percent of all nonsupervisory wage and salary workers—primarily those employed in larger firms involved in interstate commerce (manufacturing, mining, and construction). As Table 3.2 indicates, both the basic minimum wage and coverage under the minimum wage have expanded over time. Indeed by January 1, 1981, the minimum wage was set at $3.35 an hour, and about 80 percent of all nonsupervisory workers were covered by its provisions.

It is important to emphasize that the minimum wage rate is currently specified in *nominal* terms and not in terms *relative* to some other wage or price index. Historically, this definition of minimum wage has led to a pattern of minimum wage changes that can be represented by Figure 3.6, where time is plotted on the horizontal axis and the value of the minimum wage relative to average hourly earnings in manufacturing is plotted on the vertical axis. Congress initially specifies the nominal level of the minimum wage (MW_0), which, given the level of average hourly earnings that prevail in the economy (AHE_0), leads to an initial value of the minimum wage relative to average hourly earnings (MW_0/AHE_0). Now over time

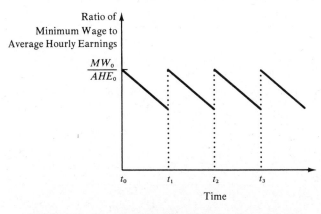

**FIGURE 3.6   Time Profile of the Minimum Wage Relative
to Average Hourly Earnings**

this relative value declines as average hourly earnings increase due to inflation or productivity growth. The reduced relative value of the minimum wage creates pressure on Congress to legislate an increase in the nominal minimum wage, and after the passage of time (point t_1 in Figure 3.6) Congress returns the relative value of the minimum wage approximately to its initial level. Over time the process is repeated, and the saw-toothed time profile of relative minimum-wage values portrayed in Figure 3.6 emerges. Although it varies from peak to peak, the value of the minimum wage relative to average hourly earnings in manufacturing after each legislated change has typically been in the range of 0.45 to 0.50 in recent years (see Table 3.2).

A Model with Uniform Coverage

Unfortunately, as with many social programs, minimum wage legislation may have unintended side effects that work against the program's goals of reducing poverty. Consider the labor market for unskilled workers and assume, initially, that all are covered by minimum wage legislation. As Table 3.2 indicates, such uniform coverage certainly would not be a reasonable assumption if we wanted to analyze minimum wage effects during the early years of the legislation. However, a model of full coverage may be more appropriate today than it once was.

Figure 3.7 represents the labor market for unskilled labor, which is in equilibrium prior to the imposition of the minimum wage with an employment level of E_0 and a *real* wage of W_0/P_0. Now suppose Congress legislates a nominal minimum wage of W_1, which is higher than W_0; this legislation will raise the real wage to W_1/P_0 and reduce the number of employees firms want to hire to E_1. Although a larger number of workers (E_2) are willing to offer their services at that wage rate, no downward pressure is exerted on the money wage because by law the wage cannot be reduced below the nominal minimum. As a result, the immediate impact of the

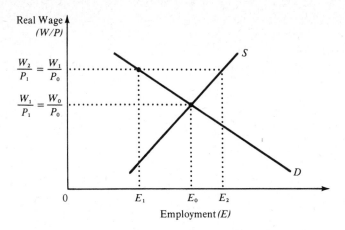

FIGURE 3.7   Minimum Wage Effects: Uniform Coverage

increase in the minimum wage is a decrease in employment and an increase in unemployment (which equals $E_2 - E_1$).[19]

Over time, the government may take actions to stimulate the economy in the hope of reducing unemployment. Such actions invariably include pursuing expansionary monetary and fiscal policy (increasing the money supply and government spending, decreasing taxes) and lead to increases in the price level. However, as the price level goes up, the real minimum wage falls, because the nominal minimum wage is being held constant. As the real wage falls, the number of workers employed increases. If Congress takes no other action but continues to pursue expansionary policies, eventually the price level will rise to P_1, where $(W_1/P_1) = (W_0/P_0)$. That is, the real value of the minimum wage will fall back to the market-clearing level, and employment will return to its initial level. While the immediate impact of the minimum wage increase was to reduce employment, over a longer period of time this employment reduction is eliminated, at the expense of a higher price level.

The story, however, does not end here. As noted above, Congress periodically increases the nominal minimum to restore its value relative to average hourly earnings. An increase, say, to W_2, where $(W_2/P_1) = (W_1/P_0)$, would again reduce employment to E_1 and create further pressure for the government to take action to reduce unemployment. What results then is a cycle of minimum wage increases

---

[19]The analysis here is somewhat oversimplified. The supply curve in Figure 3.7 indicates the number of workers who want to work at each real wage, under the assumption that any one who wants to work can find employment. However, the imposition of a minimum wage that leads to a real wage (W_1/P_0) above the market-clearing level means that not all workers who want to work at that real wage can actually find employment. This reduced probability of finding employment should reduce the actual number of workers seeking employment below the level indicated by the supply curve (E_2). As a result, the actual increase in unemployment will be less than the depicted excess supply of labor $(E_2 - E_1$ in Figure 3.7). Since this complication does not fundamentally alter any of the conclusions in this chapter, we ignore it in the analysis that follows. Jacob Mincer, in "Unemployment Effects of Minimum Wage Changes," *Journal of Political Economy* 84 (August 1976): S87–S104, has presented evidence that higher minimum wage rates do lead to reduced labor-force participation rates.

inducing short-run employment losses, inflation reducing the real value of the minimum wage and restoring employment, and then Congress increasing the nominal minimum and starting the process all over.

Periodically proposals have been introduced into Congress to tie the minimum wage to either the consumer price level or average hourly earnings; the minimum wage would automatically increase each year to maintain a constant value relative to one of these variables. If tied to the former, the net effect of the legislation would be to fix the real wage of low-skilled labor at a level such as (W_1/P_0) in Figure 3.7. Whether such a policy is desirable for low-skilled workers as a group depends upon whether the higher real wage is sufficiently high to compensate low-skilled workers for their employment losses $(E_0 - E_1)$ and upon the income support programs, such as unemployment insurance, available to unemployed workers.

What's Wrong with the Model?

Early studies of the employment effects of minimum wage legislation, conducted in the 1940s and 1950s, often found that employment *increased* after minimum wage increases. They concluded that there are no adverse effects of minimum wage legislation and that the neoclassical model presented above is all wrong.

These studies, however, do not succeed in disproving the neoclassical model for at least three reasons. First, they ignore the fact that the uniform coverage model is not applicable to the earlier period when coverage was less than complete. Second, they ignore the possibility that employers may not fully comply with increases in the minimum wage; noncompliance would reduce the employment effects of the legislated increase (the noncompliance problem will be discussed later in the chapter). Third, and most important, they ignore the fact that all the predictions from our models are made holding other factors constant. If other factors are not actually constant, changes in one or more of them may obscure the negative relationship between wages and the demand for labor.

To see the effects of such other factors, consider Figure 3.8, where for simplicity we have omitted the labor supply curve and focused on only the demand side of the market. Suppose that D_0 is the demand curve for low-skilled labor in year 0, in which year the real wage is W_0/P_0 and the employment level is E_0. Further

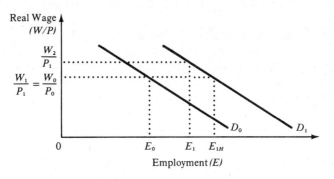

FIGURE 3.8 **Minimum Wage Effects: Growing Demand**

assume that in the absence of any change in the minimum wage, the money wage and the price level would both increase by the same percent over the next year, so that the real wage in year 1 (W_1/P_1) would be the same as that in year 0.

Now suppose that in year 1, two things happen. First, the minimum wage rate is raised to W_2, which is greater than W_1, so that the real wage increases to W_2/P_1. Second, because the economy is expanding, the demand for low-skilled labor shifts out to D_1. The result of these two changes is that employment increases from E_0 to E_1 in Figure 3.8.

Comparisons of observed employment levels, such as E_1 and E_0 above, caused early investigators to conclude that minimum wage increases had no adverse employment effects. However, this simple before/after comparison is *not* the correct one. Rather, one should ask, "How did the actual employment level in period 1 compare to the level that *would have prevailed* in the absence of the increase in the minimum wage?" Since demand grew between the two periods, this hypothetical employment level would have been E_{1H}. E_{1H} is greater than E_1, the actual level of employment in period 1, so $E_{1H} - E_1$ is the jobs loss caused by the minimum wage.

In sum, in a growing economy with complete coverage, the net effect of a one-time increase in the minimum wage is to reduce the rate of growth of employment. By focusing on only the actual employment growth, the early studies both misunderstood the implications of the neoclassical model and failed to adequately estimate the adverse employment effects of the program.[20]

A Model with Incomplete Coverage

Although minimum wage coverage has grown over time, so that today about 87 percent of all nonsupervisory workers in the private sector are covered, as recently as 1965 more than one third of private-sector workers were not covered. The major uncovered sectors then included retail trade, the service industries, and agriculture; today they include primarily employees in these industries who work for small firms. Since coverage is less than complete, it is useful to present a model of minimum wage effects under incomplete coverage. (A similar model will appear in Chapter 12 when we discuss the effects of unions on wages.)

To simplify the discussion, we shall assume:

a. That prices are constant (so we can talk interchangeably about real and money wages),
b. That the labor market for unskilled labor is characterized by a vertical supply curve such that total employment of the unskilled is E_T,
c. That this labor market has a covered and an uncovered sector, and
d. That unskilled workers move back and forth between sectors seeking jobs where the wages are highest.

---

[20]It is important to distinguish between a one-time increase in the minimum wage and recurrent increases that, because of inflation, have tended to keep the ratio of the minimum wage to the price level roughly constant after each increase in the minimum (Figure 3.7). In the case of recurrent increases, the main effect of minimum wage legislation is to decrease the average *level* of employment, rather than to decrease the average (over time) rate of growth of employment.

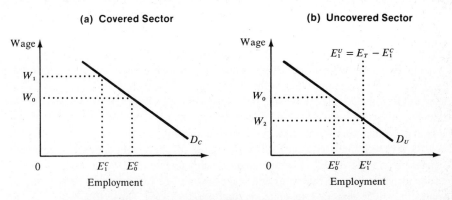

(a) Covered Sector

(b) Uncovered Sector

$$E_1^U = E_T - E_1^C$$

FIGURE 3.9   Minimum Wage Effects: Incomplete Coverage

These assumptions suggest that without a minimum wage, the wage in each sector will be the same. Referring to Figure 3.9, let us assume that this "pre-minimum" wage is W_0 and that total employment of E_T is broken down into E_0^C in the "covered" sector plus E_0^U in the other sector.

If a minimum wage of W_1 is imposed on the covered sector, all unskilled workers will prefer to work there. However, the increase in wages there, from W_0 to W_1, reduces demand, and covered-sector employment will fall from E_0^C to E_1^C. Some workers who previously had, or would have found, jobs in the covered sector must now seek work in the uncovered sector. Thus, to the E_0^U workers formerly working in the uncovered sector are added $E_0^C - E_1^C$ other workers seeking jobs there. Thus, all unskilled workers in the market who are not lucky enough to find "covered jobs" at W_1 now look for work in the uncovered sector,[21] and the supply curve to that sector becomes E_1^U $[= E_0^U + (E_0^C - E_1^C) = E_T - E_1^C]$. The increased supply of workers to that sector drives down the wage there from W_0 to W_2.

As with most laws, a partial-coverage minimum wage produces both winners and losers. The winners are those covered-sector workers who kept their jobs after the imposition of the minimum and now receive the higher minimum wage. The losers are those low-skilled workers who lost their jobs in the covered sector and now are paid lower wages in the uncovered sector. The losers also include those low-skilled workers in the uncovered sector who kept their jobs but now find their real wages depressed by the increased supply of labor to that sector. Hence, even in the context of this model, in which there are no overall employment effects, it is not obvious that the legislation is desirable on balance. The gains won by some groups must be weighed against the losses suffered by other groups before an unambiguous conclusion can be reached.

---

[21]Under some circumstances it may be rational for these unemployed workers to remain unemployed for a while and to search for jobs in the covered sector. We shall discuss this possibility—which is discussed by Jacob Mincer in "Unemployment Effects of Minimum Wage Changes," *Journal of Political Economy* 84 (August 1976): S87–S104—in Chapter 12. At this point we simply note that if it occurs, unemployment will result.

Social Losses

Besides predicting that minimum wage laws produce both gainers and losers among the poor, this chapter also predicts that such laws will create losses for society as a whole. In the case of full coverage, where government-mandated increases in the real wage create unemployment, the losses of potential output from those who are unemployed is obvious. However, there are also social losses in cases where, as in our Figure 3.9 example of partial coverage, total employment remains constant. To understand this point requires a quick review of profit-maximization principles.

A firm will hire labor until labor's marginal revenue product equals the money wage rate. In the partial coverage example above (Figure 3.9), unskilled labor— prior to imposition of the minimum wage—would be hired in both sectors to the point at which marginal revenue product equalled W_0. Thus, if a worker were transferred from one sector to the other, the value of total output would go down by W_0 in the "sending" sector and up by W_0 in the "receiving" sector. Overall output would remain unchanged by such a transfer.

After the minimum wage is imposed on the covered sector, however, employment is reduced there until labor's marginal revenue product equals W_1. Wages in the uncovered sector, in contrast, fall to W_2; employment in that sector will thus increase until labor's marginal revenue product equals W_2. The marginal revenue product in the uncovered sector is now *below* that in the covered sector (W_2 is less than W_1), so that if a worker were transferred from the uncovered to the covered sector, output could be increased! (The value of output lost in the uncovered sector by this transfer would be W_2, while the value of output gained in the covered sector would be W_1.)

Since W_1 exceeds W_2, *the value of output* could be increased by transferring labor from the uncovered to the covered sector. This transfer would occur naturally if there were no minimum wage, because workers seeking the higher-paying jobs in the covered sector would bid down wages there and employment in that sector would expand. Transfers of labor would stop when the wages in each sector were equalized—and as we have shown above, when wages are equal in both sectors of the unskilled labor market, there are no further gains to be made by transfers of labor between the two sectors of that market.

With a minimum wage, however, labor *cannot* transfer out of the sector with the lower wage (and lower marginal revenue product) to the higher-wage sector. Wages in the latter sector cannot legally fall, and therefore employment cannot expand there. A beneficial transfer of resources is blocked, and social losses occur. Put differently, total output could be increased with no change in our total resources merely by transferring labor from one sector to another, and the effective prevention of this transfer by the minimum wage law implies social losses.

The Effects of Monopsony

This analysis of the minimum wage law has assumed that firms are sufficiently small that their hiring decisions do not affect the market wage for low-skilled workers. That is, we have assumed there is no monopsony in the low-skilled labor market. While this assumption is probably appropriate for most employers of low-skilled labor, it is theoretically possible that monopsony exists in some communities. To

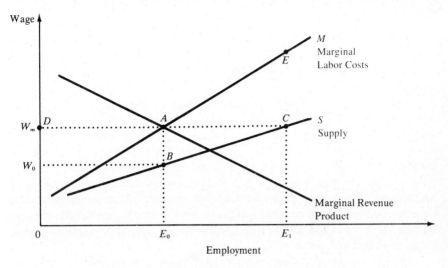

FIGURE 3.10   Minimum Wage Effects Under Monopsony

understand the effects of a minimum wage on monopsonized markets, consider a "full coverage" model (with only one employer and no uncovered sector).

You will recall from our earlier discussion of the demand for labor by monopsonists that their marginal labor costs are above the wage rate. In maximizing profits, they choose an employment level (E_0 in Figure 3.10) at which marginal labor costs equal marginal revenue product (point A in Figure 3.10). The wage corresponding to employment level E_0 in Figure 3.10 is W_0.

Suppose now that a minimum wage of W_m is set in Figure 3.10. This minimum wage prevents the firm from paying a wage less than W_m and effectively creates a horizontal portion in the supply curve facing the firm (which is now $DACS$). The firm's marginal cost of labor curve is now $DACEM$, because up to employment level E_1 the marginal costs of labor are equal to W_m. The firm, which maximizes profits by equating marginal revenues with marginal costs (which equation now occurs at point A), will still hire E_0 workers, but it will pay them W_m instead of W_0. Moreover, if the minimum were set at a wage rate *between* W_0 and W_m, wages *and* employment would increase.

The apparent conclusion that a minimum wage can increase wages without reducing employment in a monopsonized market is subject to two qualifications. First, in the context of Figure 3.10, the minimum wage cannot be set above W_m if employment is to remain at least as large as E_0. Above W_m there would be employment losses. The second qualification is that the firm must remain in business in order for employment not to fall. While an employer may be the only buyer of labor in a particular market, the employing firm may also have many competitors in its product market. If its product market is competitive, its level of profits will be "normal"—which means that if profits were to fall, the firm would find it could earn more profits in another line of business. If, in our initial example (Figure 3.10), wages rose from W_0 to W_m and employment remained at E_0, firm profits would clearly fall. If the fall were large enough, the firm might go out of business and all E_0 workers would lose their jobs.

Empirical Evidence

Labor economists have devoted much effort to empirically estimating the magnitudes of the effects of minimum wage legislation on the employment levels of various age/race/sex groups.[22] Although the precise magnitudes of the relationships have yet to be pinned down, it is now widely agreed that increases in minimum wages do reduce employment opportunities, especially among teenagers. The studies use different data and often ask slightly different questions. Virtually all agree, however, that employment opportunities for teenagers have been reduced by the minimum wage—although the size of the reduction is in doubt. A careful review of the evidence concluded that a 10 percent increase in the minimum wage would reduce teenage employment by 1 to 3 percent and the employment of young adults (ages 20 to 24) by a somewhat smaller amount.[23] There is no consensus, however, on the effects of minimum wage legislation on other adults, perhaps because far fewer adults are directly affected by the minimum wage (most have wages in excess of the minimum).

Somewhat surprisingly, most research on the minimum wage has focused on its unintended adverse outcome: reductions in employment. Very little research has addressed the question of whether minimum wage legislation is achieving its intended goal of reducing the incidence of poverty. The few studies that have considered this issue have found that minimum wage legislation has only a minor effect on the distribution of income.[24] This finding is not surprising because not all low-wage workers are members of low-income families; many low-wage workers, especially among teenagers, are second earners in middle- or upper-income families. Put another way, minimum wage legislation directly affects low-wage workers, not necessarily low-income families.

The Fair Labor Standards Act has a certain political sanctity because it was the first piece of protective labor legislation adopted at the federal level; very few people would seriously argue for the repeal of the minimum wage law today. Instead, given the estimates of the adverse effects of the legislation on youth employment opportunities, many people have recently argued that a youth differential or youth subminimum wage should be instituted. Lower wages for teens, they claim, would help alleviate the teenage unemployment problem. While there

---

[22]For a very readable, albeit critical, nontechnical survey of economic research on the minimum wage, *see* Sar Levitan and Richard Belous, *More Than Subsistence: Minimum Wages for the Working Poor* (Baltimore: Johns Hopkins Press, 1979). For a more sympathetic view, see Finis Welch, *Minimum Wages: Issues and Evidence* (Washington, D.C.: American Enterprise Institute, 1978). A more recent but somewhat more technical treatment is Charles Brown, Curtis Gilroy, and Andrew Kohen, "The Effect of the Minimum Wage on Employment and Unemployment," *Journal of Economic Literature* 20 (June 1982): 487–528.

[23]Brown *et al.*, "The Effect of the Minimum Wage on Employment and Unemployment."

[24]*See* Edward Gramlich, "Impact of Minimum Wages on Other Wages, Employment, and Family Incomes," *Brookings Papers on Economic Activity*, 1976–2, pp. 409–62. Other studies have examined the effect of minimum wages on teenagers' educational decisions, which, as we discuss in Chapter 9, have important implications for the distribution of income. See, for example, Ronald Ehrenberg and Alan Marcus, "Minimum Wages and Teenagers' Enrollment-Employment Outcomes: A Multinomial Logit Model," *Journal of Human Resources* 17 (Winter 1982):39–58.

Example 3.3

Minimum Wages in Developing Countries

Does minimum wage legislation reduce employment? The answer depends at least partially on the *level* at which the minimum is set relative to prevailing wages. While in the United States the minimum has stayed at roughly 35 to 50 percent of average hourly earnings, in developing countries the minimum is sometimes set much higher. Not surprisingly, the predictions of economic theory are often borne out in situations like the one in Zimbabwe in July 1980. As the *New York Times* reported, a Zimbabwe government decision to set a minimum wage resulted in the dismissal of thousands of workers.

SALISBURY, Zimbabwe, July 6 (Reuters)—A Government decision to set a minimum wage for workers has backfired for thousands with dismissals reported throughout the country.

Officials of the ruling party of Prime Minister Robert Mugabe said today that in the Salisbury area alone more than 5,000 workers were dismissed before the minimum wage bill went into effect last Tuesday.

Worst hit, according to the officials, were domestic servants and farm workers for whom the minimum had been set at $45 a month. Employees in the commercial and industrial sectors, where the minimum had been fixed at $105 a month, have also been dismissed. The officials said that every party office in the country was dealing with hundreds of workers each day complaining of unfair dismissal.

SOURCE: *New York Times*, July 7, 1980.

appears to be empirical support for this proposition, opponents, including organized labor, point out that reducing the wages of teenagers relative to adults would encourage employers to increase their employment of teenagers at the expense of reduced adult employment. Estimates of the likely magnitude of this substitution are required before intelligent policy decisions can be made with respect to a youth differential (see Chapter 4); in the language of some opponents, one should not substitute parents' unemployment for that of their children.

Two additional reasons may help explain why increases in the minimum wage have not had as dramatic effects on employment or the distribution of income as one might expect. First, there is no reason to suspect that all employers comply with the legislation; only limited resources are expended on enforcement of the legislation, and the penalties for employers found to be not complying (paying covered workers less than the minimum) are quite small. Indeed, certain evidence suggests that only 50 to 70 percent of covered workers who would have earned less than the minimum in the absence of the law are actually paid the minimum. The remainder are paid a wage that is illegally low.[25]

---

[25]Orley Ashenfelter and Robert S. Smith, "Compliance with the Minimum Wage Law," *Journal of Political Economy* 87 (April 1979): 335–50.

Second, our discussion has ignored the possibility that employers may respond to increases in the minimum wage by lowering other forms of nonwage compensation that are *not* covered by the minimum wage law.[26] As Chapter 11 will discuss, nonwage forms of compensation (including holiday, vacation, and sick-leave pay, health insurance, and retirement benefits) now comprise a large, and still growing, share of total compensation. To the extent that employers can respond to increases in the minimum wage by lowering the levels (or more likely the rates of growth) of these benefits, increases in the minimum will have smaller effects on total labor costs—and hence smaller employment effects—than one might have otherwise anticipated.

REVIEW QUESTIONS

1. "It is generally agreed that the volunteer army is a dismal failure—the quality of volunteers is down and the number is not sufficient to meet desired force levels. The only alternatives are to raise the pay of volunteers or to reinstitute a draft system. Since the cost to society is clearly higher in the former than in the latter case, from an economist's perspective a draft system would be preferable." Evaluate this position.
2. Suppose the government were to subsidize the wages of all women in the population by paying their *employers* 50 cents for every hour they work. What would be the effect on the wage rate women received? What would be the effect on the unsubsidized wage employers paid? (The unsubsidized wage would be the wage women received less 50 cents.)
3. The Occupational Safety and Health Administration promulgates safety and health standards. These standards typically apply to machinery, which is required to be equipped with guards, shields, etc. An alternative to these standards is to require the employer to furnish personal protective devices to employees—such as earplugs, hard hats, and safety shoes. *Disregarding* the issue of which alternative approach offers greater protection from injury, what aspects of each alternative must be taken into account when analyzing the possible *employment* effects of the two approaches to safety?
4. Assume that there are two grades of professional football players. There are a limited number of "stars," whom the fans most want to watch, and an unlimited number of "nonstars." There are too few stars to fully staff each team, but there are enough for a few to be on each team if an owner decides to hire them.
   a. Assume that football teams keep all the "gate" and TV revenues they generate and that players are free to choose their teams at the end of any season. Do stars earn more than nonstars? How are the wages of each group determined?
   b. Continue to assume that players are free to choose their teams, but assume now that teams agree to share *all* their gate and TV revenues equally (they put them into a "pool" and divide it equally among the team owners). What happens now to salaries of stars and nonstars?

---

[26]For a discussion of this point, see Walter J. Wessels, *Minimum Wages, Fringe Benefits, and Working Conditions* (Washington, D.C.: American Enterprise Institute, 1981).

SELECTED READINGS

Ashenfelter, Orley, and Smith, Robert. "Compliance with the Minimum Wage Law." *Journal of Political Economy*, April 1979.

Levitan, Sar, and Belous, Richard. *More Than Subsistence: Minimum Wages for the Working Poor*. Baltimore: Johns Hopkins University Press, 1979.

Mincer, Jacob. "Unemployment Effects of Minimum Wage Changes." *Journal of Political Economy*, August 1976.

Report of the Minimum Wage Study Commission. Washington, D.C.: U.S. Government Printing Office, 1981.

Rottenberg, Simon, ed. *The Economics of Legal Minimum Wages*. Washington, D.C.: American Enterprise Institute, 1981.

Welch, Finis. *Minimum Wages: Issues and Evidence*. Washington, D.C.: American Enterprise Institute, 1978.

APPENDIX 3A
Graphic Derivation of a Firm's Labor Demand Curve

Chapter 3 described verbally the derivation of a firm's demand-for-labor curve. This appendix will present the *same* derivation graphically. This graphic representation permits a more rigorous derivation, although our conclusion that demand curves slope downward in both the short and long run remains unchanged.

THE PRODUCTION FUNCTION

Equation (3.1) presented the "production function" as $f(L,K)$. Figure 3A.1 illustrates this production function graphically and depicts several aspects of the production process.

Consider the convex curve labeled $Q = 100$. Along this line, every combination of labor (L) and capital (K) produces 100 units of output (Q). That is, the combination of labor and capital at point $A(L_a, K_a)$ generates the same 100 units of output as the combinations at points B and C. Because each point along the $Q = 100$ curve generates the same output, that curve is called an *isoquant* (*iso* = "equal"; *quant* = "quantity").

Two other isoquants are shown in Figure 3A.1 ($Q = 150$, $Q = 200$). These isoquants represent higher levels of output than the $Q = 100$ curve. The fact that these isoquants indicate higher output levels can be seen by holding labor constant at L_b (say) and then observing the different levels of capital. If L_b is combined with K_b in capital, 100 units of Q are produced. If L_b is combined with K_b', 150 units are produced (K_b' is greater than K_b). If L_b is combined with even more capital (K_b'', say), 200 units of Q could be produced.

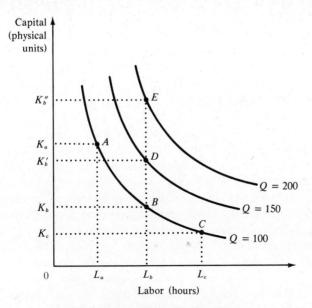

FIGURE 3A.1   A Production Function

Note that the isoquants in Figure 3A.1 have *negative* slopes, reflecting an assumption that labor and capital are substitutes. If, for example, we cut capital from K_a to K_b, we could keep output constant (at 100) by increasing labor from L_a to L_b. Labor, in other words, could be substituted for capital to maintain a given production level.

Finally, note the *convexity* of the isoquants. At point A, the $Q = 100$ isoquant has a steep slope, suggesting that to keep Q constant at 100, a given decrease in capital could be accompanied by a *modest* increase in labor. At point C, however, the slope of the isoquant is relatively flat. This flatter slope means that the same given decrease in capital would require a much *larger* increase in labor for output to be held constant. The decrease in capital permitted by a given increase in labor in order for output to be held constant is called the *marginal rate of technical substitution* (*MRTS*) between capital and labor. Symbolically, the *MRTS* can be written as

$$MRTS = \frac{\Delta K}{\Delta L} \mid \overline{Q} \qquad (3A.1)$$

where Δ means "change in" and $\overline{Q}$ means "output is held constant." The *MRTS* is *negative*, because if L is increased, K must be reduced to keep Q constant.

Why does the absolute value of the marginal rate of technical substitution diminish as labor increases? When labor is highly used in the production process and capital is not very prevalent (point C in Figure 3A.1), there are many jobs that capital can do. Labor is easy to replace; if capital is increased, it will be used as a substitute for labor in parts of the production process where it will have the highest payoff. As capital becomes progressively more utilized and labor less so, the few remaining workers will be doing jobs that are hardest for a machine to do, at which point it will take a lot of capital to substitute for a worker.[1]

DEMAND FOR LABOR IN THE SHORT RUN

Chapter 3 argued that firms will maximize profits in the short run (K fixed) by hiring labor until labor's marginal product (MP_L) is equal to the real wage (W/P). The reason for this decision rule is that the real wage represents the *cost* of an added unit of labor (in terms of output), while the marginal product is the *output* added by the extra unit of labor. As long as the firm, by increasing labor (K fixed), gains more in output than it loses in costs, it will continue to hire employees. The firm will stop hiring when the marginal cost of added labor exceeds MP_L.

The requirement that $MP_L = W/P$ in order for profits to be maximized means that the firm's labor demand curve in the short run (in terms of the *real* wage) is identical to its marginal-product-of-labor schedule (refer back to Figure 3.1). Remembering that the marginal product of labor is the extra output produced by one-unit increases in the amount of labor employed, holding capital constant, consider the production function displayed in Figure 3A.2. Holding capital constant at K_a, the firm can produce 100 units of Q if it employs labor equal to L_a. If labor is increased to L_a', the firm can produce 50 more units of Q; if labor is increased from L_a', to L_a'', the firm can produce an additional 50 units. Notice, however, that the required increase in labor to get the latter 50 units of added output, $L_a'' - L_a'$, is larger than the extra labor required to produce the first 50-unit increment ($L_a' - L_a$). This difference can only mean that as labor is increased when K is held constant, each successive labor-hour hired generates progressively smaller increments in output. Put differently, Figure 3A.2 graphically illustrates the diminishing marginal productivity of labor.

Why does labor's marginal productivity decline? Chapter 3 explained that labor's marginal productivity declines because, with K fixed, each added worker has less capital (per capita) with which to work. Is this explanation proven in Figure 3A.2? The answer is, regrettably, "No." Figure 3A.2 is drawn *assuming* diminishing marginal productivity. Renumbering the isoquants could produce a different set of marginal productivities. (To see this, change $Q = 150$ to $Q = 200$, and change $Q = 200$ to $Q = 500$. Labor's marginal productivity would then rise.) However, the logic that labor's marginal product must eventually fall as labor is increased, holding buildings, machines, and tools constant, is very compelling. Further, as Chapter 3 pointed out, even if MP_L rises initially, the firm will only stop hiring labor

---

[1] Only a decade or two ago, most long-distance telephone calls were made through operators. Over time, operators have been increasingly replaced by a very capital-intensive direct-dialing system. Those operators who remain employed, however, perform tasks that are the most difficult for a machine to perform—handling collect calls, dispensing directory assistance, and acting as "trouble shooters" when problems arise.

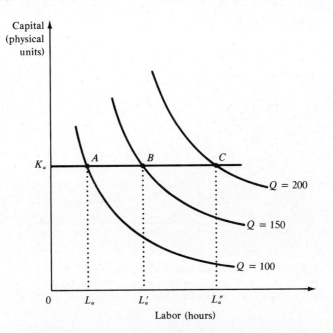

FIGURE 3A.2 The Declining Marginal Productivity of Labor

in the range where MP_L is declining; as long as MP_L is above W/P and *rising*, it will pay to continue hiring.

The assumptions that MP_L declines eventually and firms hire until $MP_L = W/P$ are the basis for the assertion that a firm's short-run demand curve for labor slopes downward. The graphic, more rigorous derivation of the demand curve in this appendix confirms and supports the verbal analysis in the chapter. However, it also emphasizes more clearly than a verbal analysis can that the downward-sloping nature of the short-run labor-demand curve is based on an *assumption*—however reasonable—that MP_L declines as employment is increased.

DEMAND FOR LABOR IN THE LONG RUN

Recall that a firm maximizes its profits by producing at a level of output (Q^*) where marginal cost equals marginal revenue. That is, the firm will keep increasing output until the addition to its revenues generated by an extra unit of output just equals the marginal cost of producing that extra unit of output. Because marginal revenue, which is equal to output *price* for a competitive firm, is not shown in our graph of the production function, the profit-maximizing level of output cannot be shown either. However, continuing our analysis of the production function can illustrate some important aspects of the demand for labor in the long run.

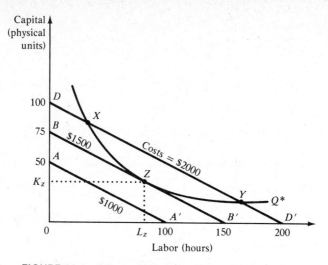

FIGURE 3A.3   **Cost Minimization in the Production of Q***
(Wage = $10 per Hour; Price of a Unit
of Capital = $20)

Conditions for Cost Minimization

In Figure 3A.3, the profit-maximizing level of output is Q^*. How will the firm combine labor and capital to produce Q^*? It can only maximize profits if it produces Q^* in the least expensive way; that is, it must minimize the costs of producing Q^*. To better understand the characteristics of cost minimization, refer to the three *isoexpenditure* lines—AA', BB', DD'—in Figure 3A.3. Along any one of these lines the costs of employing labor and capital are equal.

For example, line AA' represents total costs of $1000. Given an hourly wage (W) of $10 per hour, the firm could hire 100 hours of labor and incur total costs of $1000 if it used no capital (point A'). In contrast, if the price of a unit of capital (C) is $20, the firm could produce at a total cost of $1000 by using 50 units of capital (point A). All the points between A and A' represent combinations of L and K that, at $W = \$10$ and $C = \$20$, cost $1000 as well.

The problem with the isoexpenditure line of AA' is that it does not intersect the isoquant Q^*, implying that Q^* cannot be produced for $1000. At prices of $W = \$10$ and $C = \$20$, the firm cannot buy enough resources to produce output level Q^* and hold total costs to $1000. The firm can, however, produce Q^* for a total cost of $2000. Isoquant DD', representing expenditures of $2000, intersects the Q^* isoquant at points X and Y. The problem with these points, however, is that they are not cost-minimizing; Q^* can be produced for less than $2000.

Since isoquant Q^* is convex, the cost-minimizing combination of L and K in producing Q^* will come at a point where an isoexpenditure line is *tangent* to the isoquant (that is, just barely touches isoquant Q^* at only one place). Point Z, where labor equals L_Z and capital equals K_Z, is where Q^* can be produced at minimal cost, *given* that $W = \$10$ and $C = \$20$. No lower isoexpenditure curve touches the isoquant, meaning that Q^* cannot be produced for less than $1500.

An important characteristic of point Z is that the slope of the isoquant at point Z and the slope of the isoexpenditure line are the same (the slope of a curve at a given point is the slope of a line tangent to the curve at that point). The slope of the isoquant at any given point is the *marginal rate of technical substitution* as defined in equation 3A.1. Another way of expressing equation 3A.1 is:

$$MRTS = \frac{-\Delta K/\Delta Q}{\Delta L/\Delta Q} \qquad (3A.2)$$

Equation 3A.2 directly indicates that the *MRTS* is a ratio reflecting the reduction of capital required to *decrease* output by one unit if enough extra labor is hired so that output is tending to *increase* by one unit. (The ΔQs in equation 3A.2 cancel each other and keep output constant.) Pursuing equation 3A.2 one step farther, the numerator and denominator can be rearranged to obtain the following:[2]

$$MRTS = \frac{-\Delta K/\Delta Q}{\Delta L/\Delta Q} = -\frac{\Delta Q/\Delta L}{\Delta Q/\Delta K} = -\frac{MP_L}{MP_K}, \qquad (3A.3)$$

where MP_L and MP_K are the marginal productivities of labor and capital, respectively.

The slope of the *isoexpenditure line* is equal to the negative of the ratio W/C (in Figure 3A.3 W/C equals 10/20, or 0.5).[3] Thus, at point Z, where Q^* is produced in the minimum-cost fashion, the following equality holds:[4]

$$MRTS = -\frac{MP_L}{MP_K} = -\frac{W}{C} \qquad (3A.4)$$

Equation 3A.4 is exactly the same as equation 3.11 in the text.

The economic meaning, or logic, behind the characteristics of cost minimization can most easily be seen by stating the *MRTS* as $-\dfrac{\Delta K/\Delta Q}{\Delta L/\Delta Q}$ (see equation 3A.3) and equating this version of the *MRTS* to $-\dfrac{W}{C}$:

$$-\frac{\Delta K/\Delta Q}{\Delta L/\Delta Q} = -\frac{W}{C}, \text{ or} \qquad (3A.5)$$

$$\frac{\Delta K}{\Delta Q} \cdot C = \frac{\Delta L}{\Delta Q} \cdot W \qquad (3A.6)$$

Equation 3A.6 makes it very plain that to be minimizing costs, the cost of producing an extra unit of output by adding only labor must equal the cost of producing that extra unit by employing only additional capital. If these costs differed, the company could reduce total costs by expanding its use of the factor with which output can be increased more cheaply and cutting back on its use of the other factor. Any point where costs can still be reduced while Q is held constant is obviously not a point of cost minimization.

---

[2]This is done by making use of the fact that dividing one number by a second one is equivalent to *multiplying* the first by the *inverse* of the second.

[3]Note that 10/20 = 50/100, or $0A/0A'$.

[4]The negative signs on each side of (3A.4) cancel each other and can therefore be ignored.

The Substitution Effect

If the wage rate, which was assumed to be $10 per hour in Figure 3A.3, goes up to $20 per hour (holding C constant), what will happen to the cost-minimizing way of producing output of Q^*? Figure 3A.4 illustrates the answer that common sense would suggest: total costs rise, and more capital and less labor are used to produce Q^*. At W = $20, 150 units of labor can no longer be purchased if total costs are to be held to $1500; in fact, if costs are to equal $1500, only 75 units of labor can be hired. Thus, the isoexpenditure curve for $1500 in costs shifts from BB' to BB'' and no longer is tangent to isoquant Q^*. Q^* can no longer be produced for $1500, and the minimum-cost way of producing Q^* will rise. In Figure 3A.4 we assume that it rises to $2250 (isoexpenditure line EE' is the one tangent to isoquant Q^*).

Moreover, the increase in the cost of labor relative to capital induces the firm to use more capital and less labor. Graphically, the old tangency point of Z is replaced by a new one (Z'), where the marginal productivity of labor is higher relative to MP_X, as equation 3A.4 explained. Point Z' is reached (from Z) by adding more capital and reducing employment of labor. The movement from L_Z is L'_Z is the *substitution effect* that is generated by the wage increase.

FIGURE 3A.4   Cost Minimization in the Production of Q^* (Wage = $20 per Hour; Price of a Unit of Capital = $20)

**FIGURE 3A.5   The Substitution and Scale Effects
of a Wage Increase**

The Scale Effect

The fact that Q^* can no longer be produced for $1500, but instead involves at least
$2250 in costs, will generally mean that it is no longer the profit-maximizing level
of production. The new profit-maximizing level of production will be less than Q^*
(how much less cannot be determined unless we know something about the product
demand curve).

Suppose that the profit-maximizing level of output falls from Q^* to Q^{**} in
Figure 3A.5. Since all isoexpenditure lines have the new slope of -1 when $W =$
$20 and $C = $20, the cost-minimizing way to produce Q^{**} will lie on an
isoexpenditure curve parallel to EE'. We find this cost-minimizing way to produce
Q^{**} at point Z'', where an isoexpenditure curve *(FF')* is tangent to Q^{**}.

The *overall* response in the employment of labor to an increase in the wage rate
has been a fall in labor usage from L_Z to L_Z''. The decline from L_Z to L_Z' is called the
substitution effect, as we have noted. It results because the *proportions* of K and L
used in production change when the ratio of wages to capital prices *(W/C)* changes.
The *scale effect* can be seen as the reduction in employment from L_Z' to L_Z'' wherein
the usage of both K and L is cut back solely because of the reduced *scale* of
production. Both effects are simultaneously present when wages increase and
capital prices remain constant, but as Figure 3A.5 emphasizes, the effects are
conceptually distinct and occur for different reasons. Together, these effects lead us
to assert that the long-run demand for labor curve slopes downward.

4

Elasticities of Demand for Labor

The previous chapter stressed that the effects of various government policies on employment and wage levels depend crucially on the magnitudes of labor demand elasticities. Given the importance of these elasticities, this chapter will present an extended discussion of the determinants of the elasticities of demand for labor, will summarize the available empirical evidence on the magnitudes of these elasticities, and will then illustrate the importance of this knowledge in a number of policy applications.

ELASTICITY AND CROSS-ELASTICITY DEFINED

The Own-Wage Elasticity of Demand

Recall that the *own-wage elasticity of demand* for a category of labor is defined as the percentage change in its employment *(E)* induced by a 1 percent increase in its wage rate *(W)*:

$$\eta_{ii} = \frac{\%\Delta E_i}{\%\Delta W_i} \qquad (4.1)$$

In equation (4.1), we have used the subscript i to denote category of labor i, η to represent elasticity, and the notation $\%\Delta$ to represent "percentage change in." Since the last chapter showed that labor demand curves slope downward, an increase (decrease) in the wage rate will lead employment to decrease (increase); the own-wage elasticity of demand is a negative number. What is at issue is its magnitude. The larger its *absolute* value (its magnitude, ignoring its sign), the larger will be the percentage decline in employment associated with any given percentage increase in wages.

Labor economists often focus on whether the absolute value of the elasticity of demand for labor is greater than or less than one. If it is greater than one, a 1 percent increase in wages will lead to an employment decline of greater than 1 percent; this situation is referred to as an *elastic* demand curve. In contrast, if the absolute value is less than one, the demand curve is said to be *inelastic*; a 1 percent increase in wages will lead to a proportionately smaller decline in employment.[1] If demand is elastic, aggregate earnings (defined here as the wage rate times the employment level) of individuals in the category will decline when the wage rate increases because employment falls at a faster rate than wages rise. Similarly, if demand is inelastic, aggregate earnings will increase when the wage rate is increased.

To see the importance of the magnitude of elasticity, let us return to our analysis of the minimum wage in a world with *complete coverage.* We saw in Chapter 3 that an increase in the minimum wage would lead to a decrease in employment, if other factors affecting employment were held constant. Does this result imply, from the perspective of low-wage workers as a group, that minimum wage increases are undesirable? The answer is ambiguous; it depends upon the extent to which the higher minimum wage for those workers who keep their jobs offsets the loss in employment that occurs. There are obvious equity issues involved here that make such comparisons difficult. However, *if* the own-wage elasticity of demand for low-skilled workers is inelastic, an increase in the minimum wage will lead to an increase in aggregate earnings for this group. This increase in aggregate earnings among the low-skilled implies that those who keep their jobs could compensate those who lose them and still be better off.[2] (The fact that *low-skilled* workers, as a *group, might* be made better off by a minimum wage law does not imply that the gains to *society* as a whole would exceed the losses. Chapter 3 addressed the social losses.)

Figure 4.1 shows that the flatter of the two demand curves graphed *(D₁)* has greater elasticity than the steeper *(D₂).* Beginning with any wage (*W*, for example), given wage changes (to *W'*, say) will yield greater responses in employment with demand curve D_1 than with D_2 (compare $E_1 - E_1'$ with $E_2 - E_2'$).

To speak of a demand curve as having "an" elasticity, however, is technically incorrect. Given demand curves will generally have elastic and inelastic ranges— and while we are usually just interested in the elasticity of demand in the range around the current wage rate in any market, one cannot fully understand elasticity without understanding that it can vary along a given demand curve.

To illustrate, suppose we examine the typical straight-line demand curve that we have used so often in Chapters 2 and 3 (see Figure 4.2). One feature of a straight-line demand curve is that, at *each* point along the curve, a unit change in wages induces the *same* response in terms of units of employment. For example, at any point along the demand curve shown in Figure 4.2, a $2 decrease in wages will increase employment by 10 workers.

However, the same responses in terms of *unit* changes along the demand curve do *not* imply equal *percentage* changes. To see this point, look first at the upper end

---

[1]If the elasticity just equals -1, the demand curve is said to be *unitary elastic.*

[2]Once we include transfer payments, such as unemployment insurance, in the analysis, it becomes possible for the total income of low-skilled workers (including transfer payments) to increase even if the elasticity is greater than one. See Edward Gramlich, "Impact of Minimum Wages on Other Wages, Employment, and Family Incomes," *Brookings Papers on Economic Activity*, 2 (1976).

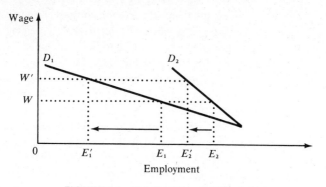

FIGURE 4.1   Relative Demand Elasticities

of the demand curve in Figure 4.2 (the end where wages are high and employment is low). A $2 decrease in wages when the base is $12 represents a 17 percent reduction in wages, while an addition of 10 workers when the starting point is also 10 represents a 100 percent increase in demand. Demand at this point is clearly *elastic*. However, if one looks at the same unit changes in the lower region of the demand curve (low wages, high employment), demand there is inelastic. A $2 reduction in wages from a $4 base is a 50 percent reduction, while an increase of 10 workers from a base of 50 is only a 20 percent increase. Since the percentage increase in employment is smaller than the percentage increase in wages, demand is seen to be inelastic at this end of the curve.

Thus, the upper end of a straight-line demand curve will exhibit greater elasticity than the lower end. Moreover, a straight-line demand curve will actually be elastic in some ranges and inelastic in others (as shown in Figure 4.2).

THE HICKS-MARSHALL LAWS OF DERIVED DEMAND

Knowledge of own-wage elasticities of demand is very important for making policy decisions. The factors that influence own-wage elasticity can be summarized by the four "Hicks-Marshall Laws of Derived Demand"—"laws" named after two distinguished British economists, Alfred Marshall and John Hicks, who are closely associated with their development.[3] These laws assert that, other things equal, the own-wage elasticity of demand for a category of labor is high under the following conditions:

1. When the price elasticity of demand for the product being produced is high,
2. When other factors of production can be easily substituted for the category of labor,
3. When the supply of other factors of production are highly elastic (that is, usage of other factors of production can be increased without substantially increasing their prices), and
4. When the cost of employing the category of labor is a large share of the total costs of production.

---

[3]John R. Hicks, *The Theory of Wages*, 2nd ed. (New York: St. Martins Press, 1966), pp. 241–47; Alfred Marshall, *Principles of Economics*, 8th ed. (London: Macmillan, 1923), pp. 518–38.

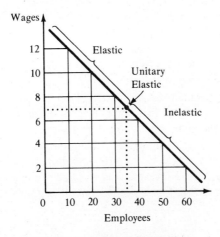

FIGURE 4.2 Different Elasticities Along a Demand Curve

Not only are these laws generally valid as an empirical proposition, but the first three can be shown to always hold. There are conditions, however, under which the final law does not hold. (Each of the laws, including the exception just mentioned, is graphically derived in the appendix to this chapter.)

In seeking to explain why these laws hold, it is useful to act as if we could divide the process by which an increase in the wage rate affects the demand for labor into two steps: First, an increase in the wage rate increases the relative cost of the category of labor in question and induces employers to use less of it and more of other inputs (the *substitution effect*). Second, when the wage increase causes the marginal costs of production to rise, there are pressures to increase product prices and reduce output, causing a fall in employment (the *scale effect*). The four laws of derived demand each deal with substitution or scale effects.

Demand for the Final Product

We noted above that wage increases cause production costs to rise and tend to result in product price increases. The greater the price elasticity of demand for the final product, the larger will be the decline in output associated with a given increase in price—and the greater the decrease in output, the greater the loss in employment (other things equal). Thus, *the greater the elasticity of demand for the product, the greater the elasticity of demand for labor will be.* One implication of this result is that, other things equal, the demand for labor at the *firm* level will be more elastic than the demand for labor at the *industry*, or market, level. For example, the product demand curves facing *individual* carpet manufacturing companies are highly elastic because the carpet of Company X is a very close substitute for the carpet of Company Y. Compared to price increases at the *firm* level, however, price increases at the *industry* level will not have as large an effect on demand because the closest substitutes for carpeting are hardwood, ceramic, or some kind of vinyl floor covering—none of which is a very close substitute for carpeting. The demand for labor is thus much more elastic for an individual carpet manufacturing firm than for the carpet manufacturing industry as a whole. (For the same reasons, the labor demand curve for a monopolist is less elastic than for an individual *firm* in a competitive industry. Monopolists, after all, face *market* demand curves for their product because they are the only seller in the particular market.)

Another implication of this first law is that *wage elasticities will be higher in the long run than in the short run*. The reason for this is that price elasticities of demand in product markets are higher in the long run. In the short run there may be no good substitutes for a product, or consumers may be locked into their current stock of consumer durables. However, after a period of time, new products that are substitutes may be introduced and consumers will begin to replace durables that have worn out.

Substitutability of Other Factors

As the wage rate of a category of labor increases, firms have an incentive to try to substitute other, now relatively cheaper, inputs for the category. Suppose, however, that there were no substitution possibilities; a given number of units of the type of labor *must* be used to produce one unit of output. In this case, there is no reduction in employment due to the substitution effect. In contrast, when substitution possibilities do present themselves, a reduction in employment owing to the substitution effect will accompany whatever reductions are caused by the scale effect. Hence, other things equal, *the easier it is to substitute other factors of production, the higher the wage elasticity of demand will be*.

Limitations on substitution possibilities need not be solely technical ones. For example, as we shall see in Chapter 12, unions often try to limit substitution possibilities by including specific work rules in their contracts (e.g., minimum crew size for railroad locomotives). Alternatively, the government may legislate limitations by specifying minimum employment levels for safety reasons (for example, each public swimming pool in New York State must always have a lifeguard present). Such collectively bargained or legislated restrictions make the demand for labor less elastic. Note, however, that substitution possibilities that are not feasible in the short run may well become feasible over longer periods of time, when employers are free to vary their capital stock. For example, if the wages of railroad workers went up, companies could buy more powerful locomotives and operate with larger trains and fewer locomotives. Likewise, if the wages of lifeguards rose, cities might build larger, but fewer, swimming pools. Both adjustments would occur only in the long run, which is another reason why the demand for labor is more elastic in the long run than in the short run.

The Supply of Other Factors

Suppose that, as the wage rate increased and employers attempted to substitute other factors of production for labor, the prices of these inputs were bid up substantially. This situation might occur, for example, if one were trying to substitute capital equipment for labor. If producers of capital equipment were already operating their plants near capacity, so that taking on new orders would cause them substantial increases in costs because they would have to work their employees overtime and pay them a wage premium, they would only accept new orders if they could charge a higher price for their equipment. Such a price increase would dampen firms' "appetites" for capital and thus limit the substitution of capital for labor.

For another example, suppose an increase in the wages of unskilled workers caused employers to attempt to substitute skilled employees for unskilled employees. If there were only a fixed number of skilled workers in an area, their wages would be bid up by employers. As in the prior example, the incentive to substitute alternative factors would be reduced, and the reduction in employment due to the substitution effect would be smaller. In contrast, if the prices of other inputs did not increase when employers attempted to increase their usage, other things equal, the substitution effect—and thus the wage elasticity of demand—would be larger.

Note again that prices of other inputs are less likely to be bid up in the long run than in the short run. In the long run, existing producers of capital equipment can expand their capacity and new producers can enter the market. Similarly, in the long run more skilled workers can be trained. This observation is an additional reason why the demand for labor will be more elastic in the long run.

The Share of Labor in Total Costs

Finally, the share of the category of labor in total costs is crucial to the size of the elasticity of demand. If the category's initial share were 20 percent, a 10 percent increase in the wage rate, other things equal, would raise total costs by 2 percent. In contrast, if its initial share were 80 percent, a 10 percent increase in the wage rate would increase total costs by 8 percent. Since employers would have to increase their product prices by more in the latter case, output, and hence employment, would fall more in that case. *Thus, the greater the category's share in total costs, the higher the wage elasticity of demand will tend to be.*[4]

The Cross-Wage Elasticity of Demand

Because firms may employ several categories of labor and capital, the demand for any one category can be affected by price changes in the others. For example, if the wages of carpenters rose, more people might build brick homes and the demand for *masons* might increase. On the other hand, an increase in carpenters' wages might decrease the overall level of home building in the economy, which would decrease the demand for *plumbers*. Finally, changes in the price of *capital* could increase or decrease the demand for workers in all three trades.

---

[4]As we noted earlier, this law does not always hold. More specifically, when it is easy for employers to substitute other factors of production for the category of labor but difficult for consumers to substitute other products for the product being produced (low price elasticity of demand), this law is reversed. A graphic demonstration of this law and its exception is given in the Appendix 4A. For a more formal treatment, see Hicks, *The Theory of Wages*.

Example 4.1

How to Finance Black Lung Benefits

In 1969 Congress passed the Coal Mine Health and Safety Act, which, among other things, made coal miners and ex-coal miners with black lung disease eligible for monthly benefits. Black lung disease, which develops when lungs become clogged with coal dust, is disabling and can lead to early death. Any coal miner found eligible in the first five years of the program was to receive benefits financed by the government, but beginning in 1974 the financing of the benefits for new recipients was to fall upon the coal-mine operator for whom the recipient last worked for at least one year.

As 1974 approached, it became clear that many coal-mine operators would buy insurance against their potential liabilities and that the insurance premiums would be charged as a fraction of the operator's *payroll* costs. These premiums, which the government feared would be large, would increase the cost of hiring labor and could have very adverse effects on the employment of coal miners. How large might these effects be?

The first step in estimating employment effects was to obtain an estimate of what the insurance premiums would be. The insurance industry estimated they would average about 11 percent of the payroll in underground mining and 7 percent of the payroll in strip (or surface) mining, where the problem of black lung disease is smaller.

The next step involved breaking the employment response into the *scale* and *substitution* effects. The share of labor in the total costs of underground mining was about 50 percent, so the insurance premiums in that sector would increase costs and prices by about 5.5 percent (in other words, there was an 11 percent increase in half of the total costs). In strip mining, labor costs were only about 25 percent of total costs, so the 7 percent premium there would increase prices by only 1.7 percent. These calculations clearly made use of data on the *labor share in total cost.*

The price increases in coal that would be caused by the insurance premiums would have two effects. First, the overall price of coal would rise and cause less of it to be used. The overall elasticity of demand for coal was estimated to be −0.5 (an inelasticity caused by difficulties in substituting oil or natural gas for coal in electric power generation). Second, because underground and strip-mined coal are good substitutes for each other, the change in their *relative* prices would cause those still using coal to increase their purchases of strip-mined coal at the expense of underground coal.

The total scale effect in the *underground-coal* sector that would take place if the 11 percent and 7 percent rates were charged was estimated to cause a 6 percent reduction in output and employment (largely because of substituting away from underground coal toward strip-mined coal). Strip mining, by virtue of the shift away from underground coal, would probably experience a 4 percent increase in employment. These calculations used estimates of the *price elasticity of demand* for both underground and strip-mined coal.

The final step in estimating the employment effects of the Black Lung Benefits Program was to estimate substitution effects. From data on the capital-labor ratios in each sector of the coal mining industry, it appeared that a 1 percent increase in the price of labor relative to the price of capital was associated with a 1 percent increase in the capital-labor ratio used in production. (Economists define the percentage change in the ratio of factor inputs associated with a 1 percent change in the relative prices of these inputs as the "elasticity of substitution.") With this information on the *substitutability of capital and labor*, it was estimated that about 4.5 percent of employment in the underground sector would be lost to capital substitution. The corresponding losses in the strip-mining sector were estimated at 3.9 percent. (The estimate of the substitution effect was made *assuming that capital prices would remain constant*. Again, this amounts to assuming that the supply curve for capital in the coal-mining industry is horizontal.)

The *overall* estimate of employment losses that would accompany the imposition of financial liability for black-lung payments on coal operators amounted to about 8.4 percent (or almost 12,000 jobs, virtually all of which were in the underground sector). This estimate implied that even if the coal industry expanded (as it did), there would be around 12,000 fewer jobs in that industry than there would otherwise have been.

The program was not implemented as originally planned, partly because there were difficulties in finding the coal-mine operators liable for benefit payments when ex-miners had last worked several years ago. The program was amended so that benefits are now paid out of a trust fund financed by the industry in general from a tax of 50 cents per ton of underground coal and 25 cents per ton of strip-mined coal.

The employment effects of a *ton tax* are different from those of an insurance premium based on wages. A ton tax would produce scale effects, of course, but because it would not raise the price of labor relative to capital, it would produce *no substitution effects*. It was estimated, in fact, that a ton tax large enough to produce the *same* revenues as the 11 percent and 7 percent payroll charges would have caused an overall job loss of only 5,200.

Saving jobs, however, is not necessarily the most appropriate criterion for choosing a means of financing the benefits. One would certainly want to use a financing scheme that provided operators with incentives to reduce the incidence of disease among their workers. One way to reduce disease is to reduce dust levels, but another is to substitute capital for labor and essentially let *machines* mine coal. An increase in payroll costs, because it does tend to increase the capital-labor ratio, might thus do more to reduce disease, other things equal, than a ton tax (assuming the machines did not create higher dust levels for those workers remaining).

SOURCE: Morris Goldstein and Robert S. Smith, "The Predicted Impact of the Black Lung Benefits Program on the Coal Industry," in Orley Ashenfelter and James Blum, eds., *Evaluating the Labor-Market Effects of Social Programs* (Princeton, N.J.: Princeton University, 1976).

The magnitude of the above effects can be summarized by examining the elasticities of demand for inputs with respect to the prices of other inputs. Recall that in the previous chapter we defined the *elasticity of demand for input j with respect to the price of input k* as the percentage change in the demand for input *j* induced by a 1 percent change in the price of input *k*. If the two inputs are both categories of labor, these *cross-wage elasticities of demand* are given by

$$\eta_{jk} = \frac{\%\Delta E_j}{\%\Delta W_k} \tag{4.2}$$

and

$$\eta_{kj} = \frac{\%\Delta E_k}{\%\Delta W_j}$$

If the cross elasticities are positive (with an increase in the price of one increasing the demand for the other), the two are said to be *gross substitutes*. If these cross elasticities are negative (and an increase in the price of one reduces the demand for the other), the two are said to be *gross complements* (refer back to Figure 3.5).

It is worth restressing that whether two inputs are *gross substitutes* or *gross complements* depends on *both* the production function and demand conditions. To see this, suppose we assume that adults and teenagers are *net substitutes,* or substitutes in production. A decrease in the teenage wage will thus have opposite effects on adult employment. On the one hand, there is a substitution effect—for a given level of output, employers will now have an incentive to substitute teens for adults in the production process and reduce adult employment. On the other hand, there is a scale effect—a lower teenage wage provides employers with an incentive to increase employment of all inputs, including adults. The magnitude of the scale effect depends on the elasticity of product demand with respect to price; the larger this elasticity is, the larger the scale effect will be.

If the scale effect proves to be smaller than the substitution effect, adult employment will move in the same direction as teenage wages and the two groups will be gross substitutes. In contrast, if the scale effect is larger than the substitution effect, adult employment and teenage wages will move in opposite directions and the two groups will be gross complements. Knowing that two groups are substitutes in production, then, is not sufficient to tell us if they are gross substitutes or gross complements.[5]

Both the sign and magnitude of cross elasticities are important for policy analysis. To return to our minimum wage example again, would the introduction of a youth subminimum, or youth differential in the minimum wage, be an effective way to increase teenage employment levels? If the own-wage elasticity of demand for youth is elastic, a youth differential of 15 percent would lead to a greater than 15

---

[5]Of course, if two groups are complements in production, both the substitution *and* scale effects suggest that a decrease in the price of one should lead to increased employment of the other. Hence, complements in production are also always gross complements.

percent increase in teenage employment.[6] The story does not end here, however, as one also needs to consider whether other groups would face adverse employment effects. If, for example, teens and adult workers were gross substitutes, employment of low-skilled adult workers would fall if a youth differential were enacted. However, if the magnitude of the elasticity were very small, the decline in adult employment would be small and this negative side effect of the policy might not be judged serious. Estimates of the cross-wage elasticity of demand of adult labor with respect to the teenage wage are thus also required to make intelligent policy decisions. As discussed below, there is evidence that the own-wage elasticity of demand for teenagers is elastic; however, evidence on the size and sign of relevant adult-teenager cross-wage elasticities is generally lacking.[7]

EMPIRICAL EVIDENCE ON WAGE ELASTICITIES OF DEMAND

Literally hundreds of studies have been published in recent years that present empirical estimates on the magnitudes of wage elasticities of demand. Some of these studies focus on the aggregate demand for labor in the economy as a whole; others focus on the demand by different industries. Some focus on the demand for different skill classes; still others focus on the demand for different age/race/sex groups. Although our knowledge in a number of these areas is not very precise, it is useful to summarize what we do know.

To draw a particular demand curve with precision requires knowledge of the factors that affect derived demand: the technological possibilities given by the production function (substitutability of capital and labor, labor share in total cost), the supply curve of capital, and the elasticity of product demand. In estimating the elasticity of demand for labor, we do not want to hold these factors constant because they are all crucial in determining the *size* of the elasticity of demand. As a practical matter, however, researchers usually have to estimate demand elasticities holding the *price of capital* constant.[8] This is tantamount to assuming that capital usage can be increased or decreased as wages change with no effect on the price at which capital is supplied; that is, capital supply curves are assumed to be horizontal. All elasticity estimates cited below make this assumption.[9]

---

[6]This actually is an overestimate since it assumes all teens earn the minimum wage. In fact, many earn significantly more; their wages would not be directly affected by a youth differential. Hence, the actual reduction in the average teenage wage would be substantially less than 15 percent.

[7]See Daniel Hamermesh and James Grant, "Econometric Studies of Labor-Labor Substitution and Their Implications for Policy," *Journal of Human Resources* 14 (Fall 1979):518–42; and Daniel Hamermesh, "The Demand for Labor in the Long Run," in Orley Ashenfelter and Richard Layard, eds., *Handbook of Labor Economics* (North-Holland Press, forthcoming).

[8]*Capital*, even in a given industry, encompasses so many machines, tools, supplies, and buildings that estimating a supply function is beyond the capability of the data usually available.

[9]Studies in which the level of *output* or the level of capital *usage* is held constant are ignored here since they assume away either scale or substitution effects.

TABLE 4.1 Representative Estimates of Long-Run Wage Elasticities of Demand, by Industry

Industry	Long-Run Wage Elasticity
Coal mining[a]	
Underground	−0.98
Surface	−0.86
Manufacturing[b]	−0.09 to −0.62
Retail trade[c]	−0.34 to −1.20
State and local government[d]	
Employees in education sector	−1.06
Noneducation employees	−0.38

[a]Derived from estimates presented in Morris Goldstein and Robert S. Smith, "The Predicted Impact of the Black Lung Benefits Program on the Coal Industry," in Orley Ashenfelter and James Blum, eds., *Evaluating the Labor-Market Effects of Social Programs* (Princeton, N.J.: Princeton University, 1976).

[b]Daniel Hamermesh, "Econometric Studies of Labor Demand and Their Applications to Public Policy," *Journal of Human Resources* (Fall 1976):507–25.

[c]Philip Cotterill, "The Elasticity of Demand for Low-Wage Labor," *Southern Economic Journal* 41 (January 1975):520–25.

[d]Orley Ashenfelter and Ronald G. Ehrenberg, "The Demand for Labor in the Public Sector," in Daniel Hamermesh, ed., *Labor in the Public and Nonprofit Sectors* (Princeton, N.J.: Princeton University Press, 1975).

The *overall*, own-wage elasticity of demand for labor in the economy as a whole is inelastic and probably in the range of −0.3.[10] This inelasticity is to be expected, because at the level of the economy *as a whole*, scale effects are likely to be small. Workers losing jobs due to wage increases will become self-employed in some cases. There are federal policies and programs designed to maintain national output and create full employment. Foreign goods and services are often very hard to substitute for domestic goods and services. For all these reasons, the *overall* wage elasticity of demand is small.

The own-wage elasticities of demand at the *industry* level tend to vary widely across industries and in the main are also inelastic. Table 4.1 presents a representative set of estimates for coal mining, manufacturing, retail trade, and the state and local government sector. That the demand for employees in underground mining (located primarily in the East) is more elastic than the demand for employees in surface or strip mining (located primarily in the West) is not unexpected. Surface mining is much more capital intensive, and labor costs are a smaller share of the total costs of production in that sector. That the estimated elasticities at the industry

[10]Daniel Hamermesh, "Econometric Studies of Labor Demand and Their Application to Policy Analysis," *Journal of Human Resources* (Fall 1976):507–25; and Hamermesh, "The Demand for Labor in the Long Run."

level tend to be in the inelastic range is also not surprising because scale effects at that level are likely to be relatively small in many cases. The elasticity of product demand *for a firm* is very high, as mentioned earlier, but *at the industry level* it is not likely to be very large.

A third set of empirical findings suggests that the own-wage elasticity of demand is higher for production workers than for nonproduction workers. This difference appears to be the result of the greater substitutability between capital and *production* labor than between capital and nonproduction workers.[11]

In general, the more substitutable with capital a group of workers is, the greater will be its elasticity of demand, other things equal. Research to date suggests that capital and unskilled labor are more easily substituted for each other in the production process than capital and skilled labor,[12] but whether this translates into a greater own-wage elasticity of demand depends upon the "other things" affecting elasticity: product demand elasticities, share of labor in total cost, and the supply curve for capital. *If* these other factors are more or less the same for skilled and unskilled workers, on average, then the own-wage elasticity of demand will tend to be greater for the unskilled. It appears, for example, that the elasticity of demand for teenage labor may be in the range of -7 to -9 and that it is much higher than the elasticity of demand for adults (who tend to be in more skilled jobs).[13]

All of the evidence cited above has concerned *own-wage* elasticities of demand. As indicated earlier, evidence on *cross-wage* elasticities of demand is generally much sketchier. We *do* have evidence that teenagers and adults, especially adult females, are substitutes in production,[14] but whether they are *gross substitutes* depends on the *scale effect* as well as on the substitution effect. In other words, we know with some certainty that if teenage wages were reduced by a youth differential in the minimum wage, teenagers would be substituted for adults (at least to some degree) in the production process. However, whether adult employment would go up or down depends also on the scale effect a youth subminimum would create. If scale effects are large, teenagers and adults *could* be gross complements (that is, as teenage wages fell, adult employment would rise despite the substitution against them in the production process). Unfortunately, it is not clear at this point whether teenagers and adults are gross complements or gross substitutes.

Similarly, there is evidence that black men and adult women are substitutes in production.[15] Hence, if women's wages fall because of their growing relative numbers in the labor force, employers are likely to substitute women for black men when producing any level of output. However, since the *scale* effect of a decrease in adult women's wages will tend to *increase* black male employment, we cannot say

---

[11]Hamermesh and Grant, "Econometric Studies of Labor-Labor Substitution."

[12]Hamermesh and Grant, "Econometric Studies of Labor-Labor Substitution."

[13]Hamermesh and Grant, "Econometric Studies of Labor-Labor Substitution."

[14]Hamermesh and Grant, "Econometric Studies of Labor-Labor Substitution," and James Grant and Daniel Hamermesh, "Labor Market Competition Among Youths, White Women and Others," *Review of Economics and Statistics* 63 (August 1981):354–66.

[15]George Borjas, "The Demographic Determinants of the Demand for Black Labor" (paper presented at the Conference on Innercity Black Youth Unemployment, Cambridge, Mass.: National Bureau of Economic Research, August 1983).

a priori if black male employment is reduced or increased by the growing female labor supply. As with teenagers and adults above, at this point it is not known whether black men and adult women are gross complements or gross substitutes.

Finally, there is some preliminary evidence that black men and Hispanics are complements in production, which in turn implies that they are gross complements (see footnote 5).[16] As a result, a decline in the Hispanic wage caused by increased immigration of Hispanics to the United States might lead to increased employment of black men. If this evidence proves correct, fears by some that black male employment prospects will be diminished by Hispanic immigration may prove unfounded (for a more complete discussion of immigration and its effects on the labor market, see Chapter 10).

APPLYING THE LAWS OF DERIVED DEMAND

Because empirical estimates of demand elasticities that may be required for making decisions are lacking in some cases, it is sometimes necessary to try to guess what these elasticities are likely to be. In making these guesses, we can apply the laws of derived demand to predict these magnitudes for various types of labor. Consider first the demand for unionized New York City garment workers. As we shall discuss in Chapter 12, because unions are complex organizations, it is not always possible to specify what their goals are. Nevertheless, it is clear that most unions value both their members' wage *and* employment opportunities. This observation leads to the simple prediction that, other things equal, the more elastic the demand for labor, the smaller will be the wage gain that a union will succeed in winning for its members. The reason for this prediction is that the more elastic the demand curve, the greater will be the percentage employment decline associated with any given percentage increase in wages. As a result, we can expect the following:

1. Unions would win larger wage gains for their members in markets with inelastic labor demand curves;
2. Unions would strive to take actions that reduce the wage elasticity of demand for their members' services; and
3. Unions might first seek to organize workers in markets in which labor demand curves are inelastic (because the potential gains to unionization are higher in these markets).

As we shall see, many of these predictions are borne out by empirical evidence (see Chapter 12).

Due to foreign competition, the price elasticity of demand for the clothing produced by New York City garment workers is extremely high. Furthermore, employers can easily find other inputs to substitute for these workers—namely, nonunion garment workers in the South (this substitution would require moving the plant to the South, a strategy that many manufacturers have followed). These facts

---

[16]Borjas, "The Demographic Determinants of the Demand for Black Labor," and George Borjas, "The Substitutability of Black, Hispanic, and White Labor," *Economic Inquiry* 21 (January 1983), 93–106.

lead one to predict that the wage elasticity of demand for New York City unionized garment workers should be very elastic, a prediction that seems to be borne out by union policies in the industry. That is, because the garment workers' union faces a highly elastic demand curve, its wage demands historically have been moderate. However, the union has also aggressively sought to reduce the elasticity of product demand by supporting policies that reduce foreign competition; in addition, it has pushed for higher federal minimum wages in order to reduce employers' incentives to move their plants to the South.

Next, consider the wage elasticity of demand for unionized airplane pilots on commercial scheduled airlines in the United States. The salaries of pilots are only a small share of the costs of operating large airplanes; they are dwarfed by the fuel and capital costs of airlines. Furthermore, substitution possibilities are limited; there is little room to substitute unskilled labor for skilled labor (although airlines can contemplate substituting capital for labor by reducing the number of flights they offer while increasing the size of airplanes). Prior to the deregulation of the airline industry that took place in 1978, many airlines also faced no competition on many of their routes or were prohibited from reducing their prices to compete with other airlines that flew the same routes. These factors all suggest that the wage elasticity of demand for airline pilots was quite inelastic. As one might expect, pilots' wages were also quite high because their union could push for large wage increases without fear that such an increase would substantially reduce pilots' employment levels. However, after airline deregulation, competition among airline carriers increased substantially, leading to a more elastic labor demand for pilots. As a result, many airlines "requested," and won, reduced wages from their pilots.

Finally, consider the wage elasticity of demand for *domestic* farm workers. This elasticity will depend heavily on the supply of immigrants, either legal or illegal, who are willing to work as farm workers at wages less than the wages paid to domestic farm workers. The successful unionization of farm workers, coupled with union or government rules that prevent illegal immigrants from accepting such employment, obviously will make the demand curve for domestic farm workers less elastic. Similarly, government regulations that either limit the quantity of foreign farm products that can be imported into the United States (quotas), place tariffs on such products, or limit foreign producers from *dumping* (selling their farm products in the United States at prices less than they charge in their own countries) will reduce the price elasticity of demand for U.S. farm products (and hence the wage elasticity of demand for domestic farm workers). This example indicates how government policies can heavily influence wage elasticities in particular labor markets.

POLICY APPLICATIONS

Knowledge of the magnitudes and signs of wage elasticities of demand are important in many policy applications, as the discussion above and the following examples illustrate.

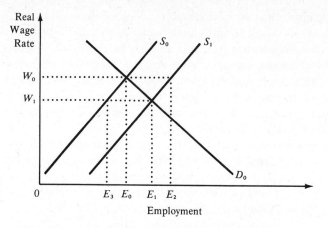

FIGURE 4.3   Market Effects of a Government Training Program

Market Effects of a Government Training Program

Suppose the labor market for typists is competitive and is initially in equilibrium. This situation is depicted in Figure 4.3; the initial demand curve is D_0, the supply curve is S_0, and E_0 typists are employed and paid the real wage rate W_0. Suppose also that there is unemployment of unskilled workers in the area and that to remedy this situation the government funds a training program to train these unemployed unskilled workers to become typists.[17] If $E_2 - E_0$ unskilled workers are trained, the supply curve of typists in the market will shift to S_1. At the old equilibrium wage (W_0), the number of typists who want to work will exceed the number that firms want to hire (by $E_2 - E_0$). Downward pressure will be placed on the wage rate and eventually equilibrium will be reestablished at the lower real wage rate of W_1 and the higher employment level of E_1.[18]

Note that even if all trainees are placed in jobs, the net impact of the program is not to increase employment of typists by the number of trainees. Employment has increased by less than the number of trainees because the reduction in the real wage rate has induced some previously employed workers to quit their jobs and drop out of the typist labor market. Also, those typists who have kept their jobs are now worse off because their wages are lower than before. Both of these market effects must be taken into account in any evaluation of a training program's effects.

Under what circumstances will both the decline in wages and the loss of jobs by previously employed typists be small? Clearly the answer is, when the wage elasticity of demand for labor is high. In this situation, a small decline in wages will lead to a large expansion in the number of employees firms want to hire. Other

---

[17]During the late 1970s and early 1980s, the major government training programs for adults were funded under the Comprehensive Employment and Training Act (CETA). This was replaced in 1982 by the Job Training Partnership Act (JPTA). See the most recent issue of the *Employment and Training Report of the President* for background data on, and a description of, current training programs.

[18]In a period of rising prices, real wages can fall without a cut in money wages. All that is required here is that prices rise more rapidly than money wages.

things equal, trainees should be trained for occupations in which the demand curves are highly elastic.

Of course, this analysis assumes that real wages are flexible in the market for typists, so that initially there is not a shortage of labor in that market. If instead the real wage could not initially rise above W_1 in Figure 4.3 (which might occur during a period in which wages were directly controlled by federal legislation), then the initial employment level would be E_3. In this situation, employment could increase by the number of trainees and the real wage might not fall. However, if the government attempted to train more than $E_1 - E_3$ new typists, the lesson learned above would apply and employment of typists would not increase by the number trained.

Investment Tax Credit to Reduce Unemployment

An *investment tax credit* allows businesses to subtract a certain percentage of the investments they make in new capital equipment from their tax bills. As such, the credit is an implicit subsidy given to employers for increasing their capital stocks. It has the effect of reducing the price of new capital equipment, which should stimulate such investments. To the extent that this increases the growth rate in the economy, such a tax credit may stimulate employment growth and reduce the unemployment rate. However, working against this scale effect is a substitution effect: the cost of capital is lower because of the tax credit, and this induces the substitution of capital for labor.

Investment tax credits have been part of federal tax legislation since the early 1960s. Indeed, as of 1984 the credit was 10 percent of the purchase price for most capital investments. A policy issue of major interest is whether increasing the level of the tax credit substantially reduces unemployment. Since the cost of the credit to the U.S. Treasury in the form of lost revenue is rather substantial, and because this lost revenue could be used to reduce unemployment in other ways, the effects of the tax credit on employment opportunities is a critical question.

Although the overall effects of an investment tax credit on employment have not been precisely pinned down, we have a fairly good idea which groups would gain or lose from an increase in the credit. As noted above, the data seem to indicate that capital and skilled labor are less substitutable than capital and unskilled labor. Hence, as increases in the investment tax credit reduce the cost of capital, one would expect greater substitution effects, which adversely affect employment levels, among the unskilled. Whether the *actual* level of employment among the unskilled would fall or not depends, as we have emphasized, on the size of the *scale* effect. However, we would expect a tax credit to cause more displacement of unskilled workers than skilled workers.

Employment Tax Credits or Wage Subsidies

As an alternative to an investment tax credit, one might institute a system of payments to employers for increasing their employment levels. When the payment is made directly to employers (for example, when employers are rebated 50 percent of their new employees' wages) the payment is called a *wage subsidy*. If the payment is implicit, in the form of a tax credit, it is called an *employment tax credit*. The analyses, and effects, of both types of payment programs are identical, however. By reducing the price the employer pays for labor, both tend to stimulate employment.

Employment tax credits, or wage subsidy schemes, can take many forms.[19] They can apply to all new hires or only to increases in firms' employment levels (in which case they are called *marginal* employment tax credits). Since firms typically hire new employees to replace employees who have quit, retired, or been involuntarily terminated, they would receive subsidies in the former case even if they maintained a constant employment level.

Employment subsidies can also be either *general* or *selective*. A general subsidy is not conditional on the characteristics of the people hired, while a selective, or *targeted*, plan makes payments conditional on hiring people from certain target groups (such as the disadvantaged).

Although European nations have had more experience with employment-tax-credit programs than the United States, both general and selective tax credit programs have been tried in the United States in recent years. For example, a New Jobs Tax Credit was part of the 1977 economic stimulus package passed by Congress. This general, marginal employment tax credit program was in effect only for 1977 and 1978. Due to limitations on the size of the credit that an employer could receive for each employee (essentially 50 percent of the workers' annual earnings up to a maximum earnings ceiling of $4200), the plan effectively gave employers a proportionately greater subsidy for hiring unskilled and part-time labor than it did for hiring skilled or full-time labor.[20] Because of this, *if* the own-wage elasticities of demand are the same or larger for unskilled or part-time labor *and* if the various skill groups are gross substitutes, one would expect the employment levels of unskilled and part-time workers to be stimulated most by the program.

Preliminary evaluations of the program indicate that it may have had some small positive effect on the overall level of employment; firms that knew of the program's existence seemed to grow more rapidly than firms that did not know.[21] However, one year into the program, less than one half of all surveyed firms actually knew that the program existed, and one might conjecture that the direction of causation ran from "plans to grow rapidly" to "knowledge of the program," rather than vice versa.[22] That is, firms that were planning to expand their employ-

---

[19]*See* Daniel Hamermesh, "Subsidies for Jobs in the Private Sector," in John Palmer, ed., *Creating Jobs: Public Employment Programs and Wage Subsidies* (Washington, D.C.: Brookings Institution, 1978) for an extended discussion.

[20]For more details of the plan, see Orley Ashenfelter, "Evaluating the Effects of the Employment Tax Credit," in U.S. Department of Labor, *Conference Report on Evaluating the 1977 Economic Stimulus Package* (Washington, D.C.: U.S. Government Printing Office, 1979).

[21]*See* Jeffrey Perloff and Michael Wachter, "The New Jobs Tax Credit—an Evaluation of the 1977–78 Wage Subsidy Program," *American Economic Review* 69 (May 1979): 173–79; John Bishop and Robert Haveman, "Selective Employment Subsidies: Can Okun's Law be Repealed?" *American Economic Review* 69 (May 1979): 124–30.

[22]Perloff and Wachter, "The New Jobs Tax Credit"; Bishop and Haveman, "Selective Employment Subsidies."

Example 4.2
The Slowdown in U.S Productivity Growth

One measure of productivity that is customarily used is *labor productivity*, or output per hour of labor employed. Between 1948 and 1973 labor productivity grew at a rate of almost 3 percent per year in the private business sector. Between 1973 and 1982, however, it grew at a rate of only about 0.7 percent per year. This slowdown in the rate of growth of productivity is particularly disturbing because, as we shall see in Chapter 16, the rate of growth of labor productivity is directly related to both the rate of growth of real wages and the rate of price inflation in the economy.

Not surprisingly, then, economists have expended considerable effort to try to understand the causes of the slowdown in productivity growth. Although the slowdown is not fully understood, a number of factors are known to contribute to it. These factors include, but are not limited to, changes in the age-sex composition of the labor force, changes in the industrial composition of employment, government mandated investments in pollution-abatement equipment (which do not lead to increases in *measured* output, since the quality of the environment is not measured in gross national product), and a decline in the capital-labor ratio that has accompanied a slowdown in normal business investment. With less capital to work with, each unit of labor is less productive.

Why has this reduction in capital investment occurred? The answer may hinge on the explosion of energy prices that followed the 1974 OPEC oil embargo. Several studies indicate that capital and energy are gross complements and that labor and energy are gross substitutes. Hence, rapid increases in the price of energy should induce employers to reduce their capital stocks and increase employment. Once we realize that energy is an input into the production process and that increases in the price of energy raise the cost of operating capital, it becomes clear why capital/labor ratios have fallen and contributed to the slowdown in measured labor productivity. Government policies to reduce the cost of capital, such as increasing the size of the investment tax credit, could offset energy price increases and stimulate investment, thus increasing labor productivity; however, as already noted, the net effect on *employment*, especially of unskilled workers, will not necessarily be favorable.

SOURCES: J. R. Norsworthy, Michael Harper, and Kent Kunze, "The Slowdown in Productivity Growth: Analysis of Some Contributing Factors," *Brookings Papers on Economic Activity* 2 (1979):387–423. Edward F. Denison, *Accounting for Slower Economic Growth: The United States in the 1970s* (Washington, D.C.: Brookings Institution, 1979). Martin N. Baily, "Productivity and the Services of Capital and Labor," *Brookings Papers on Economic Activity* (1981–1):1–50. Evidence that capital and energy are gross complements is found in Ernst Berndt and David Wood, "Technology, Prices and the Derived Demand for Energy," *Review of Economics and Statistics* 57 (August 1975):259–68, and Edward A. Hudson and Dale Jorgenson, "Energy Prices and the U.S. Economy, 1972–76," *Data Resources Review* 7 (September 1978):1.24–1.37. The findings, however, are not unambiguous. James Griffin and Paul Gregory, in "An Intercountry Translog Model of Energy and Substitution Responses," *American Economic Review* 66 (December 1976):845–57, find that capital and energy are gross substitutes.

ment, even in the absence of the program, had an incentive to learn about the program so that they could receive the subsidy.

This example again highlights the difficulties social scientists face when they attempt to evaluate the effect of social programs. It also suggests the importance of rapidly disseminating information about the existence of programs; the passage of a law, *per se*, does not guarantee that employers will know about it.

The New Jobs Tax Credit was replaced in 1979 by a Targeted Employment Tax Credit, which was a selective tax credit that subsidized the hiring of unemployed youth (18–24), handicapped individuals, and welfare recipients. Although no evaluations of the program have been published, it is possible to examine some of the evaluation issues.[23]

To the extent that the demand for teenagers is highly elastic, as the empirical estimates indicate, this program does have the potential to substantially increase youth employment. However, it will be important to examine its impact on the employment levels of the nontargeted groups—especially unskilled adults for whom teenagers may be quite close substitutes. Another problem is the lack of data on demand elasticities for the handicapped or welfare recipients. Without these data, *ex post facto* (after the fact) evaluations of the program's effects on the employment levels of the different groups will be required.

REVIEW QUESTIONS

1. Suppose Congress had just passed a permanent tax credit applicable to the purchase of machinery. What impact would this tax reduction have on the demand for labor? Under what conditions would the demand for labor be affected *most*?
2. A national study concludes that the hourly pay received by part-time workers is always less than the hourly pay received by full-time workers in comparable jobs. It also concludes that part-time workers are disproportionately women, teenagers, the elderly, and the hard-to-employ. Thus, the study suggests that Congress pass a law compelling employers offering part-time jobs to pay the *full-time* wage rate prevailing in their area for the relevant jobs. Analyze as completely as you can the effects on both part-time and full-time workers.
3. How would a youth differential in the minimum wage (i.e., a lower legal minimum for teenagers) affect the employment prospects of older workers who wanted to work part-time? How would the latter fare if the minimum wage were eliminated completely?
4. Union A faces a demand curve in which a wage of $4 per hour leads to demand for 20,000 person hours and a wage of $5 per hour leads to demand for 10,000 person hours. What is the elasticity of demand for this union's labor?

    Union B faces a demand curve in which a wage of $6 per hour leads to demand for 30,000 person hours, while a wage of $5 per hour leads to demand for 33,000 person hours.

    a. Which union faces the *more* elastic demand curve?
    b. Which union will be more successful in increasing the total income (wages times person hours) of its membership?

---

[23]For a more general discussion of problems inherent in targeted tax credits, see David O'Neill, "Employment Tax Credit Programs: The Effects of Socioeconomic Targeting Provisions," *Journal of Human Resources* 17 (Summer 1982): 449–59.

SELECTED READINGS

Borjas, George. "The Substitution of Black, Hispanic, and White Labor." *Economic Inquiry*, January 1983.

Denison, Edward F. *Accounting for Slower Economic Growth: The United States in the 1970s*. Washington, D.C.: Brookings Institution, 1979.

Hamermesh, Daniel. "Subsidies for Jobs in the Private Sector." In John Palmer, ed., *Creating Jobs: Public Employment Programs and Wage Subsidies*. Washington, D.C.: Brookings Institution, 1978.

Hamermesh, Daniel. "The Demand for Labor in the Long Run." In Orley Ashenfelter and Richard Layard, eds., *Handbook of Labor Economics*. North-Holland Press, forthcoming.

Perloff, Jeffrey, and Wachter, Michael. "The New Jobs Tax Credit—An Evaluation of the 1977–78 Wage Subsidy Program." *American Economic Review*, May 1979.

APPENDIX 4A
The Laws of
Derived Demand

Chapter 4 presented a verbal explanation of the Hicks-Marshall laws of derived demand and briefly mentioned that one of those laws does not always hold. This appendix will graphically derive and analyze these laws when the *substitution effect* is zero (that is, it will analyze the determinants of the elasticity of demand when *only* a *scale effect* occurs), and will briefly analyze the above exception when only a *substitution effect* exists.

SCALE EFFECT BUT NO SUBSTITUTION EFFECT

To begin, let us assume that labor and capital must be combined in *fixed proportions* to produce a unit of output.[1] We can assume, for example, that one secretary and one typewriter must be combined if a letter is to be typed. If more labor is added to this one typewriter, no extra output is produced—and if more typewriters are given to one secretary, no extra output is produced.[2] In graphic terms, the isoquants of a fixed-proportions technology are perpendicular lines, as shown in Figure 4A.1. Costs are minimized at the "corner" (point A for $Q = 100$), and no matter what the

---

[1]The analysis in this section leans heavily on Milton Friedman, *Price Theory: A Provisional Text* (Chicago: Aldine Publishing Company, 1962), pp. 148–55.

[2]This assumption is rather extreme and is made for analytical convenience only. We argued in Chapter 3 that adding secretaries to one typewriter *could* increase output because the extra secretaries would permit them to alternate typing and resting, to address envelopes by hand, or to otherwise expedite work. Likewise, an extra typewriter per secretary could add to output when the inevitable breakdowns occur.

**FIGURE 4A.1   Isoquants of a Fixed-Proportions
Production Function**

relative prices are of labor and capital, the same amount of each will be used to produce Q of 100. (To see that this is the case, observe two isocost curves on which point A falls. When the wage (W) = $1 and the cost of capital (C) = $1, the isocost curve runs between B and D, while when W = $2 and C = $0.50, it runs between E and F. If output of 100 is to be produced, it will be done using L^* and K^*, no matter what the relative prices of L and K. Any other input combination along the isoquant would have a higher total cost.) With this kind of production function, no substitution effect is generated by a change in wages.

An increase in wages, however, will cause a scale effect. Production costs rise as wages increase, and the profit-maximizing level of output will tend to fall. The extent of the fall, and the forces underlying the degree to which employment also falls, can be easily shown in this fixed-proportions example.

Chapter 4 emphasized that a demand curve for labor is drawn holding three underlying forces constant: the production function, the product demand curve, and the supply curve of capital. These three influences, along with the demand-for-labor curve they imply, are illustrated in Figure 4A.2 for a (hypothetical) industry that specializes in typing and mailing letters for customers. The fixed-proportions nature of the technology that we have assumed is shown along the horizontal axis. If 2,000 hours of labor and machine units are combined, 10,000 letters can be produced; if 4,000 hours of labor and capital are combined, 20,000 letters can be produced. The capital/labor combinations shown are the *only* ones that are consistent with cost minimization at any factor price ratio (W/C).

FIGURE 4A.2 Derivation of the Demand Curve for Labor
with Fixed-Proportions Technology

The product demand curve D_P is drawn against the price charged for *bundles of 5 letters*—the hourly output of a unit of labor and a unit of capital—and has the usual negative slope.[3] This demand curve can be interpreted in two mutually consistent ways: it indicates, for given prices, the quantity of output that can be sold; it also indicates, for given levels of output, the price that can be charged.

The third force underlying the demand curve for labor in Figure 4A.2 is the supply curve on capital (S_K). We initially assume that this supply curve is horizontal at C_0, meaning that additional units of capital (in our example, hours of machine usage) can be purchased at the constant price of C_0 per unit.

In deriving the demand-for-labor curve implied by the three forces above, look first at the output level of 20,000 (4,000 bundles of five). If output is 20,000, a price

---

[3]Output and factor prices must be put on the same hourly basis if they are to be useful in our graphic analysis. It is obvious that one can divide the price per bundle by 5 and get the *unit* price.

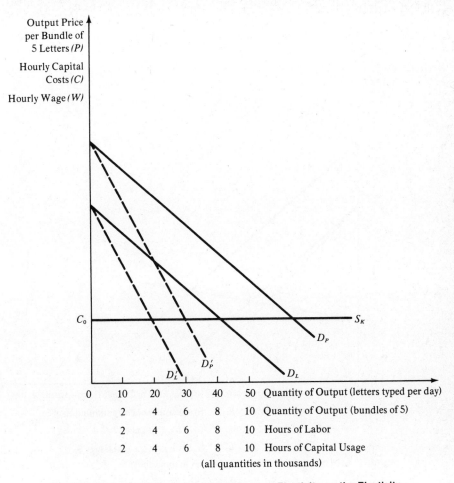

Output Price
per Bundle of
5 Letters *(P)*

Hourly Capital
Costs *(C)*

Hourly Wage *(W)*

C_0

S_K

D_P

D_P'

D_L'

D_L

0	10	20	30	40	50	Quantity of Output (letters typed per day)
	2	4	6	8	10	Quantity of Output (bundles of 5)
	2	4	6	8	10	Hours of Labor
	2	4	6	8	10	Hours of Capital Usage

(all quantities in thousands)

**FIGURE 4A.3   The Effect of Product-Demand Elasticity on the Elasticity
of Demand for Labor**

of P_H can be charged for each bundle. The *capital* cost of producing each bundle is C_0, so the maximum wage that could be paid for a labor hour at this level of output is $P_H - C_0$.[4] Point A thus becomes one point along the demand curve for labor. If 50,000 units of output are produced, P_L could be charged per bundle, and $P_L - C_0$ is the maximum wage per labor-hour that could be paid. Point B, then, is another point on labor's demand curve. D_L becomes the demand-for-labor curve implied by the technology, product demand, and capital supply curve. It shows the maximum hourly wage firms would be willing to pay at different levels of employment or the hours of labor firms would desire to employ at any given hourly wage.

Once this derivation of the demand-for-labor curve is understood for the fixed-proportions case, three of the laws of derived demand can be easily illustrated graphically. First, consider the proposition that *the less elastic is product demand, the less elastic will be the demand for labor*, other things equal. Figure 4A.3, which

---

[4]We assume that C_0 includes a normal profit for the owner.

Output Price per Bundle of 5 Letters *(P)*

Hourly Capital Costs *(C)*

Hourly Wage *(W)*

0	10	20	30	40	50	Quantity of Output (letters typed per day)
	2	4	6	8	10	Quantity of Output (bundles of 5)
	2	4	6	8	10	Hours of Labor
	2	4	6	8	10	Hours of Capital Usage

(all quantities in thousands)

FIGURE 4A.4   The Effect of the Elasticity of Supply of Capital on the Elasticity of Demand for Labor

depicts a relatively elastic product-demand curve represented by the solid curve D_P and a less elastic one represented by the dashed line D_P', illustrates this law. The labor-demand curve (D_L) derived from the relatively elastic product demand curve has a flatter slope than, and lies above, the dashed labor-demand curve (D_L'), which implies that at any level of labor usage, the dashed curve is less elastic.[5]

Next consider the proposition that *the less elastic is the supply of capital, the less elastic will be the demand for labor* (other things equal). Figure 4A.4 contains two alternative capital supply curves—the perfectly elastic S_K shown before and a

---

[5]Students should satisfy themselves that a demand curve with a steeper slope *could* be more elastic (at a given employment level) than a flatter one *if* it lies above its flatter alternative at that point. This possibility relates to the fact that equal changes in the wage rate represent smaller *percentage* changes at higher wage levels.

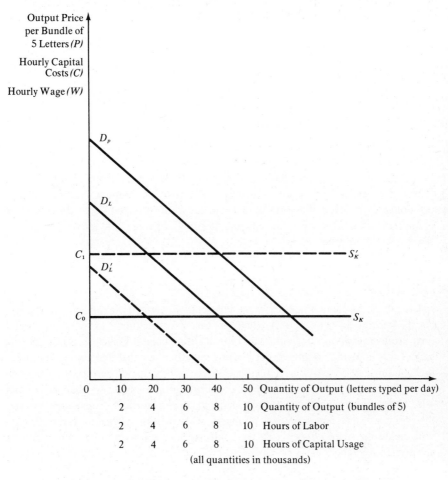

FIGURE 4A.5   The Effects of Labor Share in Total Cost on the Elasticity of Demand for Labor

less elastic (dashed) alternative, S_K'. (The product-demand curve is held constant.) It is easily seen that D_L, the demand curve consistent with S_K (the perfectly elastic supply-of-capital curve), has a flatter slope than, and lies above, its dashed alternative (D_L'). At each level of employment, then, D_L is more elastic than D_L'.

Finally, consider the law that *when there is no substitution effect, a smaller share of labor in total cost is associated with a less elastic labor-demand curve* (others things equal). Figure 4A.5 illustrates this law, showing the product-demand curve (D_P) and two *equally elastic* capital-supply curves. When capital is supplied along S_K (at a constant price of C_0), the share of labor in total cost is larger than when a unit of capital costs C_1 (see supply curve S_K'). One can readily see that D_L and D_L' have the same slope (given our assumptions about D_P, S_K, and S_K'), but that D_L' lies below D_L at each level of employment. A demand curve with the same slope as one lying above it is the less elastic of the two. Equal changes in wages (at a given employment level) call forth equal absolute and *percentage* changes in employment; however, equal changes in wages represent larger *percentage changes* in wages along the *lower* of the two curves. Since the elasticity of demand for labor is defined as

$$\frac{\text{Elasticity of Demand}}{\text{for Labor}} = \frac{\% \, \Delta \text{ Employment}}{\% \, \Delta \text{ Wages}}, \qquad (4A.1)$$

it can easily be seen that the lower of the two demand curves (D'_L in Figure 4A.5) is the less elastic, and is the one associated with the smaller labor share in total costs.[6]

Thus, three of the four laws of derived demand can be geometrically demonstrated if we assume away any substitution effects by assuming a fixed-proportions technology. However, if instead we assume that a substitution effect exists, but now ignore the scale effect, we can better understand why the law relating to labor's share does not always hold.

SUBSTITUTION EFFECT BUT NO SCALE EFFECT

In Chapter 4, footnote 4 noted that the law relating a smaller labor share with a less elastic demand curve holds only when it is easier for customers to substitute among final products than it is for employers to substitute capital for labor. Since the first half of this appendix assumed that it was *impossible* to substitute capital for labor, this condition was clearly met. To illustrate the reverse condition, in which capital/labor substitution can occur but product substitution cannot, we shall now work with an example in which the product-demand curve is vertical. Consumers will buy the product in the same amounts, no matter what the price; hence, a wage increase will create *no scale effect*. Here we shall assume, however, that capital can be substituted for labor.

The version of the labor share law that says that a *smaller labor share is associated with a more elastic demand for labor when it is easier to substitute in the production process than among final goods* is true if other things are held constant:

1. The product-demand curve, which we assume to be vertical;
2. The supply-of-capital curve, which we take to be horizontal (perfectly elastic); and
3. The *substitutability* between capital and labor in the production function.

The substitutability of capital and labor can be measured by the *elasticity of substitution*, which is defined as the percentage change in the capital/labor ratio called forth by a 1 percent change in the ratio of wages to capital costs:

$$\text{Elasticity of Substitution} = \frac{\% \, \Delta \, (K/L)}{\% \, \Delta \, (W/C)} \qquad (4A.2)$$

---

[6]Although the share of labor varied in this example because of capital prices, we would obtain the same results if we allowed it to vary for technological reasons (higher ratios of capital to labor that might be required). For example, if *two* units of capital had to be combined with a unit of labor to produce a unit of output, then the required expenditures on capital per unit of output are $2C_0$ (when each capital unit costs C_0).

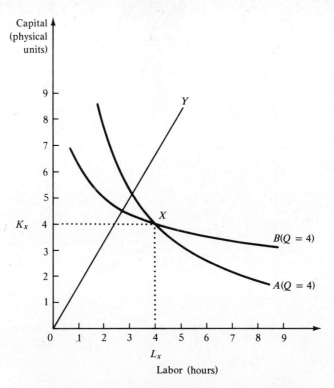

**FIGURE 4A.6   Two Production Functions With an Elasticity
of Substitution Equal to -1**

The elasticity of substitution is clearly a positive number because as W rises relative to C, capital will be substituted for labor. Expressing substitutability as an elasticity is convenient because elasticity is measured in units independent of the units in which capital and labor are measured.

Figure 4A.6 displays representative isoquants of two different (industry) production functions. *Both* these production functions have elasticities of substitution equal to $+1$. A unitary elasticity of substitution has the property that factor shares remain constant no matter what the relative prices of capital and labor. If wages rise 10 percent relative to capital prices, the use of labor falls 10 percent relative to the use of capital, and labor's share remains constant.[7]

While isoquants A and B have different shapes, it can be understood (with some work) that their elasticities of substitution are equal. Suppose, for example, that industries A and B were both operating at point X, where the capital/labor ratio equals K_X/L_X. Industry A will be at point X if wages are relatively high compared to capital costs, while B will be there if wages are relatively low (remember that the

---

[7]The production functions in Figure 4A.6 are both Cobb-Douglas production functions, meaning they have the form $Q = L^\alpha K^{1-\alpha}$, where α = labor's share and $1-\alpha$ equals capital's share. All Cobb-Douglas production functions have an elasticity of substitution equal to 1. Isoquant A is the $Q = 4$ isoquant for $Q = L^{0.5}K^{0.5}$. Isoquant B is the $Q = 4$ isoquant for $Q = L^{0.25}K^{0.75}$.

FIGURE 4A.7 **A Smaller Share of Labor in Total Costs Generates a Larger Elasticity of Demand for Labor When the Elasticity of Substitution Between Labor and Capital Exceeds the Elasticity of Product Demand**

marginal rate of technical substitution, as given by the slope of the isoquants, must equal the ratio of W to C). The equality of the elasticity of substitution for A and B means that if the factor-price ratios in each case change by the same percentage amount, their capital/labor ratios will also change by equal percentages. Since K_X/L_X held for *both* prior to the change in factor-price ratios, K/L *after* the change must also be the same. This means that K_A/L_A and K_B/L_B after adjustment must lie along the *same ray* passing through the origin of Figure 4A.6. Along a given ray (Y, for example), levels of usage of K and L vary, but the *ratio* of K to L is the same at each point. While the post-adjustment usage of capital and labor will be different in industries A and B, then, the capital/labor *ratios* will be the same if they both start at point X and experience the same *percentage changes* in W/C.

Isoquants A and B are repeated in Figure 4A.7, where it is assumed that the two industries, while having different production functions, face the *same* factor prices. Industry A responds to these factor prices by producing 4 units of output at point A', where the capital/labor ratio is K_a/L_a. Industry B responds by producing its 4 units at point B', where the capital/labor ratio is much higher (at K_b/L_b). Given that factor prices are exactly the same, the share of labor in total cost is much lower in B than A. This can easily be seen using the formula for labor share:

$$\text{Labor Share in Total Cost} = \frac{WL}{WL + CK}, \tag{4A.3}$$

where W and C are the same for each industry, but K/L is much smaller for industry B.

Figure 4A.7 can now be used to analyze the effects of labor share on the elasticity of demand for labor, given (a) completely inelastic product demand curves, (b) a completely elastic supply of capital, and (c) equal elasticities of substitution between K and L. Now suppose that originally W_0 and C_0 were such that isoexpenditure curve X held, but that wages increase to W_1 while C_0 remains constant. This increase in wages tilts the new isoexpenditure curves to Y and Y'—both of which have the same slope of W_1/C_0. Because there is no scale effect, both industries continue producing at $Q = 4$. Industry A moves from a cost-minimizing point of A' to point A'', while B moves from B' to B''. The amount of labor used by A falls from L_a to L_{aa}—a percentage drop of roughly 50 percent, as shown in Figure 4A.7. The labor used by B drops by a smaller amount in absolute terms but by a much larger percentage owing to the smaller base; the percentage decrease in B's labor is around 70 percent in the figure. Thus B, with the smaller labor share, has a more elastic demand for labor than does A.

One senses, then, that the exception to the "labor share" law of derived demand is a result of the relatively small initial usage of labor in industries where labor share is also small (other things equal). Given equal elasticities of substitution and no scale effect (or a very small one), a change in the ratio of wages to capital prices will call forth relatively larger percentage changes in employment where labor share is smaller because of the smaller initial level of employment.

5

Quasi-Fixed Labor Costs
and Their Effects on Demand

To this point in our detailed discussion of the demand for labor, we have treated all labor costs as *variable*—that is, as being strictly proportional to the length of time the employee works. Variable labor costs, such as the hourly wage rate, recur every period and, of course, can be reduced if the hours of work are reduced. Many labor costs, however, are *quasi-fixed*, in that they are not strictly proportional to hours of work. Such costs are borne by the firm on a *per-worker* basis that is largely independent of the hours each employee works. This chapter traces the effects these quasi-fixed costs have on the demand for labor.

Because quasi-fixed labor costs are generally *nonwage*, the first section discusses the nature, magnitude, and growth of nonwage labor costs. Included in our discussion are the costs to firms of hiring and training new employees, the costs of legally required social insurance programs (such as social security and unemployment compensation), and the costs of privately negotiated fringe benefits (such as health insurance, vacation and sick-leave pay, and private pensions). These nonwage costs typically exceed 20 to 30 percent of employers' payroll costs.

One important effect that quasi-fixed costs have on the demand for labor concerns the choice firms have between hiring more (or fewer) workers and employing those already on the payroll for longer (or shorter) hours. As discussed in the second section, the fact that many nonwage labor costs do *not* vary at the margin with weekly hours of work explains why some employers decide to regularly work their employees overtime at legally required premium wage rates rather than increasing the level of employment—a phenomenon that has led periodically to the proposal that the legally mandated overtime premium be increased in an effort to discourage employers from authorizing overtime and to encourage them to "spread the work." The second section concludes with a policy analysis of the federally mandated overtime pay premium.

The third section looks in detail at the nature and consequences of one important type of quasi-fixed labor cost: *investments* by firms in the hiring and training of their employees. Investments generally involve a current outlay of funds with a future payback, so that investments in workers cause firms' employment decisions to extend over multiple periods. Thus, this section discusses two critical issues: the ways current costs and future returns can be meaningfully compared, and the multiperiod criterion for profit maximization in the hiring of labor. The application of these concepts to the issue of *training* investments is made in the section that follows, in which we discuss the conditions under which these investments by a firm will meet the profit-maximizing criterion. We conclude this section with some implications for the occupational distribution of layoffs, labor hoarding, and the training effects of minimum wage laws.

Turning from training to *hiring* investments, the next section briefly discusses the choices firms face in the often costly process of selecting employees. The underlying rationale for the existence of *internal labor markets* and the use of credentials in screening employees is discussed here. Finally, we conclude with a section that analyzes some hiring practices that often appear to be discriminatory.

NONWAGE LABOR COSTS

Although simple textbook models of the labor market often refer to the hourly wage rate paid to workers as the cost of labor, substantial *nonwage* labor costs have important implications for labor market behavior. In general, they fall into two categories: hiring or training costs and fringe benefits.

Hiring and Training Costs

Firms incur substantial costs in hiring and training new employees. *Hiring costs* include all costs involved in advertising positions, screening applicants to evaluate their qualifications, and processing successful applicants who have been offered jobs. One might also include the overhead costs of maintaining employees on the payroll once they have been employed in this category of costs; these costs would include record-keeping costs, the costs of computing and issuing paychecks, and the costs of providing forms to the government (such as W-2 forms to the Internal Revenue Service) about employees' earnings.

New employees typically undergo formal or informal training and orientation programs. These programs may teach new skills, such as how to use a machine, that directly increase the employees' productive ability. Alternatively, orientation programs may simply provide newcomers with background information on how the firm is structured, such as who to call if a machine breaks down or where the rest room is. Such information, while not changing skill levels, does increase productivity by enabling workers to make more efficient use of time.

Firms incur at least three types of *training costs*:

1. The *explicit* monetary costs of employing individuals to serve as trainers and the costs of materials used up during the training process;
2. The *implicit* or opportunity costs of the trainee's time (while individuals are undergoing training, they are not producing as much output as they would if all of their time were devoted to production activities); and

3. The opportunity costs of using capital equipment and experienced employees to do the training in less formal training situations (for example, if training consists solely of an experienced employee demonstrating how he or she does a job to a new recruit, the demonstrator may work at a slower pace than normal).

Because a large share of employers' hiring and training costs are implicit, it is not surprising that detailed estimates of the magnitude of hiring and training costs in the U.S. economy do not exist. Some estimates for individual firms have been made, however, that suggest that the costs are high. For example, a study conducted by the American Management Association in 1960 concluded that *hiring* and

Example 5.1
Recruiting Strategies

The fact that recruiting and evaluating job applicants is a costly procedure induces employers to carefully select an overall hiring strategy. An employer wanting to hire *X* employees of a given quality has basically three choices. One is an *intensive-search* strategy, whereby the employer incurs substantial costs in advertising the openings and then interviewing applicants. A second choice is a *high-wage* strategy. By becoming known as a high-wage employer, an employer can generate large applicant pools very easily, and with so many applicants it can often fill its vacancies with workers who are obviously of high quality (thus saving screening costs). Finally, employers might choose a *training* strategy in which, instead of undertaking expensive efforts ensure a large pool of highly qualified applicants, they accept inexperienced applicants and train them (the two broad kinds of training offered and who pays for each are discussed later in this chapter).

Whether a given firm decides on intensive search, higher wages, or greater training as its means of recruiting personnel depends on the relative costs of each strategy to that firm. While firms differ in the strategies (or mixes of strategies) they choose, a study of recruiting in Chicago's clerical labor market revealed that intensive search, higher wages, and greater training are suitable substitutes. High-wage firms tended to hire only experienced workers and recruited their applicants through very low-cost sources (word of mouth mainly, but there was some use of newspaper ads). Low-wage firms that hired at the lowest level and trained workers for successively more skilled positions—a feasible strategy in large firms in which work can be highly specialized—tended to recruit inexperienced applicants very cheaply from local high schools. Low-wage, smaller firms that needed workers who could perform "up to speed" from the beginning spent the most on search; they tended to use employment agencies (whose fees can be high) to generate and screen pools of applicants.

SOURCE: Joseph C. Ullman, "Interfirm Differences in the Cost of Search for Clerical Workers," *Journal of Business* 41,2(April 1968):153–65.

orientation costs varied from around $200 per unskilled laborer to more than $4500 per engineer.[1] This study did not include estimates of training costs, and the costs that were included are not expressed in terms of today's prices. A 1951 International Harvester Company study[2] did include training costs and estimated that its average *hiring* and *training cost* per employee was about $380; in terms of current prices, this figure would be over $1400. Each of these estimates must be considered only suggestive, however, because the studies are old, the samples are small, and measuring some of these costs is difficult.

Fringe Benefits

We have much better data, however, on the other types of *nonwage* labor costs that firms incur. *Fringe benefits* include *legally required* social-insurance contributions and *privately provided* benefits. Examples of legally required benefits are payroll-based payments employers must make to fund programs that compensate workers for unemployment (unemployment insurance), injury (workers' compensation), and retirement (old-age, survivors', disability, and health insurance—or "Social Security"). Examples of privately provided benefits are holiday pay, vacation and sick leave, private pensions, and private health and life insurance.

Tables 5.1 and 5.2 give some idea of the magnitude and growth of these benefits. Department of Commerce data for the nation as a whole, tabulated in Table 5.1, indicate that forms of compensation other than wages and salaries rose from 6.7 percent of total compensation in 1957 to 16.3 percent in 1981. These data understate the importance of nonwage items in total compensation because they include holiday, vacation, and sick pay as wages. A more comprehensive measure, although for a more limited sample, comes from the biennial U.S. Chamber of Commerce survey of large manufacturing establishments. These data, tabulated in Table 5.2, indicate that total fringe benefits as a percent of *payroll* (which does not include pension and insurance costs) rose from 20.3 percent to 38.2 percent during 1957–80.

Both data sets indicate, then, an approximate doubling of the share of fringes in total compensation over the last 25 years or so. This increase has occurred in both legally required employer payments and privately negotiated benefits. (Chapter 11 will discuss *why* fringe benefits have increased as a fraction of total compensation.)

The Quasi-Fixed Nature of Many Nonwage Costs

The distinction between wage and nonwage costs of employment is important because many nonwage costs are *costs per worker* rather than *costs per hour worked*. That is, many nonwage costs do not vary at the margin with the number of

---

[1]See Frederick J. Gaudet, *Labor Turnover: Calculation and Costs* (New York: American Management Association, 1960). Similar data for 1965–66 for a variety of occupations and a sample of employers in the Rochester area is found in John Myers, *Job Vacancies in the Firm and the Labor Market* (New York: National Industrial Conference Board, 1969).

[2]This study is cited in Walter Oi, "Labor as a Quasi-Fixed Factor," *Journal of Political Economy* 70 (December 1962):538–55.

TABLE 5.1   Compensation of Employees, 1957–1981 (in billions of dollars)

Year	Total	Wages and Salaries (including vacation and holiday pay)	Supplements	Ratio of Supplements to Total (percent)
1957	$ 256.5	$ 239.3	$ 17.2	6.7
1959	279.6	258.9	20.6	7.4
1961	303.6	279.5	24.1	7.9
1963	342.9	313.4	29.5	8.6
1965	396.5	362.0	34.5	8.7
1967	471.9	427.5	44.4	9.4
1969	571.4	514.6	56.8	9.9
1971	652.2	581.5	70.7	10.8
1973	797.7	700.9	96.8	12.1
1975	931.1	805.9	125.2	13.4
1977	1152.3	983.8	168.5	14.6
1979	1460.9	1235.9	225.0	15.4
1981	1771.7	1482.9	288.8	16.3

Notes: "Compensation of Employees" is the income accruing to employees as remuneration for their work. "Wages & Salaries" consists of the monetary remuneration of employees, including compensation of corporate officers, commissions, tips, and bonuses, and payments in kind, which represent income to the recipients. "Supplements" to wages and salaries consists of employer contributions for social insurance and other labor income. Employer contributions for social insurance comprise employer payments under old-age, survivors', disability, and hospital insurance, state unemployment insurance, railroad retirement and unemployment insurance, government retirement, and a few other minor social insurance programs. Other labor income includes employer contributions to private pension, health and welfare, unemployment, and workers' compensation funds.

SOURCES: U.S. Department of Commerce, Bureau of Economic Analysis, *Business Statistics, 1975*, p. 6; and U.S. President, *Economic Report of the President 1982* (Washington, D.C.: U.S. Government Printing Office, February 1982), Table B-21.

TABLE 5.2   Fringe Benefits as a Percent of Payroll in Manufacturing, 1957–80

Year	Legally Required Payments (employer's share)	Pensions, Insurance	Paid Rest	Pay for Time Not Worked	Other Items	Total Fringe Benefits
1957	4.1	5.8	2.4	6.5	1.5	20.3
1959	4.5	6.1	2.7	6.7	1.6	21.6
1961	5.5	6.8	2.8	7.2	1.3	23.6
1963	5.9	6.7	2.9	7.3	1.4	24.2
1965	5.3	6.7	2.7	7.2	1.7	23.6
1967	6.4	7.0	3.0	7.3	1.9	25.6
1969	6.8	7.6	3.1	7.8	1.7	27.0
1971	6.9	9.9	3.5	8.6	1.7	30.6
1973	8.3	10.2	3.5	8.5	1.5	32.0
1975	8.8	11.6	3.7	10.1	1.9	36.1
1977	9.3	12.9	3.6	9.2	2.3	37.3
1979	10.1	12.1	3.6	8.8	2.6	37.2
1980	9.9	13.0	3.6	9.5	2.2	38.2

Note: "Payroll" (used as the denominator in calculating the above percentages) includes pay for time not worked, such as vacations and holidays, but does not include pension and insurance costs or payroll taxes. "Other items" includes profit sharing, contributions to thrift plans, bonuses, and employee educational benefits.

SOURCE: U.S. Chamber of Commerce, *Fringe Benefits and Employee Benefits* (various issues).

hours an employee works. Economists thus refer to them as *quasi-fixed*, in the sense that once an employee is hired the firm is committed to a cost that does not vary with his or her hours of work.[3]

It should be obvious that hiring and training costs are quasi-fixed; they are associated with each new employee, not with the hours he or she works after the training period. Many fringe costs, however, are also quasi-fixed. For example, in most firms holiday and vacation pay are specified as a fixed number of days per year (which may vary with seniority), and overtime hours do not affect these costs. Or to take another example, an employer's unemployment insurance payroll-tax liability is specified to be a percentage (the tax rate) of each employee's earnings up until a maximum earnings level (the taxable wage base)—which in half of all states was $7,000 in 1984. Since most employees earn more than $7,000 per year, having an employee work an additional hour per week will *not* cause any increase in the employer's payroll-tax liability.[4]

The quasi-fixed nature of many nonwage labor costs has important effects on employer hiring and overtime decisions. These effects are discussed below.

THE EMPLOYMENT/HOURS TRADE-OFF

The simple model of the demand for labor presented in the preceding chapters spoke of the quantity of labor demanded and made no distinction between the number of individuals employed by a firm and the average length of its employees' workweek. Holding all other inputs constant, however, a firm can produce a given level of output with various combinations of the number of employees hired and the number of hours worked per week. Presumably increases in the number of employees hired will allow for shorter workweeks, while longer workweeks will allow for fewer employees, other things equal.

In the short run, with capital and all other inputs fixed, the output (Q) a firm can produce is related to both its employment level (M) and its average work week per employee (H) by the following production function:

$$Q = f(M,H). \tag{5.1}$$

It is reasonable to assume that both inputs in equation (5.1) have positive marginal products ($MP_M > 0; MP_H > 0$). That is, increasing the number of employees holding hours constant—or increasing the average workweek holding employment constant—will lead to increases in output. While remaining positive, each of these marginal products must surely decline at some point. When the number of employ-

---

[3]*See* Oi, "Labor as a Quasi-Fixed Factor."

[4]This is not true for all fringe benefits. For example, the social security (OASDHI) payroll tax liability of employers is also specified as a percentage of earnings up until a maximum taxable wage base; however, this wage base is considerably higher—$37,800 in 1984. Since this level exceeds the annual earnings of most full-time employees, the employer's payroll tax liability *is* increased when a firm employs a typical employee an additional hour per week.

ees is increased, this decline may be due to the reduced quantity of capital that each employee will have to work with or the fact that the firm may be forced to employ lower-quality workers. When the hours each employee works per week are increased, the decline in marginal product may occur because after some point fatigue sets in.

Given this production function,[5] how does a firm determine its optimal employment/hours combination? Is it ever rational for an employer to work his or her existing employees overtime on a regularly scheduled basis, rather than hiring additional employees?

Determining the Mix of Workers and Hours

The fact that certain labor costs are *not* hours-related and others are makes it important to examine the marginal cost an employer faces when employing an additional *worker* for whatever length workweek other employees are working (MC_M). This marginal cost will equal the weekly value of the quasi-fixed labor costs plus the weekly wage and variable (with hours) fringe-benefit costs for the specified length of workweek. Similarly, it is important to examine the marginal cost a firm faces when it seeks to increase the *average workweek* of its existing work force by one hour (MC_H). This marginal cost will equal the hourly wage and variable fringe-benefit costs multiplied by the number of employees in the work force. Of course, if the employer is in a situation in which an overtime premium (such as time-and-a-half or double time) must be paid for additional hours, that higher rate is the relevant wage rate to use in the latter calculation.

Viewed in this way, a firm's decision about its optimal employment/hours combination is no different from its decision about the usage of any two factors of production, which was discussed in Chapter 3. Specifically, to minimize the cost of producing any given level of output, a firm should adjust both its employment level and its average workweek so that the costs of producing an added unit of output are equal for each:

$$\frac{MC_M}{MP_M} = \frac{MC_H}{MP_H} \qquad (5.2)$$

Put another way, the marginal cost of hiring an additional employee (MC_M) relative to the marginal cost of working the existing work force an additional hour (MC_H) should be equal to the marginal productivity of an additional employee relative to that of extending the workweek by an hour:

$$\frac{MC_M}{MC_H} = \frac{MP_M}{MP_H} \qquad (5.3)$$

---

[5]For estimates of such a function, *see* Martin Feldstein, "Specification of the Labor Input in the Aggregate Production Function," *Review of Economic Studies* 34 (October 1967):375–86. *See also* Sherwin Rosen, "Short-Run Employment Variation in Class-I Railroads in the U.S., 1947–1967," *Econometrica 36* (July–October 1968):511–29.

The Fair Labor Standards Act (FLSA) requires that all employees covered by the legislation receive an overtime pay premium of at least 50 percent of their regular hourly wage (time-and-a-half).[6] Now while a large proportion of overtime hours are worked because of disequilibrium phenomena—such as rush orders, seasonal demand, mechanical failures, and absenteeism—a substantial amount of overtime appears to be regularly scheduled. Equation (5.3) indicates why this scheduling of overtime may occur. Although overtime hours require premium pay, they also enable an employer to avoid the quasi-fixed employment costs associated with employing an additional worker. This point can be illustrated by considering what would happen if the overtime-wage premium were to be increased.

Policy Analysis: The Overtime-Pay Premium

Periodically proposals have been introduced in Congress to raise the overtime premium to double time.[7] The argument made to support such an increase is that even though unemployment remains a pressing national problem, the use of overtime hours has not diminished. Moreover, the argument continues, the deterrent effect of the overtime premium on the use of overtime has been weakened since the FLSA was enacted because of the growing share of hiring and training costs, fringe benefits, and government-mandated insurance premiums in total compensation (see Tables 5.1 and 5.2). As already noted, many of these costs are *quasi-fixed*, or employee-related rather than hours-related, and thus do not vary with overtime hours of work. An increase in them increases employers' marginal costs of hiring new employees relative to the costs of working their existing work forces overtime.

In terms of equation (5.3), the increase in quasi-fixed costs that has occurred causes an inequality between the ratio of marginal productivities and marginal costs at the old equilibrium employment/hours combination:

$$\frac{MC_M}{MC_H} > \frac{MP_M}{MP_H} \tag{5.4}$$

To restore the equality (and to thus minimize costs) requires increasing the right-hand side of equation (5.4). Given our assumptions of diminishing marginal productivities, if output were to remain constant, employment would have to be reduced and hours worked per employee would have to increase. It is claimed, therefore, that the growth of these quasi-fixed costs has been at least partially responsible for increased usage of overtime hours and that an increase in the

[6]In 1978, approximately 59 percent of all workers were subject to the overtime pay provisions of the FLSA. See U.S. Department of Labor, *Minimum Wage and Maximum Hours Standards Under the Fair Labor Standards Act* (Washington D.C.: U.S. Government Printing Office, October 1979). The major categories of excluded employees are executive, administrative, and professional personnel, outside salespersons, most state and local government employees, and agricultural workers.

[7]For example, Congressman John Conyers of Michigan introduced HR 1784 into Congress in February 1979. To quote a supporter of the proposal, "The AFL-CIO endorses the double-time provision as a means of generating additional jobs. The evidence is persuasive that the overtime pay requirements of the Fair Labor Standards Act have lost their effectiveness as a deterrent to regularly scheduled overtime work." (See the statement by Rudolph Oswald, Director of Research, AFL-CIO, in the minutes of the Hearings before the Subcommittee on Labor Standards on HR 1784, October 23,1979.)

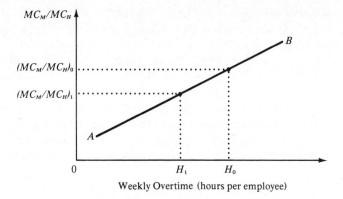

**FIGURE 5.1   Simulating the Effect of an Increase
in the Overtime Premium to Double Time**

overtime premium is required to better "spread the work."[8] Such an increase, by raising the marginal cost of overtime hours relative to the marginal cost of hiring new workers, should induce employers to substitute new employees for the overtime hours employers might otherwise schedule.

Would an increase in the overtime premium prove to be an effective way of increasing employment and reducing unemployment? A number of economists have sought to answer this question. Although the overtime premium is, for the most part, legislatively fixed at a point in time, the ratio MC_M/MC_H, varies across establishments because the weekly quasi-fixed costs and the straight-time wage rate vary across establishments. Economists have attempted to estimate the extent to which the usage of overtime hours varies across establishments with the ratio MC_M/MC_H, when all other factors are held constant.[9]

Once this relationship is known, it is possible to simulate what the effect of an increase in the overtime premium would be on overtime hours per employee. For example, suppose that the statistical analyses indicated that the relationship between overtime hours and MC_M/MC_H was given by the line AB in Figure 5.1. Consider a representative firm that faced relative marginal costs $(MC_M/MC_H)_0$ and whose employees worked an average of H_0 overtime hours per week. It is a simple matter to compute the effect on the relative marginal cost of an increase in the overtime premium to double time. If an increased premium caused a decrease to $(MC_M/MC_H)_1$, overtime hours would correspondingly fall to H_1.

Now if one *assumes* that *all* of the reduction in overtime would be converted to new full-time positions, it is possible to estimate what the effect on the employment level would be. The implied results from these studies appear in Table 5.3; these results suggest that employment increases in the range of 0.3 to 4.0 percent would

---

[8] For example, average weekly overtime hours of work in manufacturing averaged 2.56 hours per employee between 1956 and 1963. However, over the 1964–1977 period the average rose to 3.34 hours per employee, an increase of more than 30 percent. This increase undoubtedly helped stimulate the Conyers proposal mentioned in footnote 7.

[9] Since hiring- and training-costs data are not available, these studies utilize data on the other fringe benefits only.

TABLE 5.3 **Estimated Changes in Full-Time Employment Resulting from Increasing the Overtime Premium from Time-and-a-Half to Double Time**

Study	Group	Absolute Change	Percentage Change
Ehrenberg (1971)	1966 manufacturing production workers	+218,500	+1.6
Nussbaum and Wise (1977)	1968 manufacturing production workers	+491,400	+3.7
	1970 manufacturing production workers	+487,700	+3.7
	1972 manufacturing production workers	+361,900	+2.8
	1974 manufacturing production workers	+549,700	+4.0
	1968–1974 pooled manufacturing interindustry data	+320,000	+2.0
Solnick and Swimmer (1978)	1972 private nonfarm nonsupervisory workers (low estimate)	+159,264	+0.3
	1972 private nonfarm nonsupervisory workers (high estimate)	+1,521,664	+3.1

SOURCES: Ronald G. Ehrenberg, "The Impact of the Overtime Premium on Employment and Hours in U.S. Industry," *Western Economic Journal* 19 (June 1971):199–207; Joyce Nussbaum and Donald Wise, "The Employment Impact of the Overtime Provisions of the FLSA" (Final Report submitted to the U.S. Department of Labor, 1977); Loren Solnick and Gene Swimmer, "Overtime and Fringe Benefits—A Simultaneous Equations Approach" (mimeograph, 1978).

result. At first glance, then, increasing the overtime premium to double time does seem like an effective way of increasing employment and reducing unemployment.

A complete economic analysis, however, suggests that such a conclusion would be an overly optimistic assessment of the effects of a double-time premium.[10] First, these estimates *assume* that the demand for *total* labor hours is completely inelastic with respect to its cost. That is, they ignore the fact that an increase in the overtime premium raises the average cost of labor (even if overtime is eliminated), and that this may induce a shift to more capital-intensive methods of production. Further, to the extent that the cost increase is passed on to consumers in the form of higher prices, a reduction in the quantity of output will occur. Both these *scale* and *substitution effects* should lead to a decline in the number of labor hours purchased by employers; this decline will limit the employment gain associated with any given decline in overtime hours.

Second, these estimates ignore the responses of currently employed workers who would be simultaneously faced with an increase in the overtime premium and a reduction in their hours of work. Although we have yet to discuss the supply side of the labor market in detail, it should be obvious that one possible response to a reduction in overtime hours is for them to *moonlight*—to seek part-time second jobs. Moonlighting would be more likely to occur if the increase in the premium resulted in a decrease in their labor earnings.[11] If increased moonlighting occurred, the creation of new jobs for the unemployed would be further reduced.

---

[10]*See* Ronald G. Ehrenberg and Paul L. Schumann, *Longer Hours or More Jobs? An Investigation of Amending Hours Legislation to Create Employment* (Ithaca, N.Y.: New York State School of Industrial and Labor Relations, 1982).

[11]Formally, this would occur if employers' demand curves for overtime hours were elastic with respect to the overtime wage.

Third, these estimates assume that the skill distributions of the unemployed and of those who work overtime are sufficiently similar to permit all of the reduction in overtime to be converted into new full-time employment. However, *if* those working overtime were primarily skilled workers and the unemployed were primarily unskilled, potential employment gains from raising the overtime premium might be considerably smaller than these estimates.

Finally, these estimates assume that the overtime-pay provisions of the FLSA are fully complied with and that they would continue to be fully complied with after an increase in the premium to double time. However, since an increase in the overtime premium would increase the amount employers save by *not* complying with the legislation, such an increase may well lead to a reduced compliance rate, which would further reduce the positive employment effects of the legislation. A number of studies indicate that noncompliance with the overtime-pay provisions is currently at least in the 10 percent range.[12] That is, at least 10 percent of the individuals working overtime who are covered by the FLSA *fail* to receive a premium of at least time-and-a-half. Hence, the possibility of increased noncompliance cannot be dismissed.

Our analysis of the wisdom of increasing the overtime premium to double time to stimulate employment growth unfortunately reminds us that policy analysis is never as easy as one might initially hope. The world is complex and any complete analysis of a policy issue must consider a number of factors. It is in identifying what factors to consider that economic theory is so useful. Indeed, in the present case, even though the *initial* simulations suggested that a double-time premium would lead to an increase in employment, consideration of the *other* factors noted above led to a recommendation against increasing the overtime premium.[13]

FIRMS' LABOR INVESTMENTS AND THE DEMAND FOR LABOR

The models of the demand for labor given in Chapters 3 and 4 were static in the sense that they considered only *current* marginal productivities and *current* labor costs. If all of a firm's labor costs are variable each year, then its employment decisions each period are independent and it will employ labor *each period* to the point at which labor's marginal revenue product equals the wage. For a competitive firm, which takes product price as given, this condition reduces to employing labor each period up until the point at which labor's marginal product equals its real wage (the money wage divided by the price level). This condition is a straightforward generalization of the single-period decision rule expressed in equation (3.6) of Chapter 3.

---

[12]*See* Ronald G. Ehrenberg and Paul L. Schumann, "Compliance with the Overtime Pay Provisions of the Fair Labor Standards Act," *Journal of Law and Economics* 25 (April 1982):159–81.

[13]Ehrenberg and Schumann, *Longer Hours or More Jobs?*

However, once we begin to consider hiring and training costs, the analysis changes somewhat.[14] Hiring and training costs are usually heavily concentrated in the initial periods of employment and do no recur. Later on, however, these early investments in hiring and training raise the productivity of employees. Once the investments are made, it is cheaper for the firm to *continue* hiring its previous workers than to hire, at the same wage rate, new ones (who would have to be trained). Likewise, with an investment required for all *new* workers, employers have to consider not only *current* marginal productivity and labor costs, but also *future* marginal productivity and labor costs in deciding whether (and how many) to hire. In short, the presence of investment costs—hiring and training expenses— means that hiring decisions must take into account past, present, and future factors.

To illustrate the hiring decision in the face of labor-investment costs, let us consider a firm that is seeking to determine its employment level over a two-period horizon. To keep the discussion simple, we shall ignore fringe-benefit costs and the decision about how many hours employees will work; all workers employed in a period will be assumed to work for the entire period. We shall also assume that the firm is a competitive firm that takes its product price as given. Hence, as in Chapter 3, we can express all of the firm's labor costs in real terms (money costs divided by the price level).

Now suppose the firm incurs hiring and training costs only in the initial period (period 0) and that these *direct outlays* amount to Z per worker in real terms. Suppose also that during the initial period, when workers are undergoing training, their actual marginal product schedule is lowered from MP^* to MP_0 (as shown in Figure 5.2)—in other words, $MP^* - MP_0$ represents the *implicit* costs of training in real terms. In the period after training (period 1), the marginal productivity of trained employees is higher (MP_1). Finally, suppose that the real wage a firm must pay each employee, the money wage divided by the product price, is W_0 and W_1 in periods 0 and 1, respectively; for now, we take these wages as given by the market, although we shall shortly examine how they are determined.

The Concept of Present Value

In determining its optimal employment level over the two periods, the firm clearly must consider the costs of employing workers in both periods and their marginal products in both periods. A *naive* approach would be to simply add up the costs $(W_0 + W_1 + Z)$, add up the marginal products $(MP_0 + MP_1)$, and then stop hiring when the sum of the marginal products that the last worker produces over the two periods is just equal to the sum of his or her wages and hiring/training costs in real terms. This approach is naive because it ignores the fact that benefits accruing in the future are worth less to the firm than an equal level of benefits that accrue now. Similarly, costs that occur in the future are less burdensome to the firm than equal dollar costs that occur in the present.

---

[14]This section draws heavily on Gary Becker's pioneering work, *Human Capital,* 2nd ed. (New York: National Bureau of Economic Research, 1975); and on Oi, "Labor as a Quasi-Fixed Factor."

Marginal Product of Labor *(MP)*
Present Value of Marginal Product of Labor *(PVP)*
Present Value of Real Marginal Cost of Labor *(PVC)*

$$PVC = W_0 + Z + \frac{W_1}{1 + r}$$

$$PVP = MP_0 + \frac{MP_1}{1 + r}$$

MP_1 (after training)

MP^* (potential marginal productivity in the absence of training)

MP_0 (during training)

0 E^*

Employment Level

FIGURE 5.2   Multiperiod Demand for Labor

Why should this be the case? The answer hinges on the role of interest rates. A dollar of revenue earned by a firm today can be invested at some market rate of interest so that by the second period it will be worth more than a dollar. Hence, faced with a choice of employing a worker whose marginal product is 5 in period 0 and 2 in period 1, or a worker whose marginal product is 2 in period 0 and 5 in period 1, the firm would prefer the former (if wages for the two workers were equal in each period). The sooner the product is produced and sold, the quicker the firm can gain access to the funds, invest them, and earn interest.[15] Similarly, faced with the option of paying a $100 wage bill today or $100 next period, the firm should prefer the second option. It could earn interest on the $100 in the first period, make the payment in the next period, and have the interest left over. If the firm had made the payment in the initial period, it could not have earned interest income.

These examples illustrate why firms prefer benefit streams in which the benefits occur as early as possible and prefer cost streams in which the costs occur as late as possible. But how do we compare different benefit and cost streams when benefits and costs occur in more than one period? Economists rely on the concept of *present value*, which we define to be the value *now* of an entire stream of benefits or costs.

Suppose a firm receives the sum of B_0 in the current period and will receive nothing in the next period. How much money could it have in the second period if it invested B_0 at a rate of interest that equals r? It would have its original sum, B_0, plus the interest it earned, rB_0:

$$B_1 = B_0 + rB_0 = B_0 (1 + r). \tag{5.5}$$

---

[15]We are assuming here, of course, that the real price the firm receives for its product is constant and that the real rate of interest is positive.

Since assets of B_1 can be automatically acquired by investing B_0 at the market rate of interest, B_0 *now and* B_1 *next period are equivalent values.* That is, a person who is offered B_0 now or B_1 in one year would regard the offers as exactly the same as long as $B_1 = B_0 (1 + r)$.

Following this line of reasoning, suppose that the firm knows it will receive B_1 in the second period. What is the value of that sum to the firm in the first period? The firm would need to have sum X in the first period in order to invest this sum and wind up with principal plus interest equal to B_1 in period 2:

$$X (1 + r) = B_1. \tag{5.6}$$

Dividing both sides by $(1 + r)$,

$$X = \frac{B_1}{1 + r}. \tag{5.7}$$

The quantity X in equation (5.7) is called the *discounted value* of B_1 earned one period in the future.

The *present value* of the firm's earnings over two periods is equal to its earnings in the first period plus the discounted value of its earnings in the second period.[16] Returning to our two-period hiring decision example given at the start of this section, the *present value* of marginal productivity *(PVP)* can now be seen as

$$PVP = MP_0 + \frac{MP_1}{1 + r}. \tag{5.8}$$

That is, the value of a worker's marginal productivity *now* to the firm is the marginal productivity in the current period *(MP₀)* plus the marginal productivity in the second period *discounted* by $(1 + r)$. Likewise, the present value of the real marginal *cost* of labor *(PVC)* is equal to

$$PVC = W_0 + Z + \frac{W_1}{1 + r}, \tag{5.9}$$

where r is the market rate of interest. W_0 and Z are not discounted because they are incurred in the current period. However, W_1 is discounted by $(1 + r)$ because it is incurred one year in the future.

The present value calculation reduces a stream of benefits or costs to a single number that summarizes a firm's entire stream of revenues or liabilities over different time periods. For example, the *PVC* can be thought of as the answer to the question, "Given that a firm incurs costs per worker of $(W_0 + Z)$ this period and W_1 next period, how much does it have to set aside today to be able to cover both periods' costs?" The *PVC* is *less* than $W_0 + Z + W_1$ because W_1 is not owed until the second period and any funds set aside to cover W_1 can be invested now. If it sets aside $W_1/(1 + r)$ to cover its labor cost in the next period and invests this amount earning a rate of return r, the interest, $r[W_1/(1 + r)]$, plus principal, $W_1/(1 + r)$, available in the next period will just equal W_1. Similarly, the *PVP* can be thought of as the answer to the question, "Given that a worker's marginal product will be MP_0 in this period and MP_1 next period, what is the value of that output stream to the employer today?" The *PVP* is less than $MP_0 + MP_1$ because if the firm were to

---

[16]Earnings in the first period are not discounted because they are received *now*, not in the future.

attempt to borrow against the employee's future marginal product, it could borrow at most $MP_1/(1 + r)$ today and still afford to repay the principal plus interest, $r[MP_1/(1 + r)]$, out of earnings in the second period.[17]

The Multi-period Demand for Labor

The concept of present value can help clarify what determines the demand-for-labor function in our two-period model. Rather than focusing on the marginal product of labor in each period, an employee's productivity must be summarized by the *present value* of the marginal product schedule, which is drawn as the curve *PVP* in Figure 5.2. Similarly, rather than focusing on the hiring and training costs and the wage rates in each period separately, an employer must consider the *present value* of the marginal cost of labor (*PVC*). To maximize its present value of profits, a firm should employ labor up until the point that adding an *additional* employee yields as much as it costs in real terms (when both yields and costs are stated as present values):

$$PVP = PVC, \text{ or } MP_0 + \frac{MP_1}{1 + r} = W_0 + Z + \frac{W_1}{1 + r} \qquad (5.10)$$

Given the particular values of W_0, W_1, Z, and r that are specified in Figure 5.2, this proves to be the employment level E^*. More generally, the employer's demand-for-labor schedule coincides with the present value of the marginal-product-of-labor schedule.

Now equation (5.10) merely states the familiar profit-maximizing condition, that marginal returns should equal marginal costs, in a multiperiod context. If Z were zero, for example, equation (5.10) implies that profits could be maximized when labor is hired so that $MP_0 = W_0$ and $MP_1/(1 + r) = W_1/(1 + r)$, or, since $1 + r$ is the denominator on both sides of the equation, $MP_1 = W_1$. Thus, when there are no hiring or training costs ($Z = 0$), the conditions demonstrated in Chapter 3 are sufficient to guarantee profit maximization in the multiperiod context. However, when Z is positive, which means that firms make initial investments in their workers, the conditions for maximizing profits change.

To understand the change in profit-maximizing conditions suggested by equation (5.10), suppose that in the first period the real wage the worker receives (W_0)

---

[17]More generally, if the firm expects to receive benefits of B_0, B_1, B_2, . . . , B_n dollars over the current and next n periods, and if it faces the same interest rate, r, in each period, its present value of benefits *(PVB)* is given by

$$PVB = B_0 + \frac{B_1}{1 + r} + \frac{B_2}{(1 + r)^2} + \frac{B_3}{(1 + r)^3} + \cdots + \frac{B_n}{(1 + r)^n}$$

An analogous expression exists for the present value of costs. The reader should make sure that he or she understands why the denominator of B_2 is $(1 + r)^2$, the denominator of B_3 is $(1 + r)^3$, etc. If one thinks in terms of a series of one-period loans or investments, it should become obvious. For example, X_0 invested for one period yields $X_0 (1 + r)$ at the end of the period. Let us call $X_0 (1 + r) = X_1$. X_0 invested for two periods is equal to its value after one period (X_1) times $(1 + r)$—or $X_2 = X_1 (1 + r)$. But $X_1 = X_0 (1 + r)$, so $X_2 = X_0 (1 + r)^2$. To find the present value of X_2 we divide by $(1 + r)^2$, so $X_0 = X_2/(1 + r)^2$.

plus the firm's direct investment outlays *(Z)* exceed the extra worker's output *(MP$_0$)*. We can call this difference the *net cost* to the firm of hiring an additional worker in the first period *(NC$_0$)*:

$$NC_0 = W_0 + Z - MP_0 > 0. \qquad (5.11)$$

In order for the firm to maximize the present value of its profit stream, it must thus get a net *surplus* in the second period—see equation (5.10). If it does not, the firm will not have any incentive to hire the additional worker.

The discounted value of the second period's surplus *(G)* is defined as:

$$G = \frac{MP_1}{1 + r} - \frac{W_1}{1 + r} = \frac{MP_1 - W_1}{1 + r}. \qquad (5.12)$$

From equations (5.10), (5.11), and (5.12), we see that the discounted value of the second-period surplus must equal the net cost *(NC$_0$)* in the first period if the firm is to maximize profits:

$$W_0 + Z - MP_0 = \frac{MP_1 - W_1}{1 + r} \qquad (5.13)$$

A second-period surplus can *only* exist if real wages in that period *(W$_1$)* lie *below* marginal product *(MP$_1$)*. This surplus makes up for the fact that the employer's labor costs in the first period *(W$_0$ + Z)* were above the worker's marginal product *(MP$_0$)*.

To this point we have established two things. First, equation (5.10) has shown that in a multiperiod model of labor demand, the firm's demand curve is the same thing as the curve representing the *present value* of labor's marginal product over the periods of hire. Thus, the firm maximizes profits when the present value of its marginal labor costs in real terms equals the present value of labor's marginal product. Second, we demonstrated in equation (5.13) that maximizing profits when the firm's labor costs in the first period exceed the worker's first-period marginal product requires real wages in the second period to be below marginal productivity in the second period (so that a surplus is generated). The only times when a second-period surplus is not necessary to induce the hiring of an additional employee are when investment costs *(Z)* are zero in the first period or when investment costs of Z exist but the first-period real wage is decreased to such an extent that it equals $MP_0 - Z$. In the latter case, employees pay for their own training by accepting a wage in the first period that is decreased by the direct costs of training. Understanding how W_0 and W_1 are determined, then, is central to the task of analyzing the demand for labor in the presence of investment costs. To understand the level and time profile of wages, however, we must first examine the nature of job training.

TRAINING INVESTMENTS

In this section we shall consider the types of training a firm will find it profitable to undertake and trace out some important implications of training investments by firms. In the section that follows we shall analyze hiring investments.

General and Specific Training

Following Gary Becker, it is useful to conceptually distinguish between two types of training: *general training* that increases an individual's productivity *to many employers* equally, and *specific training* that increases an individual's productivity *only at the firm* in which he or she is currently employed.[18] Pure general training might include teaching an applicant basic reading skills or teaching a would-be secretary how to type. Pure specific training might include teaching a worker how to use a machine that is unique to a single employer or showing him or her the organization of the production process in the plant. The distinction is primarily a conceptual one because most training contains aspects of both types; however, the distinction does yield some interesting insights.

Suppose (continuing our two-period model) that a firm offers *general* training to its employees and incurs a first-period net cost equal to NC_0 of equation (5.11). This training increases employee marginal productivity to MP_1 in the second period, and the firm scales its wages (W_1) in the second period so that there is a surplus in that period whose present value (G) equals NC_0. What will happen? The trained employee is worth MP_1 to several other firms, but is getting paid less than MP_1 by the firm doing the training (so that it can obtain the required surplus). The employee can thus get *more* from some other employer, who did not incur training costs and thus will not demand a surplus, than he or she can from the employer offering the training. This situation will induce the employee to quit after training and seek work elsewhere. Assuming all other conditions of employment are the same, the firm would have to pay its employees MP_1 after training to keep them from quitting.

If firms must pay a wage equal to MP_1 after training, they will not be willing to pay for general training of their employees. They either will not offer training or will force trainees to bear the full cost of their training by paying wages that are less than marginal product in the period of training by an amount equal to the direct training costs (that is, NC_0 must equal zero). Exceptions to this conclusion can be found in cases in which the employee is bound to the firm in some way. For example, the federal government requires employees it has sent to college (in Master of Business Administration programs, for example) to remain in the federal service for a specified number of years or to repay the costs of the training. Similarly, firms may offer to pay for the general training of long-term employees bound to the firm by pension rights or unique promotion opportunities (see Chapter 11 for further discussion).

In contrast, consider an individual who receives *specific training* that increases marginal productivity with the *current* employer to MP_1 in the second period. Since the training is firm-specific, the trainee's marginal product in *other* firms remains at its pretraining level of MP^*. Now the firm that trains the worker *will* have an incentive to offer (and at least partially pay for) the job training because it can pay a wage above MP^* but below MP_1 in the second period.

Why will it pay above MP^* in the second period? It will do so because if it makes a first-period investment in the worker, it does not want the worker to quit. If

---

[18]Becker, *Human Capital*.

it pays $MP*$, the worker will not have much of an incentive to stay with the firm, since he or she can get $MP*$ elsewhere, too. The higher W_1 is compared to $MP*$, the less likely the worker is to quit. Why will the firm pay less than MP_1? As noted earlier, the firm must obtain a surplus in the second period to recoup its first-period investment costs. Thus, the firm prefers a *second-period* wage that is above $MP*$ and below MP_1:

$$MP* < W_1 < MP_1. \tag{5.14}$$

This second-period wage is also preferred by employees. If, for example, they were promised a wage equal to MP_1 in the second period, the lack of employer surplus would mean two things. First, employees would be required to pay the *full* cost of training in the first period, and, second, they would live in fear of being laid off. Since their second-period wage would be equal to their marginal productivity, a firm would not lose much if it laid them off—and *the workers* would lose all the investment costs incurred in the first period. However, if the workers generated a surplus for the employer, layoff would be less likely in the post-training period.

The wage scheme in equation (5.14) thus suggests that the employer and employee should be willing to share in the costs of specific training. If employees bear *all* the costs of training, there will be no second-period surplus to protect them from layoff. If employers bear *all* the costs, they may not be able to pay their employees enough in the second period to guard against their quitting. It is in their *shared* interest to foster a long-term employment relationship, which can best be done by sharing the investment costs of the first period.

Implications of the Theory

Layoffs.   One major implication of the presence of specific training is the above-mentioned reluctance of firms to lay off workers in whom they have invested. We have seen that in the post-training period, wages must be less than marginal productivity if the firm is to have any incentive at all to bear some initial training costs. This gap between MP_1 and W_1 provides protection against employee layoffs, even in a recession.

Suppose a recession were to occur and cause product demand to fall. The marginal productivity associated with each employment level would fall (from MP' to MP'' in Figure 5.3). For workers whose wage was equal to marginal productivity before the recession, this fall would reduce their marginal productivity to *below* their wage—and profit-maximizing employers would reduce employment, as shown in panel (a) of Figure 5.3, in order to maximize profits under the changed market conditions. In terms of Figure 5.3(a), employment would fall from E' to E''.

For a worker whose wage was *less* than marginal productivity, owing to past specific training, the decline in marginal productivity might *still* leave such productivity *above* the wage. Firms would not be making enough surplus in the second period to earn back their net labor costs incurred during the training period. However, these costs have already been spent and they cannot get them back. They will not hire and train *new* workers, but neither will they fire the ones they have trained. After all, these trained workers are still generating more than the company

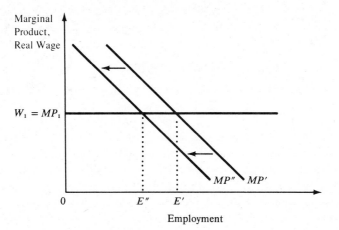

(a) General Training
A decline in *MP* will reduce employment
for those whose real wage = MP_1 initially.

(b) Specific Training
A decline in *MP* will not necessarily reduce employment
for those whose real wage < MP_1 initially.

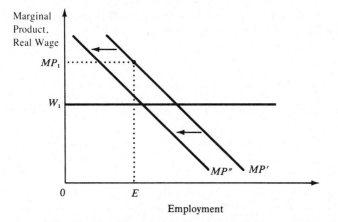

**FIGURE 5.3   The Effect of a Decline in Demand on Employment
with General and Specific Training**

is paying them, and to lay them off would only reduce profits further. Thus, as panel
(b) of Figure 5.3 shows, workers in whom their employers have invested are
shielded to some extent from being laid off in business downturns. Of course, if
marginal productivity fell to the point where it was below the wage, even trained
workers might be laid off.[19]

Thus, this model suggests that during an economic downswing firms have an

---

[19]If the downturn is expected to be short and if marginal productivity is not too much below the wage,
firms might not lay off workers and chance losing them. Why any adjustment would come in the form
of layoff, rather than by temporarily reducing wages or hours of work, is discussed in Chapter 15.

Example 5.2

Paternalism in Japan—Is It Rooted in Feudalism or Economics?

In Japan there are many large firms in which employer and employee are committed to a virtual lifetime relationship. These firms almost never lay off workers, and all of their new hires have recently left school. Employees, on the other hand, are given incentives to remain with the firm for their entire career. Wages are strongly linked to seniority, pensions and paid vacations are formulated to encourage a long job tenure, and company loyalty is encouraged through the provision of "paternalistic services," such as company housing, health care, and recreational facilities. James Abegglen describes the consequences of these employment policies:

> At whatever level of organization in the Japanese factory, the worker commits himself on entrance to the company for the remainder of his working career. The company will not discharge him even temporarily except in the most extreme circumstances. He will not quit the company for industrial employment elsewhere. He is a member of the company in a way resembling that in which persons are members of families. . . .

While the paternalistic employment relationship described above really pertains to less than half of all Japanese workers—full-time, year-round, predominantly male workers in large firms—the mere existence of such a seemingly permanent employer–employee attachment for so many workers in Japan has drawn much comment. Abegglen views this lifelong relationship as a natural outgrowth of Japan's feudal system prior to industrial development, with its emphasis on the reciprocal loyalty of lord and vassal:

> The loyalty of the worker to the industrial organization, the paternal methods of motivating and rewarding the worker, the close involvement of the company in all manner of what seem to Western eyes to be personal and private affairs of the worker—all have parallels with Japan's preindustrial social organization.

Adherents of this explanation seem to conclude that the Japanese system of industrial relations represents a continuation of an ancient elitist paternalism, rather than a system that was consciously chosen for economic reasons by rational industrialists.

An alternative view is that the Japanese system described above finds its roots in profit-maximization calculus. Those who espouse this view argue that Japan's rapid industrialization beginning around 1900 was accompanied by severe shortages of skilled factory workers. Firms competed against each other for skilled labor, and by the end of World War I this fierce competition for workers had led to annual turnover rates of 100 percent for many factories. By 1917 firms were using bribes, cash bonuses, and even physical threats to secure and retain a work force. A government report in 1919 lamented, "The virtue of long and diligent service has been supplanted by a propensity to change jobs."

Faced with such a high degree of employee turnover, firms did not find it profitable to train their own workers; these workers would be gone before they could recoup their investment costs. To reduce the need for constant recruiting, and to induce employees to have long enough job attachments to make training feasible, firms began to offer cash bonuses, company-paid pleasure trips, and shares of company profits to long-term workers. Company housing was provided, and firms took an active interest in improving the quality of worker life both on and off the job. While the "loose" labor markets of the early 1930s provided a setback, industrial growth and attendant labor shortages during and after World War II fostered the growth of the Japanese system of paternalism throughout the economy. Advocates of this alternative view of Japan's paternalism, such as Koji Taira, argue that the paternalistic system is based more on the need of employers to protect training investments than on feudal tradition.

SOURCES: James C. Abegglen, *The Japanese Factory: Aspects of Its Social Organization* (Glencoe, Ill.: The Free Press, 1958); Clark Kerr, *Industrialization and Industrial Man* (Cambridge, Mass.: Harvard University Press, 1960); Koji Taira, *Economic Development and the Labor Market in Japan* (New York: Columbia University Press, 1970).

incentive to lay off workers with either no training or general training, but that it may prove profitable for firms to retain workers who have specific training. Although it is difficult to estimate the extent to which workers have specific training "imbedded" in them, there is some evidence that layoffs are lower for workers with higher skill levels, holding all other things including their *wage rates* constant.[20] Since the divergence between skill (productivity) and wages during the post-training period can be taken as a measure of the extent of specific training, this finding provides some support for the theory.

Labor productivity. A second phenomenon our revised theory of demand can help explain is the fall in average productivity—output per labor hour—that occurs in the early stages of a recession.[21] As demand and output start to fall, firms that have invested in specific training respond by maintaining their specifically trained workers on their payrolls. Such *labor hoarding* causes measured productivity to fall. Of course, the converse of this is that when demand picks up, firms can increase their output levels without proportionately increasing their employment levels because they, in effect, maintained an *inventory* of skilled labor. Labor hoarding due to specific investments in human capital thus causes average productivity to increase in the early stages of a cyclical expansion and decrease in the early stages of a recession.

Minimum wage effects again. A third implication of our theory has to do with training effects of the minimum wage. We have seen that firms will offer *general*

---

[20]For a summary of the evidence, see Donald O. Parsons, "Models of Labor Market Turnover: A Theoretical and Empirical Survey," in Ronald G. Ehrenberg, ed., *Research in Labor Economics*, vol. 1 (Greenwich, Conn.: JAI Press, 1977). Parsons also provides evidence on the existence of a negative relationship between quit rates and specific training; as noted earlier, this is another implication of the theory.

[21]*See* the 1977 *Employment and Training Report of the President* (Washington, D.C.: U.S. Government Printing Office, 1977), pp. 23–25.

training only if the employee fully pays for it. For this to be the case, the employee must receive a first-period wage that is below actual marginal productivity by an amount equal to the direct costs of training. If the minimum wage is set so that receiving such a low wage is precluded, then employers will not offer them training. They may be willing to *hire* workers, if the minimum wage is not above their marginal productivity, but any training would have to take place off the job.

This same analysis would also hold for *specific* training. If the minimum wage prevented the *first*-period wage from going low enough, firms offering specific training might *not* be able to offer *second*-period wages that are higher than workers' alternative offers. If this is the case, trained workers will always be on the verge of quitting in the second period, which places the firm's first-period investment at risk. Under these conditions, firms will have little incentive to offer specific training. Minimum wage legislation may thus reduce the number of jobs offering training options that are available to low-skilled youths and lower their rates of wage growth. In fact, there is some evidence that this has occurred.[22]

HIRING INVESTMENTS

As pointed out earlier, firms often incur significant costs in selecting employees. These costs cause them to establish institutions or behave in ways that can be explained using the concepts we have discussed. The implications of hiring costs are the subject of this section.

Credentials or Screening Devices

Since firms often bear the costs of hiring and training workers, it is in their interests to make these costs as low as possible. Other things equal, firms should prefer to obtain a given quality work force at the least possible cost. Similarly, they should prefer to hire workers who are fast learners because such workers could be trained at less cost. Unfortunately, it may prove expensive for firms to extensively investigate the backgrounds of every possible individual who applies for a job to ascertain his or her skill level and ability to undertake training.

One way to reduce these costs is to rely on *credentials*, or *signals*, in the hiring process, rather than intensively investigating the qualities of individual applicants.[23] For example, if *on average* college graduates are more productive than high-school graduates, an employer might specify that a college degree is a requirement for the job. Rather than interviewing and testing all applicants to try to ascertain the productivity of each, the firm may simply select its new employees from the pool of

---

[22]Masanori Hashimoto, "Minimum Wage Effects and Training on the Job," *American Economic Review*, 72 (December 1982):1070–87; and Linda Leighton and Jacob Mincer, "Effects of Minimum Wages on Human Capital Formation," in Simon Rottenberg, ed., *The Economics of Legal Minimum Wages* (Washington, D.C.: American Enterprise Institute, 1981), pp. 155–73.

[23]*See* Michael Spence, "Job Market Signaling," *Quarterly Journal of Economics* 87 (August 1973):355–74. See also Appendix 9A, " 'Signaling' in the Labor Market."

applicants who meet this educational standard. Similarly, if employers believe that married men are less likely to quit their jobs than single men, or that 25-year-olds are less likely to quit than teenagers, they may give preferential treatment to married men and 25-year-olds over single men and teenagers in their hiring decisions.

Such forms of *statistical discrimination*, judging individuals by *group* characteristics, have obvious costs. On the one hand, for example, some high-school graduates may be fully qualified to work for a firm that insists on college graduates. The exclusion of them from the pool of potential applicants imposes costs on them (they do not get the job); however, it also imposes costs on the employer *if* other qualified applicants cannot be readily found. On the other hand, there may be some "lemons" among the group of college graduates, and if the employer hires them he or she may well suffer losses while they are employed. However, if the reduction in hiring costs that arises when *signals* (such as educational credentials, marital status, or age) are used is large, it may prove profitable for an employer to use them even if an occasional lemon sneaks through. Put another way, the total costs of hiring, training, and employing workers may well be lower for some firms when hiring standards are used than when such firms rely upon more intensive investigations of applicant characteristics. (Chapter 14 will return to the issue of statistical discrimination.)

Internal Labor Markets

A major problem with the use of credentials, or screening devices, to predict which applicants will become good employees is that these credentials may only be loosely related to actual productivity on the job. Such personal attributes as dependability, motivation, honesty, and flexibility are difficult to observe using credentials, yet for many jobs such attributes may be crucial. This difficulty with screening has induced some firms to adopt a policy of hiring workers at low-level jobs, observing their behavior, and filling all upper-level jobs from within the firm—that is, filling all upper-level vacancies with people whose characteristics have been carefully observed in other jobs the firm has given them to do.

This second approach to the problem of minimizing hiring costs while maximizing the productivity of employees creates an *internal labor market*, because most jobs in the firm are filled from within the ranks of current employees.[24] The hiring done from outside the firm tends to be heavily concentrated at certain low-

---

[24]For a detailed discussion of internal labor markets, *see* Peter Doeringer and Michael Piore, *Internal Labor Markets and Manpower Analysis* (Lexington, Mass.: D.C. Heath and Company, 1971). The same general concept has been identified by others as "industrial feudalism," "balkanization of labor markets," and "property rights" in a job. *See* Arthur Ross, "Do We Have a New Industrial Feudalism?" *American Economic Review*, 48, 5 (December 1958): 914; Clark Kerr, "The Balkanization of Labor Markets," in E. Wight Bakke, et. al., *Labor Mobility and Economic Opportunity* (Cambridge, Mass.: MIT Press, 1954); and Frederick Meyers, *Ownership of Jobs: A Comparative Study*, Institute of Industrial Relations Monograph Series (Los Angeles: University of California Press, 1964). Other reasons for the existence of internal labor markets are found more recently in Oliver Williamson, et al., "Understanding the Employment Relation: The Analysis of Idiosyncratic Exchange," *Bell Journal of Economics* 16 (Spring 1975):250–80.

level "ports of entry." These jobs—such as "general laborer," "machine cleaner," and "packer" for blue-collar applicants or "management trainee" for white-collar applicants—are at sufficiently low responsibility levels that a bad employee cannot do too much damage to the firm or its equipment. However, these jobs do give the firm a chance to observe *actual* productive characteristics of the employees hired, and this information is then used to determine who stays with the firm and how fast and how high employees are promoted.

The *benefits* of using an internal labor market to fill vacancies is that the firm knows a lot about the people working for it. Hiring decisions for upper-level jobs in either the blue-collar or white-collar work forces will thus offer few surprises to the firm. The *costs* of using the internal labor market are associated with the restriction of competition for the upper-level jobs to those in the firm. Those in the firm may not be the best employees available, but they are the only ones the firm considers for these jobs. Firms most likely to decide that the benefits of using an internal labor market outweigh the costs are those whose upper-level workers must have a lot of firm-specific knowledge and training that can best be attained by on-the-job learning over the years. For those firms, the number of qualified *outside* applicants for upper-level jobs is relatively small. Firms in the steel, petroleum, and chemical industries tend to rely on internal labor markets to fill vacancies, while those in the garment and shoe industries do not.[25] The former group of industries has highly automated, complicated, and interdependent production technologies that can only be mastered through years on the job. The garment- and shoe-manufacturing industries employ workers who perform certain discrete crafts, skills that are not specific to one firm.

As noted earlier, firms engaged in *specific training* will want to ensure that they obtain a stable, long-term work force, which can learn quickly and perform well later on. For these firms, the internal labor market offers two attractions. First, it allows the firm to observe workers on the job, where it can see firsthand who learns quickly, who is easily motivated, who is dependable, and so forth, and thus make better decisions about which workers will be the recipients of later, perhaps very expensive, training. Second, the internal labor market tends to foster an attachment to the firm by its employees. They know that outsiders will not be considered for upper-level vacancies and that they, therefore, have an inside track on job vacancies. If they quit the firm, they would lose this privileged position. They are thus motivated to become long-term employees of the firm. The full implications of internal labor markets for wage policies within the firm will be discussed in the chapter on compensation (Chapter 11).

POLICY APPLICATION: WHY DO EMPLOYERS DISCRIMINATE IN HIRING?

It is commonly asserted that older workers and women are not given the same preference as *prime-aged* men (men between 25 and 55) in filling many jobs,

---

[25]Doeringer and Piore, *Internal Labor Markets and Manpower Analysis*, p. 43.

Example 5.3
Coping with Fluctuations in Product Demand

The demand for a firm's product is never constant over a given period. It fluctuates from day to day, week to week, and month to month. If a firm finds it feasible to hold inventories of its finished goods, these fluctuations in demand can be absorbed by *product inventories*, thus permitting the firm to keep its employment and production levels constant during the period. That is, in periods when product demand does not absorb what is produced, the firm stores its unsold output; in periods when demand exceeds output, these stores are drawn down.

Many firms, however, find that the costs of maintaining inventories are very high. Some products are perishable; they either spoil or become obsolete very quickly. Other products are expensive to make or bulky to store, and keeping inventories of them ties up funds and building space, requires large insurance coverage, and imposes added property taxes on the firm. Still other firms produce services, which by their very nature are impossible to produce ahead of demand. How can firms with high inventory costs cope with fluctuating demand?

One way to cope is to hire workers on a temporary basis when product demand is unusually high. As indicated in the text, however, the one-time costs of advertising an opening, screening candidates, and processing the paperwork necessary to put workers on the payroll can be quite high. If the tenure of a job is relatively short, the firm may have insufficient time to recoup these costs. In this case the firm might consider "renting" workers from a temporary help service.

Temporary help services specialize in screening and hiring workers who are then put to work in client plants that need temporary workers. These workers are technically employees of, and receive their paychecks from, the temporary help service; however, they work under the direction and supervision of the client.

The temporary help service bills its clients for the time its workers spend under their direction. The hourly charges to its clients are generally *above* the wage the client would pay if it hired directly—a premium the client is willing to pay because it is spared the investment costs associated with hiring. Because obtaining jobs through the temporary help service also saves employees repeated investment costs associated with searching and applying for available temporary openings, the employees are willing to take a wage *less* than they otherwise would receive. The difference between what its clients are charged and what its employees are paid, of course, permits the successful temporary help service to cover the investment costs necessary to obtain a match of employer and employee and to earn a profit.

Hiring temporary workers is clearly not feasible if a significant amount of specific training must be undertaken before the job can be adequately performed. When job tenure is expected to be short, neither employer nor employee has enough time to recoup training costs (for this reason, temporary help services deal mainly with jobs requiring general training: typing, drafting, simple clerical skills, and so forth). When specific training is important, the firm might use *overtime* to meet fluctuations in product demand. This option, discussed at length in the text, involves paying a substantial wage premium, in some cases leads to problems associated with fatigue, and could cause problems in coordinating production in some industries.

The final option for meeting fluctuations in demand is to hire *reserve workers*—workers who are hired on a full-time basis but who are idle or partially idle some of the time. Some large plants with easily predicted absentee rates hire and train workers to fill in for absentees. What may be more common, however, is to keep everyone partially idle during normal periods by running production lines at less than maximum speed. During periods of increased demand, production rates can be increased without having to hire more labor or resort to overtime. The cost of reserve workers, of course, is associated with the fact that they are paid even when essentially idle.

Which strategy a firm will choose to cope with product demand fluctuations depends on the relative costs of each. One study, for example, found greater use of reserve workers in industries in which product inventory costs are relatively high.[1] If a firm finds that all strategies to meet product demand fluctuations are too costly, it can exercise its final option and let orders go unfilled, which runs the risk of losing both current and future customers.

[1] Roger LeRoy Miller, "The Reserve Labour Hypothesis: Some Tests of Its Implications," *Economic Journal* 81 (March 1971):17–35.

especially the better-paying ones. While this preference may be rooted in prejudice, there may also be an underlying, nondiscriminatory rationale for it. Chapter 14 will discuss discrimination, but we wish to point out here that what *appears* to be prejudice may be employer behavior designed to avoid losses on hiring and training investments.

To illustrate how the presence of hiring and training costs bears on the issue of apparent age or sex discrimination, let us assume two people apply for a job for which the employer is intending to make a first-period investment of Z in hiring and training costs. It is expected that one applicant will be with the firm for two periods, while the other will remain for three periods. Which will the firm prefer to hire?

If it were possible to find workers and train them without cost, firms would not care about the length of their tenure. If one worker quit, a replacement could easily and costlessly be found. When hiring a worker involves an initial investment by the firm, however, employers prefer to hire workers with relatively long expected tenures. The longer an employee is expected to be with the firm, the more likely it is the firm will recoup its initial investment costs. Thus, if the two applicants in our example were alike in every respect except their expected length of tenure with the firm, the one expected to remain with the firm for three periods would be preferred.

This preference can be demonstrated by referring back to equation (5.12). Equation (5.12) calculates the present value of a worker's post-training surplus *(G)* for a case in which he or she will be employed for just one period after training. To repeat, the present value of the surplus in cases in which there is *one* post-training period, which we shall call G_1, is calculated as:

$$G_1 = \frac{MP_1 - W_1}{1 + r} \qquad (5.15)$$

If there are *two* post-training periods of employment, the present value of a firm's surplus is found by adding to G_1 the discounted value of the surplus in the second post-training period. The *undiscounted* surplus in this period is the difference between marginal productivity and wages *(MP$_2$ − W$_2$)*. However, because this surplus occurs farther into the future than period one's surplus, it must be more heavily discounted when calculating present value. This is done by dividing *(MP$_2$ − W$_2$)* by $(1 + r)^2$—the rationale for which is given in footnote 17. Thus, the present value of a surplus derived over two periods (G_2) is:

$$G_2 = \frac{MP_1 - W_1}{1 + r} + \frac{MP_2 - W_2}{(1 + r)^2} \qquad (5.16)$$

It is obvious, by comparing G_2 and G_1, that the post-training surplus a firm can expect to gain from a worker increases as the expected length of the worker's tenure with the firm goes up, if other things are equal. That is, if the differences between marginal productivity and wages are the same for two workers, the one with the longer tenure will generate more post-training "surplus" for the firm.

Applicants who are very close to retirement will not be seriously considered for jobs that require large employer hiring or training investments (*unless* they accept a low post-training wage). That is, if post-training wages are equal, firms tend to prefer prime-aged applicants to equally productive older ones whenever substantial employer hiring or training investments are involved because the older applicants may retire before the firm can recoup its investment costs. Older workers could redress this imbalance in hiring preferences only by agreeing to work for a lower wage than younger applicants or by paying at least some of the hiring and training costs themselves, conditions that themselves might raise charges of discrimination!

This same reasoning can help explain why women have not had ready access to jobs requiring sizable initial employer investments. Women—or at least *married* women—have tended to enter and leave the labor force more often than men. Chapter 9 will show, for example, that many married women enter the labor force in their early 20s, drop out to care for children, and then re-enter later on. Chapter 15 will also note that the average white woman worker age 25–59 is 15 times more likely to go from having a job to being out of the labor force than a comparable male worker during a one-month period. (For blacks, the probability of going from employment to out of the labor force is 3 times higher for females.) The result of this movement in and out of the labor force among women is that the average length of job tenure for males is about twice what it is for women. That is, the average male worker in 1978 had been on his current job for 4.5 years, while the average woman had been on her job for just 2.6 years.[26]

The shorter average job tenure among women could legitimately induce employers contemplating hiring and training investments to be wary of investing in female workers. This concern has an understandable economic rationale to it, but it also offers a good example of what we earlier called *statistical discrimination* (judging individuals by the characteristics of the group to which they belong). In this case, statistical discrimination could have unfortunate consequences for women who *do* plan continuous careers outside the home. For example, single (never-married) women age 25–34 have about the same average job tenure (2.6 years) as men of that age (2.7 years). For single women age 35–44 the typical length of time on one's current job is 5.7 years, while for men it is only slightly higher (6.9 years). In contrast, the typical married woman worker age 35–44 has only been on her job for 3.5 years. Thus, women who never marry are much more likely to have job tenures equivalent to the typical male worker, but a firm using general hiring standards (such as age and sex) might not make such distinctions.

In summary, two policy-related points can be drawn from this discussion of hiring and training investments. First, employers may have legitimate economic reasons for preferring to hire employees who are expected to have relatively long job tenures *when* there are significant employer hiring or training investments involved. Thus, it is not necessarily maliciousness or prejudice that causes older workers and women to have reduced access to jobs that typically require such investments.

The second point, however, is that individuals within groups vary, and using group averages to estimate an individual's expected tenure may do a disservice to atypical members of the group. We have seen, for example, that women who never marry have much longer job tenures than married women. Taking this fact into account when screening applicants would make hiring decisions more fair to single women, but would probably entail added costs to employers. Firms would have to collect data on their applicants to attempt accurate guesses as to which of their female applicants would remain in the labor force continuously or would never marry.

REVIEW QUESTIONS

1. Both low-skilled workers and high-paid professors have high rates of voluntary quits. What do they have in common that leads to a high quit rate?

---

[26]U.S. Bureau of Labor Statistics, *Job Tenure Declines as Work Force Changes*, Special Labor Force Report No. 235 (Washington, D.C.: U.S. Government Printing Office, 1979). As families become smaller, as household duties become more evenly divided among men and women, and as more women seek *careers*, it is very likely that the labor force behavior of women and men will become more similar.

2. Wages in the U.S. Postal Service have been attacked for being higher than wages elsewhere for people of the same age and education. The Postal Service answers that it *must* pay higher wages than workers could get elsewhere in order to keep the quit rate below the quit rate in other jobs. Are there circumstances under which this argument has any merit?

3. Suppose the government wants to reduce recidivism of ex-convicts by improving their employment prospects and job stability. Suppose further that the government is considering subsidizing half of employer costs incurred in training ex-convicts for jobs. How will this subsidy affect the job prospects and stability of ex-convicts, assuming ex-convicts are the only group subsidized?

4. Unemployment insurance is financed through a payroll tax levied on the employer. Assume that taxes paid = tax rate × firm's payroll. Generally speaking, the tax rate increases when a firm lays off workers. Assuming the firm is unable to shift the tax, what effect will abolition of this tax have on the firm's decision to lay off workers? hire workers? schedule overtime work?

5. In presentations to the Democratic and Republican national platform committees, the AFL-CIO proposed the following changes to the Fair Labor Standards Act in 1976:
   a. Raise the federal minimum wage to $3.00 per hour (the minimum was then less than $3.00);
   b. Increase overtime pay to double the standard wage (it was then 1½ times the standard);
   c. Reduce the standard workweek to 35 hours (down from 40) so that overtime pay would be owed to a worker after 35 hours per week.

   Analyze the employment effects of these proposals.

SELECTED READINGS

Becker, Gary. *Human Capital.* 2nd. ed. New York: National Bureau of Economic Research, 1975.

Doeringer, Peter, and Piore, Michael. *Internal Labor Markets and Manpower Analysis.* Lexington, Mass.: D. C. Heath, 1971.

Ehrenberg, Ronald G., and Schumann, Paul L. *Longer Hours or More Jobs? An Investigation of Amending Hours Legislation to Create Employment.* Ithaca: New York State School of Industrial and Labor Relations, Cornell University, 1982.

Oi, Walter. "Labor as a Quasi-Fixed Factor." *Journal of Political Economy* 70(December 1962):538–55.

Spence, Michael. "Job Market Signalling." *Quarterly Journal of Economics* 87(August 1973):355–74.

Williamson, Oliver, et al. "Understanding the Employment Relation: The Analysis of Idiosyncratic Exchange." *Bell Journal of Economics* 16(Spring 1975):250–80.

6

Supply of Labor to the Economy: The Decision to Work

This and the next four chapters will focus on issues of *worker* behavior. That is, Chapters 6–10 will discuss and analyze various aspects of *labor supply* behavior. Labor supply decisions can be roughly divided into two categories. The first, which is addressed in this chapter and the next, includes decisions about whether to work at all, and if so, how long to work. Questions that must be answered include whether to participate in the labor force, whether to seek part-time or full-time work, and how long to work both at home and for pay. The second category of decisions, which is addressed in Chapters 8–10, deals with the questions that must be faced by a person who has decided to seek work for pay: the occupation or general class of occupations in which to seek offers (Chapters 8–9), and the geographical area in which offers should be sought (Chapter 10).

This chapter begins with some basic facts concerning labor force participation rates and hours of work and then moves on to analyze decisions to work for pay. This analytical framework is useful for structuring income maintenance programs.

TRENDS IN LABOR FORCE PARTICIPATION AND HOURS OF WORK

When a person actively seeks work, he or she is, by definition, in the *labor force*. As pointed out in Chapter 2, the *labor force participation rate* is the percentage of a given population that either has a job or is looking for one. Thus, one clearcut statistic important in measuring people's willingness to work outside the home is the labor force participation rate.

TABLE 6.1   Labor Force Participation Rates of Females over 16 Years of Age, by Marital Status, 1900–1980 (percent)

Year	All Females	Single	Widowed, Divorced	Married
1900	20.6 (100)	45.9 (100)	32.5 (100)	5.6 (100)
1910	25.5 (124)	54.0 (118)	34.1 (105)	10.7 (191)
1920	24.0 (117)			9.0 (161)
1930	25.3 (123)	55.2 (120)	34.4 (106)	11.7 (209)
1940	26.7 (130)	53.1 (116)	33.7 (104)	13.8 (246)
1950	29.7 (144)	53.6 (117)	35.5 (109)	21.6 (386)
1960	35.7 (173)	42.9 (94)	38.7 (119)	30.6 (546)
1970	41.6 (202)	50.9 (111)	39.5 (122)	39.5 (705)
1980	51.7 (250)	61.2 (133)	44.1 (136)	50.2 (896)

Note: Index numbers, with 1900 = 100, are shown in parentheses.

SOURCES: 1900–1950: Clarence D. Long, *The Labor Force Under Changing Income and Employment* (Princeton: Princeton University Press), 1958, Table A-6.

1960: U.S. Department of Commerce, Bureau of the Census, *Census of Population, 1960: Employment Status* (Subject Reports PC(2)-6A), Table 4.

1970: U.S. Department of Commerce, Bureau of the Census, *Census of Population, 1970: Employment Status and Work Experience* (Subject Reports PC(2)-6A), Table 3.

1980: U.S. President, *Employment and Training Report of the President, 1980* (Washington, D.C.: U.S. Government Printing Office, 1981), Tables A2, B1. (The data for 1980 are not strictly comparable because they are derived from a monthly survey, not the decennial census.)

Perhaps the most revolutionary change taking place in the labor market today is the tremendous increase in the proportion of women, particularly married women, working outside the home. Table 6.1 shows the extraordinary dimensions of this change. As recently as 1950 only 21.6 percent of married women were in the labor force. By 1960 this percentage had risen to 30.6 percent, and by 1980 it had increased to 50.2 percent—almost two and a half times what it had been in 1950.

We need not dwell here on the social changes that have been associated with this increasing tendency for women to seek work outside the home. Changes in family income, child-rearing practices, and the family itself are obvious. Less obvious are the effects on the demand for education by females and on the unemployment rate, which will be discussed in Chapters 9, 15, and 16. The longer life span of females is another factor that will affect labor supply and will become an important issue, for example, in funding pension plans (see Chapter 11). Of paramount concern in this chapter are the factors that have influenced this fundamental change in the propensity of women to seek work outside the home.

A second major trend in labor force participation is the decrease in the length of careers for males, as can be seen in Table 6.2. The overall labor force participation rate of men has been falling, as was noted in Chapter 2, but the really substantial decreases have been among the very young and the very old. The labor force participation rate of teenagers fell from 61.1 percent in 1900 to 35.8 percent in 1970—a 41 percent decline—althought the growth of the student labor force since

TABLE 6.2   Labor Force Participation Rates For Males, by Age, 1900–1980 (percent)

	Age Groups				
Year	*14–19*	*20–24*	*25–44*	*45–64*	*Over 65*
1900	61.1 (100)	91.7 (100)	96.3 (100)	93.3 (100)	68.3 (100)
1910	56.2 (92)	91.1 (99)	96.6 (100)	93.6 (100)	58.1 (85)
1920	52.6 (86)	90.9 (99)	97.1 (101)	93.8 (101)	60.1 (88)
1930	41.1 (67)	89.9 (98)	97.5 (101)	94.1 (101)	58.3 (85)
1940	34.4 (56)	88.0 (96)	95.0 (99)	88.7 (95)	41.5 (61)
1950	39.9 (65)	82.8 (90)	92.8 (96)	87.9 (94)	41.6 (61)
1960	38.1 (62)	86.1 (94)	95.2 (99)	89.0 (95)	30.6 (45)
1970	35.8 (59)	80.9 (88)	94.4 (98)	87.3 (94)	25.0 (37)
1980			95.4 (99)	82.2 (88)	19.1 (28)

Note: Index numbers, with 1900 = 100, are shown in parentheses.

SOURCES: 1900–1950: Clarence D. Long, *The Labor Force Under Changing Income and Employment* (Princeton: Princeton University Press), 1958, Table A-2.

1960: U.S. Department of Commerce, Bureau of the Census, *Census of Population, 1960: Employment Status* (Subject Reports PC(2)-6A), Table 1.

1970: U.S. Department of Commerce, Bureau of the Census, *Census of Population, 1970: Employment Status and Work Experience* (Subject Reports PC(2)-6A), Table 1.

1980: U.S. President, *Employment and Training Report of the President, 1981* (Washington, D.C.: U.S. Government Printing Office, 1981), Table A2. (The data for 1980 are not strictly comparable because they are derived from a monthly survey, not the decennial census. Reliable data for males under 25 are unavailable.)

World War II has slowed the decrease somewhat. The decrease for men over 65 has been even more dramatic, from 68.3 percent in 1900 to 25 percent in 1970 and down to 19 percent by 1980. Participation rates for men of "prime age" have declined only slightly, although among 45–64-years-olds there were sharp decreases in the 1930s and 1970s. Clearly, men are starting their careers later and ending them earlier than they were at the beginning of this century.

Other measures reflecting the decisions people make about work are the weekly hours of work, the fraction of people who work *part-time,* and the proportion of people who hold more than one job ("moonlight"). It is not common for people to think of *hours* of work as being a *supply* variable that is subject to *employee* choice. After all, don't employers, in responding to the factors discussed in Chapter 5, establish their hours of work? They do, of course, but this does not mean that employees have no choice of, or influence on, working hours. The *weekly* hours of work offered by employers vary to some extent, so in choosing an employer a worker can also choose hours of work. The range of choice may be limited—70 percent of all full-time plant workers normally worked a 40-hour week in 1973, for example, and most of the rest were within 5 hours of that—but choice does exist. Among full-time, nonsupervisory office workers in 1973, only 59 percent worked 40 hours a week, while 17 percent worked 37.5 hours, and 13 percent worked 35-hour weeks.[1] Moreover, firms with the same 40-hour standard workweek offer

---

[1] U.S. Department of Labor, Employment Standards Administration, *1973 Survey of Establishment Characteristics and Practices* (Washington, D.C.: U.S. Government Printing Office, 1979), Table 15.

TABLE 6.3   **Average Weekly Hours Actually Worked by Manufacturing Production Workers During the Peak Employment Years in Each Business Cycle, 1900–1979 (excluding 1940–45)**

	Average Hours Worked	*Average per Decade Decline in Hours Worked*
1901	54.3	
1906	55.0	
1913	50.9	
1919	46.1	2.2
1923	48.9	
1926	47.8	
1929	48.0	4.6
1948	38.8	
1953	38.6	
1956	38.2	0.4
1969	38.3	
1973	38.0	
1979	37.5	

SOURCE: The data for 1900–57 were taken from Ethel Jones, "New Estimates of Hours of Work Per Week and Hourly Earnings, 1900–1957," *Review of Economics and Statistics*, November 1963:374–85. Data for 1969–79 were calculated from the *Annual Survey of Manufacturers*, which contains worker hours worked (exclusive of vacations, sick leave, and holidays).

different *yearly* hours of work because of different vacation and holiday policies. Finally, *occupational* choice has a working-hours dimension. The weekly or yearly hours of work are different if one chooses to become a teacher rather than an accountant, a retail clerk rather than a traveling sales representative, or a Wall Street rather than a small-town lawyer.

Thus, employees can, in effect, exercise some choice over their hours of work in the short run by choosing their employment. In the long run, a similar mechanism gives employees some influence on working hours. If employees receiving an hourly wage of $X for 40 hours per week really wanted to work only 30 hours at $X per hour, some enterprising employer would seize on their dissatisfaction and offer jobs with 30-hour weeks—ending up with a more satisfied work force in the process. As noted below, large declines in the average hours worked per week took place in this century well before the advent of unions and federal legislation concerning hours of work.

Table 6.3 displays the historical change in *actual* weekly hours of work in this century after correcting for the fact that these hours tend to rise in prosperity and fall in recessions.[2] What the table shows is that weekly hours fell steadily until the 1940s, but since then have more or less stabilized. Overall, the typical manufacturing worker has 16 more hours of leisure each week than he or she had in 1901—virtually an entire waking day. Yet perhaps equally worth emphasizing is

---

[2]Chapter 2 noted, when defining wages and fringe benefits, that hours of *actual* work and hours for which an employee is *paid* are two different things. Since World War II, *paid* hours of work have been greater than *actual* hours of work because of the growing prevalence of paid holidays and paid vacations.

TABLE 6.4 Percentage of Employed
Persons Working Part-
Time Voluntarily, 1963 and
1977 (in percent)

Group	1963	1977
All workers	10.7	14.4
Males, 20 years and over	3.5	5.0
Females, 20 years and over	19.5	21.3
Both sexes, 16–19	37.8	45.5

Note: A part-time worker is one who works
between 1 and 34 hours a week.

SOURCE: U.S. Department of Labor, Bureau of
Labor Statistics, *Handbook of Labor Statistics 1978* (Washington, D.C.: U.S. Government Printing Office), Table 21.

that almost all of this change came in the first 45 years of this century, much of it in
the first 30 years when unions and federal legislation could not have exerted much
influence. An explanation for this must include an analysis of factors influencing
both the demand for and supply of weekly hours per worker. The supply factors
are considered in this chapter, while the demand-side influences were treated in
Chapter 5.

Table 6.4 contains data indicating that the fraction of employed workers who
voluntarily work part-time (less than 35 hours per week) has risen from 10.7 percent
in 1963 to 14.4 percent in 1977. Partly this rise has occurred because the fastest
growing groups in the labor force are teenagers and women, groups for which part-
time employment is relatively common. However, it is obvious from Table 6.4 that
all major labor force groups have experienced an increase in the proportion of their
members who work part-time.

In contrast to trends in part-time employment, there appears to be no trend in
the percentage of workers holding two or more jobs. Since 1956, the proportion of
employed workers holding two or more jobs has fluctuated around 5 percent,
achieving lows of 4.5 percent in 1959 and 1974 and a high of 5.7 percent in 1963.
In 1977 exactly 5 percent of employed workers were "moonlighters."

Because labor is the most abundant factor of production, it is fair to say that this
country's well-being is heavily dependent on the willingness of its people to work.
As we shall demonstrate, leisure and other ways of spending time that do not
involve work for pay are also important in generating well-being; however, our
economy relies heavily on goods and services produced for market transactions.
Therefore, it is important to understand the *work-incentive* effects of higher wages
and incomes, different kinds of taxes, and various forms of income maintenance
programs.

The question of work incentives, for example, will become critically important
as our population—through longer life spans and a declining birth rate—gradually
becomes older. When this happens, there will be a period when relatively few
people of working age will have to support a large number of retirees. Their ability
to do this and still maintain current standards of living obviously depends on the age
at which older people retire and the fraction of the working-age population in the
labor force.

A THEORY OF THE DECISION TO WORK

The decision to work is ultimately a decision about how to spend time. One way to use one's available time is to spend it in pleasurable leisure activities. The other major way in which people use time is to work.[3] One can work around the home, performing such *household production* as raising children, sewing, building, or even growing food. Alternatively, one can work for pay and use one's earnings to purchase food, shelter, clothing, and child care.

Because working for pay and engaging in household production are two ways of getting the same jobs done, we shall initially ignore the distinction between them and treat work activities as working for pay. We shall therefore be characterizing the decision to work as a choice between leisure and working for pay. Most of the crucial factors affecting work incentives can be understood in this context, but insight into labor supply behavior can be enriched by a consideration of household production, also; this we do in Chapter 7.

If we regard the time spent eating, sleeping, and otherwise maintaining ourselves as more or less fixed by natural laws, then the discretionary time we have (16 hours a day, say) can be allocated to either work or leisure. Since the amount of discretionary time spent on leisure is time not spent on working, and vice versa, the *demand for leisure* can be considered the reverse side of the coin labeled *supply of labor*. It is actually more convenient to analyze work incentives in the context of the demand for leisure, because one can apply the standard analysis of the demand for any good to the demand for leisure, and then simply subtract leisure hours from total discretionary hours available to obtain the *labor supply* effects.

A Verbal Analysis of the Labor/Leisure Choice

Since we have chosen to analyze work incentives in the context of the demand for leisure, it is instructive to briefly consider the factors that affect the demand for any good. Basically, the demand for a good is a function of three factors:

1. The *opportunity cost* of the good (which is often equal to *market price*),
2. One's level of *wealth,* and
3. One's set of *preferences*.

For example, heating oil consumption will vary with the *cost* of such oil; as that cost rises, consumption tends to fall unless one of the other two factors intervenes. As *wealth* rises, people generally want larger and warmer houses that obviously require more oil to heat.[4] Even if the price of energy and the level of personal wealth were to remain constant, the demand for energy could rise if a falling birth rate and lengthened life span resulted in a higher proportion of the population being aged and therefore wanting warmer houses. This change in the composition of the population amounts to a shift in the overall *preferences* for warmer houses and thus leads to a change in the demand for heating oil.

---

[3] Another category of activity is to spend time acquiring skills or doing other things that enhance one's future earnings capacity. These activities will be discussed in Chapters 9 and 10.

[4] When the demand for a good rises with wealth, economists say the good is a *normal good.* If demand falls as wealth rises, the good is said to be an *inferior good* (traveling or commuting by bus is sometimes cited as an example of an inferior good).

To summarize, the demand (D) for a "normal good" (see footnote 4) can be characterized as a function of opportunity costs (C) and wealth (V):

$$D = f(\overset{-}{C}, \overset{+}{V}), \tag{6.1}$$

where f—the particular relationship between demand and the variables C and V for an individual—depends on preferences. The notation above C and V indicates the direction in which the demand for a good is expected to go when the variable in question *increases, holding the other one constant*. The demand would move in the opposite direction if C or V were to decrease.

Note: Economists usually assume that preferences are given and not subject to immediate change. For policy purposes, the changes in C and V, not changes in the function f, are of paramount interest to us in explaining changes in demand because C and V are more susceptible to change by government policy. For the most part, we shall assume preferences are *given* and *fixed* at any point in time.[5]

To apply this general analysis of demand to the demand for leisure, we must first ask, "What is the opportunity cost of leisure?" The cost of spending an hour watching television is basically what one could earn if one had spent that hour working. Thus, the opportunity cost of an hour of leisure is very closely related to one's *wage rate*—so closely related, in fact, that to simplify the analysis we shall say that leisure's opportunity cost *is* the wage rate.[6]

Next, we must understand and be able to measure wealth. Naturally, wealth includes a family's holdings of bank accounts, financial investments, and physical property. Workers' skills can also be considered assets, since these skills can be, in effect, rented out to employers for a price. The more one can get in wages, the larger is the value of one's human assets. Unfortunately, it is not usually possible to directly measure people's wealth. It is much easier to measure the *returns* from that wealth because data on total *income* are readily available from government surveys. Economists thus often use total income as an indicator of total wealth, since the two are conceptually so closely related.[7]

If we replace the general demand function in equation (6.1) with the *demand for leisure function*, it would become equation (6.2) if leisure were a normal good:

$$D_L = f(\overset{-}{W}, \overset{+}{Y}), \tag{6.2}$$

where D_L is the demand for leisure hours, W is the wage rate, Y is total income, and f (as before) depends on preferences people have for leisure independent of W and Y. The signs over W and Y indicate what happens to the demand for leisure if the variable in question increases, holding the other variable constant.

---

[5]On occasion the government attempts to influence consumption patterns of people by changing preferences rather than prices. For example, rather than raising cigarette taxes to discourage cigarette consumption, the federal government in the 1970s prohibited cigarette manufacturers from advertising on television and even sponsored radio and television campaigns against smoking. The effectiveness of these attempts to change preferences is difficult to assess.

[6]This assumes that individuals can work as many hours as they want at a fixed wage rate. While this assumption may seem overly simplistic, it will not lead to wrong conclusions with respect to the issues analyzed in this chapter. More rigorously, it should be said that leisure's *marginal* opportunity cost is the *marginal* wage rate (the wage one could receive for an extra hour of work).

[7]The best indicator of wealth is one's *permanent,* or long-run potential, *income*. One's current income may differ from one's permanent income for a variety of reasons (unemployment, illness, unusually large amounts of overtime work, etc.). For our purposes here, however, the distinction between current and permanent income is not too important.

If income increases, holding wages (and *f*) constant, equation (6.2) asserts that the demand for leisure goes up. Put differently, *if income increases (decreases), holding wages constant, hours of work will go down (up)*. Economists call this predicted response the *income effect*. The income effect is based on the simple notion that as incomes rise, holding leisure's opportunity cost constant, people will want to consume more leisure (which means working less).

Because we have assumed that time is spent either in leisure or in working for pay, the income effect can be expressed in terms of the *supply of working hours,* as well as the demand for leisure hours. Because the ultimate focus of this chapter is labor supply, we choose to express this effect in the context of supply.

Using algebraic notation, we define the income effect as the change in hours of work (ΔH) produced by a change in income (ΔY), holding wages constant ($\overline{W}$):

$$\text{Income Effect} = \left.\frac{\Delta H}{\Delta Y}\right|_{\overline{W}} < 0. \tag{6.3}$$

We say the income effect is *negative* because the *sign* of the *fraction* in equation (6.3) is *negative*. If income goes up (wages held constant), hours of work fall. If income goes down, hours of work increase. The numerator (ΔH) and denominator (ΔY) in equation (6.3) move in opposite directions, giving a negative sign to the income effect.

Equation (6.2) also suggests that *if income is held constant, an increase (decrease) in the wage rate will reduce (increase) the demand for leisure, thereby increasing (decreasing) work incentives*. This *substitution effect* occurs because as the opportunity costs of leisure rise (income held constant), working hours are substituted for leisure hours.

In contrast to the income effect, the substitution effect is *positive*. Because this effect is the change in hours of work (ΔH) induced by a change in the wage (ΔW), holding income constant ($\overline{Y}$), the substitution effect can be written as:

$$\text{Substitution Effect} = \left.\frac{\Delta H}{\Delta W}\right|_{\overline{Y}} > 0. \tag{6.4}$$

Because numerator (ΔH) and denominator (ΔW) always move in the same direction, at least in theory, the substitution effect has a positive sign.

At times it is possible to observe situations or programs that create pure income or substitution effects. Usually, however, both effects are simultaneously present, often working against each other.

A "pure" income effect.   Winning a state lottery is an example of the income effect by itself. The winnings enhance one's wealth (income) *independent* of the hours of work. Thus, income is increased *without* a change in the compensation received from an hour of work. In this case, the income effect induces the person to consume more leisure, thereby reducing the willingness to work. (If the change in nonlabor income were *negative,* on the other hand, the income effect suggests that people would work *more*.)

A "pure" substitution effect.   In the 1980 Presidential campaign, candidate John Anderson proposed a program aimed at conserving gasoline. His plan consisted of raising the gasoline tax but offsetting this increase by a reduced Social Security tax payable by individuals on their earnings. The idea was to raise the price of gasoline without reducing people's overall spendable income.

For our purposes, this plan is interesting because it creates a pure substitution effect on labor supply. Social Security revenues are collected by a tax on earnings, so reductions in the tax are, in effect, increases in the wage rate.[8] However, for the average person, the increased wealth associated with this wage increase is exactly offset by increases in the gasoline tax.[9] Hence, wages are increased while income is held more or less constant. This program would thus create a substitution effect that induces people to work more hours.

Both effects occur when wages rise. While the above examples illustrate situations in which the income or subtitution effects are present by themselves, normally both effects are present—often working in opposite directions. The presence of both effects working in opposite directions creates ambiguity in predicting the overall labor supply response in many cases. Consider the case of a person who receives a wage increase.

The labor supply response to a simple wage change will involve *both* an income and a substitution effect. The *income effect* is the result of the worker's enhanced wealth (or potential income) after the increase. For a given level of work effort, he or she now has a greater command over resources than before (because more income is received for any given number of hours of work). The *substitution effect* results from the fact that the wage increase raises the opportunity costs of leisure. Because the actual labor supply response is the *sum* of the income and substitution effects, we cannot predict the response in advance; theory simply does not tell us which effect is stronger.

If the *income* effect is dominant, the person will respond to a wage increase by decreasing his or her labor supply. This decrease will be *smaller* than if the same change in wealth were due to an increase in *nonlabor* wealth because the substitution effect is present and acts as a moderating influence. However, when the *income* effect dominates, the substitution effect is not large enough to prevent labor supply from *declining*. It is entirely plausible, of course, that the *substitution* effect will dominate. If so, the actual response to wage increases will be to *increase* labor supply.

Should the substitution effect dominate, the person's labor supply curve—relating, say, desired hours of work to wages—will be *positively sloped*. That is, labor supply will increase with the wage rate. If, on the other hand, the income

---

[8]Social Security taxes are levied on yearly earnings up to some maximum—$37,800 in 1984. Once that maximum level is reached within a year, no more Social Security taxes are paid. People whose yearly earnings exceed the base experience no change in the marginal opportunity cost of leisure because an additional hour of work per year is not subject to Social Security taxes anyway. However, the marginal opportunity cost of leisure would be increased for many, if not most, workers.

[9]An increase in the price of gasoline will reduce the income people have left for expenditures on nongasoline consumption only if the demand for gasoline is inelastic. In this case, the percentage reduction in gasoline consumption is smaller than the percentage increase in price: total expenditures on gasoline would thus rise. Our analysis assumes this to be the case.

Example 6.1

Incentives and Absenteeism

The problem of employee absenteeism is significant and apparently growing. A 1947 study of absences in manufacturing industries suggested a daily absentee rate of about 4.3 percent, while recent manufacturing data indicate absentee rates are currently around 7 percent. Are workers becoming more sickly? Are they less motivated? Is the work place more alienating? Is management more inept? These are some of the many questions that arise concerning this problem. The concepts introduced in this chapter suggest yet another question: is absenteeism caused to some extent by the structure of compensation?

As documented in Chapter 5 (and again discussed in Chapter 11), fringe benefits form a large and increasing proportion of total compensation. What has happened over time is that employees have received an ever larger proportion of their pay increases in the form of fringe benefits rather than wages. In some cases, these fringe-benefit packages have included paid sick leave provisions, which serve as an obvious inducement for a certain amount of absenteeism. Because workers can call in sick for a specified number of days per year without losing any pay, it is not surprising that a study of absenteeism among public school teachers found that it was greater in districts with more generous paid sick leave provisions.

However, the growth of fringe benefits frequently offers incentives for greater absenteeism independent of paid sick leave. An absence often causes a worker to lose his or her daily wage, but the value of many fringe benefits is invariant with respect to an absence. (For example, the value of a worker's medical insurance policy or future pension benefits is not affected by absence from work in most cases.) Thus, when compensation is increased in the form of fringe benefits rather than wages, an *income effect* on the demand for leisure is created *without a corresponding substitution effect*.

The increased use of fringe benefits as a form of compensation has had a possibly profound effect on the incentives to come to work on days when one is feeling slightly ill, needs a "break," or has a personal problem. The increased compensation that has accompanied economic growth tends to induce greater consumption of all normal goods, including leisure; however, to the extent *wages* are not increased, the price of leisure is not raised. Thus, the changing structure of compensation suggests that relatively stronger income effects, and correspondingly weaker substitution effects, on the demand for leisure have been accompanying economic growth in recent years.

Because absenteeism is one way leisure is consumed, it may well be that rising absenteeism is at least partially caused by the increased use of fringe benefits in pay packages. Indeed, absenteeism appears to be higher when fringe benefits are more extensively used; for example, rates are higher in manufacturing than retail trade, and higher in large manufacturing plants than small ones. Moreover, a careful intraindustry statistical study has uncovered evidence that a compensation package weighted toward fringe benefits rather than wages will be accompanied by greater absenteeism.

SOURCES: Max Kossoris, "Illness Absenteeism in Manufacturing Plants in 1947," *Monthly Labor Review* 66 (March 1948): 265–67; Janice N. Hedges, "Absence from Work—Measuring the Hours Lost," *Monthly Labor Review* 100 (October 1977): 16–23; Donald Winkler, "The Effects of Sick-Leave Policy on Teacher Absenteeism," *Industrial and Labor Relations Review* 33 (January 1980): 232–40; Steven G. Allen, "Compensation, Safety and Absenteeism: Evidence from the Paper Industry," *Industrial and Labor Relations Review* 34 (January 1981): 207–18.

effect dominates, the labor supply curve will be *negatively sloped*. Economic theory cannot say which effect will dominate, and in fact individual labor supply curves could be positively sloped in some ranges of the wage and negatively sloped in others. In Figure 6.1, for example, the person's desired hours of work increase (substitution effect dominates) as wages go up as long as wages are low (below W^*). However, at higher wages, further increases result in reduced hours of work (the income effect dominates); economists refer to such a curve as "backward-bending."

While economic theory is unable to predict whether the income or substitution effect will dominate in an individual's labor supply curve, it can bring some useful insights to bear on important policy issues. The work-incentive effect of the personal income tax is an important case in point.

Tax rate cuts and "supply-side" economics.   The election of Ronald Reagan as President in1980 brought to power an administration persuaded that high rates of inflation (that is, rising prices) and lagging labor productivity could be at least partially overcome by cutting taxes in such a way that investment and work effort would be stimulated. The use of tax rate cuts and tax-related investment incentives to drive *actual output* up to its potential has long been accepted by many economists

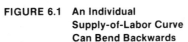

**FIGURE 6.1 An Individual
Supply-of-Labor Curve
Can Bend Backwards**

and policymakers as a technique for overcoming recessionary forces.[10] However, the use of tax rate cuts to stimulate the growth of *potential output* is central to what came to be called supply-side economics. An important element of the supply-side strategy proposed by President Reagan was the Kemp-Roth plan to make large across-the-board cuts in personal income tax rates over a three-year period.[11] It was believed that cuts in personal income tax rates would, among other things, increase the incentive of people to work:

> According to supply-siders, large tax rate cuts would cause an increase in investment and work effort that would reduce fundamental inflationary pressures.[12]

Is the belief by supply-siders that income tax rate cuts will increase work effort theoretically sound? Suppose, first, that Congress were to lower the income tax rates of lower-income workers but not cut the level of government services provided for this group. A decrease in their income tax rates would be equivalent to an increase in wages because the workers would take home more income for each hour of work. This wage increase would generate an income and substitution effect, and theoretical reasoning alone cannot predict which effect will dominate. If the substitution effect dominated, labor supply would increase; if the income effect were dominant, the tax cuts would be accompanied by a *fall* in labor supply! The issue is ultimately an empirical question.[13]

The supply-siders who claim that reducing income tax rates increases work incentives have a valid point, however, when one considers *general* income tax rate reductions. While at any point in time *individuals* or *small* groups of people can experience income effects if their wages change, workers as a *whole* cannot. The available wealth of a society is more or less fixed at any point in time by the resources and technology it has available to it, and changing the wage rates of workers does not immediately change this wealth. (If it did, we could make ourselves, as a society, arbitrarily wealthy by granting ourselves large wage increases.) Thus, income tax rate reductions for everyone would be accompanied by a *substitution* effect but *not* by an *income* effect. The cut in income tax rates would increase workers' real wage rates, if the government at the same time reduced expenditures so that inflationary pressures did not occur, but it would not immediately affect society's real wealth. There would be a substitution effect with no overall income effect, and labor supply would increase. The *aggregate* supply-of-labor curve, then, must be upward sloping, as shown in Figure 6.2. *How much* labor supply would increase as a result of any given tax rate reduction is another question, and the answer is largely unknown at the moment. However, the estimates

---

[10] A recession is said to occur when *actual* national output declines, thereby falling below potential output. A recession is accompanied by resource unemployment of both labor and capital. A widely (though not universally) accepted technique for ending a recession is for the government to spend more than it collects in taxes.

[11] The plan was named for its Congressional sponsors, Representative Jack Kemp and Senator William Roth. In the summer of 1981 Congress voted to cut taxes 25 percent over 3 years and to adjust tax brackets for inflation thereafter.

[12] "Reagan's Top Problem: Braking Inflationary Expectations," *Business Week*, December 1, 1980: 110.

[13] Later this chapter will show that the income effect may dominate for men but not for married women.

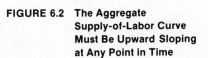

**FIGURE 6.2 The Aggregate
Supply-of-Labor Curve
Must Be Upward Sloping
at Any Point in Time**

summarized later in the chapter suggest that the increase would probably be larger for women than men.

To better understand the upward-sloping nature of the aggregate supply-of-labor curve, let us examine in more concrete terms how a general 10 percent reduction in income tax rates might be handled. While a cut in tax rates would, of course, increase workers' wage rates, it would have the *initial* effect of reducing by 10 percent the revenues available to government. Unless the government were trying to combat a recession and accompanying unemployment, it might respond to reduced revenues by cutting back on various services it formerly provided: mail delivery on Saturday, educational subsidies, and road construction funds, for example. Thus, while *wages* would be increased, real income would be held more or less constant by the cut in government services.[14] Workers would have more take-home income but fewer government-provided services.[15] There would be a substitution effect but no overall income effect.

The increase in labor supply caused by the tax cut would serve to increase people's money incomes and reduce their consumption of leisure. Some of the increased earnings would be spent on goods or services, and some would go to the government in the form of taxes.[16] However, whether the increased goods or services are provided privately or by the government, the happiness they generate is offset by the reduced consumption of leisure time. In the short run, to repeat, increased goods and services are offset by reduced consumption of leisure, leaving society equally well off.

---

[14]Some people would be more affected by the governmental spending cuts than others, but the *overall* change in real wealth would be zero.

[15]The alternative to cutting services, at least initially, is to borrow money. However, borrowing increases the money supply if it is done, as is most often the case, from banks, and this would tend to be inflationary in the absence of resource unemployment associated with a recession. A rise in *prices* would lower the real wage and mitigate any substitution effects (if before-tax money wages remained constant).

[16]Because earnings are taxed and leisure is not, a 10 percent tax cut that called forth increased labor supply would mean that government revenues would *not* fall by 10 percent in the long run.

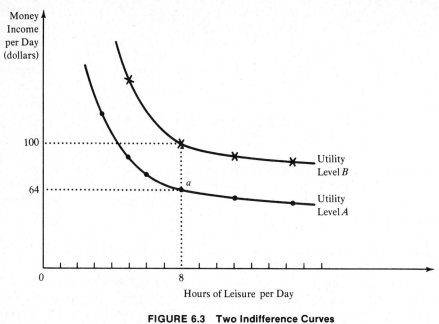

FIGURE 6.3   Two Indifference Curves for the Same Person

In the *long run,* however, real national wealth could be increased *if* the increase in goods and services were channeled into *investment* activities and not immediately consumed. Wage increases that accompany the growth of national wealth *do* generate income effects. However, real national welfare could *only* be increased in the long run and only if current investments were to increase.

The following section introduces indifference curves and budget constraints—material that may already be familiar to students with a background in these fundamentals.

A Graphic Analysis of the Labor/Leisure Choice: The Fundamentals

Graphic analysis requires a level of rigor that is more convincing than verbal analysis and incorporates visual aids that make the analysis easier to understand. The graphic analysis here, however, is simply a more rigorous, visible repetition of our verbal analysis; hence, none of the conclusions or definitions reached above will be changed in any way.

Preferences.   Let us assume that there are two major categories of goods that make people happy—leisure and money income (which can, of course, be used to buy other goods). Collapsing all goods into two allows our graphs to be drawn in two-dimensional space.

Since both leisure and money can be used to generate satisfaction (or *utility*), these two goods are to some extent substitutes for each other. If one were forced to give up some money income—by cutting back one's hours of work, for example—there would be some increase in leisure time that could be substituted for this lost income to keep the person as happy as before. A very thoughtful consumer/worker, in fact, could reveal a whole *variety* of combinations of money income and leisure hours that would yield him or her this same level of satisfaction.

To understand how preferences can be graphed, suppose a thoughtful consumer/worker were asked to decide how happy he or she would be with a daily income of $64 combined with 8 hours of leisure (point *a* in Figure 6.3). This level of happiness could be called utility level *A*. Our consumer/worker could name *other combinations* of money income and leisure hours that would *also* yield utility level *A*. Assume that our respondent named five other combinations. All six combinations of money and leisure that yield utility level *A* are represented by heavy dots in Figure 6.3. The curve connecting these dots is called an *indifference curve,* a curve connecting the various combinations of money income and leisure that yield equal utility. (The term *indifference curve* is derived from the fact that, since each point on the curve yields equal utility, a person is truly indifferent about where on the curve he or she will be.)

Our worker/consumer could no doubt achieve a higher level of happiness if he or she could combine the 8 hours of leisure with an income of $100 per day, instead of just $64 a day. This higher satisfaction level could be called utility level *B*. The consumer could name other combinations of money income and leisure that would also yield *this* higher level of utility. These combinations are denoted by the *X*s in Figure 6.3 that are connected by a second indifference curve.

Indifference curves have certain specific characteristics that are reflected in the way they are drawn:

1. Utility level *B* represents more happiness than level *A*. Every level of leisure consumption is combined with a higher income on *B* than on *A*. Hence our respondent prefers all points on indifference curve *B* to any point on curve *A*. A whole *set* of indifference curves could be drawn for this one person, each representing a different utility level. Any such curve that lies to the northeast of another one is preferred to any curve to the southwest because the northeastern curve represents a higher level of utility.

2. Indifference curves *do not intersect*. If they did, the point of intersection would represent *one* combination of money income and leisure that yielded *two* different levels of satisfaction. We assume our worker/consumer is *not* so inconsistent in stating his or her preferences that this could happen.

3. Indifference curves are *negatively sloped,* because if either income or leisure hours is increased, the other is reduced in order to preserve the same level of utility. If the slope is steep, as at segment *LK* in Figure 6.4, a given loss of income need not be accompanied by a large increase in leisure hours in order to keep utility constant.[17] When the curve is relatively flat, as at

---

[17]Economists call the change in money income needed to hold utility constant when leisure hours are changed by one unit the *marginal rate of substitution* between leisure and money income. This marginal rate of substitution can be graphically understood as the slope of the indifference curve at any point. At point *L*, for example, the slope is relatively steep so economists would say that the marginal rate of substitution at point *L* is relatively high.

FIGURE 6.4   An Indifference Curve

segment *MN* in Figure 6.4, a given decrease in income must be accompanied by a large increase in the consumption of leisure to hold utility constant. Thus, when indifference curves are relatively steep, people do not value money income as highly as when such curves are relatively flat, for when they are flat, a loss of income can only be compensated by a large increase in leisure if utility is to be kept constant.

4. Indifference curves are *convex*—steeper at the left than at the right. This shape reflects the assumption that when money income is relatively high and leisure hours are relatively few, leisure is more highly valued than when leisure is abundant and income relatively scarce. At segment *LK* in Figure 6.4, a great loss of income (from Y_4 to Y_3, for example) can be compensated for by just a little increase in leisure, whereas a little loss of leisure time (from H_3 to H_4, for example) would require a relatively large increase in income to maintain equal utility. What is relatively scarce is highly valued.

   Conversely, when income is low and leisure is abundant (segment *MN* in Figure 6.4), income is more highly valued. Losing income (by moving from Y_2 to Y_1, for example) requires a huge increase in leisure for utility to remain constant. To repeat, what is scarce is assumed to be highly valued.

5. Finally, different people have different sets of indifference curves. The curves drawn in Figures 6.3 and 6.4 were for *one person*. Another person would have a completely different set of curves. People who value leisure more highly, for example, would have had indifference curves that were generally steeper (see Figure 6.5a). People who do not value leisure highly

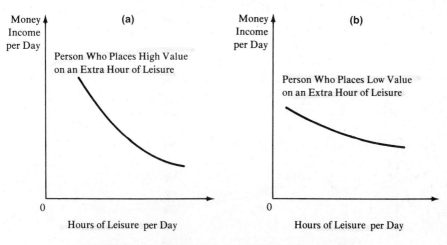

FIGURE 6.5   Indifference Curves for Two Different People

would have relatively flat curves (see Figure 6.5b).[18] Thus, individual preferences can be portrayed graphically.

Income and wage constraints.   Now everyone would like to maximize his or her utility, which could be most nicely done by consuming every available hour of leisure combined with the highest conceivable income. Unfortunately, the resources anyone can command are limited. Thus, all that is possible is to do the best one can, given limited resources. To see these resource limitations graphically requires superimposing constraints over one's set of indifference curves to see which combinations of income and leisure are available and which are not.

Suppose the person whose indifference curves are graphed in Figure 6.3 had no source of income other than labor earnings. Suppose, further, that he or she could earn $8 per hour. Figure 6.6 contains the two indifference curves drawn in Figure 6.3 as well as a straight line *(DE)* connecting combinations of leisure and income that are possible for a person with an $8 wage and no outside income. If 16 hours per day are available for work and leisure and if this person consumes all 16 in leisure, then money income will be zero (point *D* in Figure 6.6). If 8 hours a day are devoted to work, income will be $64 per day (point *M*), and if 16 hours a day are worked, income will be $128 per day (point *E*). Other points on this line, the point of 15 hours of leisure (1 hour of work) and $8 of income, are also possible. This line, which reflects the combinations of leisure and income that are possible for the individual, is called the *budget constraint.* Any combination to the right of the budget constraint is not achievable; the person's command over resources simply is not sufficient to attain these combinations of leisure and money income.

---

[18]The two curves shown in Figure 6.5 should be compared in *slope* only. Levels of utility for two people cannot be compared because happiness is not objectively measurable. Figure 6.5 simply shows that people with different preferences have indifference curves with different *slopes*.

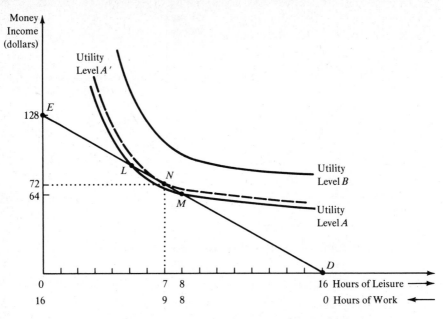

FIGURE 6.6 Indifference Curves and Budget Constraint

The *slope* of the budget constraint is a graphic representation of the wage rate. One's wage rate is properly defined as the increment in income (ΔY) derived from an increment in hours of work (ΔH):

$$\text{Wage Rate} = \frac{\Delta Y}{\Delta H}. \tag{6.5}$$

Now $\Delta Y/\Delta H$ is exactly the slope of the budget constraint (in absolute value).[19] Figure 6.6 shows how the constraint rises $8 for every one-hour increase in work: if the person works zero hours, income per day is zero; if the person works one hour, $8 in income is possible; if he or she works 8 hours, $64 in income can be achieved. The reason the constraint rises $8 for every unit increase in hours of work is because the wage rate the person commands is $8 per hour. If the person could earn $16 per hour, the constraint would rise twice as fast and therefore be twice as steep.

It is clear from Figure 6.6 that our consumer/worker cannot achieve utility level B. He or she can achieve *some* points on the indifference curve representing utility level A—specifically, those points between L and M in Figure 6.6. However, if our consumer/worker is a utility maximizer, he or she will realize that a utility level *above* A is possible. Remembering that an infinite number of indifference curves can be drawn between curves A and B in Figure 6.6, one representing each possible level of satisfaction between A and B, we can draw a curve (A') that is northeast of

---

[19]The vertical change for a one-unit change in horizontal distance is the definition for *slope*. *Absolute value* refers to the size of the slope, disregarding whether it is positive or negative.

curve *A* and just *tangent* to the budget constraint. Any movement along the budget constraint *away* from the tangency point places the person on an indifference curve lying *below A'*.

An indifference curve that is just tangent to the constraint represents the highest level of utility that the person can obtain given his or her constraint. It is the most northeast curve with an achievable point on it, and no curve superior to it can be reached. If this highest possible curve is denoted as utility level *A'* in Figure 6.6, then point *N* represents the utility-maximizing combination of leisure and income. Thus, our consumer/worker is best off, given his or her preferences and constraints, working 9 hours a day, consuming 7 hours of leisure, and having a daily income of $72. All other possible combinations, such as 8 hours of work and $64 of income, yield lower utility.

The decision not to work.   In the example discussed above and illustrated in Figure 6.6, a point of tangency *(N)* existed between the individual's indifference curve and the budget constraint. That point of tangency indicated the utility-maximizing labor/leisure combination. What happens if there is no point of tangency? What happens, for example, when a person's indifference curves are at every point more steeply sloped than the budget constraint (see Figure 6.7)?

If indifference curves that represent an individual's preferences are very steeply sloped, it indicates that the person places a very high value on extra hours of leisure (see Figure 6.5a). A very high hourly wage would be required to compensate the person for an hour of *lost* leisure (that is, an hour of work). If the increase in money

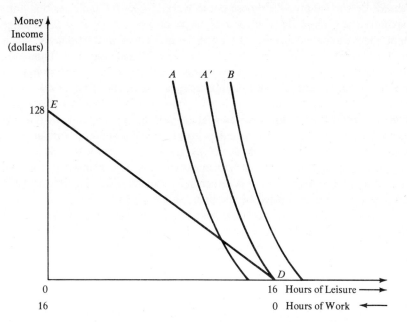

FIGURE 6.7   The Decision Not To Work Is a "Corner Solution"

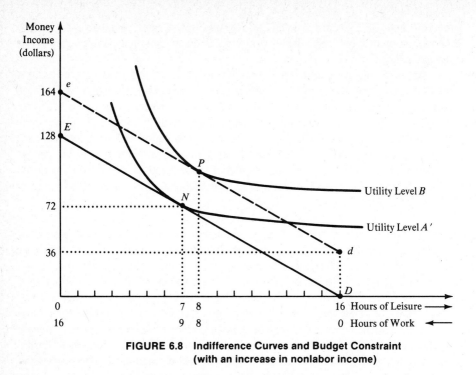

FIGURE 6.8 **Indifference Curves and Budget Constraint (with an increase in nonlabor income)**

income required to compensate the worker for an hour of work (to keep utility constant) is greater than the wage rate at every feasible number of leisure hours, then the person simply will choose not to work. Figure 6.7 indicates that utility is maximized at point *D*, a point of zero hours of work. Point *D* is *not* a tangency point; there can be no tangency if the indifference curve has no points at which the slope equals the slope of the budget constraint. Thus, utility in Figure 6.7 is maximized at a *corner*, a point at the extreme end of the budget constraint, and at this point *(D)* the person does not choose to be in the labor force.

The income effect. Suppose now that the person depicted in Figure 6.6 is lucky and falls into a source of income independent of work. Suppose, further, that this *nonlabor* income amounts to about $36 per day. Thus, even if this person worked zero hours per day, his or her daily income would be $36. Naturally, if the person worked more than zero hours, his or her daily income would be equal to $36 plus earnings (the wage multiplied by the hours of work).

The source of nonlabor income has clearly increased our person's command over resources, as can be shown by drawing a new budget constraint to reflect the nonlabor income. As shown by the broken line in Figure 6.8, the end points of the new constraint are point *d* (zero hours of work and $36 of money income) and point *e* (16 hours of work and $164 of income—$36 in nonlabor income plus $128 in earnings). Note that the new constraint is *parallel* to the old one. Parallel lines have the same slope; since the slope of each constraint reflects the wage rate, we can infer that the increase in nonlabor income has not changed the person's wage rate.

We have just described a situation in which a pure *income effect* should be observed. Income (wealth) has been increased, but the wage rate has remained unchanged. The previous section noted that if wealth increased and the opportunity cost of leisure remained constant, the person would consume more leisure and work less. We thus concluded that the income effect was *negative*; as income went up (down), holding wages constant, hours of work went down (up). This negative relationship is illustrated graphically in Figure 6.8.

When the old (solid) budget constraint was in effect, the person's highest level of utility was reached at point *N*, where he or she worked 9 hours a day. With the new (dashed) constraint, the optimum hours of work are 8 per day. The new source of income, by not altering the wage, has caused an income effect that results in one less hour of work per day.

Income and substitution effects with a wage increase.

Suppose that, instead of increasing one's command over resources by receiving a source of nonlabor income, the wage rate for another person were to be increased from $8.00 to $12.00 per hour. This increase, as noted earlier, would cause *both* an income and a substitution effect; the person would be wealthier *and* face a higher opportunity cost of leisure. Both effects can be illustrated graphically (see Figures 6.9 and 6.10).

Figures 6.9 and 6.10 illustrate the *observed effects* of the wage change as well as the two hidden *components* of the observed change: the income and substitution effects. Figure 6.9 illustrates the case in which the observed response is to increase the hours of work; in this case the substitution effect is stronger than the income effect. Figure 6.10 illustrates the case in which the income effect is stronger and the response to a wage increase is to reduce the hours of work. Both cases are plausible. Theory tells us in what direction the income and substitution effects should go, but it does not tell us which effect will be stronger. The difference between the two cases lies *solely* in the shape of the indifference curves (preferences); the budget constraints, which reflect wealth and the wage rate, are exactly the same.

Figures 6.9 and 6.10 show a new budget constraint. We are assuming that no source of nonlabor income exists for the person depicted, so both the old and new constraints in each diagram are anchored at the same place—zero income for zero hours worked. However, the new constraint rises 50 percent faster than the old constraint, reflecting the 50 percent increase in the wage rate (from $8 to $12 per hour). The left endpoint of the new constraint is now at $192 (16 hours of work times $12 per hour), rather than at $128 (16 hours times $8).

In Figure 6.9, the new constraint implies that utility level U_2 is the highest that can be reached, and the tangency at point N_2 suggests that 11 hours of work per day is the optimum. When the old constraint was in effect, the utility-maximizing hours of work were 8 per day. Thus, the wage increase has caused the person's hours of work to increase by 3 per day.

This observed effect, however, masks the underlying forces at work. These underlying forces are, of course, the income and substitution effects. These forces are not directly observable, but they are there (and working against each other) nonetheless. A physical analogy can be used to explain how these forces work.

FIGURE 6.9   Wage Change with Substitution Effect Dominating

Suppose a riderless boat is set adrift in the Mississippi River on a day in which the wind is blowing *across* the river. The river's current carries the boat downstream, but the crosswind also exerts a force that blows the boat east. We observe where the boat is when it passes under a certain bridge. While we *observe* where the boat crosses under the bridge, we cannot directly see the two independent forces that together dictate where the boat ends up. There is the influence of the current and of the wind, and for some purposes it may be useful to measure these effects separately. How would we do it?

We would measure the influence of the current by asking ourselves, "Where would the boat have passed under the same bridge if there had been no wind?" This hypothetical question holds two elements constant: the wind (zero velocity) and the bridge under which the boat passes. The answer to the question is thus designed to identify the "pure" effect of the current. The influence of the wind could be measured by· comparing where the boat actually crossed under the bridge with where it *would have crossed* had there been no wind.

Turning now to Figure 6.9, we shall identify the income effect (as we did the current effect) by asking, "What would have been the change in the hours worked if the person had reached indifference curve U_2 (the bridge) by a change in *nonlabor* income with *no* change in the wage rate (no wind)?"

We answer this question by moving the old constraint to the northeast while maintaining its original slope (reflecting the old wage of $8.00), which holds the wage constant. By definition, we must hold the wage constant when dealing with the income effect. However, moving the old constraint hypothetically allows nonlabor income to increase so that the person arrives at the new level of utility. The

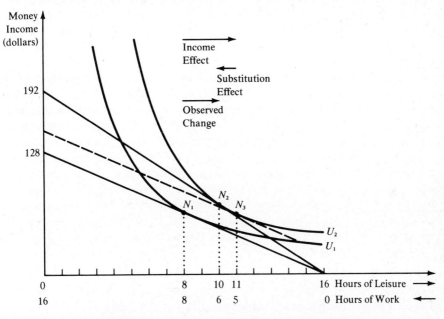

FIGURE 6.10 Wage Change with Income Effect Dominating

dashed constraint in Figure 6.9 depicts this hypothetical constraint, which is tangent to indifference curve U_2 at N_3. This tangency suggests that had the person received nonlabor income, with no change in the wage, sufficient to reach the new level of utility, he or she would have *reduced* work hours from 8 (N_1), to 7 (N_3) per day. This shift is graphic proof that the income effect is negative, assuming that leisure is a normal good.

The substitution effect can be measured once the pure effect of the wage change is known. We measure the substitution effect as the difference between where the person ends up and where he or she *would* have ended up without a wage change. *With* the wage change, the person represented in Figure 6.9 ended up at point N_2, working 11 hours a day. *Without* the wage change, the person would have arrived at point N_3, working 7 hours a day. The wage change *by itself* (holding utility, or real wealth, constant) caused work hours to increase by 4 per day. This increase demonstrates that the substitution effect is positive.

To summarize, the observed effect of raising wages from $8 to $12 per hour increased the hours of work in Figure 6.9 from 8 to 11 per day. This observed effect, however, is the *sum* of two component effects. The income effect, which operates because an increased wage increases one's real wealth, tended to *reduce* the hours of work from 8 to 7 per day. The substitution effect, which captures the pure effect of the change in leisure's opportunity cost, tended to push the person toward 4 more hours of work per day. The end result was an increase of 3 in the hours worked each day.

Figure 6.10 can be analyzed in the same way. Here the *observed* effect of the increased wage is a *reduction* in hours of work from 8 to 6 per day (points N_1 to N_2).

This change is the result of an income effect, which by itself tended to *decrease* by 3 hours the hours of work per day, and a substitution effect, which tended to *increase* working hours by 1 per day. The net result of these forces is, of course, a reduction in hours of work by 2 per day.

The differences in the observed effects of a wage increase between Figures 6.9 and 6.10 are due to differences in the shape of the indifference curves—or, in other words, to different preferences. The substitution and income effects worked in their predicted direction in both cases, but their relative strengths are a function of preferences (which are reflected in the shape and placement of indifference curves).

Although theory cannot predict whether the income or substitution effect will dominate, the income effect of any given wage change is *larger* for individuals who are *working many hours* for pay than for those who are working few hours. Changes in income represent changes in one's command over resources, and a wage increase clearly fosters greater increases in wealth the more hours one works. (In terms of our graphic analysis, it can be seen from Figures 6.9 and 6.10 that the budget constraint representing a wage of $12 per hour lies further to the northeast of the one representing an $8 wage in its upper portion, where more hours are worked.)

Empirical Findings on the Labor/Leisure Choice

This chapter has argued, both verbally and graphically, that the income effect on labor supply is negative and that the substitution effect is positive. While these predictions are often useful for policy purposes, as we saw in the discussions of the work incentive effect of the income tax, it is also important to know *how large* the two effects are. It is the *relative size* of each effect that determines the ultimate *observed* effect.

Evidence on the absolute and relative sizes of income and substitution effects can be obtained in two ways:

1. The *time-series study* can be used to look at *trends* in labor force participation rates and hours of work over time.
2. The *cross-section study* can be used to analyze the patterns of labor supply across individuals at a given point in time.

Time-series studies. Chapter 2 pointed out that real hourly wages rose fourfold from 1914 to 1980. Associated with that rise was a rather sharp decline in the labor force participation rate of older men, clearly reflecting a trend toward earlier retirement. One can also observe substantial declines in hours of work. One might be tempted to conclude from these trends that the income effect dominates the substitution effect, meaning that when wages rise, the propensity to work will fall.

There are three potential objections to, or problems with, the conclusion that the income effect is larger than the substitution effect. First, the earlier retirement of men can be seen as a function of the greater availability of pensions and/or disability payments. Pensions pay older people for not working, thereby creating incentives not to work at an elderly age. The growth in disability payments to those with health problems has been shown to affect the participation rates of older men.[20] Interestingly, however, a large part of the decline in labor force participation rates for elderly men came *before* 1940, when pensions and disability payments were virtually nonexistent.

A second disturbing fact that raises questions about the relative strength of the income and substitution effects is the much smaller decline in hours of work after World War II. Has the income effect grown weaker relative to the substitution effect? Not necessarily for at least two reasons. First, hours of work are *jointly* determined by employers and employees, and while rising real wages may be inducing employees to want to work less, a number of developments have led employers to offer incentives for workers to work longer hours (these forces were discussed in Chapter 5). It is important to remember that countervailing forces may well be coming from the *demand* side of the market in determining hours of work. Second, the increase in hours of paid work among married women can influence the working hours of their husbands independently of the male wage. We discuss this issue in Chapter 7 in the context of household production and *family* labor supply decisions.

The third problem is that, while we cannot rule out the possibility that the income effect dominates the substitution effect for males, interpreting the dramatic rise in participation rates among women becomes difficult. One possible explanation is that preferences among women changed, particularly after their heavy involvement in the labor market during World War II. For example, the stigma against working wives or mothers weakened. This change in preferences may explain some of the rising propensity of women to work, but it does not explain the *cause* of the changing preferences. Since women's attitudes may be most strongly influenced by the sheer increase in the number of working women, understanding what started the increase originally is fundamental.

Another explanation for the growing proportion of working women is based on the observation that women really have a tripartite choice of how to spend time: leisure, market work, and nonmarket (household) work (see Chapter 7 for further discussion of this tripartite choice). The inventions of automatic washers and dryers, frost-free refrigerators, and prepared foods, to name a few, have reduced the time required to perform household tasks. The ability to perform these tasks faster reduces the savings from staying home instead of working for pay. Thus, yet another force is at work affecting the incentives of women to work for pay.

Finally, since wives often work in the home more, and for pay less, than men and unmarried women, the income effect for them tends to be smaller and the substitution effect larger. The plausibility of a smaller income effect rests on the observation that, at any point in time, many married women are out of the labor force and many others are working less than full time. Thus, as noted before, a given wage increase will generate a smaller income effect than it would if virtually

---

[20]Donald O. Parsons, "The Decline in Male Labor Force Participation," *Journal of Political Economy*, February 1980, pp. 117–34.

all were working for pay full time. A larger substitution effect is plausible for married women because household and market work are close substitutes, whereas market work and leisure are not, as we argue below.

Suppose that women and men have roughly the same preferences regarding leisure and work. These two ways to spend time are substitutes, but not close substitutes. Thus, a change in the opportunity cost of leisure may not elicit a large change in the supply of working hours for either sex; leisure and work are simply too different for a large responsiveness to changes in opportunity costs to be observed. However, there are two types of *work* activity, market work (for pay) and household work, and there is a high degree of substitutability between *these* alternatives. If market work is performed, household chores are hired out to specialists (baby-sitters, cleaning services) or done by machines (frost-free refrigerators). If household work is substituted for market work, these costs of hiring out tasks are saved. Thus, doing household work oneself and working for pay and hiring out these chores represent two ways of getting the same job done. They are very close substitutes, so when the incentives to pursue one alternative change, a large response in time spent doing the other can be expected. Because married women have traditionally performed household work to a greater extent than have men and unmarried women, we would expect this second influence on the overall substitution effect (the substitution between work activities) to be more important for married women. The substitution effect observed in the above studies is thus plausibly larger for married women. (Chapter 7 will return to the issue of household and market work in more detail.)

It is easy to see that looking at *trends* in the propensity of people to work for evidence on the relative strength of income or substitution effects is not completely satisfactory. So many other factors are involved over time that affect these propensities that isolating income and substitution effects is impossible. Indeed, the growth of pensions, changes in employer desires concerning hours of work, time-saving household inventions, and changed attitudes toward working women all cloud our analysis of trends.

Cross-section studies. Numerous studies of labor supply behavior have relied on cross-sectional data. These studies basically analyze labor force participation or annual hours of work as they are affected by wage rates (the slope of the budget constraint) and unearned income (how far out the constraint lies). The most reliable and informative studies are those done on large samples of men, primarily because the labor supply behavior of women is complicated by child-rearing and household work arrangements for which data are sketchy at best. The findings discussed here are of *nonexperimental studies*—studies in which variations in wages and incomes are *observed*, rather than *generated by*, the researchers (findings from experimental studies are summarized later in this chapter in the discussion of income maintenance programs).

Most studies of male labor supply behavior indicate that the income effect dominates the substitution effect, and thus that men have (individual) negatively sloped supply curves. There is as yet no consensus about the *size* of the labor supply response. However, one careful review study[21] claims that, once various statistical and definitional problems are accounted for, the effect of raising a man's wage by 10 percent would be a 1–2 percent reduction in his labor supply. This observed effect is the result of something like a 2.5 percent reduction resulting from the income effect and roughly a 1 percent increase associated with the substitution effect.

The estimates for women are less well defined, perhaps for the reasons cited above. Nevertheless, the results of cross-sectional studies usually indicate that the *substitution* effect dominates, yielding a positively sloped labor supply curve for women.[22] Studies comparable to those for men (noted above) have generally found similar income effects among women, but the substitution effects for women are much larger than those for men, the likely reasons for which were mentioned earlier.[23]

It is interesting, and somewhat heartening, that the results of nonexperimental, statistically sophisticated cross-sectional studies generally support the observations based on trends over time. Namely, the income effect appears to dominate for males and the substitution effect appears dominant for females. As noted earlier, the relatively larger substitution effect among women probably reflects the traditional household role of married women, rather than sex-related differences in work/ leisure preferences.

POLICY APPLICATIONS

Virtually all government income maintenance programs—from welfare payments to unemployment compensation—have work incentive effects, and the direction and size of these effects are often critical issues in constructing and enacting such programs. As a society, we have decided to help those among us who are economically disadvantaged for one reason or another. However, it is important to understand how income maintenance programs can affect willingness to work. This final section will discuss the labor-supply implications of unemployment insurance, workers' compensation, and welfare programs and their alternatives.

---

[21]George Borjas and James Heckman, "Labor Supply Estimates for Public Policy Evaluation," *Proceedings of the Industrial Relations Research Association* (1978), pp. 320–31.

[22]*See* Jacob Mincer, "Labor Force Participation of Married Women," in *Aspects of Labor Economics* (Princeton, N.J.: Princeton University Press, 1962); Glen G. Cain, *Married Women in the Labor Force* (Chicago: University of Chicago Press, 1966); William G. Bowen and T. Aldrich Finegan, *The Economics of Labor Force Participation* (Princeton, N.J.: Princeton University Press, 1969).

[23]*See* Glen G. Cain and Harold W. Watts, "Toward a Summary and Synthesis of the Evidence," *Income Maintenance and Labor Supply: Econometric Studies* (Chicago: Markham, 1973). Mark Killingsworth, *Labor Supply*, Cambridge Surveys of Economic Literature (Cambridge, England: Cambridge University Press, 1983), offers a very comprehensive review of what the author calls "first- and second-generation" estimates of income and substitution effects.

Income Replacement Programs

Unemployment insurance and workers' compensation might be called *income replacement programs*. Unemployment insurance benefits are paid to workers who have been laid off, permanently or temporarily, by their employers. Workers' compensation is paid to employees who have been injured on the job. Both programs are intended to compensate workers for earnings lost while out of work.[24]

Complete replacement?   Given that both the unemployment insurance and workers' compensation programs are intended to replace lost earnings, it may seem a bit odd, if not callous, that both programs typically replace roughly just *half* of before-tax lost earnings.[25] Most benefits paid out under these programs are not taxed, so the fraction of *after-tax* earnings replaced is usually somewhat higher than 50 percent. However, lost fringe benefits are not replaced, so lost compensation is far from completely replaced. Why?

The reason for incomplete earnings replacement has to do with work incentives. Both injured and unemployed workers have some discretion over how long they will remain out of work. A man with a lacerated arm might be able to carry out his normal duties with some discomfort after a few days of recuperation, or he might choose to wait until his wound is completely healed before returning to work. An unemployed woman might accept the first offer of work she obtains, or she may prefer to wait a while and see if she can generate a better offer. In both cases the worker has the legal latitude to decide (within some limits) when to return to work. These decisions will obviously be affected by work incentives inherent in the income replacement programs affecting them.

Replacing *all* of lost income could result in *overcompensation* by generating a higher level of utility than before the loss of income,[26] and would motivate the recipients of benefits to remain out of work as long as possible. Figure 6.11 shows that before employment ceased, the person earned E_0 and had a level of utility equal to U_1. If, when employment ceases, the worker receives benefits equal to E_0 he or she will be at point T on a higher indifference curve. Before work ceased, the worker earned E_0 and had 8 hours of leisure, whereas at T he or she has E_0 in income and 16 hours of leisure per day. In this case, the recipient would be better off not working than working. Thus, full earnings replacement could clearly inhibit program beneficiaries from returning to work at the earliest possible time (see Example 6.2 for a case in which full earnings replacement would *not* completely destroy work incentives).

---

[24]For a complete description of these programs, *see* George E. Rejda, *Social Insurance and Economic Security* (Englewood Cliffs, N.J.: Prentice-Hall, 1976). We shall return to the unemployment insurance and workers' compensation programs in the chapters on unemployment (Chapter 15) and compensating differentials (Chapter 8).

[25]Both programs are run at the state level and thus vary in their characteristics across states. Benefits in both programs are bounded by minimums and maximums.

[26]We are assuming here that the psychic costs of injury or layoff are small. It could be argued that complete income replacement is justified on the grounds that it compensates for large psychic losses, but our analysis of work incentive effects would be unchanged.

**FIGURE 6.11   Full-Earnings Replacement
Overcompensates Workers**

Actual income loss vs. "scheduled" benefits.   A second issue in income
replacement programs is how to structure workers' compensation for permanent
disabilities. Should workers who are either totally or partially disabled receive
benefits that replace their *actual* lost earnings, or should they receive benefits
according to some impersonal schedule appropriate for people with their disability?
One might initially think that replacing actual losses is more fair, but in almost all
states those with permanent disabilities are compensated without reference to actual
losses. We show below that if actual losses were to be completely compensated,
such a program would create an enormous disincentive to work.

Suppose a manual worker became partially disabled by an injury on the job.
Suppose this worker lost three fingers on one hand and must now seek work in jobs
that pay less than he earned before. His new "market" budget constraint might be
the line AD in Figure 6.12. If our injured worker earned E_0 before injury and
workers' compensation replaced all earnings loss up to E_0, the workers' compensation budget constraint facing this worker would be like the solid-line constraint
($ABCD$) drawn in Figure 6.12. This income replacement constraint has a vertical
segment (AB), which indicates that if the person does not work at all, he receives a
benefit equal to E_0. If he does earn money by taking a job, the difference between E_0
and his actual earnings becomes his disability benefit. Thus, as long as his actual
earnings are below E_0, his benefit is such that his total income remains at E_0, which
is why the segment BC is horizontal at E_0. The segment CD corresponds to his
"market" (unsubsidized) constraint when earnings are above E_0.

Example 6.2

The Economics of the "Workaholic"

The text discussion of work incentives inherent in income-replacement programs has assumed that more leisure time always increases one's utility. This assumption leads to the conclusion that government income subsidies that are reduced one dollar for every dollar earned will induce people not to work. It was argued that such subsidies essentially reduce wages to zero, and that people will not work if they cannot increase their income by working.

Although the above assumption that an hour of leisure yields more in utility than an uncompensated hour at work may be true for most people, we can all think of people we know who love their work and become bored and restless when away from work. For them, work may be a "hobby," a "calling", or a means of socializing. It seems inconceivable that these people would choose *not* to work even if their money income would be the same whether they did or did not work. Can economic theory deal with these "workaholics" who derive more pleasure from work than from leisure, holding money income constant? The answer is yes.

Let us suppose that a "workaholic" places a positive value on leisure when her working hours are high, but after *L'* hours of daily leisure are consumed, any further increases in leisure cause her to be bored and restless. She places *negative* value on leisure at that point and would prefer to be at work even if she were not paid for it! A graphic representation of this woman's indifference curve is given by the curve *ACD* in the accompanying figure. Along the arc *AC*, the indifference curve is negatively sloped, which

The Work/Leisure Choice of a Workaholic

means that she would be willing to give up some income to obtain more leisure (that is, she places a positive value on leisure). Increases in leisure hours beyond L', however, place her in a range where her indifference curve is positively sloped (segment CD). In this range she places a negative value on leisure and would *give up* income if it meant she could avoid the boredom or social isolation of not working.

If our workaholic faced a budget constraint like RU in this figure, she would maximize utility at point B and work H^* hours per day. However, even if her budget constraint had a horizontal (zero-wage) segment in it (see, for example, the constraint $RSTU$ in the figure), she would work. In this case, she would maximize utility at point C and work H' hours. H' represents fewer hours than $H,^*$ but is clearly not equal to zero. Economic theory, then, *can* represent and successfully analyze the behavior of workaholics.

The interesting thing about Figure 6.12 is that, for many people, B—a point of no work at all—is the point of maximum utility. Throughout the horizontal segment, BC, the individual's net wage is zero (as reflected by BC's zero slope). If our worker were to earn an extra $10, the government would reduce his benefits by $10. In a very real sense, any earnings would be "taxed" away completely in the form of a dollar-for-dollar reduction in benefits. When people cannot increase their income by working, there is usually no incentive to work. There are exceptions, however, in which a zero wage *would* be associated with a positive level of work hours, as illustrated in Example 6.2.

**FIGURE 6.12 Budget Constraint with Actual
Income Replacement**

FIGURE 6.13   Comparing Budget Constraints of Two Disability Programs

One way to avoid the disincentives inherent in replacing *actual* lost earnings for disabled workers is to grant benefits according to some schedule drawn up with reference to the disability but without regard to the individual's actual earnings loss. For example, in the state of New York, a worker losing the first three fingers of one hand receives two thirds of his or her before-injury weekly wage for a period of 101 weeks, irrespective of his or her actual earnings during or after this 101-week period.[27] Other states compensate permanent, partial disabilities in a similar manner.

Using an impersonal schedule of disability benefits preserves at least some incentive to work because benefits are not reduced if earnings increase. The benefits received become a grant of nonwage income, and they do not alter the recipient's wage rate (price of leisure).

Figure 6.13 contains the "market" constraint (*AD*) and the "actual earnings loss" constraint (*ABCD*) previously depicted in Figure 6.12. Now assume that, instead of actual earnings loss, disability benefits for our disabled worker equal E_0 no matter how much or how little he earns after the injury. His new constraint is thus *ABE*. This new constraint is parallel to *AD*, his "market" constraint (*ABE* is everywhere E_0 higher than constraint *AD*), reflecting the fact that this form of compensation for injury does not alter his wage rate.

Figure 6.13 provides a graphic demonstration that with "scheduled" benefits there are greater incentives to work than if benefits are calculated to completely replace earnings losses. Our injured worker maximizes utility at point G rather than at point B, even though both disability benefit programs depicted pay equal benefits for those who cannot or do not choose to work.

The conclusion that scheduled payments offer stronger work incentives than benefits based on actual losses becomes even stronger if the scheduled benefits are reduced below E_0. As benefits are reduced, the constraint ABE moves closer to AD, and the point of utility maximization moves farther from G and closer to F (the utility-maximizing point in a world without disability benefits). Maximum work incentives are retained when there is no income transfer program, a situation in obvious conflict with the overall *goal* of helping workers who find themselves economically disadvantaged.[28]

While the basic aim is to restore income to disadvantaged workers, it is important to preserve work incentives as much as possible. If we take AD as the budget constraint when no benefit program exists and point F as the corresponding optimum work effort, it is easy to see from Figure 6.13 that "scheduled" benefits cause only an income effect. The constraint moves out to ABE, but it does not change slope. Work effort declines, since point G is to the right of point F, but it does not cease.[29]

On the contrary, if actual earnings loss were to become the benefit, there would be an income *and* a substitution effect, and *both* would work in the *same* direction. The benefits would simultaneously increase income while *reducing* the wage rate to zero (in the segment BC of constraint $ABCD$). The presence of a zero wage rate would reduce the price of leisure to zero and be a powerful disincentive to work. It is not surprising that payments for partial disabilities are generally "scheduled."[30]

Income Maintenance Programs

Income maintenance programs, more popularly known as "welfare" or "relief" programs, have the goal of *raising* the income of the poor to some minimum acceptable level. They thus differ from income replacement programs, which are aimed at *restoring* lost income. Because poverty is generally an income-related concept, the benefits paid out under income maintenance programs generally are affected by the level of the beneficiary's actual income. As we shall see, income-conditioned benefits inevitably reduce work incentives below what such incentives would be with no income support system for the poor. They simultaneously increase income while reducing the price of leisure (the wage rate), both of which should

---

[28]Chapter 8 will show that workers who are injured may be compensated *in advance* of injury by having higher wages (due to the risk inherent in their job) than they would otherwise have. The *compensating wage differentials* must also be taken into account when establishing programs on post-injury compensation.

[29]An exception to this statement would be a situation in which a person's indifference curves were such that a "corner solution," as in Figure 6.7, was obtained.

[30]For more details on the workers' compensation program, *see* Rejda, *Social Insurance and Economic Security*.

**FIGURE 6.14 Income and Substitution Effects
for Old Welfare System**

cause the demand for leisure to increase and the supply of labor to fall. This fact is
the root of much of the controversy welfare programs have generated over the years.
Welfare payments have taken two forms in this country, as described below.

The old welfare system. Prior to 1967, welfare took the form of a guaranteed
annual income. A welfare worker would determine the "needed" income of the
eligible person or family, based on family size, area living costs, and local welfare
regulations. Actual earnings would be subtracted from this needed level, and a
check would be received each month for the difference. If earnings went up, welfare
benefits would go down, dollar for dollar. This created a budget constraint like
$ABCD$ shown in Figure 6.14, where total income is Y_n (the "needed" income) as
long as the person is subsidized. There is no incentive to work for many people
because there is a zero wage (segment BC) over most normal hours of work.

Thus, the old welfare system served to increase income by moving the budget
constraint out from AC to ABC; this shift created an *income effect* tending to reduce
labor supply from points E to F in Figure 6.14. However, it *also* caused the wage to
effectively drop to zero: every dollar earned was matched by a dollar reduction in
welfare benefits. This dollar-for-dollar reduction in benefits induced a huge *substitution effect*, causing many to reduce their hours of work to zero (point B). The
old system clearly had strong disincentives for welfare recipients to find work.

The revised welfare system. Recognizing the nonexistent work incentives for
welfare recipients in the old system, the government restructured welfare benefits in

**FIGURE 6.15   Income and Substitution Effects
of the Revised Welfare Program**

1967 to eliminate the zero wage rate. Welfare recipients were allowed to keep the first $30 of any earnings per month and one third of the rest. Thus, ignoring the first $30, a welfare recipient who earned an extra $100 by working would have his or her benefits reduced by $67. The take-home wage rate thus became, in effect, one third of the market wage. While a take-home wage of one third the market wage clearly reduced the wage rate compared to what it would have been without welfare, it represented a significant improvement in work incentives over the zero wage rate implicit in the old system (see Figure 6.15).

Let us assume that the government had determined that the minimum needed income, Y_n, for recipient families was $16 per day. It thus guaranteed that the families would have a welfare benefit of $16 if no one worked. Suppose, however, that the family heads could earn $3 per hour if they worked, or a total of $48 per day if they worked 16 hours a day. If we ignore the first $30 of monthly earnings that could be kept completely[31] and remember that for every $3 the heads earned the government reduced their welfare benefit by $2, we can easily see that if they worked 8 hours a day, and thus earned $24, they would be taken off welfare and receive no benefit (two thirds of $24 is $16). An income of $24 thus becomes the *break-even level* of income (Y_B), the point at which a family is no longer subsidized.

For incomes higher than $24 per day, a family's budget constraint is *CD*, the

---

[31]To take into account this small sum would complicate our diagram without changing the analysis or its conclusions in any essential way.

subsidized or market constraint of which the slope's absolute value is 3 (reflecting the $3 wage). If the family earnings are zero, the welfare benefit is $16 (point *B* in Figure 6.15). If earnings are $0–24, the family is subsidized and has a total income (earnings plus subsidy) that falls along segment *BC* in Figure 6.15. Segment *BC* rises from $16 (point *B*) to $24 (point *C*) for 8 hours of work, which suggests this segment has a slope of which the absolute value is one. This slope is one third the slope of *AD*, which reflects the market wage of $3. Therefore, as long as the family is subsidized, the take-home wage rate is one third of the market wage under the revised welfare system.

If one compares constraint AD in Figure 6.15 with constraint ABCD, the revised welfare system constraint, one can see that the program increases income and reduces the take-home wage rate (because it "taxes away," in the form of reducing welfare benefits, two thirds of earnings). The increased income alone, with no change in wage, would create an *income effect* that decreases labor supply from points *G* to *E*. However, the fact that the take-home wage is reduced below the market wage creates a *substitution effect* that further reduces labor supply to point *F*.[32] Again, *both* the income and the substitution effects work in the direction of less work *compared to a world with no income subsidies*. However, comparing Figures 6.15 and 6.14, one can see that the revised welfare system had stronger work incentives for welfare recipients because welfare benefits were not reduced dollar for dollar with earnings.

The current welfare system.   In 1981 the welfare system was changed so that the budget constraints facing recipients are now a hybrid of the old and the revised systems. If a person receiving welfare finds a job, he or she faces the revised constraint (ABCD) analyzed in Fig. 6.15 for four months. That is, for the first four months of work, the recipient's earnings (above $30) are "taxed" at the rate of 67 percent. After that, earnings (less allowances for child-care costs and work-related expenses) are "taxed" at 100 percent and the person's constraint becomes ABCD in Figure 6.14. An analysis of this change in the welfare system is useful in making a further point about work incentives.

Our analysis of the welfare system so far has emphasized the work incentive effects on welfare *recipients*. It is true that for those who *continue to receive welfare*, the 1981 return to a 100 percent tax on earnings represents a reduced work incentive as compared to the revised system discussed above. However, the 1981 changes may induce some recipients who were previously employed to work longer hours and to leave the welfare rolls.

Consider Figure 6.16. For the individual whose preferences are represented there by indifference curves Z and Z', utility was maximized at point X under the revised welfare system when the constraint facing that individual was ABCD.

---

[32]Note that because of the decrease in the take-home wage, the *income effect* of the income maintenance program described becomes smaller the *more* one works (as long as income is sufficiently low to qualify for the subsidy). Graphically, segment *ABC* of the constraint in Figure 6.15 is further to the northeast of the market constraint *AD* in the region where working hours are fewest, and closest near 8 hours of work (the point where the subsidy ends).

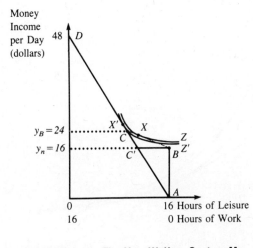

FIGURE 6.16 **The New Welfare System May Increase Work Incentives for the Working Poor**

However, after the 1981 changes, this individual faces the constraint ABC'D after four months of working and utility is now maximized at point X'. It is important to note three things about point X':

1. It is a point offering greater utility than point B for this individual (whose indifference curves are relatively flat, which means he or she values income relatively highly), so the person does not cease working;
2. It lies to the left of point X, which suggests that this individual will work longer and consume less leisure than he or she did under the revised system; and
3. The individual is now off welfare (utility is maximized along C'D, not ABC'), but his or her level of utility is reduced compared to what it was under the revised system (utility level Z is no longer possible).

The major point is that whether a given change in the welfare system increases or reduces work incentives depends on one's preferences. For people whose indifference curves are so steep (that is, their preferences for leisure are quite strong) that they were working very little under the revised system, the 1981 changes would likely reduce work incentives and those individuals would probably remain on welfare and cease working entirely. In contrast, for those whose indifference curves are relatively flat, as was illustrated in Figure 6.16, work incentives were increased under the 1981 changes. Economic theory is thus very useful in highlighting this frustrating policy problem.

Welfare dilemmas. Lest the student receive the impression that the obvious solution to this work incentive problem is to reduce the implicit tax from two thirds to some lower fraction, let us explore what would happen if this implicit tax were

FIGURE 6.17   Some May Reduce Hours of Work and Money Income Under an Income Maintenance Program

reduced to one fourth. Under this plan, the welfare recipient would be allowed to keep three of every four dollars earned. If $16 is still the daily benefit when there are no earnings, the break-even level of income becomes $64 (instead of $24). In other words, no matter what their wage rate, people who earn less than $64 per day would receive welfare benefits. Clearly, a low implicit tax rate and a reasonably generous guarantee level are inconsistent with confining welfare benefits to the needy. This dilemma pervades just about all disputes over welfare policy. That is, reducing implicit tax rates to increase the work incentive leads to an increase in the number of people eligible for benefits.

It is also worth noting here that, because the welfare subsidy is conditioned on income, and because income is to some extent under the control of an individual, some people previously above the break-even level of income might reduce their labor supply enough to qualify for the subsidy. This possibility is illustrated in Figure 6.17. Prior to the subsidy, the person depicted maximizes utility at point L, working 9 hours per day. After the subsidy is instituted and the constraint moves to $ABCD$, this person finds that utility is maximized at point M, where hours of work are much fewer. Point M is a point of lower money income than point L, but the increased leisure time more than makes up for the lost income.

Empirical studies of welfare and work incentives.   Although making welfare benefits available to people who were not previously eligible for them will clearly decrease their work incentives, the relevant policy question is: by how much will their work incentives be decreased? Some studies used estimates of income and

Example 6.3
Worker Adjustment to Incentives

The discussion of work incentives inherent in income replacement and income maintenance programs assumed that workers are well informed about program characteristics—that is, that they have some intuitive understanding of the budget constraint facing them. It also assumed that workers face a sufficiently large array of choices that they can find a set of working hours close to their utility-maximizing set. Students often have a healthy skepticism about the degree to which these assumptions approximate reality. The following example suggests that workers *do* have sufficient knowledge and choice to accommodate their behavior to a given set of work incentives.

Wisconsin, like other states, has an unemployment compensation program that pays unemployed workers a weekly benefit. These benefits are different for different recipients, depending primarily on their pre-unemployment earnings. There is a minimum and a maximum weekly benefit, but for most workers the unemployment benefit is about one half of prior earnings. Also like most other states, Wisconsin has a method of allowing for partial benefits to be paid to unemployed workers who obtain part-time or low-wage work during their period of eligibility for unemployment benefits. Unlike most other states, however, Wisconsin's partial benefit scheme is such that recipients can only receive one of three unemployment benefits: their full weekly benefit, a benefit equal to half their full weekly benefit, or zero. This partial benefit program contains some interesting work incentives.

The typical recipient of unemployment compensation in Wisconsin can earn up to one fourth of his or her pre-unemployment earnings with *no loss*

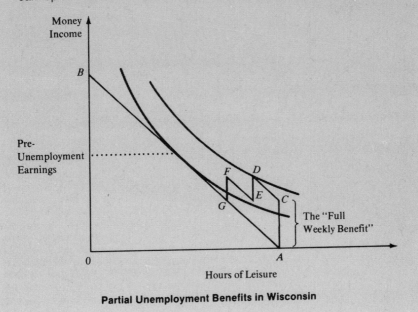

Partial Unemployment Benefits in Wisconsin

of benefits. Since recipients can, in effect, keep all their earnings up to that point, their "take home" wage rate equals their market wage. This element of the program is graphed in the first figure as segment *CD*, which is parallel to the market constraint *(AB)*.

However, once current earnings rise above the critical level of one fourth of prior earnings, benefits are reduced to one half the weekly benefit. This abrupt drop in benefits causes an equally abrupt drop in total income. Since working an extra hour past point *D* causes income to drop, the wage, in effect, becomes *negative*, as segment *DE* in the first figure illustrates.

Benefits equalling one half the full entitlement are paid, then, to recipients who earn between one fourth and one half of their prior earnings. When earnings rise just beyond the one-half point, all unemployment benefits cease and the constraint becomes the "market constraint," as segments *EF*, *FG*, and *GB* illustrate. The first figure shows a saw-toothed constraint in which the market wage alternates with extremely negative wage rates.

A quick look at the first figure indicates that, for many people, point *D* is the utility-maximizing combination of leisure hours and income. People who

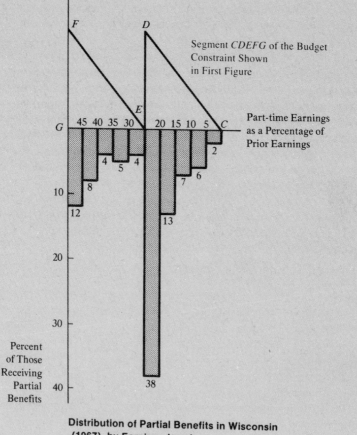

Distribution of Partial Benefits in Wisconsin (1967), by Earnings Level

are not fortunate enough to obtain a job where they can earn exactly one fourth of their prior earnings will try to choose the next best position, which is likely to be at points along the upper portions of *CD* or near point *F*. Points along most of *EF* and the lower portions of *CD* are clearly inferior, in terms of utility, to other points along the constraint running from *C* to *G*.

While it is true that most of those receiving unemployment benefits are completely unemployed, it is interesting to observe whether those who *are* able to find part-time work adjust their behavior as indicated above. In other words, *do* people tend to cluster most at point *D*, where earnings are just equal to one fourth of their prior wages? Are there more people at point *F* and the upper portions of *CD* than along the rest of the constraint running from *C* to *G*?

The answer to both these questions—at least for 1967, when a study of the questions was undertaken—is yes. In the second figure, segment *CDEFG* of the first figure's budget constraint is superimposed on the distribution of those actually receiving partial unemployment benefits, demonstrating that by far the biggest cluster of people is at point *D*, earning 20–25 percent of their prior earnings. Further, the concentrations of people increase as one moves to the upper ends of each segment (*CD* and *EF*), with two thirds of all partial-benefits recipients at either *F* or the upper half of *CD*. Thus, it appears that workers who do find partial employment while receiving unemployment benefits have the knowledge and inclination to adjust their behavior to the constraints (and the related incentives) facing them.

SOURCE: Raymond Munts, "Partial Benefit Schedules in Unemployment Insurance: Their Effect on Work Incentive," *Journal of Human Resources* 5 (Spring 1970):160–76.

substitution effects obtained from nonexperimental data in the late 1960s to answer this question. These studies imply that, for males, a guaranteed (zero earnings) benefit of about 75 percent of the poverty level (which was $3300 per year in 1967) and a 50 percent implicit tax rate would cause male labor supply to decrease by 8–15 percent.[33]

Experimental data, however, can also be used to estimate the size of income and substitution effects. Four large social experiments were conducted in New Jersey, Seattle-Denver, Gary (Indiana), and rural North Carolina in the late 1960s and early 1970s for the purpose of measuring labor supply responses to various income maintenance policies. They were conceived and funded because researchers and policymakers did not want to rely solely on estimates derived from the nonexperimental studies cited above.

While the details in each experiment varied, the welfare programs offered to the people in the experiments had benefit guarantee levels (benefits with zero earnings)

---

[33]Borjas and Heckman, "Labor Supply Estimates for Public Policy Evaluation," p. 331.

ranging from 50 to 125 percent of the poverty level.[34] The implicit tax rates in each experiment ranged from 30 to 80 percent. The typical response for males in these experiments was to reduce labor supply by 3–8 percent.[35] The somewhat smaller response than the cross-sectional prediction above is perhaps due to the known and limited duration of each experiment; responses might have been larger if recipients knew the program would be available to them indefinitely.

In examining the labor supply response of females in these experiments, it is useful to recall two facts from the nonexperimental studies. First, the estimates of income and substitution effects for women are much less precise than for men; second, the substitution effect for market work appears to be larger. Since the substitution effect of income maintenance programs induces a withdrawal of labor supply, it is not surprising that the labor supply responses of women in the experiments tended to be larger than for men and were also more varied. For wives, the responses ranged from zero decline in Gary to a 55 percent decline among Spanish-speaking wives in New Jersey, with most other estimates in the 15–30 percent range.[36] For female heads of families, the declines ranged from 11 percent in Seattle-Denver to 30 percent in Gary.

Thus, the labor supply effects of expanded welfare coverage are not likely to be innocuous. At some point, society will have to decide whether the improvements in social equity that result from more generous welfare programs are counterbalanced by the social losses attendant on reduced labor supply.[37] In making this decision, of course, society may feel quite differently about reductions in market work by some groups (say, mothers of small children) from how it feels about labor supply reductions of other groups.

---

[34]Poverty-level incomes are those below which the federal government considers a family to be living in poverty. These income thresholds are defined for farm and nonfarm families separately and are also calculated by family size and the age/sex of the household head. The threshold in each case is based on the 1963 cost of an inexpensive, but nutritionally sound, food plan designed by the Department of Agriculture. This cost was multiplied by 3, reflecting an assumption that families of three or more persons spend one third of their income on food, and has been adjusted upward each year since 1963 by changes in the Consumer Price Index. For a nonfarm family of four, the 1976 poverty threshold was $5815, up from $3128 in 1963; by 1982 changes in the Consumer Price Index implied a poverty level of around $9750 per year. (*See* U.S. Bureau of the Census, Current Population Reports, *Consumer Income,* Series P-60, No. 115, issued July 1978, for a more detailed explanation of poverty thresholds.)

[35]Minorities in the New Jersey experiment were an exception to this finding. They did not decrease their labor supply at all.

[36]For a summary of all the experiments, *see* Killingsworth, *Labor Supply,* and Robert Moffitt and Kenneth Kehrer, ''The Effect of Tax and Transfer Programs on Labor Supply: The Evidence from the Income-Maintenance Experiments,'' *Research in Labor Economics,* ed. R. Ehrenberg (Greenwich, Conn.: JAI Press, 1981).

[37]The general issue of equity vs. output considerations is treated in a readable manner by Arthur Okun, *Equality and Efficiency: The Big Trade-Off* (Washington, D.C.: The Brookings Institution, 1975).

REVIEW QUESTIONS

1. Is the following statement true, false, or uncertain: "Leisure must be an inferior good for an individual's labor supply curve to be backward-bending." Explain your answer.

2. The way the workers' compensation system works now, employees permanently injured on the job receive a payment of $X each year whether they work or not. Suppose the government were to implement a new program in which those who did not work at all got $0.5X but those who did work got $0.5X plus workers' compensation of 50 cents *for every hour worked*. What would be the change in work incentives associated with this change in the way workers' compensation payments were calculated?

3. Suppose our welfare system was structured *initially* as follows: all people earning below income $X would be given a cash grant to bring their income up to $X. *Draw a graph showing the budget constraint for this program.*

   Next, suppose we changed the welfare system to incorporate a *work test*. Persons who work *fewer* than Y hours get no welfare payment at all. Above Y hours of work, people receive a welfare payment sufficient to bring up their income to $X. *Draw in the relevant budget constraint on your graph.*

   Which system has stronger work incentives? Why?

4. Suppose the Social Security Disability Insurance (DI) program was structured so that otherwise eligible recipients lost their *entire* disability benefit if they had any labor market earnings at all. Suppose, too, that Congress was concerned about the *work disincentives* inherent in this program, and that the relevant committee was studying two alternatives for increasing work incentives among those disabled enough to qualify for it. One alternative was to *reduce* the benefits paid to all DI recipients but make no other changes in the program. The other was to maintain the old benefit levels (for those who received them) but allow workers to earn $300 per month and still keep their benefits; those who earned over $300 per month would lose all DI benefits.

   Analyze the work incentive effects of both alternatives. (The use of graphic analyses will be of great help to you.)

5. The Secretary of Labor received the following memo from a member of the President's staff:

   "The growth of interest in worker-owned enterprises raises some important questions relating to profit sharing. If workers with no previous investment income begin to receive a portion of profits, the effects on labor supply could be large. Would you please have your staff prepare an analysis of the labor supply implications of widespread worker participation in profits? The paper should cover the direction of the labor supply effects as indicated by theory and the likely ways in which these labor supply effects could be manifested. In particular, however, I am interested in a comparison of the labor supply effects of alternative bases upon which profits can be shared among workers. Which basis or bases have the smallest labor supply effects?"

   Write the paper avoiding the use of undefined jargon words. In other words, explain the concepts and hypotheses fully.

SELECTED READINGS

Bowen, William G., and Finegan, T. Aldrich. *The Economics of Labor Force Participation*. Princeton, N.J.: Princeton University Press, 1969.

Cain, Glen G. *Married Women in the Labor Force*. Chicago: University of Chicago Press, 1966.

Cain, Glen G., and Watts, Harold W., eds. *Income Maintenance and Labor Supply*. Chicago: Markham, 1973.

Killingsworth, Mark R. *Labor Supply*. Cambridge, England: Cambridge University Press, 1983.

Lewis, H. G. "Hours of Work and Hours of Leisure." *Proceedings of the Industrial Relations Research Association* (1957):196–206.

Moffitt, Robert, and Kehrer, Ken. "The Effect of Tax and Transfer Programs on Labor Supply: The Evidence from the Income Maintenance Experiments." In Ronald G. Ehrenberg, ed., *Research in Labor Economics*, 4. Greenwich, Conn., JAI Press, 1981, pp. 103–50.

Pechman, J. A., and Timpane, P. M., eds. *Work Incentives and Income Guarantees: The New Jersey Income Tax Experiment*. Washington, D.C.: The Brookings Institution, 1975.

7

Labor Supply: Household Production, the Family, and the Life Cycle

$$\mathsf{I}$$n Chapter 6 the theory of labor supply focused on *individuals* who were choosing between *labor* and *leisure*. This chapter will recast labor supply theory to take into account the interdependency of family members' decisions and the fact that much of the time spent at home is on *production*, not consumption, activities. It will also stress the interdependency of individuals' labor supply decisions across different stages of their lives. This theory of labor supply in the context of "household production" and life-cycle decisions can yield many useful insights into labor-supply behavior and related policy issues.[1]

THE THEORY OF HOUSEHOLD PRODUCTION

Although many adults are unmarried at some points in their lives, most do marry and form family units. The family thus becomes a very basic decision-making entity in society, and many important decisions concerning both consumption patterns and labor supply are made in a *family* context. Our task in this chapter is to find out in what ways the implications of the individual labor supply theory in Chapter 6 are modified or expanded by consideration of the *family*.

Throughout this chapter we shall assume that it is the *family unit* that consumes

---

[1]Models of household production are based on the pioneering work of Gary Becker, "A Theory of the Allocation of Time," *Economic Journal* 75 (September 1965):493–517. Another early study in this area is by Reuben Gronau, "The Measurement of Output of the Nonmarket Sector: The Evaluation of Housewives' Time," in Milton Moss, ed., *The Measurement of Economic and Social Performance* (New York: National Bureau of Economic Research, 1973), pp. 163–89.

and enjoys commodities; that is, we shall assume that husband and wife *jointly* derive utility from consumption. We shall also assume that many commodities the family consumes are produced, or can be produced, at home. Thus, food and energy are combined with preparation time to produce the meals from which family enjoyment is derived. A vacuum cleaner and time are combined to contribute to an orderly home. Food, clothing, and supervision time all contribute to the growth of children, whom the parents hope to enjoy. Thus, a marriage partner who stays at home may be engaged more in the production of commodities from which the family derives utility than in the direct consumption of leisure.

A Model of Household Production

Household production models explicitly recognize that both consumption and production take place in the home. The family unit, then, must make two kinds of decisions: *what* to consume and *how to produce* what it consumes. Consider the second decision first by analyzing a family that does not have to worry about what to consume because it consumes only one commodity: meals. This family derives its utility from the quantity and quality of food it eats, as well as from the general environment surrounding its meal consumption.[2]

Meals that yield equal utility can be produced in several ways. A family can eat out in a restaurant, in which case minimum time is spent in preparation and a maximum of market goods (food plus service) are consumed. The meal could be prepared at home with food bought from a market, or it could be prepared at home with food grown or made at home, which obviously represents a lot of preparation time. Since any combination of goods and household time can produce meals that are equally valuable (in terms of producing utility) to the family, we can draw a curve that represents all the time–goods combinations that can produce meals of equal utility. Such a curve can be called a utility *isoquant,* where *iso* means "equal," and *quant* means "quantity". Two isoquants are depicted in Figure 7.1 as M_0 and M_1.

Several things should be noted about the isoquants in Figure 7.1. First, along M_0, the utility provided by family meals is constant. The utility produced by the time–goods combinations along M_1 is also constant, but it is greater than the utility represented by M_0 because meals produced by such combinations generally involve more goods, more time, or both.

Second, the isoquants M_0 and M_1 are both *negative* in slope and *convex* (as viewed from below) in shape. The *negative* slope reflects an assumption that time and goods are substitutes in the production of meals. If household time is reduced, meal production can be held constant by increasing the purchase of goods. Thus, if a family decides not to grow its own food, it can buy food instead—or if it decides to spend less time cooking food, it could still maintain the same utility from meals by using a microwave oven or going out to eat.

The *convexity* of the isoquants reflects an assumption that as household meal

---

[2]We shall drop the assumption about consuming just one commodity later, but the assumption permits us to make several basic points in an easily understood fashion.

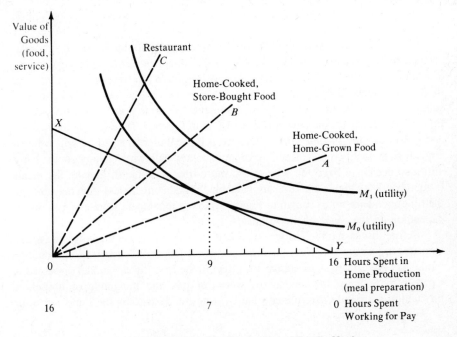

FIGURE 7.1   The Production of Family Meals

preparation time continues to fall, it becomes more difficult to make up for it with goods. If the family spends a lot of time in meal preparation, it will be easy to replace some of that time with just a few goods (store-bought food easily replaces homegrown food, for example). However, when preparation time is very short to begin with, a further cut in such time may be very difficult to absorb and still keep utility constant. Thus, it will take many goods—a large increase in food quality, for example—to substitute for reduced cooking time.

Finally, along any one ray (*A*, *B*, or *C*) emanating from the origin of Figure 7.1, the ratio of goods to household preparation time in the production of meals is constant. When time and goods are combined in the ratio along ray *A*, time-intensive meals are produced using homegrown food. Meals produced with the time–goods ratio along *B* are home-cooked, using store-bought food, and the time–goods ratio along ray *C* represents the "production" of restaurant meals.

The utility-maximizing mode of producing meals depends on the wage rate and the nonwage income and utility preferences of the producer of those meals. In Figure 7.1 the budget constraint of a woman whose husband is disabled and cannot work, who has no nonwage income, and who has a relatively low wage is depicted by *XY*. The figure suggests that the utility-maximizing mode of meal preparation is to use homegrown food, for the simple reason that when one has a low wage, time-intensive activities are relatively inexpensive. Time spent weeding, tilling, canning, and freezing does not cost a lot, in terms of forgone earnings (goods), in this case. Thus, in the example shown, nine hours a day would be spent at home, seven hours performing work for pay, and meal production on isoquant M_0 represents the highest level of utility that can be attained.

Figure 7.2 shows what will happen if the budget constraint in Figure 7.1 shifts because of an increase in *nonwage* income. What happens to the wife's propensity to work outside the home if the family begins to receive governmental payments for the husband's disability? This income grant does not change the wife's wage rate, so the new budget constraint facing the family has the same slope as constraint XY in Figure 7.1. However, the new constraint ($X'Y'$ in Figure 7.2) lies above the old one and reflects a pure *income effect*. Because it is wealthier, the family will want to enjoy higher-quality meals. It will have more money with which to buy goods, but it will also decide to have the wife spend more time at home to prepare the meals (remember, both goods and time are valuable in producing meals). She may change the time–goods ratio, as shown in Figure 7.2, by a movement from ray A to ray B, depending on the shape of the isoquants.

Before discussing the changes that result from a change in the wife's wage, let us pause to make two points. First, the income effect in this household production model has exactly the same sign as the effect in the labor/leisure model discussed in Chapter 6. Second, the amount of work for pay and the mode of household production are jointly determined; that is, they are affected by the same constraint

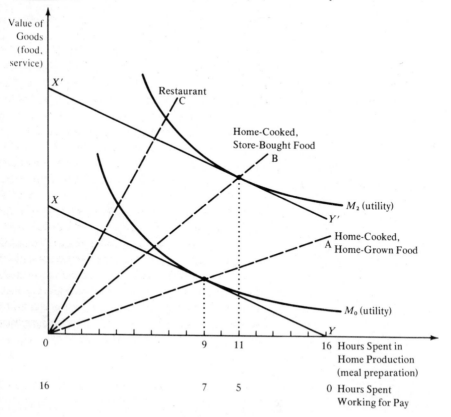

FIGURE 7.2   Production of Family Meals: The Income Effect

and are made as part of the same decision. Emphasizing household production rather than leisure, therefore, does not change our conclusion about the effects of income on labor supply in this case. Emphasizing production rather than leisure, however, does highlight the interrelated nature of decisions concerning family "household production" and decisions about labor supply.

Let us continue for a moment with our example in Figure 7.2 of a wife whose husband was disabled and unemployed. If he remained disabled but she obtained a wage increase, what would happen to her labor supply? Quite simply, there would be two opposing effects (as we found in the "leisure" model previously). The *income effect,* as above, would tend to drive her away from market work and toward more time at home, where she could spend more time in activities (meal preparation) that enhance family utility. However, the *substitution effect* would tend to push her out of the home and toward more work for pay. When her wages are increased, time spent at home preparing meals becomes more expensive than it was before. Thus, she will tend to move away from time-intensive modes of production to modes that rely more on goods, thus freeing her for more "market" work. The overall observed effect of her wage increase on her labor supply cannot be predicted based on theory alone.

Household Production and Consumption

We have just seen that when a family member is engaged in household production, an increase in the wage rate will have two effects. There will be an income effect that induces the family to consume more household "output", and tends to push the household producer out of market work and into the home. However, there is also a substitution effect that induces the family to produce its household output in a less time-intensive fashion, which tends to drive the household producer into working more for pay outside the home. Thus, *substitution in the (household) production process* occurs.

However, *another* substitution effect is also present. If we drop our assumption that the family consumes just one good, it is easy to see that when the market wage rate of the household producer changes, the family may change the *mix* of goods that it consumes. If the wife's wage, say, goes up and the prices of goods do not, the cost of very time-intensive commodities will rise more than commodities that are produced using less time. The family will tend to consume more commodities in general because it is wealthier, but it will alter the *mix* by reducing the proportion of time-intensive commodities in its consumption "basket." Thus, a change in the market wage rate of the household producer causes substitution in household *consumption* as well as in household *production*.

Recall from Chapter 6 that the substitution effect is graphically depicted by changing the slope of the budget constraint, keeping it tangent to a given indifference curve. If the relevant indifference curve is relatively flat, as in panel (a) of Figure 7.3, the substitution effect will be larger than when the indifference curve is steep, as in panel (b). What will cause it to be comparatively flat? In terms of our model, the curve will be flat when it is *easy to substitute goods for time* without loss of utility. (To prove this to yourself, ask "If an hour of time at home is given up,

(a) A Large Substitution Effect   (b) A Relatively Small Substitution Effect

FIGURE 7.3   Large vs. Small Substitution Effects

what amount of goods will have to be added to keep utility constant?'' When it is easy to substitute goods for time, it will take relatively few added goods to keep utility constant.)

Married women have traditionally been engaged in household production, as well as household consumption. Married men have tended to be less involved in household production, and a higher proportion of their time at home has been spent in consumption, or leisure, activities. As men's wages rise, they experience a substitution effect in *consumption* that tends to push them away from time-intensive forms of consumption and towards more goods-intensive consumption. When women's wages rise, however, there are substitution effects in both *production and consumption*. Women tend to consume less time-intensive commodities, but as household producers they *also* adopt less time-intensive modes of production. They substitute day care for children, frozen foods, and microwave ovens for household-production time; this substitution effect in production is more or less added to the one in consumption to yield a stronger overall substitution effect than is observed for men.

JOINT HUSBAND-WIFE LABOR SUPPLY DECISIONS

In the preceding example, we assumed that the husband was disabled and thus not very productive in either market or household production in order to analyze the labor supply decisions for the wife only. When both spouses can work inside and outside the home, the family must make decisions about who will work where. In other words, because husbands and wives are productive in two places, in the marketplace and in the household, their labor supply decisions will be jointly made.

Who Stays at Home?

Consider a utility-maximizing family trying to decide which spouse will stay home and engage in "household production" full time. This family needs to answer two questions: Who is relatively more productive at home? Who is relatively more productive in market work? The answer to the first question depends upon who can produce more commodities (more utility) for a given amount of goods and home production time. The answer to the second question depends upon who can generate the greater command over goods by working for pay. Simply put, if a utility-maximizing family decides it must have one spouse at home, it will prefer that spouse be the one who is relatively more productive there than in the marketplace.

For example, a family deciding who should stay home and perform most of the

---

Example 7.1

Household Productivity and Labor Supply in Japan

One of the fundamental insights of household production theory is that one's labor supply behavior is, in part, a function of productivity at home relative to that in the marketplace (as reflected in one's wage rate). While formal exposition of the theory is a recent development in economics, the behavior it seeks to explain is not. Many developing countries employ people in their industrial cities who have recently migrated from family farms and whose labor is valuable there at harvest time. In terms of household production theory, the harvest-related increase in their productivity back on the farm temporarily reduces the relative advantage of market (paid) work; the result is they quit or absent themselves from their factory jobs at this time of year and go back home to help out.

An example of the above behavior can be found in Japan early in this century. Many cotton-spinning mills lost 30 percent of their work force in August, stimulating factory owners to adopt countermeasures. Koji Taira describes the situation as follows:

> It was widely recognized that the seasonal fluctuations were closely related to labor requirements on farms, since the factory operatives were predominantly from farm households. From the point of view of the farm households, the value of work on the farm during busy periods was much higher than the regular wages at the factory. The essence of countermeasures on the part of the factory, therefore, was to offer such inducements as might make staying on the job more attractive than return to the farm during such periods. A variety of inducements developed that were based on this premise. One was to grant bonuses to those who stayed on their jobs during the months of peak activity on the farm. Another was a profit-sharing plan of one kind or another that was related to length of period of consecutive work. The third was a variety of devices such as company-paid pleasure trips, participation in company-sponsored lotteries, and recreational opportunities granted only to workers remaining on the job during busy seasons on the farm.

SOURCE: Koji Taira, *Economic Development and the Labor Market in Japan* (New York: The Columbia University Press, 1970), p. 122.

child rearing would, if it is going to maximize utility, consider the gains and losses attendant on either the husband or wife performing this task. The losses from staying home are related to the market wage of each, while the gains depend on their enjoyment of, and skill at, child rearing. (Since enjoyment of the parenting process increases family utility, we can designate both higher levels of enjoyment *and* higher levels of skill as indicative of greater "productivity" in child rearing.) The wage rate for women, perhaps because of discrimination, is usually below that for men. (Discrimination will be treated in Chapter 14; other reasons for male–female wage differences are dealt with in Chapters 8 and 9.) It is also likely that, because of socialization, women are more productive than men in child rearing. If a given woman's wage rate is lower than her husband's and the woman is more productive in child rearing, it is clearly better for the woman to raise the children. The family gives up less in market goods and gains more in child rearing.

Modeling the choice of who stays home to raise children as a function of relative productivities, and not just custom, emphasizes the point that child-rearing arrangements will probably change as wages and home productivities change. If discrimination against women is eliminated or if sex roles in childhood become less distinct for boys and girls, we could well observe more men rearing children in the future.

Do Both Spouses Work for Pay?

It is clearly not necessary, of course, that either husband or wife stay at home full time. Many household chores, from cooking and cleaning to child care, can be hired out or otherwise performed in a goods-intensive manner. The considerations underlying the decision about whether both should work can be best understood by

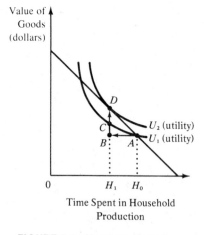

FIGURE 7.4   Home vs. Market Productivities

looking at Figure 7.4. The utility isoquants there (U_1 and U_2) represent the various combinations of household time and goods that can be used to generate family utility of two levels (level 1 and level 2).

As long as an extra hour of market work by both husband and wife creates the ability to buy more goods than are required to make up for the hour of lost home production time, both spouses will work for pay that extra hour. In terms of Figure 7.4, if a person spending H_0 hours at home decides to work an extra hour for pay, so that H_1 hours are now spent at home, he or she will gain *BD* in goods.[3] Since an increase of only *BC* in goods is required to compensate for the lost hour of home production to keep utility constant, the person is clearly better off working for pay. In other words, at point *A* the person is relatively more productive in the market-place than at home; therefore, the decision to perform more market work would be in the family's best interests. Thus, decisions about family labor supply must be made in full consideration of the market and household productivities of both marriage partners.

The Joint Decision and Cross-Effects

We have seen that family labor supply decisions are the outcomes of a process that jointly considers the household and market productivities of each spouse. However, one spouse's productivity in both production and consumption at home is affected by the *other* spouse's labor supply to the market, so that modeling the joint decision is quite complex. For example, if a married woman decides to increase her hours worked outside the home, her husband's marginal productivity for a given number of hours at home may rise as he takes over chores she once performed. Thus, if both wife and husband are *substitutes* in the household *production* of commodities, one's increased labor supply may tend to decrease the labor supply of the other.

On the other hand, both spouses may be *complementary* in the *consumption* of commodities. That is, if the woman above takes a job that involves working until 8:00 P.M. each night, her husband may decide that dinners at 6:00 P.M. have less utility than before, and as a result, he might decide that the benefits of working later outweigh the utility lost by so doing. In this case, one spouse's decision to increase hours worked for pay may induce the other spouse to likewise increase labor supply.

Theory cannot predict whether the spouses are substitutes or complements in household production and consumption; similarly, it is impossible to say which cross-effect will dominate if their signs conflict. Thus, the question of how one spouse's labor supply will respond to changes in the labor supply of the other is essentially an empirical one. As we shall show in the next section, the dominant cross-effect may vary with family circumstances. However, one study used the concept of complementarity in consumption activities to help explain why the

---

[3]We are talking here of *after*-tax spending power. The value of what one produces at home is not taxed, but earnings in the marketplace are—a difference that forces us to focus here on wages and earnings *net* of taxes.

decline in average weekly hours worked has slowed so dramatically in the postwar period (see Table 6.3). That is, the incentives for married women to work for pay have increased more rapidly in the postwar period than before, and their increased hours of paid work may have tended to induce their husbands to work longer hours than they would have otherwise.[4]

HOUSEHOLD PRODUCTION THEORY AND SOME SOCIAL ISSUES

The theory presented thus far in this chapter can be used to analyze some important social and policy issues. In this section we shall look at the effects on family labor supply of health problems, recessions, and income maintenance programs. Note that in each case, questions of the cross-effects discussed in the section above are critical.

Health and Labor Supply

An analysis of the market and household productivities of a husband and wife must consider the effects of *health* on labor supply. While a man who tires quickly because of a respiratory problem may be capable of performing market work at reduced hours or wages, his affliction renders his *market* time less productive than that of a healthy person. However, his marginal contribution to production at home, where resting in between tasks is possible, may not be affected much at all. If he and his wife are substitutes in household production, his changed relative productivity between home and the marketplace may induce him to become the principal household producer and her to become the primary wage earner. One cannot predict with any certainty that this change in roles will occur, however, for at least two reasons. First, his becoming disabled may *increase* his wife's marginal productivity at home if he needs extra care. Second, if the time of each is *complementary in consumption,* his increased time at home would tend to increase her time at home.

Here again, labor supply decisions are viewed by a utility-maximizing family as matters of choice, not custom or necessity. While custom or necessity is obviously important in some cases, viewing labor supply decisions as matters of choice provides insight into how government policies or general economic trends can change such decisions. For example, if there is discrimination against women and if this discrimination decreases so that their market wages improve relative to those for men, the labor supply withdrawal of unhealthy men might become more pronounced, for the reasons noted above. For the same reasons, it could become more common for women to be the primary breadwinners in two-adult families.

---

[4]Thomas J. Kniesner, "The Full-Time Workweek in the United States, 1900–1970," *Industrial and Labor Relations Review* (October 1976): 3–15.

The "Discouraged" vs. the "Additional" Worker

Changes in one spouse's productivity, either at home or in market work, can alter the family's basic labor supply decision. Consider, for example, a family in which market work is performed by the husband and in which the wife is employed full time in the home. What will happen if a recession causes the husband to become unemployed?

The husband's market productivity declines, at least temporarily. He may be a highly specialized worker and unable to find similar work at the moment. The drop in his market productivity relative to his household productivity (which is unaffected by the recession) makes it more likely that the family will find it beneficial for him to engage in household production. If the wage his wife can earn in paid work is not affected, the family *may* decide that, to try to maintain the family's prior level of utility (which might be affected by both consumption and *savings* levels), *she* should seek market work and *he* should substitute for her in home production for as long as the recession lasts. He may remain a member of the labor force as an unemployed worker awaiting recall, and as she begins to look for work, she becomes an "added" member of the labor force. Thus, in the face of falling family income, the number of family members seeking market work may increase. This potential response is akin to the income effect, in that, as family income falls, fewer commodities are consumed—and less time spent in consumption tends to be matched by more desired hours of work for pay.

At the same time, however, we must look at the *wage rate* someone without a job can *expect* to receive if he or she looks for work. This expected wage, denoted by $E(W)$, can actually be written as a precise statistical concept:

$$E(W) = \pi W, \tag{7.1}$$

where W is the wage rate of people who have the job and π is the probability of obtaining the job. For someone without a job, the price of an hour at home—the opportunity cost of staying home—is $E(W)$. The reduced availability of jobs that occurs when the unemployment rate rises causes the expected wage of those without jobs to fall sharply for two reasons. First, an excess of labor supply over demand tends to push down real wages (for those with jobs) during recessionary periods. Second, the chances of getting a job fall in a recession. Thus, both W and π fall in a recession, causing $E(W)$ to decline. Noting the *substitution effect* that accompanies a falling expected wage, some have argued that people who would otherwise have entered the labor force become "discouraged" in a recession and tend to remain out of the labor market. Looking for work has such a low expected payoff for them that such people decide that spending time at home is more productive than spending time in job search. The reduction of the labor force associated with discouraged workers in a recession is a force working against the "added-worker" effect—just as the substitution effect works against the income effect.

It is possible, of course, for both the "added-worker" and "discouraged-worker" effects to coexist, because "added" and "discouraged" workers will be different groups of people. Which group predominates, however, is the important question. If the labor force is swollen by "added workers" during a recession, the published unemployment rate will likewise become swollen (the added workers will increase the number of people looking for work). If workers become "discouraged" and drop out of the labor market after having been unemployed, the decline in people seeking jobs will depress the unemployment rate. Knowledge of which effect predominates is needed in order to make accurate inferences about the actual state of the labor market from the published unemployment rate.

We know that the added-worker effect does exist. Jacob Mincer, in a clever landmark study, found that the labor market behavior of wives was very sensitive to temporary changes in their husbands' income. In fact, he found that the labor supply of married women was more responsive to temporary than permanent changes in their husbands' income.[5] However, this added-worker effect is confined to the relatively few families whose normal breadwinner loses a job (the overall unemployment rate rarely goes above 10 percent). The fall in expected real wages occurs in nearly *every* household, and since the substitution effect is strong for married women, it is not surprising that the discouraged-worker effect is large and predominant. Other things equal, *the labor force tends to shrink during recessions and grow during periods of economic recovery.*

The dominance of the discouraged-worker effect creates what some call the hidden unemployed—people who would like to work but who believe that jobs are so scarce that looking for work is of no use. Because they are not looking for work, they are not counted as unemployed in government statistics. Focusing on the period 1973–1978, when the overall official unemployment rate went from 4.9 percent to 6.0 percent, can give some indication of the size of hidden unemployment.

In 1973 an average of 4.3 million people were counted as unemployed at any given time, representing 4.9 percent of the labor force. In addition, 679,000 people indicated that they wanted work but were not seeking it because they felt jobs were unavailable to them. This group constituted 1.2 percent of those adults not in the labor force. In 1978 the number of people officially counted as unemployed was 6 million, but there were 850,000 people among the "hidden" unemployed. These 850,000 people represented 1.5 percent of those adults not in the labor force. The rise in the percentage of those out of the labor market for job-related reasons is evidence of the discouraged-worker effect. Incidentally, if "discouraged workers" were counted as unemployed members of the labor force, the unemployment rate would have been 5.6 percent in 1973 and 6.8 percent in 1978.[6] To count these

---

[5]Jacob Mincer, "Labor Force Participation of Married Women," in *Aspects of Labor Economics,* A Conference of the Universities—National Bureau Committee on Economic Research (Princeton, N.J.: Princeton University Press, 1962). As more and more women become *regularly* employed for pay, the added-worker effect will tend to decline (and will increasingly be confined to teenagers).

[6]To say that including "discouraged workers" in unemployment statistics would change the published unemployment rate does not imply that it *should* be done. For a summary of the arguments for and against counting discouraged workers as unemployed, see the final report of the National Commission on Employment and Unemployment Statistics, *Counting the Labor Force* (Washington, D.C., 1979), pp. 44–49.

workers, however, would overlook the possibility that some of them desire only an intermittent labor force attachment and time their periods out of the labor force to coincide with periods when expected wages are low.

How Will an Income Maintenance Program Affect Work Incentives?

Family labor supply models can also be applied to the analysis of the effects of income maintenance programs. Our model in Chapter 6 implied that income maintenance programs clearly reduce work incentives because they simultaneously increase income and reduce the take-home wage rate. While this effect may be true for the family unit as a whole, it does *not* follow that *both* husband and wife will supply fewer hours to the labor market, primarily because of the possibility that the spouses are substitutes in household production.[7]

Consider the *wife's* response to a family income maintenance subsidy and assume she is initially the primary "household producer." The *increase* in family *income* will encourage the family to consume more of all normal goods, including "pure" leisure and other household-produced commodities. Both of these "income effects" suggest that total family hours at home will tend to rise. The *decline* in her take-home *wage rate* induces the family to adopt more time-intensive modes of household production, indicative of a substitution effect that also works in the direction of reduced family labor supply. Both effects depend, of course, on her *remaining* the primary household producer.

The income maintenance program, however, also reduces the take-home wage of her *husband,* and this change could result in the family's deciding that the *husband* should become the primary household producer. Suppose, for example, that both husband and wife have the same market wage but the wife is relatively more productive at home when just a few total hours of family time are spent there. Initially, then, the family decides that *she* should do the household production. Suppose, however, that the husband has household skills, such as carpentry and plumbing skills, that can be put to best use when time at home is substantial. When the family decides to allocate more total hours of family time to household production, his household skills become relatively more valuable, and the family may decide *he* should become the primary household producer. (The likelihood of this decision is increased if the family, for example, is renovating a very old house.) He might thus reduce his market labor supply, but she might increase hers.

Thus, it is theoretically possible that the availability of an income maintenance program could cause *overall* family labor supply to fall, while at the same time inducing one family member to *increase* his or her labor supply. To say that it is a

---

[7]For a more rigorous and complete analysis of this issue, see Mark R. Killingsworth, "Must a Negative Income Tax Reduce Labor Supply? A Study of the Family's Allocation of Time," *Journal of Human Resources* 11 (Summer 1976): 354–65.

possibility should not imply, of course, that it is a theoretical prediction *or* that it actually occurs. The empirical results on this issue are still inconclusive.[8]

LIFE-CYCLE ASPECTS OF LABOR SUPPLY

Because market productivity (wages) and household productivity vary over the life-cycle, people vary the hours they supply to the labor market over their lives. In the early adult years relatively fewer hours are devoted to work than in later years, and more time is devoted to schooling. In the very late years people fully or partially retire, though at varying ages. In the middle years most males are working full time, but many women have careers that are interrupted by years at home raising small children. While the issue of schooling is dealt with in Chapter 9, the model of household production discussed in this chapter can help us understand both the labor force behavior of married women and decisions about retirement.

The Interrupted Careers of Married Women

The basic premise of the household production model is that people are productive in two places: in the home and in a "market" job. Their decisions about whether to seek market work and for how many hours are a function of their *relative* productivities in both places. As long as an extra hour of market work allows the person to buy more goods than are required to make up for the hour of lost production time at home, the person will work for pay that extra hour.

The marginal home productivity of married women greatly increases when young children are present. In effect, the presence of young children tilts the utility isoquants of married women from U (say) in Figure 7.5 to something like U'. The important feature of U' is that an hour of home production given up is so valuable that it requires a large compensation of goods for family utility to remain constant. Since market earnings in Figure 7.5 cannot possibly provide the wherewithal to purchase those goods, the woman decides not to work. As children grow older, her indifference curves tilt back toward U, and she begins to seek more work for pay (see Example 7.2 for a discussion of how household productivity can be measured).

The Substitution Effect and When to Work Over a Lifetime

Just as deciding *who* will work at home at various stages in a family's life involves comparing market and home productivities of husband and wife, deciding *when* to

---

[8]See Chapter 6 for citations of numerous labor supply studies based on income maintenance experiments. See also T. J. Wales and A. D. Woodland, "Estimation of Household Utility Functions and Labor Supply Response," *International Economic Review* 17 (June 1976): 397–410; Thomas J. Kniesner, "An Indirect Test of Complementarity in a Family Labor Supply Model," *Econometrica* 44 (July 1976): 651–69; and Wendy Lee Gramm, "The Demand for the Wife's Non-Market Time," *Southern Economic Journal* 41 (July 1974): 124–33.

FIGURE 7.5 Household Productivity Can Change over the Life Cycle

work over the course of one's life involves comparing market and home productivities *over time*. The basic idea here is that a person will tend to perform the most market work when his or her earning capacity is high relative to home productivity. Conversely, people will engage in household production when their earning capacity is relatively low.

Suppose a sales representative working on a commission basis knows that his potential income is around $30,000 in a certain year, but that July's income potential will be twice that of November's. Would it be rational for him to schedule his vacation (a time-intensive activity) in November? The answer depends on his market productivity relative to his "household productivity" for the two months. Obviously his market productivity, his wage rate, is higher in July than November, which means that the opportunity costs of a vacation are greater in July. However, if he has children who are only free to vacation in July, he may decide that his household productivity (in terms of utility) is so much greater in July than November that the benefits of vacationing in July outweigh the costs. If he does not have children of school age, the utility generated by a November vacation may be sufficiently close to that of a July vacation that the smaller opportunity costs make a November vacation preferable.

Similar decisions are probably made over longer periods of time, perhaps one's entire life. As Chapter 9 will show, market productivity (which is reflected in one's wage) starts low in the young adult years, rises rapidly with age, then tails off and even falls in the later years, as shown in panel (a) of Figure 7.6. If home productivity is more or less constant over the years, then we should find people working (for pay) hardest in their middle years and least in the early and late years,

Example 7.2

The Value of a Homemaker's Time

The services performed by homemakers are not sold in the marketplace and thus are not counted in estimates of gross national product (GNP). The fact that they are not sold, however, does not imply they are not valuable—and for many purposes it becomes interesting to attempt to estimate the value of these services. Three approaches can be taken in evaluating these services, and household production theory can be used to compare them.

Market Prices. One method of weighing the services of homemakers is to measure how much these services would cost if they were to be purchased in the marketplace. Thus, the "market" costs of child care, cleaning, cooking, and other services are aggregated to form an overall estimate. In one careful study using this approach, Hawrylyshyn estimated that the value in 1967 of the services performed by a full-time homemaker (in a two-adult family) was $5,220. Accounting for inflation, the 1980 value of these services would be roughly $13,000. The problem with this method is that in cases in which market services are available and not purchased, the household must believe such services are *not worth their cost.* Either the price is too high or the quality too low. Thus, households that do not purchase these services clearly place a value on them that is *less* than the value assigned by the market-prices approach.

Opportunity Costs. A second method is to estimate what the homemakers would have been able to earn—net of taxes, employment, and commuting costs—if they had worked for pay. The problem here, of course, is that many married women do not work for pay at all, which implies they value the services they provide at home at *more* than their potential market earnings. Using the forgone wage to estimate the value of services performed by these women thus results in an underestimate. A recent estimate by Gronau of the value of a homemaker's services using this approach comes to about $6,800 per year in 1980 (after taxes).

Self-Employment Approach. A third method of evaluating household services is to treat homemakers as self-employed individuals. If a self-employed person, for example, increases his or her hours of self-employment by one, and decreases by one hour his or her time spent working for someone else, that person *gains* the value at which the product from that hour can be sold (the "marginal product") and *loses* the wage that could have been earned by working for someone else. If one's marginal product in self-employment exceeds one's wage, one will expand one's hours of self-employment until the marginal product and wage are equal or the person works totally for himself or herself (a corner solution reached if one's marginal product always exceeds one's wage). If the marginal product is less than the wage, the person cuts back on the hours of self-employment until the first condition is reached or until the person works totally for others. Note that if the person is self-employed part of the time and also works for someone else part of the time, theory tells us that the marginal product and wage rate must be equal.

A homemaker who performs household services will either be fully employed in the home—that is, fully self-employed—or divide the work time between self-employment and working for others. If the homemaker is fully self-employed the value of the marginal product from self-employment clearly exceeds the wage, but since this product is never priced in the market it is difficult to estimate its value. (This value may exceed the cost of employing others to do this work if the family believes that the homemaker will do a better job of cooking and raising children than someone else.)

However, for those homemakers who perform household services *and* also work for pay, we can infer from theory that the value of their *marginal* productivity at home is equal to their net market wage. Using the wage as an estimate of their marginal productivity at home, it is possible to estimate a production function for the value of household services. Applying this production function to full-time homemakers, Gronau estimated that the typical homemaker working exclusively in the home produces services worth (in 1980 terms) $15,700 to the family. Full-time married homemakers with *children under age six* were estimated to produce services worth $20,900 per year, very close to what the average male earned.

SOURCES: Oli Hawrylyshyn, "The Value of Household Services: A Survey of Empirical Estimates," *The Review of Income and Wealth* 22, 2 (June 1976):101–31.

Reuben Gronau, "Home Production—A Forgotten Industry," *Review of Economics and Statistics* 62 (August 1980):408–15.

The self-employment approach is advocated by Carmel Ullman Chiswick, "The Value of a Housewife's Time," *Journal of Human Resources* (Summer 1982):413–25.

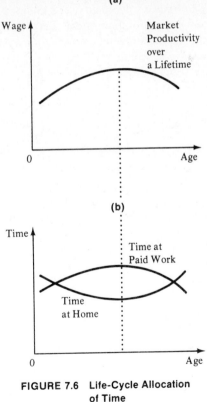

(a)

Wage — Market Productivity over a Lifetime — 0 — Age

(b)

Time — Time at Paid Work — Time at Home — 0 — Age

FIGURE 7.6 Life-Cycle Allocation of Time

as illustrated in panel (b) of Figure 7.6. Likewise, the consumption of very time-intensive commodities will occur in one's early and late years, a prediction more or less confirmed when one observes the ages of Americans traveling in Europe. That such travelers are primarily young adults and the elderly is clearly related to the fact that, for these groups, opportunity costs are lower. They make the time to go because, at these stages in their lives, time is relatively inexpensive.

The decision about *when* to do one's work for pay over the life cycle focuses on the productivity and cost of time—in other words, the *substitution effect*. Without explicitly saying so, we have been looking in this subsection at persons or families of given wealth and analyzing how they arrange market and household production over their lives in response to changing productivities in each place. In this context, the income effect is of little relevance.

For example, once one's educational level, general occupation, and probable inherited wealth are known, one's overall lifetime wealth can be foretold with reasonable accuracy. If a woman of wealth level X knows she wants to take a trip to Kenya at least once in her life, the question is not *whether* to take it, but *when*. The "when" partly depends on the factors discussed above, which emphasize substitution effects.[9]

The Choice of Retirement Age

As suggested above, some labor supply decisions are more concerned with *when* to work for pay than with *how much* work to do over a lifetime. Decisions about *when* to work largely turn on the substitution effect. Retirement decisions, however, concern the *quantity* of paid hours of work performed in a lifetime, and are clearly affected by both income and substitution effects.

A *life-cycle* perspective is necessary to correctly analyze retirement decisions, in large part because *yearly retirement benefits, lifetime* earnings, and *lifetime* expected pension benefits are all influenced by the age of retirement.[10] Thus, if one thinks of household productivity as a partial function of pension benefits (which are what one can "earn" by refraining from market work), the commodities that can be produced at the margin by staying home (retiring) varies with one's retirement age. Also, because one's market wage tends to change each year, both market and household productivity vary with the age of retirement, and as we argued earlier, it is because of these yearly variations that we must adopt a life-cycle perspective.

To simplify the analysis, we initially assume that retirement is associated with the total cessation of market work. We can then model workers' choices about retirement age as a function of their (discounted) *lifetime nonwork income* as of the earliest year in which they can retire and the *gain* in (discounted) lifetime total

---

[9]Another factor, of course, is the extent to which the trip will permanently increase her utility (through pleasant memories, for example).

[10]The analysis in this section borrows heavily from Olivia S. Mitchell and Gary S. Fields, "The Effects of Pensions and Earnings on Retirement: A Review Essay," *Research in Labor Economics,* ed. R. Ehrenberg (Greenwich, Conn.: JAI Press, 1982), pp. 115–55.

FIGURE 7.7   Choice of Optimum Retirement Age

(work plus nonwork) income that could be obtained by working longer and postponing retirement. The first factor affects the height of segment *AB* in Figure 7.7, where age 60 is assumed (for illustrative purposes only) to be the earliest possible retirement age. The second factor affects the *slope* of *BC* in Figure 7.7; for convenience, we assume the gain from working an added year to be constant and thus represent it with a straight line (we discuss this assumption below). The optimum retirement age, R^*, is clearly affected by the shape of the constraint *ABC and* the person's preferences (represented by curves U_1 and U_2) regarding income (goods) and years of retirement (household time).

When nonwork income (which includes pension benefits) at age 60 is larger, holding constant the gain in income beyond age 60, the vertical portion of the constraint is lengthened and the constraint shifts *up* to $AB'C'$. Because segment $B'C'$ is parallel to segment *BC* (by the assumption that the gain in income beyond age 60 remains constant), there is a pure income effect that induces the person to retire earlier. When AB' is one's lifetime income if age 60 is the retirement age, R'^* becomes the optimum age of retirement. Thus, we should expect wealthier people or people with more generous pension benefits as of age 60 to retire earlier, other things equal.

The gains in lifetime income from delaying retirement are represented by the slope of segment *BC,* as noted earlier. These gains are complex to calculate because they are the sum of added *working* income plus changes in *expected lifetime pension benefits*. Generally, the later one retires, the higher will be one's *yearly* pension benefit[11] but the fewer years one will collect that benefit. Table 7.1 shows the yearly and discounted lifetime Social Security benefits an average worker would anticipate at alternative retirement ages, assuming that he or she ceased all market work upon retirement (the case of Social Security recipients who work after officially retiring will be discussed in the next subsection) and that the real rate of interest is 2 percent. While yearly benefits rise with retirement age, expected total (discounted) lifetime benefits peak at age 64. While this typical worker may add more to discounted lifetime income by working than any drop in discounted lifetime pension benefits takes away, thus guaranteeing a negative slope to segment *BC* in Figure 7.7, the slope of this segment need not be a constant as we have drawn it (that is, *BC* need not be a straight line). Our graphic simplification notwithstanding, it is still interesting to see how retirement age is affected by changes in the lifetime income gains from delaying retirement.

If the above gains were to grow as a result of changes in the structures of pension plans, so that the expected present value of pensions grew with retirement age and segment *BC* took on a steeper slope, would people retire later? Theory cannot tell us, because the steeper slope to *BC* creates income and substitution effects that work in opposite directions. A greater income gain from continuing to work makes household time more expensive, and by itself this leads to a substitution effect that pushes in the direction of later retirement. On the other hand, greater lifetime income creates an income effect tending to encourage greater consumption of commodities and thus more time spent at home (earlier retirement).

Empirical estimates of responses in the age of retirement to changes in both nonwork, lifetime income at the earliest retirement age and net gains from postpon-

TABLE 7.1   Social Security Payments When Retirement Is Postponed (for an average worker, in 1982 dollars)

	Retirement Age						
	62	*63*	*64*	*65*	*66*	*67*	*68*
Yearly Social Security Benefit	$5,456	$5,964	$6,481	$7,017	$7,307	$7,605	$7,610
Discounted Value of Expected Lifetime Social Security Benefits	$68,387	$69,242	$69,515	$69,341	$66,311	$63,173	$59,928

SOURCE: Gary S. Fields and Olivia S. Mitchell, "Restructuring Social Security: How Will Retirement Ages Respond?" Final Report prepared under contract for the National Commission for Employment Policy (Washington, D.C.: U.S. Government Printing Office, April 1983): 10. These calculations assume a real discount rate of 2 percent.

[11]This is not always the case, as we shall discuss in Chapter 11. Some firms pressure employees to retire early by cutting yearly pension benefits for those who do not.

ing retirement are not abundant. One careful study, however, found that (as expected) increased lifetime nonwork income *by itself* reduces the retirement age. This same study found that increased gains from postponing retirement cause retirement age to *increase*, thus suggesting the dominance of the substitution effect.[12] However, the degree of responsiveness is rather small, so large changes in the structure of pension plans would probably have to be made to elicit much of a change in retirement age.[13]

Policy Application: The Social Security Retirement Test

The preceding subsection dealt with the choice of a utility-maximizing retirement age and assumed that retirement was associated with the cessation of all market work activities. This subsection deals with another decision retirees must make: whether to work after declaring retirement and qualifying for Social Security. Thus, we change our focus from one in which retirement age is an issue and it is assumed that people do not work after retirement, to one in which we assume people have already declared their retirement and filed for Social Security, and then must decide whether to work for pay full time, part time, or not at all.[14]

Nearly everyone who has worked for 7½ years and has reached 62 years of age qualifies for a Social Security pension. The size of the pension depends, within upper and lower limits, on the person's average monthly earnings while working and on the age of retirement—with those retiring at age 62, for example, receiving less per month than those retiring at 65 (as we saw above).[15]

One interesting feature of the Social Security system in the United States is that there is a "retirement test" that determines the benefits one can receive. To receive full benefits, one must qualify as being "retired," which in 1984 meant earning less than $6,960 per year for those 65 or older. (This limit is increased slightly each year, is lower for people under 65, and does not apply to those over age 70.) For those earning more than $6,960 per year in 1984, Social Security retirement benefits are reduced by 50 cents for every dollar earned *above* $6,960. Thus, if a person's "full" Social Security benefit is $7,000 and he or she earns $10,000 per year at age

[12]Olivia S. Mitchell and Gary S. Fields, "The Economics of Retirement Behavior," *Journal of Labor Economics,* January 1984:84–105.

[13]See Gary S. Fields and Olivia S. Mitchell, "Restructuring Social Security: How Will Retirement Ages Respond?" Final Report prepared under contract for the National Commission for Employment Policy (Washington, D.C.: U.S. Government Printing Office, April 1983).

[14]A complete analysis of retirement behavior would model the retirement-age and work-after-retirement decisions *jointly,* instead of separately as we do. This task is beyond the scope of this text because estimates of lifetime income changes must account for the effects of the "retirement test" (discussed in this subsection) on Social Security benefits. A graphic analysis thus becomes very difficult. The interested student might begin an investigation into this joint decision by reading Lawrence H. Thompson, "The Social Security Reform Debate," *Journal of Economic Literature* (December 1983):1425–67; Gary Burtless and Robert Moffitt, "The Effect of Social Security on Labor Supply of the Aged: The Joint Choice of Retirement Date and Post Retirement Hours of Work" (mimeo, Brookings Institution, October 1982); and Alan Gustman and Thomas Steinmeier, "Partial Retirement and the Analysis of Retirement Behavior" (National Bureau of Economic Research Working Paper No. 763, September 1981).

[15]For more details, see Thompson, "The Social Security Reform Debate."

65, the Social Security benefit received would be reduced by $1,520 (0.5 × $3,040) to $5,480.

The existence of the retirement test has long been a subject of controversy. Its supporters maintain that Social Security is a program to help older people without jobs meet their financial needs and that the costs of giving benefits to those older people who have a decent labor income would be burdensome to those of working age who finance the program through a payroll tax. Opponents argue that retirees have earned their benefits through years of paying a payroll tax and that they are entitled to them in old age, regardless of their circumstances. Opponents further assert that *removing* the retirement test would *increase* work incentives among the elderly.[16]

As illustrated in Figure 7.8, the retirement test separates the budget constraint facing Social Security recipients 65 and over into three segments. Along segment CD a recipient keeps his or her market earnings (which can be read off line AB) and the full Social Security benefit (AC). Once earnings reach $6,960, Social Security benefits are cut 50 cents for every additional dollar of earnings—reflected in the flatter segment DE (which has a slope half that of AB). At some point (E in Figure 7.8) earnings are so high that Social Security benefits are reduced to zero; at that point people are on the market constraint (segment EB), and although they have successfully applied for Social Security, their benefit is zero. Depending on one's preferences, the optimum hours of paid work put in by a Social Security recipient will be located along segment CD (person X in panel a), segment DE (person Y in panel b), or segment EB (person Z in panel c).

Would *eliminating* the retirement test increase work incentives? We analyze this question by first looking at the immediate effects of the elimination on people who have qualified for Social Security. We then return to a life-cycle perspective and analyze the effects on younger workers who are now only *future* Social Security recipients.

Immediate effects on Social Security recipients.

For those who qualify for Social Security benefits at or near the time when the retirement test is eliminated, any increase in benefits resulting from the change will increase wealth. These people receive added benefits but do not have to face years of increased payroll taxes to finance them (their future working years are limited).

Figure 7.8 shows that removing the retirement test will change the budget constraint facing these older people from ACDEB to ACF. This change preserves the market wage rate, essentially granting elderly people an income supplement independent of their work effort. People with preferences like X—people who earned less than $6,960 before the retirement test was removed—will be unaffected. Their work incentives are the same as before the change. People with preferences like Z have *reduced* work incentives. They face a pure income effect (their wage rate does not change), which will induce them to work less. However, for people affected by the portion of the old constraint labeled DE in panel (b),

---

[16]See, for example, Marshall R. Colberg, *The Social Security Retirement Test: Right or Wrong?* (Washington, D.C.: The American Enterprise Institute for Public Policy Research, 1978), for a review of this and other arguments concerning the retirement test.

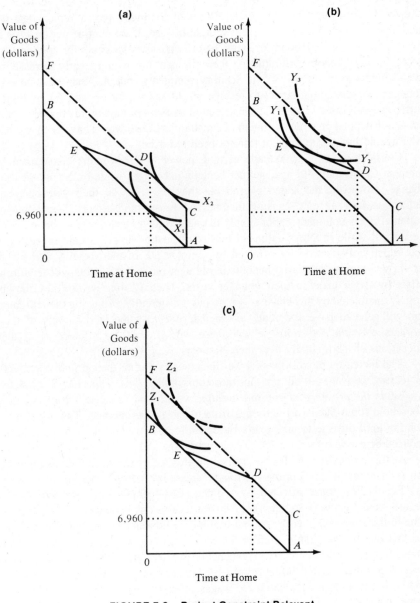

(a)

Value of Goods (dollars)

6,960

Time at Home

0

(b)

Value of Goods (dollars)

Time at Home

0

(c)

Value of Goods (dollars)

6,960

Time at Home

0

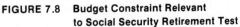

FIGURE 7.8   Budget Constraint Relevant to Social Security Retirement Test

constraint *ACF* represents a wage increase, and there is *both* an income and substitution effect. Which effect dominates cannot be foretold by theory. If the income effect dominates, people with preferences like *Y* will have *reduced* work incentives and the overall effect of eliminating the retirement test may be to reduce hours of work by the elderly. If the substitution effect dominates, labor supply by people like *Y* will increase, while the labor supply of those like *Z* might decrease. The overall effect would be unknown in advance.

Life-cycle effects. The life-cycle effects of removing the retirement test are more complicated, but still relatively straightforward, if we confine our analysis to the question of yearly hours of work before and after successfully applying for Social Security benefits. Eliminating the retirement test would clearly increase the total benefits paid out to Social Security recipients, but the increased benefits younger workers could expect to receive in old age would be paid for by higher current payroll taxes. The life-cycle effect on workers of paying this higher payroll tax would depend on which segment of constraint *ACDEB* would have been relevant after age 65 had the retirement test not been removed.

Consider workers of average earning power.[17] For workers constrained by segment *CD* in their old age, neither benefits nor wages while on Social Security change. However, the added payroll tax they must pay in their younger years reduces their wage rate, causing income and substitution effects. Depending on which effect is dominant, labor supply in one's younger years may be increased or decreased, while in the years on Social Security labor supply is unchanged.

Older workers who are affected by segment *DE* of the Social Security constraint will receive increased benefits in old age, but these benefits will tend to be offset by larger taxes in their younger years. Their *lifetime wealth* may thus be largely unaffected by this change—or, to put it differently, removing the retirement test will tend to have essentially *no income effect* on the labor supply of these workers *over their lifetime*. Where these workers will be affected is in their allocations of labor supply over their lifetimes.

The increased payroll taxes lower their wages during their prime years while increasing the wages in old age (for those on segment *DE*). This change in relative wages, *in the presence of constant wealth,* would tend to cause a reallocation of household (time-intensive) activities from old age to prime age. Thus, instead of waiting until old age to take one's European tour, some people may seize on the reduced disparity between wage rates in prime age and old age as sufficient reason to take this tour earlier in life. For the people affected by *DE*, then, labor supply will tend to *decrease* in one's prime years and increase in one's years on Social Security.

Finally, for those affected by segment *EB*—people who apply for Social Security and then work so much they do not receive any benefits—wages decrease (due to the increased payroll tax) but lifetime wealth tends to increase. The reason for this increase is simple. Before the retirement test was eliminated, they paid Social Security taxes but received no benefits; in effect, then, their taxes paid for the benefits to others. After the retirement test was eliminated, their subsidy to others ended—so that despite their reduced wages, lifetime wealth increased (as they got some of their taxes back in benefits). The reduced wages and increased lifetime wealth would drive these people toward less work at all stages in their lives.

The overall labor supply effects of removing the retirement test from the Social

---

[17]For workers with average wage rates, Social Security benefits are roughly equivalent to Social Security payroll taxes. Low-wage workers obtain proportionately higher benefits, and high-wage workers proportionately lower benefits, relative to their taxes paid out. Focusing the analysis on the average wage-earner is sufficient for our purpose, which is to illustrate the usefulness of the theory in policy analysis.

Security program cannot be predicted from theory. For some workers (such as *X*) the effects in *old age* are nil, but removing the test would create income and substitution effects in their prime years that have opposite tendencies on labor supply. For other workers, there may be some reallocation of labor from one's prime years to one's older years, but theory cannot tell us whether this shift will be one for one. For still others, lifetime labor supply may fall. What we *can* say is that people who argue that removing the retirement test will increase labor supply are being simplistic—unless, of course, they have some empirical evidence that resolves the theoretical ambiguities.[18]

REVIEW QUESTIONS

1. Suppose that 5 percent unemployment is defined as "full employment" and currently unemployment is 7 percent. Suppose further that we have the following information:

Unemployment Rate	Labor Force	Unemployment	Employment
5 percent	6000	300	5700
7 percent	5600	392	5208

    a. What is the amount of "hidden unemployment" when the unemployment rate is 7 percent?
    b. If the population is 10,000, what change occurs in the participation rate as a result of the marginal change in the unemployment rate?
    c. What is the economic significance of hidden unemployment? Should measured and hidden unemployment be added to obtain a "total unemployment" figure?

2. Several studies have indicated that for prime-age males, the income effect of a wage increase tends to dominate the substitution effect. Other recent studies point out that hourly wages tend to rise over the early stages of the life cycle (the young receive lower wages than the middle-aged) *and* young males tend to work fewer hours than middle-aged males, *ceteris paribus*. Employing a theory of life-cycle allocation of time, explain the apparent discrepancy.

3. In his first debate with President Ford, Jimmy Carter argued, "While it is true that much of the recent rise in unemployment is due to the entrance of married women and teenagers into the labor force, this influx of people into the labor force is itself a sign of economic decay. The reason these people are now seeking work is because the primary breadwinner in the family is out of work and extra workers are needed to maintain the family income." Comment.

4. Some American observers have worried about a supposed decline in the "work ethic" among U.S. workers. The thesis (as yet unproven) of these observers is that U.S. workers are less interested in working than they used to be and that in the long run our national output per capita might fail to grow if gains in productivity are offset by reductions in

---

[18]Burtless and Moffitt's careful empirical analyses suggest that the earnings test has had only modest effects on the age of retirement, but a large effect on post-retirement hours of work.

working hours or labor force participation rates. These observers conclude that "a constant per capita output of goods and services is a sure sign of economic decay. It implies that economic progress is halted—that improvements in human welfare stop. It is unthinkable that our society would tolerate such stagnation in human progress."

Suppose the *factual* premise of these observers is true. That is, suppose improvements in the marginal productivity of workers over time are offset by declining work hours and participation rates so that gross national product per capita remains constant. Use economic theory to evaluate the *conclusion* drawn by these observers that this represents a stoppage of improvements in human welfare.

5. Is the following statement true, false, or uncertain? Why? "If a married woman's husband gets a raise, she tends to work less, but if *she* gets a raise, she tends to work more."

SELECTED READINGS

Becker, Gary. "A Theory of the Allocation of Time." *Economic Journal* 75 (September 1965):493–517.

Fields, Gary S., and Mitchell, Olivia S. *Retirement, Pensions and Social Security.* Cambridge, Mass.: MIT Press, 1984.

Ghez, G. R., and Becker, G. S. *The Allocation of Time and Goods Over the Life Cycle.* New York: Columbia University Press, 1975, Chapter 3.

Gronau, Reuben. "The Measurement of Output of the Nonmarket Sector: The Evaluation of Housewives' Time." *The Measurement of Economic and Social Performance,* ed. Milton Moss. New York: National Bureau of Economic Research, 1973, pp. 163–89.

Long, Clarence D. *The Labor Force Under Changing Income and Employment.* Princeton, N.J.: Princeton University Press, 1958.

Mincer, Jacob. "Labor Force Participation and Unemployment: A Review of Recent Evidence." In *Prosperity and Unemployment,* eds. Robert A. Gordon and Margaret S. Gordon. New York: John Wiley and Sons, 1966.

Mincer, Jacob. "Labor Force Participation of Married Women." In *Aspects of Labor Economics*, A Conference of the Universities—National Bureau Committee on Economic Research. Princeton, N.J.: Princeton University Press, 1962.

Thompson, Lawrence. "The Social Security Reform Debate." *Journal of Economic Literature* (December 1983):1425–1467.

8

Compensating Wage Differentials and Labor Markets

Chapters 6 and 7 analyzed workers' decisions about *whether to seek employment* and *how long to work*. Chapters 8 and 9 will analyze workers' decisions about the industry, occupation, or firm in which they will work. This chapter will emphasize the influence on job choice of such daily, *recurring* job characteristics as working environment, length of commute from home to work, and risk of injury. The following chapter will analyze the effects of required educational *investments* on occupational choice.

This chapter will present a verbal as well as a graphic analysis of occupational choice that emphasizes the importance of both wages and nonpecuniary job characteristics in the allocation of labor to meet social needs. The empirical research on wage patterns will also be examined to see if job choices and the allocation of labor really are made along the lines suggested by these analyses. The final section applies the concepts of this chapter to two very important and controversial government programs: occupational safety and health regulation and affirmative action plans for women and minorities. An appendix considers the relationship between wages and layoffs.

A VERBAL ANALYSIS OF OCCUPATIONAL CHOICE

If all jobs were exactly alike and located in the same place, an individual's decision about where to seek work would be relatively simple. He or she would attempt to obtain a job where the expected compensation was highest. Any differences in compensation would cause workers to seek work with the highest-paying employers and avoid applying for work with the low-paying ones. The high-paying employers, having an abundance of applicants, might decide they were paying more than they had to in order to staff their vacancies. The low-paying employers would have to raise wage offers in order to compete for workers. Ultimately, if the market works without hindrance, wages of all employers would equalize.

All jobs are not the same, however. Some jobs require much more education or training than others. Some jobs are in clean, modern offices, and others are in noisy, dusty, or dangerous factories. Some permit the employee some discretion over the pace of work at various points throughout the day, while some involve highly rigid assembly-line work. Some are challenging and call for decision making by the employee; others are monotonous. While the influence of educational and training requirements will be discussed at length in the next chapter, we will discuss here the ways variations in job characteristics influence individual choice and the observable market outcomes of that choice.

Individual Choice and Its Outcomes

Suppose several unskilled workers have received offers from two employers. Employer X pays $5.00 per hour and offers clean, safe working conditions. Employer Y also pays $5.00 per hour, but offers employment in a dirty, noisy factory. Which employer would the workers choose? Most would undoubtedly choose Employer X, because the pay is the same while the job is performed under less disagreeable conditions.

Clearly, however, $5.00 is not an equilibrium wage in both firms.[1] Because Firm X finds it very easy to attract applicants at $5.00, it will "hold the line" on any future wage increases. Firm Y, however, must either clean up the plant, pay higher wages, or do both if it wants to fill its vacancies. Assuming it decides not to alter working conditions, it must clearly pay a wage *above* $5.00 to be competitive in the labor market. The extra wage it must pay to attract workers is called a *compensating wage differential* because the higher wage is paid to compensate workers for the undesirable working conditions. If such a differential did not exist, Firm Y could not attract the unskilled workers that Firm X can obtain.

Suppose that Firm Y raises its wage offer to $5.50 while the offer from X remains at $5.00. Will this 50-cent-per-hour differential—an extra $1,000 per year—attract *all* the workers in our group to Firm Y? If it did attract them all, Firm X would have an incentive to raise its wages and Firm Y might want to lower its offers a bit; the 50-cent differential in this case would *not* be an equilibrium differential.

More than likely, however, the 10 percent higher wage in Firm Y would attract only *some* of the group to Firm Y. Some people are not bothered by dirt and noise as much as others are, and these people may decide to take the extra pay and put up with the poorer working conditions.[2] Others, however, are very sensitive to noise or

---

[1] There may be a few people who really do not care about noise and dirt in the work place. We assume here that these people are so rare, or Firm Y's demand for workers is so large, that Y cannot fill all its vacancies with just those who are totally insensitive to dirt and noise.

[2] The assertion that people are affected differently by noise is documented in *Community Reaction to Airport Noise*, vol. I (report to the National Aeronautics and Space Administration prepared by Tracor, Inc., of Austin, Texas), July 1971. This study showed, for example, that around 10 percent of people are "highly susceptible" to noise annoyance, while around half are "highly adaptable" to airport noises.

allergic to dust, and they may decide that they would rather get paid less than expose themselves to working conditions that are very unpleasant. If both firms could obtain the quantity and quality of workers they wanted, the 50-cent differential *would* be an equilibrium differential, in the sense that there would be no forces causing the differential to change.

The desire of workers to avoid unpleasantness or risk, then, should force employers offering unpleasant or risky jobs to pay higher wages than they would otherwise have to pay. Put another way, in order to attract a work force, these employers will have to pay higher wages to their workers than firms that offer pleasant, safe jobs to comparable workers. This wage differential serves two related, socially desirable ends. First, it serves a *social* need by giving people an incentive to voluntarily do dirty, dangerous, or unpleasant work. Likewise, the existence of a compensating wage differential imposes a financial penalty on employers who have unfavorable working conditions. Second, at an *individual* level, it serves as a reward to workers who accept unpleasant jobs by paying them more than comparable workers in more pleasant jobs.

The allocation of labor.   Society has a number of jobs that are unavoidably nasty or would be very costly to make safe and pleasant (coal mining, deep-sea diving, and coke-oven cleaning are examples). There are essentially two ways to recruit the necessary labor for such jobs. One is to compel people to do these jobs (the military draft is the most obvious American example of forced labor). The second way is to induce people to do the jobs voluntarily.

Most modern societies rely mainly on incentives, compensating wage differentials, to recruit labor to unpleasant jobs voluntarily. Workers will mine coal, collect garbage, and bolt steel beams together 50 stories off the ground because, compared to alternative jobs for which they could qualify, these jobs pay well. The 1,500 commercial deep-sea divers in the United States, for example, who are exposed to the dangers of drowning, the rigors of construction work with cumbersome gear, a

---

Example 8.1
Coal Mining in the Soviet Union

Coal mining is a dangerous but socially necessary task the world over. Because it is difficult to recruit people to voluntarily do this unpleasant work, compensating wage differentials exist even in economies where "market" incentives are not *philosophically* recognized. In the Soviet Union, for example, the difficulties of recruiting personnel to work in the coal-mining industry have caused the average earnings of miners to be *double* those of the average factory worker. Further, miners in the most unhealthy and arduous jobs work 30 hours a week, compared to 36 hours in the other mining jobs; in addition, they receive a one-time bonus equivalent to over 25 percent of the yearly pay for manufacturing workers.

SOURCE: Radio Liberty Research, June 11, 1979 (RL 179/79).

lonely and hostile work environment, and several physiological disorders as a result of compression and decompression, made $20,000 to $45,000 per year in the mid-1970's, or about 20 to 130 percent more than the average high school graduate.

As another example, the *failure* to pay sufficiently high wages to U.S. military personnel has created occasional difficulties in recruiting and retaining such people. While the pay for military recruits with less than two years of service was 14 percent above the pay for civilian youth right after the draft was eliminated in 1973, the relative pay advantage had fallen to 2 percent by 1979. This fall in relative pay for recruits was accompanied by a severe decline in the quantity and quality of enlistees, despite the decline in civilian job opportunities that accompanied a large rise in the unemployment rate over that six-year period. By 1982 both the quality and quantity of enlistees had improved, due partly to a very high civilian unemployment rate, but probably mostly to pay raises that increased the pay for recruits to 18 percent above that for civilian youths. If the government wants to maintain armed services without resorting to the draft, it is clear that military pay must remain at a level sufficient to overcome the hazards and inconveniences of military life.[3]

Compensation for workers.   Compensating wage differentials also serve as *individual* rewards by paying those who accept bad or arduous working conditions more than they would otherwise receive. In a parallel fashion, those who opt for more pleasant conditions have to "buy" them by accepting lower pay. For example, if a person takes the $5.00 per hour job with Firm X, he or she is giving up the $5.50 per hour job with less pleasant conditions in Firm Y. The better conditions are being bought, in a very real sense, for 50 cents per hour.

Thus, compensating wage differentials become the price at which good working conditions can be purchased by, or bad ones sold to, workers. Contrary to what is commonly asserted, a monetary value *can* often be attached to events or conditions in which the effects are primarily psychological in nature. Compensating wage differentials provide the key to the valuation of these nonpecuniary aspects of employment.

In the area of occupational health and safety policy, there is continuous debate about whether to make machines safer or protect the worker from machine hazards with personal protective devices.[4] For example, high noise levels can eventually damage the hearing of workers. The Department of Labor has favored reducing noise levels through engineering changes, such as putting mufflers on or baffles around noisy machines. Employer representatives have consistently claimed that such engineering changes are inordinately expensive and that compelling workers to wear earplugs would preserve workers' hearing at much less cost. Because resources are scarce, our society would like to achieve hearing protection at

---

[3]"The Retention Problem," *The Wall Street Journal* (March 19, 1980), p. 24, and an unpublished table provided to us by Robert Lockman, Center for Naval Analyses. What is pleasant or unpleasant is determined in the market at the *margin*. For example, even if most people dislike night work, there might be enough who do not to fill night-shift jobs without a compensating wage differential.

[4]The debate about whether or not the government should be involved at all in occupational safety and health is discussed later in this chapter.

minimum cost, but we must be sure to count *all* the costs. One cost of wearing earplugs is *psychic*: they are very uncomfortable for most people to wear. The cost of this discomfort *must* be counted along with the purchase price of earplugs in arriving at the total cost of wearing earplugs.

How could we put a dollar value on earplug discomfort? A straightforward way to determine this would be to find a set of employers who *require* the use of earplugs as a condition of employment and to compare the wages they pay to those of *comparable* firms that *do not require* the wearing of earplugs. If workers find earplugs more uncomfortable than the noise, wages in the firms that require their use should be higher, and this wage differential is the estimate of what value workers place on this discomfort.

Suppose, for example, that the research showed that companies requiring earplugs pay 10 cents an hour, or $200 per year, more than *otherwise similar* firms pay for *comparable* labor.[5] Workers accepting work there are indicating by their behavior that they are willing to take $200 per year as compensation for the discomfort they must bear; that is, the cost of the discomfort to them is equal to, or less than, $200 per year. Those refusing to work at the plant place a value higher than that on their discomfort costs because $200 is insufficient to compensate them. Thus, the cost of discomfort at the margin is $200 per year (to induce one more worker to wear earplugs would require added compensation of about $200 per year).

Before concluding that the psychic costs of wearing earplugs are $200 per year, we must remember that our hypothetical findings are for the marginal worker. People differ in the amount of discomfort they feel and in the value they place on what they feel. Those most likely to take the extra pay in return for having to wear earplugs are those who are least sensitive to discomfort or most willing to trade discomfort for money. If we were to compel *all* workers in noisy factories to wear earplugs, we would be forcing earplugs on some for whom the costs of discomfort exceeded $200.

As this example illustrates, compensating wage differentials are the price at which various *qualitative* job characteristics are bought and sold. As such, they offer a way of placing a value on things most people think of as "noneconomic." This illustration, of course, does not prove that compensating wage differentials exist or that they are equilibrium prices—issues that will be discussed later in the chapter.

Assumptions and Predictions

We have seen how a simple theory of job choice by individuals leads to the *prediction* that compensating wage differentials will be associated with various job characteristics. Positive differentials (higher wages) will accompany "bad" characteristics, while negative differentials (lower wages) will be associated with "good" ones. However, it is very important to understand that this prediction can *only* be made *holding other things equal*.

---

[5]Firms may be willing to do this if they believe requiring earplugs will reduce workers' compensation claims for hearing loss in the future.

Our prediction about the existence of compensating wage differentials grows out of the reasonable assumption that if a worker has a choice between a job with "good" working conditions and a job of equal pay with "bad" working conditions, he or she will choose the "good" job. If the employee is an unskilled laborer, he or she may be choosing between an unpleasant job spreading hot asphalt or a more comfortable job in an air-conditioned warehouse. In either case, he or she is going to receive something close to the wage rate unskilled workers typically receive. However, our theory would predict that this worker would receive *more* from the asphalt-spreading job than from the warehouse job.

Thus, the predicted outcome of our theory of job choice is *not* that employees working under "bad" conditions receive more than those working in "good" conditions. The prediction is that, *holding worker characteristics constant*, employees in bad jobs receive higher wages than those working under more pleasant conditions. The characteristics that must be held constant include all the other things that influence wages: skill level, age, race, sex, union status, region of the country, and so forth. Because there are many influences on wages *other* than working conditions, our theory leads us to expect employers offering "bad" jobs to pay higher wages than employers offering "good" jobs to *comparable* workers. This theory is based on three assumptions.

Assumption 1: utility maximization. Our first assumption is that workers seek to maximize their *utility*, not their income. If workers sought to maximize income, they would always choose the highest-paying job available to them. This behavior would eventually cause wages to be equalized across the jobs open to any set of workers, as stated earlier.

In contrast, compensating wage differentials will only arise if some people do *not* choose the highest-paying job offered, preferring instead a lower-paying but more pleasant job. This behavior allows the employers offering the lower-paying, pleasant jobs to be competitive. Wages do not equalize in this case. Rather, the *net advantages*—the overall utility from the pay and the psychic aspects of the job—tend to equalize for the marginal worker.

Assumption 2: worker information. The second assumption implicit in our analysis is that workers are aware of the job characteristics of potential importance to them. Whether they know about them before they take the job or find out soon after taking it is not too important. In either case, a company offering a "bad" job with no compensating wage differentials would have trouble recruiting or retaining workers, trouble that would eventually force it to raise its wage.

It is quite likely, of course, that workers would quickly learn of dust, dirt, noise, rigid work discipline, and other obvious bad working conditions. It is equally likely that they would *not* know the *precise* probability of being laid off, say, or injured on the job. However, even with respect to these probabilities, their own direct observations or word-of-mouth reports from other employees could give them enough information to evaluate the situation with some accuracy. For example, the proportions of employees considering their work dangerous have been shown to be closely related to the actual injury rates published by the government for the industries in which they work.[6] This finding illustrates that, while workers probably cannot state the precise probability of being injured, they do form accurate judgments about the relative risks of several jobs.

Where predictions may disappoint us, however, is with respect to *very* obscure characteristics. For example, while we now know that asbestos dust is highly damaging to worker health, this fact was not widely known 40 years ago. One reason information on asbestos dangers in plants was so long in being generated is that it takes more than 20 years for asbestos-related disease to develop. Cause and effect were thus obscured from workers and researchers alike, creating a situation in which job choices were made in ignorance of this risk. Compensating wage differentials for this danger thus could not possibly arise at that time. Our predictions about compensating wage differentials, then, hold only for job characteristics that workers know about.

Assumption 3: worker mobility.   The final assumption implicit in our theory is that workers have a range of job offers from which to choose. Without a range of offers, workers would not be able to select the combination of job characteristics they desired or avoid the ones to which they did not wish exposure. A compensating wage differential for risk of injury, for example, simply could not arise if workers were able to obtain only dangerous jobs. It is the act of choosing safe jobs over dangerous ones that forces employers offering dangerous work to raise wages.

One manner in which this choice can occur is for each job applicant to receive several job offers from which to choose. However, another way in which choice could be exercised is for workers to be (at least potentially) highly mobile. In other words, workers with few concurrent offers could take jobs and continue their search for work if they thought an improvement could be made. Thus, even with few offers at any *one* time, workers could conceivably have relatively wide choice over a *period* of time, which would eventually allow them to select jobs that maximized their utility.

While there are no general data on the number of concurrent offers a typical job applicant receives, job mobility among American workers is relatively high. The reported quit rate in manufacturing is normally 1–2 percent per month, or about 12–24 percent per year. With job openings from quits and from general business expansion, manufacturing businesses newly hire 3 percent of their employees each month. Turnover is so great, in fact, that the median length of job tenure is 3.6 years, meaning that half of all workers have been on their current jobs less than three and one-half years.[7]

Another way to understand the amount of choice workers have in the job market is to look at job mobility over time. Consider male, blue-collar operatives (semiskilled workers), a group of men many feel faces the greatest restrictions on

---

[6]W. Kip Viscusi, ''Labor Market Valuations of Life and Limb: Empirical Evidence and Policy Implications,'' *Public Policy* 26 (Summer 1978):359–86.

[7]Robert E. Hall, ''The Importance of Lifetime Jobs in the U.S. Economy,'' *American Economic Review* 72 (September 1982):716–24.

job choice. Among those operatives who were over age 25 in 1965, 25 percent were working in *completely different* occupations by 1970 (10 percent had moved to skilled jobs, 4 percent had entered managerial or professional/technical occupations, 6 percent were in unskilled jobs, and the remaining changes were split among other occupational groups). The main point is that one worker in four had had a major occupational change in that five-year period.[8] Many more, of course, changed their jobs or their places of employment while still retaining semiskilled work. It is thus difficult to conclude that workers are typically lacking in job choice.

The next section will present a graphic exposition of the theory of compensating wage differentials that has just been described verbally. This graphic analysis incorporates employer behavior, which has not yet been explicitly considered, and visually illustrates some important conclusions. Economists have labeled the following analysis a *hedonic theory of wages*—that is, a wage theory based on the assumption of philosophical *hedonism* that workers strive to maximize utility (happiness).[9]

A HEDONIC THEORY OF WAGES

Business firms offer, and employees accept, jobs that may differ greatly in their level of responsibility, pace of work, security from layoff, work environment, and so forth.[10] Those job characteristics that are considered undesirable by workers should have a positive compensating wage differential associated with them, while those that are desired should be purchased by employees in the form of lower wages. To simplify our discussion, we shall analyze just one dimension—risk of injury on the job—and *assume* that the compensating wage differentials for every *other* dimension have already been established. This assumption allows us to clearly see the outcomes of the job selection process with respect to *one* undesirable dimension (injury risk); since the same analysis could be repeated for every other dimension, our conclusions are not obscured by it. To obtain a complete understanding of the job selection process and the outcomes of that process, it is necessary, as always, to consider both the employer and employee sides of the market.

Employee Considerations

Employees, it may safely be assumed, dislike the risk of being injured on the job. A worker who is offered a job for $8.00 per hour in a firm in which 3 percent of the work force is injured each year would achieve a certain level of utility from that job.

---

[8]U.S. Bureau of the Census, *Characteristics of the Population, 1970: Subject Reports: Occupation and Residence in 1965*, PC(2)7E (Washington, D.C.: U.S. Government Printing Office, 1973), Table 230. These data do not indicate what fraction of those who changed occupation also changed employers.

[9]The philosophy of hedonism is usually associated with Jeremy Bentham, a philosopher of the late 18th century who believed people always behaved in ways that they believed would maximize their happiness.

[10]The analysis in this section is adapted primarily from Sherwin Rosen, "Hedonic Prices and Implicit Markets," *Journal of Political Economy* 82 (January/February 1974):34–55.

If the risk of injury were increased to 4 percent (holding other job characteristics constant) the job would have to pay a higher wage to produce this same level of utility, since risk is considered undesirable. The added wage would compensate the worker for the increase in risk, in the sense that the level of utility would be held constant.[11]

Other combinations of wage rates and risk levels could be devised that would yield the same utility as the $8.00/3 percent-risk offer. These combinations can be connected on a graph to form an indifference curve (see the solid curve, U_2, in Figure 8.1). Unlike the indifference curves drawn in Chapters 6 and 7, those in Figure 8.1 slope upward because risk of injury is a "bad" job characteristic, not a "good" one (such as leisure, for example). In other words, if risk increases, wages must rise if utility is to be held constant.

As in the previous chapters, there is one indifference curve for each possible level of utility. Because a higher wage at a given risk level will generate more utility, indifference curves lying to the northwest represent higher utility.[12] Thus, all points on curve U_3 in Figure 8.1 are preferred to those on U_2, and those on U_2 are

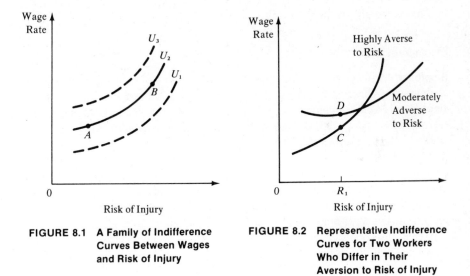

FIGURE 8.1 **A Family of Indifference Curves Between Wages and Risk of Injury**

FIGURE 8.2 **Representative Indifference Curves for Two Workers Who Differ in Their Aversion to Risk of Injury**

---

[11]Compensating wage differentials provide for *ex ante*—"before the fact"—compensation related to injury risk. Workers can also be compensated (to keep utility constant) by *ex post*—or after injury—payments for damages. Workers' compensation insurance provides for *ex post* payments, but these payments are typically incomplete. There is no way to compensate a worker for his or her own death, and workers' compensation does not cover the psychic costs of disfigurement due to permanent impairment. Moreover, the lost income associated with temporary impairments is not *completely* replaced by workers' compensation. Because not all injury-related losses are completely compensated *ex post*, compensating wage differentials must exist *ex ante* for worker utility to be held constant in the face of increased risk.

[12]When two "goods" were on the axes of our graphs, as in Chapters 6 and 7, indifference curves lying to the northeast represented higher levels of utility (people wanted more of each). When a "bad" is on the horizontal axis (as in Figure 8.1) and a "good" on the vertical axis, people with more of the "good" and less of the "bad" are unambiguously better off, and this combination is achieved by moving in a northwest direction on the graph.

preferred to U_1. The fact that each indifference curve is convex (when viewed from below) reflects the normal assumption of diminishing marginal rates of substitution. At point B of curve U_2, the person receives a relatively high wage and faces a high level of risk. He or she will be willing to give up a lot in wages to achieve a given reduction in risk because risk levels are high enough to place one in imminent danger, and the consumption level of the goods that are bought with wages is already high. However, as risk levels and wage rates fall, the person becomes less willing to give up wages in return for the given reduction in risk; the danger is no longer imminent, and consumption of other goods is not as high.

People differ, of course, in their aversion to the risk of being injured. Those who are very sensitive to this risk will require large wage increases for any increase in risk, while those who are less sensitive will require smaller wage increases to hold utility constant. The sensitive workers will have indifference curves that are steeper at any level of risk than those who are less sensitive, as illustrated in Figure 8.2. At risk level R_1, the slope at point C is steeper than at point D. Point C lies on the indifference curve of a worker who is highly sensitive to risk, while point D lies on an indifference curve of one who is less sensitive. Each person has a whole family of indifference curves that are not shown in Figure 8.2, and each will attempt to achieve the highest level of utility possible.

Employer Considerations

Employers are faced with a wage/risk trade-off of their own that derives from three assumptions. First, it is presumably costly to reduce the risk of injury facing employees. Safety equipment must be placed on machines, production time must be sacrificed for safety training sessions, protective clothing must be furnished to workers, and so forth. Second, competitive pressures will presumably force many firms to operate at *zero profits* (that is, at a point at which all costs are covered and the rate of return on capital is about what it is for similar investments).[13] Third, all *other* job characteristics are presumably given or already determined. The consequence of these three assumptions is that, if a firm undertakes a program to reduce the risk of injury, it must reduce wages to remain competitive.

Thus, forces on the employer side of the market tend to cause low risk to be associated with low wages, and high risk to be associated with high wages, *holding other things constant*. These "other things" may be fringe benefits or other job characteristics; assuming they are given will not affect the validity of our analysis (even though it may seem at first unrealistic). The major point is that if a firm spends *more on safety*, it must spend *less on other things* if it is to remain competitive.[14] The term *wages* can thus be thought of as shorthand for "terms of employment" in our theoretical analyses.

---

[13]If returns are permanently below normal, it would benefit the owners to close down the plant and invest their funds elsewhere. If returns are above normal, investors will be attracted to the industry and profits would eventually be driven down by increased competition.

[14]We *could* focus on the trade-off between safety and fringe benefits or safety and other working conditions, because certainly our theory would predict that such trade-offs exist. However, we choose to focus on the *wage* trade-off because wages are easy to measure and form the largest component of compensation.

The employer trade-offs between wages and levels of injury risk can be graphed through the use of *isoprofit curves*, which show the various combinations of risk and wage levels that yield a given level of profits (*iso* means "equal"). Thus, all the points along a given curve, such as those depicted in Figure 8.3, are wage/risk combinations that yield the *same* level of profits. Curves to the southeast represent higher profit levels because with all other items in the employment contract given, each risk level is associated with a *lower* wage level. Curves to the northwest represent, conversely, lower profit levels.

Note that the isoprofit curves in Figure 8.3 are concave (from below). This concavity is a graphic representation of our assumption that there are diminishing marginal returns to safety expenditures. Suppose, for example, the firm was operating at point *M* in Figure 8.3, a point where the risk of injury is high. The first expenditures by the firm to reduce risk will have a relatively high return because the firm will obviously choose to attack the safety problem by eliminating the most obvious and cheaply eliminated hazards. Because the risk (and accompanying cost) reductions are relatively large, the firm need not reduce wages by very much to keep profits constant. Thus, the isoprofit curve at point *M* is relatively flat. At point *N*, however, the curve is steeply sloped, indicating that wages would have to be reduced by quite a bit if the firm is to maintain its profits in the presence of a program to reduce risk. This large wage reduction is required because, at this point, further increases in safety are very costly; all the easy-to-solve safety problems have been dealt with.

As with employees, we also assume that employers differ in the ease (cost) with which they can eliminate hazards. We have just indicated that the cost of reducing risk levels is reflected in the *slope* of the isoprofit curve. In firms where injuries are costly to reduce, large wage reductions will be required to keep profits constant in the face of a safety program; the isoprofit curve in this case will be steeply sloped. The isoprofit curve of one such firm is shown as *YY'* in Figure 8.4. The isoprofit curves of firms where injuries are easier to eliminate are flatter. Note that curve *XX'*

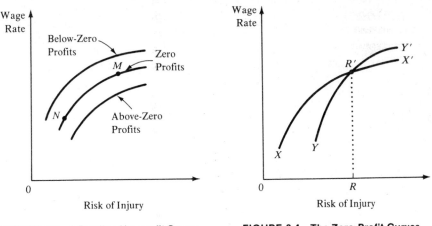

FIGURE 8.3   A Family of Isoprofit Curves for an Employer

FIGURE 8.4   The Zero-Profit Curves of Two Firms

in Figure 8.4 is flatter at each level of risk than YY'; this indicates that Firm X can reduce risk more cheaply than Firm Y.

The Matching of Employers and Employees

The aim of employees is to achieve the highest possible utility from their choice of a job. If they receive two offers at the same wage rate, they will choose the lower-risk job. If they receive two offers in which the risk levels are equal, they will accept the offer with the higher wage rate. More generally, they will choose the offer that falls on the highest, or most northwest, indifference curve.

In obtaining jobs, employees are constrained by the offers they receive from employers. Employers, for their part, are constrained by two forces. On the one hand, they cannot make outrageously lucrative offers because they would be driven out of business by firms whose costs were lower. On the other hand, if their offered terms of employment were very low, they would be unable to attract employees (who would work for other firms). These two forces compel firms in competitive markets to operate on their zero-profit isoprofit curves.

To better understand the offers firms make, refer back to Figure 8.4, where two different firms are depicted. Firm X, the firm that can cheaply reduce injuries, can make higher wage offers at low levels of risk (left of point R) than can Firm Y. Because it can produce safety (reduce risk) more cheaply, it can pay higher wages at low levels of risk and still remain competitive. Any point along segment XR' will be preferred by employees to any point along YR' because, for given levels of risk, higher wages are paid.

At higher levels of risk, however, Firm Y can outbid Firm X for employees. Firm X does not save much money if it permits the risk level to rise above R, because risk reduction is so cheap. Because Firm Y *does* save itself a lot by operating at levels of risk beyond R (it may be a sawmill where risk reduction is prohibitively costly), it is willing to pay relatively high wages at high-risk levels. Since offers along $R'Y'$ will be preferable to those along $R'X'$—again, because higher wages at any level of risk are paid by Firm Y—employees working at high-risk jobs will work for Y.

Graphing worker indifference curves and employer isoprofit curves together can show which workers choose which offers. Figure 8.5 contains the zero-profit curves of two employers (X and Y) and the indifference curves of two employees (A and B). Employee A maximizes utility by working for Employer X at wage W_{AX} and risk level R_{AX}, while Person B maximizes utility by working for Employer Y at wage W_{BY} and risk level R_{BY}.

Looking at A's choice more closely, we see that if he or she took the offer B accepted—W_{BY} and R_{BY}—the level of utility achieved would be A_1, which is less than A_2. Person A values safety very highly, and wage W_{BY} is just not high enough to compensate for the high level of risk. Person B, whose indifference curves are flatter (signifying he or she is less averse to risk) finds the offer of W_{BY} and R_{BY} on curve B_2 superior to the offer A accepts. Person B is simply not willing to take a cut in pay to W_{AX} in order to reduce risk from R_{BY} to R_{AX} because that would place B on curve B_1.

FIGURE 8.5 Matching Employers and Employees

The matching of A with Firm X and B with Firm Y is thus not accidental or random. Firm X can generate safety relatively cheaply and does not reduce cost much by operating at high-risk levels. Since X can "produce" safety more cheaply than Y, it is logical that X will be a low-risk producer who attracts employees, like A, who value safety highly. Likewise, Employer Y generates a lot of cost savings by operating at high-risk levels and can thus afford to pay high wages and still be competitive. Y attracts people like B, who have a relatively strong preference for money wages and a relatively weak preference for safety. Firm Y, then, has a comparative advantage (over X) in offering high-risk, high-paying jobs.[15]

The offer curve. The above job-matching process, of course, can be generalized beyond the case of two employees and two employers. To do this it is helpful to note that in Figures 8.4 and 8.5, the only offers of jobs to workers with a chance of being accepted lie along $XR'Y'$. The curve $XR'Y'$ can be called an "offer curve," because only along $XR'Y'$ will offers employers can afford to make be potentially acceptable to employees. The concept of an offer curve is useful in generalizing our discussion beyond two firms, because a single offer curve can summarize the potentially acceptable offers any number of firms in a particular labor market can make.

Consider, for example, Figure 8.6, which contains the zero-profit isoprofit curves of firms L through P. We know from our discussions of Figures 8.4 and 8.5 that employees will accept offers along only the most northwest segments of this set of curves; to do otherwise would be to accept a lower wage at each level of risk.

---

[15]The issue of whether society should allow Firm Y to operate at high-risk levels is examined later in this chapter.

FIGURE 8.6   An Offer Curve

Thus, the potentially acceptable offers will be found along the darkened portions of Figure 8.6, which we shall call the offer curve. The more types of firms there are in a market, the smoother this offer curve will be; however, it will always slope upward because of our twin assumptions that risk is costly to reduce and that employees must be paid higher wages to keep their utility constant if risk is increased. In some of the examples that follow, the offer curve is used to summarize the feasible, potentially acceptable offers employers are making in a labor market, because using an offer curve saves our diagrams from becoming cluttered with the isoprofit curves of many employers.

Major insights.   Our hedonic model generates two major insights. The first is that wages rise with risk, other things equal. According to this prediction, there will be compensating wage differentials for job characteristics that are viewed as undesirable by workers whom employers must attract. Second, workers with strong preferences for safety will tend to take jobs in firms where safety can be generated most cheaply. They thus tend to seek out and accept safer, lower-paying jobs. Workers who are not as averse to accepting risk will seek out and accept the higher-paying, higher-risk jobs offered by firms that find safety costly to "produce." The second insight, then, is that the job-matching process—if it takes place under the conditions of knowledge and choice—is one in which firms and workers offer and accept jobs in a fashion that makes the most of their strengths and preferences.

Before employing the above hedonic model to analyze labor market problems, it is useful to establish the empirical credibility of the theory of compensating differentials. The major empirically testable prediction of this theory is that, other things equal, wages are higher in jobs with disagreeable characteristics.

EMPIRICAL TESTS OF THE THEORY OF COMPENSATING WAGE DIFFERENTIALS

The prediction that there are compensating wage differentials for undesirable job characteristics is at least 200 years old. Adam Smith, in his *Wealth of Nations*, published in 1776, proposed five "principal circumstances which . . . make up for a small pecuniary gain in some employments, and counterbalance a great one in others." One of these, the constancy of employment, is discussed in the appendix to this chapter. Another two will be discussed in other chapters: the difficulty of learning the job (Chapter 9) and the probability of success (Chapter 11). Our discussion in this chapter, while it could draw upon any of Smith's "principal circumstances" to illustrate the concept of compensating wage differentials, will focus on his assertion that "the wages of labour vary with the ease or hardship, the cleanliness or dirtiness, the honourableness or dishonourableness of the employment."[16]

One would think that 200 years is a sufficient period of time over which to have accumulated substantial evidence concerning an important prediction. Unfortunately, the prediction has only been seriously tested in the last ten years, and then in only a limited way. The reasons for this lack of evidence are twofold. First, the prediction is that, *other things equal*, wages will be higher in unpleasant or dangerous jobs. The prediction can only be tested validly if the researcher is able to control for the effects of age, education, sex, region, race, union status, and all the other factors that typically influence wages. Only when the effects of these factors on wages are known can the researcher filter out the *separate* influence on wages of (say) injury risk.[17] Statistical procedures can control for these other factors, but these procedures require large data samples and the use of computers, and only in the last ten years or so have the necessary data and computers been widely available to researchers.

---

[16]*See* Adam Smith, *Wealth of Nations* (New York: Modern Library, 1937), Book I, Chapter 10. The fifth "principal circumstance" is "the small or great trust which be reposed in the workmen." This job characteristic has not been widely studied in the context of compensating wage differentials, but positive compensating wage differentials have been found for supervisory jobs. See, for example, Martha S. Hill, "Authority—A Job Quality with Greater Benefits for Men Than Women," Working Paper Series, Survey Research Center, University of Michigan, 1983.

[17]It is especially important to control for these other influences because safety is probably a normal good (meaning that higher-income workers desire more of it). A *simple* correlation of risk levels and earnings is thus negative—not positive as predicted by theory. However, the simple correlation fails to account for all the *other* factors that influence earnings. Only if the influence of these factors can be accounted for would we expect to obtain the predicted positive relationship between earnings and risk.

The adequacy of studies in which the wage/risk relationship is inferred from a cross-section of workers has been challenged by several authors on the grounds that there are many unmeasured characteristics whose omission from the data set could bias the results. These authors propose the use of longitudinal data in which two or more observations on each worker are recorded, permitting unmeasured, person-specific characteristics to be controlled for. See, for example, Charles Brown, "Equalizing Differences in the Labor Market," *Quarterly Journal of Economics* 94 (February 1980):113–34, and Greg Duncan and Bertil Holmlund, "Was Adam Smith Right After All? Another Test of the Theory of Compensating Wage Differentials," *Journal of Labor Economics* 1 (October 1983):366–79.

The second problem that has hindered the empirical testing for compensating wage differentials is the problem of specifying, in advance of these tests, job characteristics that are generally regarded as disagreeable. For example, while some people dislike outdoor work and would have to be paid a premium in order to accept it, others prefer such work and dislike desk jobs. Similar observations can be made about such job characteristics as repetitiveness, chances to make decisions, and amount of physical exertion. Tests of the theory require selecting job characteristics on which there is widespread agreement about what is "good" or "bad" at the margin. For this reason, many of the most credible and convincing tests of the theory have dealt with the level of *danger* on the job. While people may respond with different intensities to danger, it is difficult to believe that anyone prefers

---

Example 8.2

Compensating Wage Differentials in 19th-Century Britain

English mill towns in the mid-1800s were often beset by violence and unhealthy living conditions. Infant deaths, a common indicator of health conditions, averaged over 200 per 1000 live births in English towns—a rate well above those that typically prevail today in the poorest countries.[1] Violence was also a common part of life: crime rates were high, husbands beat wives, parents beat children, and corporal punishment was often used by factory supervisors against child laborers.

It is interesting, however, that the conditions varied from town to town and factory to factory. Infant mortality rates ranged from 110 to 344 in English towns in 1834, for example. As a further example, not all factories used corporal punishment as a means of industrial discipline. These differences in conditions have led economic historians to wonder whether workers' *information* and *choices* back then were sufficient to generate compensating wage differentials for the more unpleasant or unhealthy sectors of employment.

More specifically, workers were leaving rural areas to work in towns during this era. Towns in which conditions were very unhealthy would be less attractive to potential migrants than towns with healthier environments if the wages one could receive in each place were equal. If workers had reasonably good information on health conditions and could obtain work in several places, they would tend to gravitate toward the more pleasant places and away from the unhealthy towns. Differences in the relative supplies of migrants should have caused a wage differential to be created; that is, factories in the more squalid towns would have had to offer higher wages to compete for migrants. Likewise, factories that used corporal punishment would have had to offer higher wages than firms that did not if employees had information on working conditions and could exercise choice about where they worked.

[1]Jeffrey G. Williamson, "Was the Industrial Revolution Worth It? Disamenities and Death in 19th Century British Towns," *Explorations in Economic History* 19 (1982):221–45.

While wage and other data from the 1800s are such that research results are probably more suggestive than definitive, two intriguing findings have emerged from studies of compensating wage differentials in 19th-century England. First, it appears that once the cost of living and regional wage differences are accounted for, wages were higher for unskilled laborers in towns where infant mortality rates were greater. Results using 1834 data, replicated again using 1905 data, suggest that where infant mortality rates were 10 percent greater than average, the unskilled wage was 2–3 percent higher than average.[2] It also appears that male children who worked in factories where corporal punishment was used received wages some 16–18 percent higher than boys of the same age, experience, and literacy who worked in plants where violence was not used.[3] (Because workers receive compensating wage differentials only if employers are willing to pay them, one must entertain the notion that the threat, and use, of corporal punishment raised productivity by 16–18 percent.)

[2]Williamson, p. 233.
[3]Clark Nardinelli, "Corporal Punishment and Children's Wages in Nineteenth Century Britain," *Explorations in Economic History* 19 (1982): 283–95. We are indebted to Professor Ronald Warren, University of Virginia, for calling our attention to this article and for suggesting this general topic as an example.

injury to safety; danger is an unambiguous "bad." The risk of injury is also objectively measured from injury rates published by occupation or, more commonly, by industry.

The strongest evidence of compensating wage differentials for on-the-job danger relates to the risk of *fatal* injury. Several studies using different sets of data from the United States and Great Britain have found that wages are positively associated with the risk of being killed on the job, other things equal.[18] The results vary in magnitude and are rather sensitive to changes in the sample of workers used for estimation; however, they suggest that workers receive between $20 and $300 more per year for every one-in-ten-thousand increase in the risk of being killed on the job. (One death for every 10,000 workers is roughly the yearly average for steel mills, while a rate of 10 deaths per 10,000 workers is the average for logging camps.) While these estimates seem small, they do imply that a plant with 1,000 employees could save between $20,000 and $300,000 in wage costs *per year* if it undertook a safety program that would save one life every ten years.

The results for nonfatal injuries are not as supportive of the theory of compensating differentials. Most of these injuries are relatively minor and at least partially compensated for by workers' compensation insurance, which means that the losses incurred by workers are relatively small. Small losses probably do not generate much incentive to obtain large compensating wage differentials, so that any differ-

[18]Eight studies are reviewed in Robert S. Smith, "Compensating Wage Differentials and Public Policy: A Review," *Industrial and Labor Relations Review* 32 (April 1979):339–52. *See also* Alan Marin and George Psacharopoulos, "The Reward for Risk in the Labor Market: Evidence from the U.K. and a Reconciliation with Other Studies," *Journal of Political Economy* 90 (August 1982):827–53; Stuart Dorsey, "Employment Hazards and Fringe Benefits: Further Tests for Compensating Differentials," in *Safety and the Work Force,* ed. John D. Worrall (Ithaca, N.Y.: ILR Press, 1983); and Alan Dillingham, "The Influence of Risk Variable Definition on Value-of-Life Estimates," *Economic Inquiry,* forthcoming.

entials that do exist may simply be too small to distinguish from other forces that influence wages.[19] It is not too surprising, then, that is has been easier to observe compensating wage differentials for fatal than nonfatal work accidents. The victims of fatal accidents cannot possibly be fully compensated after the fact, so that the sheer magnitude of the losses caused by these accidents motivates those at risk to seek compensating differentials that are large enough to observe (see footnote 11).

POLICY APPLICATIONS

The insights of hedonic wage theory can be applied to some very critical social issues: the federal occupational safety and health program and affirmative action plans for hiring minorities.

Occupational Safety and Health

Are workers benefited by the reduction in risk?   In 1970 Congress passed the Occupational Safety and Health Act, which directed the U.S. Department of Labor to issue and enforce safety and health standards for all private employers. The

Example 8.3
Mandatory Risk Reduction in Coal Mining

The caution with which the government should proceed with *mandatory* risk-reduction programs is underscored by events in coal mining. The Federal Coal Mine Health and Safety Act of 1969 directs that miners be offered chest X-rays in order to detect black lung disease. (This disease is technically known as *coal workers' pneumoconiosis*—a condition in which the inhalation of coal dust eventually reduces the functional capacity of the lungs. It is progressive, disabling, and sometimes fatal.) When it appears miners have the disease, their employers must, under the law, offer them jobs in less dusty areas of the mine. These jobs are lower paid and less prestigious than the dusty jobs at the "face" of the mine. Consequently, only 10 percent of the miners offered such jobs in the 1970s accepted them. The behavior of most miners thus tells us that they were willing to undertake a known risk because the compensation (monetary and psychic) of the dangerous jobs was great enough to offset this risk. A law *compelling* them to leave the dusty jobs would clearly have reduced their welfare, at least as they saw it.

---

[19]The statistical problem is one of distinguishing the influence of injuries from all the other influences, including random ones, on wages. It is a little bit like trying to locate the position of Pluto from one's backyard. When Pluto is close to earth, the moon is merely a crescent, there is no haze, and the city is dark, it can be done. If the moon is full, Pluto is far from the earth, and ground light and haze are present, Pluto's weak light signal cannot be seen or "filtered" out from all the other stars or planets.

stated goal of the act was to ensure the "highest degree of health and safety protection for the employee."[20]

Despite the *ideal* that employees should face the minimum possible risk in the work place, implementing this ideal as social *policy* is not necessarily in the best interests of workers. Our hedonic model can show that reducing risk in some circumstances will lower the workers' utility levels. Consider Figure 8.7.

Suppose a labor market is functioning about like our textbook models, in that workers are well informed about dangers inherent in any job and are mobile enough to avoid risks they do not wish to take. In these circumstances, wages will be positively related to risk (other things equal), and workers will sort themselves into jobs according to their preferences. This market can be modeled graphically in Figure 8.7, where, for simplicity's sake, we have assumed there are two kinds of workers and two kinds of firms. Person A, who is very averse to the risk of injury, works at wage W_{AX} and risk R_{AX} for Employer X. Person B works for Employer Y at wage W_{BY} and risk R_{BY}.

Now suppose the Occupational Safety and Health Administration (OSHA), the Department of Labor agency that is responsible for implementing the federal safety and health program, promulgates a standard that, in effect, says that risk levels above R_{AX} are illegal. The effects, although unintended and perhaps not immediately obvious, would be detrimental to employees like B. Reducing risk is costly, and the best wage offer a worker can obtain at risk R_{AX} is W_{AX}. For B, however, wage W_{AX} and risk R_{AX} generate *less utility* than did Y's offer of W_{BY} and R_{BY}. Figure 8.7 shows

FIGURE 8.7   The Effects of Government Regulation
on a Perfectly Functioning Labor Market

---

[20]Section 6(b)(5) of the Occupational Safety and Health Act.

that X's offer of W_{AX} and R_{AX} lies on indifference curve B_1, whereas Y's old (now illegal) offer was on the higher curve B_2.

When the government mandates the reduction of risk in a market where workers are compensated for the risks they take, it penalizes workers like B, who are not terribly sensitive to risk and appreciate the higher wages associated with higher risk. The critical issue, of course, is whether workers have the knowledge and choice necessary to generate compensating wage differentials. Many people believe that workers are uninformed, unable to comprehend different risk levels, or immobile, and thus most do not choose risky jobs voluntarily. If this belief were true, government regulation *could* make workers better off; indeed, such conditions almost undoubtedly prevail in some markets. However, the arguments already presented concerning information and mobility and the evidence of the positive relationship between wages and risk of death should challenge the assumption that, in general, the labor market fails to generate compensating differentials.

To say that worker utility *can* be reduced by such programs does not, of course, imply that it *will* be reduced. The outcome depends on how well the unregulated market functions and how careful the government is in setting its standards for risk reduction. The following section will analyze a government program implemented in a market that has *not* generated enough information about risk for employees to make informed job choices.

How strict should OSHA standards be?   Consider a labor market, like that mentioned previously for asbestos workers, in which ignorance or worker immobility hinders labor market operation. Let us suppose also that the government becomes aware of the health hazard involved and wishes to set a standard regulating worker exposure to this hazard. How stringent should this standard be?

The crux of the problem in standard setting is that reducing hazards is costly; the greater the reduction, the more it costs. While businesses bear these costs initially, they ultimately respond to them by cutting costs elsewhere and raising prices (to the extent that cutting costs is not possible). Since labor costs constitute the largest cost category for most businesses, it is natural for firms facing large government-mandated hazard reduction costs to hold the line on wage increases or to adopt policies that are the equivalent of reducing wages: speeding up production, being less lenient with absenteeism, reducing fringe benefits, and so forth. It is also likely, particularly in view of any price increases (which, of course, tend to reduce product demand), that employment will be cut back. Some of the job loss will be in the form of permanent layoffs that force workers to find other jobs—jobs they presumably could have had before the layoff but chose not to accept. Some of the loss will be in the form of cutting down on hiring new employees who would have regarded the jobs as their best employment option.

Thus, whether it is in the form of smaller wage increases, more difficult working conditions, or inability to obtain or retain one's first choice in a job, the costs of compliance with health standards will fall on employees. Employees will bear these costs in ways that reduce their earnings below what they *would have been in the absence of OSHA*. These losses may not be immediate or very obvious, since it is hard to know what wages would have been without the OSHA standard.

However, the obscurity of this outcome of government regulation does not justify ignoring it. A graphic example can be used to make an educated guess about whether worker utility will be enhanced or not as a result of the increased protection from risk mandated by an OSHA health standard.

Figure 8.8 depicts a worker who believes she has taken a low-risk job, when in fact she is exposing herself to a hazard that has a relatively high probability of damaging her health in 20 years. She receives a wage of W_1 and *believes* she is at point A, where the risk level is R_1 and the utility level is U_1. Instead, she is in fact at point B, receiving W_1 for accepting (unknowingly) risk level R_2; she would thus experience lower utility (indifference curve U_0) if she knew the extent of the risk she was taking.

Suppose now that the government discovers that her job is highly hazardous. The government could simply inform the affected workers and let them move to other work. However, if it has little confidence in the ability of workers to understand the information or to find other work, the government could pass a standard that limits employee exposure to this hazard. But what level of protection should this standard offer?

If the government forces the risk level down to R', the best wage offer the woman in our example could obtain is W' (at point D on the offer curve). Given the market, no employer would or could pay her more at risk level R', other things equal. Point D, however, lies on indifference curve U', which represents a lower level of utility than she is in fact getting now (U_0). She would be worse off under the government-imposed standard. On the other hand, if the government forced risk levels down to a level between R_0 and R_2, she would be better off because she would be able to reach an indifference above U_0 (see shaded area of Figure 8.8).

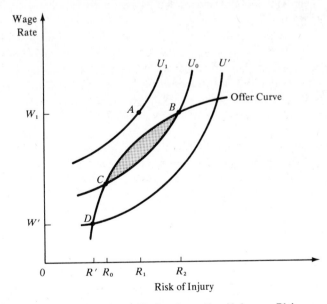

FIGURE 8.8   A Worker Accepting Unknown Risk

How can one estimate, in a practical way, how much wage loss workers would be willing to bear in exchange for a reduction in risk and still feel at least as well off as they are currently? The answer lies in estimating compensating wage differentials in markets that appear to work. Suppose, in a properly functioning market, that workers facing risk level R_1—the one our hypothetical worker *thought* she was facing in Figure 8.8—accept wage cuts (increases) of $300 per year for reductions (increases) in the yearly death rate of 1 in 10,000 (this represents the upper estimates reported on p.235). These workers appear to feel that, other things equal, $300 is a price they are willing to pay for this reduction in risk. Thus, as noted earlier in the case of earplug use, compensating wage differentials can be used to estimate the value workers place on seemingly intangible aspects of their jobs. The use of such differentials should not be oversold, because the difficulties of establishing which markets are properly functioning are considerable. However, estimating compensating wage differentials is probably the best way of finding out what value workers attach to various job characteristics.[21]

Since one cannot rule out the possibility—indeed, the likelihood—that one way or another workers will ultimately pay for the costs of their reduced workplace risks, economists argue strongly that the government should conduct studies to estimate whether the value workers place on risk reduction is commensurate with the costs of the program. These studies are called *benefit-cost* studies, and they weigh the costs of a program against the value workers (or other beneficiaries) attach to the benefits of reduced risk. Estimates of compensating wage differentials can be very useful in estimating these benefits.

Consider the OSHA standard that reduced the exposure of 90,000 asbestos workers to two fibers of asbestos per cubic centimeter of air. Inhaling airborne asbestos fibers is stongly and persuasively associated with several types of cancer; it is expected that the two-fiber standard will reduce yearly asbestos-related deaths by 4 per 1000 workers. The *lower* estimates of compensating differentials associated with the risk of death (mentioned on p. 235) suggest that asbestos workers would probably be willing to pay *at least* $800 per year for this four-in-one-thousand reduction in risk.[22] Because the yearly cost of the asbestos standard comes to roughly $800 per worker, it seems reasonably certain that the workers benefited by the standard would be willing to bear any of the program's costs that are shifted to them.[23] Thus, the asbestos standard almost certainly improves the welfare (utility) of asbestos workers.

As another example of benefit-cost analysis, consider two alternative standards limiting the exposure of chemical workers to *acrylonitrile*—a substance used in making acrylic fibers and a certain type of resin. Exposure to acrylonitrile is

---

[21]*See* E. J. Mishan, ''Evaluation of Life and Limb: A Theoretical Approach,'' *Journal of Political Economy* 79, 4(July/August 1971):687–705.

[22]The figure of $800 arises from multiplying the lower estimate of $20 for a one-in-ten-thousand reduction in death risk by a factor of 40 (to bring it up to a four-in-one-thousand reduction).

[23]Russell Settle, ''Benefits and Costs of the Federal Asbestos Standard,'' paper delivered at a Department of Labor Conference on Evaluating the Effects of the Occupational Safety and Health Program, March 18–19, 1975.

believed to increase one's chances of contracting cancer; reducing worker exposure from 20 parts per million (ppm) of air to 2 ppm would reduce the yearly risk of cancer-related deaths by 8.4 per 10,000 exposed workers. We know from our estimates of compensating differentials that the *most* we can assume workers would be willing to give up to obtain this reduction in risk is about $2,500 per year.[24] Since obtaining this new level of risk would cost $2,800 per worker (per year), it is conceivable that the standard would improve worker utility if workers bore the costs, but the costs would come very close to outweighing the benefits.

On the other hand, reducing acrylonitrile exposure to 1 ppm would reduce the death rate by 9 per 10,000 exposed workers at a yearly cost of $25,000 per worker. Given that the most workers seem willing to pay for a 9 in 10,000 reduction in risk is $2,700 per year, there is no chance that a 1 ppm standard could improve their utility if they bore the costs. Thus, while a 2 ppm standard may be worth promulgating, a 1 ppm standard would not be.[25] Perhaps because of the high costs and small benefits, OSHA chose to set the acrylonitrile standard at 2 ppm.

Judging OSHA under alternative norms.
In our analysis of OSHA above, we argued that a safety or health standard is socially desirable only if the value workers place on risk reduction is commensurate with the costs of the standard. The implicit assumptions of this analysis were that the only beneficiaries of the standard are the workers whose risk is reduced, and the benefits can best be measured by the current willingness of employees to pay for risk reduction. Neither assumption is universally accepted.

It is frequently argued that members of society who are not directly affected by the risk reduction program might be willing to pay *something* for the benefits that accrue to those who *are* directly affected. Presumably, this "willingness to pay" is strongest for family members, relatives, and close friends and weakest for strangers. However, even strangers would have some interest in reducing injury and disease if they were taxed to subsidize the medical treatment of those who are injured or become ill. Thus, it is argued, the benefits of OSHA standards extend beyond the direct beneficiaries to other external parties whose willingness to pay should also be counted.

The major issue for policymaking is not whether these external benefits exist, but how large they are and whether they are already included in the willingness to pay of those directly benefited by an OSHA standard. For example, one could plausibly argue that a worker's *family* might be heavily involved in his or her choice of jobs, so that compensating wage differentials *already* reflect family preferences. Put differently, the opinions and preferences of family members and close relatives *could* affect the indifference curves of the workers directly at risk and thus play a

---

[24]This figure is obtained by multiplying the upper estimate of $300 for a one-in-ten-thousand reduction by 8.4.

[25]This analysis is based on data reported in James Miller, "Occupational Exposure to Acrylonitrile," statement before the Occupational Safety and Health Administration on behalf of Vistron Corporation, Washington, D.C., 1978.

role in determining what jobs such workers choose at what wages. To date, no research has addressed this issue.

Also unclear at present is the degree to which medical care for job-related injuries and illnesses is subsidized by parties who are not direct beneficiaries of an OSHA standard. Workers' compensation insurance premiums, for example, are established at the *industry* level and are subject to some modification based on the experience of the individual firm in that industry; it seems unlikely that one industry's workers subsidize the medical treatment of injured workers in other industries. Since OSHA standards apply to *entire industries,* it does not appear probable that subsidies by external parties through workers' compensation are very large. However, because most occupational *illnesses* are not effectively covered by workers' compensation, treatment of those who contract a disease from their work is paid for by them, their insurance, or public subsidies (Medicare and Medicaid).[26] The likelihood that external parties subsidize the treatment of those directly at risk of occupational disease is thus very high; what is unknown at present is the magnitude of the subsidy.[27]

Another argument against using only the apparent willingness of workers to pay for risk reduction as a measure of its benefit is that workers really do not know what is best for themselves in the long run. Society frequently prohibits (or at least tries to prohibit) people from indulging in activities that are dangerous to their welfare; laws against the use of narcotics and gambling are two examples. Some argue that OSHA standards limiting exposure to dangerous substances or situations fall into the category of preventing workers from doing harm to themselves by being lured into dangerous work; therefore, it is argued that to ask how much they value risk reduction is irrelevant. The conflict between those who claim that workers know what is best for themselves and those who claim they do not can only be resolved on philosophical grounds.

However, one offshoot of the argument that workers do not know best for themselves deserves special mention. Some argue that worker preferences are molded by the environment in which they were raised and that there is no reason to take that environment as "given" or unchangeable. Once all workers at risk are required to wear protective clothing and equipment, and once they are prevented from taking certain risks on the job (in return for higher pay perhaps), their attitudes and preferences will change. A few years ago, for example, wearing hard hats was considered "sissified," but today it is not. Thus, OSHA standards are regarded as an engine for changing worker, as well as employer, attitudes and behavior.

How far one wants to go in imposing present costs on workers to induce a

---

[26]When a worker contracts lung cancer, it is usually very difficult to tell whether the cause was job related, due to personal habits, related to residential location, or a combination of all three. Because it cannot usually be proven to be job related, workers' compensation does not apply.

[27]This ignorance need not prevent us from making benefit estimates, however. We could, for example, calculate benefits in two ways: We could first assume no subsidy and use compensating wage differentials as discussed in the text. Alternatively, we could assume a 100 percent subsidy of medical costs and add to the willingness to pay implied by the compensating differentials the medical cost savings associated with the OSHA standard. These calculations would at least indicate the range into which benefits are likely to fall.

change of attitude is a philosophical issue. We should add, however, that the value judgment underlying normative economics—that of mutual benefit, or making some better off and no one else worse off—is usually interpreted as applying to *current* (observed) preferences. Thus, the policy analyses of this text, by taking indifference curves and the current set of prices (compensating wage differentials, for example) as given, have implicitly assumed that workers know what is best for themselves. This section has pointed out that *alternative* assumptions *do* exist.

Affirmative Action Planning

In an effort to end discriminatory hiring practices, all large firms doing business with the federal government are required to prepare *affirmative action plans* listing their goals for the hiring of women and minorities for the coming years. If these goals are set too low or if approved goals are not met, the firm could conceivably lose its government contracts. Thus, setting realistic goals is important.

In order to construct and evaluate a realistic affirmative action plan for hiring employees, firms must know the *availability* of women and minorities. The concept of availability used by the government has been interpreted in basically two ways:

1. The percentage of minorities or women among those who have the skills required by a specific job group or who are capable of acquiring them;
2. The percentage of minorities and women who can be expected to become available during the period [in which] the ultimate goal is to be achieved.[28]

A construction contractor seeking to hire 20 carpenters for a big job may be required to establish a goal of having six blacks among them if 30 percent of *all* carpenters in the city are black. Alternatively, an automobile manufacturer that will be hiring 20 beginning mechanical engineers may be required to set a goal of having five women among them if 25 percent of *new graduates* in mechanical engineering are female. The definition of availability to be used is the one that makes more sense in the situation.

While this flexibility in defining availability undoubtedly helps achieve the goal of setting realistic targets for firms, the government has usually ignored another aspect of availability: the *interest of workers* in a particular employer. In the case of locally recruited minority workers, for example, the government has typically used the percentage of qualified minorities in the entire city or metropolitan area as the measure of availability, regardless of how far away they may live from the place of employment. This measure of availability disregards the fact that people prefer to work near home, other things equal, and that their interest in applying for jobs diminishes as the commuting distance rises. Commuting costs, in terms of both time and money, are seen by workers as negative aspects of employment—aspects to be avoided unless adequate compensation for them is received. Failure to take them into account when trying to measure availability works against the intention of setting realistic hiring goals.

---

[28]U.S. Department of Labor, Office of Federal Contract Compliance Programs, *Compliance Manual* (October 18, 1978).

The Timken Company.   An illustration of the severity of the commuting issue arose in 1976, when the government declared the Timken Company ineligible to receive government contracts.[29] The reason for debarment was that Timken's plant in Bucyrus, Ohio, set its minority hiring goals based on a 16-mile recruiting radius, an area with a 0.6 percent minority population, and refused to include the town of Mansfield, which was 25 miles from its plant and contained 15 percent minorities. The government concluded that 25 miles—35-45 minutes by car—was a reasonable commuting distance and that Mansfield should thus be included for goal-setting purposes. Characteristically, the government's hiring goal for Timken assumed that workers in Mansfield were as interested in a job at Timken as workers in Bucyrus. The government thus calculated its measure of availability by drawing a 25-mile radius around the plant and calculating the percentage (3.5 percent) of minorities living in that entire area.

Timken took the case to court and won a reversal. The court, looking at the jobs available in Mansfield and the commuting pattern of its residents, decided that workers living in Mansfield were unlikely to want to commute to Bucyrus. In this decision, the court relied on a survey of 12 major employers in Bucyrus, none of whom restricted the geographic range of their hiring, which showed only four Mansfield residents out of 2300 workers were working in the Bucyrus firms.

While it is clear that the government was wrong in weighting Mansfield and Bucyrus residents equally in computing Timken's availability, it is not clear that the court was correct in rejecting Mansfield as part of Timken's natural recruiting area.

A hedonic model of commuting.   We asserted earlier that the cost of commuting to work is viewed by workers as a disadvantage; the higher the cost is, the greater are the disadvantages of the job. In this respect, commuting costs are like the risk of injury, to be avoided unless compensation is received. Thus, we would expect that workers, in order to keep their utility constant, would require higher wages to commute longer distances to otherwise identical jobs.

Figure 8.9 shows worker commuting preferences graphically by drawing indifference curves that are upward sloping and convex (similar to indifference curves in the analysis of risk of injury). Workers with the greatest aversion to commuting (like Employee A) have the steepest curves because they require the greatest wage increases to commute longer distances. Workers with the weakest aversion to commuting (like Employee B) have the flattest indifference curves.

On the employer side of the market, there is also a positive relationship between wages and the commuting distances of their workers. Consider a firm that is dissatisfied with its pool of job applicants and wants to enlarge this pool so it can be more selective in hiring. One solution is to raise its wage offers in order to attract more applicants. This higher wage offer will, among other things, attract applicants who live farther from the plant. The higher wage offer serves to overcome the commuting costs for these workers.

---

[29]*Timken Company* v. *Vaughn* 413 F. Supp. 1183 (N.D., Ohio 1976).

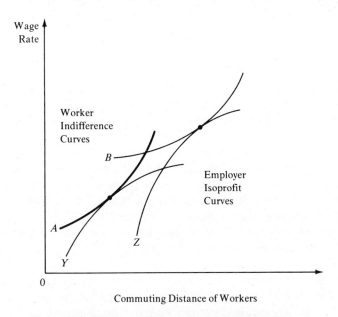

FIGURE 8.9 A Hedonic Model of Commuting

How high the firm is willing to raise its wage offer depends on how much more productive its work force will be. A large, sophisticated, assembly-line plant may be willing to raise its wages a lot to increase the size of its labor market, because it can select the most skilled *and* the most dependable workers. Unsteady workers, or those prone to absenteeism, can impose high costs on an assembly-line producer. These large, sophisticated firms have the steepest isoprofit curves (like Z in Figure 8.9). A smaller firm looking for workers of the same general skill, but lacking a highly interdependent production process may not obtain a very big increase in productivity if it hires only the most dependable workers. Thus, it may not find that increasing the size of its labor market is as beneficial; this type of small firm (like Y) has a flatter isoprofit curve.

Figure 8.9 suggests two conclusions of interest in the context of antidiscrimination programs. First, there is a *positive* relationship between wages and commuting distances, other things equal. High-wage firms will have geographically larger recruiting areas than low-wage employers.[30] What this means for affirmative action planning is that the firm's wage policy—whether its pay rate is high, average, or low for the skills it hires—should play a role in determining the size of its labor market and the availability of minorities or women.

In the Timken case, for example, Mansfield may well have been in Timken's legitimate recruiting area (even if it was not for the other twelve employers) *if*

---

[30]For a recent study on this topic, see Philip S. Borba, "Factors That Influence the Home-to-Work Dispersion of Workers in a Local Labor Market, with an Application to the External Labor Market Availability of Protected Class Workers," Unpublished Doctoral Dissertation, Cornell University, 1982.

Timken's wage rates were higher than average for the jobs involved. Mansfield workers would not, under any circumstances, be considered as available as Bucyrus workers, but an important consideration—the wage rate—was ignored by the court in defining the availability of minorities to Timken. This consideration, however, was taken into account in a 1979 court decision, wherein it was held that residents of the District of Columbia were not effectively in the labor pool of a suburban employer because, in part, the employer's wages were lower than those paid in the district.[31]

The second major conclusion suggested by Figure 8.9 is that workers select wage offers and commuting distances based on their preferences. People who place a high value on working close to home will accept lower wage offers. These lower offers serve as a compensating wage differential for the desirable characteristic of being able to commute to work quickly and cheaply.

This second conclusion is significant for antidiscrimination policy because women typically work closer to home than men. Usually having the primary family responsibilities for meal preparation and child rearing, women appear to place a premium on being able to work close to home. Figure 8.9 illustrates that their wages will be somewhat lower as a result of this preference. Thus, *some* of the gross wage differentials between men and women may well be explained by the generally shorter commutes among women. (Incidentally, our analysis here also suggests that firms' recruiting areas for women may be smaller than they are for men.)

Chapter 14 will return to a closer examination of male-female wage differences. The point here is that the role women traditionally have had as primary homemaker affects their earnings adversely. While assigning women this role may in itself be considered discriminatory by some, this form of discrimination is not the direct object of antidiscrimination programs conducted by the government. These programs by themselves cannot completely eradicate male-female earnings differences.

REVIEW QUESTIONS

1. Is the following true, false, or uncertain: "Certain occupations, such as coal mining, are inherently dangerous to workers' health and safety. Therefore, unambiguously, the most appropriate government policy is the establishment and enforcement of rigid safety and health standards." Explain your answer.

2. Statement 1: "Business executives are greedy profit maximizers, caring only for themselves." Statement 2: "It has been established that workers doing filthy, dangerous work receive higher wages, other things equal." Can both of these statements be generally true? Why?

3. It has often been claimed that an all-volunteer army would be entirely made up of soldiers from minority groups or disadvantaged backgrounds. Using what you have learned in this chapter, analyze the reasoning and assumptions underlying this claim.

---

[31]*U.S.* v. *County of Fairfax* 19 FEP Cases 753 (E.O., Va. 1979).

4. "The concept of compensating wage premiums for dangerous work does not apply to industries like the coal industry, where the union has forced all wages and other compensation items to be the same. Since all mines must pay the same wage, owners of dangerous mines will have to pay the same wage as owners of safe mines. Therefore, compensating differentials cannot exist." Is this statement correct? (Assume wages and other forms of pay must be equal for dangerous and nondangerous work and consider the implications for individual labor supply behavior.)

SELECTED READINGS

Brown, Charles. "Equalizing Differences in the Labor Market." *Quarterly Journal of Economics* 94 (February 1980):113–34.

Duncan, Greg, and Holmlund, Bertil. "Was Adam Smith Right After All: Another Test of the Theory of Compensating Wage Differentials." *Journal of Labor Economics* 1 (October 1983):366–79.

Rosen, Sherwin. "Hedonic Prices and Implicit Markets."*Journal of Political Economy* 82 (January-February 1974):34–55.

Smith, Adam. *Wealth of Nations.* (New York: Modern Library, 1937), Book I, Chapter 10.

Smith, Robert S. "Compensating Wage Differentials and Public Policy: A Review." *Industrial and Labor Relations Review* 32 (April 1979):339–52.

Smith, Robert S. *The Occupational Safety and Health Act: Its Goals and Its Achievements.* Washington, D.C.: The American Enterprise Institute for Public Policy Research, 1976.

Viscusi, W. Kip. *Employment Hazards: An Investigation of Market Performance.* Cambridge, Mass.: Harvard University Press, 1979.

Appendix 8A

Compensating Wage Differentials and Layoffs

As mentioned in the preceding text, one of the circumstances identified by Adam Smith under which compensating wage differentials would arise relates to the "constancy or inconstancy of employment." While there is evidence, as we shall see, to support this prediction, the relationship of wages to layoff probabilities is by no means as simple as Smith thought. In particular, there are three issues relevant to the analysis—all of which we shall discuss briefly.[1]

UNCONSTRAINED CHOICE OF WORK HOURS

Suppose that, in the spirit of Chapters 6 and 7, employees are free to choose their hours of work in a labor market that offers an infinite choice of work hours. Given the wage a particular worker can command and his or her nonwage income, the utility-maximizing choice of working hours would be selected. For the person depicted in Figure 8A.1, the utility maximizing hours of work is H^*, given his or her offered wage rate (W^*) and level of nonwage income (assumed here to be zero).

If H^* is thought of in terms of yearly work hours, it is easy to understand that a worker may *prefer* a job involving layoff! Suppose H^* is 1500 hours per year—or essentially three quarters of the typical "full-time" job of 2000 hours. One could work 6 hours a day, 5 days a week for 50 weeks a year, or one could work 8 hours a day, 5 days a week, for 9 months and agree to be laid-off for 3 months. Which alternative holds more appeal to any given individual depends on his or her preferences with respect to large blocks of leisure or household time, but it is clear that many people value such large blocks. Teachers, for example, typically work full time during a 9-month school year and then some of them vacation during the

---

[1]The analysis in this appendix draws heavily upon John M. Abowd and Orley Ashenfelter, "Anticipated Unemployment, Temporary Layoffs, and Compensating Wage Differentials," in Sherwin Rosen, ed. *Studies in Labor Markets* (Chicago: University of Chicago Press, 1981), pp. 141–70.

FIGURE 8A.1   Choice of Hours of Work

summer. Many other jobs, from construction trades to work in canning factories, involve predictable seasonal layoffs, and workers in these jobs may have chosen them because they value the leisure or household production time accompanying the layoffs.

Putting the point differently, the theory of compensating wage differentials suggests they will be positive only when a job characteristic is regarded as bad by the marginal worker. Predictable blocks of leisure or household time accompanying seasonal layoffs may not be regarded as bad by the marginal worker. In fact, workers in some markets may see layoffs as a mechanism through which they can best achieve their desired yearly hours of work.

CONSTRAINED HOURS OF WORK

Suppose that the worker depicted in Figure 8A.1 is offered a choice between a job offering wage W^* and hours H^*, and one offering fewer hours than desired because of a predictable layoff each year that reduces hours of work to H'. Clearly, if the wage for the latter job remains at W^*, the worker's utility will be reduced by taking the job offering H' hours because he or she will be on an indifference curve passing through point A. The job offering W^* and H^* is thus clearly preferred at W^*.

However, suppose that H' is offered at a wage of W', where W' exceeds W^* by enough so that point B can be reached. Point B, where the wage is W' and hours of work are H', is on the *same* indifference curve as point C (the utility-maximizing point when W^* is the offered wage). Point B is not a point of utility maximization at a wage offer of W',[2] but if the worker is offered an unconstrained choice of hours at wage rate W^*, or a wage of W' where working hours are *constrained* to equal H', he or she would be indifferent between the two job offers.

In the above example, $(W' - W^*)$ is the compensating wage differential that would have to arise for the worker to consider a job where hours of work were constrained to lie below those otherwise desired. Many people view layoffs as an event that prevents workers from working the number of hours they would otherwise desire to work. If this is the case, and if these layoffs are predictable and known with certainty, such as layoffs accompanying model changeovers in the auto industry, then compensating wage differentials associated with the predictable, certain layoff rate would arise in a well-functioning labor market (that is, one where workers are informed and mobile).[3]

The Effects of Uncertain Layoffs

In the above section, we assumed that layoffs were predictable and known with certainty. In most cases, however, they are not. While one might expect layoff rates to be higher in some industries than in others, they are in fact often subject to considerable random fluctuation *within* industries over the years. This *uncertainty* of layoffs is itself another aspect of affected jobs that is usually thought to be a negative feature and for which a compensating wage differential might arise.

Suppose that utility is measurable and is a function only of income, so that it can be graphed against income (Y), as in Figure 8A.2.[4] Suppose also that the person depicted is offered a job for which a wage of W' and yearly hours of H' are known *with certainty*. The utility associated with these H' hours is a function of his or her income at H' hours of work: $W'H'$ (again assuming no nonwage income).

Now suppose there is another job paying W' in which the *average* hours of work per year are H' but half the time H_h is worked and half the time H_ℓ is worked. Although we have assumed that $.5\,H_h + .5\,H_\ell = H'$, so that over the years the person averages H' hours of work, it turns out that with the convex utility function we have drawn the person's average utility is *below* $U(H')$. To understand this we must look closely at Figure 8A.2.

When the person's working hours are H_h, which is half the time, he or she earns

---

[2]It is not a point of tangency; that is, at a wage of W' the worker depicted in Figure 8A.1 would prefer to work more than H' hours if he or she were free to choose work hours. We have assumed in the discussion that the choice is *constrained* so that hours cannot exceed H'.

[3]A similar argument can be used to predict that workers will receive compensating wage differentials if they are forced to work longer hours than they would otherwise prefer. For the argument and evidence in support of it, see Ronald G. Ehrenberg and Paul L. Schumann "Compensating Wage Differentials for Mandatory Overtime," *Economic Inquiry*, December 1984.

[4]Although economists typically work with *ordinal* utility functions, which specify the relative ranking of alternatives without assigning each alternative a numerical value of utility, the analysis of choice under uncertainty requires the use of *cardinal* utility functions (ones in which each alternative is assigned a specific numerical value of utility). It is far beyond the scope of this text to fully discuss the properties of such functions; the interested reader is referred to other sources such as R. Duncan Luce and Howard Raiffa, *Games and Decisions* (New York: John Wiley, 1957). A similar analysis of another topic can be found in the appendix to Chapter 13.

FIGURE 8A.2 **The Choice Between H′ Hours with Certainty and H′ Hours on Average**

$W'H_h$, and this income yields a utility of $U(H_h)$. Thus, half the time the worker will be at point C enjoying utility level $U(H_h)$. The other half of the time, however, the person will be working H_ℓ hours, earning $W'H_\ell$ in income, and be at point A enjoying utility of $U(H_\ell)$. His or her average utility is thus $\overline{U}$, which is $\overline{U} = .5 U(H_h) + .5 U(H_\ell)$. Note that $\overline{U}$, which is midway between $U(H_h)$ and $U(H_\ell)$ in our example, lies *below* $U(H')$—the utility derived from a job paying W' and employing the person for H' *with certainty* every year.

Why is $\overline{U} < U(H')$ even though H' hours are worked on *average* in both cases? The answer lies in the convexity of the utility function, which economists define as exhibiting *risk aversion*. Moving from H' to H_h covers the same absolute distance as moving from H' to H_ℓ, but the changes in utility are not the same in *magnitude*. In particular, moving from point H' to H_h (points B to C) in the good years adds *less* to utility than moving from H' to H_ℓ (points B to A) in the bad years takes away. Put differently, the convexity of the total utility curve in Figure 8A.2 implies diminishing marginal utility of income. Thus, in the unlucky years, when hours are below H', there is a relatively big drop in utility (as compared to the utility associated with H' hours), while in the lucky years the added income increases utility by a relatively small amount.

The upshot of this discussion is that when workers are averse to risk—that is, when their utility functions are convex so that they in essence place a larger value on negative changes from a given level of income than they do on positive changes of equal dollar magnitude—they would prefer a job paying W' and offering H' hours with certainty to one paying W' and offering only H' hours on average. Thus, to compensate them for the loss in utility associated with *risk aversion*, they would require a wage above W' on the job offering H' hours only on average.

THE OBSERVED WAGE-LAYOFF RELATIONSHIP

The discussion above centered on worker preferences regarding layoffs. For compensating wage differentials to arise, of course, employers must be willing to pay them. That is, employers must profit from being able to lay off workers, and if we are to observe firms pursuing a high-wage/high-layoff strategy, their gains from layoff must exceed their costs of higher wages.

The discussion above also neglected Unemployment Insurance (UI) payments to laid-off workers. This topic is discussed in some detail in Chapter 16. Here we need note only that if UI payments fully compensate laid-off workers for their lost utility, compensating wage differentials will not arise. Compensating wage differentials will arise only if UI payments do not fully compensate laid-off workers.

One study that looked very carefully at the relationship between wages and layoffs suggests that the compensating wage differential for an average probability of layoff is around 4 percent of wages, with over 80 percent of this differential related to the aversion to risk associated with the variability (uncertainty) in layoff rates facing workers over time. Workers in the high-layoff industries of automobile manufacturing and construction received estimated compensating wage differentials ranging over the early 1970s from 6 to 14 percent and 6 to 11 percent, respectively.[5]

---

[5]These estimates are from the Abowd and Ashenfelter article cited in footnote 1 of this appendix. For those interested in how the presence of compensating wage differentials and UI benefits affect workers' choices of jobs when layoff probabilities differ across jobs, see Robert M. Hutchens, "Layoffs and Labor Supply," *International Economic Review* 24 (February 1983):37–55.

9

Investments
in Human Capital:
Education and Training

Chapters 6, 7, and 8—on the decision to work and job choice—emphasized the effects of *current* wages and psychic income on worker decisions. However, many labor supply choices require a substantial initial *investment* on the part of the worker. Recall that investments, by definition, entail an initial cost that is then recouped (hopefully) over some period of time. Thus, for many labor supply decisions, *current* wages and working conditions are not the only deciding factors. To model these decisions, one needs to develop a framework that incorporates investment behavior.

Workers undertake three major kinds of investments: education and training, migration, and search for new jobs. All three investments involve an initial cost, and all three are made in the hope and expectation that the investment will pay off well into the future. To emphasize the essential similarity of these investments to other kinds of investments, economists refer to them as investments in *human capital,* a term that conceptualizes workers as embodying a set of skills that can be "rented out" to employers. The knowledge and skills a worker has—which come from education and training, including the training that experience yields—generate a certain *stock* of productive capital. However, the *value* of this amount of productive capital is derived from how much these skills can earn in the labor market. Job search and migration are activities that increase the value of one's human capital by increasing the price (wage) received for a given stock of skills.

Society's total wealth should therefore be thought of as a combination of both human and nonhuman capital. Human capital includes accumulated investments in such activities as education, job training, and migration, whereas nonhuman wealth includes society's stock of land, buildings, and machinery. Total wealth in the United States was estimated at $15.6 trillion in 1973, or about $75,000 for every man, woman, and child. Of this, 52 percent—or $39,000 per capita—took the form of *human* wealth.[1] Thus, investments in human capital are enormously important in our society.

The expected *returns* on human capital investments are, as noted, a higher level of earnings, greater job satisfaction over one's lifetime, and a greater appreciation of nonmarket activities and interests. Generally speaking, the investment *expenditures* can be divided into three categories:

1. *Out-of-pocket* or *direct* expenses include tuition and books (education), moving expenses (migration), and gasoline (job search).
2. *Forgone earnings* are another source of cost because during the investment period it is usually impossible to work, at least full time.
3. *Psychic losses* are a third kind of cost incurred because education is difficult and often boring, because job search is tedious and nerve-wracking, and because migration means saying goodbye to old friends.

This chapter will analyze educational investments and their labor market implications. Because most such investments are closely related to the supply of labor to a particular occupation or set of occupations, this aspect of human capital theory adds more depth to the analysis of occupational choice begun in the last chapter. Chapter 10 deals with turnover and migration; other aspects of job search are treated in Chapter 15.

DEMAND FOR EDUCATION BY WORKERS

There are many ways in which workers, or potential workers, can enhance their earning capacity through education. They can attend high school, junior college, or college. They can go to a trade school or technical institute. They can enter an apprenticeship program or acquire skills on the job. The analysis of the demand for any of these types of education or training is essentially the same. Therefore, this section will analyze the demand for a college education as an illustration and application of human capital theory.

People want to attend college when they believe they will be better off by so doing. For some, the benefits may be short-term: they like the courses or the lifestyle of a student. Students attending for these reasons regard college as a *consumption good*—that is, they are going to college primarily for the satisfaction it provides during the period of attendance. Others, however, attend college because of the *long-term* benefits it provides. These benefits are partly in the form of higher earnings, partly in the form of gaining access to more interesting, challenging, or pleasant jobs, and partly in the form of prestige or enhanced enjoyment of nonmarket activities. Attendance for the long-term benefits, or *investment behavior,* is the behavior this chapter seeks to analyze.

---

[1]U.S. Congress, Joint Economic Committee, *Economic Growth and Total Capital Formation* (Washington, D.C.: U.S. Government Printing Office, February 18, 1976).

An Overview of the Benefits and Costs of an Educational Investment

Calculating the benefits of an investment over time requires the progressive discounting of benefits lying farther into the future (see Chapter 5). Benefits that are received in the future are worth less to us now than an equal amount of benefits received today for two reasons. First, if people plan to consume their benefits, they prefer to consume earlier. (One is relatively sure of being able to enjoy such consumption now, but the uncertainties of life make future enjoyment problematic.) Second, if people plan to invest the monetary benefits rather than use them for consumption, they can earn interest on the investment and enlarge their funds in the future. Thus, no matter how people intend to use their benefits, they will discount future receipts to some extent.

As Chapter 5 explained, the present value of a stream of yearly benefits (B) over time (T) can be calculated as follows:

$$\text{Present Value} = \frac{B_1}{1 + r} + \frac{B_2}{(1 + r)^2} + \frac{B_3}{(1 + r)^3} + \cdots + \frac{B_T}{(1 + r)^T} \qquad (9.1)$$

where the interest rate (or discount rate) is r. As long as r is positive, benefits into the future will be progressively discounted. For example, if $r = 0.06$, benefits payable in 30 years would receive a weight that is only 17 percent of the weight placed on benefits payable immediately ($1.06^{30} = 5.73$; $1/5.73 = 0.17$).

The costs of going to college are normally incurred over a relatively short period of time. These costs include the direct costs of tuition, fees, and books, the forgone earnings attendant on being a full-time student, and the psychic costs of studying and being examined. The total costs of going to college are thus very high, with the monetary costs alone (direct costs plus forgone earnings) in the range of $10,000–20,000 per year in 1984.

A person considering college has, in some broad sense, a choice between two streams of income over his or her lifetime. Stream A begins immediately but does not rise very high; it is the earnings stream of a high school graduate. Stream B (the college graduate) has a negative income for the first four years (owing to college tuition costs), followed by a period when the salary is less than what the high school graduate makes, but then it takes off and rises above stream A. Both streams are illustrated in Figure 9.1. (Why these streams are *curved* will be discussed later in this chapter.) The streams shown in the figure are stylized so that we can emphasize some basic points. Actual earnings streams will be shown in Figures 9.11 and 9.13.

Obviously, the earnings of the college graduate would have to rise above those of the high school graduate to induce someone to invest in a college education (unless, of course, the psychic or consumption-related returns were large). The gross benefits, the difference in earnings between the two streams, must total much more than the costs because such returns are in the future and are therefore discounted. For example, suppose it costs $15,000 per year to obtain a four-year college education and the real interest rate (the nominal rate less the rate of inflation) is 2 percent. The after-tax returns—if they were the same each year— must be $2,200 in constant-dollar terms (that is, after taking away the effects of

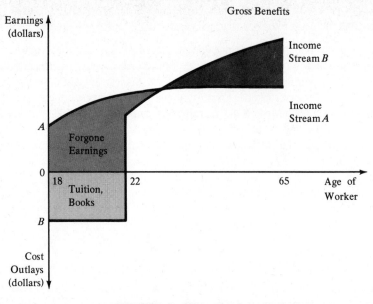

FIGURE 9.1   Alternative Income Streams

inflation) each year for 40 years in order to justify the investment on purely monetary grounds. These returns must be $2,200 because $60,000 invested at a 2 percent interest rate can provide a payment (of interest and principal) totaling $2,200 a year for 40 years.[2]

A Formal Model of Choice and Its Implications

The preceding discussion emphasized that investing in a college education is worthwhile if the present value of the benefits (monetary and psychic) is at least as large as the costs. In mathematical terms this criterion can be expressed as

$$\frac{B_1}{1 + r} + \frac{B_2}{(1 + r)^2} + \cdots + \frac{B_T}{(1 + r)^T} \geq C, \qquad (9.2)$$

where C equals the total costs of a college education and B equals the yearly differences in earnings between college and high school graduates.

There are two ways one can measure whether the criterion in equation (9.2) is met. Using the *present-value method*, one can specify a value for the discount rate,

---

[2]This calculation is made using the *annuity formula:*

$$Y = X \frac{1 - [1/(1 + r)^n]}{r},$$

where Y equals the total investment ($60,000 in our example), X = the yearly payment ($2,200), r = the rate of interest (0.02), and n = the number of years (40). In this example, we treat the costs of a college education as being incurred all in one year rather than being spread out over four—a simplification that does not alter the magnitude of required returns much at all.

r, and determine if the present value of benefits is greater than or equal to costs. Alternatively, one can adopt the *internal-rate-of-return method*, which asks, "How large could the discount rate be and still render college profitable?" Clearly, if the benefits are so large that even a very high discount rate would render college profitable, then the project is worthwhile. In practice, one calculates this internal rate of return by setting the present value of benefits equal to costs and solving for *r*. The internal rate of return is then compared to the rate of return on other investments. If the internal rate of return exceeds the alternative rates of return, the investment project is considered profitable.[3]

In deciding whether to attend college, no doubt few students make the very precise calculations suggested in equation (9.2). Nevertheless, if they make less formal estimates that take into account the same factors, four predictions concerning the demand for college education can be made:

1. Present-oriented people are less likely to go to college than forward-looking people (other things equal).
2. Most college students will be young.
3. College attendance will increase if the costs of college fall (other things equal).
4. College attendance will increase if the gap between the earnings of college graduates and high school graduates widens (again, other things equal).

Present-orientedness.   Psychologists use the term *present-oriented* to refer to people who do not weight future events or outcomes very heavily. While all people discount the future with respect to the present, those who discount it more than average—or, at the extreme, ignore the future altogether—could be considered present-oriented. In terms of equations (9.1) and (9.2), a present-oriented person is one with a very high discount rate *(r)*.

Suppose one were to calculate investment returns using the *present-value method*. If *r* is large, the present value of benefits associated with college will be lower than if the discount rate being used is smaller. Thus, a present-oriented person would impute smaller benefits to college attendance than one who is less present-oriented, and those who are present-oriented would be less likely to attend college. Using the *internal-rate-of-return method* for evaluating the soundness of a college education, one would arrive at the same result. If a college education earns an 8 percent rate of return but the individuals in question are so present-oriented that they would insist on a 25 percent rate of return before investing, they would likewise decide not to attend.

The prediction that present-oriented people are less likely to attend college than forward-looking ones is difficult to substantiate or disprove. The rates of discount

---

[3]For our purposes here, the present-value and internal-rate-of-return methods may be considered interchangeable in evaluating investment alternatives. In *some* circumstances, however, the two methods would not provide identical rankings of investment opportunities. *See* J. Hirshleifer, "On the Theory of Optimal Investment Decision," *Journal of Political Economy* 66 (August 1958):329–52.

that people use in making investment decisions are rarely available, because the decisions are not made as formally as equation (9.2) implies. However, the model does suggest that people who have a high propensity to invest in education will also engage in other forward-looking behavior. Certain medical statistics tend to support this prediction.

In the United States there is a strong statistical correlation between education and health status.[4] People with more years of schooling have lower mortality rates, fewer symptoms of disease (such as high blood pressure, high cholesterol levels, abnormal X-rays), and a greater tendency to report themselves to be in good health. This effect of education on health is independent of income, which appears to have no effect of its own on health status except at the lowest poverty levels. Is this correlation between education and health a result of better use of medical resources by the well educated? It appears not. Better-educated people undergoing surgery choose the same doctors, enter the hospital at the same stage of disease, and have the same length of stay as less-educated people of equal income.

What *may* cause this correlation is a more forward-looking attitude among those who have obtained more education. People with lower discount rates will be more likely to attend college, and they will *also* be more likely to adopt forward-looking habits of health. They may choose healthier diets, be more careful of health risks, and make more use of preventative medicine. This explanation for the correlation between education and health is not the only plausible one, but it receives some direct support from British data on cigarette smoking.[5] From 1958 to 1975, the proportion of men in the most highly educated groups who smoked fell by 50 percent. During the same time period, the proportion of smokers in the more poorly educated class remained unchanged. It is unlikely that the less-educated group was uninformed of the smoking dangers revealed during that period. It is more likely that they were less willing to give up a present source of pleasure for a distant benefit. Thus, we have at least some evidence that people who invest in education also engage in *other* forward-looking behavior.

Age.   Given similar *yearly* benefits of going to college, young people have a larger present value of *total* benefits than older workers simply because they have a longer remaining work life ahead of them. In terms of equation (9.2), T for younger people is greater than for older ones. We would therefore expect younger people to have a greater propensity than older people to obtain a college education or engage in other forms of training activity. This prediction is parallel to the predictions in Chapter 5 about which workers employers will decide to invest in when they make decisions about hiring or specific training.

---

[4] The analysis of the correlation between education and health status is taken from Victor Fuchs, ''The Economics of Health in a Post-Industrial Society,'' *The Public Interest*, Summer 1979:3–20.

[5] It could be, for example, that healthy people, with longer life spans, are more likely to invest in human capital because they expect to experience a longer payback period. Alternatively, one could argue that the higher incomes of college graduates later in life mean they have more to lose from illness than do non-college graduates.

Costs.   A third prediction of our model is that human capital investments are more likely when costs are lower. The major monetary costs of college attendance are forgone earnings and the direct costs of tuition, books, and fees. (Food and lodging are not always opportunity costs of going to college because much of these costs would have to be incurred in any event.) Thus, if forgone earnings or tuition costs fall, other things equal, we would expect an increase in college enrollments. Similarly, if offers of financial aid to college applicants rise, other things equal, we would expect more accepted applicants to enroll in college.[6]

The costs of college attendance offer an additional reason why we observe older people attending less often than younger people. As workers age, they acquire levels of experience and maturity that employers are willing to reward with higher wages. Because older workers thus command higher wages (on average), their opportunity costs of college attendance are higher than those for younger students.[7] Older people are thus doubly discouraged from attending college: their forgone earnings are relatively high and the period over which they can capture benefits is comparatively short.

The psychic costs of going to college cannot be ignored. While these costs cannot be easily observed, they are likely to be related to ability. People who learn easily and who do well in school have an easier and more pleasant time in college than people who do not.

In any set of market transactions, some people are *at the margin*, which means that they are close to the point of not transacting. For example, consider a downward-sloping demand curve for education, where the number of people attending college is drawn as a function of its money costs (see Figure 9.2). If the money costs were X_0, we would observe that N_0 people would go to college. If the costs were raised to X_1, only N_1 would decide to attend. The people deciding to drop out when costs rise to X_1 are those who were closest to not going when costs were X_0. They are the ones who had the hardest time making up their minds at X_0—in other words, those who came closest to deciding not to go when costs were X_0.

Who are the people closest to the margin regarding the decision to go to college? In part, they are people for whom the psychic costs of studying and being examined are relatively high, people who do not especially like school. This group—who, we have argued, might consist to a large extent of less-able students—is thus likely to be the most responsive to changes in the money costs of education. (See the appendix to this chapter for a fuller discussion of the signaling issue.) Indeed, studies that have analyzed the effects of college location on college attendance show that males of moderate ability are much more responsive to college location than those of high ability. That is, whether a college is available in one's

---

[6]For evidence that these relationships exist, see Charles F. Manski and David Wise, *College Choice in America* (Cambridge: Harvard University Press, 1983) and Ronald G. Ehrenberg and Daniel Sherman, "Optimal Financial Aid Policies for a Selective University," *Journal of Human Resources* 19 (Spring 1984):202–30.

[7]This discussion is related to our discussion of the life-cycle supply of labor in Chapter 7. When wages are low, people engage in time-intensive activities.

FIGURE 9.2 The Demand for a College Education

hometown seems to matter a lot more to moderate-ability students than it does to high-ability students.[8]

Earnings differentials. The fourth prediction of human capital theory is that the demand for education is positively related to the *returns*—that is, to the increases in lifetime earnings or psychic benefits that a college education allows. In practice, this prediction can be tested only with reference to money returns, since psychic returns are unobservable; however, this prediction has been used to explain the sharp fall in college enrollments that occurred in the early 1970s.[9]

Beginning around 1970, the labor market for college graduates began to exhibit signs of a surplus. Jobs in the professional fields, in which college graduates typically found employment, began to dwindle relative to the supply, and more and more college graduates had to take jobs as sales, clerical, or blue-collar workers. For example, in 1958 only 10.5 percent of recent female college graduates and 13.8

---

[8]C. A. Anderson, M. J. Bowman, V. Tinto, *Where Colleges Are and Who Attends* (New York: McGraw-Hill, 1972). Given that loans to attend college often are not always available, the *financial resources* of the investor are also an important factor in the decision to invest. Thus, people in families with modest wealth are closer to the margin regarding the educational decision, other things equal, than those with more wealth.

[9]There is evidence, although it is somewhat weak, that better-educated workers are more likely to describe themselves as satisfied with their jobs. (See Daniel Hamermesh, "Economic Aspects of Job Satisfaction," in *Essays in Labor Market Analysis*, eds. Orley Ashenfelter and Wallace Oates (New York: John Wiley and Sons, 1977), pp. 53–72. *Quantifying* job or nonjob psychic benefits, however, is still not possible.

The analysis in the succeeding paragraphs relies heavily on Richard Freeman, "Overinvestment in College Training?" *Journal of Human Resources* 10, 3 (Summer 1975):287–311.

percent of recent male college graduates were employed in nonprofessional, non-managerial jobs, such as sales, clerical, or blue-collar work. For 1970–71 college graduates, these percentages had more than doubled to 24.4 percent for women and 30.5 percent for men. The deterioration in employment prospects for college graduates was also manifest in the starting salaries for graduates with bachelor's degrees. Table 9.1 tells the story for men, for whom comparative data over time are more available and reliable than the data for women. From 1961 to 1969, starting salaries for male college graduates increased faster than wages and prices in general, indicative of a pre-existing *shortage* of college graduates (see Chapter 2 for a review of the concepts of *shortage* and *surplus*). From 1969 to 1974, starting salaries for male bachelor's graduates increased more slowly than both average wages and the price level, which is what one would expect in sectors in which labor surpluses exist.

In analyzing the potential effects of this surplus of college graduates on college enrollments, however, one must not ignore the fact that our model stresses the discounted stream of benefits *over a lifetime*, while the data just presented refer mainly to employment prospects *immediately after graduation*. Nevertheless, there are two reasons to believe that immediate post-college prospects are of crucial importance in the decision to go to college. First, being closer to the present, earnings immediately after graduation are less heavily discounted than earnings later on. Second, in the absence of any better information, people may use current employment trends for college graduates as estimates of what prospects in the more distant future will be like. If there is a surplus now, people may assume it will last long enough to render college a poor investment.

TABLE 9.1 Compound Annual Changes in the Starting Salaries of Male Bachelor Graduates, 1961–69 and 1969–74

	1961–69 Period of Relative Market Boom		1969–74 Period of Relative Market Bust	
	Annual Percent Change in Salaries	Annual Percent Change Minus Change in CPI[a]	Annual Percent Change in Salaries	Annual Percent Change Minus Change in CPI
Accountant	6.0	3.4	4.0	−2.2
Business-general	5.7	3.1	2.4	−3.8
Humanities and social science	5.3	2.7	1.1	−5.1
Aeronautic engineering	4.8	2.2	3.1	−3.1
Chemical engineering	5.8	3.2	3.8	−2.4
Civil engineering	5.7	3.1	3.9	−2.5
Electrical engineering	5.1	2.5	3.2	−3.0
Mechanical engineering	5.3	2.7	3.5	−2.7
Industrial engineering	4.7	2.1	3.3	−2.9
Physical sciences, mathematics	4.8	2.2	2.1	−4.1
Changes in annual earnings of year-round full-time workers	4.7	2.1	6.6[b]	+0.4

[a]CPI = Consumer Price Index.

[b]1974 estimated by percentage change in average hourly earnings of all private industry production workers from March 1973 to March 1974.

SOURCE: Reprinted from Richard Freeman, "Overinvestment in College Training?" *Journal of Human Resources* 10,3(Summer 1975), Table 1 (© 1975 by the Board of Regents of the University of Wisconsin System), p. 288. Reprinted by permission of The University of Wisconsin Press.

Example 9.1
Do Unskilled Jobs Cause Poor Mental Health?

It is frequently asserted that the mental health of low-skilled workers is poorer than it is for higher-skilled workers of the same age. For example, a study of factory workers in the automobile industry found that 56 percent of middle-age *skilled* workers had good mental health, while only 26 percent of middle-age workers in repetitive, semiskilled jobs exhibited good mental health. The figures were 58 percent and 10 percent, respectively, for younger workers, and for both age groups there was a steady downward fall in the percentages of those with good mental health as one moved down the skill ladder between skilled and repetitive semiskilled jobs.* The conclusion generally drawn from such findings is that the boring, uncreative nature of jobs requiring little skill causes workers to lose self-esteem and to adopt negative attitudes toward life.**

It is entirely possible, however, that the causal connection between skill level and mental health is the reverse. For example, in the above-mentioned study of automobile workers, the following characteristics were included (with others) as indicative of poor mental health: a "live for today" attitude, a belief that success is due to luck and pull, a belief that one can't do much to shape one's future, and a lack of optimism. People with these characteristics are probably much less likely to undertake costly human capital investments with distant payoffs. Lack of self-esteem raises the perceived costs of education or training, while a lack of optimism or a present orientation limits the expected benefits. Thus, workers with these characteristics are much less likely to undertake human capital investments and become skilled. While human capital theory cannot be used to prove the causation runs from poor mental health (as defined by the researchers) to lower skill levels, it *can* be used to raise questions about the standard interpretation of the observed association between skill level and measures of mental health.

---

*Arthur Kornhauser, *Mental Health of the Industrial Worker* (New York: John Wiley and Sons), 1965, p. 57.

**Kornhauser, p. 76, and George Strauss and Leonard R. Sayles, *Personnel: The Human Problems of Management* (Englewood Cliffs, N.J.: Prentice-Hall, Inc.), 1972, p. 21.

Associated with the surplus of college graduates was a decline in the proportion of young men going to college. Among males, for whom labor market conditions appeared to change most in the early 1970s, the percentage of high school graduates going to college fell from 58 percent (1969) to 50 percent (1973). Further, the proportion of 18- to 24-year-old males going to college, after rising almost steadily since 1950, fell from 35 percent (1969) to 27 percent (1973).

Among females, the enrollment response was an abrupt cessation of growth in the proportion of young women enrolled in college, rather than a decline. Nevertheless, this response did represent a significant departure from the trend in growing college attendance during the 1960s. (The failure of enrollments to fall can possibly be explained, at least in part, by the tremendous increase in the propensity of women to seek work outside the home that has occurred in recent years. The longer one expects to work outside the home, the greater are the benefits of college attendance.) One might also argue that the differential response of men and women in terms of college attendance was due to changes during the early 1970s in the draft laws, which effectively removed the incentives for men to attend college in order to avoid the draft. While the draft law changes did have an effect, the timing of the decline in enrollments makes it clear that such changes can explain only part of the decline in demand for college education among men. Declining returns to a college education were clearly a major stimulus for the changed patterns of college attendance in the early 1970s.

Earnings Differences and the Demand for Education

As we have just seen, the demand for education is influenced by the differences in earnings made possible by an educational investment. However, the returns to education are themselves affected by the number of people who attend school. To obtain an overall picture of how enrollments and returns are interrelated, it is necessary to return briefly to our simple model of the labor market.

Figure 9.3 shows the labor market demand for, and supply of, college graduates. We know why the demand curve for labor slopes downward, but why does the supply curve for college graduates in Figure 9.3 slope upward? The reason, discussed earlier in this chapter, is that college is costly. If college graduates typically earned relatively low wages, few people would want to attend college. If

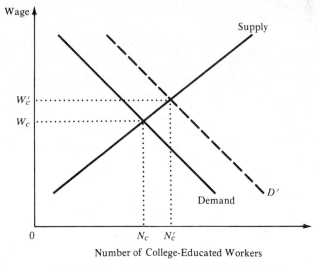

FIGURE 9.3　**The Market for College Graduates with a Shift in Demand**

the earnings of college graduates were to rise, more would want to attend college. If they were to rise still more, even greater numbers would enroll.

What would happen if the demand for college graduates were to shift outward, so that more such graduates were demanded at any given wage? Figure 9.3 illustrates that if the demand curve shifted to D', the wages of college graduates would rise from W_C to W_C'. This increase in the wages of college graduates would serve as an incentive for more people to attend college, and the number of college graduates would rise.

What would happen if, on the other hand, the supply of college graduates were to shift to the right, indicating that more people wanted to attend college for any given wage level that could be attained by graduates? Such a shift might occur, for example, if the government were to subsidize students in college or to exempt students from the military draft. Figure 9.4 shows that the outward shift in the supply of college graduates drives wages down to W_C'', a reduction that serves to moderate the increase in enrollments (as W_C falls to W_C'', the movement along S' suggests that fewer people decide to attend).

Unfortunately, the adjustment of college enrollments to changes in the returns to education is not always smooth or rapid, particularly in special fields, like engineering and law, that are highly technical. The problem is that if engineering wages (say) were to go up suddenly in 1986, the supply of graduate engineers would not be affected for three or four years (owing to the time it takes to learn the field). Likewise, if engineering wages were to fall, those students enrolled in an engineering curriculum would understandably be reluctant to immediately leave the field. They have already invested a lot of time and effort and may prefer to take their chances in engineering, rather than devote more time and money to learning a new field.

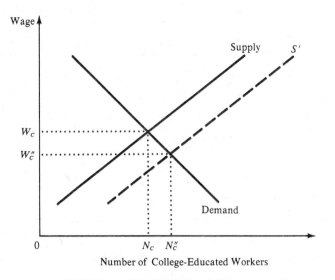

FIGURE 9.4   The Market for College Graduates with a Shift in Supply

The inability to respond immediately to changed market conditions can cause *boom-and-bust cycles* in the market for highly technical workers. If educational planners in government or the private sector were unaware of these cycles, they might seek to stimulate or reduce enrollments at times when they should be doing exactly the opposite, as illustrated below.

Suppose the market for engineers is in equilibrium, where the wage is W_0 and the number of engineers is N_0 (see Figure 9.5). Let us now assume that the demand curve for engineers shifts from D_0 to D_1. Initially, this increase in the demand for engineers does *not* induce the supply of engineers to increase beyond N_0 because it takes a long time to become an engineer once one has decided to do so. Thus, while the increased demand for engineers causes more people to decide to enter the field, the number available for employment at the moment is N_0. These N_0 engineers, therefore, can *currently* obtain a wage of W_1 (in effect, there is a vertical supply curve, at N_0, for a few years until the supply of engineering graduates is increased).

Now W_1, the *current* engineering wage, is above W_e, the new *long-run* equilibrium wage caused by the intersection of D_1 and S. The market, however, is unaware of W_e, observing only W_1. If people are myopic and assume W_1 is the new engineering wage, N_1 people will enter the engineering field (see Figure 9.6). When these N_1 all graduate, there will be a *surplus* of engineers (remember W_1 is *above* long-run equilibrium).

With the supply of engineers now temporarily fixed at N_1, the wage will fall to W_2. This fall will cause students and workers to shift *out* of engineering, but that effect will not be fully felt for a few years. In the meantime, note that W_2 is below long-run equilibrium (still at W_e). Thus, when supply *does* adjust, it will adjust too

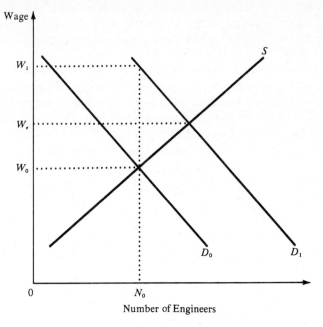

FIGURE 9.5 The Labor Market for Engineers

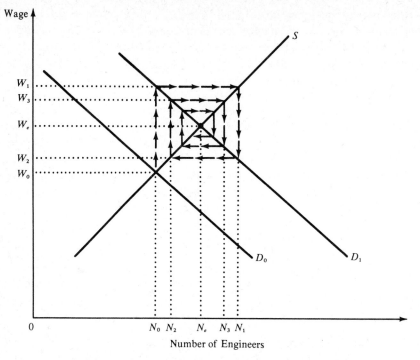

FIGURE 9.6   The Labor Market for Engineers: A Cobweb Model

much—all the way to N_2. Now there is another shortage of engineers because at W_2 there is greater demand than supply. This causes wages to rise to W_3, and the cycle repeats itself. Over time, the swings become smaller, and eventually equilibrium is reached. Because the adjustment path in Figure 9.6 looks like a cobweb, the adjustment process described above is sometimes called a *cobweb model*.[10]

Any market characterized by a cobweb adjustment process will experience alternating shortages and surpluses, and any educational institution training students for these fields will also experience booms and busts. Engineering appears to be one such field.[11] In the early 1950s people were talking of a surplus of engineers. In the late 1950s and early 1960s the discussion was of shortages. In the late 1960s there was again a surplus, followed in the 1970s by another shortage. Engineering enrollments fluctuated likewise, clearly reacting to the changed state of the market for engineers.

---

[10]Critical to cobweb models is the assumption that suppliers—in this case, workers—have static or myopic expectations about prices. In our example, they first assume that W_1 will be the prevailing wage, ignoring the possibility that the behavior of others will in 4 years drive the wage below W_1. One might expect that they would learn of their errors over time; however, as long as they assume the future prevalence of wages that oscillate above and below W_e, cobweb-type behavior will result.

[11]Richard B. Freeman, "A Cobweb Model of the Supply and Starting Salary of New Engineers," *Industrial and Labor Relations Review* 29 (January 1976):236–46.

The lesson to be learned from the cobweb model should not be lost on government policymakers. If the government chooses to take an active role in dealing with labor shortages and surpluses, it must be aware that, because supply adjustments are slow in highly technical markets, wages in those markets tend to *over*-adjust. For example, at the initial stages of a shortage when wages are rising toward W_1 (in our example), the government should be pointing out that W_1 is likely to be *above* the long-run equilibrium. If instead it attempts to meet the current shortage by *subsidizing* study in that field, it will be encouraging an even greater *surplus* later on. The moral of the story is that a complete knowledge of how markets adjust to changes in demand or supply is necessary before one can be sure that government intervention will do more good than harm.

THE EDUCATION/WAGE RELATIONSHIP

The preceding section used human capital theory to explore the demand for education, particularly college education. This section will investigate in more detail the effects of education on earnings and will explore several policy issues to which human capital theory can be applied.

A Hedonic Model of Education and Wages

The preceding section argued that the prospect of improved lifetime earnings served as a major inducement for people to invest in an education or training program. Indeed, unless education is acquired purely for purposes of consumption, people will not undertake an investment in education or training without the expectation that, by so doing, they can improve their stream of lifetime earnings or psychic rewards. However, in order to obtain these higher benefits, *employers* must be willing to pay for them. Therefore, it is necessary to examine both sides of the market to fully understand the prediction made over 200 years ago by Adam Smith that wages rise with the "difficulty and expense" of learning the job.[12]

Supply (worker) side.   Consider a group of people who have chosen selling as a desired career. These salespersons-to-be have a choice of how much education or training to invest in, given their career objectives. In making this choice they will have to weigh the returns against the costs, as pointed out in the previous section. Crucial to this decision is how the *actual* returns compare to the returns each would *require* in order to invest.

Figure 9.7 shows the indifference curves between yearly earnings and education for two workers, A and B. To induce A or B to acquire X years of education would require the assurance of earning W_x after they begin work. However, to

---

[12]See Adam Smith, *Wealth of Nations*, Book I, Chapter 10. The five "principal circumstances" listed by Smith as affecting wage were first discussed in Chapter 8.

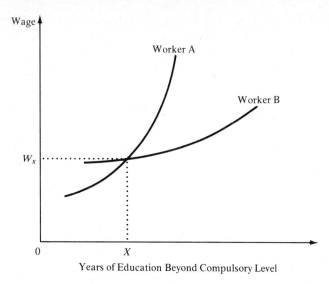

FIGURE 9.7   Indifference Curves for Two Different Workers

induce A to increase his or her education beyond X years (holding utility constant) would require a larger salary increase than B would require. A's greater aversion to making educational investments could be explained in several ways. Person A could be older than B, thus having higher forgone earnings and fewer years over which to recoup investment costs. Person A could be more present-oriented and thus more inclined to discount future benefits heavily—or could have less ability in classroom learning or have a greater dislike of schooling. Finally, A may find it more difficult to finance additional schooling. Whatever the reason, this analysis points up the important fact that people differ in their propensity to invest in schooling.

Demand (employer) side.   On the demand side of the market, employers must consider whether they are willing to pay higher wages for better-educated workers. If they are, they must also decide how much to pay for each additional year. Figure 9.8 illustrates employers' choices about the wage/education relationship. Employers Y and Z are *both* willing to pay more for better-educated sales personnel (to continue our example) because they have found that better-educated workers are more productive.[13] Thus, they can achieve the same profit level by either paying lower wages for less-educated workers or higher wages for more-educated workers. Their isoprofit curves are thus upward sloping (see Chapter 8 for a description of isoprofit curves).

The isoprofit curves in Figure 9.8 have three important characteristics:

---

[13]Whether schooling causes workers to be more productive or simply reflects—or "signals"—higher productivity is not important at this point, but we do address this issue later on.

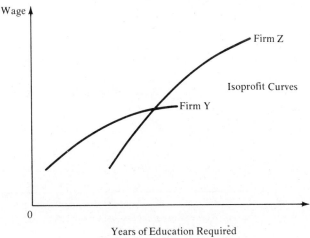

FIGURE 9.8   Isoprofit Curves for Two Different Firms

1. For each firm the curves are concave; that is, they get flatter as education increases. This concavity results from the assumption that, at some point, the added benefits to the employer of an additional year of employee schooling begin to decline. In other words, we assume that schooling is subject to diminishing marginal productivity.
2. The isoprofit curves are the *zero-profit curves*. Neither firm can pay higher wages for each level of education than those indicated on the curves; if they did so, their profits would be negative and they would cease operations.
3. The added benefits from an extra year of schooling are smaller in Firm Y than in Firm Z, causing Y to have a flatter isoprofit curve. Firm Y, for example, may be a discount department store in which "selling" is largely a matter of waiting on a counter. While better-educated people may be more productive, they are not *too* much more valuable than less-educated people; hence, Firm Y is not willing to pay them much more. Firm Z, on the other hand, may sell technical instruments for which a knowledge of physics and customer engineering problems is needed. In Firm Z, additional education adds a relatively large increment to one's productivity.

Market Determination of the Wage/Education Relationship

Putting both sides of the market for educated workers together, it is clear that the wage/education relationship will be positive, as indicated in Figure 9.9. Worker A will work for Y, receiving a wage equal to W_{AY} and obtaining X_1 years of education. The reason for this matching is simple. Firm Z cannot pay higher wages (for each level of education) than those shown on the isoprofit curve in Figure 9.9, for the

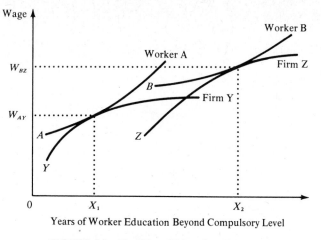

FIGURE 9.9 **The Wage/Education Relationship**

reasons noted above. Clearly, then, Worker A could never derive as much utility from Z as he or she could from Y; working for Firm Z would involve a loss of utility to Worker A. For similar reasons, Worker B will accept work with Firm Z, obtain X_2 years of schooling, and receive higher pay (W_{BZ}).

When examined from an overall social perspective, the positive wage/education relationship is the result of a very sensible sorting of workers and employers performed by the labor market. Workers with the greatest aversion to investing in education *(A)* will work for firms where education adds least to employee productivity *(Y)*. People with the least aversion to educational investment *(B)* are hired by those firms most willing to pay for an educated work force *(Z)*.

Note: If employers were unwilling to pay higher wages for more educated

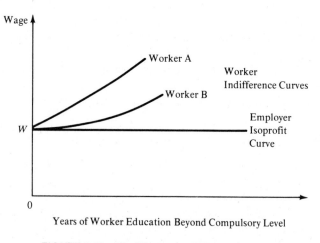

FIGURE 9.10 **Unwillingness of Firm to Pay for More Education by Employees**

workers, no education-related differentials would exist and employer isoprofit curves would be horizontal. Without a positive education/wage relationship, employees would have no incentive to invest in an education (see Figure 9.10).

The relationship between education and earnings is well documented and can be observed graphically in Figure 9.11. This figure presents *age/earnings profiles—* or lifetime earnings patterns—for males at five levels of schooling. Two conclusions are immediately obvious:

1. Better-educated males earn more than less-educated males at each post-schooling age level, as predicted by our theory. Note, however, from the (dashed) earnings profile of men with education beyond the bachelor's degree, that earnings while in school are lower than they would otherwise be (a graphic representation of the concept of forgone earnings).
2. The age/earnings profiles for workers with more education are steeper than the profiles of workers with less education. That is, the differences in

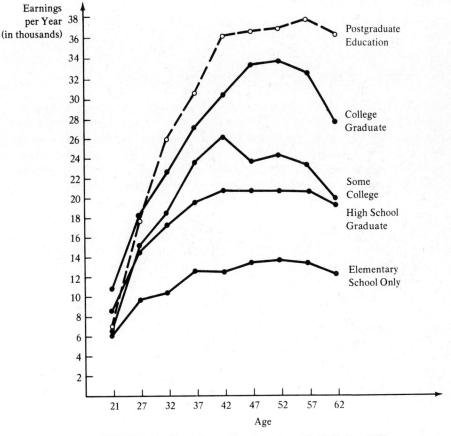

FIGURE 9.11   Total Money Earnings (mean), All Males, 1981

SOURCE: U.S. Bureau of the Census, *Money Income in 1981 of Families and Persons in the United States,* Current Population Reports, Series P-60, No. 137 (1983), Table 48.

earnings associated with education tend to widen as workers grow older. In the early years the earnings gap is small. Workers who have gone to college have not had a chance to acquire the work experience of their colleagues who have been working rather than attending college. Later, after they have had a chance to gain experience, their earnings rise much more sharply. (A more detailed discussion of *why* age/earnings profiles are steeper for more educated workers will be presented later in this chapter.)

IS EDUCATION A GOOD INVESTMENT?

It is well established that workers with more education tend to earn higher wages. However, an individual deciding whether to go to college would naturally ask, "Will I increase my monetary and psychic income enough to justify the costs of going to college?" Further, government policymakers trying to decide whether to expand educational facilities or subsidize increased enrollments must ask, "Will the benefits of improved productivity outweigh the costs?" The next two subsections deal with *individual* and *social* returns from educational investments.

Is Education a Good Investment for Individuals?

Individuals about to make an investment in a college education are typically committing themselves to costs of at least $10,000 per year. Is there evidence that this investment pays off for the typical student? Several studies have tried to answer this question by calculating the internal rates of return to educational investments. While the methods and data used vary, these studies normally estimate benefits by calculating earnings differentials at each age from age/earnings profiles such as those in Figure 9.11. (*Earnings* are usually used to measure benefits because higher wages and more stable jobs are payoffs to more education.) The *rate of return* is that discount rate that equates the present value of benefits to the cost of acquiring the level of education in question. It should be stressed that all such studies have analyzed only the monetary, and not the psychic, costs of and returns on educational investments.

The rates of return typically estimated in the above studies generally fall in the range of 5–15 percent (after adjusting for inflation). These findings are interesting because most other investments generate returns in the same range. Thus, it appears, at least at first glance, that an investment in education is about as good as an investment in stocks, bonds, or real estate. This conclusion must be qualified, however, by recognizing that there are systematic biases in the estimated rates of return to education. These biases, which are of unknown size, work in opposite directions.

The upward bias. The typical estimates of the rate of return on further schooling overstate the gain an individual student could obtain by investing in education because they are unable to separate the contribution *ability* makes to higher earnings

Example 9.2

Schooling, Earnings, and Compensation for Wrongful Death

How does a court determine the size of an award in a wrongful death case? Many states allow the family of a person killed through the negligence of another to collect from the responsible party the present value of the deceased's lost lifetime earnings. The procedure employed in calculating the size of the award often relies heavily on the victim's level of education in predicting earnings had he or she lived. This procedure is illustrated by summarizing an actual case in which one of the authors was involved.

John Doe was a 20-year-old high school graduate not yet firmly established in a career. While a passenger in a car one night in late 1976, he was killed when the car's drunk driver hit a truck while drag racing. Doe's family sued the driver of the car, seeking to collect the discounted value of his lost lifetime earnings. In evaluating his loss, the court had to decide which would be the appropriate age/earnings profile to use in estimating lost earnings, and which would be the appropriate interest rate to use in discounting these losses to the present.

It is obvious that John Doe's lifetime earnings losses are impossible to calculate precisely, but must instead be estimated. What is the most reasonable estimate? We know that people's earnings differ because of differences in both luck and unmeasurable personal characteristics, such as perseverance and the drive to succeed. Since there is no reason to believe Doe would have been exceptionally lucky or unlucky, and since unmeasurable characteristics are by definition difficult to deal with, the court was forced to assume he would have been average in these respects.

We also know that earnings vary because of education, age, race, sex, health status, union membership, region, occupation, and the industry in which employment is found. Had Doe, who was white, been reasonably settled in an occupation—carpentry, say—one could have used age/earnings profiles for the average white male carpenter. Unfortunately, Doe was not in a training program and had worked only briefly in a variety of jobs. (Indeed, occupational mobility in the United States is so high that few people remain in one occupation or industry for an entire career. Chapter 10 will return to this point.)

If evidence of a career-long job attachment is absent, the best estimate of lifetime earnings is derived from age/earnings profiles specific to the race, sex, and educational level of the individual. In the case of John Doe, earnings that would have prevailed at each age in his working life were estimated by plotting the typical age/earnings profile for white, male high school graduates in the United States for 1977. The profile applicable to Doe is summarized in the accompanying table. Assuming Doe would have retired at age 65, the simple summation of these yearly earnings totals $624,666. This figure is undiscounted and thus inappropriate for a court settlement, which pays a lump-sum payment now. However, it does give the reader an idea of the magnitude of the losses involved.

The age/earnings profile shown in the table would be appropriate to use

**Average Earnings of White,
Male High School Graduates, 1977**

Age	Earnings
18–24	$ 6,708
25–29	11,506
30–34	13,290
35–39	15,667
40–44	15,584
45–49	16,529
50–54	15,843
55–59	15,002
60–64	13,341
65	7,316

Note: Earnings shown are *median* earnings, meaning that half of all high school graduates earned
more than the amount shown and half earned
less.

SOURCE: U.S. Bureau of the Census, "Money In-
come in 1977 of Families and Persons in the
United States," *Current Population Reports*,
Series P-60, no. 118, March 1979, Table 48.

in calculating Doe's undiscounted losses only if Doe would have earned at
each age what workers currently that age were earning in 1977. There are
at least three reasons why this is unlikely. First, Doe may not have been
average in terms of luck, union membership, health status, or unmeasurable personal characteristics. We have already mentioned this problem and
suggested that assuming he would have been average is the best one
could do.

Second, inflation alone will increase money wages substantially over
one's career. However, the court can downplay inflation because the award
to Doe's family is a *lump-sum* settlement payable in the current year. Doe's
family could spend all the money in the current year at *current* prices, or
they could invest it. Because interest rates and other forms of investment
returns *tend* to reflect inflation, investing the funds would provide a natural
adjustment for inflation. (Economists often distinguish between the "real"
and "nominal" rate of interest. The *nominal* rate is the one that is quoted by
banks or bond dealers. The *real* rate is the nominal rate minus the rate of
inflation.)

Third, real wages have grown in the past and will grow in the future
because of increased productivity. The court needed to take real wage
growth into account in order to arrive at real earnings losses, so it was
assumed that real earnings would grow 1.27 percent each year—the average real wage growth during the 1953–77 period. Thus, the 1977 age/
earnings profile was adjusted to reflect estimated changes in real wages
that would have occurred over Doe's career. The undiscounted total of
lifetime earnings adjusted to reflect real wage growth amounts to $855,324.

In making its award, the court must calculate the present value of Doe's
lost earnings. The reason is probably obvious: Doe's family will receive *now*
all the income Doe would have received over his entire lifetime. If this sum

were not discounted, the returns that would be possible if the money were invested would have the effect of increasing the award beyond the level of Doe's actual lost earnings.

Choice of a discount rate is critical to the size of the award. For example, if Doe's age/earnings profile for real earnings were discounted at 7 percent, its present value would have been around $200,000. If it were discounted at 2 percent, however, its present value would be roughly twice as large. In Doe's case, earnings were discounted at 2.14 percent because this was the 1953–77 average *real rate of interest* on the safest corporate bonds. Put differently, 2.14 percent was the rate at which invested funds would grow, in real terms, if invested safely. Discounted at 2.14 percent, the present value of Doe's losses amounted to $389,000. (The case was actually settled out of court for less than discounted earnings losses.)

from the contribution made by *schooling*.[14] The problem is that (a) people who are smarter, harder-working, and more dynamic are more likely to obtain more schooling, and (b) such people might be more productive, and hence earn higher-than-average wages, even if they did not complete more years of schooling than others. When measures of ability are not observed or accounted for, the studies attribute *all* the earnings differentials associated with college to college itself and none to ability, even though *some* of the added earnings college graduates typically receive would probably be received by an equally able high school graduate who did not attend college.

Most studies attempting to identify the separate effects of ability and schooling have concluded that the effects of ability are relatively small—accounting for, at most, one fifth of observed earnings differentials.[15] However, these studies have used aptitude-test scores, such as IQ or mathematical reasoning, as measures of ability, and these measures are primarily designed to predict success in school, not in the work place. Success in the world of work is also affected by interpersonal skills, work habits, motivation, and resourcefulness—attributes that are not easily measured by a test.

---

[14]Another source of upward bias has been pointed out by C. M. Lindsay, "Measuring Human Capital Returns," *Journal of Political Economy* 79 (November/December 1971):1195–1215. Lindsay reasons that if human capital investments earn a normal rate of return, they do not change the wealth of those who invest; post-investment returns, in other words, just make up for the costs of investment. Human capital investments, however, do raise wages, and hence the price of leisure. As the principles of labor supply in Chapters 6 and 7 suggested, an increased wage with unchanged wealth would cause hours of leisure consumed to fall. Thus, human capital investments cause an increased price, and reduced consumption, of the important consumer good we call "leisure." Some of the differential in earnings we observe between those with more human capital and those with less is offset by utility lost by the former group when leisure is reduced. To count the entire earnings differential as a return on the investment without correcting for lost leisure overstates the *real gains* (that is, those expressed in terms of *utility*) to human capital investments.

[15]See, for example, Gary Becker, *Human Capital* (New York: National Bureau of Economic Research, 1975); Zvi Griliches and William M. Mason, "Education, Income, and Ability," and John C. Hause, "Earnings Profile: Ability and Schooling, " both in *Journal of Political Economy* 80, 3(May/June 1972).

One interesting attempt to control for all the unmeasured aspects of ability used data on twins.[16] When the researcher first calculated rates of return on an added year of education ignoring any controls for ability, the estimated return was 8 percent. When he looked only at earnings differences between identical twins—people with a common *genetic and environmental* background—with different levels of schooling, he found that the rate of return on schooling dropped to 3 percent. While no one study is conclusive, the results do suggest that part of earnings differentials associated with higher levels of schooling are due to inherently abler persons obtaining more schooling.[17]

The downward bias. By focusing only on the earnings differentials associated with an educational investment, the studies of returns to educational investments ignore other aspects of the returns on schooling. First, some benefits of college attendance are not necessarily reflected in higher productivity, but rather in an increased ability to understand and appreciate the behavioral, historic, and philosophical foundations of human existence. While these benefits may be difficult to measure, they exist nonetheless.

Second, most rate-of-return studies fail to include fringe benefits; they measure money earnings, not total compensation. Because fringe benefits as a fraction of total compensation tend to rise as money earnings rise, ignoring fringe benefits tends to create a downward bias in the estimation of rates of return to education. The size of this bias is largely unknown at present.[18]

Third, some of the job-related rewards of college are captured in the form of psychic or nonmonetary benefits. Jobs in executive or professional occupations are probably more interesting and pleasant than the more routine jobs typically available to people with less education. While executive and professional jobs do pay more than others, the total benefits of these jobs are probably understated when just earnings differences are analyzed.

An interesting example of the role nonmonetary costs and benefits play in schooling decisions can be seen in the fact that there is near-universal agreement that conventionally calculated rates of return fall as educational level rises. That is, the rate of return on a high school education is higher than for a college education, and higher yet than the average returns from going to graduate school. This fact can be understood when psychic benefits and costs are accounted for. Referring back to Figure 9.9, one is reminded that students who acquire the most education are, on average, the ones who dislike school the least. They may also be the ones who,

---

[16]Paul Taubman, "Earnings, Education, Genetics, and Environment," *Journal of Human Resources* 11, 4(Fall 1976): 447–61.

[17]Zvi Griliches, "Sibling Models and Data in Economics: Beginnings of a Survey," *Journal of Political Economy* 87(October 1979): S37–S64, reviews several studies attempting to estimate rates of return on schooling from data on siblings. This article suggests that much of the drop from an estimated 8 percent rate of return to an estimated 3 percent rate is a statistical artifact, rather than the result of controlling for heredity and environment.

[18]Greg J. Duncan, "Earnings Functions and Nonpecuniary Benefits," *Journal of Human Resources* 11, 4(Fall 1976): 462–83.

because of their higher learning abilities, derive the most psychic benefits from college. They thus require a smaller monetary incentive to attend college than do their less able colleagues.[19]

Selection bias.   A third source of bias in the standard estimates of rates of return on education arises from what has become known in recent years as the *selectivity* problem.[20] Briefly put, one who decides to go to college and become a manager, rather than terminate schooling with high school and become a mechanic, may do so in part because he or she has very little mechanical aptitude; thus, becoming a mechanic might yield this person *less* income than would be earned by others who chose to become mechanics rather than go to college. Likewise, those who go to college may have aptitudes that generate more income in managerial jobs than could have been earned in those jobs by terminal high school graduates if they had acquired the college education needed to qualify for the managerial jobs.

The significance of these considerations is that the measured rate of return on a college education may *understate* the actual return for those who choose to attend college. Likewise, the measured rate of return may *overstate* the return that would have been received by those terminating schooling with high school had they instead chosen to attend college. To understand these points, return to equation (9.2), where the benefits of a college education in year t were given as B_t. The term B_t is equal to the following:

$$B_t = E_{C,t}^C - E_{H,t}^H, \qquad (9.3)$$

where E_C^C represents the earnings in a college-level job of those who choose to go to college, and E_H^H represents the earnings in a high school-level job of those who choose not to go to college.

Now had the person who chose to attend college instead terminated schooling at high school, he or she would have earned $E_{H,t}^C$, where $E_{H,t}^C$ is perhaps *less* than $E_{H,t}^H$. Thus, the benefits in year t to those who chose college (B_t^C) are

$$B_t^C = E_{C,t}^C - E_{H,t}^C, \qquad (9.4)$$

—a sum *greater* than the measured benefit in equation (9.3). Thus, the benefits of going to college to those who choose to go may be greater than is indicated by the measured rate of return.

Similarly, if those who chose not to attend college were to alter their decisions, the earnings they could expect in year t would be $E_{C,t}^H$. The considerations in this subsection suggest that *their* post-college earnings ($E_{C,t}^H$) might be *less* than the earnings of those who did decide to attend college ($E_{C,t}^C$). Since the benefits of a college education to those who decided not to attend (B_t^H) are

$$B_t^H = E_{C,t}^H - E_{H,t}^H, \qquad (9.5)$$

----

[19]It may also be true that students from poor families, who lack the financial resources to obtain much education, require a higher rate of return on their educational investments than do students from families in which wealth is more abundant.

[20]The discussion in this subsection is based on Robert J. Willis and Sherwin Rosen, "Education and Self-Selection," *Journal of Political Economy* 87(October 1979):S7–S36.

it is apparent by comparing equations (9.3) and (9.5) that B_t^H is less than B_t. Thus, the potential rate of return to those who decided not to go to college may well be less than the measured rate of return.

The Willis-Rosen study mentioned in footnote 20 calculated estimates of the rate of return to schooling beyond high school for those who did not go beyond high school and those who did. Taking into account both measured differences in ability and the selectivity bias discussed in this section, they estimated a rate of return of 9.9 percent for those attending college. For those who did not go beyond high school, the rate of return they could have obtained from going to college was estimated to be 9.3 percent. While this is not a large difference, it is a reminder that when abilities are diverse, the principle of comparative advantage is an important factor in making choices about schooling and occupations.

It is difficult to summarize the findings on the question of whether education is a sensible investment for an individual. Considering only monetary costs and benefits, rates of return on educational investments are modest (once ability is accounted for), but not out of line with the "real" returns on many other types of investments. Moreover, if benefits other than money earnings were measured, the estimated returns on education would probably be higher.

Is Education a Good Social Investment?

The United States spends roughly 7 percent of its gross national product on formal education (primary, secondary, and college). If forgone earnings of high school and college students were included, this figure would rise to 10 percent.[21] In part these expenditures are justified by our need for a literate citizenry, speaking a common language and sharing a common culture. In part, however, education, especially at the secondary and college levels, is justified on the grounds that it enhances worker productivity. Interestingly, an early Soviet economist, S. G. Strumilin, wrote in 1929:

> A long time ago we had already arrived at the conclusion, that the expenditure of the state budget to raise the cultural level of the country ought to be considered along with the expenditures on technical reconstruction of production as capital expenditures and as equal in terms of their importance to our economy.[22]

There are some fields, such as mechanics and engineering, in which education clearly has a social payoff in the form of increased productivity. Recently, however, some critics have suggested that, to a large degree, education acts merely as a "sorting device." They argue that rather than making workers more productive, the

---

[21]The forgone earnings of high school and college students have been estimated to equal 60 percent of the *direct* cost outlays at those schooling levels. See Theodore Schultz, *The Economic Value of Education* (New York: Columbia University Press, 1963).

[22]Arcadius Kahan, "Russian Scholars and Statesmen on Education as an Investment," in *Educational and Economic Development*, eds. C. A. Anderson and M. J. Bowman (Chicago: Aldine Publishing Co., 1965), p. 10.

educational process is merely a screening device that reveals to employers the productive characteristics *already inherent* in prospective workers (we touched on this issue earlier in the discussion of the relationship between education and ability).

Employers, as noted in Chapter 5, are faced with the problem of ascertaining the quality of their job applicants. If they hire people for a trial period to see how they work out, they may face the costs of terminating low-quality employees and recouping the losses associated with their mistakes. An alternative procedure is to screen applicants through interviews, evaluations from previous employers, or work-related tests. These procedures themselves are costly, of course. They take time and money, and may still give imprecise readings of applicant quality.

Employers may also use data on applicant education as a screening tool. To do well in school requires both a capacity to learn and a willingness to work. The intellectual abilities required to succeed in school are obviously more closely correlated with the requirements for success in some jobs than others; however, workers who are better able to learn in school are probably easier to train and more flexible in the work place than others. The discipline required in school—promptness, willingness to follow directions, adherence to deadlines—is very similar to the discipline required to perform well in most jobs. In a real sense, schooling is the "work" of youth and may well be a good test of ability to succeed later on.

The argument of those who regard education *only* as a sorting device goes beyond the argument that employers use educational attainment to screen applicants. Such critics of education assert that schooling does *nothing* to alter productive characteristics, that it does not increase knowledge of the kind useful to employees, and that it does not impart useful attitudes or work habits. In short, they say, nothing happens to students while in school that affects productivity later on. The educational system is seen as simply a filter that has the effect of *signaling* which people are likely to be most productive.[23] (For a discussion of signaling, see the appendix to this chapter.)

It should be recognized that even if schooling were only a screening device, it could have social, as well as private, value. Employers need a reliable method with which to select employees. Obviously, sorting millions of workers into various categories of ability is an enormous job for any society, and schooling may be a very efficient means of doing this. The people most likely to acquire more schooling are the ones for whom schooling entails the least psychic cost, and as we have argued, this group will tend to be heavily populated by the most able people. Investment in schooling, then, sends a *signal* to the labor market that one has a certain level of ability. The costs of investing in schooling purely for its signaling value generate net *private* benefits if the increased wage a graduate can obtain

---

[23]If this was all schools did, they would not do much to alter the influences of family background, and thus would not be terribly useful in breaking down existing class distinctions or providing a vehicle for social mobility. For an elaboration of this point, see Samuel Bowles and Herbert Gintis, *Schooling in Capitalist America: Educational Reform and the Contradictions of Economic Life* (New York: Basic Books, 1976).

outweighs the costs. Schools in this case would have net *social* value if the decision to attend and the success one attained in school sent accurate signals about productive characteristics to employers in the least costly way.

Whether schooling is purely a sorting device or adds to productivity is not a particularly important question for individuals. Whatever role schools play, additional schooling does enhance one's lifetime income. Where the issue of screening is important is at the social level. If the only purpose of schools is to screen, why encourage the expansion of schooling? If 40 years ago being a high school graduate signaled above-average intelligence and work discipline, why incur the enormous costs of expanding college attendance only to find out that now a bachelor's degree signals above-average intelligence and work habits? The issue is of even more importance in less-developed countries, where mistakes in allocating extremely scarce capital resources could be disastrous (see Example 9.3).

Unfortunately, direct evidence on the role schooling plays in society is almost impossible to obtain. Advocates of the screening viewpoint, for example, assert that the fact that rates of return for college *graduates* are higher than for college *dropouts* is evidence that schooling is a screening device.[24] They argue that what is learned in school is proportional to the time spent there and that an added bonus (rate of return) just for a diploma is proof of the screening hypothesis. Advocates of the view that schooling enhances human capital counter that one who graduates after four years probably has learned more than four times what the freshman dropout has learned. They argue that dropouts are more likely to be poorer students—the ones who overestimated their returns on schooling and quit when they discovered their mistake. Thus, their relatively low rate of return is associated not with their dropping out but with their *reason* for dropping out.[25]

To take another example, proponents of the human capital view of education sometimes argue that the fact that earnings differentials between college and high school graduates continue to grow supports their view. They argue that if schooling were just a screening device, employers would rely on it *initially* but as they accumulated direct information from experience with their employees schooling would play a smaller role in determining earnings. Screening advocates could counter that continued growth in earnings differentials and the continued association of schooling and earnings only illustrate that educational levels are a *successful* sorting device; in other words, workers with higher levels of attainment in school do make more productive workers.

Finally, it has been argued that the 1940–65 change in skill requirements for a large number of jobs was very small, yet the educational requirements for obtaining those jobs rose dramatically.[26] Thus, while shoe salespeople in 1965 performed the

---

[24]Dropouts naturally have lower incomes than graduates, but because they have also invested less, it is not clear that their *rates of return* should be lower.

[25]See Barry Chiswick, "Schooling, Screening, and Income," in *Does College Matter?* ed. Lewis Solomon and Paul Taubman (New York: Academic Press, 1973), and Charles F. Manski and David Wise, *College Choice in America*, Chapter 8.

[26]See Ivar Berg, *Education and Jobs: The Great Training Robbery* (New York: Praeger Publishers, 1970).

Example 9.3

The Socially Optimal Level of Educational Investment

In addition to asking whether schooling is a good social investment, we could also ask, What is the socially optimal *level* of schooling? The general principle guiding our answer to this question is that society should increase or reduce its educational investments until the marginal rate of return (to society) equals the marginal rate of return on other forms of capital investment (investment in physical capital, for example).

The rationale for the above principle is that if society has some funds it wants to invest, it will desire to invest them in projects yielding the highest rates of return. If an investment in physical capital yields a 20 percent rate of return and the same funds invested in schooling yield (all things considered) only a 10 percent return, society will clearly prefer to invest in physical capital. As long as the two rates of return differ, society could be made better off by reducing its investment in low-yield projects and increasing them in those with higher rates of return.

The text has discussed many of the difficulties and biases inherent in estimating rates of return to schooling. However, the general principle of equating the rates of social return on all forms of investments is still a useful one to consider. It suggests, for example, that capital-poor countries should invest in additional schooling only if the returns are very high—higher, in all probability, than the rates of return required for optimality in more capital-rich countries. Indeed, the rates of return to both secondary schooling and higher education appear to be generally higher in less-developed countries than in developed countries. One study estimated that the rate of return on secondary schooling investments was 9.5 percent for a developed country (on average), while for a less-developed country it was 15.2 percent. Comparable rates of return on investments in higher education were 9.4 percent and 12.3 percent, respectively.

SOURCE: George Psacharopoulos, *Returns to Education* (San Francisco: Jossey-Bass, 1973), p. 67.

---

same job as in 1940, they were required to have more education because of the general inflation in levels of educational attainment. While this seems like persuasive evidence in favor of the screening hypothesis, it ignores the fact that the real earnings of sales personnel rose. While the job requirements were the same—fitting and selling shoes—the salesperson of the 1960s needed a higher marginal product than his or her counterpart of the 1940s. This higher marginal productivity could have been achieved by harder work and improved store layout or it could have been the result of more knowledgeable sales personnel. Exactly how the increase was obtained is unknown, but one cannot rule out improvements in human capital as a partial cause.

Thus, just about any evidence offered to support one side of the argument can be accommodated by the other side. Perhaps the best resolution of this issue relies on economic reasoning. We know that college, for example, is very expensive and that to induce students to attend requires a reasonable return on their investment. Thus, to obtain college graduates, employers must pay them wages high enough to compensate them for their investment. If their investment costs are $60,000, employers must pay them wages whose present value is at least $60,000 higher than if they did not attend.[27] In short, a college graduate costs an employer at least $60,000 more than hiring a high school graduate in present-value terms.

Now the college graduate may in fact be worth $60,000 more because of his or her productive characteristics. However, if these characteristics existed prior to college and were unaffected by college, it would pay the firm to find its own method of sorting high school graduates in order to find the best potential workers. As long as the methods it used were as reliable and cost less than a college education ($60,000 per worker), it would be profitable to adopt them. The firm could pay lower wages to their workers because these workers would be spared the expense of college.

The fact that firms have not generally substituted their own screening devices for the educational requirements widely used suggests one of two things. Either education *does* enhance worker productivity or it is a *cheaper* screening tool than any other that firms could use. In either case, the fact that employers are willing to pay a high price for an educated work force *seems* to suggest that education produces social benefits.[28]

Government Training Programs

Questions about the social benefits and costs of educational investments can be extended from general schooling to *particular* job training programs, where the questions are generally easier to answer.

Beginning in the early 1960s, the federal government became heavily involved in programs to increase worker skills. In 1978, for example, 856,000 workers were enrolled in federally funded classroom or on-the-job training programs, at a cost of close to $2,000 per trainee on the average. One need not be a hard-bitten cynic to ask, "Are these programs worth their cost?" At times the answer seems to be a clear-cut "No."

During the 1960s, one government training program was aimed primarily at blacks in the poverty-stricken Mississippi-delta area. When delta training programs were geared to produce more than 8,000 trainees a year, available jobs for trainees were opening up at a rate of 3,000 per year.[29] Given this lack of job openings the

---

[27]If some of the benefits of college attendance are *consumption* goods, the investment costs that employees must recoup are, of course, less than $60,000.

[28]For an interesting test of whether educational investments contain a screening component, see John G. Riley, "Testing the Educational Screening Hypothesis," *Journal of Political Economy* 87 (October 1979):S227–S252.

[29]Michael J. Piore, "Negro Workers in the Mississippi Delta: Problems of Displacement and Adjustment," in *Perspectives on Poverty and Income Distribution*, ed. James G. Scoville (Lexington, Mass.: D.C. Heath, 1971), pp. 151–57.

programs became, in effect, welfare programs—valued for the stipend they paid trainees rather than their future benefits. Trainees had no incentive to graduate and tried to stay in the program as long as possible.

While it can be argued that enhancing the incomes of poor delta blacks is itself a worthy enterprise, training programs are not efficient means of doing this. They require society to pay the salaries of instructors (who are not poor) and to purchase capital equipment, funds which might better be used if they were given directly to the poor.

The intent of a properly conceived job skills training program is to enhance private and social productivity by training workers to do jobs that are in demand. Some policymakers have followed a *personnel planning* approach in deciding how many workers, in what fields, to train. This personnel planning approach asks employers how many persons with certain kinds of qualifications they will need, projects the numbers likely to be supplied by other sources, and recommends filling the gap with government training programs. While this method, if successfully used, should avoid the problems mentioned in the case of the delta trainees, it does suffer the fatal flaw of ignoring *costs:*

> The manpower planner who plans supply to match demand asks the *wrong* questions. He asks, "What is the absorptive capacity of the economy for persons with different skills and educational attainments?" and does not consider the costs of schooling at all. If employers say (or his calculations lead him to believe) that an extra graduate would be hired, the manpower planner directs the education system to produce an extra graduate. He does not ask, "What is the nature of the work the graduate will perform and what benefits will he confer on society?" Nor does he ask, "How much will it cost society to educate another graduate? Do the benefits justify the costs?"[30]

The only way one can be sure that investments in training programs are socially productive is to weigh their costs against the increases in productivity they permit. Since theory implies that marginal productivity and wages are roughly equal, one can look at the wage increases of trainees to obtain an approximation of productivity increases. For example, if a worker would have earned $8,000 per year had she not had training and earns $8,600 a year after training, the program has pretty clearly increased her productivity by $600 per year. This yearly benefit to her (and society) must then be weighed against the cost of training in order to see if the rate of return is as large as it would be if the funds had been invested elsewhere.

Weighing costs against returns is not an easy job, primarily because one must find some way of estimating what trainees would have earned in the absence of the program. One way to make such an estimate is to project the earnings based on past earnings trends, taking note of earnings trends among comparable workers who did not enter the training program. A comprehensive study of 13,000 people who received training in 1964 under the federal Manpower Development and Training Act (MDTA) found that, for males, yearly increases in earnings were in the $150–

---

[30]Gary S. Fields, "Private and Social Returns to Education in Labour Surplus Economies," *Eastern Africa Economic Review* 4, 1 (June 1972): 43.

Example 9.4
Communists or (Human) Capitalists?

The concepts of human capital theory are neither unknown nor ignored in the Soviet Union. A study of wages in the American, German, Dutch, Italian, and Russian steel industries, for example, found that the wage premiums skilled workers in Russia command over unskilled workers are much larger than in the other countries. In fact, the range of wages paid to blast-furnace and open-hearth workers in the Soviet Union is roughly twice the range paid to comparable American workers. Why do these large wage differentials exist in a country supposedly dedicated to the ideal of equality?

According to the Soviet managers, the Soviet Union places extraordinary emphasis on the education and training of its workers:

> The Soviet government recognizes that such training costs the individual effort and time, and it is willing to reward him by promotion to distinctly higher-paying jobs. . . . In other words . . . the big wage-rate differentials are part and parcel of a tremendous effort to raise the qualifications and performance of workers in the Soviet iron and steel industry.

SOURCE: M. Gardner Clark, "Comparative Wage Structures in the Steel Industry of the Soviet Union and Western Countries," *Proceedings of the Thirteenth Annual Meeting, Industrial Relations Research Association* (Madison, Wis.: IRRA, 1961), pp. 266–88.

---

500 range, with the effects declining by half over a five-year post-training period. For females the gains were in the $300–600 range, with no decline over time.[31]

Do these returns justify the costs? The costs per student in this program were $1,800. If a 10 percent rate of return on this investment were to be earned indefinitely, the gains would have to amount to $180 a year. The results for men roughly meet this standard, while those for women clearly exceed it. Thus, the MDTA program appears to have been a good investment in 1964, although the results indicate that training for females was a better investment and should, therefore, have been expanded. (Later classes of trainees did not experience as high a rate of return as the 1964 class.)

APPLICATIONS OF HUMAN CAPITAL THEORY

The theory of human capital can be used to explain several interesting phenomena in the labor market. This section will apply the theory to post-school investments in training, the labor force behavior of women, and the distribution of earnings.

---

[31]Orley Ashenfelter, "Estimating the Effect of Training Programs on Earnings," *Review of Economics and Statistics* 60, 1 (February 1978): 47–57. Evidence of the effects of more recent training programs is found in Lauri J. Bassi, "The Effects of CETA on the Postprogram Earnings of Participants," *Journal of Human Resources* 18(Fall 1983): 539–57.

Post-Schooling Investments and Age/Earnings Profiles

Schooling is largely a full-time, formally organized activity. However, there are less formal kinds of human capital investments that are more difficult to observe. These investments take the form of training that normally occurs in the work place. Some of this "training" is *learning by doing* (as one hammers nails month after month, one's skills naturally improve), but much of it takes place on the job, under close supervision, or consists of a formal program in the work place. All forms of training are costly in the sense that the productivity of learners is low, and all represent a conscious *choice* on the part of the employer to accept lower current productivity in exchange for higher output later. It has been estimated that the average worker acquires the equivalent of at least two years of college in on-the-job training and that the annual cost of such training amounts to 3 percent of gross national product![32]

Who bears the cost of on-the-job training? You will recall that Chapter 5 argued that the cost of *specific training,* training of use *only* to one's employer, is shared by the worker and firm. The employee might be paid a wage greater than marginal product *(MP)* during the training period, but after training the employee's wage is below *MP* (but above what the employee could get elsewhere). In the case of general training, in which employees acquire skills they can use elsewhere, they alone pay the training costs.

How do employees pay the costs of general training provided by their employer? They work for a wage lower than they would get if they were not receiving training. Their wage is equal to their *MP,* which is, of course, decreased during the training period when trainees require close supervision or time off the job to engage in classroom learning. Why do employees accept this lower wage? They accept it for the same reason that some decide to obtain schooling: in the expectation of improving the present value of their lifetime earnings. In other words, employees incur current investment costs (lower wages) to obtain increased earnings later.

The timing of post-schooling investments.   This chapter has demonstrated that if people are going to invest in themselves, they will tend to undertake most of the investment at younger ages for two reasons:

1. Investments made at younger ages have a longer period over which to capture returns and thus tend to have higher total benefits.
2. One big cost of investing in education and training is forgone earnings, and this cost rises as one gets older and earnings become higher (if for no other reason, because of learning by doing).

Consequently, putting off human capital investments lowers the returns on such investments.

It is not surprising to find, then, that schooling, largely a full-time activity, is

---

[32]Jacob Mincer, "On-the-Job Training: Costs, Returns, and Some Implications," *Journal of Political Economy* (Supplement 1962), pp. 50–79.

followed by on-the-job training, which is normally a part-time activity. Further, we also find that job training declines with age, being most heavily concentrated in one's early years on the job when opportunity costs are lower. However, in the case of job training, where scholarships and loans are not available and where the training is part time, investment will not take place all at once. Too much current consumption would have to be forgone by the ordinary worker if one's entire lifetime amount of job training were acquired completely in the first two years of one's career. Thus, employees tend to parcel out their job training over a number of years but gradually reduce such training as time goes by.

Timing of investment and age/earnings profiles.

The above theory of post-schooling investments helps explain why age/earnings profiles are concave: rising more rapidly at first, then flattening out, and ultimately falling (see Figure 9.12). Earnings, low at first because of training investments, rise quickly as new skills are acquired. However, as workers grow older, the pace of training investment slows and so does the rate at which productivity increases. At the end of one's working life skills may have depreciated, as a result of lack of continued investment and the aging process, to the extent that retirement, semiretirement, or a change in jobs is necessary for many workers. This depreciation contributes to the downturn in *average* earnings near retirement age.

The fanning out of age/earnings profiles by education.

As noted earlier in this chapter, the differences in average earnings between people of the same age but different educational levels increase over time (see Figure 9.11). This phenomenon is also consistent with what human capital theory would predict.

The answer to the question "Who will invest most in post-school training?" should be familiar by now. Those who expect the highest benefits and learn most quickly will do the most investing in job training. The fact that they learn rapidly shortens the training period, which both reduces investment costs and increases the duration of benefits. But who are these fast learners? They are most likely the people who, because of their abilities, were best able to reap benefits from formal schooling! Thus, human capital theory leads us to expect workers who invested more in schooling to also invest more in post-schooling job training.

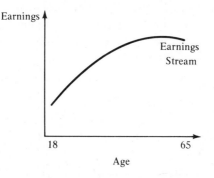

FIGURE 9.12   Age/Earnings Profile

The tendency of the better-educated workers to invest more in job training explains why their age/earnings profiles start low, rise quickly, and keep rising after the profiles of their less-educated counterparts have leveled off. Their earnings rise more quickly because they are investing more heavily in job training, and they rise for a longer time for the same reason. In other words, people with the ability to learn quickly select the ultimately high-paying jobs where much learning is required and thus put their abilities to greatest advantage.

Women and the Acquisition of Human Capital

As implied in Chapters 6 and 7, the career pattern of many married women has tended to consist of distinct stages. First there is a period of employment preceding childbirth. Following the birth of the first child is a period of nonparticipation in the labor force, followed by a return to labor market participation, often on a part-time or temporary basis. A study conducted on data collected in the 1960s found that the first stage of participation usually lasted 3 or 4 years and that the second stage of nonparticipation usually lasted 7 years,[33] although it is likely that the former period has lengthened and the latter shortened.

The interrupted nature of many women's careers has profound implications for the acquisition of education and training. First, because women's careers are usually shorter than men's, they have less time to reap the rewards of investments in human capital. This lowers the benefits of such investments as schooling and training, rendering women less likely than men to invest.

Second, the interruptions add further incentives to avoid costly investments. During the period of nonparticipation in the labor market, skills depreciate and the continuity of experience is broken. Previous investments in human capital may become almost useless, especially in highly technical, ever-changing fields such as law, medicine, engineering, and research. Thus, many women in the prematernal years might be expected to avoid investments that will lose their value during the years of child rearing, thereby avoiding occupations that require continuity of experience or training to be successful.

Human capital theory therefore predicts that women will acquire less schooling and less training than men. The evidence is generally consistent with these predictions, but rapid changes have been occurring. The above predictions of human capital theory, it must be remembered, are for "traditional" women—those who have, or expect to have, interrupted labor-market careers. To the extent that women's expectations concerning their jobs are changing, these predictions will be less and less supported by the data.

Women and schooling.   When one considers the reduced benefits traditional women receive from a human capital investment relative to those for men, it is not surprising that, historically, relatively fewer of them attended college. Table 9.2

---

[33]These data are taken from Jacob Mincer and Solomon Polachek, "Family Investments in Human Capital: Earnings of Women," *Journal of Political Economy* 82,2(March/April 1974):S76–S108.

TABLE 9.2   Percentages of Women in Selected Educational Categories, 1971 and 1980

Category	1971	1980
Graduating seniors, high school	50.4	50.8
College students	41.8	51.4
Graduating seniors, bachelor's degree	43.4	49.0
Graduating with master's degree	40.1	49.4
Graduating with doctoral degree	14.3	29.7

SOURCES: U.S. National Center for Education Statistics, *The Condition of Education* (1983), Tables 1.23, 2.1, 2.19; U.S. National Center for Education Statistics, *Digest of Education Statistics 1973* (1974), Table 67.

demonstrates that as late as 1971, females—who made up 50–51 percent of high school graduates—made up only about 42 percent of college students. Slightly fewer women went on to obtain master's degrees, and far fewer women obtained doctoral degrees. By 1980, however, women and men were almost equally represented among high school, college, and master's graduates. Only at the doctoral level were women severely underrepresented in 1980, and even there the proportion of women had doubled in nine years.

The data in Table 9.2 thus suggest a marked change in the relative benefits and costs of investments in higher education among younger women. Sex differences in major fields of study persist, though, suggesting that young women are still more likely than men to choose occupations in which interrupted careers are less damaging. For example, Table 9.3 reveals that in 1980 women were much more likely than men to major in education and much less likely to major in business or engineering. However, shifts away from tradition can be seen even here, with a rise in female business majors from 1969 to 1980.

TABLE 9.3   Percentages of Bachelor's and Master's Degrees Conferred, by Selected Major Field of Study and Sex, 1969 and 1980

	1969				1980			
	Bachelor's		Master's		Bachelor's		Master's	
	Men	Women	Men	Women	Men	Women	Men	Women
Business	21	3	16	1	26	14	28	8
Engineering	10	a	12	a	13	1	10	1
Education	9	36	27	53	7	19	20	49
Health professions	1	5	2	3	2	12	3	8
All majors	100	100	100	100	100	100	100	100

aNegligible.
SOURCES: U.S. National Center for Education Statistics, *Digest of Education Statistics 1970* (1970), Table 117; *Digest of Education Statistics 1982* (1982), Table 108.

Women and job training. Besides reduced incentives to invest in schooling, women have had fewer incentives than men to invest in job training. As a result, women have not typically found themselves in jobs with steep age/earnings profiles. While we lack the data necessary to track the earnings of individual women through time, we can plot (as we did for men) average earnings of each age group. As Figure 9.13 shows, the age/earnings profiles for women are very flat: older women do not appear to earn much more than younger women. We can conclude from this that experience-related increases in productivity have not been a big influence on women's wages, which implies that the acquisition of job training has not been very widespread among women.

One reason for the lack of job training among traditional women may be their shorter and more interrupted careers, which reduces both their incentives and the incentives of their employers to engage in such training. Another reason, however, may be various forms of discrimination (see Chapter 14, "Discrimination," for

FIGURE 9.13   Total Money Earnings (mean), Full-Time Female Workers, 1981

SOURCE: U.S. Bureau of the Census, *Money Income in 1981 of Families and Persons in the United States*, Current Population Reports, Series P-60, No. 137 (1983), Table 48.

further discussion of women's earnings). Nevertheless, at least some of the differences between the earnings of men and women are due to differences in the acquisition of human capital. The magnitude of these differences will be addressed in Chapter 14.

Human Capital and the Distribution of Earnings

Society is often as interested in the *distribution* of income as it is in the average *level* of income. For example, it is frequently asserted that the United States is a rich country but one in which advantaged workers are rewarded handsomely while those less fortunate receive a very small portion of the national wealth. To evaluate this assertion that the outcome of our market system is unfair requires data on the *distribution* of income. Such distribution data are needed to answer questions like, "How much more does the top 10 percent of the population make than the bottom 10 percent?"

This section presents a few basic facts about the distribution of both family *income* and individual *earnings* in the United States and uses human capital theory to explain certain characteristics of the distribution of *earnings*. Earnings are considered separately from income because income can include rents, dividends, interest, and income maintenance payments that are not the result of labor market transactions and are therefore not the subject of human capital theory.[34]

Statistical concepts.   To understand certain basic concepts related to the distribution of income (or the distribution of earnings) it is helpful to think in graphic

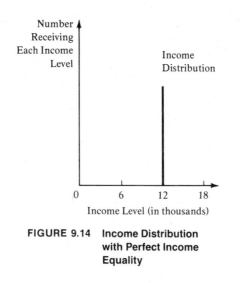

FIGURE 9.14   **Income Distribution with Perfect Income Equality**

---

[34]Because the availability of loans for human capital investments is imperfect, students from wealthy families face fewer constraints in making such investments than others. Thus, financial and human wealth are interconnected to some extent.

terms. Consider a simple plotting of the number of people receiving each given level of income. If everyone made the same income—say $12,000 per year—there would be no dispersion or disparities in income. The graph of the income distribution would look like Figure 9.14.

If there *were* disparities in the income people received, these disparities could be relatively large or relatively small. If the average level of income received was $12,000 and virtually all people received incomes very close to the average, the *dispersion* of incomes would be small. If the average was $12,000 but some made much more and some much less, the dispersion of incomes would be large. In Figure 9.15 two hypothetical income distributions are illustrated. Distribution *A* exhibits smaller dispersion than distribution *B*. Incomes in *A* are more closely bunched and do not show wide differences. We could conclude that, because of its smaller dispersion, distribution *A* exhibits a *greater degree of equality*.

While for most purposes the degree of income dispersion is of most importance in judging equality, it is also interesting to inquire if the distribution of incomes (or earnings) is *symmetric* or not. If the distributions are symmetric, as in Figure 9.15, then as many people earn $X less than average as earn $X more than average. Put differently, the dispersion of incomes for the poorest half of society mirrors the dispersion for the richest half if the distribution is symmetric. If the distribution is not symmetric, we say it is *skewed*, meaning that one part of the distribution is bunched together and the other part is relatively dispersed (see Figure 9.16). In fact, the actual distributions of income and earnings in the United States are skewed to the right, meaning that they are bunched at the left (at the lower levels of income) and widely dispersed at the higher income levels.

Skewness is an important characteristic of the distribution of income or earnings because the concept suggests another dimension of fairness. For example, many less-developed countries do not have a sizable middle class. Such countries

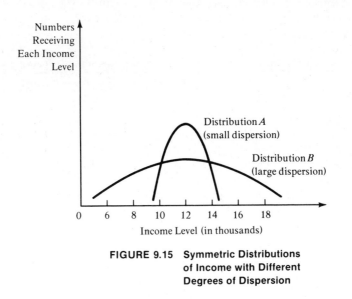

FIGURE 9.15   Symmetric Distributions of Income with Different Degrees of Dispersion

FIGURE 9.16   Skewed Distribution
of Income

have a huge number of very poor families and a tiny minority of very wealthy families. Thus, the distribution of income in these countries, normally considered unfair, is highly skewed to the right.

While dispersion and skewness in the distribution of earnings are indicators of inequality in labor market outcomes, their presence can be at least partially explained by investments in human capital.

Dispersion.   Although incomes in the United States are disparate, there is no evidence of a recent trend toward greater equality. Note from Table 9.4 that the 20 percent of families that have the lowest incomes obtain about 5 percent of the total income received, while the top 20 percent obtain more than 40 percent of the total income. Neither figure has changed very much since 1947. This pattern of income dispersion is not unique to the United States; Table 9.5 gives similar data on the

TABLE 9.4   **Distribution of Income Among Families at Different Income Levels, 1947–1981**

	Percent of Aggregate Income Received					
Income Level	*1947*	*1957*	*1967*	*1973*	*1977*	*1981*
Total families	100.0	100.0	100.0	100.00	100.0	100.0
Lowest fifth	5.0	5.1	5.5	5.5	5.2	5.0
Second fifth	11.9	12.7	12.4	11.9	11.6	11.3
Third fifth	17.0	18.1	17.9	17.5	17.5	17.4
Fourth fifth	23.1	23.8	23.9	24.0	24.2	24.4
Highest fifth	43.0	40.4	40.4	41.1	41.5	41.9
Top 5 percent	17.5	15.6	15.2	15.5	15.7	15.4
Median family income (in 1981 dollars)	$12,342	$17,660	$23,721	$25,521	$24,782	$23,873

Note: The income (before taxes) boundaries of each fifth of families, arranged by income in 1981, were: lowest fifth, under $10,918; second fifth, $10,918 to $18,552; third fifth, $18,553 to $26,528; fourth fifth, $26,529 to $37,547; highest fifth, over $37,457; top 5 percent, over $58,554.
SOURCE: *Money Income of Households, Families, and Persons in the United States, 1981,* Current Population Reports, Series P-60, No. 137 (1983), Tables 16 and 17.

TABLE 9.5   Percentage of National Income Received by the
Lowest- and Highest-Income Families in Seven
Countries, 1973

| | Percentage of National Income Received by | |
Country	Lowest 20 Percent	Highest 20 Percent
Australia	6.8	39.7
Denmark	5.6	44.5
France	5.1	42.5
Germany	6.0	46.7
Japan	3.8	46.2
Sweden	6.0	40.5
United Kingdom	5.6	40.2

SOURCE: Paolo Roberti, "Income Inequality in Some Western
Countries: Patterns and Trends," *International Journal of Social
Economics* 5(1978):22–41.

percentage of national income received by the lowest and highest 20 percent of
families in seven other countries for 1973.

Another way to measure inequality is by comparing the incomes of those whose
income ranks at the 20th percentile (where 80 percent of the population has a higher
income) with those whose income ranks at the 80th percentile (where only 20
percent of the population has a higher income). In 1981 those families at the 80th
percentile received an income of $37,457—3.4 times higher than the $10,918
received by those at the 20th percentile. The absolute difference in income between
the two groups was over $26,000.

As noted earlier, this chapter is interested *not* in the distribution of *income* but
in the distribution of *earnings*. Three major factors could cause the distribution of
income to be different from that of earnings:

1. The owners of financial capital (stocks, bonds, real estate) are probably
   people who also have high earnings, a situation that would cause the
   distribution of income to be even more unequal than the distribution of
   earnings.
2. Many income maintenance programs redistribute income in favor of those
   with low earnings, this time making the distribution of income more equal
   than the distribution of earnings.
3. Many families have more than one wage-earner. If high-earning men tend to
   marry high-earning women, the distribution of family income would tend to
   be more unequal than the distribution of earnings.

The 1981 distribution of earnings for men aged 25–64 is graphed in Figure
9.17. (The distribution of earnings for men of this age group is less affected by
variations in hours of work and labor force participation status than the earnings of
any other group.) It is obvious from Figure 9.17 that there is considerable dispersion
(as well as skewness) in the earnings of this group. However, this dispersion turns
out to be slightly less than that noted above for family income. For example, the
ratio of *incomes* at the 80th percentile to those at the 20th percentile was 3.4 to 1,
while the corresponding ratio for male *earnings* is 2.3 to 1. The absolute difference
in earnings between males at these two percentiles, $30,000 at the 80th and $13,000

FIGURE 9.17   Distribution of Earnings, Men 25–64, 1981

SOURCE: U.S. Bureau of the Census, *Money Income of Households, Families, and Persons in the United States: 1981* (1983), Table 50.

at the 20th percentile, is also smaller. It would appear, therefore, that the forces tending to make earnings *more* equal than incomes are somewhat dominant.

It is not surprising, of course, that earnings vary. This chapter, for example, has shown that much of the higher earnings received by the well-educated and highly trained is a return on their investments in human capital. In fact, in any society in which people can make themselves more productive only through a costly investment of time and money, we would expect to observe earnings differentials. Not *all* the observed dispersion in earnings is related to the normal returns on human capital investments, but *some* dispersion is to be expected when these investments are being made by some people and not others.

A portion of the overall dispersion in earnings among men aged 25–64 is the result of combining men of different ages in the same distribution. We know that productivity increases over time, so older men typically earn more than younger men. This source of dispersion is probably not of much concern to society because everyone's income follows the pattern of being relatively low in the younger years.

What may be of more concern is the dispersion of earnings *within* age groups. Here human capital theory offers a clear-cut prediction. When people are young, the job training in which some people are investing keeps their earnings close to (or below) what those who are not investing receive. As time passes, however, the earnings of those who have invested are raised considerably above the earnings of others. We noted this phenomenon when we examined age/earnings profiles: earnings "fan out" with age. Hence, due to the acquisition of more human capital by some than others, the dispersion of earnings among older workers is expected to be greater than among younger workers.

Human capital theory can thus help explain the presence and patterns of dispersion in earnings. Can it also help explain why the earnings distribution is skewed?

Skewness. It has long been a puzzle to people why the distribution of earnings is skewed. *If* ability is distributed symmetrically and is reflected in productivity, it would seem that earnings should be symmetrically distributed. Human capital theory suggests at least two reasons why, even if there *were* a symmetric distribution of ability, one would expect to find earnings skewed to the right.

First, it is true that *if* ability were symmetrically distributed and no one invested in education or training in order to enhance their productivity, the earnings distribution would be symmetric. However, the people who make investments that increase their earnings later in life tend to be high-ability people. Thus, while low-ability people tend to go through their careers with their productivity relatively unchanged by investment, high-ability people augment their productivity by investments. The more ability they have, the more they tend to invest. Thus, education and training tend to increase the earnings of workers in some rough proportion to their abilities, which extends—or *skews*—the distribution at the upper earnings levels.

Second, the discounting process aids the above forces in skewing the distribution of earnings. A person attending graduate school for one year after graduating from college incurs a greater cost and has a shorter time over which to obtain benefits than a person deciding to attend an extra year of college. The graduate student has higher opportunity costs and is also older and just that much closer to retirement. Therefore, those considering ever-larger investments in schooling will require ever-larger payoffs per year (in the form of earnings increments). This need for ever-larger payoffs in order to encourage greater investments in human capital tends to skew the distribution of earnings. In effect, the larger costs and smaller remaining career life discourage most people from continuing to invest, which serves to handsomely reward those who do undertake the investment (since they are "scarce"). Since these latter people tend to be those of highest ability (they are the ones who can learn with the most ease), the "rich get richer" and the distribution becomes skewed.

While one may be tempted to conclude from this analysis that human capital investments make the distribution of earnings more unequal than it would otherwise be, one must first consider two mitigating factors. First, human capital theory suggests that some of the inequality observed in earnings is a normal return on a prior investment; that is, it is compensation for an earlier period in one's life when earnings were low due to the acquisition of human capital. Second, if access to colleges were severely limited, the lucky few able to advance themselves would reap very large rewards. This limitation on opportunities would impart an extreme skewness to the earnings distribution (very few would get a lot, and most would earn very little). Thus, although human capital acquisitions will impart a rightward skew, widespread availability of educational and training opportunities serves to reduce the skewness relative to what it would be with only limited access to these opportunities.

Policy Application: Human Capital and Earnings in Regulated Industries

Human capital theory can be useful in analyzing policy issues related to employee earnings. One such issue arises in the state regulation of monopolies. State commissions that regulate public utilities (such as telephone, electric, and gas companies) must decide whether all the costs that the utilities incur should be legitimately charged to consumers. It would be obvious to the commission that some costs should not be charged to consumers. For example, if an executive of a company had chartered a plane to take his family on a winter vacation to the Bahamas, surely that cost would be disallowed. Or if a construction contract were awarded to the friend of the president of a local utility without being submitted to competitive bidding, a commission might want to examine that contract closely to make sure the price charged was comparable to what other contractors in the area would have charged.

Deciding whether or not labor costs should be charged to consumers is more difficult. On the one hand, it is often conjectured that employers in regulated industries have less of an incentive to "bargain tough" with the unions that may represent their employees than do employers in nonregulated industries because historically regulatory commissions have allowed utilities to pass all labor cost increases on to consumers (in the form of higher utility prices). If such an argument is valid, it would indicate the need for commissions to carefully scrutinize utilities' wage settlements. On the other hand, it is difficult to decide upon what wage rates a commission should consider "just and reasonable." A utility's work force includes a number of different skill categories, as does the work force of other employers in an area, and making simple comparisons using raw wage-rate data would fail to take into account qualitative differences between work forces.

The human capital framework suggests a more appropriate comparison. According to this framework, better-educated workers receive higher wages than less-educated workers and more-experienced workers get paid more than less-experienced workers. By statistically controlling for such worker characteristics as education and experience, it should be easier to see if employees in a regulated industry are paid more than employees in other firms. When such a comparison was made for telephone workers in New York State, it was found that the utility's employees were paid approximately 9–12 percent more than were other employees with comparable education and experience levels in the state in 1970.[35]

Such evidence in itself does not imply that a public commission should prevent a utility from passing all its labor cost increases on to consumers in the form of higher prices. For example, the wage premium might in some cases be seen as a compensating differential paid to the utility's employees for more difficult jobs or less favorable working conditions, as discussed in Chapter 8. Nevertheless, the human capital framework does provide a useful starting point for public utility commissions seeking to address the labor cost issue. In the case mentioned above,

---

[35]Ronald G. Ehrenberg, *The Regulatory Process and Labor Earnings* (New York: Academic Press, 1979).

the commission decided not to limit the permissible wage increase but did reserve the right to limit future wage "pass-throughs" if similar comparative studies illustrated the need for such limits.

REVIEW QUESTIONS

1. Why do women receive lower wages, on average, than men of equal age? Why does the discrepancy between earnings for men and women grow with age?
2. Suppose financial aid to college students were financed by income taxes on the general population and the President cut this aid significantly (correspondingly cutting taxes). Analyzing the likely *labor market* effects of these cuts, identify the various groups that would *gain* and *lose* from these cuts over their lifetimes. Discuss your reasoning concerning each in turn. Then analyze the likely effects on the retirement ages of these groups.
3. Many crimes against property (burglary, for example) can be thought of as acts that have immediate gains but entail long-run costs (sooner or later the criminal may be caught and imprisoned). If imprisoned, the criminal loses income from both criminal and noncriminal activities. Using the framework for occupational choice in the long run, analyze what kinds of people are most likely to engage in criminal activities. What can society do to reduce crime?
4. Suppose education provided no *social* benefits of any kind; that is, it did not enhance worker productivity and did not accurately "signal" who was already more productive. What conditions would have to hold for there to be a positive *individual* return to education in this circumstance?
5. Why do those who argue that more education "signals" greater ability believe that the most able people will obtain the most education?

SELECTED READINGS

Becker, Gary. *Human Capital*. New York: National Bureau of Economic Research, 1975.

Berg, Ivar. *Education and Jobs: The Great Training Robbery*. New York: Praeger Publishers, 1970.

Blaug, Mark. "Human Capital Theory: A Slightly Jaundiced Survey." *Journal of Economic Literature* 14 (September 1976):827–55.

Freeman, Richard B. *The Overeducated American*. New York: Academic Press, 1976.

Manski, Charles F., and Wise, David A. *College Choice in America*. Cambridge: Harvard University Press, 1983.

Mincer, Jacob. "On-the-Job Training: Costs, Returns, and Some Implications." *Journal of Political Economy* Supplement 1962:50–79.

Mincer, Jacob. *Schooling, Experience and Earnings*. New York: National Bureau of Economic Research, 1974.

Mincer, Jacob, and Polachek, Solomon. "Family Investments in Human Capital: Earnings of Women." *Journal of Political Economy* 82(March/April 1974):S76–S108.

Schultz, Theodore. *The Economic Value of Education*. New York: Columbia University Press, 1963.

Spence, Michael. "Job Market Signaling." *Quarterly Journal of Economics* 87 (August 1973):355–74.

APPENDIX 9A

"Signaling" in the Labor Market

Chapter 9 discussed both the private and social benefits of education and stressed that individuals will undertake an educational investment if the long-run gains to them outweigh the monetary and psychic costs. *Societal* decisions to invest in education should likewise be made only if the social gains outweigh the social losses; however, Chapter 9 noted that there is a rather lively debate about the nature and extent of the social benefits of formal education. Some believe that education *enhances* worker productivity, while others believe that, at best, education simply *reveals*—or "signals"—the inherent productivity of workers.

This appendix will delve into the signaling aspect of formal education in greater depth.[1] It will analyze the benefits and costs of educational signaling to workers and firms in an example in which it is assumed that education does *not* enhance productivity. Initially, however, it is important to understand just what *signaling* is and why it exists.

An employer seeking to hire workers is never completely sure of the actual productivity of any applicant, and in many cases the employer may remain unsure long after an employee is hired. What an employer *can* observe are certain *indicators* that firms have found (or otherwise believe) to be correlated with productivity: age, race, sex, experience, education, and other personal characteristics. Some

---

[1]This appendix is based on Michael Spence, "Job Market Signaling," *Quarterly Journal of Economics* 87 (August 1973):355–74.

of these indicators—such as race and sex—are immutable. Others, like formal schooling, can be *acquired* by workers. Indicators that can be acquired by individuals can be called *signals;* our analysis will focus on the signaling aspect of formal education.

THE FIRM'S DESIRE FOR SIGNALS

Let us suppose that firms trying to hire new employees in a particular labor market know there are two groups of applicants that exist in roughly equal proportions. One group has a productivity of 2, let us say, and the other group has a productivity of 1. In the absence of screening or applicant signaling, firms would be forced to assume that workers in this market had average productivities of 1.5 and would offer wages up to 1.5.

While workers in this simple example would be receiving what they were worth on *average,* any one firm could increase its profits if it were possible (at no cost) to distinguish between the two groups of applicants. When wages equal 1.5, workers with productivities equal to 1 are receiving more than they are worth. If these applicants could be identified, a firm could increase profits by rejecting their applications and hiring only those with a productivity of 2. These gains might be short-lived if other firms did the same and drove the wage for the more productive workers up to 2. However, the individual firms in a competitive market cannot control or affect the behavior of competitors, and screening would occur as each sought to obtain maximum profit.[2]

WORKER SUPPLY OF SIGNALS

To continue with our example, suppose that firms believe that if an applicant has acquired e^* or more years of schooling, he or she has a productivity of 2. If the applicant has less than e^* years of formal education, it is believed he or she has a productivity of 1. Let us also assume that education does *not* enhance productivity. In what situations, if any, could this use of schooling as a screening device be productive? The answer is that educational signaling can only be useful if the costs to the worker of acquiring the signal are negatively related to productivity.

If firms use e^* as a hiring standard, applicants with schooling of e^* or greater will be preferred if wages for all workers are equal; their wages will eventually be driven up to 2, while those with less than e^* will obtain wages of 1 (see Figure 9A.1). If all applicants could acquire e^* at no cost, they would obviously do so and this screening device would fail; workers of both productivity levels would have at least e^* years of schooling. As we argued in Chapter 9, however, formal schooling

---

[2]The phenomenon here is very similar to the entry of firms into markets with excess profits. The gains from entry are short-lived because the entry of others will drive profits down to the normal level. Individual firms, however, react to the presence of excess profits nevertheless, expecting to catch "a piece of the action" and hoping no one else will be quite as smart as they are!

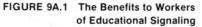

FIGURE 9A.1   **The Benefits to Workers
of Educational Signaling**

is not costless. Furthermore, we also argued that the *psychic* costs of education are probably inversely related to one's ability: those who learn easily can acquire the educational signal (of e^* in this case) more cheaply than others. *If*—and this is crucial—those who have *lower* costs of acquiring education are *also* more productive on the job, then educational signaling can be useful.

To understand the role of costs in signaling, refer to Figure 9A.2, in which the reward structure from Figure 9A.1 is reproduced. If we assume that each year of education costs those with less productivity C and those with greater productivity $C/2$, the fundamental influences on worker choices concerning education are easily seen. Workers will want to choose a level of education at which the difference between benefits (wages) and educational costs are maximized. For those with a productivity of 1 and educational cost of C, the difference between wages and costs is greatest when years of schooling equal zero (distance $A0$). For those whose educational costs are $C/2$, this difference is maximized at e^* (where it equals BD, which is greater than $A0$). Thus, only those with costs of $C/2$—the workers with productivities of 2—acquire e^* years of school.

THE USEFULNESS OF EDUCATIONAL SIGNALING

Several points should be made about our simple example of signaling above. First, workers may not think of themselves as acquiring a signal if they attend school, even though in our example they are. All most workers will know is that by obtaining more education they can increase their wages, and their decision about how much education to acquire depends on the costs and returns to them.

Second, our simple example demonstrated how education could have signaling value even if it did not directly enhance worker productivity. It is necessary to stress, though, that for education to have signaling value in this case, on-the-job productivity and the costs of education must be *negatively* related. This negative relationship is by no means universally accepted, and there are even those who

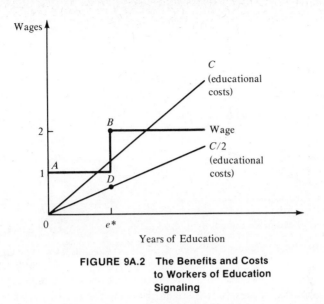

Years of Education

**FIGURE 9A.2 The Benefits and Costs
to Workers of Education
Signaling**

assert that better-educated workers are actually *less* productive.[3] However, if education is *not* a good signal for productivity, firms should eventually find this out and stop using formal schooling as a screening device! (The argument that education will survive as a signal for productivity only if it is an accurate indicator does not suggest, of course, that firms will learn about signaling errors immediately.)

Third, if the signal required by firms were reduced from e^* to e' (in Figure 9A.3), the signaling value of education would be lost. Workers of both productivity levels would find it beneficial to acquire the signal of e' because the distance $A0$ is exceeded by GD for the less productive and by BD for the more productive. Education would cease to be a good screening device for employers to use. A signal of e' could not be an equilibrium signal in the long run because employers would eventually learn that not all workers with e' years of education have a productivity of 2. They would either have to give up on screening and pay a wage of 1.5 or increase hiring standards.

Fourth, increases in the educational signal beyond e^* in our example are not productive. A look back at Figure 9A.2 indicates that individual workers with educational costs of $C/2$ have no incentives to obtain more schooling than e^* because such schooling is costly but results in no higher wage offer. Moreover, if firms increased their minimum hiring standard from e^* to e'' (Figure 9A.3), the signaling value of education would again be lost. Even the more productive workers would not have incentives to acquire an education (because $A0$ exceeds FE), and firms could not distinguish between the two kinds of workers.

---

[3]See Ivar Berg, *Education and Jobs: The Great Training Robbery* (New York: Praeger Publishers, 1970), pp. 85–104, which questions the social value of educational investments.

FIGURE 9A.3 Signaling Failures   FIGURE 9A.4 The Optimum
                                                                Educational Signal

Finally, there *is* an optimum educational signal in our example: the minimum schooling level that successfully distinguishes between the two types of workers. Optimality is reached *just to the right of e*** in Figure 9A.4. A required signal of just beyond *e*** is one that will be acquired by workers of productivity 2, but it will not be acquired by those with productivity 1. If the required signal were reduced below *e***, both kinds of workers would acquire it and signaling value would be lost. If the required signal were increased much beyond *e***—to *e**, say—the signal would still be accurate but would cost more than necessary. Put differently, if *e** were required, the more productive workers would acquire it and the less productive ones would not. However, the extra *e*–e*** years in school would entail social costs for which there were no benefits because *e*** distinguishes between the two types of workers just as well as *e**. The critics of education mentioned in Chapter 9 argue that the escalation of educational standards occurs for jobs in which work requirements are largely unchanged. These critics can be understood as saying that firms require *e** when *e*** would distinguish between workers just as well and be much less costly.[4]

Are there market forces pushing the required signal toward *e***? We have argued that a required signal below *e*** would be unable to discriminate between applicants and would eventually be abandoned by employers. However, if the required signal were initially *e**, there would *also* be forces pushing it back to *e***, although these influences take us outside of our simple model with its fixed wages. Workers who have acquired *e** years of education will be more costly to hire than workers acquiring *e*** because they will want to recoup their educational costs. Noting their higher asking wage, some firms may experiment and hire applicants with only *e*** years of schooling. If these latter workers proved to be just as productive as those with *e** years of schooling, the firms that experimented would be rewarded with extra profits. Other firms would eventually follow, and *e*** would become the equilibrium hiring standard.

---

[4]See Berg, *Education and Jobs*, pp. 38–60.

10

Worker Mobility:
Turnover and Migration

A salient fact about the U.S. economy is the high degree of mobility among its workers. The monthly quit rate in manufacturing industries is 1–3 percent per month, which implies a yearly turnover rate of 12–36 percent. Chapter 8 noted that 25 percent of semiskilled male workers over age 25 in 1965 were employed in *completely different* occupations by 1970. Roughly 25 percent of all workers change the industry in which they work over a three-year period.[1] Moreover, in many cases job mobility is accompanied by geographic mobility. Between 1975 and 1980, for example, 13.6 million people over 20 years of age—9.2 percent of the total—moved between states; 15.5 million more (10.5 percent) moved to a different county within a state. Thus, one fifth of the adult population made a major move in just a five-year period, and the fraction rises to one third when one focuses only on those in their twenties.[2] Finally, the United States admits about 500,000 legal immigrants each year, and the discrepancy between the numbers who want to come and the numbers permitted by law is so great that hundreds of thousands more enter illegally. As of 1980, most experts believed that at least 4 million illegal immigrants were living in this country.

This mobility is not without its costs. Sometimes a temporary loss of income occurs between the time one job is given up and a new one, perhaps in a new place, is obtained. There are direct moving costs when migration occurs. Psychic costs are associated with leaving a familiar job or place and having to become acquainted with a new environment. There can be no doubt, then, that large monetary and psychic costs are borne each year by large numbers of people wanting to improve

---

[1]Lowell E. Gallaway, *Interindustry Labor Mobility in the United States, 1957 to 1960,* Social Security Administration Research Report No. 18 (Washington, D.C.: U.S. Government Printing Office, 1967), p. 29.

[2]U.S. Bureau of the Census, Current Population Reports, *Geographical Mobility: March 1975 to March 1980,* Population Characteristics, Series P-20, No. 368 (December 1981), Table 6.

their lot in life. In this sense mobility represents a significant investment in human capital. Costs are borne in the short run so that benefits will be possible in the long run. The human capital model of mobility described in this chapter offers some clear-cut implications about who invests in mobility and where they go.

The basic human capital model of mobility is a model of "voluntary" mobility undertaken by workers who perceive mobility to be in their self-interest. The factors influencing employer-initiated mobility—layoffs, for example—are quite different, as discussed in Chapter 5.[3] The determinants of voluntary mobility are discussed first, and later in the chapter the testable implications of human capital theory for both migration and job-quitting behavior are analyzed. The chapter will conclude with an economic analysis of immigration and its implications for national policy.

THE DETERMINANTS OF WORKER MOBILITY

The human capital model presented in Chapter 9 can be used to understand and predict worker-initiated mobility. This model views voluntary mobility as an investment in which costs are borne in some early period in order to obtain returns over a longer period of time. If the present value of the benefits associated with mobility exceeds the costs, both monetary and psychic, we assume that people will decide to change jobs or move, or both. If the discounted stream of benefits is not as large as the costs, then people will decide against such a change.

What determines the present value of the net benefits of mobility—that is, the benefits minus the costs—determines the mobility decision. These factors can be better identified by writing out the formula one would use if one were to precisely calculate these net benefits:

$$\text{Present Value of Net Benefits} = \sum_{t=1}^{T} \frac{B_{jt} - B_{ot}}{(1 + r)^t} - C \qquad (10.1)$$

where:

B_{jt} = the utility derived from the new job (j) in the year t;
B_{ot} = the utility derived from the old job (o) in the year t;
T = the length of time (in years) one expects to work at job j;
r = the rate of discount;
C = the utility lost in the move itself (direct and psychic costs); and
Σ = a summation—in this case the summation of the yearly discounted net benefits over a period running from year 1 to year T.

Clearly, the present value of the net benefits of mobility will be larger the greater is the utility derived from the new job, the less happy one is in the job of origin, the smaller are the immediate costs associated with the change, and the longer one expects to be in the new job or live in the new area (that is, the greater is T). These observations lead to some clear-cut predictions about which groups in

---

[3]The distinction between "employee-" and "employer-initiated" mobility is more apparent than real, as we point out later in this chapter.

Example 10.1

Job Satisfaction: An Alternative View

In the last decade or so, managers and researchers have expressed much interest in job satisfaction, and most are inclined to view dissatisfaction as a result of *employer* policies concerning job tasks, working conditions, or compensation. Economists, however, view the phenomenon of job satisfaction somewhat differently. Workers are viewed as making choices of jobs and employers from among competing alternatives; if they are unhappy in a particular occupation or with a particular employer, they will be motivated to seek other employment. Moreover, as noted in Chapter 8, pecuniary and nonpecuniary aspects of jobs are viewed as substitutes for each other; higher wages, for example, might compensate for poor working conditions and lead to overall satisfaction with one's job. Thus, economists tend to view job satisfaction as an outcome of the employer-worker *matching* process and not solely as the result of employer policies. If the matching process is impeded by factors inhibiting mobility, workers may be "stuck" in jobs they dislike. If workers are aware of alternatives and are able to leave jobs that are unsatisfactory for them, they should eventually find something close to their best option.

A survey of job satisfaction around 1970 found that 47 percent of all workers were "very satisfied" with their jobs and 38 percent were "somewhat satisfied," while only 15 percent were either "not too satisfied" or "not at all satisfied." A more sophisticated statistical analysis of job satisfaction responses in this survey found that workers were more likely to indicate feelings of satisfaction as they became older and as their *actual* earnings exceeded an estimate of their *alternative* earnings.

Taken together, the above results offer some support for economists' views. The small number of people who report themselves even mildly dissatisfied, coupled with the finding that dissatisfaction falls with age, suggests that job mobility may be an antidote for dissatisfaction. It appears that employees "try out" occupations and employers and leave situations they dislike. If they realize that the job they have is on the whole better-paying than their alternatives, they express greater satisfaction and are presumably less likely to leave it. Thus, a trial-and-error process, fueled by information about one's alternatives, may well be at work producing generally satisfactory matches between workers and jobs in the long run.

SOURCE: Daniel S. Hamermesh, "The Economics of Job Satisfaction," Technical Analysis Paper No. 22, Office of the Assistant Secretary for Policy, Evaluation, and Research, U.S. Department of Labor (May 1974), Appendix. A revised version of this paper, without the appendix, was published with the same title in Orley Ashenfelter and Wallace Oates, eds., *Essays in Labor Market Analysis* (New York: John Wiley and Sons, 1978).

society will be most mobile and about the *patterns* of mobility one would expect to observe. These predictions are analyzed in the following sections on migration and quit behavior.

GEOGRAPHIC MOBILITY

When people are asked about their reasons for moving, 70–85% of them cite economic reasons. While about one third of those who moved to a different area in the late 1960s or early 1970s stayed with their current employers, in about two thirds of the cases a change in employer took place. Taking into account those who say their moves were motivated by economic factors and who also changed jobs, it appears that one third to one half of all moves are caused by the decision to change jobs.[4] This emphasis on job change suggests that the implications of the human capital theory for migration can be tested in the labor market.

Comparing Wages and Employment Opportunities

If job changes are the dominant factor motivating mobility, then we should observe people migrating from areas where wages and employment opportunities are relatively poor to areas where they are relatively good. Three interrelated patterns of internal migration can be observed in the United States over the recent decades: rural-to-urban shifts, the movement of blacks, and the interregional flows of people.

Rural-to-urban movements.   Huge movements of people from rural to urban areas have occurred in this century as farming jobs have diminished in number.[5] In 1910, 54 percent of the U.S. population lived in rural areas—that is, areas with less than 2,500 inhabitants. By 1980 this percentage had stabilized at 26 percent. In the 1960s alone, farming employment fell by 40 percent, and the rural areas of California, the Dakotas, Nebraska, and Kansas experienced population losses of 10–16 percent. Interestingly enough, the *overall* rural population fell by only 0.9 percent during the 1960s, while it rose by the same percentage (11 percent) as the urban population in the 1970s. This recent change reflects, to a large degree, the extension of suburban areas into neighboring rural counties and thus does not contradict our observation that people move to where the jobs are.

Migration of blacks.   A dramatic characteristic of rural-urban migration in this century has been the massive movement of blacks out of the rural South to urban areas in the non-South. This movement began during World War I, when wartime production created jobs in the urbanized, industrial states in the North. In the 1920s this migration continued as 800,000 blacks left the South, headed primarily for big cities in the North. This flow was cut in half during the 1930s, when the Great

---

[4]Ann P. Bartel, "The Migration Decision: What Role Does Job-Mobility Play?" *American Economic Review* 69(December 1979):775–86. See also Larry Schroeder, "Interrelatedness of Occupational and Geographical Labor Mobility," *Industrial and Labor Relations Review* 29(April 1976):405–11.

[5]Data in this section are from the *Manpower Report of the President* (Washington, D.C.: U.S. Government Printing Office, 1974), pp.77–78, and U.S. Bureau of the Census, *1980 Census of the Population, U.S. Summary* PC80-1-A1 (1983), Table 3.

Depression diminished job opportunities in the industrial sector, but rose to 1.6 million during the war-dominated 1940s. In the essentially prosperous decades of the 1950s and 1960s, 2.9 million more blacks left the South.

Undoubtedly part of the migration of blacks reflects the decline in farming employment. Many southern states have also experienced outflows of whites. More whites left the states of Alabama, Kentucky, Oklahoma, and West Virginia during the 1950s and 1960s than entered them, while Arkansas, the Carolinas, Georgia, Mississippi, and Tennessee experienced out-migration of whites in the 1950s but net in-migration of whites during the 1960s.

That the migration of blacks out of the South is not completely due to the decline in agricultural jobs is clearly indicated by the fact that while blacks were *leaving* the South during the 1960s, whites were, on balance, *flowing into* the South as jobs there expanded. Because basic federal civil rights laws concerning segregation and voting were not passed until the mid-'60s and programs aimed at eliminating job discrimination were not implemented until the late '60s, it is not farfetched to speculate that much of the black migration out of the South was induced by perceptions of greater freedom and opportunities elsewhere. As discrimination lessened in the 1970s, however, and blacks began to share in the general economic expansion underway in the South, there was, on balance, a movement of blacks *into* the South. Between 1970 and 1980 there was a net influx of 209,000 blacks into the South—the first time this had occurred in the 20th century. Interestingly, migration of blacks to the South during the 1970s was far greater than to any other region.[6]

Regional migration.

Further evidence to support the view that people move from regions where opportunities are poor to regions where they are better can be found by examining regional migration. The older, slow-growing industrial states of New York, Pennsylvania, Ohio, Illinois, and Michigan are experiencing outmigration, while the faster-growing states in the South and West are the recipients of an influx of migrants. During 1975–80, for example, the northeast and northcentral states had a net outflow of 2.5 million people, while the South and West had net inflows of 1.8 million and 700,000, respectively. The net inflow to the South is a complete turnaround from the 1950s, when the region was largely rural and offered relatively few job opportunities. As the South has industrialized and opportunities have inproved, it has become the region with the most net in-migration.

Human capital theory predicts that people will move from areas of relatively poor earnings possibilities to places where opportunities are better. While the general regional flows of people support this prediction, the prediction can also be tested by looking at the characteristics of more specific areas from which and to which people move. In general, the results of such studies suggest that the "pull" of good opportunities in the areas of destination are stronger than the "push" of

---

[6]U.S. Bureau of the Census, *Statistical Abstract of the United States: 1982–83* (December 1982), Table 13. Other data in this section were obtained from the *Manpower Report of the President,* 1974, pp. 90–97, and U.S. Bureau of the Census, *Statistical Abstract of the U.S.,* 99th ed. (Washington, D.C.: U.S. Government Printing Office, 1978), Table 26.

poor opportunities in the areas of origin. In other words, while people are more attracted to places where earnings are expected to be better, they do not necessarily come from areas where opportunities are poorest.

The most consistent finding in these detailed studies is that people are attracted to areas where the real earnings of full-time workers are highest. One might also expect that the chances for obtaining work in a new area would also affect that area's attractiveness. One way to measure job availability in an area is to use the unemployment rate, but the studies find no consistent relationship between unemployment and in-migration, perhaps because the number of people moving with a job already in hand is three times as large as the number moving *to look* for work.[7] If one already has a job in a particular field, the *overall* unemployment rate is irrelevant.

Most studies have found that, contrary to what one might expect, the characteristics of the place of origin do not appear to have much net influence on migration. One reason for this finding is that while those in the poorest places have the greatest *incentives* to move, the very poorest areas also tend to have people with lower levels of wealth, education, and skills—the very people who seem least *willing* (or able) to move. To understand this phenomenon, we must turn from the issue of *where* people go to a discussion of *who* is most likely to move.

Personal Characteristics of Movers

Migration is highly selective in the sense that it is not an activity in which all people are equally likely to be engaged. To be specific, mobility is much higher among the young and the better-educated, as human capital theory would suggest.

Age.   Age is the single most important factor in determining who migrates. The peak years for mobility are the ages 22–24, when nearly 20 percent of the population migrates across county or state lines. By age 32 the rate of migration is half what it was in the early twenties, and by age 42 migration is only one fourth as high as it was in the twenties.

There are two explanations for the fact that migration is an activity primarily for the young. First, the younger one is, the greater the potential returns from any human capital investment. As noted earlier, the longer the period over which benefits from an investment can be obtained, the larger is the present value of these benefits.

Second, a large part of the costs of migration are psychic—the losses associated with giving up friends, community ties, and the benefits of knowing one's way around. When one is starting out as an adult, these losses are comparatively small because one is not well established in the adult world. However, as one grows

---

[7]John B. Lansing and Eva Mueller, *The Geographic Mobility of Labor* (Ann Arbor, Mich.: Survey Research Center, University of Michigan, 1967), p. 37. For a review of empirical findings on migration, see Michael Greenwood, "Research on Internal Migration in the United States: A Survey," *Journal of Economic Literature* 13(June 1975):397–433.

older, community ties become stronger and the losses associated with leaving loom larger, thus inhibiting mobility. This line of reasoning is underscored by the fact that, within age groups, unmarried people are more likely to migrate than married ones, and married people without children are more mobile than those with children.[8]

Education. While age is probably the best predictor of who will move, education is the single best indicator of who will move *within* an age group. As can be seen from Table 10.1, more education does make one more likely to move; however, it is a *college* education that makes the probability of migrating rise most. The labor markets for college-educated workers are more likely to be regional or national than are the labor markets for those with less education.

One cost of migration is that of ascertaining *where* opportunities are and *how good* they are likely to be. If one's occupation has a national labor market, for example, it is relatively easy to find out about opportunities in distant places. Jobs are advertised in national newspapers. Recruiters from all over visit college campuses. Employment agencies make nationwide searches. In cases such as these, people usually move with a job already in hand.

However, if the relevant labor market for one's job is localized, it is difficult to find out where opportunities might be better. For a janitor in Beaumont, Texas, to find out about employment opportunities in the northcentral region is like looking for the proverbial needle in a haystack. That such moves occur at all, let alone in reasonably large numbers, is testimony to the fact that people are able to acquire information despite the obstacles.

TABLE 10.1 Annual Migration Rates for Men and Women 30–34, by Educational Level, 1975–1980 (percent)

Educational Level (in years)	Moving Between Counties Within States		Moving Between States	
	Men	Women	Men	Women
0–8	11.7	10.0	6.3	7.6
9–11	12.7	10.1	12.0	8.7
12	13.8	12.6	10.1	10.6
13–15	15.6	15.8	14.2	16.0
16	19.9	19.0	18.8	17.7
17 or more	18.0	19.8	25.0	21.6

SOURCE: U.S. Bureau of the Census, *Geographical Mobility: March 1975 to March 1980*, Population Characteristics, Series P-20, No. 368, Table 24.

---

[8]See Jacob Mincer, "Family Migration Decisions," *Journal of Political Economy* 86,5(October 1978):749–73.

The Role of Distance

Human capital theory clearly predicts that as migration costs rise, the flow of migrants will fall. The costs of moving increase with distance for two reasons. First, as noted above, for people in local labor markets, acquiring *information* on opportunities elsewhere can be very difficult (costly). Surely it is easier to find out about employment prospects closer to home than farther away; newspapers are easier to obtain, phone calls are cheaper, friends and relatives are more useful contacts, and knowledge of employers is greater. Second, the *money costs* of transportation for the move and for trips back to see friends and relatives, and hence the *psychic costs* of the move, obviously rise with distance. Thus, one would clearly expect to find that people are more likely to move short distances than long distances.

In general, people *are* more likely to move shorter than longer distances. One study published in the late 1960s found that 34 percent of all moves were of less than 100 miles and 51 percent were of less than 200 miles. In contrast, only 17 percent were of distances between 200–400 miles and only 10 percent were between 400 and 600 miles in length.[9] Thus, moves over 600 miles accounted for only 22 percent of all moves. Clearly, the propensity to move far away is smaller than the propensity to stay close to home.

Related to the desire to minimize psychic and informational costs is the fact that people tend to migrate to areas where friends or relatives have previously migrated. This *chain migration* is especially evident in the stream of migration from Puerto Rico to the mainland: most Puerto Ricans go to Chicago and to the tristate area of New York–New Jersey–Connecticut.

Interestingly, lack of education appears to be a bigger deterrent to long-distance migration than does age (other influences held constant), a fact that can shed some light on whether it is information costs or psychic costs that are the primary deterrent. As suggested by our arguments in the previous subsection, the age deterrent is closely related to psychic costs, while educational level and ease of access to information are closely linked. The apparently larger deterrent of educational level suggests that information costs have more influence on the relationship between migration and distance.[10]

The Individual Returns to Migration

The previous section discussed the fact that the people most likely to move are the ones with the most to gain and the least to lose by migration, and that they move to areas where their net gains are likely to be largest. Another way to test our human capital theory of migration is to see if the incomes of people who migrate are higher than they would have been without migration.

---

[9]Lansing and Mueller, *The Geographic Mobility of Labor,* p. 28. Some of the moves of less than 100 miles may not have been accompanied by a job change; the explanation for these moves lies outside the realm of human capital theory.

[10]Aba Schwartz, "Interpreting the Effect of Distance on Migration," *Journal of Political Economy* 81(September/October 1973):1153–67.

The post-immigration earnings patterns of foreign-born workers have been of interest to economists in recent years and provide an informative test of the theory. In general, the wages of immigrants are initially low relative to what native-born Americans of the same races and levels of education make, but they tend to grow very rapidly. One study, for example, found that five years after immigration white men earned 10 percent less than otherwise comparable native-born males, but 13 years after immigration their earnings were equal, and at 20 years their earnings exceeded those of native-born men by 6 percent. Similar patterns have been found for most other immigrant groups, although some make more rapid progress than others.[11]

The above earnings pattern invites two comments. First, it would appear that hiring newcomers is regarded as a risky proposition by employers, either because they find it hard to evaluate immigrants' backgrounds or because immigrants' productivity is lowered by language and cultural problems. During the first years after immigration, the foreign-born invest heavily in themselves by acquiring experience in the culture and with the language, and this investment eventually pays off. A recent study, for example, shows a very strong relationship between the wages of Hispanic men and their proficiency in English.[12]

Second, the reason that immigrants seem to eventually surpass their native-born counterparts in earning ability is because they are not average people. They are people with enough drive to accept the costs of immigration to "get ahead." Interestingly, the strong work orientation of first-generation immigrants seems to carry over to their children. For example, white native-born sons of immigrants earn 5 percent more than other males of comparable education and age. However, the characteristics that raise wages appear to be absent in the third generation.[13]

Given the poverty of the countries from which less-skilled workers generally come, the fact that they do well here clearly implies eventual gains from immigration for them as individuals. Can the same conclusion be reached concerning migrants *within* the United States? Studies have found that, as a general rule, migrants do earn more than they would have earned if they had not moved. The exact size of the typical earnings differential is unclear, but earnings increases in the 10–20 percent range have been found for blacks moving out of the South.[14] There may be no *immediate* increases in income for migrants within the United States, but increases after five years are found and turn out to be large—a finding more or less

---

[11]See Barry Chiswick, "The Economic Progress of Immigrants: Some Apparently Universal Patterns," *Contemporary Economic Problems,* William Fellner, ed. (Washington, D.C.: American Enterprise Institute, 1979); and George Borjas, "The Earnings of Male Hispanic Immigrants in the United States," *Industrial and Labor Relations Review* 35(April 1982):343–53.

[12]Walter McManus, William Gould, and Finis Welch, "Earnings of Hispanic Men: The Role of English Language Proficiency," *Journal of Labor Economics* 1(April 1983):101–30.

[13]Barry Chiswick, "Immigrants and Immigration Policy," in *Contemporary Economic Problems,* William Fellner, ed. (Washington, D.C.: American Enterprise Institute, 1978), and Geoffrey Carliner, "Wages, Earnings and Hours of First, Second, and Third Generation American Males," *Economic Inquiry* 18(January 1980):87–102.

[14]Michael J. Greenwood, "Research on Internal Migration in the United States: A Survey."

consistent with the finding for foreign-born migrants. Thus, the studies of returns accruing to *individual* moves confirm the findings of research on the relationship between area-wide incentives and the *general flow* of migrants.

One other finding regarding the individual returns on migration is that the gains to *wives* from migration are much lower than the gains to husbands. For example, one study of husband-wife families who moved across state lines in 1971–72 found that the changes in present value of earnings over the next four years were $4254 for husbands and −$1716 for wives. (These figures compare to increases of $1648 and $160, respectively, for nonmovers.)[15] The reason for this disparity is found in the way that family migration decisions have traditionally been made. The husband's earnings opportunities have probably been given primary weight in the decision about whether (and where) to move. The husband is thus free to move where his earnings potential is best, and it would only be by coincidence that this same place would be optimal for his wife (in terms of earnings). Thus, while *family* income seems to rise after a move, it is the husband's income that increases the most. The wife's earnings, as shown by this one study, may actually decline when migration takes place. Example 10.2 elaborates on the problems raised by *family* migration.

Return Migration

To say that, on average, migration is a good investment for those who decide to undertake it does not imply that it is a good investment for all. Clearly, most people *do not* migrate in any year, presumably because they believe that, for them, it would not be a good investment. It is equally clear, however, that some migrants find out they have made a mistake. What they thought would be a good investment may turn out not to be. In these cases people will seek to leave where they are and move elsewhere, and it is understandable that they might seek to minimize costs by moving back to an area with which they are familiar.

Twenty percent of all moves are to an area in which the person had *previously* lived, and about half of these are back to one's birthplace.[16] Thus, *return migration*—migrating to a place from which one originated in some sense—is an important phenomenon of geographic mobility. Not all return migration may be the result of a failed investment. After all, people do leave home to acquire training or experience with the intent to return. However, much return migration may be a response by those who find that job opportunities were not what they had expected or that the psychic costs of living without the social or economic "safety net" of friends and family were higher than they had anticipated. Return migration, then, serves to remind us that, as with other forms of investments, investments in human capital can also fail to be profitable.

---

[15]Solomon W. Polachek and Francis W. Horvath, "A Life-Cycle Approach to Migration: Analysis of the Perspicacious Peregrinator," in *Research in Labor Economics,* ed. Ronald Ehrenberg (Greenwich, Conn.: JAI Press, 1977), pp. 128–29. For a study with similar findings, see Steven Sandell, "Women and the Economics of Family Migration," *Review of Economics and Statistics* 59(November 1977):406–14.

[16]Lansing and Mueller, *The Geographic Mobility of Labor,* p. 34. For an econometric analysis of return migration, see John Vanderkamp, "Migration Flows, Their Determinants and the Effects of Return Migration," *Journal of Political Economy* 79(September/October 1971):1012–31.

Example 10.2

The New Economics of Job Rotation

It is the practice of many large employers to systematically rotate employees through positions in various plant or office locations. These employers believe that such rotation creates employees with broad, flexible, company-wide perspectives who bring fresh points of view to each job. Often, however, an employee who accepts a new position (usually because it is perceived as a path to success) must also move to a new geographic location, so these transfers are accompanied by the costs of uprooting one's family.

In families in which one spouse is considered the primary earner, locational decisions are not normally influenced much by the job considerations of the secondary earner. Typically, this has meant that wives follow their husbands in geographic moves, and many of the jobs dominated by women are ideally suited to people in a "follower" role. For example, unlike many occupations, the occupations of teacher, nurse, and secretary—all heavily female—can be found in virtually every community in which one might move. Moreover, because all three occupations require little firm-specific training, human capital losses are not imposed on employers if the employee must leave the area; thus, employers do not have great incentive to discriminate against people in a "follower" position when hiring in these jobs.

Despite the occupational adaptation of most wives to their "follower" status, the economic losses they sustain from a move may not be insignificant. For example, the wives of military personnel (who are required to move to a new duty station every 4 years or so) are just as likely to work as other wives, but they are much more likely to work in part-time jobs. It is also clear that in the year of a move, most military wives who normally work throughout the year are employed for only part of the year. Nevertheless, when wives' earnings are small and only supplementary to the primary earnings of their husbands, the changes in overall *family* income from a potential move usually correspond relatively closely to changes in just the *husband's* earnings. Thus, as was found in a study mentioned earlier in this chapter, the mobility-related gains in husbands' incomes far exceed the corresponding losses sustained by wives—a situation that strongly suggests a "traditional" decision-making process concerning geographic location.

Recently, however, more women have begun to seek careers in higher-paying management or professional occupations, with four important consequences. First, if women pursuing these careers marry, their earnings may well equal or exceed the earnings of their husbands. Second, many managerial and professional jobs are not ubiquitous; employment for chemical engineers, for example, is not normally found in small communities and may not exist in very many larger cities. Third, it may not be possible to change geographic locations without sustaining large losses even when one has an occupation with ubiquitous alternatives. Opportunities for lawyers and doctors exist in all communities, for example, but changing communities means losing one's clientele.

Fourth, family locational decisions are enormously complicated if both spouses are pursuing careers because a geographic area ideal for one career may not be optimal for the other. One of the marriage partners must normally compromise, and more often than not it is the wife who does. One study of wives pursuing professional careers in small cities, for example, estimated that their earnings were 8 percent less than they would have been if they had chosen their optimal locations and their husbands had compromised.

Fifth, there is some evidence of a positive relationship between geographic moves and marital dissolution. While some cases of divorce may prompt one of the former spouses to move, in other cases of divorce a failure to agree upon geographic location may have played a part in the dissolution.

For wives pursuing higher-paying managerial or professional careers, then, the costs of being a "follower" can be high. Further, as wives' earnings approach equality with those of their husbands, the losses they sustain from a "follower" status have a greater effect on overall *family* income. Once having found a satisfactory geographic area in which to pursue dual careers, the family will be very reluctant to leave. Thus, to the extent that *both* spouses pursue these careers, their willingness to move from area to area will be reduced, and employers' reliance on job rotation as a managerial or developmental tool will undoubtedly have to be curtailed. Put differently, as the costs of family mobility rise, it will cost employers more to induce their employees to move to new areas, and this added cost will probably reduce the incidence of employee transfers in the future.

SOURCES: Louis Jacobson, "Research to Quantify the Effect of Permanent Change of Station Moves on Wives' Wages and Labor Supply," Center for Naval Analyses, Alexandria, Virginia, December 1982; Solomon W. Polachek and Francis W. Horvath, "A Life-Cycle Approach to Migration: Analysis of the Perspicacious Peregrinator," in *Research in Labor Economics*, ed. Ronald Ehrenberg (Greenwich, Conn.: JAI Press, 1977), pp. 103–49; Robert Frank, "Why Women Earn Less: The Theory and Estimation of Differential Overqualification," *American Economic Review* 68(June 1978):360–73. Jacob Mincer, "Family Migration Decisions," *Journal of Political Economy* 5(October 1978):749–75, demonstrates the reduction in family mobility associated with the wife's attachment to the labor force and includes some data on mobility and marital dissolution.

VOLUNTARY TURNOVER

While most workers who experience geographic mobility also change jobs (although perhaps not employers), these migrants are but one part of a wider group of workers who change jobs each year with or without a change of residence. Some of this job changing is voluntary in the sense that it is initiated by the employee; the remainder is said to be involuntary because it is employer initiated. Voluntary separations are termed *quits* and involuntary separations are *layoffs*. Layoffs can be temporary separations for economic reasons or permanent discharges, whether for cause (firing) or for economic reasons.

The human capital model outlined in this chapter focuses on *worker-initiated* mobility and contains the same types of implications for this wide class of voluntary job mobility as it did for geographic mobility. This section will focus on *voluntary turnover*—deciding whether or not to quit; some major determinants of employer-initiated turnover were discussed in Chapter 5. The related decision of *how long to search* for a new job once one has quit his or her former job is discussed in Chapter 15.

Wage effects.   Human capital theory predicts that, *other things equal,* a given worker will have a higher probability of quitting a low-wage job than a higher-paying one. That is, workers employed at lower wages than they could obtain elsewhere are most prone to quitting. Indeed, a very strong and consistent finding in virtually all studies of worker quit behavior is that, holding worker characteristics constant, employees in industries with lower wages have higher quit rates.[17] In fact, the relationship between wages and quit rates is so strong that we argued in Chapter 2, and shall argue again in Chapter 13, that an unusually low quit rate is often a reliable signal of an above-equilibrium wage rate.

In thinking about the relationship between quit rates and wages, it is useful to bear in mind a constant theme throughout this text: that market outcomes are the result of both worker *and* employer behavior. While workers may decide to quit if their wages fall below what they could get elsewhere, *employers* often have incentives to reduce quits by raising wages. While we may talk of a quit as "worker-initiated," the fact that an employer did not choose to take steps to retain potential quitters would seem to imply that the employer believed keeping them was not worth the cost. Thus, the distinction between "worker-initiated" and "employer-induced" quits is quite ambiguous. To expand on this point, we shall briefly discuss the relationship between quit rates and firm-specific human capital investments in the context of both *firm-size* and *sex* differences in quit rates.

From Table 10.2, it can be seen that *quit rates tend to decline as firm size*

TABLE 10.2   Monthly Quit Rates (per 100 Workers) by Firm Size, Selected Industries, 1977–81 Averages

| | Number of Employees | | | |
Industry	< 250 Employees	250–499	500–999	1000 and Over
All manufacturing	3.28	3.12	2.40	1.50
Food and kindred products	3.46	4.11	3.95	2.28
Fabricated metal products	3.33	2.64	2.12	1.20
Electrical machinery	3.81	3.12	2.47	1.60
Transportation equipment	3.90	2.78	2.21	1.41

SOURCE: Walter Oi, "The Durability of Worker-Firm Attachments" (report to the U.S. Department of Labor, Office of the Assistant Secretary for Policy, Evaluation, and Research, March 25, 1983), Table 1.

---

[17]Donald O. Parsons, "Models of Labor Market Turnover: A Theoretical and Empirical Survey," in *Research in Labor Economics,* ed. Ronald Ehrenberg (Greenwich, Conn.: JAI Press, 1977), pp. 185–223. George Borjas and Sherwin Rosen, "Income Prospects and Job Mobility of Younger Men," also in *Research in Labor Economics,* Ronald Ehrenberg, ed. (1980, pp. 159–81), found that the gains to job changers were larger than the gains that *would* have been received by those who did *not* change jobs *if* they had decided instead to quit and take other jobs. This finding is similar to that cited in footnote 21 of Chapter 9 relating to "selection bias" in returns on education.

increases. One explanation offered for this phenomenon is that large firms offer more possibilities for transfers and promotions.[18] Another, however, builds on the fact that large firms generally pay higher wages.[19] This explanation asserts that large firms tend to have highly mechanized production processes, where the output of one work team is highly dependent on that of production groups preceding it in the production "chain." Larger firms, it is argued, have greater needs for dependable and steady workers because employees who shirk their duties can impose great costs on a highly interdependent production process. Large firms, then, establish "internal labor markets" for the reasons suggested in Chapter 5; that is, they hire workers at entry-level jobs and carefully observe such hard-to-screen attributes as reliability, motivation, and attention to detail. Once having invested time and effort in selecting the best workers for its operation, a large firm finds it costly for such workers to quit. Thus, large firms pay high wages to reduce the probability of quitting because they have substantial firm-specific screening investments in their workers.[20]

It is well established that *female workers have higher propensities toward quitting* than male workers—a fact at least partially revealed by the data in Table 10.3, which show the generally lower levels of job tenure among women. In large part, this differential propensity probably reflects lower levels of firm-specific human capital investments. We argued in Chapter 9 that the interrupted careers of "traditional" women workers rendered all forms of human capital investment less beneficial than would otherwise be the case, and reduced levels of firm-specific training could account for lower wages, lower job tenures, and higher quit rates.[21]

TABLE 10.3   Job Tenure by Age and Sex, 1978

Age	Percent with Less Than 1 Year with Employer		Percent with More Than 10 Years with Employer		Median Job Tenure (years)	
	Men	Women	Men	Women	Men	Women
25–29	32.6	36.3			2.5	1.6
30–34	22.3	32.0	14.0	8.1	3.7	2.6
35–39	17.1	27.5	29.8	13.0	5.9	2.7
40–44	15.1	22.5	42.5	18.3	8.0	3.7
45–49	11.5	18.9	50.2	27.0	10.0	5.6
50–54	9.5	15.0	56.9	35.2	12.5	6.7
55–59	9.3	12.1	60.1	40.7	14.3	7.9
60–64	8.1	10.9	61.7	47.8	14.9	9.4

SOURCE: Walter Oi, "The Durability of Worker-Firm Attachments," Tables 2A, 2B.

---

[18]Arthur M. Ross, "Do We Have a New Industrial Feudalism?" *American Economic Review* 48(1958):903–20.

[19]Walter Oi, "The Fixed Employment Costs of Specialized Labor," *The Measurement of Labor Cost,* Jack E. Triplett, ed. (Chicago: University of Chicago Press, 1983).

[20]This argument is developed more fully and elegantly in Walter Oi, "The Durability of Worker-Firm Attachments" (report prepared for the U.S. Department of Labor, Office of the Assistant Secretary for Policy, Evaluation, and Research, March 25, 1983).

[21]Jacob Mincer and Boyan Jovanic, "Labor Mobility and Wages," in Sherwin Rosen, ed., *Studies in Labor Markets* (Chicago: University of Chicago Press, 1981).

In fact, once the lower wages and shorter careers of women are controlled for, there appears to be no difference between the sexes in the propensity to quit a job.[22]

Cyclical effects. Another implication of the theory is that workers will have a higher probability of quitting when it is relatively easy for them to obtain a better job quickly. Thus, when labor markets are *tight* (jobs are more plentiful relative to job-seekers), one would expect the quit rate to be higher than when labor markets are *loose* (few jobs are available and many workers are being laid off). This prediction is confirmed in studies of time series data.[23] Quit rates tend to rise when the labor market is tight and fall when it is loose. One measure of tightness is the unemployment rate; the negative relationship between the quit rate and unemployment can be readily seen in Figure 10.1. Another measure of labor market conditions is the layoff rate, which tends to rise in recessions and fall when firms are expanding production. It, too, is inversely correlated with the quit rate (see Figure 10.1).

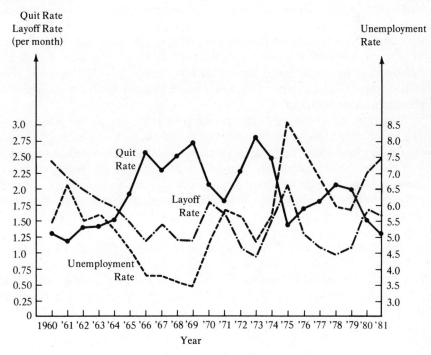

FIGURE 10.1   The Quit Rate and Labor Market "Tightness"

SOURCE: U.S. President, *Employment and Training Report of the President* (1982), Tables A-28 and C-13.

---

[22]Francine Blau and Lawrence Kahn, "Race and Sex Differences in Quits by Younger Workers," *Industrial and Labor Relations Review* 34(July 1981):563–77, and W. Kip Viscusi, "Sex Differences in Worker Quitting," *Review of Economics and Statistics* 62(August 1980):388–98. See also Andrew Weiss, "Determinants of Quit Behavior," *Journal of Labor Economics* 2(July 1984):371–87.

[23]Parsons, "Models of Labor Market Turnover," pp. 185–223.

Unexpected outcomes.   While human capital theory predicts that, on average, workers will flow from jobs with lower wages to those with higher wages (other things equal), it does not imply that mistakes are never made. Like other investments, human capital investments involve a substantial element of risk. A person might quit a job thinking better opportunities are abundant only to find that he or she was misinformed. The risk of turnover, however, can be decreased if a worker who intends to quit lines up another job first. One study of "quitters" in 1966–67 found that those who quit only after another job had been obtained—about 50–60 percent of all quitters—increased their wages by 10.7 percent on average.[24] This same study found that for those who quit one job and were unemployed for a while, the average wage increase was almost nil. While the utility of the latter group of quitters could still have been increased by *nonwage* factors, it does seem likely that at least some of this group received returns below what they expected.

Age.   Earlier this chapter argued that people tend to invest more heavily in human capital early in their careers. In many cases younger people have lower opportunity costs and a longer period over which to recoup such costs. The data on all forms of job mobility clearly indicate that turnover falls as age rises, but is this true for *voluntary* mobility? The answer appears to be yes. Studies that have investigated differences in quit rates among various industries have generally found that, other things (wages, for example) equal, quit rates are higher when the proportion of younger workers is greater.[25]

The relationship between age and worker mobility can also be inferred from data on job tenure (the length of time an employee has been with an employer). As can be seen from Table 10.3, the percentage of male workers who have been with their employers for less than one year falls with age, while the median number of years with one's current employer rises with age. By retirement age, over 60 percent of all male workers have been with their employers for 10 years or more. While the data for female workers show much lower job tenure, a similar relationship between mobility and age can be seen.

What appears to prevail, then, is a pattern suggested in Example 10.1. Namely, there is very high mobility when workers are young as mutually satisfactory worker-firm attachments are being sought; however, once these attachments are formed, mobility decreases markedly. One study, for example, found that most employees work for about ten employers in the course of their careers, with eight of these jobs being held before the age of 40.[26]

Costs of quitting.   Another prediction of human capital theory is that quit rates will be higher when the costs of quitting are lower. For example, workers in rural

---

[24]J. Peter Mattila, "Job Quitting and Frictional Unemployment," *American Economic Review* 64(March 1974):235–39.

[25]Parsons, "Models of Labor Market Turnover," p. 209; Farrell E. Bloch, "Labor Turnover in U.S. Manufacturing Industries," *Journal of Human Resources* 14(Spring 1979):236–46.

[26]Robert Hall, "The Importance of Lifetime Jobs in the U.S. Economy," *American Economic Review* 72(September 1982):716–24.

Example 10.3

A Positive and Normative Theory of Quitting in 19th-Century Japan

Is modern labor economics, in both its positive and normative modes, culture bound? Does the theory presented in this book pertain only to circumstances as they are now in the United States? Despite our emphasis on the analysis of current American policy issues, economic behavior is so general, and the need for markets so pervasive, that the theory presented here as *modern labor economics* is neither American nor necessarily modern.

For example, in the years just before 1900 when Japan was just beginning to industrialize, labor turnover rates (as noted in Example 5.2) were very high owing to persistent labor shortages. In 1898 a conference of business and government leaders was held to discuss the problems underlying this high turnover and the need for legislation concerning it. In the course of those discussions, Shoda Heigoro, a Mitsubishi executive, articulated the "modern" theory of job quitting behavior—in both its positive *and* normative aspects:

> Since it is the nature of man to be tempted by better opportunities, it is impossible to keep workers without adequate provisions. That is, if a worker desires to go to another factory because of better pay there, his present employer should allow him to go. If the employer wanted to keep the worker, he should raise wages so that the worker would see no reason to move. Were I censured for this statement on the ground that the competitive spiraling of wages would damage the profits of factory owners and retard industrial progress, I would rebut by calling attention to the simple logic of demand and supply in the market. Factory operatives, engineers, machinists, and other workers in modern industries are scarce in Japan today, because these occupations unlike the traditional crafts emerged only recently. It is true that their relative scarcity enables them to command relatively higher wages than other types of labor. But this very fact of high wages also induces more workers to flow into these occupations. . . .
>
> Therefore, if the forces of demand and supply worked normally, the increase in their number would in time reduce their wages. But this subsequent decrease in their wages would spell no hardship for them, because workers would move into these occupations only insofar as the advantages there were sufficient to make them willing to move. . . . Thus, in my opinion, it is highly necessary that factory owners should acquiesce in the economic motives of workers in seeking high wages and better occupations. . . .

SOURCE: Koji Taira, *Economic Development and the Labor Market in Japan* (New York: Columbia University Press, 1970), p. 118.

areas who change employers may well have to move their residences if they want to find a job in the same industry or occupation. Job-changers who live in large cities have a much wider choice of jobs in their fields and have a much lower probability of having to move. Because job changing is thus less costly for residents of large cities, one would expect turnover to be higher in these large cities. Indeed, we do find that industries in which employment is more concentrated in larger cities have higher quit rates, other things (wages and ages of worker, for example) equal.[27]

NATIONAL IMMIGRATION POLICY

Nowhere are the analytical tools of the economist more important than in the area of immigration policy; the lives affected by immigration policy number in the millions each year. After a brief outline of the history of U.S. immigration policy, this section will analyze in detail the consequences of illegal immigration, a problem currently attracting widespread attention.

U.S. Immigration History

The United States is a rich country—a country whose wealth and high standard of living make it an attractive place for immigrants from nearly all parts of the world. For the first 140 years of our history as an independent country, the United States followed a policy of essentially unrestricted immigration (the only major immigration restrictions were placed on Orientals and convicts). The flow of immigrants was especially large after 1840, when industrialization here and political and economic upheavals in Europe made immigration an attractive investment for millions. As one can see from Table 10.4, officially recorded immigration peaked

TABLE 10.4 Officially Recorded Immigration: 1820 to 1980

Period	Number (in thousands)	Annual Rate (per thousand of U.S. population)	Year	Number (in thousands)	Annual Rate (per thousand of U.S. population)
1820–1980	49,655	3.5			
1820–1830	152	1.2	1971	370	1.8
1831–1840	599	3.9	1972	385	1.8
1841–1850	1,713	8.4	1973	400	1.9
1851–1860	2,598	9.3	1974	395	1.9
1861–1870	2,315	6.4	1975	386	1.8
1871–1880	2,812	6.2	1976	399	1.9
1881–1890	5,247	9.2	1977	462	2.1
1891–1900	3,688	5.3	1978	601	2.8
1901–1910	8,795	10.4	1979	460	2.0
1911–1920	5,736	5.7	1980	531	2.3
1921–1930	4,107	3.5			
1931–1940	528	0.4			
1941–1950	1,035	0.7			
1951–1960	2,515	1.5			
1961–1970	3,322	1.7			

SOURCE: U.S. Immigration and Naturalization Service, *Annual Report.*

---

[27]Parsons, "Models of Labor Market Turnover"; Bloch, "Labor Turnover in U.S. Manufacturing."

in the first decade of the 20th century, when the *yearly* flow of immigrants was more than 1 percent of the population.

In 1921, however, Congress adopted the Quota Law, which set annual quotas on immigration on the basis of nationality. These quotas had the effect of reducing immigration from eastern and southern Europe. This act was followed by other laws in 1924 and 1929 that further restricted immigration from southeastern Europe. These various revisions in immigration policy were motivated, in part, by widespread concern over the alleged adverse impact on native employment of the arrival of unskilled immigrants from eastern and southern Europe.

In 1965 the passage of the Immigration and Nationality Act abolished the quota system based on national origin that so heavily favored northern and western Europeans. Under this new law, overall ceilings were established for the eastern and western hemisphere, with no more than 20,000 coming from any one country. Within these limits, however, first preference is given to family reunification (74 percent of all immigrant visas). Sixteen percent of visas are reserved for professionals or artists of exceptional ability and for workers in occupations for which labor is scarce. An immigrant in the latter categories must obtain a labor certificate approved by the U.S. Department of Labor after an investigation to verify that the applicant is qualified for the job, that there is a shortage of workers for that job in the area, and that the terms of employment are average or better.

While the 1965 change in immigration policy did achieve its goal of making immigration less overtly discriminatory, the policy still imposes a ceiling on immigrants that is far below the numbers who wish to come. The fact that immigration to the United States is viewed as a very worthwhile investment for many more people than are allowed to take advantage of it has created incentives for people to enter the country illegally.

One way in which entry is made illegally is for the immigrant to come to this country as a student or visitor. Once here, the foreigner can look for work, although it is illegal to work at a job under a student's or visitor's visa. If the "student" or "visitor" is offered a job, he or she can apply for an "adjustment of status" to become a permanent resident (based on the existence of a labor certificate). Emigrants from the eastern hemisphere are allowed to remain in the United States while their adjustment-of-status application is being evaluated.

Residents from the western hemisphere are required to return home while their adjustment-of-status applications are being processed. The backlog of people awaiting entry is such that, in recent years, the delay in re-entering the United States as a legal permanent resident has been about two and one-half years. Since most job offers will not wait that length of time, the affected immigrants understandably take the jobs and work here illegally while awaiting approval of their status change.

Roughly 7 million people enter the United States every year under nonimmigrant visas. Since many leave without informing U.S. officials, it is impossible to say how many of these 7 million overstay their periods of admission, but government officials believe that the numbers range from 10 to 20 percent.[28] If half of these

---

[28]Walter Fogel, "Illegal Alien Workers in the United States," *Industrial Relations* 16,3(October 1977):250.

visa abusers intend to immigrate illegally, the number of illegal immigrants would at least be equal to, and perhaps double the size of, the number of legal immigrants.

Moreover, there are other ways of illegally immigrating to the United States. Immigrants from the Caribbean often enter through Puerto Rico, whose residents are U.S. citizens and thus allowed free entry to the mainland. Others walk across the Mexican border. Still others are smuggled into the United States or use false documents to get through entry stations. The value of immigration as a human capital investment is indicated by the fact that *coyotes,* people who help illegal aliens cross the border and find jobs, could command $300 per head in 1978,[29] or roughly 8 months of pay for the average Mexican peasant.

No one knows how many illegal immigrants are in the United States. In 1977 the Immigration and Naturalization Service apprehended and deported more than 1 million illegal aliens, and many believe that for every person apprehended two make it into the country successfully.[30] The report of the Select Commission on Immigration and Refugee Policy, submitted in 1981, places the total number of illegal residents at below 6 million, possibly in the range of 3.5–5 million.[31] While not all "illegals" are in the labor market, the profile of the typical illegal alien is that of a young, unattached male who is seeking work and unaccompanied by nonworking family members.

Despite the lack of precise knowledge about the dimensions of illegal immigration, the fact remains that by the early 1980s it had become a very prominent policy issue. The Secretary of Labor estimated in late 1979 that if only *half* of the jobs held by illegal aliens were given to U.S. citizens, the unemployment rate would drop from 6 percent to 3.7 percent. Similar beliefs led both houses of Congress in 1984 to pass bills that would make it illegal for employees to hire undocumented immigrants (as of late 1984 the two bills had not been reconciled and signed into law). Support for this legislation was by no means unanimous, and many claimed that the employment of these immigrants served useful purposes. The policies people advocate are based on their beliefs about the consequences of immigration. Nearly everyone with an opinion on this subject has an economic model implicitly or explicitly in mind when addressing these consequences; the purpose of the remainder of this chapter is to make these economic models explicit and to evaluate them.

Naive Views of Immigration

There are two opposing views of illegal immigration that can be considered naive. One view, which is widely held in the government, is that every illegal immigrant deprives a citizen or legal alien of a job. For example, a Department of Labor official told a House committee studying immigration, "I think it is logical to conclude that if they are actually employed, they are taking a job away from one of

---

[29]Edwin P. Reubens, "Aliens, Jobs, and Immigration Policy," *Public Interest* 51(Spring 1978):126.

[30]Reubens, "Aliens, Jobs and Immigration Policy," p. 126.

[31]Select Commission on Immigration and Refugee Policy, *U.S. Immigration Policy and the National Interest* (Washington, D.C.: U.S. Government Printing Office, 1981), p. 36.

Example 10.4
"Economic" vs. "Political" Immigrants

Individuals who immigrate to a country like the United States presumably do so because they believe they will be improving their well-being. For some the decision is motivated primarily by economic considerations, and the timing of the move is both voluntary and planned. These individuals may be referred to as "economic" migrants. Others, however, may be forced to flee their countries because of *political* upheavals, and for these individuals the decision is likely to be less motivated by economic factors, not planned far in advance, and somewhat less voluntary (given the life-threatening prospects they may face). The latter may be referred to as "political" migrants.

What differences might we expect in the economic success of the two groups when they arrive in the United States? On the one hand, since the "economic" migrants' decisions were motivated by expectations of improved economic welfare, one might expect that they would initially earn more than the "political" migrants, who were less prepared for the move. On the other hand, members of the latter group do not have the option of ultimately returning to their homelands as the "economic" migrants do. Because return migration is precluded for "political" migrants, they have stronger incentives than economic migrants to make human capital investments that have payoffs only in the United States ("economic" migrants may want to preserve skills that will be useful to them if they return to their homelands). In addition, "political" migrants often leave all their physical or financial assets behind when they flee their homelands; as a result, they may prefer to concentrate a greater share of their subsequent investments in human (rather than physical) capital. For both reasons, one might expect "political" migrants to have steeper earnings profiles—more rapid earnings growth with years in the United States—than "economic" migrants.

In a carefully conducted study, George Borjas found substantial evidence to support these expectations. Other factors (such as age and education) held constant, Cuban male immigrants to the United States, many of whom fled their homeland after Fidel Castro came to power, appear to have lower earnings than other Hispanic male immigrants (primarily Mexicans and Puerto Ricans) in the early years after both groups arrive in the United States; however, in subsequent years they exhibit more rapid rates of earnings growth.

SOURCE: George Borjas, "The Economic Status of Male Hispanic Migrants and Natives in the U.S.," in R. Ehrenberg, ed., *Research in Labor Economics* vol. 6 (Greenwich, Conn.: JAI Press, 1984), pp. 65–122.

our American citizens."[33] According to this view, if x illegal aliens are deported and others kept out, the number of unemployed Americans would decline by x.

---

[32]Elliott Abrams and Franklin S. Abrams, "Immigration Policy—Who Gets In and Why?" *Public Interest* 38(Winter 1975):25.

At the opposite end of the policy spectrum is the equally naive argument that the illegals perform jobs no American citizen would do:

> You couldn't conduct a hotel in New York, you couldn't conduct a restaurant in New York . . . if you didn't have rough laborers. We haven't got the rough laborers anymore. . . . Where are we going to get the people to do that rough work?[33]

Both arguments are simplistic because they ignore the slopes of the demand and supply curves. Consider, for example, the labor market for the job of "rough laborer"—any job most American citizens find distasteful. Without illegal immigrants, the restricted supply of Americans to this market would imply a relatively high wage (W_1 in Figure 10.2). N_1 citizens would be employed. If illegal aliens entered the market, the supply curve would shift outward and perhaps flatten (implying that immigrants were more responsive to wage increases for rough laborers than citizens). The influx of illegals would drive the wage down to W_2, but employment would increase to N_2.

Are Americans unwilling to do the work of rough laborers? Clearly, at the market wage of W_2, many more aliens are willing to work at the job than U.S. citizens. Only N_3 citizens would want these jobs at this wage, while the remaining supply (N_2-N_3) is made up entirely of aliens. If there were no immigrants, however, N_1 Americans would be employed at wage W_1 as rough laborers. Wages would be higher, as would the prices of the goods or services produced with this labor, but the

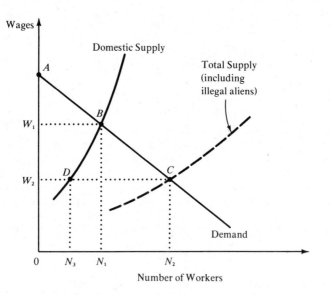

FIGURE 10.2   Demand and Supply of Rough Laborers

[33]Abrams and Abrams, "Immigration Policy—Who Gets In and Why?" p. 26.

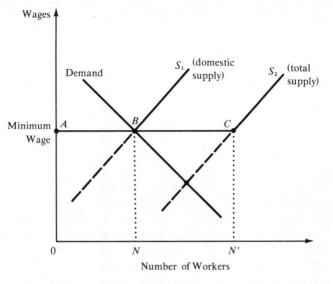

**FIGURE 10.3   Demand and Supply of Rough Laborers
with a Minimum Wage**

job would get done. The only "shortage" of American citizens is at the low wage of
W_2; at W_1 there is no shortage (see Chapter 2 for further discussion of labor
shortages).

Would deporting those illegal aliens working as rough laborers create the same
number of jobs for U.S. citizens? The answer is clearly no. If the N_2–N_3 aliens
working as laborers were deported and all other illegal aliens were kept from the
market, the number of Americans employed as laborers would rise from N_3 to N_1
and their wages would rise from W_2 to W_1 (Figure 10.2). N_2–N_1 jobs would be
destroyed by the rising wage rate associated with deportation. Thus, while deportation would increase the employment and wage levels of Americans in the laborer
market, it would certainly not reduce unemployment on a one-for-one basis.

There is, however, one condition in which deportation *would* create jobs for
American citizens on a one-for-one basis: when the federal minimum wage law
creates a surplus of labor. Suppose, for example, that the supply of American
laborers is represented by ABS_1 in Figure 10.3 and the total supply is represented by
ACS_2. Because an artificially high wage has created a surplus, only N of the N'
workers willing to work at the minimum wage can actually find employment. If
some of them are illegal aliens, sending them back—coupled with successful efforts
to deny other aliens access to these jobs—would create jobs for a comparable
number of Americans. However, the demand curve would have to intersect the
domestic supply curve (ABS_1) at or to the left of point B to prevent the wage level
from rising (and thus destroying jobs) after deportation. In addition, all laborers
would have to be paid the minimum wage, an unlikely eventuality given the lack of
compliance noted in Chapter 3.

An Analysis of the Gainers and Losers

Some claim that, while perhaps not reducing citizen-held jobs one for one, large immigrant flows are indeed harmful to American workers. This view is probably the dominant force behind our restrictive immigration policy and the consequent concern about illegal immigration.

The argument is based primarily on a single-market analysis like that contained in Figure 10.2, where only the effects on the market for rough labor are examined. As far as it goes, the argument is correct. When immigration increases the supply of rough laborers, both the wage and employment levels of American citizens working as laborers are reduced. The total wage bill paid to American laborers falls from $W_1 0 N_1 B$ in Figure 10.2 to $W_2 0 N_3 D$. Thus, some American workers leave the market in response to the reduced wage, and those who stay earn less. If the Americans employed as laborers are, for example, minorities or members of some other group that is the target of antipoverty efforts, the influx of immigrants could substantially frustrate such efforts.

It would be a mistake, however, to conclude from the above analysis that, because immigration is harmful to domestic *laborers,* it is therefore necessarily harmful to Americans as a *whole.* First, immigration of "cheap labor" clearly benefits consumers using the output of this labor. As wages are reduced and employment increases, the goods and services produced by this labor are increased in quantity and reduced in price.

Second, employers of rough labor (to continue our example) are obviously benefited, at least in the short run. In Figure 10.2, profits are increased from $W_1 A B$ to $W_2 A C$. This rise in profitability, however, should serve to attract more people to become employers, which in the long run will reduce profits back down to normal levels. As employers or managers become more numerous, opportunities for workers who would have been neither in the absence of immigration are expanded. (For example, a supply of cheap labor may induce a cook to open his own diner or a janitor to open her own cleaning service.)

Third, our analysis of the market for laborers assumed that the influx of immigrants had no effect on the demand curve (which was held fixed in Figure 10.2). This is not a bad assumption when looking at just one market because the fraction of earnings immigrant laborers spend on the goods and services produced by rough labor is probably small. However, immigrants do spend money in the United States, and this added demand may create job opportunities or higher wages (or both) for more-skilled workers (see Figure 10.4). Thus, workers who are not close substitutes for unskilled immigrant labor may benefit from immigration because of the increase in consumer demand attendant on this addition to our working population.

(Note: Recall from Chapter 3 that if the demand for skilled workers increases when the wage of unskilled labor falls, the two grades of labor would be *gross complements.* Assuming skilled and unskilled labor are substitutes in the production process, the only way they could be gross complements is if the *scale effect* of a decline in the unskilled wage dominated the substitution effect. In the case of immigration one may suppose the scale effect to be very large, because as the working population rises, aggregate demand is increased. While theoretical analysis

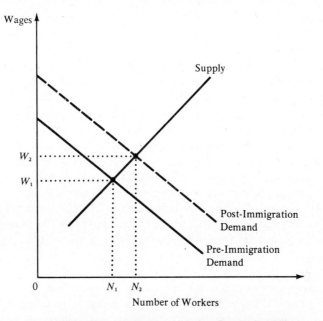

FIGURE 10.4   Market for All Labor Except Unskilled

cannot *prove* that the demand for skilled workers is increased by unskilled immigration if the two grades of labor are substitutes in the production process, it can offer the above observation that an increase in demand for skilled workers remains a distinct possibility. Of course, for any type of labor that is *complementary* with unskilled labor in the production process—supervisory workers, for example— immigration does represent a clear-cut gain.)[34]

The Effect of Immigration on the "Native" Population

Thus far we have concluded that illegal immigration is harmful to the interests of native unskilled workers but increases the real incomes of owners and possibly of skilled workers as well. However, it is also interesting and important to inquire whether the *aggregate income of native Americans* is increased. If it is, the gainers (skilled workers and owners) gain more than the losers lose. There would thus be large enough gains that the losers could be compensated for their losses, by income maintenance or job training programs, and the gainers would still come out ahead. In this case, policymakers might choose to pursue a policy of ignoring illegal immigration.

If immigrants are paid a wage equal to the value of their marginal product (*MP*) and are not subsidized by native taxpayers, then the aggregate income of U.S. citizens *will* increase as a result of immigration. Recall that total product—the area under the marginal product curve—is greater than wages paid. Only for the last unit

---

[34]For an interesting empirical investigation of the substitutability between immigrants and nonimmigrant labor, see Jean B. Grossman, "The Substitutability of Natives and Immigrants in Production," *Review of Economics and Statistics* 64(November 1982):596–603.

of labor employed, where MP = Wage, is there no surplus or profit generated. Thus, as long as immigrants get paid a wage equal only to their MP, the aggregate income of the native-born population cannot be reduced.

One way in which the native-born population, taken as a whole, *can* lose from immigration is if the immigrants obtain government services or payments in excess of the payroll, income, sales, and property taxes they pay. Because many government programs are essentially aids to the poor—public health, welfare, and unemployment insurance, to name just three—there is a distinct possibility that legal immigrants could be receiving net subsidies.[35] On the other hand, *illegal* immigrants tend to be young, unattached males—people without children in school who do not generally qualify for other government programs because they are undocumented. Moreover, the taxes these workers do pay, directly or indirectly, also serve to reduce the burden of certain "overhead" expenses to U.S. citizens—expenses, like those of national defense and road maintenance, which the presence of immigrants does not increase. Thus, illegal immigration is likely to increase the aggregate income of the native-born populace.

If the aggregate income of the resident population is increased by immigration, then the gainers gain more than the losers lose. You will recall from Chapter 1 that when the gains are larger than the losses, a mutually beneficial transaction is possible. The immigrants gain from their move to this country and, on balance, the resident population gains. In fact, the gains are large enough that the beneficiaries could compensate those who lose from immigration and *still* be better off.

Whether a policy of unrestricted immigration would be advisable probably depends on three factors:

1. The possibility that those hurt by it could actually receive compensation,
2. The probability that immigrants would remain unsubsidized, and
3. The desirability of programs designed to reduce or deny subsidies to immigrants.

Since many social programs are aimed at the poor, compensation to unskilled workers for their losses associated with immigration of the unskilled may be fairly automatic, coming in the form of unemployment compensation, public housing, food stamps, job retraining, and welfare payments. Compensation to skilled workers (if the immigrants are predominantly skilled) would be less automatic and might have to take the form of a special program.[36]

The reservations many have about unrestricted immigration center on points 2 and 3, especially as they relate to immigration of those most likely to receive public subsidies: the unskilled. Illegal immigrants *are* denied access to certain public

---

[35] A recent study suggests that immigrants are substantially less likely to receive public transfer payments than "natives" of equal age and education. See Francine Blau, "The Use of Transfer Payments by Immigrants," *Industrial and Labor Relations Review* 37(January 1984):222–39.

[36] Such a program already exists for those hurt by foreign imports. The Trade Adjustment Assistance Program identifies those hurt and compensates them through job retraining, subsidies to move to other areas, and special unemployment insurance payments. While this program has been criticized as generally unsuccessful in several respects, it does serve as an example of a program specifically designed to compensate those who lose as a consequence of a public policy.

Example 10.5

Indentured Servitude and Human Capital Investments

Obtaining the funds necessary to make an investment is a common problem for would-be investors. The problem is especially formidable for those who would invest in human capital because loans for human capital investments are not widely made. Unlike loans for investments in physical capital (cars, homes, machines), which can be secured by the asset purchased, loans for human capital investments must generally be unsecured and thus are more risky to the creditor.

In colonial days, indentured servitude was an institution that permitted poor immigrants to obtain passage to the New World using funds provided by a creditor and to secure this "loan" with all they had: their labor. British emigrants would sign an indenture with a British merchant or sea captain that specified the colony to which they would be sent and the length of time they would be bound to their master. The merchant or sea captain was then responsible for feeding, clothing, and transporting the servant to the colony. Upon arrival at the colony, the contract would be sold to a colonial farmer or planter and the servant would be bound to this employer for the specified length of time, presumably long enough to pay back the expenses connected with immigration plus interest.

The market for indentures was apparently competitive. There were enough British agents selling these indentures, and the potential servants were well enough informed, that genuine bargaining took place. The "price" of an indenture was its length, which varied from 2 to 10 years. A long indenture was obviously costly to the servant, but it could bring a high price in the colonies to the agent. A short indenture was less profitable to the agent and a better deal for the servant.

A look at the length of British indentures during the period 1718–1759 offers striking confirmation of the general implications of human capital theory presented in Chapter 9. Literate and experienced workers were able to obtain the shortest indentures—while younger, less experienced, or illiterate workers had to sign for longer periods of indenture. (Women were able to obtain slightly shorter indentures than men, other things equal, a fact that the reader is free to interpret.) There is also evidence of compensating differentials. Indentures to be sold in the West Indies were shorter than those to be sold in the mainland colonies, where environmental conditions were more healthy and post-servitude opportunities were considered better.

SOURCE: David Galenson, "Immigration and the Colonial Labor System: An Analysis of the Length of Indenture," *Explorations in Economic History* 14(1977):360–77.

welfare programs because of their undocumented status, but they also represent what some view as an "underclass" who cannot vote and who do not have full citizenship rights. An alternative used in Europe—"guest worker" programs—

also denies permanent residence and citizenship rights to immigrants; in addition, these workers can be required to leave the country at the government's will. Thus, ensuring that poor, unskilled immigrants remain unsubsidized means denying them the rights of other citizens and legal aliens. While the immigrants themselves are obviously willing to pay the price when they immigrate, some worry that they or their foreign-born children may not be willing to pay this price indefinitely.

The Consequences of Emigration

The consequences of emigration are generally the reverse of those for immigration. The country loses a productive resource, and those remaining are deprived of the surplus (total product less wages) produced by the emigrants. The groups most competitive with the emigrants are helped by their departure, but the aggregate income of the residents who remain will be smaller, with two important exceptions.

First, if the emigrants are owners of capital and are forced by the government to leave this capital behind, the remaining population could benefit (in much the same way the Black Death benefited the survivors, as pointed out in Chapter 2). Some governments, most notably Cuba's, have permitted middle-class workers to leave under these conditions. A drawback, however, is that workers (such as doctors) with sizable amounts of financial capital may also have sizable amounts of *human* capital that *does* leave with them, making it necessary for those remaining to invest in programs to train replacements.

The second exception applies to economies in which there is a permanent labor surplus. Many believe that in very poor countries the supply of labor is so large relative to demand that the equilibrium wage is below a socially acceptable minimum (perhaps the subsistence level). If the minimum must be paid, a labor surplus is created (see Figure 10.5). If surplus workers leave, the country obviously gains.

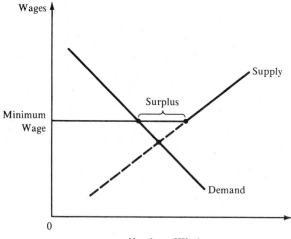

FIGURE 10.5   A "Labor-Surplus" Market

These workers were not producing anything, but they had to be kept alive by transfer payments from others. Emigration is a clear-cut help to those who remain.

Labor surpluses in less-developed countries can also be created by the high wages paid in the industrial, urban sector. These wages are set high to attract foreign labor with the requisite skills and must by law be paid to native workers also. Hoping to be lucky enough to obtain these jobs, migrants flock to the cities, where they form sizable groups of unemployed, surplus workers. If a country were not willing to let the industrial wage for native workers fall to the point of market equilibrium, emigration would be an attractive solution to the resulting problem of a labor surplus.

REVIEW QUESTIONS

1. The following four paragraphs were taken from an Associated Press story on December 8, 1979:

   > WASHINGTON (AP)—Treasury Secretary G. William Miller said Friday that the Senate Banking Committee version of the Chrysler aid bill is "unworkable," in part because the automaker might lose many of its best workers.
   >
   > Miller said the most objectionable feature of the committee bill is a requirement that Chrysler workers accept a three-year wage freeze in exchange for $1.25 billion in federal loan guarantees for Chrysler.
   >
   > "Under the proposed bill, efforts to aid Chrysler would fail, because conditions of the bill simply could not be met," he said, adding that the wage freeze would impose "a disproportionate financing burden on the workers of the company."
   >
   > "The terms of the bill would substantially impair the operations of the Chrysler Corporation, risk loss to the company of many of its most able employees, and seriously damage the morale and productivity of the workers essential to the company's future success," he said.

   Suppose you are a staff worker for an important senator trying to evaluate Secretary Miller's contention that a wage freeze would cause Chrysler to lose its best employees. Write an essay evaluating Miller's contention. Start with a coherent statement of the theory relevant to Miller's assertion and then analyze all the conditions necessary for Miller's assertion to be true.

2. As you know, thousands of illegal immigrants are working in the United States. Suppose the United States increases the penalties for illegal immigration to include long jail sentences. Analyze the effects of this increased penalty on the wages and employment levels of *all* affected groups of workers.

3. Suppose a Presidential commission on immigration policy were to make the following report:

   > "As a compromise between those on our commission who wish to make it illegal for an employer to hire 'undocumented' (that is, illegal) aliens and those who wish to continue the current practice (where it is not illegal), we propose that
   >
   > (a) a tax be placed on any employer who hires an undocumented alien in the amount of $1.00 for every hour that alien is employed, and
   >
   > (b) the revenues be used to finance job training programs for American citizens who have low skill levels."

Assume that the program above could be carried out feasibly. Analyze the effects the program would have on employment and earnings of both illegal aliens and American citizens. (In writing your answer, assume it is not currently illegal to hire undocumented workers and only limited job training is available.) Would this proposal tend to reduce the influx of illegal immigrants? Why?

SELECTED READINGS

Borjas, George. "The Earnings of Male Hispanic Immigrants in the United States." *Industrial and Labor Relations Review* 35(April 1982):343–53.

Chiswick, Barry. "The Economic Progress of Immigrants: Some Apparently Universal Patterns." In *Contemporary Economic Problems*, ed. William Fellner. Washington, D.C.: The American Enterprise Institute for Public Policy Research, 1979. Pp. 357–99.

Chiswick, Barry. "The Effect of Americanization on the Earnings of Foreign-Born Men." *Journal of Political Economy* 86(October 1978):897–921.

Greenwood, Michael J. "Research on Internal Migration in the United States: A Survey." *Journal of Economic Literature* 8, 2(June 1975):397–433.

Parsons, Donald O. "Models of Labor Market Turnover: A Theoretical and Empirical Survey." In *Research in Labor Economics*, ed. Ronald Ehrenberg. Greenwich, Conn.: JAI Press, 1977. Pp. 185–223.

Pencavel, John. *An Analysis of the Quit Rate in Manufacturing Industry*. Princeton, N.J.: Industrial Relations Section, Princeton University, 1970.

Piore, Michael J. "The 'New Immigration' and the Presumptions of Social Policy." *Proceedings of the Industrial Relations Research Association*. Madison, Wis.: Industrial Relations Research Association, 1974. Pp. 350–58.

Reder, Melvin. "The Economic Consequences of Increased Immigration." *Review of Economics and Statistics* 45,3(August 1963):221–30.

11

The Structure of Compensation

Chapters 6 and 7 examined factors influencing the decision to work for pay and the desired hours of work. Chapters 8 and 9 analyzed the day-to-day and human capital aspects, respectively, of occupational choice. Chapter 10 discussed human capital aspects of voluntary job and geographic mobility. We now turn to a discussion of yet another set of factors influencing job choice and work effort decisions: employer compensation policies both at one point in time and over several periods of time.

What ultimately matters to workers in making labor supply decisions is the total compensation they receive per unit of time worked. This total compensation paid to employees consists of far more than hourly, weekly, or monthly pay for time worked. There are numerous *fringe benefits* offered in varying combinations by employers, which have value to employees but are not paid to them in the form of currently spendable cash. Employers can also offer, explicitly or implicitly, different bases for computing or timing pay over one's career. These various forms of compensation affect employee behavior and labor market outcomes in interesting ways.

This chapter will begin by describing and analyzing the consequences of fringe benefits. Of particular policy importance is the issue of pension fund regulation by the federal government. The chapter will also discuss various ways to arrange compensation in order to provide strong incentives for employees to maximize their productivity and remain attached to a firm for long periods of time. These forms of compensation offer different ways to *compute* current pay, but they also include a certain element of choice in *timing* a worker's pay over his or her career with a firm—choices that are particularly available in the context of an internal labor market.

THE ECONOMICS OF FRINGE BENEFITS

As noted in Chapter 5, the proportion of total compensation coming in the form of cash payments to workers has fallen over time as the use of fringe benefits has risen. According to the data presented in Table 11.1, the most common fringe benefits are paid vacations, medical insurance, maternity leaves, pensions, life insurance, and paid sick leave. Less common, but still available to large numbers of workers, are company-paid education or training; discounted meals, merchandise, or work clothing; dental care, eye care, or legal benefits; stock options or savings plans; and maternity leave with pay. In addition to these private fringes, there are also publicly mandated benefits that employers must fund, at least in part: social security, workers' compensation, and unemployment insurance.

One way to grasp the growth and composition of fringe benefits is to look at their cost to employers. Table 11.2 contains two sets of data on employer costs for specific benefits as percentages of total compensation for workers in manufacturing industries. One set of data derives from Chamber of Commerce surveys, which are heavily weighted with larger firms.[1] The other data were obtained from a more representative sample of manufacturing firms.

TABLE 11.1.   Fringe Benefits Available to Workers

Fringe Benefit	Percentage of Workers Reporting the Availability of the Benefit in 1977[a]
Paid vacation	80.8
Medical, surgical, or hospital insurance that covers any illness or injury that might occur *off* the job	78.1
Maternity leave with full re-employment rights	74.5
Retirement program	67.4
Life insurance that would cover a death occurring for reasons *not* connected with job	64.1
Sick leave and full pay	62.8
Training (or education) program to improve skills	49.0
Thrift or savings plan	39.8
Free or discounted merchandise	34.3
Dental benefits	29.4
Maternity leave with pay	29.4
Eyeglass or eye-care benefits	21.8
Profit sharing	19.8
Stock options	17.6
Work-clothing allowance	16.8
Free or discounted meals	16.3
Legal aid or services	10.3
Day-care facilities	2.2

[a]Includes only wage and salaried workers.

SOURCE: From *The 1977 Quality of Employment Survey* by Robert P. Quinn and Graham L. Staines. Copyright © 1979 by The University of Michigan. Reprinted by permission of the Institute for Social Research of The University of Michigan.

---

[1]These data are based on information contained in Table 5.2. The data in Table 5.2, however, calculated fringe benefits as a percentage of *wage and salary* payments; the data in Table 11.2 state fringes as a percentage of *total compensation*.

TABLE 11.2.   Comparisons of Employer Expenditures for Compensation, 1959, 1977, 1980

	Percentage of Employer's Total Compensation Expenditures				
	(a) Production and Related Workers in Manufacturing		(b) All Employees in Larger Manufacturing Firms		
Categories of Compensation	*1959*	*1977*	*1959*	*1977*	*1980*
Pay for working time	85.4	74.8	82.2	72.8	72.4
Pay for leave time (vacations, holidays, sick leave, personal days)	5.4	7.3	7.7	9.3	9.5
Private pension plans	2.2	4.2 ⎫	5.1	9.4	9.4
Life, accident, and health insurance	2.0	5.5 ⎭			
Government-required contributions to Social Security, workers' compensation, and unemployment insurance	4.1	7.4	3.7	6.8	7.1
Other	0.5	0.8	1.3	1.7	1.6
Total fringe benefits	14.6	25.2	17.8	27.2	27.6
Total compensation	100.0	100.0	100.0	100.0	100.0

SOURCES: (a) U.S. Department of Labor, Bureau of Labor Statistics, *Handbook of Labor Statistics 1980*, Bulletin 2070 (Washington, D.C.: U.S. Government Printing Office), 1980.
(b) U.S. Chamber of Commerce, *Fringe Benefits and Employee Benefits* (1959, 1977, 1980).

Table 11.2 provides a number of insights. First, the proportion of total compensation devoted to fringe benefits rose about 10 percentage points from 1959 to 1977 in each data set, and the rise appears to have continued, although at a slower pace, through 1980. Second, the most costly fringes are paid leave time and the government-mandated benefits, which together account for 59 percent of all fringe benefit costs. Life and health insurance and private pension plans account for roughly 35 percent of fringe benefit costs. Third, it is clear from the data in Table 11.2 that fringe benefits are a greater proportion of total compensation in large firms than in small ones.

Table 11.3, which compares office and nonoffice employees of all but the smallest firms in the private sector, illustrates another interesting fact: fringe benefits as a percentage of compensation are slightly, but not markedly, higher for office than nonoffice workers. Further, government-required fringes and pay for nonworking time comprise the two largest components of the fringe package in both cases.

What accounts for the growth and size of fringe benefits? What are the consequences of this growth and size? To answer these questions, we must examine both the employee and employer sides of the market.

Employee Preferences

The distinguishing feature of all fringe benefits is that they compensate workers in a form *other* than currently spendable cash. In general, there are two broad categories of such benefits. First and largest are *payments in kind*—that is, compensation in the form of some commodity. As we have seen, it is very common for employers to at

TABLE 11.3. **Employee Compensation for Private, Nonagricultural Workers, 1977 (in percent)**

	Percentage of Employer's Total Compensation Expenditures	
	Office Workers	Nonoffice Workers
Pay for working time	75.8	77.5
Pay for leave time (vacations, holidays, sick leave, personal days)	7.9	6.2
Private pension plans	4.8	3.5
Life, accident, and health insurance	3.6	4.3
Government-required contributions to Social Security, workers' compensation, and unemployment insurance	5.6	7.9
Other	2.3	0.6
Total compensation	100.0	100.0

Note: The data are for workers in plants with 20 or more employees.

SOURCE: U.S. Department of Labor, Bureau of Labor Statistics, *Handbook of Labor Statistics 1980*, Bulletin 2070 (Washington, D.C.: U.S. Government Printing Office), 1980.

least partially buy insurance policies of one kind or another on behalf of their employees. Slightly less obvious as payments in kind are paid vacations and holidays. A woman earning $15,000 per year for 2,000 hours of work can have her hourly wage increased from $7.50 to $8.00 by either a straightforward increase in current money payments or a reduction in her working hours to 1,875 with no reduction in yearly earnings. If her raise comes in the form of an increase in money payments, she will receive $1,000 (before taxes) more in yearly income that she can use to buy a variety of things (she could even buy time off by giving money back to her employer in exchange for days off). However, if she receives her raise in the form of paid vacation time, she is in fact being paid in the form of a commodity: leisure time.

The second general type of fringe benefit is *deferred compensation*, compensation that is earned now but will be paid in the form of money later on. Pension benefits make up the largest proportion of these fringes.

Payments in kind. It is a well-established tenet of economic theory that, *other things equal*, people prefer to receive $X in cash to receiving a commodity that costs $X. The reason is simple. With $X in cash the person can choose to buy the particular commodity, but he or she can also buy a variety of other things. Cash is thus the form of payment that gives the recipient the most discretion and the most options in maximizing utility. In-kind payments are inherently more restrictive, and while they generate utility, they do not ordinarily generate as much as cash payments of equal monetary value.

As might be suspected, however, "other things" are not equal. Specifically, in-kind payments offer employees a sizable tax advantage because, for the most part, they are not taxable under current income tax regulations. The failure to tax important in-kind payments is a factor that tends to offset their restrictive nature in affecting employee demands for in-kind payments. A worker may prefer $1,000 in cash to $1,000 in some in-kind payment, but if his or her income- and payroll-tax rates total 25 percent, the comparison is really between $750 in cash and $1,000 in the in-kind benefit.

Deferred compensation. Like payments in kind, deferred compensation schemes enjoy a tax advantage over current cash payments. With deferred payments the tax advantage is that the compensation is not taxed until it is received by the worker. In the case of pensions, for example, employers contribute currently to a pension fund, but employees do not obtain access to this fund until they retire. Neither the pension fund *contributions* made on behalf of employees by employers nor the *interest* that compounds when these funds are invested is subject to the personal income tax. Only when the retirement benefits are received does the ex-worker pay taxes, but because of lower income and special tax advantages given the elderly, the tax rates actually paid are relatively low.

Because of the above-noted tax advantages accorded to pension fund contributions, employees wishing to save for old age have incentives to do so through a pension fund, rather than receiving cash payments and saving from that (although employees can now establish their own Individual Retirement Accounts). Saving through a pension fund defers the taxation of part of one's compensation (the pension fund contributions) until old age and permits funds for retirement to accumulate on a tax-free basis. What one *loses* with saving through a pension fund is the ability to currently control one's assets: by putting money into a pension fund, one is forgoing the ability to use that money now for routine or emergency needs.

Again, then, two opposing forces are at work on the demand for fringe benefits by employees. With both kinds of benefits there is a loss of discretion in spending one's total compensation, which tends to render fringes inferior to cash payments in generating utility. On the other hand, special tax advantages are accorded to both kinds of benefits as compared with cash payments, which tends to increase the demand for fringes.[2]

Before turning to a discussion of employer preferences regarding fringe benefits, it is interesting to note that the presence of labor unions appears to increase the share of total compensation devoted to fringe benefits.[3] As we mention when discussing this issue in Chapter 12, one possible reason for this effect is that unions may be able to more effectively identify the desire for a given fringe benefit among workers than can an employer. It may also be that by raising wages, unions place their members in higher tax brackets and make it more likely that they will become permanently attached to the firm, both of which should increase the desirability of fringe benefits. Moreover, if union leaders are politically more responsive to the preferences of older, longer-term members than younger, more mobile workers, the preferences of the former group will tend to dominate in the negotiating process.[4]

---

[2]Stephen Woodbury, "Substitution Between Wage and Nonwage Benefits," *American Economic Review* 73(March 1983):166–82, shows that wages and fringe benefits (especially pensions) are viewed by workers as very good substitutes, and that tax rate increases play a large role in explaining the growth of fringe benefits.

[3]Richard B. Freeman, "The Effect of Unionism on Fringe Benefits," *Industrial and Labor Relations Review* 34(July 1981):489–509.

Thus, while tax advantages may be the driving force behind the relatively recent growth of fringe benefits, unions appear to facilitate this growth.

Employer Preferences

Suppose employers are totally indifferent about whether to spend $X on wages or $X on fringes. Both expenditures are of equal sums of money and are equally deductible as a business expense. If so, the composition of total compensation is a matter of indifference to them; only the level of compensation is of concern.

The easiest way to depict the willingness of a firm to offer fringe benefits is through the use of isoprofit curves (introduced in Chapter 8). Suppose a firm offers a certain type of job for which it must pay at least $X in total compensation to attract workers. Suppose also that if it paid more than $X, its profits would fall below zero. Thus, it must compensate its workers $X per year to remain competitive in both the labor and product markets. However, if the *composition* of total compensation is a matter of indifference to the firm, it will be willing to offer any combination of wages and fringes that totals $X in value. The various compensation packages a firm is willing to offer fall along the zero-profit isoprofit curve drawn between wages and fringes (see Figure 11.1).

Any combination of wages and fringes along the isoprofit curve shown in Figure 11.1 would yield the firm equal profits (assuming it could recruit workers). Thus, it is willing to offer $X in wages and no fringe benefits, fringes that cost (say) $300 and wages that equal $(X - 300), or any other combination totaling $X in cost. The slope of the isoprofit curve is *negative,* reflecting the fact that the firm can only increase fringes if it reduces wages (again, because of competitive pressures). Further, in this case the isoprofit curve has a slope of -1, which reflects employer indifference about the composition of compensation. If employees want a health insurance policy costing $300, it will cost them $300 in wages.

There are some reasons to expect that firms might offer fringe benefits to their employees on something other than the dollar-for-dollar basis assumed above. For one, by increasing compensation in the form of fringes rather than wages, employers can often avoid taxes and required insurance payments that are levied as a fraction of payroll. Social security taxes and workers' compensation premiums are examples of costs that generally increase with salaries and wages but not with fringe benefits, thus making it more costly for an employer to increase compensation by increasing salaries than by increasing benefits.[5] Payroll taxes thus tend to flatten the offer curve shown in Figure 11.1 (a $300 increase in fringes could be accompanied by a reduction in wages of only $280, and the firm would be equally profitable).

---

[4]For evidence on this issue, see Stanley M. Nealey, "Pay and Benefit Preference," *Industrial Relations* 3(October 1963):17–28. Other evidence that the preferences of younger and older workers diverge can be found in Jonathon Eaton and Harvey Rosen, "Agency, Delayed Compensation and the Structure of Executive Remuneration," Industrial Relations Section, Princeton University, Working Paper 153 (September 1982).

[5]The argument that the presence of social security taxes levied on the employer increases the costs of granting salary increases holds only for workers who earn less than the maximum taxable earnings base, which in 1984 was $37,800. Earnings beyond $37,800 in 1984 were not subject to the social security tax.

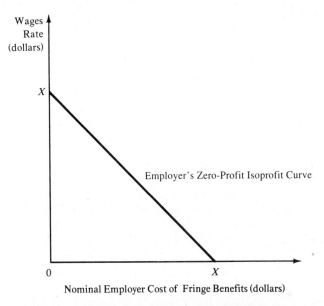

FIGURE 11.1   An Isoprofit Curve Showing the Wage/Fringe Offers a Firm Might Be Willing to Make to Its Employees: A Unitary Trade-off

There are also more subtle factors that might cause firms to offer fringes to their employees on something other than the dollar-for-dollar basis in Figure 11.1. Some fringe benefits allow firms to attract a certain kind of worker in situations in which the use of wage rates would be of questionable legal validity. For example, suppose a firm prefers to hire mature adults, preferably those with children, in the hopes of acquiring a stable, dependable work force. An employer attempting to attract these people by offering them higher wages than single, younger, or much older adults would risk charges of discrimination. Instead, the firm can accomplish the same effect by offering its employees fringe benefits that are of much more value to the group it is trying to attract than to others. For example, offering *family* coverage under a health insurance plan has the effect of compensating those with families more than others because single or childless people cannot really take advantage of the full benefit. Offering dental insurance covering orthodontic work or tuition assistance for children who attend college accomplishes similar purposes. Thus, at times fringe benefits allow the firm to give preferential treatment to a group it wants to attract without running afoul of discrimination laws.

The preferential treatment given to some groups of workers, however, has become of increasing concern to employees as fringes have grown in importance. Many families, for example, have dual earners and have no need of two family medical insurance policies. In a move to take into account employee dissatisfaction with biases in fringe benefits, some 100 firms have adopted *cafeteria plans* that allow workers to elect their own fringe benefits up to some dollar limit. Instead of receiving a redundant medical insurance policy, for example, a worker already covered by a spouse's insurance policy could elect to receive a longer paid vacation.

One firm implementing such a plan found that only 10 percent of its employees elected to receive the same benefits offered by its old program.[6]

Another subtle reason why a firm may prefer to put an extra dollar of compensation into fringe benefits rather than wages (and thus have a flatter offer curve than is shown in Figure 11.1) is found whenever the government regulates profits or controls wages. Regulated monopolies or governmental bodies, for example, fearing that the granting of large wage increases would call forth an investigation or outrage public opinion, could hide an increase in compensation by granting increases in fringe benefits that are difficult to cost out: a nicer work environment, shortened days in the summer, time off for religious observances, top-quality food in the company cafeteria for bargain prices, low-cost loans to employees for buying a home, and so forth.[7] Similar behavior will occur among firms that are having trouble recruiting employees during a period when the government is attempting to control wages to fight inflation. Wages are easy to observe and measure. Many fringe benefits are very difficult to observe and quantify, and can thus be used to increase compensation without violating wage controls.[8] Examples of fringes that are difficult for wage control boards to monitor are increased rest times on the job, rules increasing crew sizes in dangerous activities, and better recreational facilities for employees.

On the other hand, as noted earlier in Example 6.1, some fringe benefits could conceivably increase absenteeism, thus reducing the firm's profitability. Life insurance, health insurance, and pensions, for example, are all awarded to current employees regardless of their actual hours of work during the year (assuming they work enough to keep their jobs). If an increase in compensation comes in the form of increasing one of these benefits, workers' *incomes* are increased in the sense that they need to save less for "rainy days" and are thus freer to spend their cash income. However, this increase in income is accomplished without an increase in the price of leisure because the hourly wage has not risen. Recall from Chapter 6 that an increase in income with no change in the price of leisure causes people to want to work less. In this case workers will not quit their jobs, but they may be absent from work more often.[9] The connection between absenteeism and a fringe benefit is even more obvious in the case of paid sick leave.[10]

---

[6]"Making Job Benefits Flexible," *The New York Times,* March 13, 1981, pp. D1, D3; Hay/Higgins *Bulletin* (June 1984).

[7]For further arguments along this line, *see* Armen Alchian and Reuben Kessel, "Competition, Monopoly, and the Pursuit of Money," *Aspects of Labor Economics,* ed. H. G. Lewis (Princeton, N.J.: Princeton University Press, 1962). *See also* our discussion in Chapter 13 of fringe benefits in the public sector.

[8]For a brief discussion of the difficulties inherent in controlling fringe benefits, *see* John Dunlop, "Wage and Price Controls as Seen by a Controller," *Proceedings of the Industrial Relations Research Association* (Madison, Wis.: Industrial Relations Research Association, 1975), pp. 457–63.

[9]Although there has not been much empirical work on this issue, a study of absenteeism in the paper and box industry found it was positively related to pensions and negatively related to wage rates. *See* Steven G. Allen, "Compensation, Safety, and Absenteeism: Evidence from the Paper Industry," *Industrial and Labor Relations Review* 34(January 1981):207–18. *See also* his "An Empirical Model of Work Attendance," *Review of Economics and Statistics* 63(February 1981):77–87.

[10]For evidence on teacher absenteeism, *see* Donald R. Winkler, "The Effects of Sick-Leave Policy on Teacher Absenteeism," *Industrial and Labor Relations Review* 33,2(January 1980):232–40.

Wage Rate (dollars)

X

A

Alternative Isoprofit Curves

B

0

X

Nominal Employer Cost of Fringe Benefits (dollars)

FIGURE 11.2 Alternative Isoprofit Curves Showing the Wage/Fringe Offers a Firm Might Be Willing to Make to Its Employees: Nonunitary Trade-offs

Aside from the possibility of contributing to absenteeism, some fringe benefits compress the differentials in compensation between skilled and unskilled workers, thereby reducing the incentives of employees to obtain training for skilled positions.[11] Fringes such as medical insurance and free or discounted merchandise are of equal value to people of similar-size families, no matter how much they earn. Because their value thus represents a larger percentage of a low-wage worker's compensation, such benefits tend to compress earnings differentials between skilled and unskilled workers.

The major point of our analysis of fringes from the employer's perspective is that a dollar spent on fringes could cost employers more or less than a dollar nominally spent on wages or salaries.[12] When fringes enhance productivity more than a similar expenditure on wages would, the isoprofit curve in Figure 11.1 will flatten. Figure 11.2 shows this as isoprofit curve *A*. When fringes increase other costs or reduce productivity, the isoprofit curve will steepen. In this case (curve *B* in Figure 11.2) a $300 fringe benefit would have to be accompanied by a $320 fall in wages, say, to keep profits constant.

---

[11]*See* Chapter 9 for the complete argument on how wage differentials affect the incentives of workers to acquire human capital.

[12]Many fringe benefits, like pensions and paid vacations, become more generous as the worker's tenure with the firm increases. In fact, in most firms, workers are not even eligible to receive retirement benefits unless they have worked at least 10 years for the firm. These policies are clearly designed to reduce costly turnover, but they are more a matter of the *timing* of compensation than anything else. We shall discuss issues regarding the timing of compensation later in this chapter.

The Joint Determination of Wages and Fringes

The offer curve in a particular labor market can be obtained by connecting the relevant portions of each firm's zero-profit isoprofit curve, as done in Chapter 8 (see Figure 8.5). When all firms have isoprofit curves with a slope of -1, the offer curve is a straight line with a negative and unitary slope. One such offer curve is illustrated in Figure 11.3, and the only difference between this curve and the zero-profit isoprofit curve in Figure 11.1 is that the latter traced out *hypothetical* offers *one* firm could make, while this one traces out the *actual* offers made by *all* firms in this labor market. Of course, if firms have isoprofit curves whose slopes are different from -1, the offer curve will not look like that depicted in Figure 11.3. However, whatever its shape or the absolute value of its slope at any point, it will slope downward.

Employees, then, face a set of wage-fringe offers that imply the necessity for making trade-offs. Those employees (like Y in Figure 11.3) who attach relatively great importance to the availability of currently spendable cash will choose to accept offers in which total compensation comes largely in the form of wages. Employees who may be less worried about current cash income but more interested in the tax advantages of fringe benefits will accept offers in which fringe benefits form a higher proportion of total compensation (see the curve for Worker Z in Figure

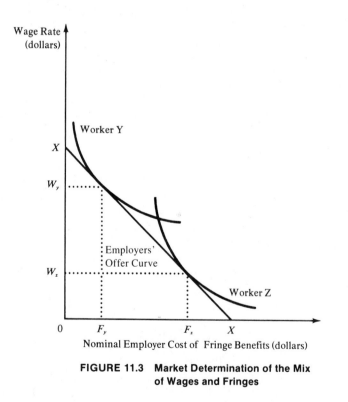

**FIGURE 11.3   Market Determination of the Mix
of Wages and Fringes**

11.3).[13] Thus, employers will tailor their compensation packages to suit the preferences of the workers they are trying to attract. If their employees tend to be young, poor, or present-oriented, for example, their compensation packages may be heavily weighted toward wages and include relatively little in the way of pensions and insurance. Alternatively, if they are trying to attract people in an area where family incomes are high and hence fringe benefits offer relatively large tax savings, firms may offer packages in which fringe benefits constitute a larger proportion of the total.

Figure 11.3 shows that workers receiving more generous fringe benefits pay for them by receiving lower wages, other things being equal. Further, if employer isoprofit curves have a unitary slope, a fringe benefit that costs the employer $1 to provide will cost workers $1 in wages. In other words, economic theory suggests that workers pay for their own fringe benefits.

Actually observing the trade-off between wages and fringe benefits is not easy. Because firms that pay high wages usually also offer very good fringe benefits, it often appears to the casual observer that wages and fringes are *positively* related. Casual observation in this case is misleading, however, because it does not allow for the influences of *other factors,* such as the demands of the job and the quality of workers involved, that influence total compensation. The other factors are most conveniently controlled for statistically, and the few statistical studies on this subject tend to support the prediction of a negative relationship between wages and fringe benefits.[14]

The policy consequences of a negative wage/fringe trade-off are enormously important because government legislation designed to improve fringe benefits might well be paid for by workers in the form of lower future wage increases.

Policy Application: Pension Reform Legislation

Pension plans provided by employers are of two general types: *defined contribution* plans and *defined benefit* plans. The less common are *defined contribution* plans, in which the employer merely promises to contribute a certain amount each year to a

---

[13]The indifference curves in Figure 11.3 are drawn with the typical convexity. One assumption underlying this convexity is that as *fringes* increase, the decrease in currently spendable cash that one is willing to bear declines, owing to the loss of discretionary control in spending one's income. The other assumption is that as *current wages* increase and workers advance into higher income tax brackets, the tax advantages offered by fringe benefits become ever more attractive (which causes the indifference curves to steepen).

[14]Empirical studies of the trade-offs between wages and pensions are as yet few in number. Many of the studies that do exist indicate workers pay, perhaps dollar for dollar, for their pensions in the form of lower wages. For a review of these studies, see Ronald Ehrenberg and Robert Smith, "A Framework for Evaluating State and Local Government Pension Reform," in *Public Sector Labor Markets,* eds. Peter Mieszkowski and George E. Peterson (Washington, D.C.: The Urban Institute, 1981). However, not all studies done in this area have found the predicted trade-offs, perhaps because of data problems. For a discussion of data requirements for estimating these trade-offs, see Robert Smith and Ronald Ehrenberg, "Estimating Wage-Fringe Trade-Offs: Some Data Problems," in *The Measurement of Labor Cost,* ed. Jack E. Triplett, National Bureau of Economic Research, Conference on Research in Income and Wealth, Studies in Income and Wealth, vol. 48 (Chicago: University of Chicago Press, 1983).

Example 11.1

The Wage/Fringe Trade-off in the Collective Bargaining Process

At times, the wage/fringe trade-off can be directly observed in the collective bargaining process, although management and unions are usually reluctant to explicitly acknowledge that workers might be paying for their own fringe benefits. In 1950, however, the United Automobile Workers (the UAW) called a strike against Chrysler over the issue of pensions. Chrysler had promised a pension benefit to its workers for the first time, but it had not promised to put aside current funds to *guarantee* retirees that they would obtain benefits in the future. Fearing that Chrysler could become bankrupt in the future, the UAW wanted this pension promise to be backed up with current funding, and it called a strike. (In the early 1980s Chrysler did teeter on the edge of bankruptcy, although by 1983 the company was again solvent.) The union's last offer to Chrysler before the strike is an excellent illustration of a wage/fringe trade-off: it asked Chrysler either to pay 6 cents per hour (per worker) to a pension fund and 4 cents to buy medical insurance or to give workers a 10-cents-per-hour raise in wages.

SOURCE: *The Daily Labor Report*, January 17, 1950, p. A-17.

---

fund to which the employee has access upon retirement. The fund is increased each year by employer, and perhaps also employee, contributions and by returns from investments made by the fund's managers. One's retirement benefits depend solely on the size of the fund at the age of retirement.

More common are *defined benefit* pension plans, in which the employer promises employees a certain benefit upon retirement. This benefit may be a fixed sum per month or a fixed fraction of one's earnings prior to retirement. In either case employers guarantee the size of the pension benefit, and it is up to them to make sure that the funds are there when the promised benefits need to be paid.

The *vesting* provisions of any pension plan are the rules about who becomes eligible to receive a pension. If a plan is unvested, any worker who quits the company before retirement age loses all rights to a pension benefit. Once workers are vested, they can receive a pension from Company X even if they quit X before retirement age and work elsewhere. How much they receive from X at retirement, of course, depends on their length of service with X and their preretirement earnings; however, the point is that they receive *something* from X upon retirement if they are vested.

In 1974 Congress passed the Employee Retirement Income Security Act (ERISA), which, among other things, required private-sector employers to adopt liberalized vesting rules. The intent of the legislation was to help employees by making it more likely that they would receive pensions in their old age. However, as we have seen with other programs designed to help workers, good intentions can sometimes be undone by unintended side effects. What are the side effects of ERISA's vesting provisions?

From the employees' perspective, rules that entitle them to become vested, or vested sooner, enhance their welfare if nothing else in the compensation package is changed. They are not penalized as much for voluntarily leaving an employer, nor are they as economically vulnerable to being fired. However, the value different workers attach to liberalized vesting may vary widely. Suppose ERISA forced a plant to vest its employees after 10, rather than 15, years of work. Employees who plan on working for a given employer less than 10 years do not benefit at all from the liberalized vesting mandated by ERISA; neither do workers who have more than 15 years of service with the company. On the other hand, workers who might want to change employers after 10–15 years of service, or who might be fired during that period, stand to gain from liberalized vesting.

From the employers' perspective, ERISA's vesting rules impose costs because they make it possible for more workers to qualify for pensions. For example, it was estimated that the pension costs of nonvesting employers would rise by 3–26 percent as a result of ERISA's vesting rules.[15] Will firms simply absorb these costs, or will they force workers to pay for their more liberal pension benefits in the form of lower wages?

Our theory suggests that employers probably will not—and in a competitive market cannot—absorb the added pension costs. Those firms for which pension costs are increased will have to hold the line on future wage increases to remain competitive in the product market, and over time the wages they pay will fall below the level that would have held had it not been for the pension reform legislation.[16]

Unfortunately, the decline in wages that will occur in the firms affected by ERISA's vesting rules does *not* simply mean that worker welfare is unchanged. Indeed, it can be shown (see Figure 11.4) that *if* the workers employed by firms with illiberal vesting are both *informed* and *mobile,* their utility will be negatively affected by the ERISA vesting regulation. Suppose, for example, that before ERISA Person A worked for a nonvesting employer, receiving the relatively high wage of W_1 and a low level (P_0) of expected retirement benefits owing to the slim chances of receiving a pension. Person B, who obviously cares more than A about pensions, as can be seen by the different indifference curve, takes a job promising a relatively large and secure pension (P_1) but paying a lower current wage (W_0). Suppose also that ERISA in effect makes all levels of expected pension benefits below P_1 illegal by forcing employers with pension plans to provide vesting after 10 years.

Competitive pressures force all wage/pension offers to lie along the offer curve, *XX,* in Figure 11.4. Thus, when the pension promises of A's employer are forcibly increased to P_1, the wage offer in that firm will eventually fall to W_0. For Person A, a person who is not willing to give up much in the way of current compensation to obtain a better pension, utility is reduced from A_1 to A_0. In other words, the effect of

---

[15]Norman Ture, *The Future of Private Pension Plans* (Washington, D.C.: The American Enterprise Institute for Public Policy Research, 1976), p.89.

[16]The two studies that have looked at the effects of vesting on wages have both found that nonvesting (public) employers pay higher wages, other things equal, than ones who vest. See Ehrenberg and Smith, "A Framework for Evaluating State and Local Government Pension Reform," for more details.

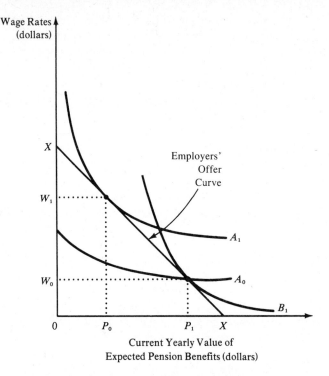

Wage Rates (dollars)

Employers' Offer Curve

X

W_1

A_1

W_0

A_0

B_1

0   P_0 P_1 X

Current Yearly Value of
Expected Pension Benefits (dollars)

**FIGURE 11.4   The Effects of ERISA in a Properly
Functioning Market**

a law that increases pension benefits may well be to reduce wages, with the consequence that it reduces the utility of people who have the strongest preferences for current, as opposed to deferred, income.

Under certain circumstances, however, the ERISA vesting rules would enhance worker welfare. For example, suppose people with preferences like Person C in Figure 11.5 *thought* they were working for an employer who, while perhaps not vesting their pension rights, would in fact employ them until they retired. Later they find out that this employer is more likely than they thought to fire them before retirement and that, if so, they will lose their entire pensions. These people *believe* themselves to be at point L, receiving P_1 in expected pensions, W_1 in wages, and C_2 in utility. In actuality, they are, at point M, receiving P_0 in expected pension benefits and C_0 in utility. If ERISA forces the expected pension level to rise to P_1 by requiring vesting, their *actual* utility will increase from C_0 to C_1 despite the fact that their wages fall from W_1 to W_0 (they move in actuality from point M to N in Figure 11.5). ERISA would also improve the welfare of people like C if they were at point M and, because of a lack of mobility, could not find a job with another employer that would place them at point N.

The major point of this discussion is that if product markets are competitive and firms are forced to operate on their zero-profit isoprofit curves, workers will pay for ERISA-mandated increases in pension benefits in the long run. Workers immobilized by ignorance or lack of choice may be better off with government-mandated floors on pension benefits, despite the downward pressure on their wages. However,

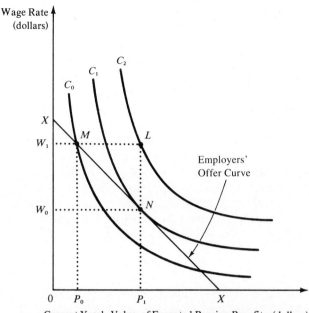

FIGURE 11.5   **Effects of ERISA in an Uninformed Market**

there are also circumstances in which workers would be made worse off by the mandated increases in expected pension benefits. Careful study in advance of reform legislation may be desirable to avoid hurting the people the government is intending to help.

IMPLICIT CONTRACTS, EXPLICIT CONTRACTS, AND ASYMMETRIC INFORMATION

The agreements between employers and employees concerning job duties and compensation can be considered as contracts, whether or not they are formally written. An *explicit contract,* such as a formal written agreement between a union and a firm, specifies what transactions or events will occur when some contingency arises. Thus, such contracts may spell out how the firm is to respond if layoffs are necessary or what is to be done when a job vacancy occurs.

Nonunion employees, however, typically do not work under explicit contracts. These employees, who constitute a majority of American workers, have relationships with their employers that are governed by *implicit contracts.* An implicit contract is a set of shared, informal understandings about how firms and workers will respond to contingencies.[17]

---

[17]For a more detailed analysis of implicit contracts, see Michael Riordan and Michael Wachter, "What Do Implicit Contracts Do?" *Proceedings of the Industrial Relations Research Association,* (1982):291–98, or Robert Flanagan, "Implicit Contracts, Explicit Contracts and Wages," *American Economic Review, Papers and Proceedings,* 74(May 1984):345–49.

The major difference between explicit and implicit contracts is that provisions of the former are legally enforceable while, although some rules in implicit contracts *may* be legally enforceable, others are not. This distinction, however, may not be quite as significant as it first appears because the *market* could provide a means for enforcing implicit contracts. More specifically, if either employer or employee acquires a reputation for breaking the promises inherent in implicit agreements, others will be less willing to transact with them in the future. Thus, differences between the two contracts in enforceability are mostly a matter of degree. Moreover, since drawing up a list of all forseeable contingencies and specifying rules for responding to them would be very costly to both parties, even employment relationships governed largely by explicit contracts remain implicit to some extent.

Over the years, but especially lately, labor economists have been interested in the forces that shape some fundamental characteristics common to explicit and implicit contracts in the labor market. For example, economic theory has been used to explain the following compensation practices:

1. Wages are typically tied to hours of work, rather than to units of output produced;
2. Nominal wages are rarely reduced, even in the nonunion sector, so when the demand for labor curve shifts left during a recession, the labor market typically adjusts through layoffs; and
3. Workers typically receive higher wages as they become older, but are then required—or offered a large "bribe" (a pension)—to fully retire from their companies at a specified age.

Analyses of these phenomena tend to stress three themes: there are costs associated with agreeing upon or adjusting contract provisions; the two parties may have different attitudes toward fluctuations in income; and there are costs associated with enforcing contractual promises. The implications of enforcement costs have received much attention in recent years, and we shall briefly examine this theme here.

Each party to a contract is interested in holding the other to its promises; thus, it is very important to know when a contingency covered by the contract has really occurred. A contract may specify, for example, that employees who steal or shirk their duties can be fired, but a given firm might find it very difficult to prove who has violated rules on stealing or shirking, or to what extent. Likewise, a contract may permit the wage rate to be reduced during times of economic distress, but workers, lacking access to the company's records, may find it difficult to ascertain just how much distress their employer is facing.

Put differently, one of the problems facing each party in enforcing a contract is that the other party may have greater information about a particular contingency. In this respect, access to information is *asymmetric*. Moreover, the party with the greater information may have incentives to mislead the other: a firm that is actually prospering during a recession may claim it is being hurt so it can reduce wages, just as a shirking worker will attempt concealment. Because this asymmetry of information makes cheating possible, and because monitoring by the other party is often very costly, ways must be found to make contracts *self-enforcing*. That is, incentives must be built in to labor contracts that induce both parties to refrain from cheating the other when each has the opportunity to do so.

In the remainder of this chapter we shall examine economic analyses of phenomena 1 and 3 above. That is, we shall consider why labor contracts typically pay workers for their time instead of their output, and why workers at age 64 (say), who appear to be highly paid, highly valued members of a production team, are suddenly required or strongly urged to retire at age 65. We shall defer our consideration of phenomenon 2—nominal wage inflexibility over a business cycle— until Chapter 15. In analyzing each of these compensation phenomena, we shall bring one or more of the three themes mentioned above to bear.

THE BASIS OF PAY

The agreements between employers and employees concerning job duties and compensation can be considered as *contracts,* whether or not they are formally written. As mentioned briefly in Chapter 1, there are two basic types of pay provisions in labor contracts. One rewards employees for the *time* they work, and the other rewards them for some *result* of their work.[18] Some contracts, however, contain a hybrid system of rewards.

The most common reward structure is payment for time worked, with about 86 percent of U.S. employees paid either by the hour or by the month. When employees are paid for time at work, it becomes management's challenge to motivate them not to shirk during that time. An alternative that would appear to alleviate the problem of shirking is payment by results, or incentive pay. In some industries, particularly the garment industry, workers are paid for each piece of output produced. In other firms, a *standard time*—60 minutes, say—is allowed for a given task. If the task is completed *within* that time the employee is paid for the full 60 minutes, regardless of the actual time spent on the task; however, if the worker takes longer than 60 minutes to complete the job, he or she is paid for the *actual* time spent. In still other instances, workers share in the profits of the firm or receive a fraction of the value of the items they sell *(commissions).* In all these cases, workers are paid at least somewhat proportionally to their output or to the degree their employer prospers. Because such payment schemes serve as an obvious incentive to work industriously, one is led to wonder why only 14 percent of U.S. workers are paid on an incentive basis. Selecting the basis for pay is ultimately a matter of satisfying the interests of both employer and employee.

Employee Preferences

If employees were told that their average earnings over the years under a time payment system would be equal to their earnings under an individual incentive-pay

---

[18]This distinction concerning labor contracts is analyzed in Herbert A. Simon, "A Formal Theory of the Employment Relationship," *Econometrica* 19,3(July 1951):293–305, and more recently in Joseph E. Stiglitz, "Incentives, Risk, and Information: Notes Toward a Theory of Hierarchy," *Bell Journal of Economics* 6(Autumn 1975):552–79.

scheme, they would probably choose to be paid on a *time* basis. Why? Earnings under a piece-rate or commission system depend on the thought and energy one is able to bring to the job. There are days and even weeks in any person's life when one is depressed, preoccupied, tired, or otherwise distracted from maximum work effort. There are other periods when one is exceptionally productive. If employees are paid on a piece-rate basis, their earnings could be highly *variable* over time because of the somewhat uncontrollable swings in productivity. The variability in income could cause anxiety owing to the possibility that several low-productivity months could be strung together, making it difficult to meet mortgage payments and other obligations.

Because of this anxiety about less productive periods of time, employees might prefer the certainty of time-based pay to the uncertainty of piece-rate pay if both schemes paid the same average wage over time. In order to induce employees to accept piece-rate pay, employers would have to pay higher average wages over time; that is, a compensating differential would have to exist to compensate workers for the anxiety associated with variations in their earnings. Conversely, to obtain more certainty in their stream of earnings, employees would probably be willing to accept a somewhat lower average wage.

Employer Considerations

The willingness of employers to pay a premium in order to induce employees to accept piece rates depends on the costs and benefits to employers of incentive-pay schemes. If workers are paid on a *time* basis, the *employer* accepts the risk of variations in their productivity. When they are exceptionally productive, profits increase; when they are less productive, profits decline. Employers, however, may be less anxious about these *variations* than employees are. They typically have more assets and can thus weather the lean periods more comfortably than can individual workers. More important, perhaps, employers usually have several employees, and the chances are that not all will suffer the same swings in productivity at the same time (unless there is a morale problem in the firm). Thus, employers may not be as willing to pay for income certainty as are workers.

Employers must also consider, however, that incentive-pay schemes, such as piece rates, may reduce the variations in profits over time, but they will also increase the *level* of productivity. Because workers directly benefit from their own diligence in a piece-rate system, they may work much harder. A full analysis of these productivity-related incentives and the costs of implementing them must take into account differences between *individual* and *group* incentive-pay plans.

Individual Rewards: Piece Rates and Commissions

The Bureau of Labor Statistics found in 1973 that nearly half of the production workers in U.S. auto-repair shops were paid incentive rates.[19] Roughly one quarter received some fraction of the labor costs charged to the customer (they were paid by

---

[19]Sandra King, "Incentive and Time Pay in Auto Dealer Repair Shops," *Monthly Labor Review* 98,9(September 1975):45–48.

commission, in essence), and the other quarter were paid a flat rate (*piece rate*) for each kind of repair performed. The big advantage of these compensation schemes from the employer's perspective is that they induce employees to adopt a set of work goals that are consistent with those of their employer. Employees paid a piece rate are motivated to work quickly, while those paid by commission are induced to very thoroughly evaluate the servicing needs of the firm's customers. Moreover, these inducements exist without the need for, and expense of, close monitoring by the firm's supervisors. Auto-repair shops, however, provide a specific example of several general disadvantages to individually based incentive-pay schemes. These general problems include maintaining quality standards, misusing equipment, setting the rate, and measuring output.

Maintaining quality standards. Workers paid by the job are motivated to work quickly, but they are also motivated to have minimal regard for quality. Workers paid by commission are motivated to be so thorough in ferreting out servicing needs that they may fix things that are not broken. Both bases for compensation thus create a need for close supervisory attention to the quality of work performed, a need and an expense that in many cases will offset the supervisory savings associated with incentive pay.

Equipment misuse. Allied to the problem of work quality is the problem of equipment misuse. Workers receiving incentive pay are motivated to work so quickly that machines or tools are often damaged or otherwise misused. It is often asserted, for example, that piece-rate workers disengage safety devices on machinery in their desire to maximize output. This problem is mitigated to the extent that equipment damage causes *downtime* that results in lost employee earnings.

Setting the rate. A third problem, probably more associated with piece rates than with commissions, is setting the rate. For example, it may be standard practice in the auto-repair industry to assume that an engine tune-up will require two hours of work and to translate this time requirement into a "per job" piece rate. Suppose, however, some new tool or electronic device is adopted that reduces the time required for a tune-up. A new piece rate will have to be adopted, but how do the shop's owners determine the standard time requirement for tune-ups now? The best way may be to observe mechanics using the new devices, but if these workers know they are being observed for purposes of setting a new rate, they will probably deliberately work slowly so that the time requirement is overestimated in order to drive up the piece rate. The problem is compounded in industries facing frequent changes in products or technology. In the women's apparel industry around the turn of the century, for example, it was common to have seasonal strikes over piece rates coinciding with seasonal changes in fashions.[20]

---

[20]Louis Levine, *The Women's Garment Workers* (New York: B. W. Huebsch, 1924), p. 42. The observation that a stable technology is important for the success of an incentive-pay system is also made by Sumner H. Slichter, James J. Healy, and E. Robert Livernash, *The Impact of Collective Bargaining on Management* (Washington: The Brookings Institution, 1960), p. 519.

Measuring output. A fourth reason why individual incentive-pay schemes are not more widely used is the problem of measuring and motivating individual *output*. The output of an auto mechanic, salesperson, or a dressmaker is relatively easy to measure in terms of quantity, but what about that of an office manager or auto assembly-line worker? The manager has a number of duties and deals with a multitude of problems; combining them into a single index of output would be next to impossible. Assembly-line workers, on the other hand, may have an easily counted output, but it is not individually controlled. In both cases, *individual* incentive pay would be arbitrary or useless; however, *group* incentives might be attractive in these situations.

Group Incentive Pay

When individual output is hard to monitor or control, group incentive-pay schemes have sometimes been adopted to bring the interests of workers in line with those of the employer.[21] The forms these pay systems take are analogous to the schemes discussed above. In some cases work groups are paid by the piece for output produced *by the group*. In other cases employees share in the profits of the firm each year—a close analogue to the commission basis for individual pay. In still other cases workers might *own* the firm and split the profits among themselves, or more commonly, be partially compensated in shares of company stock.[22]

One drawback to group incentives is that groups are composed of individuals, and it is at the individual level that decisions about shirking are ultimately made. A person who works very hard to increase group output or firm profits winds up splitting the fruits of his or her labor with everyone else in the firm. Very little of the person's extra efforts are captured by him or her; most go to other people, who may not have put out extra effort. Group incentives, then, are sometimes no incentive at all. People come to realize that they can reap the rewards of someone else's hard work without doing any extra work of their own, and that if they do put out extra work, the rewards mainly go to others. Such schemes thus give workers incentives to cheat on their fellow employees by shirking.

In very small groups, however, cheating may be easy to detect, and group punishments, such as ostracism, can be effectively used to eliminate it. In these cases, group incentive-pay systems can accomplish their aims (subject, of course, to all the drawbacks of individual incentive-pay systems noted above). However, if the group of workers receiving incentive pay is large, cheating (shirking) probably

---

[21]Pay based on company profits also represents a way firms have of controlling their real wage costs. When the product price of a given firm goes up with prices in general, firms may seek to adopt a policy of tying their wage increases to some aggregate measure of prices (such as the Consumer Price Index). However, when an industry's product prices are declining relative to prices in the aggregate, firms in the industry may find profit-sharing plans advantageous. Under these plans the compensation of their workers is closely tied to the firm's profitability, and increases are granted only if the firm is profitable.

[22]For a detailed treatment of worker-owned enterprise, the most widespread example of which is in Yugoslavia, see Jaroslav Vanek, *The General Theory of Labor-Managed Market Economies* (Ithaca, N.Y.: The Cornell University Press, 1970).

cannot be effectively handled. Group incentive-pay schemes thus become less effective as group size increases.

As suggested by Example 11.2, the *basis* upon which group incentive payments are made is very important in determining the overall profitability of the firm. For example, consider a firm wishing to maximize profits over the *long run* and trying to decide how to compensate its executives in such a way that this long-term goal will be achieved. If it adopts a yearly profit-sharing plan in which a fraction of year-end profits is given to each executive, its executives may be induced to pursue strategies designed to maximize profits in the current period. These short-run strategies may not be consistent with long-run profit-maximization, but the executives involved may use their short-run performances to obtain positions with other firms before the long-run consequences of their strategies are fully observed.

Perhaps for these reasons, 40 percent of the 200 largest industrial companies in the United States give their executives rights to future payments that are directly tied

---

Example 11.2

Incentive Pay and Output—or "You Get What Your Pay For"

Paying workers for a given output can lead to unexpected uses of employee resources and time. As noted in this chapter, piece rates tend to induce workers to emphasize quantity over quality, but the total effects of piece-rate schemes also depend on just what "output" is being paid for.

There is a (probably apocryphal) story that when Soviet farm labor was compensated according to the number of acres planted, plowing was done too hastily and seeds were sown too far apart for high productivity. In an effort to improve output, the Soviet Union began to compensate farm workers on the basis of yield per acre. This caused farmers to invest too many resources (time, fertilizer) per acre and not plant extensively enough, and costs rose. Only when they seized upon the idea of paying farmers on the basis of the difference between the value of output and the costs of production (that is, *profit*) did farmers have the incentive to take into account output and costs.

Another example of the importance of understanding how incentive pay can affect output comes from Great Britain. Instead of compensating dentists on the basis of "contact hours" with patients, The British National Health Service decided (for a while) to compensate dentists on the basis of cavities filled. The result was that the incidence of tooth decay identified by dentists increased substantially and the time it took to fill cavities dropped from 18 to 6 minutes per filling. It is obvious that this new basis for compensation was of questionable benefit to the patient.

SOURCES: Assar Lindbeck, *The Political Economy of the New Left* (New York: Harper & Row, 1971), p. 71; John Pencavel, "Piecework and On-the-Job Screening" (New York: Department of Economics, Stanford University, June 1975), p. 4

to company performance over a *multiyear* period.[23] Ninety-five percent of all these long-term "performance attainment" plans base their awards on some measure of company prosperity over a period of 3–5 years, apparently in the belief that a period of less than 3 years is too short to measure long-term performance, while more than 5 years would represent so long a delay in receiving rewards that their motivational effects would be weakened. As of now, little is known about the effects of these plans.[24]

Earnings Under Piece and Time Rates

Two observations lead to the prediction that workers on incentive pay earn more per hour than comparable workers paid on a time basis. First, if workers have a preference for being paid on a time basis, employers will have to pay a premium, a compensating wage differential, to induce them to accept an incentive-pay scheme. This earnings differential would compensate workers for accepting the risks associated with incentive pay. Second, the workers most likely to accept a job with incentive pay are those most likely to be successful at it: the fastest, most intense workers.

Although there are few studies of this issue, the prediction that incentive-pay workers earn more appears to hold up. A 1960s study of punch-press operators in Chicago found that piece-rate workers earned about 9 percent more per hour of work than did those paid an hourly wage.[25] More recent research by the Bureau of Labor Statistics found that auto-repair workers paid on an incentive basis earned 20–50 percent more per hour than those paid on a time basis.[26]

Other Kinds of Incentive Pay

Although used relatively infrequently, firms have also devised incentive pay schemes other than piece rates, commissions, and profit sharing to solve particular production problems. These plans usually provide for the payment of some kind of bonus if a desired outcome is achieved. For example, a firm attempting to induce employees to avoid injuries on the job might give a quarterly bonus to any worker who remained uninjured during that quarter.

---

[23]Lawrence C. Bickford, "Long-Term Incentives for Management; Part 6: Performance Attainment Plans," *Compensation Review,* Third Quarter, 1981:14–29. A related paper is Jonathon Eaton and Harvey Rosen, "Agency, Delayed Compensation, and the Structure of Executive Remuneration."

[24]That executive performance is affected by executive incentives was shown by Robert Masson, "Executive Motivations, Earnings, and Consequent Performance," *Journal of Political Economy,* November/December 1971:1278–93. His study showed that firms whose executives received company stock as part of their compensation package exhibited better stock-market performance during the 1947–66 period.

[25]John Pencavel, "Work Effort, On-the-Job Screening, and Alternative Methods of Remuneration," in *Research in Labor Economics,* vol. 1, ed. Ronald Ehrenberg (Greenwich, Conn.: JAI Press, 1977), pp. 225–58.

[26]King, "Incentive and Time Pay in Auto Dealer Repair Shops," p. 46.

Some of the most imaginative incentive pay systems have been directed at the problem of absenteeism. Two in particular have achieved notice in the oral tradition of labor economics. A manufacturing plant during the 1940s coped with absenteeism by holding a daily raffle. The prizes were various consumable and durable items of special value to householders during those shortage-prone years. However, to have a chance to win, a worker had to be present. Absenteeism apparently fell dramatically.

Another scheme was adopted by an automobile manufacturer. This involved awarding daily points to each employee who was present for work—points which could be accumulated and redeemed for prizes, such as tickets to popular vacation attractions. The wrinkle in this plan was that the points were not given to the worker, but to the worker's spouse. With the spouse helping to monitor work behavior, it is said that absenteeism problems were greatly reduced.[27]

INTERNAL LABOR MARKETS AND THE TIME PATTERN OF COMPENSATION

Given the difficulties and disadvantages of implementing the common forms of individual or group incentive pay, firms might consider methods of motivating workers using a time-based pay system. Time-based approaches to motivation usually offer delayed rewards to workers only *after* diligent effort has been expended by the worker and observed by the employer over a long period. The prospect of these rewards gives workers incentives to work hard. The rewards may come either in the form of a bonus after years of loyal effort or in the form of a promotion. However, a common requirement for both forms of rewards is a *long-term relationship* between employer and employee.

That many workers, after a period of "job shopping," establish a long-term relationship with an employer was suggested in Chapter 10. It has been estimated, for example, that over half of all men and one fourth of all women find employers for whom they will work at least 20 years. Moreover, 8 percent of men in the 45–59-year age group have worked for only one employer over their entire work history.[28] Most of the long-term employment that characterizes much of the American labor market is found in large firms with *internal labor markets*, wherein higher-level jobs are exclusively or primarily filled from within the organization.

---

[27]We are grateful to Walter Oi for this example. This fringe benefit is an excellent illustration of how such benefits can be tailored to attract certain groups of workers. Giving points to spouses is only of benefit to married workers, and if married workers tend to be more dependable, absenteeism could be reduced by attracting members of this group to the plant.

[28]Robert E. Hall, "The Importance of Lifetime Jobs in the U.S. Economy," *American Economic Review* 72(September 1982):716–24. See also George Ackerloff and B. G. M. Main, "An Experience Weighted Measure of Employment and Unemployment Durations," *American Economic Review* 71 (December 1981):1003–11, and Walter Oi, "The Durability of Worker-Firm Attachments," a report prepared for the U.S. Department of Labor, Office of the Assistant Secretary for Policy, Evaluation, and Research, March 25, 1983, p. 16.

Internal Labor Markets and Delayed Rewards

Recall from Chapter 5 that firms sometimes create an *internal labor market*, wherein hiring is done only at certain *entry-level jobs*, and all other jobs are filled from within the firm. This hiring and promotion system serves in part as a substitute for the difficult task of screening job applicants with respect to crucial personal characteristics. Workers are hired at low levels of responsibility and then observed over time to determine their actual productive characteristics. As we argued in Chapter 10, once the firm has discovered who the productive, dependable workers are, it wants to retain them. Internal labor markets can be useful in constructing a system of deferred compensation for retaining and motivating employees. The long-term association between employer and employee fosters opportunities for both deferred payments and the long-term monitoring of employee behavior necessary to make the system work.

If employees are hired with the expectation that they will spend an entire career with a firm—an expectation that is certainly encouraged by a policy of promoting only from within—then the critical element in their choice of an employer is the *present value of their career earnings*. That is, they will be concerned about their likely earnings over their entire *career* and not just the pay on the job for which they are initially hired. A firm with an internal labor market must offer a *stream* of earnings over time whose overall present value is equivalent to that offered by other firms competing in the same labor market.

To say that the present value of an earnings stream must be equivalent to that paid elsewhere does *not* imply that the wages offered for each job or at each stage in one's career must be exactly equal to those paid by other firms. Firms that pay low wages initially but offer high earnings later on may be very competitive with firms offering initially higher wages but not raising them much over time.

For example, suppose a firm offered a 10-year job sequence where the workers were paid $15,000 in each of the first five years and $18,000 for the next five years. Using a discount rate of 2 percent, an income stream with the same present value could be achieved by a labor market competitor who offered $10,000 for each of the first five years and paid $23,500 per year for the last five! Thus it should be clear that firms offering workers *careers*, and not just jobs, have a fairly wide latitude in the way they sequence compensation within the constraint of having to offer career earnings whose present value is comparable to that paid by other firms for the same type of worker. It is this latitude, of course, that allows these firms to defer some of a worker's compensation until the end of his or her career.

Employment Contracts and the Sequencing of Pay

Thus, employers with internal labor markets have options for *sequencing* workers' pay while still offering jobs with the same *present value* of career compensation as paid by the market generally.[29] In such a setting, it may be beneficial to both employer and employee to arrange workers' pay over time so that employees are

---

[29]Our discussion here draws on Edward Lazear, "Why Is There Mandatory Retirement?" *Journal of Political Economy* 87,6(December 1979):1261–84.

Example 11.3

Compensation Schemes to Modify Worker Behavior in Other Times and Places

Employers, like psychologists, confront the problem of whether positive or negative incentives—rewards or punishments—are the better approach to changing behavior. Farmers in colonial America, for example, faced the problem of inducing their indentured servants not to run away before the end of their contractual period (and thus before the farmers' investment costs had been recouped). They adopted several negative incentives for runaways; extension of the indenture period or corporal punishment were the most common forms of penalty. However, they also used the positive incentive of *freedom dues*, a lump-sum payment of cash or property paid to servants at the end of their indenture period that would be forfeited if the servant ran away. The use of freedom dues illustrates how deferred compensation can be used to motivate employee cooperation over long periods of time.

The same dilemma of whether to use positive or negative incentives also confronted Japanese employers in the early 1900s, when they were faced with the vexing problem of absenteeism. At times, absent employees were sought out and subjected to physical torture; in other cases, wages were confiscated unless a certain consecutive number of days were worked. As argued in Chapter 8, however, employers offering disagreeable conditions of employment will have more difficulties attracting workers in a competitive labor market than will employers offering comparable jobs without the unpleasant conditions. Thus, harsh penalties for *unwanted* behavior are not costless for employers, which has often led them to adopt positive rewards for *wanted* behavior. In Japan, for example, payments in addition to regular wages were frequently made to workers who had worked without absence for an entire month. Sometimes the bonuses were sent to the workers' families in an attempt to induce parents to encourage regular work attendance among their children. At other times the bonuses were paid to *groups* of workers with good group attendance records; often these bonuses took the form of improved dormitory facilities for the work group.

These compensation schemes in other times and other places indicate that the careful structuring of pay for the purpose of changing worker behavior is not the invention of modern management science.

SOURCES: David Galenson, "The Market Evaluation of Human Capital: The Case of Indentured Servitude," *Journal of Political Economy* 89, 3 (June 1981):446–67; Koji Taira, *Economic Development and the Labor Market in Japan* (New York: Columbia University Press, 1970), pp. 120–21.

"underpaid" early in their careers and "overpaid" later on. This sequencing of pay will increase worker productivity and enable firms to pay *higher* present values of compensation than otherwise for two reasons. An understanding of these reasons takes us back to the problem of creating self-enforcing contracts in the presence of asymmetric information.

First, employment contracts that underpay workers in the early years of their careers and overpay them later on will appeal most to workers who intend to establish long-term relationships with their employers and work diligently enough to avoid being fired before their deferred rewards can be collected. Thus, in the absence of knowledge by employers of which applicants are diligent and not apt to quit, a pay scheme featuring deferred compensation appears to be a clever mechanism to force employees to reveal information about themselves that employers otherwise could not obtain.[30]

Second, a company that pays poorly to begin with but well later on increases the incentives of its employees to work industriously. Once in the job, an employee has incentives to work diligently in order to qualify for the later overpayment. The employer need not devote as many resources to supervision each year as would otherwise be the case because the firm has several years in which to identify shirkers and withhold from them the reward. Workers are less likely to take chances and shirk their responsibilities because the penalties for being caught and fired are forfeiture of a large reward. Because all employees work harder than they otherwise would, their total compensation tends to be higher also.

One feasible compensation sequencing scheme would pay workers *less* than their marginal product early in their careers and *more* than their marginal product later on. This scheme, however, must satisfy two conditions. First, the present value of the earnings streams offered to employees must be at least equal to alternative streams offered to workers in the labor market; if not, the firm cannot attract the workers it wants. Since pay that is deferred into the future is discounted, deferred sums must be larger the higher is the discount rate (or *present-orientedness*) of workers (see Chapter 9). Second, the scheme must also satisfy the equilibrium conditions that firms maximize profits and do not earn supernormal profits. If profits are not maximized, the firm's existence is threatened; if firms make supernormal profits, new firms will be induced to enter the market. Thus, in neither case would equilibrium exist.

These two conditions will be met if hiring is done until the present value of one's career-long marginal product *(MP)* equals the present value of one's career earnings stream. (This career-long condition is the multiyear analogue of the single-year profit conditions discussed in Chapter 3 and the two-year profit maximization criteria discussed in Chapter 5.) Thus, for firms choosing the "underpayment now, overpayment later" compensation scheme to be competitive in both the labor and product markets, the present value of the yearly amounts by which *MP exceeds* compensation early on must equal the present value of the later amounts by which *MP falls short* of pay.

The above compensation plan is diagrammed in Figure 11.6. We assume that *MP* rises slightly over one's career, but that in the first t^* years of employment compensation remains below *MP*. At some point in one's career with the firm—year t^* in the diagram—compensation begins to exceed *MP*. From t^* onward are the years in which diligent employees are rewarded by receiving compensation in excess of what they could receive elsewhere (namely, their *MP*). For the firm to be

---

[30]Walter Oi, "The Durability of Worker-Firm Attachments," pp. 41–45.

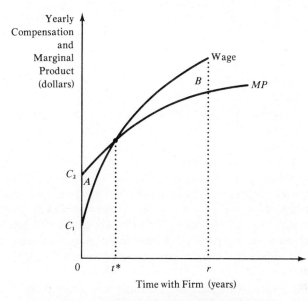

FIGURE 11.6   A Compensation Scheme Designed
to Increase Worker Motivation

competitive in both the labor and product markets, the *present value* of area A in the diagram must equal the *present value* of area B. (Area B is larger than area A in Figure 11.6 because sums received farther in the future are subjected to heavier discounting when present values are calculated.)

To be sure, there are risks to both parties in making this kind of agreement. Employees agreeing to this compensation scheme take a chance that they may be fired without cause or that their employer may go bankrupt before they have collected their reward in the years beyond t^*. It is easy to see that employers will have some incentives to renege since older workers are being paid a wage that exceeds their immediate value (at the margin) to the firm.

On the other hand, employers who do not wish to fire people face the risk that older, "overpaid" employees will stay on the job longer than is necessary to collect their reward—that is, stay on longer than time r in Figure 11.6. Knowing that their current wage is greater than the wage they can get elsewhere, since it reflects payment for more than current output, older employees will have incentives to keep working longer than is profitable for the firm.

A partial solution to these problems of risk is to agree on a formal employment contract that has two elements. One element protects older employees from arbitrary discharge by stipulating the grounds under which employees can be discharged and guaranteeing "seniority rights" for older workers. According to these seniority provisions, workers with the shortest durations of employment with the firm are usually laid off first when the firm cuts back its work force. Without these seniority rights, firms might be tempted to lay off older workers, whose wages are greater than *MP*, and keep the younger ones, who are paid less than *MP* at this point in their careers.

The second element of a formal employment contract designed to reduce the risk inherent in this compensation plan is some form of retirement clause. Unless firms can induce workers to retire before the present value of area *B* in Figure 11.6 exceeds that of *A*, or unless they can force older employees to accept wage cuts so that after year *r* their wages equal *MP*, employers will not agree to the compensation-sequencing plan under discussion.

In some instances, formal employment contracts have included a mandatory retirement age, which prior to 1978 was normally set at age 65. Under these agreements employees had to retire at age 65, whether they wanted to or not. In other cases there may be inducements offered for voluntary early retirement. For example, the 1965 contract between the automakers and the United Automobile Workers permitted workers to retire as early as age 55 if they had 30 years of service. Moreover, the monthly pension benefit before age 65 was much larger than after 65, yielding an average present value of early retirement benefits equal to $18,365, compared to a present value of $9,700 associated with retirement at age 65.[31] (A study of pension plans in 190 of the largest companies in the United States found that it is common for the present value of pension benefits to decline as retirement is postponed.)[32]

In making an early retirement decision, one must compare the utility generated by one's income and leisure streams if retirement occurs at 65 (say) with that generated by early retirement and its associated streams of leisure and pension income. When the stream of pension income associated with early retirement is increased in some way, the utility associated with early retirement is enhanced. Inducing early retirement by essentially bribing people to retire makes economic sense when older employees are paid more than they are currently worth.

Formal, explicit agreements cannot remove risks altogether, however. There is, on the employee side, no assurance that the firm will be in business during the employee's older years. Even large, once-profitable firms go bankrupt, close down plants, or are bought out by other firms—all of which can have the effect of reducing jobs or wage opportunities for older workers in the firm. While most *pension* promises are backed up by a separate fund that remains even if the employer goes bankrupt, there is really nothing to back up a promise of future pay increases. On the employer side, mandatory retirement agreements can be, and have been, voided by federal legislation. Amendments made to the Age Discrimination in Employment Act in 1978, for example, outlawed agreements that contained age 65 as the minimum age of mandatory retirement. Age 70 is now the earliest anyone can be forced to retire.

Thus, *explicit* contracts safeguarding the deferral of earnings to late in one's career are not riskless. Even more risky are *implicit contracts*, which are understood to exist but which have not been formally written and signed by both parties. In

---

[31]See Richard Burkhauser, "The Pension Acceptance Decision of Older Workers," *Journal of Human Resources* 14(Winter 1979):63–75.

[32]Edward Lazear, "Severance Pay, Pensions, and Efficient Mobility," National Bureau of Economic Research, Working Paper No. 854 (February 1982).

these contracts the employee is protected from arbitrary dismissal mainly by the need for the employer to recruit *other* workers. If a certain employer gains a reputation for firing older workers despite an implicit agreement not to do so, that employer will have trouble recruiting new employees (as noted earlier), which is some incentive to adhere to the implicit contract. However, if the company is in permanent decline, if it faces an unusually adverse market, or if information on company employment policies is not easily or accurately available to applicants, the incentives to renege on implicit contracts are probably very strong.

Pensions as Deferred Payments

One way to ensure employees receive their delayed reward is to provide a pension. According to statistics published by the American Council of Life Insurance, the average yearly retirement benefit paid by private pension plans in 1981 was $2,064.[33] While this sum is not overwhelmingly large, a yearly payment of this size beginning at age 65 and lasting 15 years (the average life expectancy of a 65-year-old) requires a fund of $26,300 to finance it at a 2 percent rate of interest. Thus, giving pensioners $2,064 per year from age 65 until death is equivalent to giving the average retiree a lump-sum payment of $26,300. If the pension benefits were more generous, the lump-sum equivalent would increase proportionately. For example, the average city employee in Pennsylvania received $3,800 per year in retirement benefits in 1976, with a lump-sum equivalent of $48,830 (at a 2 percent interest rate).

It is obvious, then, that pensions represent the equivalent of a deferred payment to workers at the end of their careers. Under ERISA, the money to finance this payment must be set aside each year by the employer in a separate fund so that employees have some assurance of receiving their reward even if the firm goes bankrupt. As discussed in this chapter, firms offering their employees pensions must pay lower wages, other things equal, to remain competitive. Thus, pensions offer a mechanism whereby spendable pay is low during one's working years but a reward is received later on.

The strongest incentives for diligence under a pension scheme would exist if the pension were not vested. Nonvested employees can be threatened with loss of a pension up to the day before retirement. Vesting, however, modifies the incentive effects of this compensation scheme somewhat. Most private-sector employees with pensions become vested after 10 years, so that the threat of losing all rights to their pension is, strictly speaking, only there for the first 10 years. This in itself may be a long enough time to motivate and observe reliable work habits, but even being fired after becoming vested entails loss. A vested worker fired by Firm X may be able to obtain a pension from X at retirement, but this pension will be smaller to the extent that one's tenure with X is shorter. To receive a *full* pension benefit would require

---

[33]American Council of Life Insurance, *Pension Facts 1982* (Washington, D.C.: American Council of Life Insurance, 1982), p. 13.

the worker to qualify for a pension with *another* firm—a process that will normally take 10 more years. Thus, while vesting softens the threat of being fired for cause after 10 years, it does not remove all the incentive to work honestly and diligently throughout one's career.

Promotion Lotteries

Another form of worker motivation within the context of internal labor markets might best be called a *promotion lottery*. Suppose a group of entering management trainees were hired with the expectation that *one* of them would become a high-ranking corporate officer and make an extraordinary sum of money each year. The employees who did not make it to the top would be guaranteed a spot in the firm somewhere, but they would not achieve such high earnings.

Now if everyone knew in advance who would be promoted, this scheme would not be incentive-producing nor would it have aspects of a lottery. However, if no one knew in advance who would "win" but all were told that winning the top job depended on hard work, all would be attracted by the large salary (or prestige) and work hard to get it. Here, as in the previous schemes, the prospect of obtaining large sums toward the end of one's career offers incentives for diligent work throughout earlier years.

In this scheme, however, not all diligent workers get the prize at career's end; only the winner does. Further, once the prize has been awarded and the losers are known, they no longer have the same strong incentives to work hard. Moreover, the employer, knowing the losers have reduced incentives, has every reason to want to get rid of them. Dangling a lucrative job in front of everyone increased the incentives of all, even the eventual losers, to work hard; once the prize has been awarded, the losers are of substantially less value to the firm.

The problem for the employer is that employees may not be willing to enter this lottery unless even the losers are treated relatively well. A firm known for firing older mid-level managers may not be able to attract a large enough group of young management trainees from which to produce an excellent corporate officer in the future. For this reason, a firm may be tempted to agree to essentially guarantee the losers desirable jobs somewhere in the organization.

Since workers whose wages are less than or equal to their marginal product do not need any guarantee of job security, it is most likely true that the losers of promotion lotteries have wages or salaries that *exceed* marginal product. If this is the case, the employer will obviously want to offer strong incentives for these employees to retire at a certain point. Again, then, a mandatory retirement clause may be an essential ingredient in the running of a promotion lottery.

Hypothesizing that promotion lotteries exist helps explain three phenomena that are widely observed in the labor market. First, it helps explain why, after a number of candidates are carefully considered for a top executive job, one is selected and paid perhaps three times what the others receive. Is it because he or she is three times as productive as the others? If so, the others would not have been serious contenders for the job. The huge pay differential most likely exists to serve as an incentive for younger employees to work hard so they can win the next lottery.[34] Second, the existence of promotion lotteries helps explain why corporations sometimes tolerate *deadwood*, older employees who obviously are not going to be promoted and who clearly are not as productive as they used to be. Such deadwood is the unfortunate cost to the firm of running a successful lottery. Third, because deadwood can be tolerated for a while but not indefinitely, there have arisen mandatory retirement rules or other inducements for employees to retire before they might otherwise decide to do so.

Federal Policy on Mandatory Retirement Reconsidered

This chapter has argued that "underpaying" employees in the early stages of their careers and "overpaying" them later serves as an incentive for employees to work industriously. Because workers are more productive, employers can offer them an income stream whose present value is increased over what it would otherwise be. While employees can command more compensation because they, as individuals, work harder, they benefit *additionally* by a system that causes *other* employees to also work more diligently.

As we have pointed out, however, overpaying workers is something a firm cannot tolerate indefinitely. Thus, for this payment scheme to work—and it must work for both parties in order for each to have incentives to agree to it— firms must be able to terminate the overpayment at the point where it is no longer profitable in the long run.

One way to end the overpayment is to reduce the wage rate of older workers after a certain age to a wage that more closely corresponds to their marginal product. Reducing the wage rate in this way would almost surely raise charges of age discrimination, reflecting a prevailing social value that workers' nominal wages should not be reduced under any but the most extraordinary circumstances. Why society has adopted this particular value is an interesting—and open—question.[35]

A social "rule" against wage cutting suggests that the "underpay now, overpay later" scheme will be adopted only if older workers can be fired—or, more politely, subjected to mandatory retirement—by their employers. In most cases such retirement will mean no work at all; in other cases the employees might be able to find work at a lower wage rate with some other employers. In either case the affected employees have absorbed wage cuts, and because these cuts—when seen from the workers' perspective in old age—have been forced on them, they are likely to feel worse off. They may even support legislation to outlaw mandatory retirement, which is exactly what happened with the 1978 amendments to the Age Discrimination in Employment Act, which raised the minimum age for mandatory retirement from 65 to 70.

---

[34]This argument is advanced by Edward Lazear and Sherwin Rosen, "Rank-Order Tournaments As Optimum Labor Contracts," *Journal of Political Economy* 89(October 1981):841–64.

[35]Chapter 15 discusses the related question of why employers react to decreases in demand by laying off workers rather than cutting their wages.

Who gains and who loses from this mandated increase in the age for mandatory retirement? It is clear that employers lose, but is it equally clear that employees gain? Surely people who are currently near retirement gain. However, their gain lies in the fact that governmental authority has been used to break a key element of a contract from which they benefited in the past. The fact that firms can no longer enforce a critical element of their old contracts removes from them the incentive to agree to future contracts of the same type. Thus, younger employees may be harmed by the provisions of the 1978 act. In fact, the gains to older employees occur only *once*—to the group that is allowed to break its contract. Future generations of older workers do not gain, since their employment contracts and compensation schemes will be made under the new rules of the game.[36]

REVIEW QUESTIONS

1. There is a law that compensation of federal government employees must be comparable to that of private-sector employees of similar skills who perform similar duties. Suppose that pay in the two sectors were compared by measuring salaries or wages of a "typical" worker in each sector (one, say, with 10 years of experience). In what respects would this approach be deficient?

2. In 1981 the President's Commission on Pension Policy proposed that every employee in the country be covered by a Minimum Universal Pension (MUP). This pension would vest immediately and would be fully *portable*. (That is, all workers would qualify for a pension no matter how many employers they worked for in their lifetime or how long they worked for each. Currently, employees are not eligible to receive any private pension benefits at age 65 unless they work for an employer 10 years.) What impact would an MUP have on labor costs and productivity?

3. Suppose mandatory retirement laws were abolished and firms undertook various strategies to induce *voluntary* retirements at age 65. Some of these possible strategies are listed below. The firm's objectives are to unambiguously increase the incentives for people over 65 to retire, but to do so in a way that offers the strongest incentives to the *least productive* of the older workers to retire. (For our purposes, the least productive will be defined as the workers no other firm would want at anything close to their current wage. Productive workers, even though elderly, could get jobs elsewhere at close to their current wage.) Evaluate each of the following strategies to determine whether it will accomplish the firm's objectives:
   a. Cut the wages of all workers after the age of 60.
   b. Provide a large lump-sum payment to anyone who quits his or her employment *at the firm* at age 65.
   c. Increase the monthly pension benefit of anyone who *retires* (and does not work elsewhere) at age 65.

---

[36]For further analysis of the winners and the losers, see Ronald G. Ehrenberg, "Retirement Policy, Employment, and Unemployment," *American Economic Review* 69,2(May 1979):131–36.

SELECTED READINGS

Allen, Steven G. "Compensation, Safety and Absenteeism." *Industrial and Labor Relations Review* 34(January 1981):207–18.

Doeringer, Peter, and Piore, Michael. *Internal Labor Markets and Manpower Analysis.* Lexington, Mass.: D. C. Heath and Company, 1971.

Ehrenberg, Ronald, and Smith, Robert. "A Framework for Evaluating State and Local Government Pension Reform." In *Public Sector Labor Markets*, ed. Peter Mieszkowski and George E. Peterson. Washington, D.C.: The Urban Institute, 1981.

Lazear, Edward. "Why Is There Mandatory Retirement?" *Journal of Political Economy* 87(December 1979):1261–84.

Pencavel, John. "Work Effort, On-the-Job Screening, and Alternative Methods of Remuneration." In *Research in Labor Economics*, Vol. 1, ed. Ronald Ehrenberg. Greenwich, Conn.: JAI Press, 1977. Pp. 225–58.

Riordan, Michael, and Wachter, Michael. "What Do Implicit Contracts Do?" *Proceedings of the Industrial Relations Research Association* 1982:291–98.

Simon, Herbert A. "A Formal Theory of the Employment Relationship." *Econometrical* 19,3(July 1951):293–305.

Stiglitz, Joseph E. "Incentives, Risk and Information: Notes Toward a Theory of Hierarchy." *Bell Journal of Economics and Management Science* 6(Autumn 1975):552–79.

12

Unions and
Collective Bargaining
in the Private Sector

Our analysis of the workings of labor markets has, for the most part, omitted any mention of the role of labor unions and collective bargaining. Because many people have strong and conflicting opinions about the role of unions in our society, it is often difficult to remain objective when discussing them. Some individuals view labor unions as forms of monopolies that, while benefiting their members, impose substantial costs on other members of society. In contrast, other individuals view unions as *the* major means by which working persons have improved their economic status and as important forces behind much social legislation.

In recent years approximately 20 percent of all individuals in the labor force and 25 percent of all employees on nonagricultural payrolls have been union members (see Table 12.1). This percentage is considerably lower than that found in most other Western countries. In addition, the United States is one of the few Western countries in which labor unions are not intimately and uniformly associated with one political party (such as the Labour Party in England, which is dominated by trade unionists). While unions play an important role in our society, their influence is probably not as pervasive as either their supporters or opponents would have us believe.

This chapter initially presents a brief discussion of the nature of unions and the collective bargaining process and the major pieces of labor legislation that have shaped collective bargaining in the private sector in the United States. (Public sector labor markets and collective bargaining will be discussed in Chapter 13.) The chapter then presents a simple conceptual model of the forces that influence the level of unionization and shows how this model can be used to explain the historical pattern of union membership in the United States.

The chapter will then discuss how unions seek to achieve their bargaining goals. After reviewing the Hicks-Marshall laws of derived demand, initially dis-

TABLE 12.1 Union and Association Membership in the United States, 1930–1980

	Union Membership Only			Union and Association Membership		
Year	Total (in thousands)	Percentage of Labor Force	Percentage of Nonagricultural Employment	Total (in thousands)	Percentage of Labor Force	Percentage of Nonagricultural Employment
1930	3,401	6.8	11.6			
1932	3,050	6.0	12.9			
1934	3,088	5.9	11.9			
1936	3,989	7.4	13.7			
1938	8,034	14.6	27.5			
1940	8,717	15.5	26.9			
1942	10,380	17.2	25.9			
1944	14,146	21.4	33.8			
1946	14,395	23.6	34.5			
1948	14,300	23.1	31.9			
1950	14,300	22.3	31.5			
1952	15,900	24.2	33.3			
1954	17,022	25.4	33.7			
1956	17,490	25.2	33.2			
1958	17,029	24.2	33.2			
1960	17,049	23.6	31.5			
1962	16,586	22.6	29.9			
1964	16,841	22.2	28.9			
1966	17,940	22.7	28.1			
1968	18,916	23.0	27.9	20,721	25.2	30.5
1970	19,381	22.6	27.3	21,248	24.7	30.0
1972	19,435	21.8	26.4	21,657	24.3	29.4
1974	20,119	21.7	25.8	22,809	24.5	29.1
1976	19,634	20.3	24.5	22,662	23.4	28.3
1978	20,246	19.7	24.0	22,880	22.3	27.1
1980				22,366	20.9	24.7

SOURCE: U.S. Bureau of Labor Statistics, *Directory of National Unions and Employee Associations, 1979.* Bulletin 2079 (Washington, D.C.: U.S. Government Printing Office, 1980); U.S. Bureau of the Census, *Historical Statistics of the United States: Colonial Times to 1970* (Washington, D.C.: U.S. Government Printing Office, 1975); Bureau of National Affairs, *Directory of U.S. Labor Organizations, 1982–83 ed.* (Washington, D.C.: BNA Books, 1982).

cussed in Chapter 4, to analyze the factors that limit a union's ability to improve the economic well-being of its members without causing a substantial fraction of them to lose their jobs, the chapter will turn to a discussion of how, given such constraints, unions can translate their bargaining goals into actual outcomes. (An appendix to the chapter addresses the issue of whether the wage/employment combinations that result under collective bargaining tend to lie on, or off of, employers' demand for labor curves.)

The chapter also examines the effects unions have had on wage *and* nonwage outcomes. Neoclassical economists have traditionally focused on estimating the amount by which unions have increased the wages of their members *relative* to the wages of comparable nonunion workers and they have argued that such wage differentials lead to inefficiencies that have a negative effect on society. Recently, however, analytical labor economists have begun to rediscover the variety of roles that unions play and concluded that unions may play many positive roles that leave society as a whole better off.[1] This chapter contrasts the evidence that supports both views of unions' effects.

Returning to our earlier example (in Chapter 9) of wage determination in a heavily unionized, regulated industry, we shall conclude the chapter by noting that there may be a fundamental inconsistency between a policy that seeks to promote the collective bargaining rights of workers and one that seeks to minimize the prices paid by consumers for products produced in regulated industries, such as public utilties. Policymakers often face the dilemma that different policy goals may be mutually inconsistent.

UNIONS AND COLLECTIVE BARGAINING

Labor unions are collective organizations whose primary objectives are to improve the pecuniary and nonpecuniary conditions of employment of their members. Unions can be classified into two types: an *industrial* union represents most or all of the workers in an industry or firm regardless of their occupations, and a *craft* union represents workers in a single occupational group. Examples of industrial unions are the unions representing automobile workers, steel workers, bituminous coal miners, and rubber workers; while craft unions include the unions representing the various building trades, printers, and dock workers.

Although most unions are members of the American Federation of Labor–Congress of Industrial Organizations (AFL-CIO), this federation of unions is not involved in the collective bargaining process *per se*.[2] In some industries—for example, automobile and steel—bargaining is done primarily at the *national* level. In others, such as construction, bargaining is done at the *local* level. In either case, bargaining can be *multiemployer,* in which case an agreement is reached simultaneously with a number of employers, or bargaining can take place separately with individual employers. The structure of bargaining in our economy influences both the ability of unions to accomplish their objectives and the inflationary process.

Collective bargaining typically covers a much wider range of issues than simply the issue of wage rates. Among the issues usually included are other pecuniary conditions of employment (such as vacation pay, health insurance, pensions, and the like), as well as nonpecuniary conditions of employment, including job security provisions (such as seniority rules or rules governing layoffs) and working conditions (such as workplace safety, rights to refuse overtime, and methods of production). Unions also help employers administer the provisions of union contracts while collective bargaining agreements are in effect and provide individual employees with a means of communicating their concerns to management. The tendency of some observers to focus on the pecuniary aspects of collective bargaining agreements to the neglect of the nonpecuniary aspects and the roles unions play while a contract is in effect can lead to an incomplete analysis of the effects of unions.

---

[1] This "new" view of unions is summarized by two of its exponents in a nontechnical fashion in Richard B. Freeman and James L. Medoff, "The Two Faces of Unionism," *Public Interest* 57(Fall 1979): 69–93.

[2] As of 1984, the Teamsters was the only major national union not in the AFL-CIO.

Modern Labor Legislation in the United States

Public attitudes and federal legislation have not always been favorably disposed toward labor unions and the collective bargaining process. For example, during the early part of the 20th century, employers were often able to claim that unions acted like monopolies in the labor market and hence were illegal under existing antitrust law. Such employers were often able to get court orders or injunctions that prohibited union activity and aided them in stopping union organization drives. In addition, employers were often able to require potential employees to sign *yellow dog contracts,* contracts in which employees agreed not to join a union as a condition of accepting employment. Given this environment, it is not surprising that the fraction of the labor force that were union members stood at less than 7 percent in 1930 (see Table 12.1).

Since that date, four major pieces of federal labor legislation have shaped the collective bargaining process in the private sector, the ability of unions to increase their membership, and the way unions operate. These laws and some of their salient provisions are listed in Table 12.2.

Two laws were products of the Depression. The *Norris-LaGuardia Act,* enacted in 1932, for all practical purposes outlawed the antiunion practices of employers discussed above. The *National Labor Relations Act* (NLRA), or *Wagner*

TABLE 12.2 Major Pieces of Federal Labor Legislation Governing Collective Bargaining in the Private Sector

Date	Law	Some Salient Provisions
1932	Norris-LaGuardia Act	1. Restricted employers' uses of court orders and injunctions as weapons to combat union-organizing drives. 2. Prohibited "yellow dog" contracts, contracts in which potential employees had to agree *not* to join a union as a condition of employment.
1935	National Labor Relations (Wagner) Act	1. Defined unfair labor practices for both employers and employees. In particular, employers are required to bargain with unions representing the majority of their employees, and may not interfere with employees' right to organize. 2. The National Labor Relations Board (NLRB) was established to settle many labor-management disputes. The NLRB was given power to investigate alleged unfair labor practices, to order violators to cease and desist, and to have its orders enforced by the courts. The NLRB was also given the right to conduct elections to see which unions, if any, employees wanted.
1947	Labor-Management Relations (Taft-Hartley) Act	1. Restricted some aspects of union activity. Section 14B permits states to pass right-to-work laws; these prohibit the requirement that persons become (or refrain from becoming) union members as a condition of employment.
1959	Labor-Management Reporting and Disclosure (Landrum-Griffin) Act	1. Designed to protect the rights of union members, it increases union democracy. It includes provisions for periodic reporting of union finances and provisions that regulate union elections.

Act, of 1935 went far beyond the earlier act by requiring employers to bargain with unions that represented the majority of their employees and by asserting that it was illegal for employers to interfere with their employees' right to organize collectively. The National Labor Relations Board (NLRB) was established by the NLRA and given power both to conduct elections to see which union, if any, employees wanted to represent them and to investigate claims that employers were either violating election rules or refusing to bargain with elected unions.[3] In the event violations were found, the NLRB was given further power to order violators to "cease and desist"; these orders were to be enforced by the courts.

After World War II the pendulum shifted decidedly in an antiunion direction. The *Taft-Hartley Act* of 1947 restricted some aspects of union activity. Perhaps its most famous provision is Section 14B, which permits individual states to pass *right-to-work laws*. These laws prohibit the requirement that a person become, or promise to become, a union member as a condition of employment. By 1980 some 20 states, located primarily in the South, Southwest, and Plains areas, had passed such laws.

Finally, in 1959 Congress passed the *Landrum-Griffin Act.* This law, which was designed to protect the rights of union members in relation to their leaders, contained provisions that increased union democracy. As argued below, such provisions may well have had the side effect of increasing the level of strike activity in the economy.

A Model of the Level of Unionization

Table 12.1 presents data on union membership from 1930 through 1980. For the last decade the table also includes data on membership in employee associations, such as the National Education Association (NEA). The primary purposes of employee associations historically have not related to collective bargaining; for example, the NEA has long been primarily concerned with professional standards and improving the quality of education students receive. However, these associations have become increasingly involved in the collective bargaining process.

Data on union membership are notoriously poor; nevertheless, Table 12.1 yields some striking patterns. First, union membership, in both absolute terms and as a percentage of the labor force (and of nonagricultural employment), grew steadily during both the 1930s and World War II. The former result was somewhat surprising to analysts, since prior to the 1930s periods of high unemployment were typically associated with declining union strength.[4] After a slight dip in the immediate postwar period, union strength reached a peak of 25 percent of the labor force in the mid-1950s. However, since that time the share of union members in both total nonagricultural employment and the labor force has declined steadily.

---

[3] Actually, the NLRA was much less pro-labor than our brief discussion indicates; the NLRA also gave the NLRB power to investigate employers' claims that their employees, or unions, were violating provisions of the act.

[4] For evidence and a discussion of the pre-1930s view, see John R. Commons, *The History of Labor in the United States*, vol. III (New York: Macmillan, 1918).

Indeed, by 1978 union membership stood at about 20 percent of the labor force—a 30-year low. While inclusion of employee association members in Table 12.1 raises this estimate somewhat, it does not alter the underlying trend.

Further evidence of this trend can be found in the National Labor Relations Board certification and decertification vote data for 1970–1980, which are found in Table 12.3. These data indicate that, while the number of elections in which unions have sought the right to represent unorganized workers has fluctuated between 8000 and 9500 a year, the *share* of the elections that the unions actually won has fallen steadily during the period, from 55 to 46 percent. Furthermore, the annual number of *decertification votes*—votes in which union claims to represent a majority of workers in a firm were challenged—more than doubled, with the share of these votes lost by unions increasing slightly to more than 70 percent during this period.

A simple model of the demand and supply of union activity can be used to explain the forces that influence union strength.[5] On the demand side, employees' demand to be union members will be a function of the "price" of union membership; this price includes monthly dues, initiation fees, the value of the time an individual is expected to spend on union activities, etc. Other things equal, the higher the price, the lower the fraction of employees that will want to be union members, as represented by the demand curve D_0 in Figure 12.1.

It is costly to represent workers in collective bargaining negotiations and to supervise the administration of union contracts. Moreover, union-organizing campaigns require resources, and as unions move from organizing workers who are the most favorably inclined towards unions to those who are the least favorably inclined, the cost of making a sufficiently strong case to win a union representation election increases. As such, it is reasonable to conclude that, other things equal, on

TABLE 12.3   Results of Representation Elections and Decertification Polls Supervised by the National Labor Relations Board

Fiscal Year	Union Elections	Percent Won by Union	Decertification Votes	Percent Lost by Union
1970	8,074	55.2	301	69.8
1971	8,362	53.2	401	69.6
1972	8,923	53.6	451	70.3
1973	9,369	51.1	453	69.5
1974	8,858	50.0	490	69.0
1975	8,577	48.2	516	73.4
1976	8,638	48.1	611	72.8
1977	9,484	46.0	849	76.0
1978	8,240	46.0	807	73.6
1979	8,043	45.0	777	75.0
1980	8,198	45.7	902	72.7

SOURCE: *Annual Report of the National Labor Relations Board*, Appendix Tables (various years).

---

[5]This model is based upon the approach found in Orley Ashenfelter and John Pencavel, "American Trade Union Growth, 1900–1960," *Quarterly Journal of Economics* 83(August 1969):434–48; and John Pencavel, "The Demand for Union Services: An Exercise," *Industrial and Labor Relations Review* 24(January 1971):180–91.

the supply side of the market the willingness of unions to provide union services is an upward-sloping function of the price of union membership, as represented by the supply curve S_0 in Figure 12.1. The intersection of these demand and supply curves yields an equilibrium percentage of the work force that is unionized (U_0) and an equilibrium price of union services (P_0).

What are the forces that determine the *positions* of the demand and supply curves? Anything that causes either the demand curve *or* supply curve to shift to the right will increase the level of unionization in the economy, other things equal. Conversely, if either of these curves shifts to the left, other things equal, the level of unionization will fall. Identifying the factors that shift these curves enables one to explain *changes* in the level of unionization in the economy over time.

On the demand side, it is likely that individuals' demand for union membership is positively related to their perceptions of the *net benefits* from being union members. For example, the larger the wage gain they think unions will win for them, the further to the right the demand curve will be and the higher the level of unionization. Another factor is *tastes;* if individuals' tastes for union membership increase, perhaps because of changes in social attitudes or the introduction of labor legislation that protects the rights of workers to join unions, the demand curve will also shift to the right.

On the supply side, anything that changes the *costs* of union-organizing activities will affect the supply curve. Introduction of labor legislation that makes it easier (harder) for unions to win representation elections will shift the supply curve to the right (left). Changes in the industrial structure that make it more difficult to organize the work force will also shift the curve to the left and reduce the level of unionization.

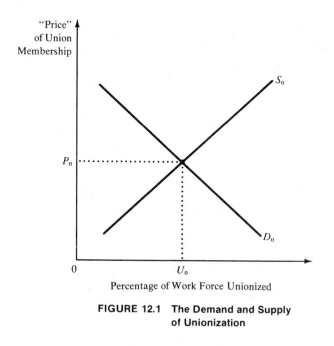

**FIGURE 12.1   The Demand and Supply
of Unionization**

The rapid growth in unionization that took place during the 1930s was a product of both the changing legal environment (Norris-LaGuardia and Wagner Acts) and changing social attitudes towards unions induced by the Great Depression—changes that shifted both the demand and supply curves to the right.[6] The growth continued during the World War II years as low unemployment rates reduced workers' fears of losing their jobs if they indicated pro-union sentiments (shifting the demand curve to the right). Unemployment increased after the end of World War II, shifting the demand curve back to the left, while the passage of the Taft-Hartley Act made it more difficult for unions to increase membership in right-to-work states and shifted the supply curve further to the left. Both shifts served to decrease the percentage unionized.

The decline in union membership since the mid-1950s can be at least partially explained by two factors discussed in earlier chapters. First, the fraction of the labor force that is female has increased substantially (see Chapter 6), and women historically have tended not to join unions. The benefits from union membership are a function of individuals' expected tenure with firms; seniority provisions, job security provisions, and retirement benefits are not worth much to individuals who expect to be employed at a firm for only a short while. *In the past,* women tended to have shorter expected job tenure than men and to have more intermittent labor force participation. As a result, their expected benefits from joining unions were lower; an increase in their share in the labor force would shift the aggregate demand curve for union membership to the left.[7]

The second factor in the decline of union membership is the shift in the industrial composition of employment, discussed in Chapter 2. The last 25 years have seen a substantial decline in the relative employment shares of manufacturing, mining, construction, transportation, and public utilities and, conversely, a substantial increase in the share of employment in wholesale and retail trade, finance, insurance, real estate, and the service industries. Indeed, the former group fell from 48.7 percent of nonagricultural payroll employment in 1955 to 35.3 percent by 1978. During the same period the latter group rose from 37.6 to 46.7 percent.[8] As Table 12.4 indicates, the industries in the former group are the most heavily unionized in the private sector, while the industries in the latter group are the least unionized. The shifting industrial composition of employment has led to a distribution that is weighted more heavily towards industries that are not heavily unionized.

---

[6]It is difficult to identify the effect of the laws per se, as they are determined by societal attitudes themselves. However, as noted both above and below, prior to and after the Depression, periods of high (low) unemployment have been associated with weakening (growing) union membership, which leads one to suspect that the changing legal environment induced by the Depression, which reduced employees' fears of being fired for union activities, did have a substantial effect on union growth during the 1930s.

[7]We emphasize "in the past" here. Changing labor force patterns, with a greater share of women now having permanent attachment to the labor force, will likely increase their propensity to become union members.

[8]U.S. Department of Labor, *1979 Employment and Training Report of the President* (Washington, D.C.: U.S. Government Printing Office, 1979), Table C-1. We defer discussion of government employment until Chapter 13.

TABLE 12.4   Union and Association Membership by Industry in 1978

Industry	Number of Union Members (in thousands)	Number of Employees on Payrolls (in thousands)	Percentage of Employees That Are Union Members
Manufacturing	8,119	20,476	39.7
Mining	428	851	50.3
Construction	2,884	4,271	67.5
Transportation and public utilities	2,651	4,927	53.8
Wholesale and retail trade	1,713	19,499	8.8
Finance, insurance, and real estate	51	4,727	1.1
Service	1,990	16,220	12.3
Federal government	1,420	2,753	51.6
State and local government	4,674	12,723	36.7

SOURCE: U.S. Bureau of Labor Statistics, *Directory of National Unions and Employee Associations*, Bulletin 2079 (Washington, D.C.: U.S. Government Printing Office, 1980), Table 16; U.S. Bureau of Labor Statistics, *Handbook of Labor Statistics, 1980*, Bulletin 2070 (Washington, D.C.: U.S. Government Printing Office, 1980).

Why does the latter set of industries tend not to be unionized? These industries tend to be highly competitive ones, with high price elasticities of demand. As discussed in Chapter 3, other things equal, industries with high price elasticities of demand also have high wage elasticities of demand. High wage elasticities limit unions' abilities to increase their members' wages without substantial employment declines also occurring. As such, the net benefits individuals perceive from union membership may be lower in these industries, and an increase in their importance in the economy would shift the demand for union services to the left in Figure 12.1, thereby reducing the percentage of the work force that is unionized.[9]

One additional factor that may have contributed to the decline in union strength is the movement in population and employment that has occurred since 1955 from the industrial Northeast and Midwest—the "Snowbelt"—to the "Sunbelt" of the South. As noted earlier, the Taft-Hartley Act permitted states to pass right-to-work laws. Such laws raise the costs of increasing union membership, since individuals who accept employment with a firm cannot be compelled to become union members as a condition of employment. In terms of Figure 12.1, these laws shift the supply curve of union services to the left, thereby reducing the level of unionization. Most Sunbelt states have right-to-work laws.

---

[9]These industries also tend to be populated by small establishments. The demand for unionization is thought to be lower for employees who work in small firms, since they often feel less alienated from their supervisors. Similarly, since it is more costly to try to organize 1000 workers spread over 100 firms than it is to organize 1000 workers at one plant, it is often thought that the supply of union services would shift down as the share of employment going to small firms increases. Both of these factors tend to suggest (in terms of Figure 12.1) that unionization will decline as the share of employment occurring in small establishments increases, providing another reason why the shift in industrial distribution of employment has affected the extent of unionization.

TABLE 12.5   Percent of Nonagricultural Employees That Are Union
or Association Members, 1980

Right-to-Work States	Union or Association Members (percent)	Other States	Union or Association Members (percent)
Alabama	21.8	Alaska	33.7
Arizona	16.0	California	27.0
Arkansas	16.0	Colorado	18.1
Florida	11.8	Connecticut	23.0
Georgia	15.1	Delaware	25.2
Iowa	22.2	Hawaii	28.0
Kansas	15.4	Idaho	18.4
Louisiana	16.4	Illinois	30.4
Mississippi	16.2	Indiana	30.4
Nebraska	18.1	Kentucky	24.0
Nevada	23.8	Maine	24.1
North Carolina	9.6	Maryland-D.C.	22.8
North Dakota	17.1	Massachusetts	24.9
South Carolina	7.8	Michigan	37.3
South Dakota	14.8	Minnesota	26.2
Tennessee	19.3	Missouri	27.6
Texas	11.4	Montana	29.2
Utah	17.7	New Hampshire	15.8
Virginia	15.0	New Jersey	25.7
Wyoming	18.9	New Mexico	19.0
		New York	38.8
		Ohio	31.3
		Oklahoma	15.3
		Oregon	26.1
		Pennsylvania	34.6
		Rhode Island	28.3
		Vermont	18.0
		Washington	34.4
		West Virginia	34.4
		Wisconsin	28.5

SOURCE: Bureau of National Affairs, *Directory of U.S. Labor Organizations, 1982–83 ed.*
(Washington, D.C.: BNA Books, 1982), Table 21.

Table 12.5 presents data on the extent of unionization that existed in 1980 in right-to-work and other states. The data indicate quite clearly that right-to-work states are the ones in which union strength is the lowest. In 17 of the 20 right-to-work states, the proportion of nonagricultural employees that were union or employee association members was less than 20 percent. In contrast, in 24 of the other 30 states, the proportion exceeded 20 percent. While right-to-work states are not uniformly identical to those in the Sunbelt, there is considerable overlap. As a result, between 1955 and 1980 the proportion of employees working in right-to-work states increased from 24.1 to 30.1 percent. This shifting geographic distribution of the work force, coupled with the existence of these laws, undoubtedly had a depressing effect on union membership.

It is not at all obvious, however, that the decline in unionization occasioned by the move to the Sunbelt can be attributed to right-to-work laws *per se*. The extent of unionization in right-to-work states tended to be lower than that in other states even prior to the passage of the laws. These laws may only reflect attitudes towards unions that already exist in these communities.[10] The increasing influx of "Snow-belters" into the Sunbelt may eventually lead to a change in public attitudes *and* the repeal of some of these laws.

Two lessons follow from this discussion. First, population shifts to the Sunbelt may not imply a permanent weakening of the union movement in the United States. Second, and more generally, the effects of legislation may be more political than economic; the environmental factors that shape legislation might also cause the same economic outcomes to occur (in this case union strength) even in the absence of the legislation.[11]

HOW UNIONS ACHIEVE THEIR OBJECTIVES

Union Policies to Ease Market Constraints

Many theories of union behavior attempt to formalize the view that unions are organizations that seek to maximize some well-defined objective function.[12] Indeed, recently several studies have even attempted to econometrically estimate the parameters of such an objective function.[13] As noted above, unions play many roles in addition to negotiating wage rates for their members; hence, it is not surprising that there is no widespread agreement as to what specifically is a union's objective

---

[10]Numerous econometric studies have sought to estimate the effect of right-to-work laws on union strength, wages, and industrial conflict. Studies that conclude that these laws have little or no effect on union membership levels include Keith Lumsden and Craig Peterson, "The Effect of Right-to-Work Laws on Unionization in the United States," *Journal of Political Economy* 83(December 1975):1237–48; William Moore and Robert Newman, "On the Prospects for American Trade Union Growth: A Cross-Section Analysis," *Review of Economics and Statistics* 57(November 1975):435–45; Barry T. Hirsch, "The Determinants of Unionization: An Analysis of Interarea Differences," *Industrial and Labor Relations Review* 33(January 1980):147–61; and Henry Farber, "Right-to-Work Laws and the Extent of Unionization," *Journal of Labor Economics* 2(July 1984):319–52. In contrast, David Ellwood and Glenn Fine, in "The Impact of Right-to-Work Laws on Union Organizing" (National Bureau of Economic Research Working Paper no. 1116, May 1983), find a substantial effect from the laws.

[11]Social legislation may also reduce unionization if it leads to the government's providing workers with benefits that previously were provided only through collective bargaining. See George Neumann and Ellen Rissman, "Where Have All the Union Members Gone?" *Journal of Labor Economics* 2(April 1984):175–92, for evidence that this may be occurring in the United States.

[12]See Wallace Atherton, *Theory of Union Bargaining Goals* (Princton, N.J.: Princeton University Press, 1973), for an extensive discussion of the various theories. A classic debate took place more than 35 years ago between John Dunlop, *Wage Determination Under Trade Unions* (New York: Macmillan, 1944), and Arthur Ross, *Trade Union Wage Policy* (Berkeley, Calif.: University of California Press, 1948), with respect to whether it was meaningful to analyze unions in terms of how they maximize well-defined objective functions. Dunlop argued yes and Ross no, the latter articulating an alternative political model of union behavior. Here we shall follow in Dunlop's footsteps, although we shall return to the Ross view below.

[13]See Henry Farber, "Individual Preferences and Union Wage Determination: The Case of the United Mine Workers," *Journal of Political Economy* 86(October 1978):923–42; J. N. Dertouzos and J. H. Pencavel, "Wage and Employment Determination Under Trade Unionism: The International Typographical Union," *Journal of Political Economy* 89(December 1981):1162–81; and John Pencavel, "The Trade-off Between Wages and Employment in Trade Union Objectives," *Quarterly Journal of Economics* 99(May 1984):215–31.

function. Nevertheless, it is generally agreed that in most cases unions value the wage and fringe benefits and working conditions they can achieve for their members *and* their members' employment levels. As a result, the position and wage elasticity of the labor demand curve are fundamental *market constraints* that limit the ability of unions to accomplish their objectives.

To see this, ignore fringe benefits and working conditions for the moment and consider Figure 12.2, which shows two demand curves, D_e^0 and D_i^0, that intersect at an initial wage W_0 and employment level E_0. Suppose a union seeks to raise the wage rate of its members to W_1. To do so would require employment to fall to E_e^1 if the union faced the relatively elastic demand curve D_e^0, or to E_i^1 if it faced the relatively inelastic demand curve D_i^0. Other things equal, the more elastic the demand curve for labor is, the greater the reduction in employment that will be associated with any given increase in wages.

Suppose now that the demand curve D_i^0 shifts out to D_i^1 while the negotiations are under way, due perhaps to growing demand for the final product. If the union succeeds in raising its members' wage to W_1, there will be no absolute decrease in employment in this case. Rather, the union will have only slowed the rate of growth of employment to E_i^2 instead of E_i^3. More generally, other things equal, the more rapidly the labor demand curve is shifting out (in), the smaller (larger) will be the reduction *in employment* or the reduction *in the rate of growth of employment* that will be associated with any given increase in wages. Hence, the unions' ability to raise their members' wages will be strongest in rapidly growing industries with

FIGURE 12.2 Effects of Demand Growth and Wage Elasticity of Demand on Market Constraint Faced by Unions

inelastic labor demand curves. Conversely, unions will be weakest in industries in which the wage elasticity of demand is highly elastic and in which the demand curve for labor is shifting in.

Many actions that unions take are direct attempts to relax the market constraints that they face: either to increase the demand for union labor or to reduce the wage elasticity of demand for their members' services. The laws of derived demand discussed in Chapter 4 implied that three important determinants of the wage elasticities of demand were the price elasticity of demand for the final product, the ease of substituting other inputs for union members in the production process, and the responsiveness of the supply of other inputs to their prices. Other things equal, if price elasticities of demand for the final product are less elastic, if it is difficult to substitute other inputs for union labor, and if the supply schedules of other inputs are unresponsive to their prices, a more inelastic demand for union labor will result.

As noted in Chapter 4, the wage elasticity of demand for labor is more elastic in the long run. In the short run there may be only limited foreign competition in the output market while, as American automobile manufacturers realized in the late 1970s and early 1980s, in the long run foreign competition may increase, increasing the price elasticity of demand for output. In the short run production technologies may be fixed; in the long run labor-saving technologies may be introduced. Finally, in the short run the supplies of alternative inputs may be fixed, while in the long run—because of immigration, the training of other nonunion workers, or the production of new capital equipment—they may be more responsive to price. As a result, the market constraints unions face are more severe in the long run than in the short run; large wage gains won today may lead to substantial employment losses in the future. Such constraints are the primary reason why the economic gains that unions have won for their members are, in fact, relatively modest. (This discussion has assumed that unions and employers will always agree to wage/employment combinations that lie on the demand-for-labor curve. The appendix to the chapter discusses why this might not occur.)

Altering the Demand for Union Labor

Attempts by unions to shift the demand curve for union labor to the right and to reduce the wage elasticity of demand have taken many forms. Many of these attempts have *not* occurred through the collective bargaining process per se. Rather, they have occurred through union support of legislation that at least indirectly achieved union goals and through direct public relations campaigns to increase the demand for products produced by union members.

Turning first to policies to shift the demand for the final product, at times unions have lobbied for quotas or tariffs on foreign-produced goods that would limit the amount of these goods sold in the United States. Both the steelworkers and the automobile workers sought such forms of protection during the late 1970s and early 1980s. Other unions have sought to directly influence people's tastes for the products they produce. The International Ladies Garment Workers' Union (ILGWU) continually seeks to encourage people to "Buy American," featuring the song "Look for the Union Label" in some of its television ads.

Unions have also sought, by means of legislation, to pursue strategies that

Example 12.1
The Davis-Bacon Act

The Davis-Bacon Act was passed in the midst of the Depression, in 1931. Its goal was to maintain local wage standards by requiring subcontractors and contractors on federally financed projects to pay employees wage rates established by private industry in the locality. The legislation was enacted in response to a situation in which federal construction contracts to help offset unemployment in depressed areas were being won by contractors from other areas who were underbidding local builders by importing low-wage workers. The act was designed to assure that the federal funds would go to the unemployed workers in the targeted areas.

The Davis-Bacon Act undoubtedly served a useful function during the 1930s. However, since that time almost 100 statutes have been passed, in fields such as education, health, housing, and transportation, that include similar *prevailing-wage* clauses for federally assisted projects as well. Furthermore, 35 states have passed "little Davis-Bacon statutes" covering state construction expenditures as well. As noted above, the net effect of these provisions today is to increase the labor costs of school construction, public housing projects, hospitals, and mass transit projects because these provisions effectively preclude nonunion contractors from bidding on such projects.

This example illustrates how social legislation that is desirable at one point in time may prove to be undesirable at a later date. For this reason, social legislation and programs should be continually reexamined and evaluated to make sure that their social benefits continue to exceed their social costs.

increase the costs of other inputs that are potential substitutes for union members. For example, as noted in Chapter 3, labor unions have been among the primary supporters of higher minimum wages.[14] While such support may be motivated by their concern for the welfare of low-wage workers, increases in the minimum wage raise the relative costs to employers of less-skilled nonunion workers, thereby increasing the costs of the products they produce and reducing employers' incentives to substitute nonunion workers for more-skilled union workers.

An example of such a strategy is union support for the Davis-Bacon Act and other forms of prevailing-wage legislation. These require that wages paid to construction workers on projects that are federally financed or federally assisted through loans, or whose financing is insured by the federal government, be set at

---

[14]For evidence that union support for minimum wage legislation is often transformed into pro-minimum wage votes by members of Congress, see James Kau and Paul Rubin, "Voting on Minimum Wages: A Time-Series Analysis," *Journal of Political Economy* 86(April 1978):337–42; Jonathan Silberman and Garey Durden, "Determining Legislative Preferences on the Minimum Wage," *Journal of Political Economy* 84(April 1976):317–30; and James Cox and Ronald Oaxaca, "The Determinants of Minimum Wage Levels and Coverage in State Minimum Wage Laws," in *The Economics of Legal Minimum Wages* (Washington, D.C.: American Enterprise Institute for Public Policy Research, 1981).

least equal to the prevailing wage in the area as determined by the Secretary of Labor. Since typically the prevailing wage has been set equal to the union wage scale, the net effect is to eliminate any cost advantage the nonunion construction workers may have, thereby increasing the demand for union labor.[15]

A final example of how unions can inflluence the demand for union labor is the union position on immigration policy. The AFL-CIO has been quite explicit, both historically and in recent years, about its concern that immigrants depress wages and provide competition for unionized American workers. Indeed, with respect to the problem of illegal immigration in the early 1980s, the AFL-CIO asserted that,

> while the nation should continue its compassionate and humane immigration policy, it is apparent that large numbers of illegal immigrants are being exploited by employers, thus threatening hard-won wages and working conditions. U.S. immigration policy should foster re-unification of families and provide haven for refugees from persecution, while taking a realistic view of the job opportunities and the needs of U.S. workers.[16]

It is not surprising, then, that unions have historically supported legislation restricting immigration, especially during recessionary periods.[17]

Union attempts to restrict the substitution of other inputs for union labor typically occur by means of the collective bargaining process. Some unions, notably those in the airline, railroad, and printing industries, have sought and won guarantees of minimum crew sizes (for example, at least three pilots are required to fly certain jet aircrafts). Such *staffing requirements* prevent employers from substituting capital for labor.[18] Other unions have won contract provisions that prohibit employers from *subcontracting* for some or all of the services they provide. For example, a union representing a company's janitorial employees may win a contract provision preventing the firm from hiring external firms to provide it with janitorial services. Such provisions may limit the substitution of nonunion for union workers. Craft unions, especially those in the building and printing trades, often negotiate specific contract provisions that restrict the functions that members of each individual craft can perform, thereby limiting the substitution of one type of union labor for another. Finally, craft unions also limit the substitution of unskilled union labor for skilled union labor by establishing rules about the maximum number of *apprentice* workers—workers who are learning the skilled trades—that can be employed relative to the experienced *journeymen* workers.

Apprenticeship rules also limit the supply of skilled workers to a craft. Indeed,

---

[15]See Robert Goldfarb and John Morrall III, ''The Davis-Bacon Act: An Appraisal of Recent Studies,'' *Industrial and Labor Relations Review* 34(January 1981):191–207, and Steven Allen, ''Much Ado About Davis-Bacon: A Critical Review and New Evidence,'' *Journal of Law and Economics* (forthcoming) for a more complete discussion of the act and analysis of its effects.

[16]*The AFL-CIO Platform Proposals: Presented to the Democratic and Republican National Conventions 1980* (Washington, D.C.: AFL-CIO, 1980), p. 14.

[17]F. Ray Marshall, Allan King, and Vernon Briggs, *Labor Economics: Wages, Employment, and Trade Unionism,* 4th ed. (Homewood, Ill.: Richard D. Irwin, 1980), p.196.

[18]In cases in which these requirements call for the employment of employees whose functions are redundant—for example, fire stokers in diesel-operated railroad engines—*featherbedding* is said to take place. For an economic analysis of this phenomenon, see Paul Weinstein, ''The Featherbedding Problem,'' *American Economic Review* 54(May 1964):145–52.

Example 12.2
Concession Bargaining and the Airlines

Institutional changes do not always increase union power. As noted in Chapter 4, prior to 1978 regulation of the airline industry both prohibited price competition between airlines that flew the same route and granted airlines that had no competitors on a route a form of monopoly power by limiting the entry of new carriers. Such regulation tended to reduce the price elasticity of demand for each airline's flights, which in turn reduced the wage elasticity of demand for airline pilots. In conjunction with the other forces described above and in Chapter 4, this led to very inelastic demand curves for airline pilots and, not surprisingly, the union representing the pilots historically was able to win large wage increases for its members.

The *Airline Deregulation Act of 1978,* however, opened up the industry to competition. Price competition was permitted on routes with more than one carrier and new airlines, which were often nonunion and had lower labor costs, began to compete with the existing carriers. As a result, profits of many of the established carriers dropped dramatically. Indeed, during the recession of the early 1980s, many suffered substantial losses.

This led these airlines to "request" that their unions make *concessions,* in the form of reduced wages and fringes and longer work weeks, in exchange for at least implicit promises that employment levels would be maintained. In some cases concessions were made voluntarily by the unions, in the sense that new contracts were written that agreed to temporary or permanent concessions (such *concession bargaining* also occurred in the automobile and steel industries during the early 1980s as unions attempted to trade off wage concessions for employment guarantees in the face of increased foreign competition). In at least one case, however, an airline (Continental) filed for bankruptcy and unilaterally reduced its employees' wages by almost 50 percent in an attempt to compel the unions to negotiate new contracts.

SOURCE: "Airlines in Turmoil," *Business Week,* October 10, 1983, pp. 98–102.

they represent only one of several ways in which unions or employee associations may restrict entry into an occupation. Another way is to control the accreditation of outside institutions that provide training; the American Medical Association's accreditation of medical schools is an example. A third way of restricting entry into an occupation is to lobby for state occupational licensing laws.[19]

From Market Constraints to Bargaining Power

How do unions convince employers to agree to changes that reduce the wage elasticity of demand or shift the demand curve for union labor to the right? Given

---

[19]See, for example, Alex Maurizi, "Occupational Licensing and the Public Interest," *Journal of Political Economy* 82(March/April 1974):399–413.

the elasticity and position of demand curves, how are unions able to bargain for, and win, real wage increases when in most cases an increase in the price of an input reduces a firm's profits?[20]

In some cases a union and an employer may agree to a settlement in which real wages are increased in return for the union's agreeing to certain work rule changes that will result in increased productivity. If such an agreement is explicit and tied to the resulting change in productivity, the process is often referred to as *productivity bargaining.*[21] More typically, however, unions are able to win management concessions at the bargaining table because of the unions' ability to impose costs on management. These costs typically take the form of work slowdowns and strikes. A *strike* is an attempt to deny the firm the labor services of all union members. Craft unions often have the added weapon of explicitly controlling the labor supply curve that firms face by means of previously negotiated or legislated entry restrictions described above.

Whether a strike, or a threat of a strike, will enable a union to win a concession from management depends upon the following factors:

1. The profitability of the firm and its ability to raise prices without losing its market (clearly unions in concentrated industries will be better off than those in competitive industries on this score);
2. The ability of the union to impose costs on the firm, which depends on whether the firm can stockpile its product in anticipation of a strike (thus avoiding the loss of customers during a strike), and whether nonunion supervisory employees can operate a plant during a strike;
3. Whether the firm has the financial resources to withstand the losses it would incur during a strike; and
4. Whether the union members have the financial resources to withstand their loss of income during a strike.[22]

If strikes involve costs to both union members and employers, why do they ever occur? It would seem that if both parties were aware of these costs, they would have an incentive to reach a settlement before a strike results. In fact, most models of the collective bargaining process focus on the likely division of the spoils between management and employees and ignore the determinants of strike activity.

The first, and also simplest, model of the bargaining process was developed by Sir John Hicks.[23] Suppose that management and labor are bargaining over only one issue—the size of the wage increase to be granted. How would the percentage

---

[20]It is easy to show in the context of a simple textbook model of firm behavior that an increase in the price of labor will reduce a firm's profits. However, this conclusion takes the firm's production function as given and does not consider other ways in which unions may increase productivity.

[21]See Allan Flanders, ed., *Collective Bargaining* (Baltimore, Md.: Penguin Books, 1969), pp. 317–68, for a description of productivity bargaining.

[22]In this regard it is often alleged, although there is no strong empirical evidence, that the level of strike activity is higher in the two states, New York and Rhode Island, that allow workers on strike to collect unemployment insurance benefits (after a waiting period) than would otherwise be the case.

[23]John R. Hicks, *The Theory of Wages*, 2nd ed. (New York: St. Martin's Press, 1966), pp. 136–57.

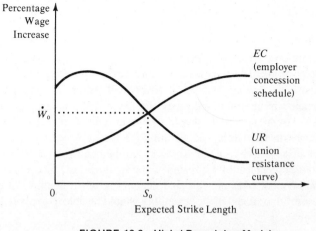

FIGURE 12.3 **Hicks' Bargaining Model
and Expected Strike Length**

increase that the union demands and the increase that the employer is willing to grant vary with the expected duration of a strike?

On the employer side of the market, the longer a strike lasts, the more costly it becomes in terms of lost customers. This increasing cost suggests that, as a strike progresses, an employer should be willing to increase the wage offer; this willingness is denoted by the upward-sloping *employer concession schedule, EC*, in Figure 12.3.

On the employee side, union members' attitudes may harden and they may actually increase their wage demands during the early part of a strike. However, after some point the loss in income they are suffering begins to color their attitudes, and they should begin to reduce their wage demands. This reduction is indicated by the *union resistance curve, UR*, in Figure 12.3, which eventually becomes downward sloping.

As the strike proceeds, the union's demands decrease and the employer's offer increases until at strike duration S_0 the two coincide. At this point a settlement can be reached, the parties may agree upon a wage increase of $\dot{W}_0$, and the strike may be terminated. Of course, *if* each party were aware of the position and shape of the other party's curve, each would know in advance of the strike what the size of the ultimate settlement would be. In this case, it would make sense to agree to a settlement of $\dot{W}_0$ *prior* to the strike so that *both* parties could avoid incurring the costs associated with the strike.

If such a settlement could be made in advance, why would strikes ever occur? One reason is that information is actually imperfect; one or both sides in the negotiation often fail to convey the true shape and position of their schedule to the other party.[24] A second reason is that, to enhance their bargaining positions and

---

[24]In the words of Hicks, "The majority of strikes are doubtless the results of faulty negotiations" (Hicks, *The Theory of Wages*, p. 146).

retain the credibility of the threat of a strike, unions may have to periodically use the weapon; a strike may be designed to influence *future* negotiations.[25] Finally, strikes may be useful devices by which the internal solidarity of a union can be enhanced against a common enemy—the employer.[26]

The major problem with these explanations of when strikes occur is that they do not enable one to predict whether a strike will occur in a particular contract negotiation and, more important, they do not offer any insights into why the aggregate level of strike activity should vary over time. Table 12.6 presents data on work stoppages in the United States during a recent 26-year period. These data suggest that strike activity, as measured by the percentage of workers involved in strikes or the percentage of estimated working time lost, is cyclical, increasing when unemployment rates are low and decreasing when unemployment rates are high. To be useful, a model of strike activity should be able to explain this observed pattern of behavior.

A Political Model of Strike Activity

Although there is no universally accepted model of strike activity, Orley Ashenfelter and George Johnson have built upon Arthur Ross's earlier work and developed what is essentially a political model of strike activity.[27] Their approach illustrates

TABLE 12.6   Work Stoppages in the United States, 1953–1979

Year	Number of Strikes	Workers Involved Number (in thousands)	Workers Involved As Percentage of Employed	Estimated Percentage of Working Time Lost	Unemployment Rate
1953	5,091	2,400	4.7	0.22	2.9
1955	4,320	2,650	5.2	0.22	4.4
1957	3,673	1,390	2.6	0.12	4.3
1959	3,708	1,880	3.3	0.50	5.5
1961	3,367	1,450	2.6	0.11	6.7
1963	3,362	941	1.1	0.11	5.7
1965	3,963	1,550	2.5	0.15	4.5
1967	4,595	2,870	4.3	0.25	3.8
1969	5,700	2,481	3.5	0.24	3.5
1971	5,138	3,280	4.6	0.26	5.9
1973	5,353	2,251	2.9	0.14	4.9
1975	5,031	1,746	2.2	0.16	8.5
1977	5,600	2,300	2.8	0.17	7.0
1979	4,800	1,700	1.6	0.15	5.8

SOURCE: U.S. Bureau of Labor Statistics, *Handbook of Labor Statistics, 1980*, Bulletin 2070 (Washington, D.C.: U.S. Government Printing Office, 1980), Tables 28 and 167.

---

[25]Lest one carry this "rusty weapon" argument too far, the reader should consider its implication for the use of nuclear weapons.

[26]Richard Walton and Robert McKersie, *A Behavioral Theory of Labor Negotiations* (New York: McGraw-Hill, 1965), p. 32.

[27]Arthur Ross, *Trade Union Wage Policy* (Berkeley, Calif.: University of California Press, 1948), and Orley Ashenfelter and George Johnson, "Bargaining Theory, Trade Unions, and Industrial Strike Activity," *American Economic Review* 59(March 1969):35–49. A more recent test of the model is found in Henry Farber, "Bargaining Theory, Wage Outcomes, and the Occurrence of Strikes," *American Economic Review* 68(June 1978):262–71.

how the maximization models of economists can be generalized to incorporate noneconomic variables and allows us to analyze the effects of the Landrum-Griffin Act on the level of strike activity.

The Ashenfelter-Johnson model is based upon the premise that it is inappropriate to view the collective bargaining process as involving only two parties, an employer and a union. Rather, they acknowledge that different members of the union will have different, and sometimes conflicting, objectives. Their focus is on the divergence in objectives between union members and union leaders. While union members are concerned primarily with their pecuniary and nonpecuniary conditions of employment, union leaders are also concerned about the survival and growth of the union *and* their own personal political survival.

Union leaders, who have been actively involved with management in the bargaining process, have much better information than rank-and-file union members about the employer's true financial position and the maximum wage settlement the union will be able to extract. If this settlement is smaller than the settlement the membership wants, the union leaders face two options.

On the one hand, union leaders can return to their members, try to convince them of the employer's true financial picture, and recommend that management's last offer (the maximum that they know they can achieve) be accepted. The danger they face with this option is that the members may vote down the recommendation, accuse the leaders of selling out to management, and ultimately vote them out of office.

On the other hand, union leaders can return to their members and recommend that the members go out on strike. This recommendation will allow them to appear to be strong, militant leaders, even though the leaders themselves know that the strike will not lead to a larger settlement. However, after a strike of some duration, in accordance with the notion of the union resistance curve in Figure 12.3, union members will begin to moderate their wage demands and ultimately a settlement for which the union leader will receive credit will be reached. Since the latter strategy is the one that is more likely to maintain the union's strength *and* keep the leaders in office, it is the strategy leaders may opt for even though it is clearly not in their members' best interests in the short run (the members have to bear the costs of the strike).

This model can provide insights into the forces that affect the frequency and duration of strike activity. In panel (a) of Figure 12.4, curve *UR* represents union members' minimum acceptable percentage wage increase ($\dot{W}$) as a function of the length of a strike; this curve is nothing more than the Hicks' union resistance curve. To simplify the discussion, we have assumed that curve *UR* always declines with strike length. In this diagram $\dot{W}$ is the union members' initial wage demand (the amount they would settle for without a strike) and $\dot{W}_m$ is the minimum amount they would ever settle for. Depending upon economic conditions and the members' hostility to management, $\dot{W}_m$ may be positive, zero, or even negative; the last possibility would occur if union members felt they had to take a pay cut to preserve their jobs.

Panel (b) of Figure 12.4 plots the employer's present value of profits (*PVP*) as a function of the length of a strike. An increase in strike duration has two offsetting effects. In the immediate period, the employer loses profits because the firm loses

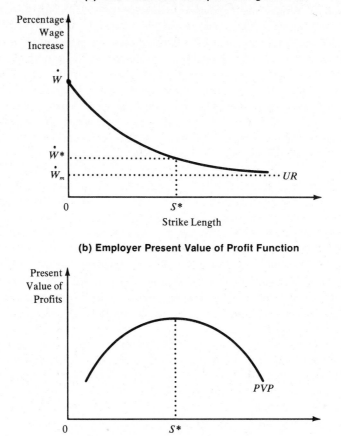

(a) Union Members' Acceptable Wage Increase

(b) Employer Present Value of Profit Function

FIGURE 12.4 Graphic Representation of Ashenfelter-Johnson Model of Strike Activity

some sales. However, in the future the firm's profits may be higher because the longer strike means that the employees will be willing to settle for smaller wage increases [from panel (a) of Figure 12.4]. In panel (b), initially the second effect dominates, but ultimately—since the union wage demands fall less rapidly (in absolute terms) and lost sales begin to mount up—the former effect dominates. That is, the employer's present value of profits first increases and then decreases with strike duration.

Suppose the employer's goal is to maximize the firm's present value of profits, and suppose the employer knows the position and shape of the curves in Figure 12.4. The employer can maximize the firm's present value of profits by offering the union a wage increase of $\dot{W}*$ after a strike of length $S*$. At that point the union members will accept the offer and the strike will end. If the PVP curve in Figure 12.4 were always negatively sloped, the employer would either settle prior to a strike or go out of business if paying $\dot{W}$ would cause the firm to suffer losses.

Changing the model's parameters influences the probability of occurrence and expected duration of a strike. For example, if the union's initial wage demand $(\dot{W})$ increases, other things equal, a strike will have a greater payoff to the employer and the expected duration will increase. Similarly, an increase in the rate at which the union's wage demands decline over time, other things equal, will increase the employer's payoff from prolonging the strike. In contrast, an increase in the union members' minimum acceptable wage demand $\dot{W}_m$ (sometimes called the union's *resistance point*) will reduce the employer's gain from incurring a strike, other things equal, and will reduce the probability of a strike occurring.

The Ashenfelter and Johnson model—which assumed that the above parameters are influenced by the unemployment rate in the economy, by past changes in wage rates and prices, and by the profit rates of corporations—is able to explain why increases in the unemployment rate lead to reduced strike activity.[28] In the context of their model, an increase in the unemployment rate is assumed to reduce the initial wage demands of unions, $\dot{W}$, because it reduces the probability that workers can find temporary part-time jobs while on strike.

Ashenfelter and Johnson also found that, after statistically controlling for the unemployment rate, profits, and past wage and price changes, the level of strike activity (as measured by the number of strikes per year) tended to decline during 1952–67. However, the decline took a particular form: while the pattern was downward from 1952 to 1959, the number jumped up in 1959 before resuming its downward trend (see Figure 12.5).[29]

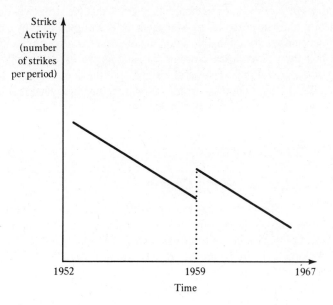

FIGURE 12.5   Ashenfelter and Johnson's Estimated Time Trend in Strike Activity

---

[28]Ashenfelter and Johnson, ''Bargaining Theory,'' pp. 42–46.
[29]Ashenfelter and Johnson, ''Bargaining Theory,'' p. 47.

The general decline in strike activity in the U.S. economy has been attributed by many observers to the maturation of industrial relations in the United States; fewer strikes are now caused by the parties' misunderstanding each other's intentions or by the need to use a strike today to enhance bargaining power tomorrow.[30] The increase in 1959 coincided with the passage of the Landrum-Griffin Act. By increasing union democracy, this act increased the chances that union leaders would be voted out of office if they failed to satisfy union members' expectations at contract negotiation time. In the context of the model presented here, making union leaders more accountable to membership would increase the probability that leaders would recommend going on strike to their members, rather than trying to sell the rank and file on an unacceptable contract. To return to a previous theme, social programs and legislation often have unintended side effects; the Landrum-Griffin Act may well have unintentionally led to an increase in the level of strike activity in the economy.

The model presented in this section does not pretend to be the ultimate model of strike activity. It focuses only on strikes that result from disagreements over economic issues and ignores strikes that may result from conflict over recognition procedures, grievance procedures, unsafe working conditions, and the like. It also makes certain assumptions that, while sometimes plausible, are unlikely to always be true. For example, in essence this model suggests that union leaders and management implicitly collude to the detriment of union members. Union leaders are assumed to be willing to recommend a strike that will impose costs (in the form of lost income) on members, even though they know that the strike will not increase management's ultimate wage offer. Management is assumed to fully know union members' resistance curve. Finally, union members are assumed to be ignorant, in the sense that they never learn how the bargaining process is actually working. Nonetheless, the model provides useful insights into the bargaining process and an explanation of why the Landrum-Griffin Act and the unemployment rate should be expected to influence the level of strike activity.

THE EFFECTS OF UNIONS

The Theory of Union Wage Effects

Suppose one had data on the wage rates paid to two groups of workers who were identical in every respect except for the fact that one group was unionized and the other was not. Let W_u denote the wage paid to union members and W_n the wage paid to nonunion workers. If the difference between the two could be attributed solely to the presence of unions, then the *relative wage advantage* that unions would have achieved for their members would be given, in percentage terms, by

$$R = (W_u - W_n)/W_n \tag{12.1}$$

---

[30]It is hard to discern a trend in any of the measures of strike activity over the 1953–79 period in the *raw* data presented in Table 12.6. One must remember, however, that during the period all the other variables (unemployment, wage and price changes, profits) were changing. The trends Ashenfelter and Johnson observe are found after one statistically controls for these other factors.

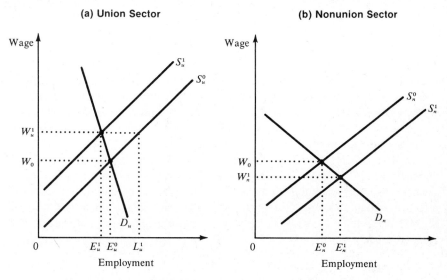

(a) Union Sector

(b) Nonunion Sector

FIGURE 12.6   Spillover Effects of Unions on Wages and Employment

Contrary to what one might expect, this relative wage advantage does *not* represent the absolute amount, in percentage terms, by which unions would have increased the wages of their members because unions both directly and indirectly affect *nonunion* wage rates also. Moreover, one cannot *a priori* state whether estimates of R will overstate or understate the absolute effect of unions on their members' real wage levels. (This chapter, as noted before, focuses on the union effects on wage *levels;* Chapter 16 will discuss union effects on the *rate of wage change.*) Figure 12.6 presents a simple two-sector model of the labor market. Except for the fact that the labor supply curves are upward sloping in both sectors, this model is identical to the one used in Chapter 3 to analyze the effects of the minimum wage in the presence of incomplete coverage; the analyses here will proceed along similar lines.[31]

Panel (a) is the union sector and panel (b) is the nonunion sector. Suppose initially, however, that both sectors are unorganized. If mobility is relatively costless, workers will move between the two sectors until wages are equalized between them. With demand curves D_u and D_n, workers will move between sectors until the supply curves are S_u^0 and S_n^0, respectively. The common equilibrium wage will be W_0, and employment will be E_u^0 and E_n^0, respectively, in the two sectors.

Now suppose a union succeeds in organizing the workers in the first sector and also succeeds in raising their wage to W_u^1. This increased wage will cause employ-

---

[31]Much of the discussion in this section is based upon the pioneering work of H. G. Lewis, *Unionism and Relative Wages in the United States* (Chicago: University of Chicago Press, 1963). In Figure 12.6 and those that follow, our analysis employs a two-sector model with labor supply curves to each sector. Remember that a labor supply curve to one sector is drawn holding the wages in other sectors (the "alternative wages") constant; whenever the wage in one sector changes, the labor supply curve to the other sector may shift. We *sometimes* ignore this complexity below to keep our exposition as simple as possible and to highlight the various behaviors that might occur in either sector in response to unionization.

ment to decline to E_u^1 workers in the union sector, resulting in $L_u^1 - E_u^1$ unemployed workers in that sector. These workers have several options; one is to seek employment in the nonunion sector. If all the unemployed workers *spill over* into the nonunion sector, the supply curves in the two sectors will shift to S_u^1 and S_n^1, respectively. Unemployment will be eliminated in the union sector; however, in the nonunion sector an excess supply of labor will exist at the old market-clearing wage, W_0. As a result, downward pressure will be exerted on the wage rate in the nonunion sector until the labor market in that sector clears at a *lower* wage, W_n^1, and a higher employment level E_n^1.

In the context of this model, the union has succeeded in raising the wages of its members who kept their jobs. However, it has done so by shifting some of its members to lower-wage jobs in the nonunion sector and, because of this spillover effect, by actually lowering the wage rate paid to individuals initially employed in the nonunion sector. As a result, the observed union *relative wage* advantage (R_1), computed as

$$R_1 = (W_u^1 - W_n^1)/W_n^1, \tag{12.2}$$

will tend to be greater than the true *absolute* effect of the union on its members' real wage. This true absolute effect (A_1), stated in percentage terms, is computed as

$$A_1 = (W_u^1 - W_0)/W_0. \tag{12.3}$$

The relative effect will not necessarily be larger than the absolute effect, however, because there are several other responses that employees or employers can make. Employers in the nonunion sector may be concerned that unions will subsequently try to organize their employees, and may view a union as undesirable if unionization both increases their wage costs and limits their managerial flexibility. As such, they may try to "buy off" their employees by offering them wage increases to reduce the probability that the employees will vote for a union.[32] Because of the costs associated with union membership, noted earlier, some wage less than W_u^1 but higher than W_0 would presumably be sufficient to assure employers that the majority of their employees would not vote for a union (assuming that the employees are happy with their nonwage conditions of employment).

The implications of such *threat effects*—nonunion wage increases resulting from the threat of union entry—are traced in Figure 12.7. The increase in wage in the union sector, and resulting decline in employment there, is again assumed to cause the supply of workers to the nonunion sector to shift to S_n^1. However, in response to the threat of union entry, nonunion employers are assumed to *increase* their employees' wages to W_n^*, which lies between W_0 and W_u^1. This wage increase causes employment to decline to E_n^*; at the higher wage nonunion employers demand fewer workers. Moreover, since the nonunion wage is now not free to be bid down, an excess supply of labor, $L_n^* - E_n^*$, exists, resulting in unemployment.

---

[32]For a more formal discussion of this possibility, see Sherwin Rosen, "Trade Union Power, Threat Effects, and the Extent of Organization," *Review of Economic Studies* 36(April 1969):185–96.

Nonunion Sector

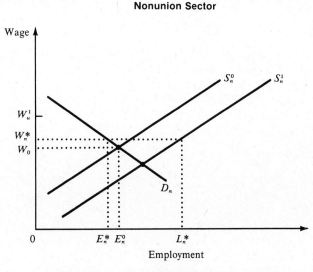

FIGURE 12.7   **Threat Effects of Unions on Wages
and Employment**

Finally, because the nonunion wage is now higher than the original wage, the observed union relative wage advantage,

$$R_2 = (W_u^1 - W_n^*)/W_n^*, \tag{12.4}$$

is smaller than the absolute effect of unions on their members' real wages.

One might question whether workers who lose their jobs in the union sector as a result of the union's increasing the wage rate will necessarily seek jobs in the nonunion sector. Even with a fixed employment level in the union sector, job vacancies occur as a result of retirements, deaths, and voluntary turnover (including quits to take other jobs in the same area, geographic migration, and temporary departures from the labor force). It may pay union members to remain attached to the union sector *and* temporarily unemployed if they will ultimately obtain a job in the union sector. Indeed, it may actually pay some employed nonunion workers to quit their jobs and move to the union sector if they might obtain a relatively higher-paying union job in the future. Such decisions lead to *wait unemployment:* workers rejecting lower-paying nonunion jobs and waiting for higher-paying union jobs to open up.[33]

Workers will move between the union and nonunion sector until their *expected earnings* in each are equal. If one ignores complications such as the costs of union membership, the presence of unemployment insurance benefits for some unem-

---

[33]See Jacob Mincer, "Unemployment Effects of Minimum Wages," *Journal of Political Economy* 84(July/August 1976, Part 2):S87–S104. Although Mincer discusses minimum wage effects, union-imposed "minimum wages" can be analyzed analogously.

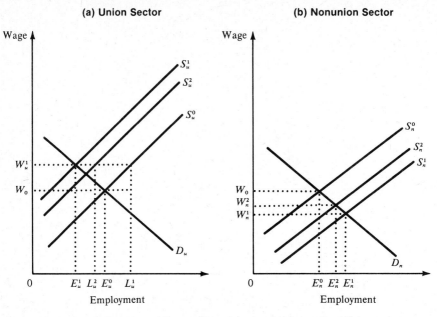

FIGURE 12.8   Wait Unemployment (nonunion wage falls)

ployed workers, fringe benefits, and the like, expected earnings will be equal when the wage rate paid in each sector multiplied by the fraction of each period *(F)* that individuals in the sector expect to be employed are equal, or when

$$W_u F_u = W_n F_n. \tag{12.5}$$

Figure 12.8 illustrates the process. If threat effects are ignored, the consequences of an increase in the union wage to W_u^1 would be a decline in employment in the union sector to E_u^1, a shift in the supply curves to S_u^1 and S_n^1, and a resulting decrease in nonunion wages to W_n^1 and increase in nonunion employment to E_n^1. Since there is no unemployment in this situation, F_u and F_n are both equal to unity. Hence, labor market equilibrium, as indicated in equation (12.5), would require that wages be equal in the two sectors. But they are *not;* W_u^1 is greater that W_n^1. Hence, individuals' expected earnings are higher in the union sector.

The above difference in expected earnings would induce some individuals to move from the nonunion sector to wait for jobs in the union sector. This movement leads to an increase in the expected earnings in the nonunion sector (as supply decreases there, wages are bid up) and a decrease in expected earnings in the union sector (as supply increases there, the probability of obtaining a job in that sector decreases). Eventually expected earnings are equalized between the two sectors by this process.

We have *assumed* that expected earnings are equalized in Figure 12.8 at the points at which the supply curves in the two sectors are S_u^2 and S_n^2. The resulting wage in the nonunion sector is W_n^2, and the resulting employment level is E_n^2. *Wait unemployment* now exists in the union sector; its level is given by $L_u^1 - E_u^1$. Finally, although W_n^2 is greater than W_n^1, W_n^2 is less than W_0. Thus, if the union relative wage advantage is measured as

$$R_3 = (W_u^1 - W_n^2)/W_n^2, \tag{12.6}$$

it will again be larger than the true absolute effect of the union on its members' real wage levels.

Of course, we have assumed that the expected earnings would be equalized as indicated in Figure 12.8. Under certain assumptions, the equalization may not occur until after the supply of labor to the union sector has shifted to the *right* of its initial position and after the supply of labor in the nonunion sector has shifted to the *left* of its initial position. This situation is more likely to occur if the demand curve in the union sector is inelastic. An inelastic demand curve would cause *expected earnings* $(W_u^1 F_u)$ in the union sector to increase immediately after the increase in the union *wage* because employment losses are so small. This immediate rise in expected earnings induces employees to migrate from the nonunion to union sector.[34] As Figure 12.9 indicates, supply in the union sector shifts right (to S_u^3) and supply in the nonunion sector shifts left (to S_n^3). In this situation wait unemployment would increase to $L_u^3 - E_u^1$, and the nonunion wage would increase to W_n^3, which is greater than W_0. The union relative wage advantage in this case, which is computed as

$$R_4 = (W_u^1 - W_n^3)/W_n^3, \tag{12.7}$$

would be less than the absolute effect of unions on their members' real wages.

One final case will complete our discussion. Suppose the union increases its members' wages by means of increasing the demand for union labor, using any of the methods discussed in the previous section. Figure 12.10 illustrates an increase in the demand for labor in the union sector to D_u^1. If this increase comes at the expense

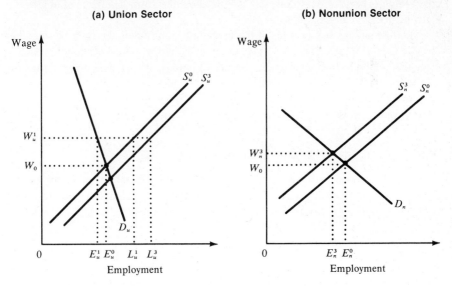

(a) Union Sector   **(b) Nonunion Sector**

FIGURE 12.9 Wait Unemployment (nonunion wage increases)

---

[34]*See* Mincer, "Unemployment Effects of Minimum Wages," and Edward Gramlich, "The Impact of Minimum Wages on Other Wages, Employment, and Family Incomes," *Brookings Papers on Economic Activity*, 1976–2, pp. 409–51, for a more complete discussion of when this is likely to occur.

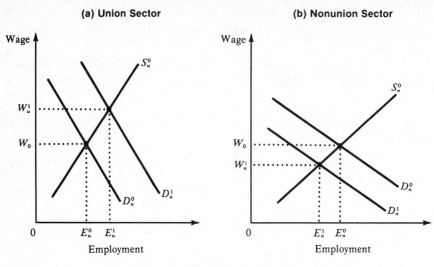

FIGURE 12.10   Union "Shifts" the Demand Curve

of the demand for labor in the nonunion sector, the latter curve will fall, say to D_n^1. Initially the effect is to increase both wages (W_u^1) and employment (E_u^1) in the union sector and decrease wages (W_n^1) and employment (E_n^1) in the nonunion sector. The ultimate change in the nonunion wage, however, will depend upon the extent to which threat effects or wait unemployment are important. So again, estimates of the union *relative* wage effects alone tell us little about the *absolute* effects of unions on their members' real wage levels.

Because unions *are* present in the economy, at any point in time all one can observe are the union and nonunion wage rates (W_u and W_n). One can*not* observe the wage that would have existed in the absence of unions, W_0. Hence, direct estimates of a union's effects on the absolute level (A_1) of its members' real wages—refer back to equation (12.3)—cannot be obtained. Care must be taken not to mistake relative wage effects for absolute wage effects.[35]

Evidence of Union Wage Effects

In recent years, economists have expended considerable effort to estimate the extent to which unions have raised the wages of their members relative to the wages of comparable nonunion workers in the private sector.[36] These studies have tended to

---

[35]This discussion has assumed a partial equilibrium model. Once one considers a general equilibrium framework and allows capital to move between sectors, even more possibilities may exist. On this point, see Harry Johnson and Peter Mieszkowski, "The Effects of Unionization on the Distribution of Income: A General Equilibrium Approach," *Quarterly Journal of Economics* 84(November 1969):539–61.

[36]See C. J. Parsley, "Labor Unions and Wages: A Survey," *Journal of Economic Literature* 18(March 1980):1–31; and Richard Freeman and James Medoff, "The Impact of Collective Bargaining: Can the New Facts Be Explained by Monopoly Unionism?" *Research in Labor Economics,* Supplement 2(1983):293–332.

use data on large samples of individuals and have attempted to separate wage differentials caused by unionization from wage differentials caused by differences in personal characteristics and differences in industry and occupation of employment. That is, these economists have sought to ascertain how much more union members get paid than nonunion workers, after controlling for any differences between the two groups in other factors that might be expected to influence wages.[37]

The various studies use several data bases that span various years, and they often employ different statistical methodologies. As such, they do not yield a single unambiguous estimate of the extent to which union members' wages exceed the wages of comparable nonunion workers in the private sector. Perhaps the best estimate is that the union relative wage advantage, on average, has fallen to the range of 10 to 20 percent in recent years. These union wage effects, however, are neither constant over time nor constant across groups.

For example, a study by Orley Ashenfelter, summarized in Table 12.7, suggests that the estimated union relative wage advantage in the private sector rose substantially between 1967 and 1975, from 11.6 to 16.8 percent. The year 1967 was one of low unemployment; the year 1975 was one of high unemployment. Since unionized workers' wages tend to be less responsive to labor market conditions than nonunion workers' wages (see Chapter 16), this result is not surprising; the union relative wage advantage tends to be larger during recessionary periods.[38]

The estimates in Table 12.7 also suggest that unions have helped improve the relative economic positions of black males. On the one hand, the estimated relative wage effects are larger for black men than white men; being a union member enhances black men's earnings by more than it does white men's. On the other hand, the percentage of black men that are union members also appears to be

TABLE 12.7   Estimated Union/Nonunion Relative Wage Effects, 1967, 1973, and 1975

	Percentage Union Wage Effect			Percentage Unionized		
	1967	*1973*	*1975*	*1967*	*1973*	*1975*
All workers	11.6	14.8	16.8	23	26	25
White men	9.6	15.5	16.3	31	33	31
Black men	21.5	22.5	22.5	32	37	37
White women	14.4	12.7	16.6	12	14	14
Black women	5.6	13.2	17.1	13	22	22

SOURCE: From "Union Relative Wage Effects" by Orley Ashenfelter in *Econometric Contributions to Public Policy*, by Richard Stone and William Peterson (eds.). Copyright © 1978 International Economic Association. Reprinted by permission of St. Martin's Press, Inc., and Macmillan, London and Basingstoke.

---

[37]Some of the more ambitious studies also attempt to control for the fact that unionization and wages may be simultaneously determined; as noted earlier, workers' decisions to join a union are partially based on the expected gains from union membership. See, for example, Lung-Fei Lee, "Unionism and Wage Rates: A Simultaneous-Equations Model with Qualitative and Limited Dependent Variables," *International Economic Review* 19(June 1978):415–33.

[38]Lewis, *Unionism and Relative Wages,* provides evidence that this relationship appeared to hold during the 1930–60 period as well.

slightly larger than the comparable percentage for white men. On balance, then, in spite of well-publicized conflicts between some unions and civil rights organizations over union seniority rules and the use of racial quotas, unions appear to have improved the economic well-being of black men relative to white men.

In contrast, Table 12.7 emphasizes that female workers are considerably less likely to be union members than are males. Although in some years women who are union members appear to have gained as much as *white* men who are union members compared to their nonunion counterparts, on balance the *overall* effect of unions is to reduce women's wages relative to men's, perhaps by as much as 2.9 percent in 1975.[39]

The estimates cited above are of the relative wage advantage (*R*) that unions have achieved for their members in comparison to nonunion workers. These estimates do not indicate what effects unions have had on the absolute real wage levels of their members. In other words, the estimates do not reveal how unions have influenced *nonunion* workers' wages. The limited evidence on this point, although ambiguous, suggests that unions may well depress the wages of nonunion workers; the *spillover effect* described in Figure 12.6 appears to dominate over the *threat* and *wait-unemployment effects* described in Figures 12.7 and 12.9.[40] That is, other things equal, the wages of nonunion workers are lower in cities in which the percent of workers who are union members is high. Thus, estimates of the relative wage effects of unions may well be greater than their effects on the absolute level of their members' real wages.

One might think that the above evidence suggests that unions increase the dispersion of labor earnings, increasing the wages of high-paid union members and decreasing the wages of lower-paid nonunion workers. In fact, however, several studies indicate that unions actually tend on balance to *decrease* the dispersion of labor earnings. For example, it is now well known that rates of return on education and job training are lower in the union than nonunion sector; these lower payoffs in the union sector cause the earnings there to be more equal among workers with different human capital investments than would otherwise be the case.[41] Other studies find that union wage policies designed to standardize wage rates within and across establishments significantly reduce the extent of wage dispersion among workers covered by union contracts,[42] and that unions also reduce the relative wage advantage of white-collar workers over blue-collar workers. Indeed, one study suggests that these effects dominate over the more widely known union effects on union/nonunion worker wage differentials, in the sense that, on balance, unions

---

[39]Ashenfelter, "Union Relative Wage Effects."

[40]Lawrence Kahn, "The Effect of Unions on the Earnings of Nonunion Workers," *Industrial and Labor Relations Review* 31(January 1978):205–16.

[41]Farrell Bloch and Mark Kuskin, "Wage Determination in the Union and Nonunion Sectors," *Industrial and Labor Relations Review* 31(January 1978):183–92; and Greg M. Duncan and Duane E. Leigh, "Wage Determination in the Union and Nonunion Sectors: A Sample Selectivity Approach," *Industrial and Labor Relations Review* 34(October 1980):24–35.

[42]Richard Freeman, "Union Wage Practices and Wage Dispersion within Establishments," *Industrial and Labor Relations Review* 36(October 1982):3–21.

Example 12.3

Codetermination and Union Relative Wage Gains in West Germany

Since the early 1950s, legislation has encouraged greater employee participation in management in West Germany. These *codetermination laws* give employees in the German iron-steel and mining industries one half of the seats on company boards of directors and give employees in all other industries (save for shipping and air transport) one third of the seats. The position of labor director has also been established on management boards in the steel and mining industries; this director cannot be approved or dismissed without a majority vote of the employee representatives to a company's board of directors.

German employee representatives on boards of directors participate in decisions about industrywide collective bargaining agreements. One might assume that these laws have increased labor's bargaining power, especially in the iron-steel and mining industries, and thus increased the size of observed wage differentials between unionized workers in these industries and other employees in the economy. A recent study concluded that codetermination has increased the earnings of the average unionized German iron-steel and mining employee by roughly 6.2 percent relative to the earnings of primarily nonunion employees in the textile industry. The effects of unions on relative wages clearly depend upon the prevailing institutional arrangements.

SOURCE: Jan Svejnar, "Relative Wage Effects of Unions, Dictatorship, and Codetermination: Econometric Evidence from Germany," *Review of Economics and Statistics* 63(May 1981):188–97.

appear to reduce wage dispersion in the United States.[43] Finally, another study suggests that, other things equal, inequality of earnings within metropolitan areas tends to be less widespread in areas in which the extent of unionization is high.[44]

Evidence of Union Total Compensation Effects

Estimates of the extent to which the wages of union workers exceed the wages of otherwise comparable nonunion workers may prove misleading for two reasons. First, such estimates ignore the fact that wages are only part of the compensation package. It has often been argued that fringe benefits, such as paid holidays, vacation pay, sick leave, and retirement benefits, will be higher in firms that are

---

[43]Richard Freeman, "Unionism and the Dispersion of Wages," *Industrial and Labor Relations Review* 34(October 1980):3–23.

[44]Thomas Hyclak, "The Effects of Unions on Earnings Inequality in Local Labor Markets," *Industrial and Labor Relations Review* 33(October 1979):77–84.

unionized than in nonunion firms. The argument states that, because tastes for the various fringe benefits differ across individuals and because there is no easy way to communicate the preferences of the average employee to the employer in a nonunion firm, nonunion firms tend to pay a higher fraction of total compensation in the form of money wages.[45] Recent empirical evidence tends to support this contention; fringe benefits and the share of compensation that goes to fringe benefits do appear to be higher in union than in nonunion firms.[46] Ignoring fringes may therefore understate the true union/nonunion total compensation differential.

In contrast, ignoring nonpecuniary conditions of employment may cause one to overstate the true effect of unions on their members' total compensation compared to nonunion workers. For example, recent studies have shown that for blue-collar workers, unionized firms tend to have more structured work settings, more hazardous jobs, less flexible hours of work, faster work paces, and less employee control over the assignment of overtime hours than do nonunion firms.[47] This situation may arise because production settings that give rise to interdependence among workers and the demand for specific work requirements by employers also give rise to unions. That is, the decision to vote for unions may be heavily influenced by these nonpecuniary conditions of employment. While unions often strive to affect these working conditions, they do not always succeed. Part of the estimated union/nonunion earnings differential may be a premium paid to union workers to compensate them for these unfavorable working conditions. Indeed, one study estimates that two fifths of the estimated union/nonunion earnings differential reflects such compensation, suggesting that the observed union/nonunion earnings differential may overstate the true union/nonunion total compensation differential.[48]

The true union/nonunion total compensation differential may also be overstated when comparisons are made between unionized and nonunion employees *at a point in time* if unobserved (to the researcher) differences in ability systematically exist between the two groups. That is, if unionized workers tend to be more able but this fact cannot be controlled for in the statistical analyses, part of the measured compensation differential will reflect the greater ability of union workers, rather than union power. Attempts to handle this problem have included using *longitudinal data*—data on individuals for a number of periods—and observing how compensation changes with changes in union status. Such studies tend to find smaller but still positive union/nonunion total compensation differentials.[49]

---

[45]This line of reasoning goes back at least as far as Richard Lester, "Benefits as a Preferred Form of Compensation," *Southern Economic Journal* 33(April 1967):488–95.

[46]Richard Freeman, "The Effect of Trade Unions on Fringe Benefits," *Industrial and Labor Relations Review* 34(July 1981):489–509; and William Alpert, "Unions and Private Wage Supplements," *Journal of Labor Research* 3(Spring 1982):179–90.

[47]Greg Duncan and Frank Stafford, "Do Union Members Receive Compensating Wage Differentials?" *American Economic Review* 70(June 1980):355–71; and J. Paul Leigh, "Are Unionized Blue-Collar Jobs More Hazardous Than Nonunionized Blue-Collar Jobs?" *Journal of Labor Research* 3(Summer 1982):349–57.

[48]Duncan and Stafford, "Do Union Members Receive Compensating Wage Differentials?"

[49]Wesley Mellow, "Unionism and Wages: A Longitudinal Analysis," *Review of Economics and Statistics* 63(February 1981):43–52; and Jacob Mincer, "Union Effects: Wages, Turnover, and Job Training," *Research in Labor Economics* Supplement 2 (1983).

The Traditional View of Union Effects on Productivity and Output

According to the traditional neoclassical view of unions, although they may improve the welfare of their members by improving their pecuniary and nonpecuniary conditions of employment, on balance, their effects on the economy at large are negative. Three reasons are given to support this view.

First, to the extent that unions succeed in driving a wedge between the wage rates of comparable quality workers who are employed in the union and nonunion sectors, there is a loss of output. Recall from Chapter 3 that the demand curves for labor reflect the marginal product of labor. If the "spillover" model in Figure 12.6 holds, the union wage, W_u, exceeds the nonunion wage, W_n, and the marginal product of labor is higher in the union sector than in the nonunion sector. Consequently, output could be increased if labor were reallocated from the nonunion sector to the union sector, where its marginal product is higher. Put another way, unions cause a misallocation of workers: too many workers are employed in the nonunion sector and too few in the union sector. Of course, if the union wage gain also induces some unemployment (see Figures 12.7, 12.8, and 12.9), the loss of output due to these idled resources must also be considered.

Second, union-negotiated contract provisions that establish staffing requirements or other restrictive work practices limit firms from employing capital and labor in the most efficient ways and may cause output losses. Several examples of such provisions include minimum crew sizes in jet aircrafts, maximum apprentice/journeymen ratios in construction, provisions limiting subcontracting or mandatory assignment of overtime, and requirements that redundant employees be employed (fire stokers in diesel-operated railroad engines, typesetters in printing plants where type is set by computer). By limiting substitution possibilities or forcing firms to use redundant inputs, unions reduce output below its maximum achievable level.

Third, unions are thought to reduce output because strikes called either at the time that collective bargaining is occurring (to influence the settlement) or during the term of a contract (to protest the way the contract is being administered) result in lost work days. In this view, if strikes were eliminated, output would increase.

Actual empirical estimates of the magnitudes of these alleged losses are few and far between. In an often cited study, Albert Rees estimated that society lost no more than 0.3 percent of gross national product because of the creation of wage differentials between comparable quality union and nonunion workers.[50] Rees also estimated that the loss of output due to restrictive work practices was at least as large. Finally, Table 12.6 indicated that the estimated percentage of working time lost due to strikes over the 25-year period from 1953 to 1977 averaged 0.2 percent. Summing these three figures yields a ballpark estimate of a loss in output of less

---

[50]Albert Rees, "The Effects of Unions on Resource Allocation," *Journal of Law and Economics* 6(October 1963):69–78. Rees's estimate also included condsideration of output losses due to union effects on intra-industry wage differentials—for example, requiring all unionized firms in an industry to pay the same wage. A more recent study on the output losses associated with union wage effects finds them to be about half the size of the Rees estimates. See Robert H. DeFina, "Unions, Relative Wages, and Economic Efficiency," *Journal of Labor Economics* 1(October 1983):408–29.

than 0.8 percent due to these three factors. Of course, whether one considers this an acceptable or unacceptable cost depends upon the benefits that one believes society as a whole receives from unionization.

An Alternative View of Union Effects on Productivity and Profits

Recently labor economists have begun to rediscover the possibility that unions may also have positive influences on productivity.[51] The analyses of Richard Freeman and James Medoff and their associates are based heavily upon the assumption that unions function as institutions of *collective voice* operating within structured internal labor markets.[52] That is, because unions can communicate the preferences of workers on various issues directly to management and can help establish work rules and seniority provisions in the context of structured internal labor markets, they can contribute to increases in productivity in a number of ways.

First, by providing workers with a direct means to voice their discontent to management and by establishing job rights based upon seniority, unions may reduce worker discontent, thus reducing voluntary turnover (quit rates). As discussed in Chapter 5, reductions in job turnover increase employers' incentives to provide their employees with *firm-specific training,* which will lead to increased productivity. Considerable evidence suggests that unions do in fact reduce quit rates.[53] Moreover, seniority systems weaken the rivalry between inexperienced and experienced employees and consequently increase the amount of informal on-the-job training that the latter are willing to give to the former.[54]

Second, by increasing the economic rewards of employment and providing grievance mechanisms, unions may directly enhance productivity by increasing worker morale, motivation, and effort. Third, unions provide an explicit mechanism by which labor can point out possible changes in work rules or production techniques that will benefit both labor and management.

---

[51]For a discussion of the evidence supporting this view, see Richard B. Freeman and James L. Medoff, "The Two Faces of Unionism," *Public Interest* 57(Fall 1979):69–93. A more detailed discussion is found in their *What Do Unions Do?* (New York: Basic Books, 1984). Note that, to the extent that employers react to induced union wage gains by restricting employment and substituting capital for labor, labor's marginal product will rise (although total production costs will also rise). The discussion below considers whether there are additional union-induced effects on labor's marginal productivity.

[52]Albert Hirschman, *Exit, Voice and Loyalty* (Cambridge: Harvard University Press, 1973), and Richard Freeman, "Individual Mobility and Union Voice in the Labor Market," *American Economic Review* 66(May 1976):361–68, provide discussions of unions' role as institutions of collective voice. Oliver Williamson, Michael Wachter, and Jeffrey Harris, "Understanding the Employment Relation: Analysis of Idiosyncratic Exchange," *Bell Journal of Economics* 6(Spring 1975):250–80, emphasize the interrelationship between unions and internal labor markets.

[53]See Richard B. Freeman, "The Exit-Voice Trade-Off in the Labor Market: Unionism, Job Tenure, Quits, and Separations," *Quarterly Journal of Economics* 94(June 1980):644–73; and James Medoff, "Layoffs and Alternatives Under Trade Unions in United States Manufacturing," *American Economic Review* 69(June 1979):380–95.

[54]See Peter Doeringer and Michael Piore, *Internal Labor Markets and Manpower Analysis* (Lexington, Mass.: D. C. Heath, 1971).

Several studies have been undertaken in recent years that attempt to estimate the net effect of unions on productivity. These studies are summarized in Table 12.8. The methodological approach used in all but the Clark study is to estimate the extent to which value of output per worker (*value added*) is associated with the level of unionization in an industry or establishment at a point in time, after controlling for other factors expected to influence productivity.[55] (The Clark study uses data on the physical volume of output and also looks at how productivity changes after a plant becomes unionized.)

These studies suggest that union workers are more productive than nonunion workers in manufacturing. Indeed, the size of the productivity differential appears to be large enough to offset the estimated union/nonunion wage differential; that is, the unit labor cost of unionized manufacturing workers does not appear to exceed the unit labor cost of nonunion workers. This result provides an explanation of how high-wage union firms and lower-wage nonunion firms can coexist in a competitive industry.

In the bituminous coal industry, positive union productivity differentials were found in 1965 but substantial negative ones appeared in 1975. Indeed, in 1975 unionized workers were estimated to be 20 to 25 percent *less* productive than nonunion workers in the industry. This decline in relative productivity has been attributed to the well-known breakdown of the United Mine Workers' (UMW) national leadership that occurred in the late 1960s and early 1970s, which resulted in deteriorating industrial relations practices, including increased occurrence of *wildcat* (unauthorized) strikes over local issues.[56] These results emphasize that the effects of unions on productivity are neither constant nor always positive; they vary across industries and time periods as industrial relations practices vary.

The Allen study cited in Table 12.8 finds surprisingly large union productivity differentials in construction—surprising because in the construction industry unions were widely thought to have adverse effects on productivity owing to their restrictive work rules (limits on apprentice/journeymen ratios, limits on the jobs members of each craft can do, etc.).[57] He attributed the differential, however, to better training at union apprenticeship programs, changes in the occupational mix induced by unions, and reduced screening and recruitment costs for contractors.

On balance, then, the studies summarized in Table 12.8 suggest that unions have *increased* productivity in certain industries.[58] There is no consensus yet, however, as to whether these increases more than offset the losses of gross national product caused by union effects on wage structures and union strike activity. These

---

[55]Value added is the difference in dollar terms between the sales price of a product and the value of the materials that went into making it.

[56]Richard Freeman, James Medoff, and Marie Connerton, "Industrial Relations and Productivity: A Case Study of the U.S. Bituminous Coal Industry" (Cambridge, Mass.: Harvard University mimeo, 1979).

[57]Steven Allen, "Unionized Construction Workers Are More Productive," *Quarterly Journal of Economics* 99(May 1984):251–74.

[58]Some economists question the findings of these studies. See, for example, John Addison, "Are Unions Good for Productivity?" *Journal of Labor Research* 3(Spring 1982):125–38.

TABLE 12.8   **Estimates of the Impact of Unionism
on Productivity in U.S. Industries**

Industry/Year of Data	Estimated Impact of Unions on Productivity (percent)
(a) All U.S. Manufacturing, 1972	20 to 25
(b) Wooden Household Furniture, 1972	15
(c) Cement, 1953–76	6 to 8
(d) Underground Bituminous Coal, 1965	25 to 30
(e) Underground Bituminous Coal, 1975	-20 to -25
(f) Construction, 1972	17 to 22

SOURCES OF ESTIMATES: (a) Charles Brown and James Medoff, "Trade Unions in the Production Process," *Journal of Political Economy* 86 (June 1978):355–78. (b) John Frantz, "The Impact of Trade Unions on Productivity in the Wood Household Furniture Industry" (Honors Thesis, Harvard University, 1976). (c) Kim Clark, "The Impact of Unionization on Productivity: A Case Study," *Industrial and Labor Relations Review* 33(July 1980):451–69. (d)-(e) Richard Freeman, James Medoff, and Marie Connerton, "Industrial Relations and Productivity: A Case Study of the U.S. Bituminous Coal Industry" (mimeo, Harvard University, 1979). (f) Steven Allen, "Unionized Construction Workers Are More Productive" *Quarterly Journal of Economics*, May 1984.

studies suggest, however, that like most questions in economics, whether unions have had a net positive or negative effect on output is an empirical question. The answer is not as obvious as either the supporters or opponents of unions would have one believe.

It is interesting to note that some of these studies suggest that unions increase productivity more than wages, which leads to the possibility that profitability is greater in firms that are organized by unions. This intriguing possibility does not accord well with the substantial efforts of most firms to oppose demands for recognition by unions and of employer organizations to oppose proposed labor law reforms that might facilitate the process of union organization. If unions improve the competitive position of firms, why are they not welcomed by managers?

One hypothesis is related to the fact that unions place substantial constraints on the prerogatives and discretion that managers value. Managers may therefore oppose unionization, despite its potentially beneficial productivity effects, to protect their power and discretion. Since it is difficult for shareholders to monitor managerial performance, it may be possible for managers to take actions (such as resisting unions and their beneficial effects) that may be in their best interests but not the interests of the shareholders.

Two ways to resolve this issue are to examine the evidence on both the effects shareholders expect unions to have on the performance of a firm and the actual effects of unions on profitability. With respect to shareholder behavior, there is considerable evidence that new publicly available information on factors influencing the profitability of a corporation is quickly reflected in stock prices. Therefore, announcements of union-organizing drives and victories in representation elections should increase the equity value of the firm (if the effect on profitability is believed to be positive) or decrease the stock price (if the effect is believed to be negative). One study of 253 NLRB representation elections between 1962 and 1980 found that stock prices fell in response to both the announcement that a petition for election had been filed with the NLRB and the certification of a union as bargaining agent.[59]

With respect to the profitability of union and nonunion firms, it is important to distinguish between different product market structures. If the effect of unions is to reduce the profitability of firms in a competitive industry, those firms will earn less than normal profits and an exodus of firms from the industry will continue until the product price increases sufficiently to restore a normal rate of return. In equilibrium, therefore, the profitability of the unionized firms that survive this process and nonunion firms should be the same. In concentrated industries, however, firms may earn excess profits in equilibrium and a union may be able to capture some of these profits. One recent study indicated that unions in fact do reduce profits (consistent with the shareholder expectations discussed above), but in equilibrium the reduction of profits is observed only in concentrated industries.[60] While some of the evidence is still preliminary, it appears that the general impact of unions is to reduce profits and that stockholders are aware of this impact.

UNIONS IN REGULATED INDUSTRIES: CONFLICTING POLICY GOALS

This chapter concludes by returning to a policy issue originally discussed in Chapter 9—namely, whether wage increases negotiated by unions in regulated industries should automatically be passed on to consumers in the form of higher utility prices.[61] Chapter 9 used the human capital framework to derive a standard by which public utility commissions could judge wage levels to be "just and reasonable." In particular, it was suggested that a reasonable standard would be to ask, after controlling statistically for the worker characteristics that are expected to influence earnings, if the unionized employees in the regulated industries are paid more than otherwise comparable workers employed elsewhere. This chapter will try to show how fraught with difficulties such comparisons would be.

Part of any estimated wage premium paid to unionized workers in regulated industries may be justified as a differential to compensate them for having relatively unfavorable working conditions or more difficult jobs than employees in other industries. Wage comparisons may not accurately reflect total compensation comparisons because they ignore fringe benefits. They also may neglect the potential positive effects that the union and a high-wage policy might have. These positive effects include, as noted earlier, reduced employee turnover (and, hence, reduced

---

[59]Interestingly, the fall in the stock price when a petition was filed (before the campaign and election) was larger in cases in which the union ultimately won the election than in cases in which the union lost, a result that the authors interpret as indicating that the market is able to anticipate the outcome of the election. See Richard S. Ruback and Martin B. Zimmerman, "Unionization and Profitability: Evidence from the Capital Market," Sloan School of Management, MIT (October 1982).

[60]Richard B. Freeman, "Unionism, Price-Cost Margins, and the Return to Capital," National Bureau of Economic Research (January 1983).

[61]Our discussion again draws heavily on Ronald G. Ehrenberg, *The Regulatory Process and Labor Earnings* (New York: Academic Press, 1979).

training costs), reduced loss of output since strike activity will be lower, and, in general, increased productivity. To accurately judge whether any union-negotiated wage increase should be passed on to consumers in the form of higher prices, one must evaluate all the above factors, which is no easy task. It has been suggested that it would be better to establish a set of incentives to encourage utilities to keep their costs down than to do "after-the-fact" statistical studies to ascertain if wage increases negotiated by utilities are acceptable.[62]

This policy issue poses a fundamental dilemma. On the one hand, ever since passage of the National Labor Relations Act, the explicit intent of the federal government has been to encourage free collective bargaining. In fact, the NLRA forbids any interference by states in the collective bargaining process that has the effect of influencing the terms of the settlement. On the other hand, state utility commissions have the explicit goal of holding down consumers' utility costs.

A commission decision to disallow part of any collectively bargained wage settlement from being passed on to consumers would not violate the NLRA since it would not affect the terms of the settlement.[63] However, it would undoubtedly affect management willingness to grant the union large wage increases in the future; if the commission refuses to grant price increases to cover cost increases, the firms' profits must fall. In other words, the commission intervention would affect the environment in which bargaining takes place and the relative bargaining power of the union. Thus, implicitly, the commission action would affect future wage settlements.

We should also note, however, that commissions that allow all labor cost increases to be passed on to consumers will also affect the environment in which bargaining takes place—by increasing the relative bargaining power of unions. This outcome, which corresponds closely to the status quo in most states, is not necessarily more desirable. In any case, it should be clear that it is difficult for government to remain neutral; its mere presence, whether or not it takes any action, affects labor markets.

REVIEW QUESTIONS

1. Suppose that a proposal for tax reductions associated with the purchase of capital equipment is up for debate. Suppose, too, that union leaders are called upon to comment on the proposal from the perspective of how it will affect the welfare of their members as workers (not consumers). Will they all agree on the effects of the proposal? Explain your answer.

2. The head of a large national union is trying to decide where he should concentrate his efforts at organizing a union. He perceives three options: Firm A, Firm B, or Firm C. The three firms are identical except that:

---

[62]Ehrenberg, *The Regulatory Process*, Chapter 4. See Chapter 16 for further discussion of such incentive schemes.

[63]Ehrenberg, *The Regulatory Process*, pp.118–22.

a. Firm A faces a perfectly elastic (horizontal) supply curve of labor and a rather inelastic demand curve for its output.

b. Firm B behaves as a monopsonist (faces an upward-sloping supply curve of labor) and faces a perfectly elastic (horizontal) demand curve for its output.

c. Firm C faces a perfectly elastic supply curve of labor and a perfectly elastic demand curve for its output.

This union head would like to know where a new union will pay off in large wage gains and small reductions in numbers of workers. Rank the three options from best to worst, giving reasons for your ranking.

3. Is the following statement true, false, or uncertain? "The host of empirical studies that indicate that unions raise the wages of their members by 10 to 15 percent relative to the wages of comparable nonunion workers imply that unions have a negative effect on national output." Explain your answer.

4. Unionized plumbers are in unions that control the size of their membership. Wages are kept high by keeping membership highly qualified and therefore small. Employers needing or wanting to employ union labor must hire from the ranks of union membership. Suppose there is a plumbers' union in each of two cities. City A has a ordinance that states that all plumbing installations and repairs must be performed by union members. City B has no such ordinance. Analyze as completely as you can the effects of City A's ordinance on workers, consumers, and the general well-being of society. (*Hint:* you can gain insight into this question by comparing Cities A and B.)

5. The Jones Act mandates that at least 50 percent of all U.S. government-financed cargo must be transported in U.S.-owned ships and that any U.S. ship leaving a U.S. port must have at least 90 percent of its crew composed of U.S. citizens. What would you expect the impact of this act to be on the demand for labor in the shipping industry and the ability of unions to push up the wages of their members?

SELECTED READINGS

Ashenfelter, Orley, and Johnson, George. "Bargaining Theory, Trade Unions, and Industrial Strike Activity." *American Economic Review* 59(March 1969):35–49.

Ashenfelter, Orley, and Pencavel, John. "American Trade Union Growth, 1900–1960." *Quarterly Journal of Economics* 83(August 1969):434–48.

Atherton, Wallace. *Theory of Union Bargaining Goals*. Princeton, N.J.: Princeton University Press, 1973.

Brown, Charles, and Medoff, James. "Trade Unions in the Production Process." *Journal of Political Economy* 86(June 1978):355–79.

Freeman, Richard B., and Medoff, James L. "The Two Faces of Unionism." *Public Interest* 57(Fall 1979):69–93.

Freeman, Richard B., and Medoff, James L. "The Impact of Collective Bargaining: Can the New Facts Be Explained by Monopoly Unionism?" *Research in Labor Economics* Supplement 2(1983):293–332.

Lewis, H. G. *Unionism and Relative Wages in the United States: An Empirical Inquiry*. Chicago: University of Chicago Press, 1963.

Lewis, H. G. *Union Relative Wage Effects: A Survey*. Chicago: University of Chicago Press, 1985.

Parsley, C. J. "Labor Unions and Wages: A Survey." *Journal of Economic Literature* 18(March 1980):1–31.

APPENDIX 12A

"Monopoly Unions" or "Efficient Contracts"?

In our discussion of how unions achieve their objectives, we assumed that unions value their members' compensation and employment levels and that their ability to achieve their objectives is constrained by the labor demand curve. It is straightforward to formalize the notion of a union's maximizing a utility function subject to the constraint of a labor demand curve, just as one can formalize the idea of a consumer's maximizing a utility function subject to a budget constraint. However, as we shall see, the solution to such a maximization process is not an *efficient contract* in the sense that it is not *pareto optimal*. That is, there are alternative wage-employment combinations that will leave *both* the employer and the union better off.[1]

Figure 12A.1 shows the demand curve D for union members as a function of their wage; for simplicity we ignore all other pecuniary (fringes) and nonpecuniary (working conditions) characteristics of employment. We assume that the union values both the wages and employment of its members and that it can aggregate its members' preferences so we can meaningfully speak of a union utility function that depends on these two variables. This utility function is summarized in Figure 12A.1 by the family of indifference curves U_0, U_1, U_2, U_3. Each curve represents a locus of employment-wage combinations about which the union is indifferent. The indifference curves are negatively sloped because to maintain a given utility level the union must be compensated for a decline in one variable (employment or wages) by an increase in the other. They exhibit the property of diminishing marginal rates of substitution (they are convex to the origin) because it is assumed that the rate at which the union is willing to trade off wages for employment along an indifference curve declines as employment of its members increases. Finally, higher indifference curves represent higher levels of union utility.

Suppose that, in the absence of a union, market forces would cause the wage to be W_0 and employment to be E_0 (point a in Figure 12A.1). How does collective bargaining affect this solution? One possibility is that the union and employer will agree on a higher wage rate and then, given the wage rate, the employer will

---

[1] This point was noted many years ago by Wassily Leontief, "The Pure Theory of the Guaranteed Annual Wage Contract," *Journal of Political Economy* 54(February 1946):76–79, and stressed recently by Ian McDonald and Robert Solow, "Wage Bargaining and Employment," *American Economic Review* 71(December 1981):896–908.

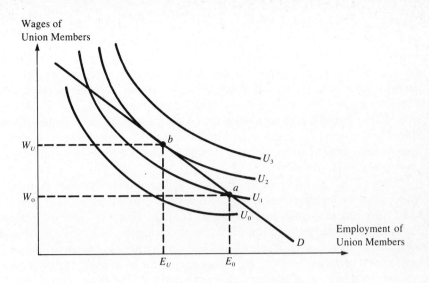

Wages of
Union Members

Employment of
Union Members

**FIGURE 12A.1   Union Maximizes Utility Subject to
the Constraint of the Demand for Labor Curve**

determine the number of union members to employ. Given a bargained wage rate, the employer will maximize profits and determine employment from the demand curve. Since the union presumably knows this, its goal is to maximize its utility function subject to the constraint that its wage-employment combination will lie on the demand curve.

In terms of Figure 12A.1, the union will seek to move to point *b,* where indifference curve U_2 is just tangent to the labor demand curve. At this point wages would be W_U and employment E_U. Given the constraint of the labor demand curve, point *b* represents the highest level of utility the union can attain.

This model, in which the union sets the wage subject to the knowledge that the employer will then determine employment from the demand curve, is often referred to as the *monopoly union* model. Since unions negotiate over wages in many collective bargaining negotiations, but not explicitly over employment levels, some economists feel it may be a useful analytic tool. What bothers other economists, however, is that point *b* is *not* an *efficient contract* in the sense that it is not *pareto optimal.* That is, there are a whole set of wage-employment combinations that at least one of the two parties to the contract would prefer and that also leave neither party worse off than it is at point *b.*

To see this, we must recall from Chapter 3 that the labor demand curve is defined by the employer's choosing the employment level to maximize profits at each wage rate. Now starting at a point like point *a* on the demand curve with the wage set at W_0, if the employer were to expand or contract employment, profits would fall. To keep profits from falling would require a lower wage rate. Expanding or contracting employment further would require a still lower wage rate to keep profits at the same level.

One can formalize this by reintroducing the concept of *isoprofit curves* that was first discussed in Chapter 8. Here an isoprofit curve is a locus of wage-employment combinations along which an employer's profits are unchanged. Figure 12A.2 shows three isoprofit curves for the employer whose labor demand curve is D. As discussed above, each curve reaches a maximum at its intersection with the demand curve; as we move along a given isoprofit curve in either direction away from the demand curve, wages must fall to keep profits constant. A higher isoprofit curve represents a lower level of employer profits because the wage associated with each level of employment is greater along the higher curve. So, for example, the employer would prefer any point on I_0, which includes the original wage-employment combination (point a), to any point on I_2, which includes the monopoly union wage-employment solution (point b).

Figure 12A.3 superimposes the family of employer isoprofit curves from Figure 12A.2 onto the family of union indifference curves from Figure 12A.1 and illustrates why the monopoly union solution, point b, is not an *efficient contract*. Suppose, rather than locating at point b, the parties negotiated a contract that called for them to locate at point d, where the wage rate, W_d, would be lower but employment of union members, E_d, higher. At point d the union would be better off since it would now be on a higher indifference curve, U_3, while the employer would be no worse off, since he still would be on isoprofit curve I_2.

Similarly, suppose rather than negotiating a contract to wind up at b, the parties agreed to a contract that called for them to locate at point e, with a wage rate of W_e and an employment level of E_e. Compared to the monopoly union solution (point b) the union is equally well off, since it remains on indifference curve U_2, but now the employer is better off because he has been able to reach isoprofit curve I_1. Because I_1 lies below I_2, it represents a higher level of profits.

In fact, there is a whole set of contracts that both parties will find at least as

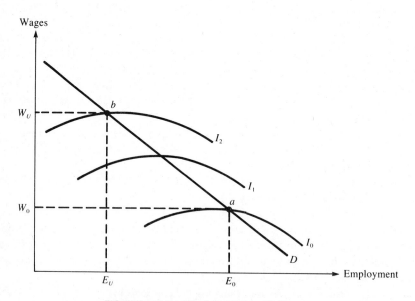

FIGURE 12A.2   Employer Isoprofit Curves

FIGURE 12A.3   The Contract Curve—The Locus of "Efficient Contracts"

good as point *b;* these are represented by the shaded area in Figure 12A.3. Among this set, the ones that are *pareto optimal* (or efficient contracts)—contracts in which no party can be made better off without hurting the other—are the ones in which employer isoprofit curves are just tangent to union indifference curves, such as points *d* and *e*. Indeed, there is a whole locus of such points and they are represented in the figure by the positively sloped curve *ed*. Each point on this curve represents a tangency of a union indifference curve and an employer isoprofit curve, a point where the rates at which the employer and the union are willing to substitute wages for employment at the margin are equal.

All of the points on *ed*, which is often called the *contract curve* (or locus of efficient contracts) will leave both parties at least as well off as at point *b*, and at least one party better off. However, the parties are not indifferent to where along *ed* the settlement is reached. As one moves from point *e* to point *d*, wages and employment both rise, increasing union members' utility but decreasing the employer's profits. Obviously the union would prefer to be close to *d* and the employer close to *e*. Where on the contract curve a settlement actually occurs in this model depends upon the bargaining power of the parties.[2]

How realistic is the *efficient-contract* model as a description of the wage-determination process in unionized work places in the United States? The efficient contract model requires that unions bargain over *both* wages and employment levels. Now some labor contracts in the United States do explicitly cover employ-

---

[2]For an attempt to model how bargaining power affects the nature of contract settlements, see Jan Svejnar, "Bargaining Power, Fear of Disagreements, and Wage Settlements: Theory and Empirical Evidence from U.S. Industry," *American Economic Review* (forthcoming).

ment levels as well as wages. For example, many contracts that cover public school teachers specify maximum class size or minimum teacher/student ratios. However, the vast majority of union contracts in the private sector contain no explicit provisions guaranteeing employment levels.[3]

To say that no *explicit* employment level guarantees exist is not to say, however, that *implicit* agreements are not present. In a world of uncertain future labor demand, it may be very difficult to specify in a written contract exactly how employment will be contingent during the contract period on future labor demand.[4] Instead, it is likely that the negotiations over wages will contain some implicit understandings between the employer and the unions about how both parties expect employment will be influenced by the wage settlement. Hence, even in the absence of explicit contract guarantees with respect to employment, it is conceivable that the process of collective bargaining does lead to efficient contracts.

If one cannot use data on the existence of explicit employment guarantees in labor contracts to evaluate whether the efficient contract model is correct, how can one decide whether the efficient contract or monopoly union model is a better representation of the unionized wage-determination process? The answer is that the two models sometimes yield different implications about how the equilibrium wage will vary in response to changes in variables that affect either the demand curve for labor or union preferences. Indeed, two recent papers that studied wage outcomes for unionized printers in the newspaper industry provided evidence in favor of the efficient contracts model there.[5] One should stress, though, that this result is only for a single industry. The "correct" model for other industries may differ.

---

[3]In 1980, only 11 percent of major private-sector collective bargaining agreements had such guarantees. See U.S. Bureau of Labor Statistics, *Characteristics of Major Collective Bargaining Agreements, January 1, 1980,* Bulletin 2095 (Washington, D.C.: U.S. Government Printing Office, May 1981).

[4]The demand for teachers throughout any one school year is quite predictable once fall enrollment figures are known, which may explain the frequency of employment guarantees (in the form of class size provisions) in teachers' contracts.

[5]Orley Ashenfelter and James Brown, "Testing the Efficiency of Employment Contracts" (mimeo, Princeton University, 1983); Thomas McCurdy and John Pencavel, "Testing Between Competing Models of Wage and Employment Determination" (mimeo, Stanford University, 1983).

13

Public Sector Labor Markets

W_{hy} does the study of public sector labor markets in the United States warrant a separate chapter in this text? One reason is that federal, state, and local governments differ from most private sector employers in that profit maximization is unlikely to be an objective of governmental units.[1] As such, labor market models based upon the assumption of profit maximization are clearly inappropriate for the government sector; alternative models must be developed. As this chapter will show, it is *not* necessary to assume profit maximization in order to deduce that the demand for public employees is a downward-sloping function of their wage rate.

A second reason is that employment expanded more rapidly between 1951 and 1975 in the state and local government (SLG) sector than in any other sector of the economy. While civilian employment by the federal government (when expressed as a percentage of total nonagricultural employment) actually declined slightly during the period, SLG employment rose from 8.5 percent to 15.5 percent of total nonagricultural payroll employment (see Table 13.1). Indeed, the absolute number of state and local government employees almost tripled during this period, rising from 4.1 to 11.9 million. Although the share of SLG employment in total employment has declined slightly since 1975, the absolute number rose to over 13 million in the early 1980s. The importance of the sector suggests that attention should be directed to analyses of it.

A third reason is that the pattern of unionization and the laws governing collective bargaining, dispute resolution, and wage determination differ between the public and private sectors. In contrast to the decline in the fraction of private sector workers who are union members, which was discussed in Chapter 12, union membership is growing rapidly in the public sector in both absolute and percentage terms. For example, between 1964 and 1978 the proportion of federal employees

---

[1]For an interesting analysis of the private not-for-profit or voluntary sector, see Burton Weisbrod, *The Voluntary Nonprofit Sector: An Economic Analysis* (Lexington, Mass.: Lexington Books, 1977).

TABLE 13.1 Government Employment in the United States: 1951–83

Year	Total Nonagricultural Payroll Employment (in thousands)	Federal Civilian Employment (in thousands)	State and Local Government Employment (SLG) (in thousands)	Federal Government as Percentage of Total	SLG as Percentage of Total
1951	47,819	2,302	4,087	4.8	8.5
1953	50,202	2,305	4,340	4.6	8.6
1955	50,641	2,187	4,727	4.3	9.3
1957	52,853	2,217	5,399	4.2	10.2
1959	53,268	2,233	5,850	4.2	11.0
1961	53,999	2,279	6,315	4.2	11.7
1963	56,653	2,358	6,868	4.2	12.1
1965	60,765	2,378	7,696	3.9	12.7
1967	65,803	2,719	8,672	4.1	13.2
1969	70,384	2,758	9,437	3.9	13.4
1971	71,214	2,696	10,185	3.8	14.3
1973	76,790	2,663	11,068	3.5	14.4
1975	76,945	2,748	11,937	3.6	15.5
1977	82,471	2,721	12,399	3.3	15.0
1979	89,823	2,773	13,174	3.1	14.7
1981	91,156	2,772	13,259	3.0	14.5
1983	89,986	2,753	12,994	3.1	14.4

SOURCE: *1982 Employment and Training Report of the President* (Washington, D.C.: U.S. Government Printing Office, 1982), Table C-1, and *1984 Economic Report of the President* (Washington, D.C.: U.S. Government Printing Office, 1984), Table B-37.

who belonged to unions increased from 38.2 percent to 50.2 percent.[2] Similarly, the proportion of SLG employees belonging to unions rose from 7.7 percent to 17.4 percent during the same period (see Table 13.2). If one includes membership in bargaining organizations, which include professional organizations such as the National Education Association (NEA) that over time have behaved more and more like unions, an even more rapid increase is observed, with the percentage of SLG employees rising to 36.2 percent in 1978.

One factor that affected this growth in public sector unionization was a change in public attitudes and legislation governing bargaining in the public sector. Unlike the private sector, where the rights of workers to organize and bargain collectively have been guaranteed since the National Labor Relations Act, laws governing bargaining in the public sector are of much more recent vintage. Executive Order 10988 issued by President John F. Kennedy in 1962 legitimized collective bargaining in the federal sector for the first time, providing federal workers with the rights to join unions and bargain over working conditions, but not wages. While this executive order has been modified several times, most federal employees' wages are

[2]John F. Burton, Jr., "The Extent of Collective Bargaining in the Public Sector," in *Public Sector Bargaining,* ed. Benjamin Aaron et al. (Washington, D.C.: Bureau of National Affairs, 1979), pp.1–43, Table 3. Changes in the way the data were reported after 1978 make later years' data noncomparable so we have ceased our comparisons as of that date.

TABLE 13.2 State and Local Government Employees Belonging to Unions or Bargaining Organizations or Covered by Union Contracts

| Year | SLG Employees Belonging to Unions | | SLG Employees Belonging to Bargaining Organizations | | Percentage of SLG Employees Covered by a Formal Contract |
	Number (in thousands)	Percent	Number (in thousands)	Percent	
1964	556	7.7			
1966	664	7.8			
1968	804	8.8	2,466	27.1	
1970	947	9.6	2,668	27.1	
1972	1,105	10.4	3,137	29.4	
1974	1,529	13.4	3,911	34.1	
1976	1,710	14.0	4,521	37.0	27.7
1978	2,243	17.4	4,674	36.2	
1980	n.a.	n.a.	3,956		

SOURCE: John F. Burton, Jr., "The Extent of Collective Bargaining in the Public Sector," in *Public Sector Bargaining*, ed. Benjamin Aaron et al. (Washington, D.C.: Bureau of National Affairs, 1979), pp. 1–43, Tables 2 and 4; and U.S. Bureau of Labor Statistics, *1979 Directory of National Union and Employee Associations* (Washington, D.C.: U.S. Government Printing Office, 1980).

still not determined by the collective bargaining process.[3] Instead, they are determined via comparability legislation, first passed in 1962, which ties the wages of most federal civilian workers to the results of government surveys of wages of "comparable" private workers, subject to possible Presidential or congressional modification.[4] The influence of federal unions on wages operates, then, primarily through the political pressure they can exert on the President and Congress to approve wage increases that the surveys suggest are warranted.

Favorable state legislation for SLG employee collective bargaining began with a 1959 law in Wisconsin; prior to that date collective bargaining was effectively prohibited in the state and local sector. By the late 1970s most industrial states had adopted statutes that permitted SLG employees to participate in determining their wages and conditions of employment, although not all employees in each state were covered by the laws.[5] While these statutes were being adopted, and at the same time

---

[3]There were some major exceptions—namely, postal workers and employees of federal government authorities, such as the Tennessee Valley Authority (TVA). In each of these cases the prices of the products or services produced (mail delivery, hydroelectric power) can be raised to cover the cost of the contract settlement, unlike other federal agencies, where salaries are paid out of general revenues.

[4]See Sharon Smith, *Equal Pay in the Public Sector: Fact or Fantasy* (Princeton, N.J.: Princeton University, 1977), for a more complete description of the comparability process in the federal sector. Federal blue-collar workers' wages are also determined, in the main, by the comparability process, with comparisons in this case being made at the local labor market level.

[5]See B. V. H. Schneider, "Public-Sector Labor Legislation: An Evolutionary Analysis," in *Public Sector Collective Bargaining*, ed. Benjamin Aaron et al. (Washington, D.C.: Bureau of National Affairs, 1979), pp. 191–223, for a more complete discussion of the evolution of legislation governing bargaining in the public sector.

TABLE 13.3   **Private- and Government-Employee
Earnings Comparisons**

Year	(1)	(2)	(3)	(4)	(5)
1954	$1.65	$1.78	$ 306	1.03	1.11
1956	1.80	1.95	334	1.03	1.11
1958	1.95	2.11	365	1.04	1.12
1960	2.09	2.26	398	1.06	1.14
1962	2.22	2.39	440	1.10	1.19
1964	2.36	2.53	470	1.11	1.19
1966	2.56	2.72	515	1.14	1.21
1968	2.85	3.01	603	1.20	1.27
1970	3.23	3.35	693	1.24	1.28
1972	3.70	3.82	764	1.20	1.24
1974	4.24	4.42	894	1.21	1.27
1976	4.86	5.22	1,016	1.17	1.25
1978	5.69	6.17	1,132	1.10	1.19
1980	6.66	7.27	1,337	1.20	1.10

(1) Average hourly earnings of private nonagricultural non-supervisory workers during the year (in dollars).

(2) Average hourly earnings of manufacturing production workers during the year (in dollars).

(3) Average monthly earnings of full-time state and local government (SLG) employees in October of the year (in dollars).

(4) Average annual earnings of SLG workers divided by average annual earnings of private nonagricultural, non-supervisory workers.

(5) Average annual earnings of SLG workers divided by average annual earnings of manufacturing workers.

SOURCE: Based on U.S. Department of Labor, *Employment and Earnings* (various issues), and U.S. Bureau of Census, *Public Employment in (Year)* (various issues).

that employment and unionization were growing in the SLG sector, SLG employees' earnings also started to rise relative to the earnings of private sector employees (see Table 13.3). From the mid-1950s to 1970, SLG employees' average earnings improved relative to those of private employees by 15–20 percent.[6] (However, during the 1970s the trend was reversed, and SLG employees' earnings fell relative to those of their private sector counterparts.)[7]

---

[6]Note that 1.24 divided by 1.03 equals 1.20—column (4), and 1.28 divided by 1.11 equals 1.15—column (5), which imply 20 percent and 15 percent increases, respectively.

[7]The comparisons in Table 13.3 are subject to a number of qualifications. They focus only on wages and ignore fringe benefits and differences in working conditions. Furthermore, they do not control for differences in skill level or occupational mixes between the public and private sectors. When the average earnings of workers in the two sectors are compared, we find that in 1954 the average annual earnings of SLG employees exceeded that of manufacturing production workers by 11 percent (column (5)). This percentage tells us nothing about how the earnings of a worker with a given skill level would compare in the two sectors. Average earnings in the SLG sector might exceed those in the private sector, even if the wage rate paid in each occupation were the same in both sectors, simply because the public sector tends to employ relatively more high-skilled workers. Similarly, when one observes changes in the ratios in columns (4) and (5), one should be aware that they may reflect changes in the relative occupational mixes across the two sectors, as well as changes in the relative compensation levels.

The growth in the relative earnings position of SLG employees during the 1960s, coupled with the growing strength of public employee unions, their increased militancy, and the trend towards allowing SLG employees to bargain over wage issues, led to fears that inflationary wage settlements would continue in the sector and aggravate the financial problems faced by state and local governments. These fears were explicitly based upon the belief that many public services are essential, and this implied that the wage elasticity of demand for public employees was very inelastic. To many, the logical conclusion was that, in the absence of market constraints that would limit the wage demands of public employees, limitations should be placed on the collective bargaining rights of these groups.[8]

Although by 1981 eight states did grant the right to strike in one form or another to selected public employee groups, most continued historic prohibitions against strikes.[9] The states that prohibited strikes, however, often provided assistance to local governments and unions in settling contract disputes, with a number of states adopting forms of binding arbitration as the terminal stage in their impasse procedures. How these alternative institutional arrangements operate and affect economic outcomes is, of course, worthy of discussion.[10]

A final reason why public sector labor markets warrant separate treatment is that they represent an area toward which much of our public policy has recently been directed. To take one example, during the 1970s and early 1980s attempts were made to reduce unemployment by means of public service employment (PSE) programs. Starting with the Emergency Employment Act of 1971 and continuing under the Comprehensive Employment and Training Act (CETA), the federal government provided funds to state and local governments to increase their employment levels, in the hope that the availability of extra public sector jobs would provide job opportunities for the unemployed. By 1978, 569,000 individuals were reported employed on PSE program funds; these employees comprised some 3.3 percent of total SLG employment. While this program was terminated by the Reagan Administration in 1982, it is important to know what its effects were.

To take another example, growing concern over the fiscal condition of state and local governments and the increased state and local tax burden borne by taxpayers

---

[8]See, for example, H. Wellington and R. Winter, "The Limits of Collective Bargaining in Public Employment," *Yale Law Journal* 69(June 1969):1107–27.

[9]For more details on dispute resolution in the public sector, see Thomas Kochan, "Dynamics of Dispute Resolution in the Public Sector," in *Public Sector Bargaining,* ed. B. Aaron et al. (Washington, D.C.: Bureau of National Affairs, 1979), pp. 150–90.

[10]Some definition of terminology may be useful. An *impasse* is a situation in which the parties cannot agree on the terms of a collective bargaining agreement. State public employment relations agencies provide three types of assistance to the parties. *Mediators* are individuals who attempt to assist the parties to negotiate with each other by serving as intermediaries when personal conflicts prevent negotiations from occurring or by making suggestions that both parties may find acceptable. *Factfinders,* after hearing both parties' positions, issue oral or written statements to the parties about the types of settlements they believe are justified by the evidence (facts). Such positions taken by impartial third parties often influence the positions taken by the parties in the negotiations. Finally, *arbitrators* issue formal rulings about what they believe the settlement should be; in many cases state laws or prior agreement by the parties dictate that if the negotiations go to arbitration, the arbitrator's decision will be binding.

led to the passage of expenditure- and tax-limitation legislation in a number of states in the late 1970s. The most notable was Proposition 13 in California, which drastically reduced local property taxes and limited the ability of all governmental units in the state to increase their revenues.

For all these reasons, the objective of this chapter is to present a simple analytical framework that can be used to discuss public sector labor markets and to then use the framework to analyze the following:

1. Why SLG employment grew so rapidly between 1950 and 1975, but fell in relative terms since then.
2. Why the relative earnings of SLG employees followed a similar pattern.
3. Why the growth of unionization has been so rapid in the SLG sector.
4. What the effects of unions have been on wage and nonwage outcomes in the SLG sector.
5. What the effects of comparability legislation have been on federal employees' wages.
6. Whether the form of impasse procedure used affects the size of wage settlements in the SLG sector and what determines whether the procedure is used by the parties.
7. What the likely effects of expenditure- and tax-limitation legislation on public sector labor markets will be.
8. What the net job-creation effects of public employment programs have been.

A MODEL OF A PUBLIC SECTOR LABOR MARKET

What are the forces that affect the level of employment and wages in a given governmental unit? Turning first to the demand side of the market, we have already indicated that profit maximization is an untenable assumption to make when analyzing the public sector. Suppose instead that there is a single decision-maker (or group of decision-makers) who makes decisions on the level and cost of governmental services in accordance with the wishes of voters who elect him or her to office.[11] Presumably voters are concerned with both the level of public services they receive and the resources left to them, after paying for these services through taxes or user charges, that can be used to consume private goods and services. Assume also, for

---

[11]There is extensive literature in economics on how decisions are made in the public sector. Under certain conditions in an open democratic political system, the preferences of the median voter on an issue will become the preferences of the decision-makers. See Anthony Downs, *An Economic Theory of Democracy* (New York: Harper & Row, 1957), and Gordon Tullock, *Towards a Mathematics of Politics* (Ann Arbor, Mich.: University of Michigan Press, 1967). However, not all economists believe that public sector decision making can be modeled in such a way. See, for example, Melvin Reder, "The Theory of Employment and Wages in the Public Sector" in *Labor in the Public and Private Nonprofit Sectors*, ed. Daniel Hamermesh (Princeton, N.J.: Princeton University Press, 1975), pp. 1–48.

simplicity, that the level of public services is proportional to the number of public employees who are hired.[12]

Decisions made by the representative public decision-maker in an effort to maximize a utility function form the basis for the demand for public employees. The decision-maker weighs the level of public services provided against the burden financing this level places on taxpayers, subject to a budget constraint that takes into account the prices of both public and private goods and services and the total resources available to the community. Without going through the details of such a maximization problem, it should be obvious that an increase in the cost of public services should reduce the quantity of services demanded (other things equal), just as an increase in the price of a consumer good leads a consumer to reduce his or her purchase of that good. Hence, an increase in the wage rate of public employees should lead governmental employers to demand fewer of them. Put another way, other things equal, the demand for public employees *is* a downward-sloping function of their wage rate despite its departure from an assumption of profit maximization.

Figure 13.1 shows a representative public sector labor demand curve (D_0). This

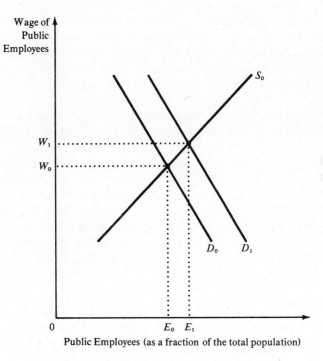

**FIGURE 13.1   The Public Sector Labor Market
and the Growth of Public Employment**

---

[12]Such an assumption, which ignores the possibility of substituting capital for labor in producing public services, is made only for expository purposes and does not affect our final conclusion.

curve has been drawn in *per capita* terms (public employees as a percentage of the population) in recognition of the fact that the flow of public services that an individual citizen receives from a given number of public employees depends upon the number of other individuals in the community that he or she has to "share" these public services with. [13] The position of the demand curve depends on a number of factors. Increases in the total resources available in the community, as measured perhaps by per capita family income or per capita grants from higher levels of governments, will shift the demand for public employees to the right. Similarly, factors that increase the community's tastes for public services, such as a rise in the school-age population, will also shift the demand curve to the right.

Turning to the supply side, one can treat the supply of individuals to public sector jobs in the same framework used in Chapters 2 and 8 to analyze labor supply to other occupations or industries. Other things equal, the higher the wage paid to public employees, the greater the fraction of the population that would be willing to work for the local government, as indicated by the upward-sloping labor supply curve (S_0) in Figure 13.1. The position of this curve is presumably determined by individuals' tastes for jobs in the public sector, by the wages and nonwage conditions of employment that are offered by other governmental and private employers, and by the nonwage conditions of employment offered by the particular governmental units. One important condition of employment, to which we shall return later, is job security. If the probability of being laid off in the future were to increase, for example, one would expect fewer people to be willing to work for the governmental employer, in which case the labor supply curve would shift to the left. [14]

Given the demand curve, D_0, and the supply curve, S_0, E_0 public employees per capita are hired and are paid a wage of W_0. At any wage less than W_0, the demand for public employees would exceed the supply, governmental units would have unfilled positions (job vacancies), and pressure would be exerted to raise the wage to attract more applicants. At any level of wages above W_0, there would be an excess supply of applicants and astute public employers would realize that they could attract the desired work force at a lower real wage. Since funds used to hire public employees have alternative uses in the public and private sectors, this excess supply would create downward pressure on the real wage. Hence, the wage/employment combination (W_0, E_0) would be an equilibrium one. [15]

---

[13] In the case of some government goods or services, however, one citizen's consumption does not reduce the amount available to others. National defense is an example of such a *pure public good*.

[14] See Orley Ashenfelter, "Demand and Supply Functions for State and Local Government Employment," in *Essays in Labor Market Analysis,* ed. Orley Ashenfelter and Wallace Oates (New York: Halstead Press, 1979), pp. 1–16.

[15] As noted in Chapter 3, there is some evidence that, *outside* of metropolitan areas, a monopsony model of public sector labor markets may be the relevant one to use. In general, however, the simple demand-and-supply model presented in the text is sufficient for our purposes. In major metropolitan areas in which scores of different local governments may employ workers in the same occupation (such as teachers), it is clear that the monopsony model is not relevant. Later the chapter does consider the possibility that the existence of excess supplies of applicants will not put downward pressure on public sector wages.

Suppose the demand curve for public employees were to shift out to D_1 in Figure 13.1. As indicated there, *both* public employees' wages and their per capita employment levels would increase. Between 1950 and 1970 median family income, measured in 1974 dollars, increased substantially in real terms from $6,800 to $12,531, as did per capita federal grants to state and local governments (from $33 to $137). Both of these factors should have increased the demand for SLG employees. Similarly, the proportion of the population that was of elementary-school age through college age (5 through 21) increased from 26.1 to 32.9 percent during the period, which should have increased the demand for SLG educational employees.[16] Together, these three forces were undoubtedly largely responsible for most of the growth in employment and relative wages of SLG employees that occurred during the period (see Tables 13.1 and 13.3). However, between the mid-1970s and the early 1980s the school-age population declined as a proportion of the population and real family incomes did not increase substantially. In retrospect, then, it is not surprising that the relative employment level and wages of SLG employees both declined during the latter period.

THE GROWTH AND EFFECTS OF PUBLIC SECTOR UNIONS

The simple demand-and-supply model of union membership presented in Chapter 12 (see Figure 12.1) can be used retrospectively to provide some insight into why unionization in the public sector has grown so rapidly since the 1960s. On the one hand, changing public attitudes and the evolution of labor legislation relating to collective bargaining in the public sector, which were described earlier in the chapter, reduced the costs of organizing public employees (shifting the supply of union services to the right) and probably increased the benefits public employees perceived from union membership (shifting the demand for union membership to the right). Both forces would lead to an increase in union strength. On the other hand, the decline in the relative earnings position of SLG employees that occurred in the mid-1970s, along with the slowdown in the rate of growth of employment and the imposition of expenditure- and tax-limitation legislation in several states, may have strengthened the desires of public employees to turn to unions in the hopes of regaining their former relative earnings positions and winning job security clauses in their contracts. Because these forces all increased the net benefits public employees perceived from union membership, they shifted the demand for unions further to the right.

This analysis naturally leads one to wonder what the effects of unions have been on wages and nonwage contract outcomes in the SLG sector. As in the private sector, a key determinant of public sector unions' ability to raise their members' wages is the wage elasticity of demand for SLG employees. If a public sector union succeeds in raising wages above the market-clearing level (W_0) to W_u in Figure

---

[16]These data come from the U.S. Bureau of the Census, *Statistical Abstract of the United States, 1975* (Washington, D.C.: U.S. Government Printing Office, 1975).

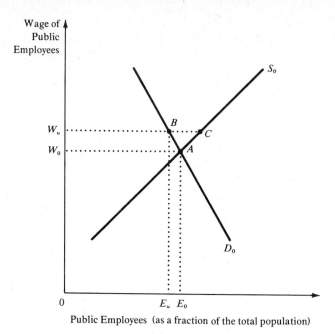

FIGURE 13.2   **The Effects of Unions in the Public Sector: Excess Applicants**

13.2, the result will be a loss of jobs of $E_0 - E_u$; the magnitude of this loss will depend upon the wage elasticity of demand. The larger this loss, the less likely it is that those unions which value both the wages and employment levels of their members will push for large wage gains. Of course, if the demand for labor were shifting out rapidly in the SLG sector, as it was through the mid-1970s, fear of job loss would be less likely to constrain the wage demands of SLG employees' unions.

Wage Elasticity of Demand

As noted earlier, the conventional wisdom has been that, because many forms of public services are both essential and monopolized, the demand for public employees was wage inelastic. This supposed wage inelasticity of demand implies that market forces would not constrain public employees' wage demands. However, one can easily think of possibilities for substituting capital for labor in the provision of public services (for example, police patrol cars could be substituted for officers on the beat or snowblowers could be substituted for snow-removal workers with shovels). Further, private firms can provide the same services as now provided publicly (for example, garbage pick-up could be subcontracted to private employers or private companies could be hired to handle janitorial services in public buildings). Moreover, given the limited resources that state and local governments can command, an increase in the relative price of one service should lead a government to substitute other services that would become relatively cheaper (for example, minimally supervised playground programs could be substituted for summertime instructional programs in sports or crafts). In other words, while a local government does not have the option of moving its plant to a nonunion area (that is, fleeing to the Sunbelt), it can substitute capital for labor, change its services, or subcontract with private firms if it feels its labor costs are too high. Hence, it is *not* obvious *a priori* that the wage elasticities of demand for all categories of state and local government employees are inelastic.

Four studies have presented estimates of the wage elasticities of demand for 11 functional categories of state and local government employees, and these studies are summarized in Table 13.4.[17] In the main, these estimates suggest that demand curves for labor in the SLG sector *are* inelastic. However, the estimated elasticities do not appear substantially lower in absolute value than the private sector wage elasticities of demand that were summarized in Table 4.1. Regardless of these estimates, one should remember that public employees are also voters and, through the political process, seek to increase (shift) the demand for their own services.[18] To

**TABLE 13.4   Estimates of Wage Elasticities of Demand
for Labor in the State and Local Sector**

Category	(1)	(2)	(3)	(4)
Education	−1.06	−0.08 to −0.57	−0.57 to −0.82	−.89
Noneducation	−0.38			
Streets and highways	−0.09	−0.44 to −0.64		
Public welfare	−0.32	−0.33 to −1.13		
Hospitals	−0.30	−0.30 to −0.51		
Public health	−0.12	−0.26 to −0.32		
Police	−0.29	−0.01 to −0.35		
Fire	−0.53	−0.23 to −0.31		
Sanitation and sewage	−0.23	−0.40 to −0.56		
Natural resources	−0.39	−0.39 to −0.60		
General control and financial administration	−0.28	−0.09 to −0.34		

SOURCES:

(1) Orley Ashenfelter and Ronald Ehrenberg, "The Demand for Labor in the Public Sector," in *Labor in the Public and Nonprofit Sectors*, ed. Daniel Hamermesh (Princeton, N.J.: Princeton University Press, 1975), Table 6.

(2) Ronald G. Ehrenberg, "The Demand for State and Local Government Employees," *American Economic Review* 63(June 1973):366–79.

(3) Robert J. Thornton, "The Elasticity of Demand for Public School Teachers," *Industrial Relations* 18(Winter 1979):86–91.

(4) Hui S. Chang and Yu Hsing, "A Note on the Demand for Faculty in Public Higher Education," *Industrial Relations* 21(Spring 1982):256–60.

---

[17]Orley Ashenfelter and Ronald G. Ehrenberg, "The Demand for Labor in the Public Sector," in *Labor in the Public and Nonprofit Sectors,* ed. Daniel Hamermesh (Princeton, N.J.: Princeton University Press, 1975), pp. 55–74; Ronald G. Ehrenberg, "The Demand for State and Local Government Employees," *American Economic Review* 63(June 1973):366–79; Robert Thornton, "The Elasticity of Demand for Public School Teachers," *Industrial Relations* 18(Winter 1979): 86–91; and Hui Chang and Yu Hsing, "A Note on the Demand for Faculty in Public Higher Education," *Industrial Relations* 21(Spring 1982):256–60.

[18]For a recent treatment of this point, see Paul Courant, Edward Gramlich, and Daniel Rubinfeld, "Public Employee Market Power and the Level of Government Spending," *American Economic Review* 69(December 1979):806–17.

the extent that they are successful, the employment loss that would be associated with any wage increase would be smaller than if the demand curve had not been shifted out.

Union Wage Effects

Numerous studies have attempted to estimate what the effect of SLG employee unions has been on their members' wages relative to the wages of otherwise comparable nonunion public employees. A detailed study using data from 1967 for noneducational municipal employees suggested that average monthly earnings of municipal employees represented by unions or employee associations exceeded those of otherwise comparable nonorganized employees by 2–16 percent.[19] These estimates are no higher, and are perhaps even lower, than the union relative wage effects observed in the private sector. Numerous studies, which use data from later periods and include analyses of educational employees' earnings, confirm this result. That is, unions in the SLG sector appear to have had more moderate effects on the relative wages of their members than unions in the private sector.[20]

As emphasized, however, wages are not identical to total compensation. In addition to those reasons presented in the previous chapter, there are other reasons to believe that the effects of public sector unions on nonwage benefits may well exceed their effects on wages. On the one hand, public employees' wages are much more visible to the public than are their fringe benefits. The public may be more aware of the cost of a $200 increase in annual starting salaries, which is well publicized, than they are of an increase in health insurance costs (due to an increase in premiums or improved coverage) that will also cost $200 per employee. As such, it may be politically easier for governmental negotiators to make concessions on fringe benefit items than on wages.

On the other hand, while the costs of increased wages must be borne in the present, the costs of improved fringe benefits are often not known at the time of settlement or are borne in the future. For example, the true cost of agreeing to pay 100 percent of employees' health insurance costs depends upon future increases in health insurance rates. To take another example, if public employee pension plans

---

[19]Ronald G. Ehrenberg and Gerald S. Goldstein, "A Model of Public Sector Wage Determination," *Journal of Urban Economics* 2(April 1975):223–45. This study also showed that the magnitude of the union relative wage effect for a given category of municipal employees (such as police) depended upon the extent of unionization of other categories of municipal employees (such as firefighters) in the city *and* the extent of organization of municipal employees in neighboring cities. That is, both occupational and geographic wage spillovers appear to occur. In the context of our public sector labor market model, one can explain these results by noting that the supply curve of, say, police to City A will shift to the left as the wages of police in a neighboring city, or the wages of other categories of municipal employees in City A, increase. This shift would, other things equal, increase the wages of police in City A. These occupational and geographic spillovers may result, then, from the impact of other unions on the supply of police in City A.

[20]For a survey of recent studies, see Ronald G. Ehrenberg and Joshua L. Schwarz, "Public Sector Labor Markets," in Orley Ashenfelter and Richard Layard, eds., *Handbook of Labor Economics* (Amsterdam: North Holland, in press).

are not fully funded, the costs of agreeing to more generous retirement provisions today will become evident only in the future, when employees begin to take advantage of these provisions.[21] Since government officials' tenures in office are often short, and since they typically depart from office well before the true costs of such fringe benefits become known, it is in their *short-run* political interests to win favor with public employee unions by agreeing to increased fringes, since the short-run costs of such agreements to taxpayers may well be small.[22]

For both of these reasons then, one might expect that the effects of public sector unions on fringe benefits would be larger than their effects on wages. Although the limited empirical evidence on this point is ambiguous, it does suggest that this has occurred.[23]

Union Effects on Productivity

Although it is often difficult to measure productivity in the public sector, a number of recent studies have sought to estimate what the effects of public sector collective bargaining have been on productivity. One study that focused on municipal public libraries found no union/nonunion productivity differentials for a variety of measures of library output.[24] Another study found that teachers' unions appeared to be associated with higher test scores for average students but lower test scores for below- and above-average students.[25] Finally, another study adopted a more indirect approach and found that teacher absenteeism tended to be higher in school districts where union contracts called for a generous sick leave policy.[26] Clearly, as with the private sector studies discussed in Chapter 12, there is no consensus about how public sector unions affect productivity.

---

[21]That most public retirement systems are not fully funded (that is, they do not have assets sufficient to meet their accrued liabilities) is well known. For example, one study found that in 1975 state and local government pension funds had assets equal only to 38 percent of their accured liabilities. See U.S. House of Representatives, *Pension Task Force Report on Public Employee Retirement Systems* (Washington, D.C.: U.S. Government Printing Office, 1978). See Example 13.1.

[22]We say short run because in the long run facts become known. The best example of this occurred in New York City, where Mayor Lindsay agreed to generous fringe benefit packages for New York City employees during the late 1960s and early 1970s. Many people subsequently blamed him for all the financial problems the city experienced in the mid-1970s, and when he ran for U.S. Senator in the Democratic primary in 1980, he finished well behind the winner.

[23]See Casey Ichniowski, "Economic Effects of the Firefighters' Union," *Industrial and Labor Relations Review* 33(January 1980):198–211; and David Rogers, "Municipal Government Structure, Unions, and Wage and Nonwage Compensation in the Public Sector" (unpublished Cornell University M.S. thesis, 1979).

[24]Ronald G. Ehrenberg, Daniel R. Sherman, and Joshua L. Schwarz, "Unions and Productivity in the Public Sector: A Study of Municipal Libraries," *Industrial and Labor Relations Review* 36(January 1983):199–213.

[25]Randall Eberts and Joe Stone, *Unions and Public Schools: The Nonwage Effect of Collective Bargaining in American Education* (Lexington, Mass.: D.C. Heath, forthcoming).

[26]Donald Winkler, "The Effect of Sick Leave Policy on Teacher Absenteeism," *Industrial and Labor Relations Review* 33(January 1980):232–40.

THE EFFECTS OF ARBITRATION STATUTES ON THE WAGES OF STATE AND LOCAL GOVERNMENT EMPLOYEES

One reason why the effect of SLG employee unions on their members' wages is not substantially larger may be that SLG employees' rights to strike are seriously limited. Many states explicitly prohibit strikes by SLG employees, substituting alternative forms of impasse resolution. Some states have adopted *binding arbitra-*

Example 13.1

Pension Underfunding in the Government Sector

The assertion that government officials tend to concentrate on labor costs in the short run can be illustrated by the extent to which public employee retirement systems are underfunded (that is, these systems lack the assets to meet their accrued liabilities). Pension funds in the *private* sector must by law be fully funded in advance, which means that private employers must put enough money per worker into their pension funds each year so that, when invested, these funds grow large enough to finance the expected pension liability of the worker upon retirement. These funds are necessary to guarantee the pension promises made to workers in the event employers become insolvent. Although most public sector pension systems nominally require advance funding, the typical public employee pension fund had only *half* the assets it should have had to be fully funded in 1975. In other words, the typical public sector pension system would have had to receive a one-time contribution equal to about $12,000 per employee to become fully funded in 1975, implying an overall level of underfunding amounting to more than $120 billion in the state and local government sector.

How did this state of affairs arise? In some cases the contributions required to fund pension promises have been deliberately understated. For example, many public sector pension funds have not taken into account the fact that pension benefits will increase as *salaries* increase; they have, in effect, assumed salaries will remain constant over the preretirement years of each worker.

A 1975 investigation of the New York City Employees' Retirement System found that the actuarial assumptions being used about retirees' life expectancy came from New York City's records of experience during the *1908–1914* period. Since life expectancy has increased substantially over the last 70 years, it is not surprising that in 1970 the actual mortality rates of male and female retirees were only 74 percent and 62 percent, respectively, of what the system projected they would be. This underestimate of retirees' life expectancy led to an underestimate of the revenue necessary to pay for their pensions, and thus to underfunding of the system.

The two sources of underfunding mentioned above cause an understatement of the officially reported liabilities (obligations) of public sector pension funds. If these errors were corrected, it is estimated that reported unfunded pension liabilities in the state and local government sector would be closer to $175 billion than to $120 billion. The other major source of underfunding is the simple refusal of employers to contribute sufficient funds to the pension systems. Underfunding is clearly used as a means of balancing current operating budgets, suggesting that short-term considerations take priority over long-run consequences when government employers put together compensation packages.

SOURCES U.S. House of Representatives, *Pension Task Force Report on Public Employee Retirement Systems* (Washington, D.C.: U.S. Government Printing Office), March 15, 1978; and State of New York, *Report of the Permanent Commission on Public Employee Pension and Retirement Systems—Financing the Public Pension Systems Part I: Actuarial Assumptions and Funding Policies* (New York, 1975).

tion as the final stage of their impasse procedure for some categories of public employees, most notably those in the essential police and firefighter areas.[27]

Such binding arbitration legislation is typically opposed by municipal government officials, who argue that arbitration takes the final decision over public employees' wages out of the hands of elected officials and leads to inflated wage settlements. Several studies have analyzed the consequences of arbitration statutes and concluded that the use of arbitration may compress differentials across cities (since arbitrators tend to award larger increases in cities in which public employees are paid relatively low wages than they do in cities in which public employees' wages are relatively high), but that, on average, the wage settlements that go to the arbitration stage are no higher than the wage settlements in otherwise comparable cities that do not go to arbitration.[28] That is, if the average percentage wage settlement in cities that went to arbitration, $\dot{W}_A$, in a particular bargaining round is compared to the average percentage wage settlement in otherwise comparable cities that did not go to arbitration, $\dot{W}_N$, the difference *(D)* is roughly zero:

$$D = \dot{W}_A - \dot{W}_N = 0 \qquad (13.1)$$

One might be tempted to conclude that the arbitration process *per se* has had no effect on the size of the average wage settlement in the public sector. However, this conclusion assumes that the rates of wage increase in cities in which negotiations did not go to arbitration *(W$_N$)* are the same as they would have been in the absence of the arbitration statute, which is not necessarily correct. The existence of the arbitration statute *per se* may well alter the size of wage settlements even in cities that do not go to arbitration.

---

[27]By 1979 at least 18 states had adopted some form of binding arbitration for police and firefighters contract dispute resolution. See Thomas Kochan, "Dynamics of Dispute Resolution in the Public Sector," in *Public Sector Bargaining,* ed. B. Aaron et al. (Washington, D.C.: Bureau of National Affairs, 1979).

[28]See, for example, Thomas Kochan et al., *Dispute Resolution Under Factfinding and Arbitration* (New York: American Arbitration Association, 1979). A review of many of these studies is found in Ronald Ehrenberg and Joshua Schwarz, "Public Sector Labor Markets."

For example, if municipal government labor negotiators fear that there is some chance that arbitrators will award settlements that are substantially more generous than would otherwise occur, they may try to induce a settlement prior to the arbitration stage by offering their employees a wage package in excess of what they would have offered in the absence of the statute.[29] Such an action would cause the estimated differential *D* to *understate* the effect of the arbitration statute on wages. Conversely, if public employers believed, and public employee unions concurred, that arbitrators were likely to award low settlements, management might offer—and unions might accept—an offer less than what management would have offered in the absence of the statute. While we cannot ascertain *a priori* whether the existence of the arbitration statute *per se* increases or decreases the size of wage settlements in cities that do not go to arbitration, it is very likely that the presence of an arbitration statute *does* affect the negotiations when settlement is made prior to arbitration.[30]

Of course the question of why contract negotiations are ever resolved prior to arbitration remains. In bargaining situations in which strikes are permitted, it is the costs that a strike will impose on both parties that provide them with an incentive to agree on a contract prior to a strike. What types of costs do the parties avoid by settling prior to arbitration when a strike is not permitted? The answer appears to be that uncertainty about the decision an arbitrator will make provides the parties with an incentive to settle on their own. That is, both parties may prefer to achieve a certain outcome on their own, rather than bear the costs associated with not knowing with certainty the decision that an arbitrator will make. This point is developed much more completely in the appendix to this chapter.

PUBLIC VS. PRIVATE PAY COMPARISONS

As noted early in the chapter, the pay of most federal government white-collar workers is determined through a comparability process that ties their wages to the results of a government survey of wages of "comparable private workers," subject to possible Presidential and congressional modification. As a result of this process, however, do comparably qualified workers performing comparable work in the public and private sectors receive equal total compensation?[31] This question is difficult to answer because the comparability survey currently focuses on wages and ignores both nonwage benefits and nonpecuniary forms of compensation. Moreover, the jobs performed in the public and private sectors are not always directly comparable, and subjective decisions must often be made as to how a job should be classified.

---

[29]The union might agree to such a settlement even if it expected that, on average, an arbitrated settlement would be higher because of its uncertainty about how the arbitrator would rule (that is, there is some chance that his or her settlement would be lower). Put another way, "a bird in the hand may well be worth two in the bush." This phenomenon is discussed in more detail in the appendix to this chapter.

[30]For a more complete discussion of this point in the context of a simple bargaining model, see Henry S. Farber and Harry C. Katz, "Interest Arbitration, Outcomes, and the Incentive to Bargain," *Industrial and Labor Relations Review* 33(October 1979):55–63.

[31]This discussion draws heavily on Sharon P. Smith, *Equal Pay in the Public Sector: Fact or Fantasy* (Princeton, N.J.: Princeton University, 1977).

Instead of focusing on the earnings of workers with comparable *job character-istics*, which (as noted above) is often impossible to do, one could focus on the earnings paid to workers who have comparable *measured personal characteristics*, such as education and experience, in the public and private sectors. In the most detailed empirical study on the subject to date, Sharon Smith used a framework analogous to the one noted in Chapter 9 which contrasted earnings in regulated and nonregulated industries.[32] Smith's comparisons, which pertain to state and local government employees as well as federal employees, are summarized in Table 13.5. As of 1975, individuals who worked for the federal government appeared to receive wages that were 13–20 percent higher than the wages received by private sector workers with comparable personal characteristics. The differentials for state and local government employees in relation to private sector employees were much more modest, and, in the case of white males the differentials were actually negative. That is, white males employed in the state and local sector appeared to receive lower wages than workers with comparable measured personal characteris-tics in the private sector.

As noted in our discussion of relative earnings in regulated and nonregulated industries (see Chapter 9), earnings comparisons like those in Table 13.5 may not accurately reflect total compensation comparisons because they ignore fringe benefits and other nonpecuniary conditions of employment. For example, they do not take into account the possibility that public employees may have more (or less) difficult jobs, better (or worse) fringe benefits, and higher (or lower) job stability than their private sector counterparts.[33] Furthermore, they do not take into account

TABLE 13.5   Implied Estimated Percentage Differences Between the Wages of Government and Private Sector Employees in 1975

	Percentage Difference Between Wages of		
Category	*Federal and Private Employees*	*State and Private Employees*	*Local Government and Private Employees*
By Sex			
Male	13 to 15	−3 to −11	−4 to −9
Female	18 to 20	6 to 7	1 to 2
By Race and Sex			
White Male	16	−4	−7
Nonwhite Male	17	12	3
White Female	25	7	1
Nonwhite Female	21	9	4

SOURCE: Based on Sharon P. Smith, *Equal Pay in the Public Sector: Fact or Fantasy* (Princeton, N.J.: Princeton University, 1977), Tables 3.7 and 6.4.

---

[32]Smith, *Equal Pay in the Public Sector*. More recent results are reported in Sharon Smith, "Are State and Local Government Workers Overpaid?" in Werner Hirsch and Anthony Rufolo, eds., *The Economics of Municipal Labor Markets* (Los Angeles: UCLA Press, 1983), pp. 59–89.

[33]The limited evidence available suggests that, other things equal, both fringe benefits and job stability are higher in the government than private sectors. See, for example, Smith, *Equal Pay in the Public Sector*; Farrell Bloch and Sharon Smith, "Human Capital and Labor Market Employment," *Journal of Human Resources* 12(Fall 1977):550–60; and Joseph F. Quinn, "Pension Wealth of Government and Private Sector Workers," *American Economic Review* 72(May 1982):283–87. Thus, the compari-sons in Table 13.5 may *understate* the public/private total compensation differentials.

the possibility that public employers may deliberately pursue a high-wage policy to reduce turnover and increase productivity.

Nevertheless, it is interesting to ask why the wage premium paid to public employees in relation to private employees appears to be larger in the federal than the state and local sectors. One possible explanation is that taxpayer information about the effect on tax rates of a wage increase for public employees is much more easily obtained and understood at the state and local level than at the federal level. It may also be easier to hold local politicians accountable for such financial decisions; each federal legislator is just one out of hundreds of representatives who vote on scores of issues besides federal pay legislation. Pressure to hold down public employee wage scales may thus be greater at the state and local level than it is at the federal level.

One may also ask whether equal pay for equal work in the public and private sectors is a reasonable criterion upon which to base federal employee compensation. If one defines *pay* to include all current and expected future wage and nonwage benefits and all conditions of employment, it is likely that, with free mobility of labor, workers will allocate themselves across sectors until pay is equalized. However, it does not follow that *current wage rates* should thus be equalized. Indeed, if public employees received wages equal to or higher than private employees and had more desirable nonwage benefits and conditions of employment, one should expect to see queues of applicants lined up for public sector jobs and very low quit rates for existing public employees. Although occasionally there are reports of job vacancies in the public sector, in the main one's impression is that there are fairly long lists of applicants for most public sector jobs.[34] Furthermore, there is some evidence that quit rates in the public sector are lower than quit rates in the private sector, even after one adjusts for differences in the characteristics of individuals employed in the two sectors.[35] Long queues of applicants and very low quit rates are both consistent with the notion that government workers receive higher pay than comparable private sector workers.

THE EFFECT OF EXPENDITURE- AND TAX-LIMITATION LEGISLATION

In June 1978 California voters overwhelmingly adopted Proposition 13, a state constitutional amendment that rolled back property taxes and drastically limited the ability of all levels of government in the state to increase their tax revenues in the future. Since that date, attempts to limit state and local government spending or

---

[34]For example, Sharon Smith in *Equal Pay in the Public Sector* reports that in September 1974 over 42,000 individuals had passed tests to become police officers in New York City and were awaiting assignment (p. 20). To take another example, the *New York Times* reported that more than 10,000 people lined up to apply for 70 Social Security Administration jobs in Baltimore in September 1980 ("10,000 Line Up in Baltimore Seeking 70 Federal Jobs," *New York Times*, September 16, 1980). Finally, the *Wall Street Journal* reported on March 24, 1981, that the New York City Postmaster had received 225,000 applications for 2,500 jobs that paid starting salaries of $9.05 an hour.

[35]James E. Long, "Are Government Workers Overpaid? Alternative Evidence," *Journal of Human Resources* 17(Winter 1982):123–31.

taxing have proliferated, and in a number of cases these attempts have been successful.[36]

The simple demand-and-supply model developed in this chapter can help illustrate the likely effects of such legislation on public sector labor markets.[37] Suppose that initially the demand and supply of public employees were D_0 and S_0, respectively, in Figure 13.3. In this case, ignoring for the moment the effect of union-won increases in wages (and queues for public jobs), equilibrium would be at point A, with the wage/employment combination (W_0, E_0).

The first-round effect of expenditure- or tax-limitation legislation is no different from the effect of any other decline in a community's ability, or willingness, to pay for public employees. The demand for public employees will decline to, say, D_2; if nothing else occurred, equilibrium would be reached at point B with the lower wage and employment combination (W_2, E_2).

This is not the end of the story, however. Expenditure- and tax-limitation legislation undoubtedly reduces public employees' expectations about the level of

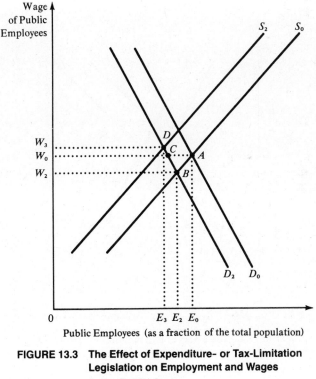

FIGURE 13.3   **The Effect of Expenditure- or Tax-Limitation Legislation on Employment and Wages in the Public Sector**

[36]For a discussion of the causes and effects of such legislation, see "Proceedings of a Conference on Tax and Expenditure Limitations," *National Tax Journal* 32 (June 1979).

[37]See Ronald G. Ehrenberg, "The Effect of Tax Limitation Legislation on Public Sector Labor Markets," *National Tax Journal* 32(June 1979):261–66, for a more complete discussion.

their *future* wages and also increases the probability that they will be laid off for financial reasons in the future. These changes reduce the desirability of being a state- or local-government employee. As a result, the supply curve shifts to S_2; equilibrium now occurs at point D, with the wage/employment combination (W_3, E_3). Although employment has *fallen* still further, public employees' wages have now *risen* above W_2.

Whether the final wage, W_3, is greater or less than the initial wage, W_0, is an open question and depends upon whether the shift in supply dominates the shift in demand. If the supply shift does dominate, as in Figure 13.3, public employees' wages will actually rise above their initial level; their employment, however, will fall by more than the shift in the demand curve (point D lies to the left of point C). Although the legislation *may* serve to reduce public employees' wages, it unambiguously reduces their employment levels and the flow of public services.[38]

Figure 13.4 introduces public employee unions into the analysis. Suppose at the outset that a public employee union had succeeded in keeping the wage rate at W_u,

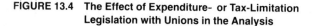

Public Employees (as a fraction of the total population)

FIGURE 13.4   The Effect of Expenditure- or Tax-Limitation Legislation with Unions in the Analysis

---

[38]This last statement ignores the possibility that public employee productivity might increase in response to the legislation. See Ehrenberg, "The Effect of Tax Limitation Legislation," for a discussion of why this might occur. See also Daniel Mitchell, "The New Climate: Implications for Research on Public Sector Wage Determination and Labor Relations," *Proceedings of the 1983 Spring Meeting of the Industrial Relations Research Association* (Madison, Wisconsin: IRRA, 1983) for evidence of the short- and long-term effects of Proposition 13 on public employees' wages in California.

which lies above the equilibrium level. In this case employment would initially be E_u^0. The fall in demand to D_2 caused by the expenditure- or tax-limitation legislation would cause public employment to fall to E_u^1, but unless the union agreed to a reduced wage scale, wages would remain at W_u. As drawn, the reduction in labor supply to S_2 would have *no* effect on wages or employment; it would serve only to reduce the excess supply of labor. Of course, if the leftward shift in supply were large enough, employment would fall still further and wages would rise above the level set by the union.

While public employee unions could still push for higher wages at the expense of lower employment levels, the expenditure- or tax-limitation legislation would reduce their ability to use the political process to shift out the demand for public employees.[39] One could reasonably project, then, that an additional effect of such legislation may be to reduce the size of the union relative wage effects observed in the state and local sector.

PUBLIC SECTOR EMPLOYMENT PROGRAMS

The final focus of this chapter is on the *net job-creation effects* of public employment programs, or the extent to which funds provided to state and local governments by the federal government to increase their employment levels actually serve to expand employment. As noted earlier, these funds were provided during the decade of the 1970s, first under the *Emergency Employment Act of 1971* and then under the *Comprehensive Employment and Training Act* (CETA).

Ignoring for a moment private sector labor markets, suppose that all the unemployed workers in the economy have attached themselves to the public sector labor market and that the wage in that market is rigid downward in the *short run*. Figure 13.5 shows that, at the prevailing SLG employee wage (W_0), the supply of workers to the SLG sector exceeds the demand for SLG employees; employment is E_0, and $L_0 - E_0$ individuals who want work cannot find it. If, through a public employment program, such as that administered under CETA, the federal government provides funds to SLGs to expand their employment, the demand for labor will shift to the right (to, say, D_1). SLG employment will expand to E_1, and unemployment will be reduced.[40]

The key issue in evaluating such a program is the extent to which the demand curve actually shifts to the right in response to the program. If, given the prevailing public sector wage, W_0, funds are provided to create 100 new SLG positions, will

---

[39]Not surprisingly, public employees are overwhelmingly against expenditure- and tax-limitation legislation. See Paul Courant et al., "Why Voters Support Tax Limitation Amendments: The Michigan Case," *National Tax Journal* 33(March 1980):1–20.

[40]If the demand curve should shift horizontally by more than $L_0 - E_0$, or if the initial SLG employee wage were a market-clearing one, the reader should be able to show that the SLG employee wage would also increase. Surprisingly, only one study has attempted to analyze the effect of these programs on public sector wage levels, and that study proved inconclusive. See Lauri Bassi, "Estimating the Impact of Job Creation Programs on Public Sector Wages" (Princeton University Working Paper, 1979).

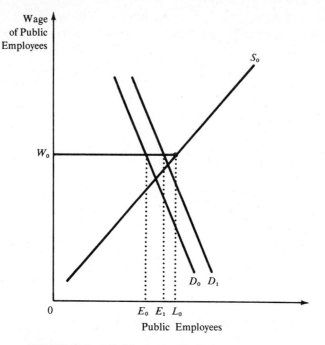

FIGURE 13.5   A Public Sector Employment Program

the demand curve actually shift to the right by 100 positions? The answer in general is no. Since SLG decision-makers have other goals in addition to increasing public employment expenditures—goals such as increasing other government expenditures, reducing local taxes, and reducing local debt—it is logical to hypothesize that they will use at least a portion of the public employment program funds to hire people they would have hired even in the absence of the program (thus freeing up their own resources for the above-mentioned alternative uses). Put another way, the public employment program funds might at least partially *displace* regular SLG expenditures on public employees, thereby reducing the net job-creation effect of the program.[41]

One may wonder how such a *displacement effect* (or *fiscal substitution*) could occur if by law the public employment program funds can be used only to expand SLG employment levels. The answer is that as long as SLG officials would have planned to expand their employment even in the absence of the program, program monitors have no direct way of ascertaining whether the jobs created by the program

---

[41]Even if such displacement is complete, program funds will still have a stimulative impact, even if they are implicitly spent on nonlabor items, used to retire a local debt, or used to reduce local taxes. If the funds have this stimulative impact, the effects of the program will be similar to any other general increase in government spending or decrease in taxes. However, they will not necessarily benefit the unemployed workers at which such programs are targeted.

would have been created in its absence.[42] Since the annual growth of SLG employment exceeded the increase in the number of public employment program positions in every year covered by Table 13.1, it is possible that such displacement or fiscal substitution occurred.

Numerous attempts have been made to estimate the displacement effects of public employment programs. A number of empirical studies have used either aggregate time-series data or cross-section data on local government employment to estimate the effects of various factors on the demand for SLG employees, including such factors as public employee wage rates, community income levels, *and* the number of public employment positions funded. Although the estimated effects of the program vary widely with the models and data used in these studies, a reasonable consensus would be that at least 30 to 50 percent of program funds ultimately displace local government funds.[43] That is, no more than 50 to 70 percent of these funds actually go towards increasing SLG employment.[44]

So far, however, our analysis of the net employment-creation effects of a public employment program has ignored the private sector. After considering the interaction between public and private labor markets, one can see that the net job-creation effects may be even less than the 50 to 70 percent figure cited above. Our analysis of this issue assumes the existence of an above-equilibrium, downward-rigid wage in the public sector and the accompanying presence of "wait unemployment" there.

In Figure 13.6, simple demand and supply models have been drawn for private and public sector labor markets. Suppose that the demand and supply curves in the private sector are initially given by D_{PR}^0 and S_{PR}^0, respectively, and that equilibrium occurs at the market-clearing wage-employment combination (W_{PR}^0, E_{PR}^0). Suppose also that the public sector demand and supply curves are given by D_{PB}^0 and S_{PB}^0,

---

[42]There are literally thousands of state and local governments in the United States, and it would be nearly impossible to obtain direct information on their planned employment levels in the absence of the public employment programs. Clearly, local officials have no incentive to report that they planned to expand employment; such an action would limit their ability to implicitly shift public employment funds to other uses.

[43]See, for example, George Johnson and James Tomola, "The Fiscal Substitution Effects of Alternative Approaches to Public Service Employment," *Journal of Human Resources* 12(Winter 1977):3–26; Michael Borus and Daniel Hamermesh, "Estimating Fiscal Substitution by Public Service Employment Programs," *Journal of Human Resources* 13(Fall 1978):561–65; and Charles Adams et al., "A Pooled Time-Series Analysis of the Job Creation Impact of Public Service Employment Grants to Large Cities," *Journal of Human Resources* 18(Spring 1983):283–94. The Johnson-Tomola paper provides an interesting case study of how research affects public policy. Later studies (such as Borus and Hamermesh) showed its precise estimates of displacement to be incorrect. However, the study was well publicized in Washington and the mere fact that Johnson and Tomola raised the displacement issue stimulated Congress to redesign the CETA program in an effort to minimize displacement (essentially by limiting individuals' participation in part of the public-employment program to a fixed term). Later studies, such as Adams et al., found that the redesign did tend to reduce displacement. As this example demonstrates, the publicity that a study gets is often as important as its scientific substance.

[44]Researchers using alternative methodologies have concluded that the net job-creation effects may be larger. See, for example, Richard Nathan et al., *Public Service Employment* (Washington, D.C.: Brookings Institution, 1981). These estimates are based on subjective perceptions of trained field observers of what local government employment would have been in the absence of the program.

respectively. The public sector wage rate, however, is again assumed to be fixed in the short run at the level W_{PB}^0. As a result, employment will initially be E_{PB}^0 in the public sector, and the excess supply of labor to the public sector is given by $L_{PB}^0 - E_{PB}^0$.

In order to have an equilibrium situation, in the sense that unemployed workers in the public sector have no incentive to search for jobs in the private sector, the expected level of earnings (ignoring all nonwage forms of compensation) must be the same in both sectors. Therefore, the wages in each sector multiplied by the fraction of time that individuals attached to each sector *(F)* expect to be employed must be equal:

$$W_{PB}^0 F_{PB}^0 = W_{PR}^0 F_{PR}^0. \tag{13.2}$$

Since there is an excess supply of labor in the public sector, F_{PB}^0 is less than one, while the market-clearing assumption in the private sector guarantees (in this framework) that F_{PR}^0 is equal to one. As a result, it must be initially true that the public sector wage exceeds the private sector wage:

$$W_{PB}^0 > W_{PR}^0. \tag{13.3}$$

Suppose that the federal government now provides funds to SLGs to expand their employment levels and that the result of this public employment program is to shift the demand curve in the public sector to D_{PB}^1. The first-round effect of the program is to increase SLG employment to E_{PB}^1, eliminating the excess supply of labor. This shift, however, also eliminates the equality in equation (13.2). Since the elimination of the excess supply of labor in the public sector increases the fraction of time that workers attached to that sector expect to be employed, it must now be true that

$$W_{PB}^0 F_{PB}^1 > W_{PR}^0 F_{PR}^0, \tag{13.4}$$

where F_{PB}^1 is the fraction of time employees attached to the *SLG* sector now expect to be employed. (In our simple model where there is no unemployment when demand equals supply, F_{PB}^1 would equal one.)

The situation depicted in equation (13.4) is not an equilibrium; the expected earnings level is now higher in the public than in the private sector. Therefore, some *employed* private sector workers have an incentive to quit their jobs to search for the now relatively more attractive public sector jobs. This quitting behavior is reflected by a leftward shift in the supply curve of labor to the private sector and a rightward shift in the supply curve to the public sector. As a result, an excess demand for labor in the private sector now exists at W_{PR}^0, and employers there are forced to bid up wages and to reduce employment levels. The shift out in the labor supply curve to the public sector creates an excess supply of labor there, reducing the expected fraction of the period that workers attached to the public sector will find employment. These shifts continue until equilibrium is restored and expected earnings are again equal in the two sectors:

$$W_{PB}^0 F_{PB}^2 = W_{PR}^1 F_{PR}^1. \tag{13.5}$$

This equilibrium is shown in Figure 13.6 as occurring when the supply curves are S_{PB}^1 and S_{PR}^1 in the two sectors.

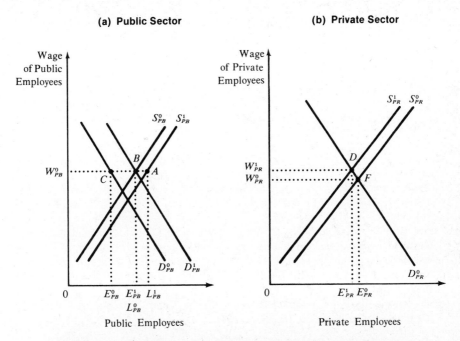

(a) Public Sector

(b) Private Sector

FIGURE 13.6 **An Analysis of the Effects of a Public Employment Program:** **Responsive Supply in the Private Sector**

Note that the increase in *total* (public plus private) employment that results is less than the increase in SLG employment because some private sector employees have quit their jobs to search (or wait) for jobs in the SLG sector. The net employment effects of the program are overestimated, then, if one focuses only on what happens to SLG employment and fails to measure employment changes in the private sector that are induced by the program. Note also that the market reactions to the program have induced higher private sector wages. Is it at all surprising, then, that business organizations, especially those that represent employers whose work forces might find public employment program positions desirable, are vocal opponents to such legislation? Such programs are simply not in these employers' self-interest.

REVIEW QUESTIONS

1. Explain why the demand curve for public sector employees slopes downward. Do your explanations hold for both the long run and short run?
2. You have been asked to oversee a study of the comparability of federal government and private sector employee compensation. List and explain the factors this study should take into account.
3. Referring to the four factors influencing the elasticity of demand for labor, spell out why the labor demand curve in the public sector is likely to be more or less elastic than demand curves in the private sector.
4. Congresswoman X states, ''I support the granting of federal funds to our cities for the purpose of hiring additional city workers. Last year the federal government authorized

payments to support 200 additional police officers in City Y, bringing its total force to 2200. This can only mean that City Y's residents were being given 10 percent more protection than they would otherwise have received, and that 200 more people were employed in City Y than would otherwise have been employed.'' Analyze Congresswoman X's conclusions about the effects of federal grants.

SELECTED READINGS

Ehrenberg, Ronald G. "The Demand for State and Local Government Employees." *American Economic Review* 63(June 1973):366–79.

Ehrenberg, Ronald G. and Schwarz, Joshua L. "Public Sector Labor Markets." In Orley Ashenfelter and Richard Layard, eds. *Handbook of Labor Economics*. Amsterdam: North Holland Publishing Co., in press).

Farber, Henry S., and Katz, Harry C. "Interest Arbitration, Outcomes, and the Incentive to Bargain." *Industrial and Labor Relations Review* 33(October 1979):55–65.

Johnson, George, and Tomola, James. "The Fiscal Substitution Effects of Alternative Approaches to Public Service Employment." *Journal of Human Resources* 12(Winter 1977):3–26.

Smith, Sharon. *Equal Pay in the Public Sector: Fact or Fantasy*. Princeton, N.J.: Industrial Relations Section, Princeton University, 1977.

APPENDIX 13A

Arbitration and the Incentive to Bargain

What incentive do the parties to collective bargaining negotiations have to settle their negotiations on their own, rather than to go to arbitration and have an outside party impose a settlement? The answer may well be that the uncertainty about an arbitrator's likely decision imposes costs on both parties and that these costs provide them with an incentive to come to an agreement on their own. This appendix provides a simple model that illustrates this proposition; it highlights the roles of both *uncertainty* about an arbitrator's likely decision and the parties' *attitudes towards risk* in determining whether a negotiation will wind up in arbitration.[1]

Consider a simple two-party bargaining problem in which the parties, A and B, are negotiating over how to split a "pie" of fixed size. Each party's utility function depends only on the share of the pie that it receives. Figure 13A.1 plots the utility function for party A. When A's share of the pie is zero, A's utility is assumed to be zero, and as A's share (S_A) increases, A's utility increases. Crucially, this utility function is also assumed to exhibit the property of *diminishing marginal utility;* equal increments in S_A lead to progressively smaller increments in U_A.[2] As we shall show below, this is equivalent to assuming that the party is *risk averse,* which means that the party would prefer having a given share of the pie with certainty to an uncertain outcome that, on average, would yield the same share.

Now suppose party A believes that, on average, the arbitrator would award it one half of the pie if the negotiations went to arbitration. If it knew with certainty that the arbitrator would do this, party A's utility from going to arbitration would be $U_A(\frac{1}{2})$—or point *a* in Figure 13A.1. Suppose, however, that party A is uncertain about the arbitrator's decision and instead believes the arbitrator will assign it one quarter of the pie with probability one half or three quarters of the pie also with probability one half. Utility in these two states is given by $U_A(\frac{1}{4})$, point *b,* and $U_A(\frac{3}{4})$, point *c,* respectively. Although, on average, party A expects to be awarded one half of the pie, its average or *expected* utility in this case is $.5U_A(\frac{1}{4}) + .5U_A(\frac{3}{4})$—which, as Figure 13A.1 indicates, is *less* than $U_A(\frac{1}{2})$. This reflects the fact that party A is risk averse, and prefers a certain outcome to an uncertain outcome tnat yields the same expected share.

Note that if party A were awarded the share S_A^0 with certainty, it would receive the same utility level as it receives under the uncertain situation, where it expects, with equal probability, the arbitrator to award it either one quarter or three quarters

---

[1] The discussion here is a simplified version of some of the material found in Henry S. Farber and Harry C. Katz, "Interest Arbitration, Outcomes, and the Incentive to Bargain," *Industrial and Labor Relations Review* 33(October 1979):55–63.

[2] Refer to Appendix 8A, especially note 4, for an introduction to this use of cardinal utility functions.

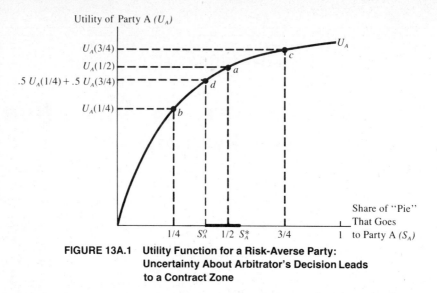

FIGURE 13A.1 Utility Function for a Risk-Averse Party: Uncertainty About Arbitrator's Decision Leads to a Contract Zone

of the pie. Indeed, it would prefer any certain share above S_A^0 to bearing the cost of the uncertainty associated with having to face the arbitrator's decision. The set of contracts it would potentially voluntarily agree to, then, is the set S_A such that

$$S_A^0 \le S_A \le 1 \qquad S_A^0 < \tfrac{1}{2} \qquad (13A.1)$$

Suppose party B is similarly risk averse and has identical expectations as party A about what the arbitrator's decision will look like. It should be obvious, using the same logic as above, that the set of contracts, S_B, that party B would potentially voluntarily agree to is given by a similar expression:

$$S_B^0 \le S_B \le 1 \qquad S_B^0 < \tfrac{1}{2} \qquad (13A.2)$$

Now any share that party B voluntarily agrees to receive implies that B is willing to give party A one minus that share. Since the minimum share B would agree to receive, S_B^0, is less than one half, it follows that the maximum share B would voluntarily agree to *give* A in negotiations, S_A^* (which equals $1-S_B^0$), is greater than one half. Party B potentially would be willing to voluntarily agree to any settlement that gives party A a share of less than S_A^*.

Referring to Figure 13A.1, observe that party A would be willing to voluntarily agree to contracts that offer it at least S_A^0, while party B would be willing to agree to contracts that give party A S_A^* or less. Hence, the set of contracts that *both* parties would find preferable to going to arbitration and *potentially* would voluntarily agree to is given by all the shares for A (S_A) that lie between these two extremes:

$$S_A^0 \le S_A \le S_A^* \qquad (13A.3)$$

This set of potential voluntary solutions to the bargaining problem is indicated by the bold line segment on the horizontal axis of Figure 13A.1 and is called the *contract curve*. As long as both parties are risk averse and are uncertain what the arbitrator will do, a contract curve will exist.

The extent of the parties' *uncertainty* about the arbitrator's decision and the extent of their *risk aversion* are important determinants of the size of the contract curve. To see this, first suppose that party A continues to expect that, on average, the arbitrator will assign it one half of the pie, but now believes that this will occur by receiving shares of one eighth and seven eighths with equal probability. Figure 13A.2 indicates its utility in each of these states (points e and f) and shows that, while its expected share is still one half, the greater uncertainty (or "spread" of possible outcomes) has led to a reduction in its expected utility. Indeed, now party A would be as happy to receive the share S_A^1 with certainty as it would to face the risks associated with going to arbitration. Since S_A^1 is less than S_A^0, the size of the contract curve has increased. Hence, increased uncertainty about the arbitrator's decision leads to a larger contract curve.

Next consider Figure 13A.3, where we have drawn a utility function for a *risk-neutral* party. A risk-neutral party has a linear utility function because its utility depends only on its expected share, not the uncertainty associated with the outcome. So, for example, in Figure 13A.3 individual A gets the same utility from having a share of one half with certainty, as it does from facing an arbitrated outcome in which the arbitrator will award it either a share of one quarter or three quarters with equal probability. As a result, faced with the possibility of going to arbitration, there is no share less than one half that party A would voluntarily agree to settle for prior to arbitration. If party B had similar expectations about the arbitrator's behavior and was similarly risk neutral, it also would refuse to settle for any share of less than one half, which on average is what it expects to win from the arbitrator. Hence, the contract curve would reduce to one point, the point where both parties receive a share of one half. The only voluntary agreement the parties will reach is what they expect to receive on average if they go to arbitration. (This illustrates how the arbitration process *per se* may influence the nature of negotiated settlements.)

More generally, one can show that as a party's risk aversion increases (the utility function becomes "more curved"), the size of the contract curve will increase. Hence, increases in either the parties' risk aversion or uncertainty about the arbitrator's decision will increase the size of the contract curve.

Larger contract curves mean that there are more potential settlements that *both*

FIGURE 13A.2   Increased Uncertainty About Arbitrator's Decision Increases Size of Contract Zone

**FIGURE 13A.3   Utility Function for a Risk-Neutral Party:
Contract Zone Is Reduced to a Single Point**

parties would prefer to an arbitrated settlement, and some people have argued that this increased "menu" of choices increases the probability that the parties would settle on their own prior to going to arbitration.[3] An immediate implication of this result is that, if one believes it is preferable for the parties to settle on their own, the arbitration system should be structured so that the arbitrator's behavior does *not* become completely predictable. That is, the parties must face some uncertainty about the arbitrator's potential decisions.

Remember, however, that the implications of the model are derived from the assumption that the probability of reaching a negotiated settlement is positively related to the size of the contract curve. Not all economists agree with this view.[4] To see why, suppose that there is only one point on the contract curve—only one bargaining outcome that both parties consider preferable to an arbitrated solution. Some argue that it should be easier for the parties to agree on that point than it would be for them to agree on one point out of 500 on a contract curve, all of which differed in their distribution of the pie between the parties. Without the assumption of the positive correlation between the size of the contract zone and the probability of reaching a negotiated settlement, many of the model's results concerning when negotiations are likely to go to arbitration vanish.[5]

---

[3]Farber and Katz, "Interest Arbitration, Outcomes, and the Incentive to Bargain."

[4]Vincent Crawford, "Arbitration and Conflict Resolution in Labor-Management Bargaining," *American Economic Review* 71(May 1981):205–10.

[5]Models of the type described above can be generalized to address a variety of additional issues. These include how arbitrators' notions of intrinsic fairness influence the offers the parties are willing to make in bargaining, whether *conventional* arbitration or *final-offer* arbitration (where the arbitrator must choose one of the party's offers as his decision) provides greater incentives for the parties to bargain, and how differences in the degree of risk aversion between the two parties will influence the fraction of the arbitrated awards each party wins and the size of the arbitrated awards. For these models, the interested reader is referred to Henry Farber, "An Analysis of Final-Offer Arbitration," *Journal of Conflict Resolution* 24(December 1980):683–705, and Farber, "Splitting the Difference in Interest Arbitration," *Industrial and Labor Relations Review* 35(October 1981):70–77. An empirical paper based on these frameworks is found in Orley Ashenfelter and David Bloom, "Models of Arbitrator Behavior: Theory and Evidence," *American Economic Review* 74(March 1984):111–24.

14

The Economics of Discrimination

We have learned that wages differ across
individuals or jobs for numerous reasons. They vary with the amount of general or
specific training, with job and locational characteristics, and with age. They also
vary with fringe benefits and compensation schemes, and, of course, they vary with
the extent of unionism. Many of these sources of wage differentials may be
regarded either as necessary in the allocation of labor or as socially legitimate on
other grounds. There are, however, sizable wage differentials that appear to be
associated solely with race and sex, and these differentials are often thought to be
synonymous with widespread discrimination against minorities—especially blacks
and Hispanics—and women. This chapter discusses the evidence and theories of
discrimination and concludes with an analysis of government policy in this area.

WHAT IS DISCRIMINATION?

The term *discrimination* is often used imprecisely because the relationship between
prejudice and discrimination often is unclear. One might assert, for example, that a
firm with two racially segregated branch offices is discriminating by failing to
integrate both offices, even if workers in both branches are paid the same wages and
have the same opportunities for advancement. This assertion raises the question of
whether discrimination is always present when there is prejudice or just when some
harm comes from this prejudice. Conversely, some people allege discrimination
exists in cases in which prejudice may not. For example, a firm offering specific
training may prefer to hire younger workers who will stay with the firm long enough
for it to recoup training costs. Is this age discrimination or good business?

Another confusing issue is whether discrimination can be identified by inequality of *achievement* or inequality of *opportunity*. Is an accounting firm located in a
small, mostly white town guilty of discrimination if it has no black auditors on its
staff? Would the answer change if the firm could show it had advertised job

openings widely and had made the same offers to blacks as to whites, but that the offers to blacks had been rejected?

Finally, just what standards are to be used to judge equality? Consider the data on college teachers in the humanities contained in Table 14.1. The overall average salary paid to black professors is slightly below the salaries paid to whites for at least two reasons. First, a lower proportion of blacks have received doctorate degrees, and, of those who have, fewer were obtained at distinguished universities. The relatively lower levels of educational attainment among blacks thus holds down their average salary. Second, among those teachers without doctorates, blacks receive lower salaries than whites. However, if one looks at salaries among professors with doctorates in the humanities from distinguished universities, we see that blacks earn *more* than whites. The same is true among those with doctorates from less distinguished universities.

Do the data in Table 14.1 suggest that blacks in academia are discriminated against? One could answer yes, because they earn less overall, because they have lower levels of preparation for their jobs, or because there are so few blacks in college teaching (2.5 percent of college professors are black, whereas blacks constitute about 8 percent of the overall employed population at large). Others might argue that there is no evidence of discrimination against blacks with doctorates once one controls for quality of preparation.

It is obvious from the questions raised by Table 14.1 that discrimination can occur in many forms and places. If it occurs in the labor market, workers with equal preparation and productivity receive different wages. If it occurs among educational institutions, students of equal ability are treated differently and emerge from formal schooling with unequal educations. If it occurs in childhood, young children with equal potential are raised with quite different aspirations and attitudes. Discrimination can also occur in a variety of other places: the housing market, various product markets, and treatment under the law.

The kind of discrimination this chapter will analyze in most depth is discrimination in the labor market. This emphasis should not imply that other forms of

TABLE 14.1   Mean Annual Salaries of Full-Time College Faculty in the Humanities, 1972 and 1973

	Black		White	
	Number	*Salary (dollars)*	*Number*	*Salary (dollars)*
All full-time faculty	2,177	15,034	85,904	15,572
Doctorate from distinguished university	89	20,259	9,765	16,832
Doctorate from other universities	173	17,262	17,894	15,790
No doctorate	1,915	14,590	58,245	15,293

SOURCE: American Council on Education.

discrimination are unimportant or unrelated to labor market discrimination. Indeed, *past* labor market discrimination may have been instrumental in causing the poverty or attitudes that are *now* manifest in child-rearing practices, school achievement levels, and career or sex role aspirations. However, since the focus of our analysis is on *current labor market discrimination,* we shall lump all *other* forms of discrimination into a more general category we shall call *premarket differences.*

An operational definition of *current labor market discrimination* is "the valuation in the labor market of personal characteristics of the worker that are unrelated to productivity."[1] This definition recognizes that one's value in the labor market depends on all the demand *and* supply factors affecting marginal productivity. However, when factors that are *unrelated* to productivity acquire a positive or negative value in the labor market, discrimination can be said to occur. Race and sex are currently the most prominent of these factors alleged to be unrelated to productivity, but physical handicaps, religion, sexual preferences, and ethnic heritage are also on the list.

Three points should be noted about the above definition. First, the emphasis in identifying discrimination is on measurable market outcomes, such as earnings, wages, occupational attainment, or employment levels. While prejudicial attitudes may be felt by members of one group toward those of another, these feelings must be accompanied by some *action* that results in a different market outcome for us to assert that discrimination is present.

Second, we are not concerned with the routine random differences in outcomes that are matters of luck. Rather, the concept of discrimination encompasses only those differences that are so systematic that they do not cancel each other out within large groups.

Finally, our definition of labor market discrimination suggests an operational way to distinguish between *labor market* and *premarket* factors that cause earnings differentials. Differentials that derive from differences in average *productivity* levels across race or sex groups, for example, can be categorized as *premarket* in nature. Differentials that are attributed to race or sex, *holding productivity constant,* can be said to be evidence of labor market discrimination.

It is very important for policy purposes to measure the relative size of labor market and premarket factors that lead to systematic earnings differences among various population groups. Any attempts to combat discrimination must be grounded in accurate information concerning the *source* of that discrimination; otherwise, effective antidiscrimination programs cannot be formulated. If the evidence points to a significant amount of labor market discrimination, programs aimed at employers and the hiring/promotion process may be effective. If, however, most of any systematic earnings differences related to race or sex appear to be rooted in premarket factors, then programs aimed at education, training, and the process of socializing children will be required.

---

[1]Kenneth J. Arrow, "The Theory of Discrimination," *Discrimination in Labor Markets,* ed. Orley Ashenfelter and Albert Rees (Princeton, N.J.: Princeton University Press, 1973), p. 3.

EARNINGS DISPARITIES BY RACE, ETHNICITY, AND SEX

There have been, and continue to be, strikingly large income disparities between most minorities and whites and between men and women. These differences are a cause of widespread social concern about discrimination, its sources, and possible remedies. This chapter will analyze various theories and their consequences for antidiscrimination policies after first describing the race and sex differences in earnings that actually exist. (We focus below on *earnings* differences for the practical reason that data on *total compensation,* which would be preferable because of the inclusion of fringe benefits, are not generally available by race and sex.)

Racial and Ethnic Differences

Blacks.   In 1981 the earnings of the typical male, year-round black worker were 71 percent of his white counterpart's. While this disparity in incomes is large and has varied considerably in the recession-plagued years after 1975, there is a gradual trend toward greater equality over time. As indicated in Table 14.2, the 1981 ratio was 5–7 percentage points higher than in the 1960s and 3–4 points higher than in the early 1970s. At no point since 1974 has the ratio fallen below what it was before 1974.

Similar patterns for women can be observed from the data in Table 14.2, although much greater equality has been achieved among women. Black and white women who worked full time at year-round jobs had virtually the same income

TABLE 14.2   Black/White Ratio of Median Income for Full-Time, Year-Round Workers

	Black/White Income Ratio	
Year	*Males*	*Females*
1959	0.61	0.66
1961	0.66	0.67
1963	0.66	0.64
1965	0.64	0.71
1967	0.64	0.74
1969	0.66	0.80
1971	0.68	0.88
1973	0.67	0.85
1974	0.70	0.91
1976	0.72	0.93
1977	0.69	0.93
1978	0.77	0.93
1980	0.70	0.93
1981	0.71	0.90

SOURCES: U.S. Bureau of the Census, *Current Population Reports: Consumer Income,* Series P-60 (relevant years). Data before 1980 refer to persons aged 14 or older; data for 1980–81 refer to ages 15 or older.

ratios as did men in the early 1960s (around .65). However, in the mid-1960s the ratio for women began to rise until by 1981 black women who worked full time earned, on average, 90 percent as much as full-time white women workers.

While these ratios and their trends are very interesting and important, they do not help us identify the immediate *source* of the disparities. Are the differences primarily due to *current labor market discrimination,* or are they the result of *premarket factors?* Blacks, for example, tend to be younger and less educated, on average, than whites.[2] Further, it may well be that the average *quality* of schooling received by blacks is lower than the average for whites.[3] We know that earnings rise with both education and experience, so *some* of the black/white earnings differences are surely attributable to these characteristics. How much of the overall differential in average earnings is due to differences in the characteristics that affect productivity and how much is due to labor market discrimination?

To measure the extent of market discrimination, one must answer the following question: "What would be the black/white earnings ratio if blacks and whites had the same productive characteristics?" In other words, if blacks (on average) had the same education, training, experience, turnover rate, health and marital status, and region of residence as whites, what would be the ratio of their earnings to those of whites? The answers to this question vary with the data sample and methodology employed, but they do establish a range within which the true ratio probably lies.

Two studies using data from the late 1960s estimated that 60–75 percent of the overall black/white disparity in wage rates for males was attributable to premarket differences[4]—implying that, in the absence of measurable differences in productive characteristics, black males would have earned between 85 and 90 percent of what white males earned. A study using data from the mid-1970s suggests that, in the absence of premarket differences, black males would have earned wages that were 88 percent of those earned by white males.[5] Finally, research using 1980 data indicated that black male high school graduates earned from 83 to 94 percent as much as comparable white males (the percentages varied with age, but not systematically).[6] Interestingly, the latter study found that for male college graduates under 30 years of age in 1980, blacks earned from 10 to 18 percent *more* than their white counterparts.

The finding that from 50 to 80 percent of the difference in average earnings can be explained by differences in productive characteristics implies that current labor

---

[2] As noted in Chapter 9, one's choice of education is influenced by expected labor market earnings over the life cycle. Hence, ensuring that market discrimination against blacks is reduced or eliminated should serve as an incentive for blacks to stay in school longer.

[3] *See* Finis Welch, "Education and Racial Discrimination," in *Discrimination in Labor Markets,* ed. Orley Ashenfelter and Albert Rees, pp. 43–81.

[4] Robert J. Flanagan, "Labor Force Experience, Job Turnover, and Racial Wage Differentials," *Review of Economics and Statistics* 56(November 1974):521–29; and A. S. Blinder, "Wage Discrimination—Reduced Form and Structural Estimates," *Journal of Human Resources* 8(Fall 1973):436–55.

[5] Mary Corcoran and Greg Duncan, "Work History, Labor Force Attachment, and Earnings Differences Between the Races and Sexes," *Journal of Human Resources* 14,1(Winter 1979):3–20.

[6] Saul Hoffman and Charles Link, "Selectivity Bias in Male Wage Equations; Black and White Comparisons," *Review of Economics and Statistics* 66(May 1984):320–24.

market discrimination *may* account for 20–50 percent of the overall differential, suggesting a rather significant role for antidiscrimination programs or policies in the labor market. However, the figures of 20–50 percent may be biased estimates of the extent of labor market discrimination because researchers simply do not have complete data on the productive characteristics of individuals or groups. Researchers can measure age, education, and, in many cases, experience, but they rarely have data on school quality, work habits, aspirations, degree of alienation, and other intangibles that clearly affect one's productivity. These intangibles, moreover, *may* vary across race (or sex) owing to such premarket factors as social treatment, socioeconomic status of one's parents, and cultural background. If the unmeasured characteristics tend to depress the productivity of minorities or women relative to white males, attributing all of the unexplained difference in average earnings to current labor market discrimination will clearly overstate the extent of that discrimination. *Some* of the unexplained 20–50 percent may be the result of unmeasured productive characteristics and thus more appropriately labeled *premarket* in nature. Of course, if the unmeasured characteristics tend to raise the productivity of minorities or women relative to white men, attributing all the differences in earnings to current labor market discrimination will understate the extent of that discrimination.

After estimating the portion of the *average* race/sex earnings differential that is explained by differences in average productive characteristics, one is left with a residual, or unexplained, portion. One part of the residual may be the result of current labor market discrimination, but the effects of any unmeasurable (or at least unmeasured) differences in average productive characteristics show up in the residual also. Because of this methodological defect, which is mainly the result of the difficulties of measuring all characteristics that affect productivity, accurate measures of the extent of labor market discrimination do not exist. Assuming *all* the unexplained residual is due to discrimination, we can estimate the effects discrimination *might* have; however, we are unable to say if actual labor market discrimination is below or above these estimates.

Hispanics. In 1975 ratios of the average wages of male Hispanics to those of non-Hispanic whites were as follows:

Mexicans: 0.72
Puerto Ricans: 0.76
Central and South Americans: 0.83
Cubans: 0.89

However, as suggested by our discussion of immigrants in Chapter 10, to estimate what fractions of these wage differences are due to differences in productive characteristics we need to control for proficiency in English, time in the United States, or both. Studies controlling for these factors, in addition to other human capital characteristics, have recently been done, and they suggest that current market discrimination is not as severe against Hispanics as against blacks.

One study, for example, estimated that if differences in productive characteristics (including English language proficiency) were eliminated, the foregoing earnings ratios would rise to approximately 0.94, 0.88, and 0.85 for Mexicans, Puerto

Example 14.1

Age and the End of Discrimination

Our discussions of investments in human capital, presented in Chapters 5, 8, and 9, suggest that if discrimination diminishes over time, it will diminish first with young adults. Job training—whether it is specific or general, on-the-job or given formally—takes place most often in one's young adult years, so it is this group that will be favored by any expansion of occupational opportunities. Young adults are also the group most likely to adjust to new opportunities by paying for their own education or training. Thus, human capital theory suggests that the eradication of discrimination's effects may be a long process that will tend to favor each successive generation of new workers over their older counterparts.

Tests of the notion that young adults are helped the most by antidiscrimination programs must take into account the fact that the age/earnings profiles of women and minorities tend to be flatter than those of white males, reflecting the smaller amounts of on-the-job training offered (or induced among) these groups. Thus, the ratio of earnings among these groups to similar-age white males tends to fall as age increases. The fact that the black/white earnings ratios in both columns of the table fall with experience reflects the more steeply sloped age/earnings profile for white male high school graduates, not the effects of antidiscrimination efforts on younger workers.

Male Black/White Earnings Ratios for High School Graduates of Various Experience, 1960 and 1970

Years of Experience	Black/White Ratio of Average Weekly Earnings	
	1960	1970
1–5	0.714	0.806
6–10	0.714	0.791
11–15 } 16–20 }	0.685	0.749 0.750
21–30	0.648	0.698
31–40	—	0.690

SOURCE: James P. Smith and Finis R. Welch, "Black-White Male Wage Ratios: 1960–70," *American Economic Review* 67(June 1977):323–38 (Table 1).

The pattern of reductions in earnings disparities can best be seen by comparing *changes* in the earnings ratios between 1960 and 1970 in the table. These comparisons can be made in two ways. First, let us follow the same groups of workers over time to see how their earnings ratios change. For example, males with 1–5 years of experience had a black/white earnings ratio of 0.714 in 1960. In 1970 this same group—then having 11–15 years of experience—had an earnings ratio of 0.749. Following the arrows in the table, we can see that each age group of black males experienced improvement relative to white males as they aged over the decade of the 1960s. Although those with 1–10 years of experience in 1960 gained to a greater extent than those with 11–20 years, those with 21–30 years of experience in 1960 gained to an even greater degree. Looked at this way, the young adults do not appear to have been the biggest group of gainers among black male high school graduates.

There is a second way of looking at the changes from 1960 to 1970, however. Instead of following the same group of workers over time, we could look to see how groups with the same experience in the two years fared. Beginning workers, for example, had an earnings ratio of 0.714 in 1960 but 0.806 in 1970. Those with 6–10 years of experience had a ratio of 0.714 in 1960, while the group 10 years behind them (with 6–10 years of experience in 1970) had a ratio of 0.791. This method suggests that the relative earnings position of the youngest blacks did improve the most.

What we can conclude from our two ways of comparing 1960 and 1970 is that while each group of black males improved in its own economic status from 1960 to 1970, the improvements were even larger for the groups 10 years their junior. To see this, look at those with 1–5 years of experience in 1960. The 1960 ratio for this group was 0.714, and in 1970 it had risen to 0.749 for the same group. However, the ratio for new workers (1–5 years of experience) in 1970 was an even higher 0.806. For those with 21–30 years of experience in 1960, the earnings ratio rose from 0.648 to 0.690; for those 10 years their junior (having 21–30 years of experience in 1970), however, the 1970 earnings ratio was 0.698.

Thus, it appears that while each age group of black males experienced relative improvement in earnings in the 1960s, the gains made by the groups that *followed* them were larger. A sobering aspect of the way in which these changes are taking place is that overall wage equality between blacks and whites will occur some 40 years after wage parity for *new* workers is attained. (It requires 40 years to "flush" the system of discrimination's victims if discrimination is first ended among younger workers.)

Ricans, and Central/South Americans, respectively.[7] The earnings of Cuban males did not appear to be adversely affected by labor market discrimination; if they acquired the same measured productive characteristics, on average, as non-Hispanic white males, it is estimated that they would earn about 6 percent more. Another study found that language proficiency explains virtually all the Hispanic/non-Hispanic wage differences.[8]

---

[7]Cordelia W. Reimers, "Labor Market Discrimination Against Hispanic and Black Men," *Review of Economics and Statistics* 65(November 1983):570–79. The findings are generally corroborated by an earlier study by James D. Gwartney and James E. Long, "The Relative Earnings of Blacks and Other Minorities," *Industrial and Labor Relations Review* 31(April 1978):336–46. *See* also Geoffrey Carliner, "Returns to Education for Blacks, Anglos, and Five Spanish Groups," *Journal of Human Resources* 11(Spring 1976):172–84; George Borjas, "The Earnings of Male Hispanic Immigrants in the United States," *Industrial and Labor Relations Review* 35(April 1982):343–53; and Gilles Grenier, "The Effects of Language Characteristics on the Wages of Hispanic-American Males," *Journal of Human Resources* 19(Winter 1984):35–52.

[8]Walter McManus, William Gould, and Finis Welch, "Earnings of Hispanic Men: The Role of English Language Proficiency," *Journal of Labor Economics* 1(April 1983):101–30.

Asians.　The issue of discrimination against Asians in the United States has not attracted much attention, probably because of their small numbers and generally high incomes. For example, as can be seen below, the earnings of male Asians (except Filipinos) tend to exceed those of whites. The ratios of earnings among males of Asian ancestry to the earnings of white males in 1970 were as follows:[9]

All Asians: 1.03
Chinese: 1.08
Japanese: 1.06
Filipino: 0.74

These data do not rule out current labor market discrimination against males of Chinese or Japanese ancestry because they do not control for productive characteristics. (Males in both groups, for example, tend to be better educated than the average white male.) Once these differences are accounted for, however, there appear to be no differences between the weekly earnings of whites and those of Chinese ancestry and only a 4 percent differential (in favor of whites) for males of Japanese ancestry. Filipinos, however, earn about 15 percent less per week than comparable white males. Thus, as with Hispanics, there appear to be considerable earnings differences among Asian groups even after controlling for productive characteristics.

Sex Differences

Differences in earnings between female and male workers are large. The average white, female, full-time worker earns roughly 60 percent of what her male counterpart earns. As one can see from Table 14.3, this ratio is down from what it was in 1955 and essentially unchanged since 1964. Further, women earn substantially less than men in each of the major occupational categories, with the ratios running from 42 percent in sales work to 76 percent among professionals. Not even in government work do women's incomes rise above 70 percent of men's, and among the self-employed the ratio is at its lowest (38 percent).

There are several factors other than labor market discrimination that could cause these large disparities. First, because the market-work life of a woman historically has been shorter than that of a man, women have had fewer incentives to invest in schooling and post-schooling training that is specifically oriented to the labor market.[10] (They, in essence, prepare for two careers—one at home and one in the labor market—and are thus typically less specialized than men.) The lack of on-the-job training, as noted in Chapter 9, is one reason why the age/earnings profiles for women are so flat, creating a greater disparity between women's and men's earnings as they grow older. Shorter working lives also mean that, within each occupational grouping, women are likely to be less experienced than men.

---

[9]Barry Chiswick, "An Analysis of the Earnings and Employment of Asian-American Men," *Journal of Labor Economics* 1(April 1983):197–214.

[10]In 1970 the expected years of lifetime work for pay were 40.1 for men and 22.9 for women. Thus, an average woman would be expected to work only 57 percent as long as an average man. These figures are changing rapidly, however; in 1960 the corresponding percentage was 48.6. See Howard Fullerton and James Byrne, "Length of Working Life for Men and Women, 1970," *Monthly Labor Review* 99(February 1976):31–35.

TABLE 14.3   **Ratio of Female/Male Wage and Salary Income for Year-Round, Full-Time White Workers**

Year	Ratio of Female/Male Income
1955	0.65
1964	0.59
1967	0.58
1970	0.59
1973	0.56
1977	0.58
1978	0.59
1980	0.59
1981	0.60
Private sector (1977)	
Professional-technical workers	0.76
Managerial	0.52
Sales	0.42
Clerical	0.64
Craft	0.59
Operatives	0.58
Laborer	0.64
Service	0.63
Government workers (1977)	
Federal—public administration	0.66
Federal—professional	0.68
State and local—public administration	0.60
State and local—professional	0.70
Self-employed, nonagricultural (1977)	0.38

SOURCES: 1955: U.S. Bureau of the Census, *Current Population Reports, Consumer Income,* Series P-60, No. 22 (September 1956), Table 7; 1964: U.S. Bureau of the Census, *Current Population Reports, Consumer Income: Income in 1964 of Families and Persons in the United States*, Series P-60, No. 47 (September 1965), Table 18; 1967–73: U.S. Bureau of the Census, *Current Population Reports, Consumer Income: Money Income in 1973 of Families and Persons in the United States*, Series P-60, No. 97 (January 1975), Table F; 1977: U.S. Bureau of the Census, *Current Population Reports, Consumer Income: Money Income in 1977 of Families and Persons in the United States*, Series P-60, No. 118 (March 1979), Table 55. 1978: U.S. Bureau of the Census, *Current Population Reports, Consumer Income: Money Income in 1978 of Families and Persons in the United States*, Series P-60, No. 123 (June 1980), Table 59. 1980: U.S. Bureau of the Census, *Current Population Reports, Consumer Income: Money Income of Households, Families, and Persons in the United States: 1980*, Series P-60, No. 132 (July 1982), Table 58. 1981: U.S. Bureau of the Census, *Current Population Reports, Consumer Income: Money Income and Poverty Status of Families and Persons in the United States: 1981*, Series P-60, No. 134 (July 1982), Table 11.

Second, because of traditional home responsibilities, women are less likely than men to work overtime or to choose occupations that offer jobs with high pay but long hours.[11] Home responsibilities also mean that women usually work closer to home than do men, a fact (as argued in Chapter 8) that implies lower wages.

---

[11]"Protective" labor legislation at the state level until recently often limited the maximum hours per week a woman could work, thus closing women out of overtime opportunities available to men.

Finally, historically women have tended to "follow" husbands when the husbands decided on the geographic location of their jobs (a fact noted in Chapter 10 and more explicitly in Example 10.2). Husbands, in effect, have been relatively free to choose their best offer, while wives have usually done the best they could *given* their geographical location. This sort of family decision-making behavior has also tended to reduce women's earnings.[12]

While the above *premarket* differences are not immediately generated by *labor market* discrimination, they will be *affected* by the presence of such discrimination. If current market discrimination exists, the resulting lower wage for women strengthens incentives for them to be the ones who engage in *household production*. The expectation that women will be the ones to stay home with children, for example, is probably the major reason behind each of the three premarket forces above. Anything that reduces the disproportionate share of women in household production will tend to increase their incentives to acquire human capital, work longer hours for pay, and select their jobs from a wider area. Thus, even though premarket differences are clearly important and deeply rooted in factors other than current labor market discrimination, measuring the extent of labor market discrimination and taking steps to end it is of obvious importance.

One way to obtain a sense of the extent of market discrimination is to look at the relative earnings of women who have never married. These women are not engaged in raising children and, unless involved in caring for a parent or sibling, do not have the household duties that usually befall married women. They tend to work almost as many hours per year as the average man, and they also exhibit concave age/earnings profiles.[13] Despite these closer similarities to men, however, the average income of never-married women age 25–64 is just 65 percent of that earned by the average man in that age group (as compared to 56 percent for married women).[14]

Before concluding that market discrimination is immediately responsible for most of the earnings gap between men and women, however, it is important to remember that the typical never-married person age 25–64 is probably younger and thus less experienced than the typical married person. It is also important to realize that human capital decisions are based on *expected* career life, and many never-married women may have expected to beome married when basic schooling or occupational decisions were made. In short, previously prevailing social expecta-

---

[12]Evidence that geographic migration usually causes husbands' earnings to rise but wives' earnings to fall was cited earlier (Chapter 10) based on Polachek and Horvath, "A Life Cycle Approach to Migration," *Research in Labor Economics* (Greenwich, Conn.: JAI Press, 1977). Other articles on the same topic are Robert H. Frank, "Why Women Earn Less: The Theory and Estimation of Differential Overqualification," *American Economic Review* 68(June 1978):360–73; and Mincer and Polachek, "Family Investments in Human Capital." Of course, increased female labor market attachment suggests that such patterns will not necessarily persist in the future.

[13]Victor Fuchs, "Differences in Hourly Earnings Between Men and Women," *Monthly Labor Review* 94,5(May 1971):9–15.

[14]These ratios are for full-time, year-round whites age 25–64 in 1977. *See* U.S. Bureau of the Census, *Current Population Reports: Money Income in 1977 of Families and Persons in the United States*, Series P-60, No. 118 (March 1979), Table 45.

tions about women's role in household production may also have influenced the human capital decisions of women who ultimately decided not to marry, causing their earnings to be lower than otherwise. Finally, the group of never-married adults is likely to contain a higher proportion of disabled persons than is found in the married group. Thus, while *some* of the 35 percent earnings differential for never-married women may be due to current labor market dicrimination, it is unlikely that *all* of the difference can be so attributed.

The best way to estimate the effects of market discrimination on the basis of sex is to perform the same kind of analysis reported earlier for black and white males. Thus we must ask, "What would the female/male earnings ratio be, on average, if women had the same education, training, experience, hours of work, commuting distance, turnover rate, and other productive characteristics as their male counterparts?" Studies that have attempted to answer this question have generally concluded that differences in education, training, turnover, and experience—but primarily experience—account for one third to two thirds of the earnings differences between men and women.[15] Thus, it appears that *labor market* discrimination can account for no more than two thirds of the earnings gap between men and women.

One aspect of alleged labor market discrimination against women is *occupational segregation*—the reservation of some jobs for men and others (mostly lower-paying ones) for women. Some dimensions of this segregation and its effects can be seen in Table 14.4, which presents for 1970 and 1981 the share of women in a variety of high-paying and low-paying occupations. Two things are especially notable in the table. First, very few of the high-paying occupations employed women to an extent even close to their overall proportion among all employed workers (43 percent in 1981). On the other hand, women were heavily *over-represented* in the low-paying occupations. Second, in the eleven years from 1970 to 1981, the proportion of women in most of the high-paying jobs rose much faster than their overall proportion among the employed, while their proportions in the lower-paying fell.

How much of the market discrimination against women takes the form of occupational segregation and how much takes the form of different wages *within* given occupations? A crude answer to this question can be obtained by estimating the wage women would make if they had productive characteristics similar to the average male. Comparing this estimated wage to the average male wage will yield an estimate of overall market discrimination. If we then estimate the wage women would receive if they had the same productive characteristics *and* the same *occupational* distribution as men, we can calculate the wage disparities caused solely by occupational differences. The most widely quoted study of the effects of occupational segregation suggests that equalizing the occupational distribution of men and

---

[15]Corcoran and Duncan, "Work History, Labor Force Attachment, and Earnings Differences Between the Races and Sexes"; Mincer and Polachek, "Family Investments in Human Capital: Earnings of Women"; and Sharon P. Smith, *Equal Pay in the Public Sector: Fact or Fantasy* (Princeton, N.J.: Industrial Relations Section, Princeton University, 1977).

TABLE 14.4   Representation of Women in Ten High-Paying and Ten Low-Paying Occupations, 1970 and 1981

	Percent Female	
Occupation	*1970*	*1981*
High-paying		
Stock and bond sales agents	8.6	17.1
Managers and administrators, n.e.c.[a]	11.6	19.6
Bank officials and financial managers	17.4	36.5
Sales representatives, manufacturing	8.5	16.0
Designers	23.5	23.9
Personnel and labor-relations workers	31.2	48.7
Sales representatives, wholesale	6.4	10.7
Computer programmers	22.7	28.4
Low-paying		
Practical nurses	96.3	97.3
Hairdressers and cosmetologists	90.4	85.3
Cooks, except private household	62.8	50.9
Health aides, except nursing	83.9	82.7
Nurses' aides	84.6	84.3
Sewers and stitchers	93.8	96.7
Farm laborers	13.2	12.3
Child-care workers, except private household	93.2	86.7
All occupations	37.7	43.0

[a]The initials n.e.c. mean "not elsewhere classified."

SOURCES: Sharon Smith, "Men's Jobs, Women's Jobs and Differential Wage Treatment," *Job Evaluation and EEO: The Emerging Issues*, papers presented at the Industrial Relations Counselors Colloquium, September 14–15, 1978, Atlanta, Georgia (New York: Industrial Relations Counselors, 1979), pp. 67–84; Nancy R. Rytina, "Earnings of Men and Women: A Look at Specific Occupations," *Monthly Labor Review* 105(April 1982):25–31.

women with the same education and years of experience would reduce the earnings gap by 9 percentage points.[16]

It would appear, then, that perhaps half of the overall 40 percent differential between the earnings of men and women is due to premarket factors. Of the remaining 20 percent, which could be due to current market discrimination, roughly half again (9 percentage points) appears to be the consequence of occupational segregation. The effect of occupational segregation *could* be larger than this, however, because the "occupations" referred to in the study are very general categories, such as professional-technical worker, manager, clerical worker, skilled

---

[16]Ronald Oaxaca, "Male-Female Wage Differentials in Urban Labor Markets," *International Economic Review* 14,3(October 1973):693–709. For other studies related to occupational segregation and its effects, see Julianne M. Malveaux, "Moving Forward, Standing Still: Women in White-Collar Jobs," in *Women in the Workplace*, ed. Phyllis A. Wallace (Boston: Auburn House Publishing Company, 1982), pp. 101–34, and Andrea H. Beller, "Occupational Segregation by Sex: Determinants and Changes," *Journal of Human Resources* 17(Summer 1982):371–92.

craft worker, and so forth. Not captured in the analysis, then, are the effects of segregation *within* these broad groupings. For example, an insurance company that was later the object of a sex discrimination lawsuit had, between 1964 and 1970, hired men and women with college degrees to be "claims adjustors" and "claims representatives." The educational requirements for each job were the same, but only men were hired as "adjustors," and almost all "representatives" were women. Claims adjustors received $2,500 more in yearly salary to begin with, and only adjustors could be promoted to higher-level supervisory positions. Both positions are in the same general occupational class, but both pay and future opportunities were much better for the male workers.[17]

One study of professional-technical employees in a large corporation found that men and women with the same job level and the same characteristics received equal pay. However, in most cases women were assigned to lower job levels than equally qualified men. While one cannot generalize from the experience of a single corporation, the results of *this* study suggest that most sex discrimination may be due to occupational segregation.[18]

Note, however, that not all occupational segregation is the result of current employer practices that exclude qualified women from higher-paying jobs. Premarket forces, beginning early in childhood, instill beliefs in women and men alike that some occupations are "women's work" and some are "men's work." These beliefs keep women out of many low-paying laborer jobs and exclude them from high-paying jobs as well. These notions will probably change over time as alternative role models become available, but not *all* these feelings can be attributed to *current* employer practices.

THEORIES OF MARKET DISCRIMINATION

As argued in the previous section, one cannot rule out the presence of substantial discrimination against women and minorities in the labor market. Before one can design policies to end discrimination, one must understand the *sources* and *mechanisms* causing it. The goal of this section is to lay out and evaluate the different theories of discrimination proposed by economists.

Three general sources of labor market discrimination have been hypothesized, and each source suggests an associated model of how discrimination is implemented and what its consequences are.[19] The first source of discrimination is *personal prejudice,* wherein employers, fellow employees, or customers dislike associating

---

[17]Barbara Bergmann, "Reducing the Pervasiveness of Discrimination," in *Jobs for Americans,* ed. Eli Ginzburg (Englewood Cliffs, N.J.: Prentice-Hall, Inc., 1976).

[18]Burton G. Malkiel and Judith A. Malkiel, "Male-Female Pay Differentials in Professional Employment," *American Economic Review* 63(September 1973):693–705.

[19]Two of the three general models were labeled by Kenneth Boulding, "Toward a Theory of Discrimination," in *Equal Opportunity and the AT&T Case,* ed. Phyllis Wallace (Cambridge, Mass.: The MIT Press, 1976).

with workers of a given race or sex.[20] The second general source is *statistical prejudgment,* whereby employers project onto *individuals* certain perceived *group* characteristics. Finally, there are models according to which the desire for, and use of, *monopoly power* is the source of discrimination. While all the models generate useful, suggestive insights, none has been convincingly established as superior.

Personal Prejudice

Employer discrimination.   Suppose that white male *employers* are prejudiced against women and minorities but that (for sake of simplicity) customers and fellow employees are not prejudiced. This prejudice may take the form of aversion to associating with women and minorities, it may be manifest as a desire to help fellow white males whenever possible, or it may be motivated by status considerations and take the form of occupational segregation. In whatever form, this prejudice is assumed to result in the discriminatory treatment of women and minorities. Further, we assume for the purposes of this model that the women and minorities in question have the same productive characteristics as white males. (This assumption directs our focus to market discrimination by putting aside premarket factors.)

   If employers have a decided preference for hiring white males in high-paying jobs despite the availability of equally qualified women and minorities, they will act *as if* the latter were less productive than the former. By virtue of our assumption that the women and minorities involved are equally productive in every way, the devaluing of their productivity by employers is purely subjective and is a manifestation of personal prejudice. The more prejudiced an employer is, the more actual productivity will be discounted.

   Suppose that MP stands for the actual marginal productivity of all workers in a particular labor market and d represents the extent to which this productivity is subjectively devalued for minorities and women. In this case, market equilibrium for white males is reached when their wage (W_M) equals MP:

$$MP = W_M. \tag{14.1}$$

   For the women and minorities, however, equilibrium is achieved only when their wage (W_F) equals their *subjective* value to firms:

$$MP - d = W_F, \text{ or} \tag{14.2}$$

$$MP = W_F + d. \tag{14.2a}$$

Since the actual marginal productivities are equal by assumption, equations (14.1) and (14.2a) are equal to each other, and one can easily see that W_F must be less than W_M:

$$W_M = W_F + d, \text{ or} \tag{14.3}$$

$$W_F = W_M - d. \tag{14.3a}$$

---

[20]The models of personal prejudice are based on Gary S. Becker, *The Economics of Discrimination,* 2nd ed. (Chicago: University of Chicago Press, 1971).

What this says algebraically has a very simple economic logic: if the actual productivity of women and minorities is devalued by employers, workers in these groups must offer their services at lower wages than white males to compete for jobs.

This model of employer discrimination has two major implications, as illustrated by Figure 14.1, which is a graphic representation of equation (14.2a). Figure 14.1 shows that a discriminating employer faced with a wage rate of W_F for women and minorities will hire N_0, for at that point $MP = W_F + d$. *Profit-maximizing* employers, however, will hire N_1; that is, they will hire until $MP = W_F$. The effects on profits can be readily seen in Figure 14.1 if one remembers that the area under the MP curve represents total product (or total revenues) of the firm, with capital held constant. Subtracting the area representing the wage bill of the discriminating employer $(OEFN_0)$ yields profits for these employers equal to the area $AEFB$. Profits for a nondiscriminating employer, however, are AEG. These latter employers hire women and minorities to the point where their marginal product equals their wage, while the discriminators end their hiring short of that point. Discriminators thus give up profits in order to indulge their prejudices.

The second implication of our employer discrimination model concerns the size of the gap between W_M and W_F. The determinants of this gap can best be understood using a graph of the supply of jobs to women or minorities (see Figure 14.2). In a labor market in which workers of equal productivity are seeking jobs, the supply of job opportunities for women and minorities will be a function of the gap $(W_M - W_F = d)$ between their wages and those of white males. As shown in Figure 14.2, some employers will hire women and minorities even if their wages equal W_M $(d = 0)$.

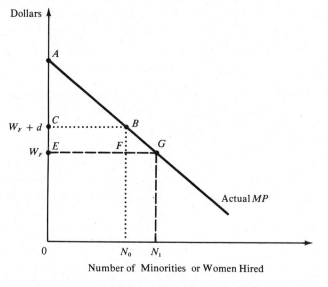

**FIGURE 14.1   Equilibrium Employment of Women
and Minorities in Firms That Discriminate**

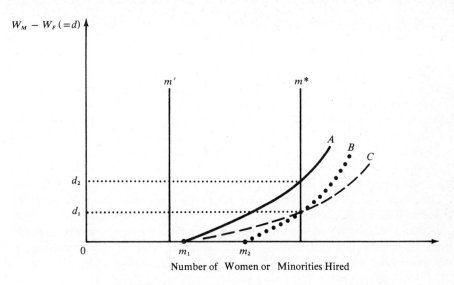

FIGURE 14.2   The Supply of Jobs to Women and Minorities

These are the nondiscriminating (profit-maximizing) employers, and supply curve $0m_1A$ assumes they account for m_1^- jobs in the market. If there are less than m_1 minorities or women seeking employment in that labor market (m', say), they would all be hired by the nondiscriminators and no discrimination would be evident. W_F would equal W_M, and women and minorities would not have to deal with those who devalued their services.

If the supply of women and minorities were greater than the number that could be absorbed by the nondiscriminating employers (m^*, say), then a wage gap would have to arise for all of them to become employed. Curve $0m_1A$ shows that if the number of women and minorities seeking jobs were to increase from m' to m^*, the required gap would rise from zero to d_2. Thus, the gap depends in part on the sheer size of the groups against whom there is personal prejudice. If the number of women or minorities seeking jobs were to rise beyond m^*, the difference between W_M and W_F would become greater than d_2.

The equilibrium gap between W_M and W_F, however, also depends on the distribution and extent of employer prejudice against women or minorities. If the number of nondiscriminatory employers grew (or if the number of jobs offered by such employers grew), the supply-of-jobs curve in Figure 14.2 would shift to the right from $0m_1A$ to $0m_2B$. This shift would reduce the observed wage disparity at m^* from d_2 to d_1. The same reduction in market discrimination could also occur if the number of nondiscriminators stayed constant but the *discriminatory preferences* of the others were *reduced*. If this were to happen, discriminatory employers would require less of a wage disparity to hire a given level of women or minorities, and the supply-of-jobs curve would shift to something like $0m_1C$ in Figure 14.2.

The most disturbing implication of the employer discrimination model is that discriminators seem to be maximizing *utility* (satisfying their prejudices) instead of *profits*. This practice should immediately raise the question of how they survive. Firms in competitive labor markets *must* maximize profits just to make a normal rate of return on invested capital. Those who do not make this return will find they can earn a better return by investing some other way—a way, perhaps, that does not involve hiring workers. Conversely, since profit-maximizing (nondiscriminating) firms would normally make more money from a given set of assets than would discriminators, we should observe nondiscriminatory firms buying out others and gradually taking over the market. In short, if competitive forces were at work, employers who discriminate would be punished and discrimination should gradually disappear.

An implication of the employer discrimination model, then, is that wage disparities will lessen naturally over time—an implication that appears to be contradicted by the facts. The figures on race and sex wage disparities in Tables 14.2 and 14.3 show great stability over many years; recent improvements for blacks can be seen, but these improvements are coincident with the adoption of various *governmental* programs aimed at ending poverty and discrimination.

Does this apparent inconsistency with the facts mean that the employer discrimination model is inappropriate or wrong? Some have suggested that the model really applies only to monopolistic or oligopolistic employers who are shielded from market forces. It is argued that these firms do not have to maximize profits to survive, so they are freer to indulge in the "luxury" of discrimination. There is some evidence that blacks are disproportionately employed in industries that are competitive and are not very well represented in large, higher-paying, oligopolistic firms.[21] However, very large firms tend to have higher skill requirements than competitive firms anyway, and that alone could explain the underrepresentation of blacks in those firms. Further, the sector most insulated from the pressures of costs and competition is the government, and as Table 14.3 showed for women, wage disparities in this sector are less than in the private sector. Thus, serious questions must be raised about how applicable this model of employer discrimination is in explaining labor market discrimination.

Customer discrimination.   A second personal prejudice model stresses *customer* prejudice as a source of discrimination. Customers may prefer to be served by white males in some situations and by minorities or women in others. If their preferences for white males extend to jobs requiring major responsibility—such as physician, stockbroker, or airline pilot—and their preferences for women and minorities are confined to less skilled jobs—nurse or flight attendant, say—then occupational segregation that works to the disadvantage of women and minorities will occur. Further, if women or minorities are to find employment in the jobs for which customers prefer white males, they must either accept *lower wages* or be

---

[21]Becker, *The Economics of Discrimination*, p. 48; Ray Marshall, "The Economics of Racial Discrimination: A Survey," *Journal of Economic Literature* 12(September 1974):864; and David P. Taylor, "Discrimination and Occupational Wage Differences in the Market for Unskilled Labor," *Industrial and Labor Relations Review* 21(April 1968):375–90.

more qualified than the average white male. The reason for this is that their value to the firm is lower than that of *equally qualified* white males because of customers' preferences for white males.

A major implication of the theory of customer discrimination is that women or minorities in jobs that involve no customer contact or who work for employers who have no competition should face very little, if any, discrimination. Those with the most customer contact are the most vulnerable to discrimination, as manifested by unequal wages for equally qualified people, occupational segregation, or both. The evidence to support this model is somewhat ambiguous. For example, the overall ratio of black-to-white earnings for full-time male workers in the private sector was 0.67 in 1977. Operatives, most of whom are factory workers with little public contact, fare better than average in the private sector (0.81), while there are so few blacks in sales jobs that comparable black/white ratios are not even published. Self-employed black males earn incomes that are 41 percent of self-employed whites.[22] Table 14.3 tells much the same story for women. Operatives and government workers do better than self-employed or sales workers; however, operatives do slightly worse than those in occupations that may have more public contact.

There are obviously serious drawbacks to the above figures as measures of discrimination. Self-employed white males may own retail stores or electronics factories, and self-employed minorities or women may own magazine stands or janitorial services. Women in the sales field may be department-store clerks, while men may be involved with higher-technology sales. Black operatives may be much more heavily unionized than average.[23] It is thus obvious that the gross ratios given above do not take into account human capital or other important differences.

Studies that *do* take into account individual productive characteristics have been done for federal government and private sector employees of different races and sexes. These studies find that differences in productive characteristics between white males and other workers do not explain all the earnings differentials that exist in either sector. However, as one might expect if customer discrimination were present, the "unexplained" differential tends to be smaller in the federal sector (which has no competitors and is not run for profit).[24]

The existence of unexplained race and sex earnings differentials in the federal sector, despite their smaller size than in the private sector, suggests the *possibility* of labor market discrimination in the federal sector. Interestingly, the racial *composition* of federal employment follows a pattern that is also consistent with the *customer* discrimination model. Agencies that serve heavily minority-oriented constituencies hire greater fractions of minorities than agencies whose constituents are

---

[22]The ratios quoted are for 1977 and are obtained from U.S. Bureau of the Census, *Current Population Reports, Consumer Income: Money Income in 1977 of Families and Persons in the United States,* Series P-60, No. 118 (March1979), Table 55.

[23]Orley Ashenfelter, "Discrimination and Trade Unions," in *Discrimination in Labor Markets,* ed. Orley Ashenfelter and Albert Rees.

[24]Smith, *Equal Pay in the Public Sector;* and James E. Long, "Employment Discrimination in the Federal Sector," *Journal of Human Resources* 11,1(1976):86–97.

mainly white: employment with the Department of Housing and Urban Development is 27 percent minority, while that with the Department of Agriculture is 10 percent minority.[25] Whether this political version of the customer discrimination hypothesis will stand up under further testing remains to be seen. While federal administrators may be sensitive to voter prejudices, the issues on which their elected superiors run are so diverse that one may legitimately wonder just how voter prejudices are communicated and enforced. At the moment, though, the existence of customer discrimination in the labor market cannot be ruled out on logical or empirical grounds.

Employee discrimination.

A third source of discrimination based on personal prejudice might be found on the supply side of the market, where white male workers may avoid situations in which minorities or women fill certain jobs they consider inappropriate. For example, they may resist taking orders from a woman, sharing responsibility with a minority member, or working where women or minorities are not confined to low-status jobs.

If white male workers have these discriminatory preferences, they will tend to quit (or avoid) employers who employ women or minorities on a nondiscriminatory basis. Employers, if they wish to hire or retain white males, will have to pay them more than they would if they confined women and minorities to their "traditional," lower-status jobs. In some cases employers may be able to avoid the higher cost of employing white males by running racially or sexually segregated plants. Segregated plants, however, are not always feasible because of the wide range of occupations required and the fact that workers of different races and sexes are not evenly distributed in each occupation.

It is interesting to note that this model of employee discrimination predicts that white males working in integrated environments will receive higher wages than those with exactly the same productive characteristics who work in segregated environments. If we could observe areas in which there were no minority workers, say, we would expect white men's wages in these areas to be pretty much the same for people embodying comparable human capital. However, in areas where blacks are found in sufficient numbers that many whites must work in integrated plants, we should observe that the wages received by white males of equal human capital will *vary* according to whether they work in segregated or integrated firms. Thus, the theory suggests that the wages received by white males within any given human capital category will show *greater similarity* when integrated work forces are rare than when some whites work in integrated environments and some do not. When one looks at U.S. data, one does in fact find that, other things equal, white men's wages are more similar in states where the minority population is small—and where, presumably, few whites work in integrated plants—than they are where the

---

[25]For an analysis of this subject, see George J. Borjas, "The Politics of Racial Discrimination in the Federal Government," *Journal of Law and Economics* 25(October 1982):271–99.

minority population is large. Moreover, this finding seems to be true of both Northern and Southern states considered separately.[26]

The interesting thing about the above finding is that neither the employer nor the customer models of discrimination predict that *white* men's wages will become *less similar* if discrimination exists. If white males are preferred for particular higher-paying jobs, their wages will be higher than if discrimination were nonexistent. However, the fact that their wages are *higher* does not imply they are more *dissimilar*. White males who, in the absence of discrimination, would have wages clustering around some lower level instead have wages clustering around some higher level. The point is that their wages continue to cluster. However, the above finding offers only indirect support for the employee discrimination model, and it is also consistent with predictions of the "monopoly power" model outlined below. Hence, convincing evidence for the existence of employee discrimination cannot be claimed.

Statistical Discrimination

Another source of discrimination might be the kind and quality of information used in making hiring decisions.[27] Employers must try to *guess* the potential productivity of applicants, but rarely will they know what actual productivity will be. The only information available to them at the time of hire is information that is thought to be *correlated* with productivity: education, experience, age, test scores, and so forth. These correlates are imperfect predictors of actual productivity, however, and employers realize this. To some extent, then, they supplement information on these correlates with a subjective element in making hiring decisions, and this subjective element could *look* like discrimination even though it might not be rooted in personal prejudice.

Statistical discrimination can be viewed as a part of the *screening problem*, which arises when observable personal characteristics that are correlated with productivity are not perfect predictors. By way of example, suppose two types of workers apply for a secretarial job: those who can type 70 words per minute (wpm) over the long haul and those who can type 40 wpm. These actual productivities are unknown to the employer, however. All the employer observes are the results of a 5-minute typing test administered to all applicants. What are the problems created by the use of this test as a screening device?

---

[26]Barry R. Chiswick, "Racial Discrimination in the Labor Market: A Test of Alternative Hypotheses," *Journal of Political Economy* 81,6(November 1973):1330–52. It should be noted that the inequality of *minority* earnings does not vary according to their proportion in the population, a finding that seems to rule out the existence of some other, unmeasured force causing greater inequality in high-minority states.

[27]The considerations developed in this section are more formally and completely treated in Dennis J. Aigner and Glen G. Cain, "Statistical Theories of Discrimination in Labor Markets," *Industrial and Labor Relations Review* 30,2(January 1977):175–87. A similar theory is developed in M. A. Spence, "Job Market Signaling," *Quarterly Journal of Economics* 87,3(August 1973):355–74.

The problems relate to the fact that some typists who can really type only 40 wpm on the job will be lucky and score higher than 40 on the test. Others who can really type 70 wpm on the job will be unlucky and score less than 70 on the test. The imperfection of test as a predictor will cause two kinds of errors in hiring decisions: some "good" applicants will be rejected, and some "bad" workers will be hired.

Figure 14.3 shows the test-score distributions for both groups of workers. Those who can actually type 70 wpm score 70 on average, but half score less. Likewise, half of the other group scores better than 40 on the test. If an applicant scores 55, say, the employer does not know if the applicant is a good (70 wpm) or bad (40 wpm) typist. If those scoring 55 are automatically rejected, the firm will be rejecting some good workers, and if it needs workers badly, this policy will entail costs. Likewise, if it accepts those scoring 55, some bad workers will be hired.

In an effort to avoid the above dilemma, suppose the employer does some research and finds out that applicants from a particular business school are specifically coached to perform well on 5-minute typing tests. Thus, applicants who can actually type X words per minute over a normal day will tend to score *higher* than X wpm on a 5-minute test due to the special coaching (that is, they will appear better than they really are). Recognizing that students from this school are likely to have test scores above their long-run productivity, the firm might decide to reject all applicants from this school who score 55 or below (on the grounds that, for most, the test score overestimates their ability), even though some who score less than 55 really can do better.

The general lesson of this example is that, in effect, firms will use both *individual* data (test scores, educational attainment, experience) and *group* data in making hiring decisions when the former are not perfect predictors of productivity. However, this use of group data can give rise to market discrimination because people with the same *measured productive characteristics* (test scores, education, etc.) will be treated differently on a systematic basis depending on *group* affiliation.

The relevance of the above discussion to the problem of discrimination against

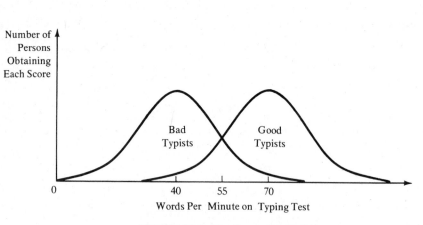

FIGURE 14.3 The Screening Problem

minorities and women is that race and sex may well be the group information used to supplement individual data in making hiring decisions. If the group data bear no relationship, on average, to actual productivity, then we really have a case of discrimination rooted in personal prejudice or monopoly power. However, we have shown that the use of group data to modify individual information may be based on nonmalicious grounds. Might these grounds legitimately apply from an employer's perspective to minorities and women?

Suppose that, *on average,* minorities with high school educations are discovered to be less productive than white males with high school educations owing to differences in schooling quality. Or suppose that, because of shortened career lives, women with a given educational level are, *on average,* less valuable to firms than men of equal education (refer back to our discussion of women and job training in Chapter 5). Employers might employ this group information to modify individual data when making hiring decisions, just as they did in our hypothetical example of the business school above. The result would be that white males with given measured characteristics would be systematically preferred over women or minorities with the same characteristics, a condition that would be empirically identified as labor market discrimination.

One unfortunate side effect of using group data to supplement individual data is that, while it could lead employers to the correct hiring decisions on average, it assigns a group characteristic to people who may not be typical of the group. There are women who will have long, uninterrupted careers, just as there undoubtedly would be graduates from the business school mentioned above who do not test well and thus perform more poorly on tests than they could do on the job. There will also be minority high school graduates of substantial ability who would have gone to college had not family poverty intervened. These atypical group members are stigmatized by the use of group data. They may have actual productivity equal to those who get hired but because of the group association do not get the job.[28]

Thus, *statistical discrimination* could lead to a systematic preference for white males over others with the same *measured* characteristics, and it could also create a situation in which minorities or women who are the equals of white males in *actual* productivity are paid less because of the above-mentioned group stigma. Both problems are caused by the use of group data in making hiring decisions, but this use need not be motivated by prejudice. The results, however, have the same appearance and effects as if prejudice were present.

An important implication of this model of statistical discrimination is that the use of group data will become a more costly screening device as members of each group become more dissimilar. For example, as greater proportions of women desire to work in full-time, year-round careers—and do not intend to drop out of the labor force to raise children—employers using sex as a handy index of labor force attachment will find themselves making costly mistakes. They will reject many

---

[28]The discussion here has obvious relevance to the ''signaling'' issue discussed in Chapter 9. Minorities, for example, may be *too poor* to acquire the necessary ''signal'' in many cases where their ability would indicate they should.

female applicants who have a permanent labor force attachment (in whom an investment in specific training would be very worthwhile), and they may accept male applicants who are less productive. In either case, firms using incorrect screening devices will have lower profits than those that adopt appropriate screens. Thus, as *premarket* differences between the races or sexes narrow, the use of race or sex *group* data should lessen and statistical discrimination should gradually disappear.

Monopoly Power Models

The persistence of large race/sex earnings disparities has led some labor economists to wonder whether the above models are really appropriate. These economists are dissenters from the orthodox view that labor markets are essentially competitive; instead, they advance *monopoly power theories* of discrimination. Inherent in these more radical views of the labor market is the assertion that discrimination exists and persists because it is *profitable* for the discriminators.

While monopoly power theories of discrimination vary from each other in emphasis, they tend to share the feature that race or sex is collectively used to divide the labor force into *noncompeting* groups, creating or perpetuating a kind of worker caste system. These theories clearly suggest that competitive forces fail to operate in the labor market.[29] Three versions of these models are outlined below.

Crowding. Occupational segregation, especially by sex, is pervasive. In 1974, for example, men were significantly overrepresented in 163 of 267 major occupations (61 percent) and women in 85 (or 32 percent); in only 19 occupations (7 percent) were men and women represented in proportions close to their proportions in the work force.[30] Moreover, over 40 percent of all employed women were found in just 10 occupations (secretary, retail trade, sales worker, elementary school teacher, waitress, typist, cashier, sewer and stitcher, cashier, registered nurse). These facts have caused some to argue that, because the occupations available to women are relatively limited, those who want to work for pay are in *crowded* labor markets and as a result face lower wages.

Graphically, the "crowding hypothesis" is very simple and can be easily seen in Figure 14.4. Panel (a) illustrates a market in which supply is small relative to demand and the wage (W_H) is thus relatively high. Panel (b) depicts a market in which crowding causes supply to be large relative to demand, resulting in a wage (W_L) that is comparatively low.

---

[29]For a summary of these views, *see* Glen G. Cain, "The Challenge of Segmented Labor Market Theories to Orthodox Theory: A Survey," *Journal of Economic Literature* 14(December 1976):1215–57.

[30]The data in this paragraph are from Andrea Beller, "Occupational Segregation by Sex: Determinants and Changes," *Journal of Human Resources* 17(Summer 1982):371–92. A sex group is considered overrepresented if its share in the occupation is 5 percentage points above its share in the employed labor force.

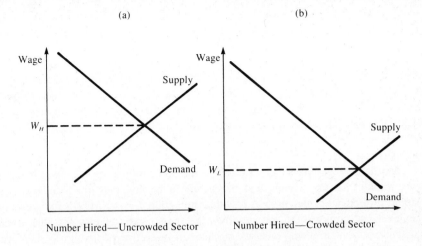

FIGURE 14.4   Labor Market "Crowding"

While the effects of crowding are easily seen, the phenomenon of crowding itself is less easily explained. If men and women were equally productive in a given job or set of jobs, for example, one would think that the lower wage of women would make it attractive for firms now employing men to seek out female workers instead, and this profit-maximizing behavior would eventually eliminate any wage differential. The failure of crowding, or occupational segregation, to disappear suggests the presence of noncompeting groups, as we noted above, but we are still left with trying to explain why such groups exist. Over the last 70 years various possible explanations have been put forth: the establishment of some jobs as "male" and others as "female" through social custom,[31] differences in aptitude that are either innate or acquired,[32] and different supply curves of men and women to noncompeting (monopsonistic) employers.[33] None of these explanations is complete in the sense of getting at the ultimate source of discrimination.[34]

Dual labor markets.   A variant of the crowding hypothesis with more recent origins is the view, held by some economists, that there is a *dual labor market*.

[31]Millicent Fawcett, "Equal Pay for Equal Work," *Economic Journal* 28(March 1918):1–6.

[32]F. Y. Edgeworth, "Equal Pay to Men and Women for Equal Work," *Economic Journal* 32(December 1922):431–57.

[33]Joan Robinson, *The Economics of Imperfect Competition* (London: MacMillan and Co., Ltd., 1934), pp. 301–4.

[34]An excellent history of crowding theories is provided in Janice F. Madden, *The Economics of Sex Discrimination* (Lexington, Mass.: Lexington Books, 1973), pp. 30–36. The crowding hypothesis is nicely advanced also in Barbara Bergmann, "The Effect on White Incomes of Discrimination in Employment," *Journal of Political Economy* 79(March–April 1971):294–313.

Dualists see the overall labor market as divided into two noncompeting markets: a *primary* and a *secondary* market.[35] Unlike the primary labor market, the secondary market offers low-wage, unstable, dead-end jobs. Workers relegated to these secondary jobs, it is believed, are tagged as unstable, undesirable workers and can never have much hope of acquiring a job in the primary sector. Since a large number of minorities and women are in the secondary market, discrimination against them tends to be perpetuated. Minorities and women, it is argued, are discriminated against because they tend (as a group) to have unstable work histories, but these histories are themselves a result of being unable to break into the primary labor market.

The dual labor market description of discrimination does not really explain what initially caused women and minorities to be confined to secondary jobs. Rather, it offers an explanation of why discrimination *persists*. It calls into question the levels of competition and mobility that exist and suggests that the initial existence of noncompeting race/sex groups will be self-perpetuating. In short, the dual labor market hypothesis is consistent with any of the models of discrimination analyzed above; what it does suggest is that if any of these theories *are* applicable, we cannot count on natural market forces to eliminate the discrimination that results.

Collusive action.   Other nonorthodox theories claim that white employers collude and become monopsonists with respect to the hiring of minority labor. Minorities are subjugated and held immobile while monopsonistic wages are forced on them.[36] One of the more cogent and complete *power theories* of discrimination argues that prejudice and the conflicts it creates are inherent in a capitalist society because they serve the interests of owners.[37] Even if the owners of capital did not conspire to *create* prejudice, they nevertheless find that if it continues they can enhance their profits. Workers divided by race or sex are harder to organize, and if they *are* unionized, are less cohesive in their demands. Further, antagonisms on the shop floor deflect attention from grievances related to working conditions. Hence, it is argued that owners of capital gain, while *all* workers—but particularly minorities and women—lose from discrimination.

Two pieces of evidence are cited to support this theory. First, in areas in which black/white earnings differentials are largest, the income inequality among *whites* is also greatest, other things equal (the greater inequality of white incomes is attributed to *owner/worker* income disparities). This kind of finding was mentioned above when we discussed employee discrimination, and there the greater inequality among whites was attributed to wage differences among white *workers*. Thus, this

[35]Michael J. Piore, "Jobs and Training: Manpower Policy," in *The State and the Poor,* ed. S. Beer and R. Barringer (Cambridge, Mass.: Winthrop Press, 1970).

[36]Lester Thurow, *The Economics of Poverty and Discrimination* (Washington, D.C.: The Brookings Institution, 1969).

[37]Michael Reich, "The Economics of Racism," in *Problems in Political Economy: An Urban Perspective,* ed. David M. Gordon (Lexington, Mass.: D. C. Heath and Company, 1971), pp. 107–13.

first piece of evidence seems more or less consistent with a theory of employee discrimination, as well as the power model.[38]

The second piece of evidence cited to support this power theory is that where black/white earnings differences are greatest, the percentage of the labor force that is unionized tends to be smallest. The strength of this argument decreases, however, when one realizes that the *causation* might be *reversed*. Rather than more racism causing less unionization, it could be that more unionization causes race discrimination to diminish. Evidence on this point was mentioned in Chapter 12 and is discussed later in this chapter.

Like the orthodox theories of discrimination, then, the monopoly power theories can muster only weak empirical support. They also share with the orthodox theories problems of logical consistency or completeness. If discrimination is created or at least perpetuated by capitalists, how does one account for its existence in precapitalist or socialist societies? It may be true that if all white employers conspire to keep women and minorities in low-wage, low-status jobs, they can all reap monopoly profits. However, if Employers A through Y adhere to the agreement, Employer Z will always have incentives to *break* the agreement! Z can hire women or minorities cheaply because of the agreement among *other* employers not to hire them, and Z can enhance profits by hiring these otherwise equally productive workers to fill jobs that A through Y are staffing with high-priced white males. Since each and every other employer has the same incentives as Z, the conspiracy will tend to break down unless cheaters can be disciplined in some way. The dual labor market and power theorists do not tell us how the conspiracy is maintained and coordinated among the millions of U.S. employers. Thus their theories, like the orthodox ones, are less than completely satisfactory.

Evaluation of Discrimination Theories

Our analysis of the different theories of discrimination suggests that if discrimination persists, it is the result of forces that hinder *competition* or labor market *adjustments* to competitive forces. Some theories—the "power" models—postulate the existence of noncompetitive or monopoly elements at the outset. The "orthodox" theories do not, but they have trouble explaining why discrimination *would* persist. The market should punish employers who discriminate or who fail to change their screening methods as the average characteristics of minorities or women change. A competitive market should drive employers to adopt *segregated* work places if employee discrimination exists; if customer discrimination exists,

---

[38]A major difference between the Chiswick study of employee discrimination and Reich's test of the power model is that the former related white income inequality to the percentage of nonwhites in the population, while the latter related it to the ratio of nonwhite to white earnings. Which is the more appropriate test is a matter beyond the scope of this text; however, we should note that observed earnings ratios can reflect human capital differences as well as current discrimination. This issue illustrates the importance of *theoretical* analysis in both the execution and interpretation of empirical studies.

customers who discriminate will be punished by having to pay the higher prices associated with being served only by white males.

It would thus appear that all models of discrimination agree on one thing: any persistence of labor market discrimination would be the result of forces or motivations that are blatantly noncompetitive or very slow to adjust to competitive forces. While no one model can be demonstrated superior to the others in explaining the facts, the various theories and the facts they seek to explain suggest that government intervention could be useful in eliminating the noncompetitive (or sluggish) influences.

STATE FAIR EMPLOYMENT PRACTICE LEGISLATION

Since the 1930s, about 30 states have enacted *fair employment practice laws* prohibiting discrimination in employment on the basis of race, creed, color, or national origin. (Unlike the federal legislation discussed below, the state laws did not address employment discrimination by sex.) These state laws normally established enforcement commissions and provided for fines and/or imprisonment for violators of the law.

Under state fair employment practice legislation, it is normally illegal for an organization to do at least one of the following: refuse employment or discharge employees because of race, or discriminate in compensation or other terms of employment by race. Our discussion of theories of market discrimination earlier in the chapter suggests that if a law contains only one of these provisions, it is likely to be ineffective in reducing labor market discrimination. That analysis predicted that even prejudiced employers would hire minority workers if they could be "compensated" by paying minorities less than their marginal product. Therefore, a state law that does not address discrimination in compensation permits prejudiced employers to comply with the law by hiring minorities but paying them less than other workers of comparable quality. On the other hand, an equal-pay-for-equal-work law that only forbids wage discrimination is likely to reduce the relative employment of minorities (and increase their relative unemployment or reduce their rate of labor force participation) unless it is accompanied by a requirement forbidding employment discrimination, since prejudiced employers will be less willing to hire minorities if they are unable to practice wage discrimination. With sufficient enforcement, laws that forbid both employment and wage discrimination may reduce discrimination in the labor market by raising the cost of such actions to violators.

How effective have state fair employment practice laws been in reducing discrimination? Some studies have found that, after accounting for differences in human capital between whites and nonwhites, the relative wages and occupational positions of nonwhites are higher in states with fair employment practice laws than in states that have not passed such laws. However, such findings raise a basic question of causality when they do not consider the way legislation is established.

Fair employment practice laws are passed by the vote of legislators, who must represent the preferences of their constituencies to remain in office. When we find that the relative earnings of minorities are higher in states with fair employment practice laws, does that represent the impact of the law or a tendency of such laws to be passed in states where prejudice is relatively low (reflected in part by the higher relative wages received by minorities)? There is some evidence that it represents the latter. Indeed, the existence of state fair employment practice legislation appears to have little or no effect on racial earnings differentials, once independent measures of prejudice and the extent of unionization in a state are controlled for. (A measure of prejudice independent of earnings differentials is clearly needed to sort out the issue of causation; one measure used is electoral support for political candidates who are known to oppose civil rights or equal opportunity legislation. Unions have been shown to increase the relative earnings of minorities, and because fair employment laws tend to be found in states with above-average levels of unionization, studies attempting to find the separate effects of fair employment practice laws must filter out the effects of unions on earnings differentials.)[39]

FEDERAL PROGRAMS TO END DISCRIMINATION

The federal govenment has enforced two sets of rules in an attempt to eliminate market discrimination. One is a *nondiscrimination* requirement made of almost all employers. The other is a requirement that federal contractors engage in *affirmative action*—that is, to actively seek out minorities and women to staff their vacancies.

Equal Pay Act of 1963

Over the years prior to the 1960s, sex discrimination was officially sanctioned by so-called *protective labor laws,* which limited women's total hours of work and prohibited them from working at night, lifting heavy objects, and working during pregnancy. Not all states placed all these restrictions on women, but the effect of these laws was to limit the access of women to many jobs. These laws were overturned by the Equal Pay Act of 1963, which also outlawed separate pay scales for men and women using similar skills and performing work under the same conditions.

The act, however, was seriously deficient as an antidiscrimination tool because it said nothing about equal opportunity in hiring and promotions. This flaw can be easily understood by a quick review of our theories of discrimination. If there is prejudice against women from whatever source, employers will treat female em-

---

[39]*See* William M. Landes, "The Economics of Fair Employment Laws," *Journal of Political Economy* 76(August 1968):507–52.

ployees as if they were less productive or more costly to hire than equally productive males. The market response is for female wages to fall below male wages, because otherwise women cannot hope to be able to successfully compete with men in obtaining jobs. The Equal Pay Act took a step toward the elimination of wage differentials, but by so doing it tended to suppress a market mechanism that helped women obtain greater access to jobs.[40] The act failed to acknowledge that if labor market discrimination is to be eliminated, legislation must require *both* equal pay *and* equal opportunities in hiring and promotions for people of comparable productivity.

Title VII of the Civil Rights Act

Some defects in the Equal Pay Act of 1963 were corrected the next year. Title VII of the Civil Rights Act of 1964 made it unlawful for any employer "to refuse to hire or to discharge any individual, or otherwise to discriminate against any individual with respect to his compensation, terms, condition, or privileges of employment, because of such individual's race, color, religion, sex or national origin." Union practices were also addressed by the new legislation. Historically, it had been very difficult for racial minorities to obtain admission into certain craft unions representing workers in the skilled trades—an exclusion that denied minorities access to both the skills training provided through union apprenticeship programs and the employment opportunities dispensed through union hiring halls. Unions representing workers in large industries were generally more integrated, although in a few unions the quality of representation in collective bargaining and in the administration of the labor agreement varied by race. Title VII made it unlawful for any labor organization to exclude individuals from membership, to segregate membership, to refuse to refer for employment, or to discriminate in admission to apprenticeship programs on the basis of race, color, religion, sex, or national origin.

This broad statement of a national policy favoring nondiscriminatory employment practices was qualified in certain respects, however. First, Title VII is not retroactive; it was written to apply to acts of discrimination occurring after its effective date of July 1, 1965. Second, the law permits exceptions to its general requirement of nondiscrimination "where religion, sex, or national origin is a bona fide occupational qualification reasonably necessary to the normal operation of a business." In practice this applies to a limited number of situations (for example, certain jobs in religious organizations, nursing homes in which the patients are of predominantly one sex, etc.). Third, Title VII permits an employer to differentiate wages and other employment conditions "pursuant to a bona fide seniority system . . . provided that such differences are not the result of an intention to discriminate." Finally, no party subject to the statute is required to grant preferential

---

[40]Some critics of the Equal Pay Act of 1963 argued that its motivation was to help men compete with lower-paid women. *See* Nancy Barrett, "Women in the Job Market: Occupations, Earnings, and Career Opportunities," in *The Subtle Revolution,* ed. Ralph E. Smith (Washington, D.C.: The Urban Institute, 1979), p.55.

treatment to any group because of existing imbalances in the work force. As will become clear below, the last two qualifications have raised difficult issues for the application of the law.

Title VII applies to all employers in interstate commerce with at least 25 employees and is enforced by the Equal Employment Opportunity Commission (EEOC), which has the authority to mediate complaints, encourage lawsuits by private parties or the U.S. Attorney General, or (since 1972) bring suits itself against employers that have violated the law. In order to expand the impact of the law, the courts permitted individual plaintiffs to expand their suits into "class actions" in which the potential discriminatory impact of an organization's employment practices on an entire group of workers is assessed by the courts.

Over the years, the federal courts have fashioned two standards of discrimination that may be applied when discriminatory employment practices are alleged—*disparate treatment* and *disparate impact*. Disparate treatment occurs under Title VII if individuals are treated differently (for example, paid different wages or benefits) because of their race, sex, color, religion, or national origin, and if it can be shown that there was an intent to discriminate. While this is probably the more obvious approach to defining discrimination, it is not the definition that the courts have relied on most frequently. The difficulty raised by this standard is that personnel policies that appear to be neutral in the sense that they ignore race, sex, etc., may nevertheless perpetuate the effects of past discrimination. For example, word-of-mouth recruiting (a seemingly neutral policy) in a plant with a largely white work force would be suspect under Title VII even if the selection of new employees from among the applicants was done on a nondiscriminatory basis, since the racial composition of the applicants is likely to be influenced by the recruiting method.

The concern with addressing the present effects of past discrimination led to the "disparate impact" standard. Under this approach it is the result, not the motivation, that matters. Personnel policies that appear to be neutral but lead to different impacts by race, sex, etc., are prohibited under Title VII unless they can be related to job performance.[41] Employers, for example, may use tests and educational standards to screen applicants, but these tests must be validated against job performance. In the words of the Supreme Court, "Tests must measure the person for the job; not the person in the abstract." Job application forms may ask about *convictions* but not *arrests* (arrest rates among minorities tend to be higher, but the courts reason that it is conviction that is important to the employer). Marital status cannot be used as a screening device unless it is applied uniformly to both sexes and is clearly a job-related requirement. In interpreting Title VII, the federal courts have generally taken the position that neutral (for example, colorblind or sexblind) personnel practices that carry forward the effects of past discrimination constitute present discrimination. As a result, plaintiffs, employers, and the courts have become interested in how closely the race or sex composition of groups selected for

---

[41]Willie S. Griggs *v.* Duke Power Company 401 U.S. 424 (1971).

employment, promotion, training, or termination accords with the race or sex composition of the pool of workers available for selection.

The adoption of the disparate impact standard by the courts as a standard of discrimination has mounted a significant challenge to employer personnel screening devices. As noted in Chapter 5, employers have an incentive to rely on screening devices, which sort job applicants on the basis of the "average" characteristics of a group, rather than according to individual merit, when it is extremely costly to ascertain the qualifications of individual applicants. While the use of screening devices often results in lower costs of personnel administration, it also gives rise to the statistical discrimination discussed earlier in this chapter. In taking the position that workers must be judged on the basis of their individual abilities, rather than average group characteristics, the courts have launched a strong assault against mechanisms of statistical discrimination, and one consequence of this assault has been higher private costs of human resource management.[42]

In certain instances, the application of the disparate impact standard and other efforts to combat labor market discrimination have been limited by some of the express qualifications written into Title VII. In recent years two particularly difficult issues have arisen in the application of the law: the treatment of seniority arrangements perpetuating the effects of past discrimination and the adoption of a "comparable worth" standard by which to judge pay equality when occupations are segregated.

Seniority.   Most unionized firms and many nonunion firms use seniority as a consideration in allocating promotion opportunities. Moreover, employees are frequently laid off in order of reverse seniority, the least senior first, in a recession. It was partially in recognition of the historically important role of seniority in American personnel arrangements that Congress appeared to exempt seniority systems from challenge under Title VII. Yet seniority systems have the strong potential for perpetuating the effects of past discrimination. We have seen how occupational segregation—the tendency of women or minorities to be restricted to relatively low-wage jobs despite qualifications for higher positions—has been one historical mechanism of discrimination in the labor market.

In many instances, particularly in the South, job segregation was accompanied by departmental seniority arrangements. That is, seniority was computed as time employed in a department, not as time employed in the plant or company. When companies sought to break down historical patterns of job segregation to comply with Title VII, two types of adjustments occurred: women and minorities were moved within a company from low-wage jobs to higher-wage jobs in other departments, and women and minorities were hired by companies into some jobs for the

---

[42]One must be careful to distinguish here between the costs to employers (*private* costs) and the costs to society (*social* costs) of statistical discrimination. Although employers' private costs for human resource management may be low because of statistical discrimination, the costs to society may be high if qualified applicants are rejected simply because of the group they are members of. While prohibiting statistical discrimination may increase the private costs of human resource management, it may decrease the social costs.

first time. Under either mechanism, women and minorities ended up with relatively low seniority under departmental seniority systems.

Many of these adjustments occurred during the late 1960s, when the general demand for labor was high. With the less favorable economic circumstances of the 1970s, however, firms began to lay off workers, and under departmental seniority arrangements a disproportionate number of those laid off were minorities and women. In many of these cases, individuals with very little departmental seniority had more *plant* seniority than workers who retained their jobs in the high-wage departments and might have been able to retain their jobs if they had the seniority that they had accrued in their former departments. Departmental seniority arrangements resulted in a disparate impact on women and minorities and perpetuated the effects of past discrimination. The resulting Title VII litigation presented the courts with a quandry. Under the disparate impact standard, the seniority systems were discriminatory, but the language of Title VII explicitly permitted "bona fide seniority systems." The lower courts tended to resolve the quandry by taking the position that a seniority system was not "bona fide" if it discriminated, and that under the prevailing definition of discrimination, only plant-wide seniority systems were "bona fide." When the Supreme Court considered the issue, however, it reversed the appellate courts and held that the language in Title VII permitted even departmental seniority systems that perpetuated the effects of discrimination.[43]

Minorities and women who were hired for the first time following passage of Title VII were susceptible to layoff under either plant or departmental seniority. Some were individuals who had been victims of hiring discrimination prior to the passage of the law or who did not apply for employment because the company had a reputation for discriminating. In litigation arising out of these cases, plaintiffs often argued that the appropriate remedy was an award of seniority retroactive to the date when the individual would have been hired if the company had not practiced discrimination. (This is sometimes referred to as "fictional seniority.") On this issue the Supreme Court has ruled that fictional seniority is an appropriate remedy for individuals who can demonstrate that they were victims of unlawful discrimination. However, the Supreme Court has argued that it is not appropriate to dismiss current employees as part of the remedy for past discrimination.[44]

Comparable worth.   We noted earlier in this chapter how women are disproportionately employed in certain jobs and occupations in which wages are relatively low. Some have argued that the wages in these jobs are low because they are filled to a large extent by women, who are the victims of market discrimination. To the extent that the labor market is biased against women, it is argued further that discrimination is perpetuated by using the market as a basis for paying, say, clerical workers (a job historically filled largely by women) less than, say, maintenance

---

[43]International Brotherhood of Teamsters *v.* United States 431 U.S. 324, 14 FEP 1514 (1977).

[44]Franks *v.* Bowman Transportation 424 U.S. 747, 12 FEP Cases 549 (1976), and Fire Fighters Local 1784 *v.* Stotts, U.S. Sup Ct, No. 82–206, June 12, 1984.

workers (a job historically filled largely by men). The remedy proposed is to pay women or minorities their "comparable worth"—that is, the intrinsic value of their jobs. However, the intrinsic value of a job would be established by comparison of its importance to some other (presumably more highly paid) job predominantly held by males, rather than by reference to market wages. (See the appendix to this chapter for more details on procedures for making these comparisons.)

The comparable worth idea has proved difficult to define precisely. How much of the wage difference between two jobs can be attributed to the fact that one is largely staffed by women and the other by men? The evidence reviewed earlier in this chapter indicates that a significant portion of the wage difference between men and women reflects differences in human capital investments and other qualifications. The amount of the difference that might be attributed to discrimination is likely to vary from job comparison to job comparison. Another important influence on wage differences between jobs was discussed in Chapter 8—nonpecuniary conditions of work. To the extent that working conditions vary substantially between jobs held predominantly by men and women, one would expect the wages to vary as well. All these factors must be considered in estimating how much of the wage differential between "male" jobs and "female" jobs is the result of market discrimination. A further difficulty in trying to construct an operational approach to the proposed comparable worth remedy is evaluating the intrinsic worth of different job requirements or characteristics. Existing job evaluation procedures may not be free of bias in the weights they assign to these characteristics.[45]

In addition to the operational difficulties with the comparable worth concept, the concept raises several fundamental policy questions. For example, is it likely to be more effective to use the law to break down occupational barriers caused by discriminatory job segregation or to develop a compensation scheme (via comparable worth) that may leave job segregation unchanged? Will raising the wage rates of traditional "female" occupations reduce women's incentives to seek occupational advancement? Will raising women's wages have an adverse effect on female employment levels?[46] Answers to these questions will be important components of any complete evaluation of comparable worth.

As of yet, the major push for comparable worth has come not in the private sector, but rather in state and local government. A number of state and local

---

[45]See Donald J. Treiman and Heidi L. Hartmann, eds., *Women, Work and Wages: Equal Pay for Jobs of Equal Value* (Washington, D.C.: National Academy Press, 1981). For a more recent discussion of comparable worth that spans a variety of disciplines, and both proponents and opponents, see Heidi L. Hartmann, ed. *New Directions for Research on Comparable Worth* (Washington, D.C.: National Academy Press, 1984).

[46]In general, we have seen in this text that increasing the wage rate for a group should lead to a decline in the group's employment. The one exception to this rule is if employers behave as monopsonists; we showed in the context of our discussion of the minimum wage (Chapter 3) that in this situation one could set a minimum wage above the current wage (within a certain range) without suffering any employment losses. A number of studies cited in Chapter 3 also suggest that registered nurses and public school teachers, both traditionally female occupations, have their wages depressed because their employers have some monopsony power. For these groups, at least, comparable worth wage adjustments might not lead to employment losses.

Example 14.2

Comparable Worth and the University

Some of the difficulties involved with the concept of *comparable worth* can be illustrated by an example in which gender does not even enter. Consider the labor market for university professors in the fields of computer science and English, and suppose that initially the demand and supply curves for both are given by D_{oc} and S_{oc}, and D_{oe} and S_{oe}, respectively. As the figure indicates, in this circumstance the same wage, W_o, will prevail in both markets, and E_{oc} computer science professors, and E_{oe} English professors will be hired. Suppose also that in some objective sense the quality of the two groups of professors is equal.

Presumably this is a situation that advocates of comparable worth would applaud. Both types of professors require the same amount of training, represented by a Ph.D., and both are required to engage in the same activities, teaching and research. Unless one is willing to assign different values to the teaching and research produced in different academic fields, one must conclude that the jobs are truly comparable. Hence, if the two groups are equal in quality, equal wages would be justified according to the concept of comparable worth.

Suppose now, however, that the demand for computer science professors rises to D_{lc} as a result of the increasing numbers of students who want to take computer science courses. Suppose at the same time the demand for English professors falls to D_{le} because fewer students want to take elective courses in English. At the old equilibrium wage rate there is an excess demand for computer science professors of $E_{lc} - E_{oc}$ and an excess supply of English professors of $E_{oe} - E_{le}$.

How can universities respond? One possibility is to let the market work;

The Market for Computer Science and English Professors

the wage of computer science professors will rise to W_{lc} and that for English professors will fall to W_{le}. Employment of the former will rise to E_{2c} while employment of the latter will become E_{2e}.

Another possibility is that the wages of the two groups of professors be kept equal at the old wage rate of W_o. Universities could respond to the excess demand for computer scientists and the excess supply of English professors by lowering hiring standards for the former and raising them for the latter. Since the average quality of English professors would then exceed the average quality of computer scientists, the wage paid per "quality-unit" would now be higher for the computer scientists. Hence, true comparable worth—equal pay for *equal-quality* workers performing comparable jobs—would not be achieved. Moreover, employment and course offerings in this situation would not change to meet changing student demands.

Alternatively, some advocates of comparable worth might argue that universities should respond by raising the wages of *all* professors to W_{lc}. While this would eliminate the shortage of computer science professors, it would exacerbate the excess supply of English professors, raising it to E_{4e} − E_{3e}. Universities would respond by drastically reducing the employment of English professors even further to E_{3e} (and reducing course offerings). Moreover, the excess supply again would permit universities to raise hiring standards for English professors, so again average quality would rise. As a result, once more the wage per quality-unit of English professors would be less than that of computer science professors and again true comparable worth would not be achieved.

The message one takes away from this example is that it is difficult to "trick the market." In the face of changing relative demand conditions, either wage differentials for the two types of professors must be allowed to arise or quality differentials will arise. In neither case, however, can comparable worth be achieved. Put another way, the value of a job cannot be determined independently of market conditions.

governments have conducted, or are in the process of conducting, formal job evaluation surveys to see if "female" occupations are "underpaid"; the appendix to this chapter illustrates in a simplified fashion how this is done. Other state or local governments have begun to implement comparable worth salary adjustments through the collective bargaining process.[47] Finally, in one major case a federal district court judge ordered the state of Washington to implement the wage adjustments that a comparable worth job evaluation survey suggested were in order.[48]

---

[47]See *Who's Working for Working Women? A Survey of State and Local Government Pay Equity Activities and Initiatives* (Washington, D.C.: National Committee on Pay Equity, 1984) and Alice Cook, "Comparable Worth: Recent Developments in Selected States," *Proceedings of the 1983 Spring Meeting of the Industrial Relations Research Association* (Madison, Wis.: Industrial Relations Research Association, 1983).

[48]See "Immediate Halt to Bias in Wages in State of Washington Is Ordered," *New York Times*, December 15, 1983. The cost of implementing the judge's order was estimated by some observers to be as high as $1 billion and the state appealed the ruling.

The Federal Contract Compliance Program

In 1965 the Office of Federal Contract Compliance Programs (OFCCP) was established to monitor the hiring and promotion practices of federal contractors (firms supplying goods or services to the federal government). OFCCP requires contractors above a certain size to analyze the extent of their underutilization of women and minorities and to propose a plan to remedy any such underutilization. Such a plan is called an *affirmative action plan.* Contractors submitting unacceptable plans or failing to meet their goals are threatened with cancellation of their contracts and eligibility for future contracts, although these drastic steps are rarely taken.

Affirmative action planning is intended to commit firms to a schedule for rapidly overcoming unequal career opportunities afforded women and minorities. Such planning affects both *hiring* and *promotion* practices, but it also raises numerous philosophical and practical questions that tend to make the planning process highly controversial.

Suppose an insurance company is attempting to construct an affirmative action plan with regard to secretaries. Its first step in setting hiring goals is to decide what number of minorities are "available" and what fraction they constitute of all available workers. If blacks, say, constitute 9 percent of the labor supply available to the firm, then it might seem to be a simple matter of setting a goal of 9 percent. However, the planner must resolve some serious questions.

First, should the pool of black secretaries be estimated based on the firm's *actual applicant* pool? The answer is probably no, since any discriminatory practices in the past will discourage black applicants currently. Further, affirmative action planning is intended to force companies to *change* their hiring practices. On the other hand, as was pointed out in Chapter 8, a firm's location within a city can attract more or less black applicants, depending on how far from the firm blacks live and the level of compensation offered. Moreover, as we saw in Chapter 11, the mix of *fringe benefits* in the total compensation package can alter the attractiveness of an employer to women, the young, and the poor.[49] Thus, to some extent the potential pool of *interested* applicants is a legitimate consideration.

Should the potential pool be estimated from the fraction of all *trained secretaries* in the area who are black? If we are interested in eradicating *market* discrimination, this may be the logical measure, since it would force firms to hire black secretaries in the same proportion as they are found in the labor market. However, years of discrimination may have induced blacks to avoid training for this occupation, with the result that blacks may be substantially underrepresented in the secretarial labor market.

Should firms then be compelled to hire black secretaries in proportion to their numbers in the adult *population* of the city at large? This goal implicitly sets out to eliminate all discrimination, both market and premarket, but if blacks are underre-

---

[49]For a review of the economic factors affecting "availability", see Ronald Ehrenberg and Robert Smith, "Economic and Statistical Analysis of Discrimination in Hiring," *Proceedings of the Thirty-Fifth Annual Meeting of the Industrial Relations Research Association* (Madison, Wisc.: Industrial Relations Research Association, 1984).

presented in the occupation, the attainment of this goal is impractical in the short run. Firms attempting to hire more black secretaries than are available would have two choices. They could hire black high school graduates and train them in secretarial skills. Remember, however, that such training is *general* in nature, so the firms would not offer it unless the workers involved paid for it in some way. Without training as an option, firms would simply try to bid against each other for the services of existing black secretaries, which would drive up their wages. The higher wage rates would induce more blacks to seek secretarial training, and their underrepresentation in the occupation would disappear in the long run.

While population-based goals would appear to fight both kinds of discrimination, they might in fact fight neither. It stands to reason that if hiring goals are set beyond the immediate reach of firms, each will individually fail to meet them. Can the government reasonably punish firms for failing to hire beyond the numbers currently available? If it cannot, then failure to meet goals will not result in punishment, which seems to remove the incentive for firms to take energetic steps to integrate their work force.

A final issue in hiring has to do with how the goals are applied. If black secretaries, to continue our example, are 9 percent of the available pool, does that mean that 9 percent of all *newly hired* secretaries should be black? This goal might seem reasonable from a firm's point of view, but if labor turnover is low it would take a very long time for the 9 percent of *new hires* to accumulate to the point where blacks were 9 percent of the firm's total secretarial work force. Since the Civil Rights Act of 1964 prohibits workers of one race from being fired to make room for those of another, getting rid of employment imbalances must occur through new hiring. However, only if aggrieved groups are *favored* in hiring can the effects of past discrimination be eradicated quickly.

Favoritism in hiring not only raises the issue of *reverse discrimination*, wherein whites or males can assert they are being discriminated against because of race or sex, but also raises the issue of how firms, as a whole, can hire women or blacks in proportions greater than their current availability. The courts have yet to resolve the considerable tension between Title VII's standard of nondiscrimination, which protects all groups from disparate treatment, and the OFCCP's standard of affirmative action. (See Example 14.3.)

It is testimony to these difficult questions about affirmative action planning that the government's requirements for calculating "availability" are rather vague. The OFCCP has proposed that, for purposes of affirmative action planning, federal contractors compute availability of minorities and women using either of two methods: the "civilian labor force" method or the "four-factor" method.[50] Under the former alternative, availability is estimated from the percentages of women and minorities in the *metropolitan area's* civilian labor force. The "four-factor" alter-

---

[50]Bureau of National Affairs, Labor Relations Reporter, *Fair Employment Practices Manual* 401:5005. OFCCP's proposal is a revision of its 1974 guidelines for federal contractors, under which eight factors were considered. As of this writing the revised guidelines have not yet been implemented.

Example 14.3

Is Affirmative Action Consistent with Equal Employment Opportunity?

One of the more difficult problems facing the implementation of public policy against discrimination is the difficulty of overcoming the present effects of past discrimination. One purpose in efforts to get employers to take "affirmative action" to increase the representation of minorities and women at all levels of the occupational structure is to overcome the residual effects of past discrimination. However, affirmative action efforts raise the potential for conflict with a law such as Title VII of the Civil Rights Act that sets a general nondiscrimination standard. By the mid-1970s the Supreme Court held that whites, males, and other "majority" groups are protected from race or sex discrimination by Title VII.* But does this mean that affirmative action plans are generally prohibited under Title VII? The Supreme Court addressed this question in the following case.

The Kaiser Aluminum and Chemical Corporation operated a plant in Gramercy, Louisiana, an area in which, in the early 1970s, about 39 percent of the labor force was black. Prior to 1974, Kaiser hired only workers with previous craft experience to fill the craft positions in the plant. This employment practice virtually restricted the craft positions to white workers, since blacks had historically been excluded from the craft unions, which were sources of training through apprenticeship programs. As a result, only 5 of 273 skilled craft employees (less than 2 percent) at the Gramercy plant were black.

In 1974 Kaiser signed a collective bargaining agreement with the United Steelworkers of America that included an affirmative action plan designed to eliminate these racial imbalances. As a part of the plan, Kaiser agreed to train its production workers to fill craft positions (rather than hiring from the outside). Selection for the training program was on the basis of seniority, subject to the provision that at least half the trainees would be black until the percentage of black craft workers in the plant was similar to the percentage in the outside labor force. (See the next example for an indication of how long this process might take.) In 1974, 7 black and 6 white production workers at Kaiser were selected for the training program, but some of the white workers whose applications for the program were rejected had more seniority than some of the blacks who were selected. One of the white workers, Brian Weber, filed a legal action alleging that the affirmative action plan violated Title VII of the Civil Rights Act because the plan discriminated against (white) workers on the basis of race. The lower courts agreed with Weber, and the company and the union appealed the case to the U.S. Supreme Court.

In a controversial decision, the Supreme Court held that Title VII does not forbid "private employers and unions from voluntarily agreeing upon bona fide affirmative action plans that accord racial preferences in the manner and for the purpose" provided in the Kaiser plan. Yet the court did not rule out the possibility that some affirmative action plans might favor minorities to an extent that violated Title VII, and refused to "define a line of demarcation between permissible and impermissible affirmative action plans." It found instead that while Title VII does not require *preferential treatment*, it permits such treatment when arrived at voluntarily. Moreover, in the Kaiser case the purpose of the affirmative action plan was to break down historical patterns of occupational segregation by race—clearly an objective of Title VII—and the plan did not "trammel the interests of white employees," since none were discharged and some were admitted to the training program. While it is true, as the Court noted, that a broad prohibition on such plans would bring about a result at variance with the purpose of Title VII, the extent to which affirmative action plans can grant preferential treatment without violating Title VII is still far from certain.

*McDonald v. Santa Fe Trail Transportation Co., 427 U.S. 273 (1976).

SOURCE: United Steelworkers v. Weber, 443 U.S. 193 (1979).

native would require the contractor to devise estimates by taking into account the following considerations:

1. The percentage of minorities and women in the civilian labor force in the *immediate labor area* (defined as the geographic area from which employees and applicants may reasonably commute to the establishment);
2. The percentage of minorities and women with requisite skills in the *immediate labor area*;
3. The percentage of minorities and women with requisite skills in the *relevant recruitment area* (defined as the geographic area from which the contractor may reasonably recruit its employees, including areas not contiguous to the immediate labor area);
4. The percentage of minorities and women among those promotable or transferable within the contractor's organization.

Contractors can assign weights of their own choosing (including weights of zero) to each of the four factors, as long as the weights are justified in writing and sum to 100 percent.

A brief analysis of the above requirements will show that they raise several questions. First, the civilian labor force method differs from factor 1 of the "four-factor" method in the definition of geographic area over which to calculate populations. Which is the less arbitrary definition for availability purposes: the metropolitan area or the "immediate labor area" (which may be larger or smaller than the metropolitan area)? Also, given the various costs of commuting discussed at the end of Chapter 8, should everyone in the defined area be assumed equally "available" for work at a given plant?

Second, factors 1 and 2 under the "four-factor" alternative differ in the attention given to *existing* skills, raising the issue discussed above concerning the goals of the contract compliance program. Is the aim of the program to eliminate only current *market* discrimination against those already in a given skill group, or should it directly address the issue of *premarket* differences in skill acquisition among race or sex groups?

Third, factor 3 is intended to apply to firms hiring in occupations that have regional or national labor markets. However, if contractors are required to adopt, as a matter of course, nontraditional hiring practices that are likely to yield more female or minority applicants, is it unreasonable to expect them to recruit regionally or even nationally for workers they normally recruit locally?

Finally, several questions can be raised about factor 4. If few minorities or women are at the office-manager rank in an organization, is the firm obliged to offer special managerial training courses for them? Should such training be equally available to interested white males? What if the interest in managerial positions varies by race or sex? Are companies supposed to promote on a nondiscriminatory basis, with the result that imbalances in its *higher*-level jobs will remain for years into the future? Instead, must employers hurry women and blacks along the promotional ladder faster than normal so that these higher-level imbalances will go away more quickly? These are the dilemmas inherent in the government's contract compliance program.

Effectiveness of Federal Antidiscrimination Programs

A question of obvious interest is just how effective the two federal antidiscrimination programs have been in increasing the relative earnings of minorities and women. The question is not easy to answer, however, because we must make some guesses as to what earnings differentials *would have been* in the absence of these programs.

As we have seen, the ratio of black to white incomes has risen since 1960 (see Table 14.2), especially in the mid-1970s. Has this rise in the ratio been a result of government efforts, or have other forces been working to accomplish this result? Three other forces are commonly cited. First, an improvement in the educational *attainment* of black workers relative to whites during this period is thought to have played an important role in raising the ratio of black to white income.[51] Second, the evidence that the *quality* of schooling received by blacks improved from 1960 to 1970 more than it did for whites lends further impetus to the increase in relative earnings.[52] Finally, blacks have historically experienced relative gains in periods of low unemployment and suffered disproportionately in periods of economic distress. The late 1960s were a period of very full employment, which could have helped increase the black/white earnings ratio from 1960 to 1970. However, general business conditions in the 1970s were not as good as in the late 1960s, so the continued improvement in that decade is unlikely to be solely the result of overall business conditions.

Two types of studies have attempted to distinguish the effects of the govern-

---

[51]Orley Ashenfelter, "Changes in Labor Market Discrimination Over Time," *Journal of Human Resources* 5,4(Fall 1970):403–30; Richard Freeman, "Black Economic Progress After 1964: Who Has Gained and Why?" in Sherwin Rosen, ed., *Studies in Labor Markets* (Chicago, Ill.: University of Chicago Press, 1981); Barry R. Chiswick and June A. O'Neill, eds., *Human Resources and Income Distribution: Issues and Policies* (New York: W. W. Norton, 1977), pp. 20–21.

[52]Finis Welch, "Black-White Differences in Returns to Schooling," *American Economic Review* 63,5(December 1973):893–907.

ment programs from the other factors that affect relative earnings: time series studies and analyses of federal contractors.

Time series studies.   There seems to have been a significant upturn in the black/white earnings ratio after the EEOC was created in 1964—an upturn that was independent of both the effects of *educational* gains by blacks and changes in the *unemployment rate*.[53] However, it also appears that the labor force participation rate of blacks fell relative to whites after 1964, a year in which many income maintenance programs began to become more generous.[54] If, as seems likely, the blacks with the lowest wages were the ones who left the labor market, their exit would increase the average wage paid to blacks and give the *appearance* of improvement. Some—probably less than half—of the post-1964 improvement is due to this latter factor.[55] Thus, there seems to be at least *some* evidence that post-1964 government efforts to lessen discrimination helped blacks.

Analysis of federal contractors.   If the contract compliance program administered by OFCCP is effective, we should observe that the economic status of blacks improves faster among federal contractors than noncontractors. Several studies have tested this hypothesis, and some have even distinguished whether or not the contractors involved had been subjected to a compliance review by the government (the government does not have the resources to inspect the affirmative action plans of *all* its contractors). The results suggest that blacks have made faster gains in contractor firms, although the gains are relatively small.[56]

One problem in assessing the *overall* effects of OFCCP, however, is that because the contract compliance program relates only to *some* employers (contractors), the gains in black employment among these firms may come at the expense of losses among noncontractors. Eligible blacks may just be bid away from noncontractors, although it should be pointed out that anyone successfully bid away from a former employer must have experienced an expected gain in utility. Perhaps more serious is the problem that becoming or remaining a federal contractor is a voluntary

---

[53]*See* Freeman, "Changes in the Labor Market for Black Americans," and (a study which updates Freeman) Richard Butler and James Heckman, "The Government's Impact on the Labor Market Status of Black Americans: A Critical Review," *Equal Rights and Industrial Relations* (Madison, Wis.: Industrial Relations Research Association, 1977), pp. 235–80.

[54]Butler and Heckman, "The Government's Impact on the Labor Market Status of Black Americans."

[55]Charles Brown, "The Federal Attack on Labor Market Discrimination: The Mouse That Roared?" in Ronald Ehrenberg, ed., *Research in Labor Economics* 5(1982):33–68. Evidence that Title VII lawsuits have played a significant role in increasing black employment is found in Jonathan S. Leonard, "Antidiscrimination or Reverse Discrimination: The Impact of Changing Demographics, Title VII, and Affirmative Action on Productivity," *Journal of Human Resources* 19(Spring 1984):145–74.

[56]For a summary of the four studies done on the early 1970s, *see* Butler and Heckman, "The Government's Impact on the Labor Market Status of Black Americans." For generally comparable results in a study of the late 1970s, *see* Jonathon S. Leonard, "Employment and Occupational Advance Under Affirmative Action," *Review of Economics and Statistics* 1984, forthcoming.

Example 14.4

How Fast Can Discrimination Be Eradicated?

To illustrate the possible rate of progress in minority employment within a firm, let us take a numerical example. Suppose there is a job group that contains 1600 employees, 100 (6.25 percent) of whom are black. Suppose, further, that this is an entry-level job group (so that all replacements come from new hires) and that the yearly turnover rate is 20 percent. Finally, assume that blacks represent 12 percent of the firm's available labor pool for this job.

The firm in question must hire 320 new workers for this job group each year. If 12 percent (about 38) of those hired each year are black, how long will it take before 12 percent (192) of the 1600-person work group is black? Another, perhaps more significant, question is how fast will the racial composition of the work group change? These questions have no obvious answers, because if blacks and whites have the same turnover rate (of 20 percent), the organization is both losing and hiring blacks each year.

One way to answer the above questions is to simulate employee turnover each year. The accompanying table shows that in the first year 20 blacks quit and 38 (12 percent of the 320 new hires) are hired. The net gain in blacks raises their level of employment in the group to 118 and their percentage of employment to 7.37 (from 6.25). In year 2, 38 blacks are again hired and about 24 quit, representing a net gain of 14, and by the end of the year the work group is 8.25 percent black. As this process continues, there are net additions to the black component of the work force each year, but these additions get smaller and smaller.

Of special interest in this example is the fact that it takes about 10 years of *nondiscriminatory hiring* for the percentage of blacks in the work group to get close to the goal of 12 percent. (The rate of progress would be approximatetly cut in half if the turnover rate were 10 percent instead of 20 percent.) Thus, if the proportion of blacks among new hires is equal to their proportion in the available labor pool and if their turnover rates are no lower than those of whites, the long-run goal of employment equality will take many years to achieve once nondiscriminatory hiring is begun. This mathematical fact illustrates why those charged with administering antidiscrimination programs are simultaneously besieged by shouts of frustration and calls for patience.

Change in the Racial Composition of a 1600-Person Job Group
(20% Yearly Turnover Rate)

	Year						
	0	*1*	*2*	*3*	*4*	*5*	*10*
Number of blacks							
Loss		20	24	26	29	31	36
New hires		38	38	38	38	38	38
Net gain		18	14	12	11	7	2
Cumulative level	100	118	132	144	155	162	181
Percent black	6.25	7.37	8.25	9.00	9.69	10.12	11.31

decision. Firms that perceive the costs of affirmative action to be high may simply choose not to be contractors. The contract compliance program may end up concentrating its efforts on the firms within which discrimination is a relatively small problem.

A final reason to temper optimism about the government's efforts to end discrimination is that it appears that the gains of blacks among contractors have come at least partially at the expense of white women. The growth of white female employment relative to total employment has been slower among federal contractors than among noncontractors, both in the early 1970s (before women were a focus of the contract compliance program) and later.[57] The reasons for this finding have not yet been convincingly explained; however, there is other evidence that women have been helped by the contract compliance program. One study, for example, looked at *quit rates,* rather than wages or employment ratios, as an index of perceived well-being. What it found (for 1978–79) was that, in industries in which federal contracts comprised a larger fraction of total sales and the OFCCP had initiated more compliance reviews, women had lower quit rates than would be expected, given their wages and other factors affecting quits.[58] The inference is that women in these industries perceived themselves to be better off than women elsewhere.

In summary, it appears that some of the gains registered by blacks since 1964 may be due to efforts by the EEOC and OFCCP, but the effects of these programs on women appear mixed. Effects on other minorities have not been extensively studied.

REVIEW QUESTIONS

1. Assume that women live longer than men, on the average. Suppose an employer hires men and women, pays them the same wage for the same job, and contributes an equal amount per person toward a pension. However, the promised monthly pension after retirement is smaller for women than men because the pension funds for them have to last longer. According to the *Manhart* decision by the Supreme Court, the above employer would be guilty of discrimination because of the unequal monthly pension benefits after retirement.
   a. Comment on the Court's implicit definition of discrimination. Is it consistent with the definition normally used by economists? Why or why not?
   b. Analyze the economic effects of this decision on men and women.

---

[57]Morris Goldstein and Robert S. Smith, "The Estimated Impact of the Antidiscrimination Program Aimed at Federal Contractors," *Industrial and Labor Relations Review* 29,4(July 1976):523–43; and Leonard, "Employment and Occupational Advance Under Affirmative Action."

[58]Paul Osterman, "Affirmative Action and Opportunity: A Study of Female Quit Rates," *Review of Economics and Statistics* 64(November 1982):604–12. Corroborating evidence is found in Andrea Beller, "The Impact of Equal Opportunity Policy on Sex Differentials in Earnings and Occupations," *Proceedings of the American Economic Association* 72(May 1982):171–75.

2. Assume there is a central city school district in which the student population is predominantly black. Surrounding the central city are predominantly white suburban school districts. Together, the central city and suburban school districts can be thought of as a local labor market for teachers. Other things being equal, black teachers in this labor market are equally willing to work in central city and suburban schools, but white teachers prefer suburban schools and are reluctant to accept jobs in the central city. There are too few black teachers to completely staff central city schools, and teachers generally have choices in the jobs they can accept.

   If federal law requires equal salaries for teachers of all races *within* a given school district but allows salaries to vary across school districts, will black teachers earn more, less, or the same salary as they would if white teachers were not prejudiced against black students? (Note: the prejudice of white teachers extends only to students, not to black teachers as co-workers. Note also: the chain of reasoning required in this answer should be made explicit in your answer.)

3. Suppose government antidiscrimination laws require employers to disregard marital status and sex in screening and hiring workers.
   a. Disregarding the employers who are engaged in discrimination, which employers will be most affected by this ruling?
   b. What alternatives do these employers have in coping with the problems created by this decision?
   c. What are the likely consequences of each alternative on employment levels and job stability among these employers?

4. Suppose the government has two methods of awarding contracts to firms. One is competitive, with the award going to the lowest bidder (who cannot then charge more than his or her bid). The other is noncompetitive, with the award going to a selected contractor who is reimbursed for actual costs incurred plus a certain percentage for profits. Suppose, too, that government contractors must hire a certain quota of minorities, many of whom require general training to be fully productive. Suppose also that federal legislation prevents the employer from shifting the costs of this general training to the minority employees. If you were an already-trained minority worker, which method of contract award would you prefer? Why?

SELECTED READINGS

Aigner, Dennis J., and Cain, Glen G. "Statistical Theories of Discrimination in Labor Markets." *Industrial and Labor Relations Review* 30(January 1977):175–87.

Arrow, Kenneth J. "The Theory of Discrimination." In *Discrimination in Labor Markets,* ed. Orley Ashenfelter and Albert Rees. Princeton, N.J.: Princeton University Press, 1973.

Becker, Gary. *The Economics of Discrimination.* 2nd ed. Chicago: University of Chicago Press, 1971.

Brown, Charles. "The Federal Attack on Labor Market Discrimination: The Mouse That Roared?" in *Research in Labor Economics,* ed. Ronald Ehrenberg. Vol. 5, Greenwich, Conn.: JAI Press, 1982. Pp. 33–68.

Cain, Glen G. "The Challenge of Segmented Labor Market Theories to Orthodox Theory: A Survey." *Journal of Economic Literature* 14(December 1976):1215–57.

Chiswick, Barry R., and O'Neill, June A., eds. *Human Resources and Income Distribution: Issues and Policies.* New York: W. W. Norton, 1977.

Ehrenberg, Ronald, and Smith, Robert. "Economic and Statistical Analysis of Discrimination in Hiring." *Proceedings of the Thirty-fifth Annual Meeting of the Industrial Relations Research Association*. Madison, Wisc.: Industrial Labor Relations Research Association, 1984.

Freeman, Richard. "Black Economic Progress After 1964: Who Has Gained and Why?" In *Studies in Labor Markets,* ed. Sherwin Rosen. Chicago: University of Chicago Press, 1981. Pp. 247–94.

Madden, Janice F. *The Economics of Sex Discrimination*. Lexington, Mass.: Lexington Books, 1973.

Marshall, Ray. "The Economics of Racial Discrimination: A Survey." *Journal of Economic Literature* 12(September 1974):849–71.

Reich, Michael. "The Economics of Racism." In *Problems in Political Economy: An Urban Perspective,* ed. David M. Gordon. Lexington, Mass.: D. C. Heath and Company, 1971. Pp. 107–13.

APPENDIX 14A

Estimating "Comparable Worth" Earnings Gaps: An Application of Regression Analysis

Although many economists have difficulty with the notion that the "worth" of a job can be established independently of market factors, formal job evaluation methods have existed for a long time. The state of Minnesota is one of the few states that has actually begun to implement "comparable worth" pay adjustments for its employees based on such an evaluation method. The purpose of this appendix is to give the reader an intuitive feel for how one might use data from job evaluations to estimate whether discriminatory wage differentials exist.[1]

Minnesota, in conjunction with Hay Associates, a prominent national compensation consulting company, began an evaluation of state government jobs in 1979. Initially evaluated were 188 positions in which at least 10 workers were employed and which could be classified as either *male* (at least 70 percent male incumbents) or *female* (at least 70 percent female incumbents) positions. Each position was evaluated by trained job evaluators and awarded a specified number of *Hay Points* for each of four job characteristics or factors: required know-how, problem-solving, accountability, and working conditions. The scores for each factor were then added to obtain a total Hay Point, or job evaluation, score for each job. These scores varied across the 188 job titles from below 100 to over 800 points.

Given these objective job evaluation scores, the next step is to ask what the relationship is between the salary (S_i) each male job pays and its total Hay Point (HP_i) score. Each dot in Figure 14A.1 represents a male job and this figure plots the monthly salary for each job against its total Hay Point score. On average, it is clear that jobs with higher scores receive higher pay.

Although all these points obviously do not lie on a single straight line, it is natural to ask what straight line fits the data best. An infinite number of lines can be drawn through these points and some precise criterion must be used to decide which line fits best. The procedure typically used by statisticians and economists is to choose that line for which the sum (across data points) of the squared vertical

---

[1]For a more complete discussion of the Minnesota job evaluation and comparable worth study, see *Pay Equity and Public Employment* (St. Paul, Minn.: Council on the Economic Status of Women, March 1982).

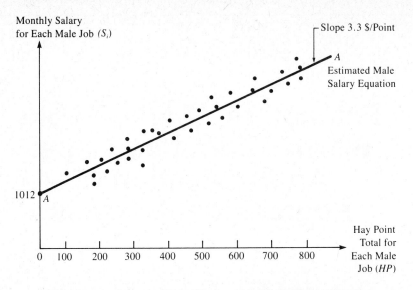

FIGURE 14A.1   Estimated Male "Comparable Worth" Salary Equation

distances between the line and the individual data points is minimized. The line estimated from the data using this method—the *method of least squares*—has a number of desirable statistical properties.[2]

Application of this method to data for the *male* occupations contained in the Minnesota data yielded the estimated line[3]

$$S_i = 1012 + 3.3 \, HP_i. \tag{14A.1}$$

So, for example, if male job i were rated at 200 Hay Points, we would predict that the monthly salary associated with job i would be $1012 + (3.3)(200)$ or $1672. This estimated male salary equation is drawn in Figure 14A.1 as line AA.

Now if the value of a job could be determined solely by reference to its job evaluation score, one would expect that, in the absence of wage discrimination against female jobs, male and female jobs rated equal in terms of total Hay Point scores would pay equal salaries (at least on average). Put another way, the same salary equation used to predict salaries of male jobs could be used to provide predictions of salaries for female jobs, and any inaccuracies in the prediction would be completely random. Hence, a test of whether female jobs are discriminated against is to see if the salaries they pay are systematically less than the salaries one

[2]These include that, on average, you get the correct answer, the estimates are the most precise possible among a certain class of estimators, and the sum of the positive and negative vertical deviations of the data points from the estimated line will be zero (i.e., on average, you get the correct prediction). For a more formal treatment of the method of least squares, see any statistics or econometrics text. A good introduction for the reader with no statistical background is David Sjoquist, Larry Schroeder, and Paula Stephan, *Interpreting Linear Regression Analysis: A Heuristic Approach* (Morristown, N.J.: General Learning Press, 1974).

[3]These estimates are obtained in Ronald Ehrenberg and Robert Smith, "Comparable Worth in the Public Sector" (paper presented at the National Bureau for Economic Research Conference on Public Sector Labor Markets, Williamsburg, Va., November 1984). They are not contained in the study cited in footnote 1.

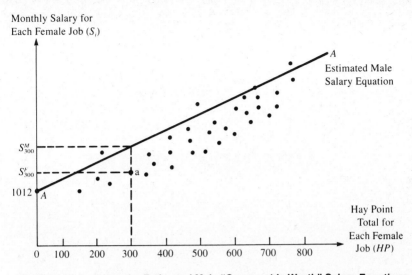

FIGURE 14A.2   Using the Estimated Male "Comparable Worth" Salary Equations to Estimate the Extent of Underpayment of Female Jobs

would predict they would pay, given their Hay Point scores and the salary equation for male jobs.

Figure 14A.2 illustrates how this is done. Here each dot represents a salary-Hay Point combination for a female job. Superimposed on this scatter of points is the estimated male job salary equation, *AA,* from Figure 14A.1. The fact that the vast majority of the data points in Figure 14A.2 lie below the male salary line suggests that female jobs tend to be underpaid relative to male jobs with the same number of Hay Points. For example, the female job that is rated at 300 Hay Points (point *a*) is paid a salary of S_{300}^{F}. However, according to the estimated male salary line, if that job were a male job it would be paid S_{300}^{M}. The difference in percentage terms between S_{300}^{M} and S_{300}^{F} is an estimate of the "comparable worth" earnings gap—the extent of underpayment—for the female job. Indeed, calculations suggest that the average (across all the female occupations) "comparable worth" earnings gap in the Minnesota data is over 16 percent.[4]

This brief presentation has glossed over a number of complications that must be addressed before such estimates can be considered estimates of wage discrimination against female jobs.[5] These include issues relating to the reliability and/or potential sex bias in the evaluation methods, whether salaries and Hay Point scores may be related in a nonlinear fashion, whether the composition of any given total Hay Point score (across the four sets of job characteristics) affects salaries, and whether variables other than the job evaluation scores can legitimately affect salaries. Nonetheless, it should give the reader a sense of how "comparable worth wage gap" estimates are computed.

---

[4]See Ehrenberg and Smith, "Comparable Worth in the Public Sector."

[5]For a more complete discussion of these issues, see Ehrenberg and Smith, "Comparable Worth in the Public Sector."

15

Unemployment

As noted in Chapter 2, the population can be divided into those people in the labor force *(L)* and those not in the labor force *(N)*. The labor force consists of those people who are employed *(E)* and those who are unemployed but would like to be employed *(U)*. The concept of unemployment is somewhat ambiguous since in theory virtually anyone would be willing to be employed in return for a generous enough compensation package. Economists tend to resolve this dilemma by defining unemployment in terms of an individual's willingness to be employed at some prevailing market wage. Government statistics take a more pragmatic approach, defining the unemployed as those who are on temporary layoff waiting to be recalled by their previous employers or those who have actively searched for work in the previous month (of course, "actively" is not precisely defined).

Given these definitions, the unemployment rate **(u)** is further defined as the ratio of the number of the unemployed to the number in the labor force:

$$\mathbf{u} = \frac{U}{L}. \tag{15.1}$$

Much attention is focused on how the national unemployment rate varies over time and how unemployment rates vary across geographic areas and age/race/sex groups.

It is important, however, to understand the limitations of unemployment rate data. They *do* reflect the proportion of a group that, at a point in time, actively wants to work but is not employed. They *do not,* however, necessarily provide an accurate reflection of the economic hardship that members of a group are suffering, for a number of reasons.[1] First, individuals who are not actively searching for work,

---

[1] This discussion draws heavily on the final report of the National Commission on Employment and Unemployment Statistics, *Counting the Labor Force* (Washington, D. C.: U.S. Government Printing Office, 1979); and Glen G. Cain, "Labor-Force Concepts and Definitions in View of Their Purposes," in *Concepts and Data Needs* (Appendix Volume I to the Commission's final report).

including those who searched unsuccessfully and then gave up, are not counted among the unemployed (see Chapter 7). Second, unemployment statistics tell us nothing about the earnings levels of those who are employed, including whether these exceed the poverty level. Third, a substantial fraction of the unemployed come from families in which other earners are present—for example, many unemployed are teenagers—and the unemployed often are not the primary source of their family's support. Fourth, a substantial fraction of the unemployed receive some income support while they are unemployed, either in the form of government unemployment compensation payments or private supplementary unemployment benefits (*SUBs*). Finally, unemployment rate data give us information on the fraction of the labor force that is not working, but tell us little about the fraction of the population that is employed.

To emphasize the last point, Table 15.1 contains data on the aggregate unemployment rate, the labor force participation rate, and the *employment rate*—the last being defined as employment divided by *population*—for 1948, 1958, 1968, and 1978. Although the unemployment rate rose from 3.9 percent in 1948 to 6.8 percent in 1958, because the aggregate labor force participation rate also rose by 1.5 percentage points during the period, the employment rate (the fraction of the population that is employed) fell only slightly. Focusing on the change in the employment rate suggests less of an economic downturn in 1958 than does focusing on the change in the unemployment rate. In contrast, while between 1968 and 1978 the unemployment rate once again rose (this time from 3.6 to 6.0 percent), the employment rate actually *rose* during the decade because of the relatively large increase in the labor force participation rate (3 percentage points) that occurred during 1968–78. In this case, focusing only on the movements in the employment rate suggests that an economic expansion took place.

Nonetheless, the unemployment rate remains a useful indicator of labor market conditions. This chapter will be concerned with why *anyone* is unemployed; with why the unemployment rate varies over time, regions, or age/race/sex groups; and with how various government policies affect, either in an intended or unintended manner, the level of unemployment.

TABLE 15.1 Labor Force Participation, Employment, and Unemployment Rates

Year	Unemployment Rate (U/L)	Labor Force Participation Rate (L/POP)	Employment Rate (E/POP)
1948	3.9	58.9	56.6
1958	6.8	60.4	56.3
1968	3.6	60.7	58.5
1978	6.0	63.7	59.9

U = number of people unemployed.
L = number of people in the labor force.
E = number of people employed.
POP = total population.

SOURCE: Based on U.S. Department of Labor, *1979 Employment and Training Report of the President* (Washington, D.C.: U.S. Government Printing Office, 1979), Table A1.

The next section begins with a simple conceptual model of a labor market that emphasizes the importance of considering the *flows* between labor market states (for example, the *movement* of people from employed to unemployed status) as well as the *number* of people in each state (for example, the *number* of the unemployed). Knowledge of the determinants of these flows is crucial to any understanding of the causes of unemployment.

The chapter will then move on to discuss how unemployment arises. Economists conceptually categorize unemployment as being *frictional, structural, demand-deficient,* or *seasonal* in nature. After defining each type of unemployment and discussing its causes, we shall focus on policy issues that are raised by the discussion. Among the issues that will be considered are how the unemployment insurance system and unemployment are interrelated, why unemployment rates vary across age/race/sex groups, why the "full employment" unemployment rate has risen since 1960, and why firms lay off workers rather than reducing their wages in a recession. The chapter will conclude by discussing some normative issues relating to unemployment, including whether teenagers who were unemployed suffer long-run losses from such experiences.

A STOCK-FLOW MODEL OF THE LABOR MARKET

Data on the number of people who are employed, unemployed, and not in the labor force are provided each month from the national *Current Population Survey (CPS).*[2] As Figure 15.1 indicates, in 1976 (when the overall unemployment rate averaged 7.7 percent) there were 87.5 million employed, 7.3 million unemployed, and 61.2 million adults age 16 and over not in the labor force during a typical month. The impression one gets when one traces these data over short periods of time is that of relative stability; for example, it is highly unusual for the unemployment rate to change by more than a few tenths of a percentage point from one month to the next.

Focusing only on these *labor market stocks* and their net month-to-month changes, however, masks the highly dynamic nature of labor markets. Each month a substantial fraction of the unemployed leave unemployment status, either finding a job or dropping out of the labor force. For example, in each month of 1976 approximately 1.6 million unemployed individuals found employment (the flow denoted by *UE* in Figure 15.1) and 1.4 million of the unemployed dropped out of the labor force (the flow denoted by *UN*). These numbers represent the proportions 0.219 *(P_{ue})* and 0.192 *(P_{un})* of the stock of the unemployed, respectively; thus, one can conclude that approximately 40 percent of the individuals who were unemployed in a given month in 1976 left unemployment by the next month. These individuals were replaced in the pool of unemployed by roughly equivalent flows of individuals into unemployment from the stocks of employed individuals (the flow

---

[2]The next two paragraphs draw heavily on Ralph E. Smith, "A Simulation Model of the Demographic Composition of Employment, Unemployment, and Labor Force Participation," in *Research in Labor Economics,* vol. I, ed. Ronald Ehrenberg (Greenwich, Conn.: JAI Press, 1977).

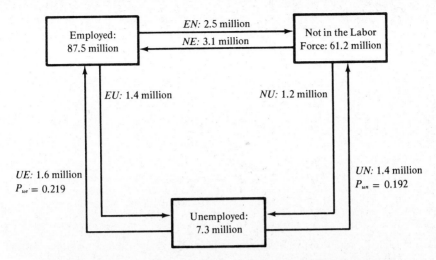

FIGURE 15.1   Labor Market Stocks and Flows: 1976 Monthly Averages

SOURCE: Ralph E. Smith and Jean E. Vanski, "Gross Change Data: The Neglected Data Base," in National Commission on Employment and Unemployment Statistics, *Counting the Labor Force,* vol. II (Washington, D.C.: U.S. Government Printing Office, 1979), appendix.

EU) and those not in the labor force (the flow *NU*).[3] The flow *EU* consists of individuals who voluntarily left or involuntarily lost their last job, while the flow *NU* consists of people entering the labor force. Finally, Figure 15.1 also indicates that each month there is considerable direct movement between employment and out-of-labor-force status.

When one thinks of the unemployed, the image of an individual laid off from his or her previous job often springs to mind. However, the view that such individuals comprise all, or even most, of the unemployed is incorrect. Table 15.2 provides some data that bear on this point for a period during the 1970s and early 1980s in which the unemployment rate varied between 4.9 and 9.7 percent. Only in the high unemployment years of 1980 and 1982 were more than half of the unemployed job losers. In each year, more than one third of the unemployed came from out-of-labor-force status—that is, they were individuals who were either entering the labor force for the first time (*new entrants*) or individuals who had some previous employment experience and were reentering the labor force after a period of time out of the labor force (*reentrants*). Indeed, although the vast majority of individuals who quit their jobs obtain new jobs prior to quitting and never pass through unemployment status, in each year (save for 1982) at least 10 percent of the unemployed were voluntary job-leavers.[4]

---

[3]Actually, in 1976 the flows of people into unemployment from both the stocks of the employed and those not in the labor force were less than the flows out of unemployment into these stocks (see Figure 15.1). As might be expected, then, the unemployment rate was declining during most of the year.

[4]For evidence that most quits do not involve a spell of unemployment, see J. Peter Mattila, "Job Quitting and Frictional Unemployment," *American Economic Review* 64(March 1974):235–39.

TABLE 15.2   Categories of Unemployment

Year	Unemployment Rate	Percent of Unemployed Who Are:			
		Job Losers	Job Leavers	Reentrants	New Entrants
1970	4.9	44.3	13.4	30.0	12.3
1972	5.6	43.1	13.1	29.8	13.9
1974	5.6	43.5	14.9	28.4	13.2
1976	7.7	49.8	12.2	26.0	12.1
1978	6.1	41.6	14.1	30.0	14.3
1980	7.1	51.9	11.6	25.2	11.4
1982	9.7	58.7	7.9	22.3	11.1

SOURCE: U.S. Department of Labor, *1982 Employment and Training Report of the President* (Washington, D.C.: U.S. Government Printing Office, 1982), Table A-36, and U.S. Department of Labor, *Monthly Labor Review*, March 1983, Table 7.

Similarly, when one thinks of an individual on layoff, one may envision an individual who has permanently lost his or her job and who finds employment with a new employer only after an exhaustive job search and long period of unemployment. However, the evidence suggests that a substantial fraction of those individuals who *lost* their last job are on *temporary layoff* and ultimately return to their previous employer, many after only a relatively short spell of unemployment.[5] Why some individuals "cycle" between employed and unemployed status, maintaining attachment to a single employer, will be discussed below.

Although ultimately public concern focuses on the level of unemployment, to understand the determinants of this level one must analyze the flows of individuals between the various labor market states. A group's unemployment rate might be high because its members have difficulty finding jobs once unemployed, because they have difficulty (for voluntary or involuntary reasons) remaining employed once a job is found, or because they frequently enter and exit the labor force. The appropriate policy prescription to reduce the unemployment rate will depend upon which one of these labor market flows is responsible for the high rate.

Somewhat more formally, one can show that if labor markets are roughly in balance, with the flows into and out of unemployment equal, the unemployment rate (**u**) for a group depends upon the various labor market flows in the following manner:

$$\mathbf{u} = F(P_{eu}^{+}, P_{en}^{+}, P_{nu}^{+}, P_{ue}^{-}, P_{un}^{-}, P_{ne}^{-}). \tag{15.2}$$

Here F means "a function of," P_{ij} represents the fraction of the group in labor market state i that moves to labor market state j during the period, and the subscripts n, e, and u represent the states "not in the labor force," "employed," and

---

[5]For evidence on the magnitude of temporary layoffs, see Martin Feldstein, "The Importance of Temporary Layoffs: An Empirical Analysis," *Brookings Papers on Economic Activity*, (1975–3); and Robert Topel, "Inventories, Layoffs and the Short-Run Demand for Labor," *American Economic Review* 72(September 1982):769–88.

"unemployed," respectively. So, for example, if there were initially 100 employed individuals in a group and 15 of them became unemployed during a period, P_{eu} would equal 0.15. [The exact formula for equation (15.2) and its derivation, found in the appendix to this chapter.]

A + over a variable in equation (15.2) means that an increase in that variable will increase the unemployment rate, while a − means that an increase in the variable will decrease the unemployment rate. The equation thus asserts that, other things equal, increases in the proportions of individuals who voluntarily or involuntarily leave their jobs and become unemployed (P_{eu}) or leave the labor force (P_{en}) will increase a group's unemployment rate, as will an increase in the proportion of the group that enters the labor force without first having a job lined up (P_{nu}). Similarly, the greater the proportion of individuals who leave unemployment status, either to become employed (P_{ue}) or to leave the labor force (P_{un}), the lower a group's unemployment rate will be. Finally, the greater the proportion of individuals who enter the labor force and immediately find jobs (P_{ne}), the lower a group's unemployment rate will be.[6]

The various theories of unemployment discussed in subsequent sections all essentially relate to the determination of one or more of the flows represented in equation (15.2). That is, they provide explanations for why the proportions of individuals who move between the various labor market states vary over time, across geographic areas, or across age/race/sex groups. Equation (15.2) can help explain why unemployment rates rise in recessions, how and why unemployment rates are influenced by the unemployment insurance system, and why unemployment rates vary across age/race/sex groups.

Equation (15.2) and Figure 15.1 also make clear that social concern over any given level of unemployment should focus on both the incidence of unemployment (on the fraction of people in a group who become unemployed) and the duration of spells of unemployment. Society is probably more concerned if small groups of individuals are unemployed for long periods of time than if many individuals rapidly pass through unemployment status. Up until recently, it was widely believed that the bulk of measured unemployment could be attributed to many people experiencing short spells of unemployment. However, recent evidence suggests that, while many people do pass quickly through the unemployed state, most unemployment is due to prolonged spells of unemployment for a relatively small number of individuals.[7]

---

[6]For an intuitive understanding of why each of these results holds, recall the definition of the unemployment rate in equation (15.1). A movement from one labor market state to another may affect the numerator or the denominator, or both, and hence the unemployment rate. For example, an increase in P_{en} does not affect the number of unemployed individuals directly, but it does reduce the size of the labor force. According to equation (15.1), this reduction leads to an increase in the unemployment rate.

[7]Kim B. Clark and Lawrence H. Summers, "Labor-Market Dynamics and Unemployment: A Reconsideration," *Brookings Papers on Economic Activity*, 1979–1, pp. 13–60.

TYPES OF UNEMPLOYMENT AND THEIR CAUSES

Frictional Unemployment

Suppose a competitive labor market is in equilibrium in the sense that, at the prevailing market wage, the quantity of labor demanded just equals the quantity of labor supplied. Figure 15.2 shows such a labor market, in which the demand curve is D_0, the supply curve is S_0, employment is E_0, and the wage rate is W_0. Thus far the text has treated this equilibrium situation as one of full employment and has implied that there is no unemployment associated with it. However, this implication is not completely correct. Even in a market equilibrium or full employment situation there will still be some *frictional unemployment* because some people will be "between jobs."

Frictional unemployment arises because labor markets are inherently dynamic, because information flows are imperfect, and because it takes time for unemployed workers and employers with job vacancies to find each other. Even if the size of the labor force is constant, in each period there will be new entrants to the labor market searching for employment while other employed or unemployed individuals are leaving the labor force. Some people will quit their jobs to search for other employment. Moreover, random fluctuations in demand across firms will cause some firms to lay off workers at the same time that other firms will be seeking to hire new employees. Because information about the characteristics of those searching for work and the nature of the jobs opening up cannot instantly be known or evaluated, it takes time for job matches to be made between unemployed workers

FIGURE 15.2   The Full-Employment Rate of Unemployment:
A Decline in Demand Leads
to Increased Unemployment

and potential employers. Hence, even when, in the aggregate, the demand for labor equals the supply, frictional unemployment will still exist.

The level of frictional unemployment in an economy is determined by the flows of individuals into and out of the labor market and the speed with which unemployed individuals find jobs. This speed is determined by the prevailing economic institutions, and institutional changes can influence the level of frictional unemployment. For example, instituting a computerized job bank system in which job applicants at the U.S. Employment Service are immediately informed of all listed jobs for which they are qualified might reduce the time it takes them to find jobs. This system would increase the probability that an unemployed worker would become employed in any period (increase P_{ue}) and hence, as indicated by equation (15.2), would *decrease* the unemployment rate. On the other hand, one should be aware that if the time it takes unemployed workers to find jobs decreases, more employed workers may consider quitting their jobs to search for better-paying employment, thereby *increasing* P_{eu} and the unemployment rate. (This example should remind us again that well-intentioned social programs often have unintended adverse side effects.)

Structural Unemployment

Structural unemployment arises when changes in the pattern of labor demand cause a mismatch between the skills demanded and supplied in a given area or cause an imbalance between the supplies and demands for workers across areas. *If* wages were completely flexible *and* if costs of occupational or geographic mobility were low, market adjustments would quickly eliminate this type of unemployment. However, in practice these conditions may fail to hold, and structural unemployment may result.

Our by now familiar two-sector labor market model, represented by Figure 15.3, can be used to illustrate this point. For the moment we shall assume the sectors refer to markets for skill classes of workers; later we shall assume that they are two geographically separate labor markets. Suppose that Market A is the market for semiskilled workers in the shoe industry and Market B is the market for skilled computer programmers, and suppose that initially both markets are in equilibrium. Given the demand and supply curves in both markets [(D_{0A}, S_{0A}) and (D_{0B}, S_{0B})], the equilibrium wage/employment combinations in the two sectors will be (W_{0A}, E_{0A}) and (W_{0B}, E_{0B}), respectively. Because of differences in training costs and nonpecuniary conditions of employment, the wages need not be equal in the two sectors.

Now suppose that the demand for semiskilled shoe workers falls to D_{1A} as a result of foreign import competition, while the demand for computer programmers rises to D_{1B} as a result of the increased use of computers. If real wages are inflexible downward in Market A because of union contract provisions, social norms, or government legislation, employment of semiskilled shoe employees will fall to E_{1A}. Employment and wages of computer programmers will rise to E_{1B} and W_{1B}, respectively. Unemployment of $E_{0A} - E_{1A}$ workers would be created in the short run.

If shoe-industry employees could costlessly become computer programmers, these unemployed workers would "move" to Market B, where we assume wages

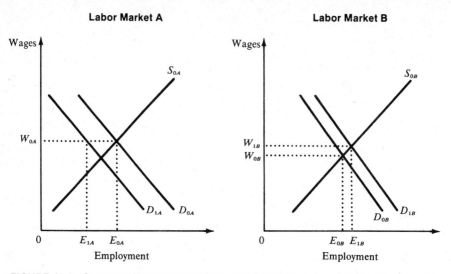

FIGURE 15.3   Structural Unemployment Due to Inflexible Wages and Costs of Adjustment

are flexible, and eventually all the unemployment would be eliminated.[8] Structural unemployment arises, however, when costs of adjustment are sufficiently high to preclude such movements. The cost to displaced individuals—many in their fifties and sixties—may prove to be prohibitively expensive, given the limited time horizons they face. Moreover, it may be difficult for them to borrow funds to finance the necessary job training.

Geographic imbalances can be analyzed in the same framework. Suppose we now assume that Market A refers to a Snowbelt city and Market B refers to a Sunbelt city, both employing the same type of labor. When demand falls in the Snowbelt and unemployment increases because wages are not completely flexible, these unemployed workers may continue to wait for jobs in their city for at least three reasons. First, information flows are imperfect, so workers may be unaware of the availability of jobs thousands of miles away. Second, the direct money costs of such a move, including moving costs and the transaction costs involved in buying and selling a home, are high. Third, the psychological costs of moving long distances are substantial because friends and neighbors and community support systems must be given up. As noted in Chapter 10, such factors inhibit geographic migration, and migration tends to decline with age. These costs are sufficiently high that many workers who become unemployed as a result of plant shutdowns or permanent layoffs express no interest in searching for jobs outside their immediate geographic area.[9]

---

[8]Actually, this statement is not quite correct. As Chapter 12 noted when analyzing the effects of unions using a similar model, *wait unemployment* may arise. That is, as long as the wage rate in Market A exceeds the wage rate in Market B and unemployed workers in Market A expect that normal job turnover will eventually create job vacancies in A, it may be profitable for them to remain attached to Market A and wait for a job in that sector. Wait unemployment is another example of frictional unemployment.

[9]See, for example, Robert Aronson and Robert McKersie, *Economic Consequences of Plant Shutdowns in New York State* (Ithaca, N.Y.: New York State School of Industrial and Labor Relations, 1980).

Structural unemployment arises, then, because of changing patterns of labor demand that occur in the face of both rigid wages and high costs of occupational or geographic mobility.[10] In terms of Figure 15.1, structurally unemployed workers have a low probability of moving from unemployed to employed status (low P_{ue}), and any social policies that increase this probability should reduce the level of structural unemployment (other things equal). Examples of such policies include the provision of subsidized training, the provision of information about job market conditions in other areas, and the provision of relocation allowances to help defray the costs of migration.

Each of these policies is part of the *Trade Adjustment Assistance Program,* which was initiated under the Trade Expansion Act of 1962 and expanded under the Trade Act of 1974. This program was designed to aid individuals who became unemployed because of changes in product demand brought about by foreign competition, and it also provided for an expanded form of unemployment compensation benefits (the effects of unemployment compensation on unemployment will be discussed later in the chapter). The available evidence indicates, however, that, perhaps because of restrictive eligibility rules, this program has had little effect on increasing the probability that these structurally unemployed workers will find employment.[11]

On a more general level, since the early 1960s the federal government has been heavily involved in policies to reduce structural unemployment. These policies include the provision of relocation allowances to unemployed workers residing in depressed areas (under the *Area Redevelopment Act of 1959*), the provision of classroom and on-the-job training to both disadvantaged and unemployed workers (under the *Manpower Development and Training Act of 1962*), the provision of both training and public sector employment opportunities (under the *Comprehensive Employment and Training Act of 1973*), and, most recently, an emphasis on public/private cooperation in the provision of training (under the *Job Training Partnership Act of 1982*). Indeed, in fiscal year 1981 more than 3.3 million individuals were enrolled at some time during the year in federally funded employment and training programs.[12] Although evidence on the effectiveness of these programs is mixed, several studies suggest that some have succeeded in increasing the earnings or employment probabilities of those individuals who were enrolled in the programs.[13]

---

[10]For recent evidence on the magnitude of structural unemployment in the U.S. economy, see Katherine Abraham, "Structural/Frictional vs. Deficient Demand Unemployment," *American Economic Review* 83(September 1983):708–24; and David Lilien, "Sectoral Shifts and Cyclical Unemployment," *Journal of Political Economy* 90(August 1982):777–93.

[11]See, for example, George R. Neumann, "The Labor Market Adjustment of Trade-Displaced Workers: The Evidence from the Trade Adjustment Assistance Program," in *Research in Labor Economics,* vol. 2, 1978; and Walter Corson and Walter Nicholson, "Trade Adjustment Assistance for Workers: Results of a Survey of Recipients Under the Trade Act of 1974," in *Research in Labor Economics,* vol. 4, 1981.

[12]*1982 Employment and Training Report of the President,* Table F-1.

[13]See, for example, Orley Ashenfelter, "Estimating the Effects of Training Programs on Earnings," *Review of Economics and Statistics* 60(February 1979):47–57; Nicholas Kiefer, "The Economic Benefits from Four Government Training Programs," in *Research in Labor Economics,* Supplement I, 1979; and Lauri Bassi, "The Effect of CETA on the Post-Program Earnings of Participants," *Journal of Human Resources* 18(Fall 1983):539–57.

Demand Deficient Unemployment

Frictional and structural unemployment can arise even when, in the aggregate, the demand for labor equals the supply. Frictional unemployment arises because labor markets are dynamic and information flows are imperfect; structural unemployment arises because of geographic or occupational imbalances in demand and supply. *Demand-deficient unemployment* occurs when the *aggregate* demand for labor declines in the face of downward inflexibility in real wages.

Returning to our simple demand and supply model of Figure 15.2, suppose that a temporary decline in aggregate demand leads to a shift in the labor demand curve to D_1. If real wages are inflexible downward, employment will fall to E_1 and $E_0 - E_1$ additional workers will become unemployed. This employment decline occurs when firms temporarily lay off workers (increasing P_{eu}) and reduce the rate at which they replace those who quit or retire (decreasing P_{ne} and P_{ue}). That is, flows into unemployment increase while flows into employment decline.[14]

One appropriate government response to demand-deficient unemployment is to pursue macroeconomic policies to increase aggregate demand; these policies include increasing the level of government spending, reducing taxes, and increasing the rate of growth of the money supply. Another policy is to use labor market programs that focus more directly on the unemployed. Examples here include temporary employment tax credits for firms and public sector employment programs, which were discussed in Chapters 4 and 13, respectively.

Of course, it still remains for us to explain *why* employers respond to a cyclical decline in demand by temporarily laying off some of their work force rather than reducing their employees' real wages. If the latter occurred, employment would move to E_2 and real wages to W_2 in Figure 15.2. Although employment would be lower than its initial level, E_0, there would be no measured demand-deficient unemployment because $E_0 - E_2$ workers would have dropped out of the labor force in response to this lower wage.

According to one explanation for rigid money wages, employers are not free to unilaterally cut money wages because of the presence of unions. However, this cannot be a complete explanation because less than one quarter of American workers are represented by unions (see Chapter 12), and unions could, in any case, agree to temporary wage cuts to save jobs instead of subjecting their members to layoffs. Why they fail to make such arrangements is instructive.[15] A temporary wage reduction would reduce the earnings of all workers, while layoffs would affect, in most cases, only those workers most recently hired. Since unions represent their entire membership, not just the newly hired, and since union leaders are not likely to be drawn from the ranks of new members, unions tend to favor a policy of layoffs rather than one that reduces wages for all members.

Layoffs do occur in nonunion firms, although less frequently than in union

---

[14]See Steven T. Marston, "Employment Instability and High Unemployment Rates," *Brookings Papers on Economic Activity,* 1976-1, pp. 169–203, for evidence on this point.

[15]See James Medoff, "Layoffs and Alternatives Under Trade Unions in United States Manufacturing," *American Economic Review* 69(June 1979):380–95, for the following argument and evidence.

firms, and there are three additional reasons why both union and nonunion employers might prefer temporary layoffs to reductions in real wages.[16] First, employers may have better information than employees on the true state of demand conditions faced by the firm. If a firm requests its employees to take a wage cut in periods of low demand, the employees may believe that the employer is falsely stating that demand is low and, noting that the employer loses nothing by the wage cut, resist the request. In contrast, if a firm instead temporarily lays workers off, it loses the output these workers would have produced, and workers may therefore accept such an action more readily. Put another way, the *asymmetry of information* between employers and employees makes layoffs the preferred policy.[17]

Second, in the presence of investments in firm-specific human capital, which often lead to structured internal labor markets (see Chapter 5), employers have incentives both to minimize voluntary turnover and to maximize their employees' work effort and productivity. Across-the-board temporary wage reductions would increase all employees' incentives to quit and could lead to reduced work effort on their part. In contrast, layoffs affect only the least experienced workers, the workers in whom the firm has invested the smallest amount of resources. It is likely, then, that the firm will find choosing the layoff strategy a more profitable alternative.[18]

Third, if potential job applicants and existing employees are aware that a firm is pursuing a temporary layoff rather than a temporary wage cut strategy, they may be willing to work for a lower *average* wage rate. Individuals are typically assumed to be *risk-averse;* that is, they are assumed to prefer a constant earnings stream to a fluctuating one.[19] In effect, a system of layoffs in which the newest employees are laid off first provides an *implicit contract* (a guarantee or form of insurance to experienced workers) that they will be immune to all but the severest declines in demand. Put another way, after an initial period when the risk of layoff is high, earnings are likely to be very stable over time. To the extent that experienced employees value stable earnings streams, they should be willing to pay for this stability by accepting lower wages in such situations, thereby reducing employers' costs. Of course, during the initial period, workers will be subject to potential

---

[16]See Medoff, "Layoffs and Alternatives Under Trade Unions," for evidence that layoff rates are higher in union than nonunion firms, other things equal. When a recession gets very severe, so that many union members are threatened by layoffs, unions agree to wage cuts. For evidence that this occurred in the early 1980s, see Robert J. Flanagan, "Wage Concessions and Long-term Union Flexibility," *Brookings Papers on Economic Activity* 1984-1:183–216.

[17]See, for example, Sanford Grossman, Oliver Hart, and Eric Maskin, "Unemployment with Observable Aggregate Shocks," *Journal of Political Economy* 91(December 1983):907–28; Sanford Grossman and Oliver Hart, "Implicit Contracts, Moral Hazard and Unemployment," *American Economic Review* 71(May 1981):301–7; and Costas Azariadis, "Employment with Asymmetric Information," *Quarterly Journal of Economics* 98(Supplement, 1983):157–72.

[18]An alternative explanation for the presence of temporary layoffs in employment situations that involve specific human capital, which stresses the inability to specify contracts that are fully contingent on all states of the world, is found in Robert Hall and Edward Lazear, "The Excess Sensitivity of Layoffs and Quits to Demand," *Journal of Labor Economics* 2(April 1984):233–59.

[19]This line of reasoning follows that in Costas Azariadas, "Implicit Contracts and Underemployment Equilibria," *Journal of Political Economy* 83(December 1975):1183–1202; and Martin Bailey, "Wages and Employment Under Uncertain Demand," *Review of Economic Studies* 41(January 1974):37–50.

Example 15.1

International Unemployment Rate Differentials

Comparisons of unemployment rates across nations are difficult because the exact definition of unemployment differs across nations. For example, in the United States "discouraged workers" who leave the labor force are not counted among the unemployed, while in Italy they are. Nevertheless, it is possible to adjust the unemployment data reported by various industrial countries so that the data correspond approximately to the U.S. definition of unemployment. These adjusted unemployment rates are reported in the table below for ten industrial nations and three years during the 1970s and 1980s.

Nation	1974	1977	1981
United States	5.6	7.0	7.6
Canada	5.3	8.1	7.6
Australia	2.7	5.6	5.8
Japan	1.4	2.0	2.2
France	2.9	5.0	7.7
Germany	1.6	3.6	4.2
Great Britain	3.1	6.2	11.3
Italy	2.8	3.4	4.2
Sweden	2.0	1.8	2.5
Netherlands	3.8	5.1	8.9

Note: The definitions of unemployment have been adjusted to approximate the U.S. concept of unemployment.

SOURCE: Joyanna Moy, "Unemployment and Labor Force Trends in Ten Industrial Nations: An Update," *Monthly Labor Review* 105(November 1982):17–21, Table 2.

This table indicates that there are large differences in the adjusted unemployment rate across these nations in each year; in 1977 the adjusted unemployment rate varied from 1.8 percent in Sweden to 8.1 percent in Canada. Part of the difference results from differences in aggregate demand across nations; labor markets were tighter in Sweden than they were in Canada in 1977. Another part of the difference, however, reflects differences in social and institutional forces that affect the underlying labor market flows.

The adjusted unemployment rate in Japan, for example, is typically lower than that in the United States. As we first saw in Chapter 5, a large sector of the Japanese labor market is characterized by a system of long-term, often lifelong, employment relations between employers and employees. Employees in this sector rarely quit their jobs voluntarily and their employers rarely lay off workers during economic downswings. As a result, the proportions of employed workers who voluntarily leave or involuntarily lose their jobs each period and enter unemployment status (P_{eu}) are low in Japan relative to the United States, as are the proportions who leave the labor force (P_{en}). As equation (15.2) indicates, the low levels of P_{eu} and P_{en} cause the Japanese unemployment rate to be lower than the American unemployment rate, other things equal.

How are Japanese employers able to maintain almost all their employees on their payrolls during economic downswings? A *Monthly Labor Review* article suggests one way:

> A number of Japanese enterprises with underutilized skilled labor (such as steel mills, shipbuilders, or textile producers) have adopted a novel method of maintaining employment for their regular workers. Excess workers are "loaned" for a specified period of no longer than 6 months to enterprises experiencing current labor shortages (such as automobile manufacturers). The workers maintain their affiliation with and receive their full wages from the lending company. The borrowing company usually pays temporary-worker wages to the lending company and the difference in wages plus benefits is made up by the lending employer. Thus, the borrowing company is able to temporarily increase its labor force with workers whose turnover rate is close to zero, while the lending company is able to maintain its regular work force at reduced cost.

SOURCES: Masanori Hashimoto, "Bonus Payments, On-the-Job Training, and Lifetime Employment in Japan," *Journal of Political Economy* 87(October 1979):1086–1104, presents evidence to support the contention that P_{eu} and P_{en} are lower in Japan than in the United States (for each age group male job tenure is seen to be higher than in the United States); Joyanna Moy, "Recent Labor Market Trends in Nine Industrial Nations," *Monthly Labor Review*, 102(May 1979):14.

earnings variability and may demand higher wages then to compensate them for these risks. However, if the fraction of the work force subject to layoffs is small, on average employers' costs should be reduced.

The incentives for both employers and employees to prefer temporary layoffs to fluctuations in real wages is magnified by two characteristics of the unemployment insurance (UI) system: the *tax treatment of UI benefits* and the system's *method of financing benefits*.[20] The unemployment insurance system is actually a system of individual state systems and, although the details of the individual systems differ, one can easily sketch the broad outlines of how they operate.

Today virtually all private sector employees are covered by a state UI system. When such workers become unemployed, their eligibility for unemployment insurance benefits is based upon their previous labor market experience and reason for unemployment. With respect to their experience, each state requires unemployed individuals to demonstrate "permanent" attachment to the labor force, by meeting minimum earnings or weeks-worked tests during some base period, before they can be eligible for UI benefits. In all states covered workers who are laid off *and* meet these labor market experience tests are eligible for UI benefits. In some states

---

[20]A more complete description of the characteristics of the UI system is found in Daniel S. Hamermesh, *Jobless Pay and the Economy* (Baltimore: Johns Hopkins University Press, 1977). The connection between temporary layoffs and these characteristics of the UI system was pointed out in Martin Feldstein, "Temporary Layoffs in the Theory of Unemployment," *Journal of Political Economy* 84(October 1976):937–58; empirical evidence on the relationship was provided in Martin Feldstein, "The Effect of Unemployment Insurance on Temporary Layoffs," *American Economic Review* 68(December 1978):834–40; and Robert Topel, "On Layoffs and Unemployment Insurance," *American Economic Review* 83(September 1983):541–59.

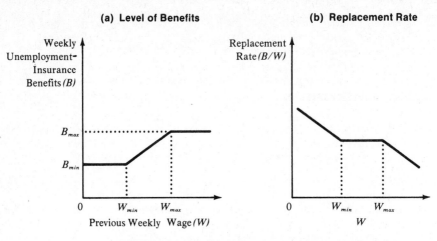

FIGURE 15.4   Weekly Unemployment Insurance Benefits as a Function of Previous Earnings

workers who voluntarily quit their jobs are eligible for benefits, while in only two states (New York and Rhode Island) are strikers eligible for benefits. Finally, new entrants or reentrants to the labor force and workers fired for cause are, in general, ineligible for benefits.

After a waiting period, which is one or two weeks in most states, an eligible worker can begin to collect UI benefits. The structure of benefits is described in Figure 15.4, where it can be seen that benefits are related to an individual's previous earnings level.[21] As shown in panel (a), all eligible unemployed workers are entitled to at least a minimum benefit level, B_{min}. After previous earnings rise above a critical level, W_{min}, benefits increase proportionately with earnings up to a maximum earnings level W_{max}, past which benefits remain constant at B_{max}. Eleven states also have dependents' allowances for unemployed workers, although in some of these states the dependents' allowance cannot increase an individual's weekly UI benefits above B_{max}.

An implication of such a benefit structure is that the ratio of an individual's UI benefits to his or her previous earnings varies according to his or her past earnings— see panel (b). This ratio is often called the *replacement rate,* the fraction of previous earnings that the UI benefits replace. Over the range between W_{min} and W_{max}, where the replacement rate is constant, most states aim to replace around 50 percent of an unemployed worker's previous earnings. It is important to stress that up until 1978 *UI benefits were not subject to the federal income tax;* since then, however, UI benefits received by those whose family incomes exceed a specified level are taxed. This level has declined over the years and in 1984 it stood at $18,000 ($12,000) for individuals filing joint (individual) tax returns.

---

[21]Benefits are calculated across states in at least three ways: as a percentage of annual earnings, as a percentage of previous weekly earnings, and as a percentage of an individual's earnings during his or her "high" earnings quarter during the past year. For our purposes, such distinctions are unimportant.

Once UI benefits begin, an unemployed individual's eligibility for continued benefits depends upon his or her making continual "suitable efforts" to find employment; the definition of suitable efforts varies widely across states. In addition, there is a maximum duration of receipt of benefits that is of fixed length in some states and varies in other states with a worker's prior labor market experience (workers with "more permanent attachment" being eligible for more weeks of benefits). Periodically Congress also passes temporary legislation that extends the length of time unemployed workers can receive benefits in states in which the unemployment rate is high, but the maximum total duration of eligibility for benefits did not exceed 65 weeks in all of the 1970s and early 1980s.

The benefits paid out by the UI system are financed by a payroll tax. Unlike the social security payroll tax, in all but four states the UI tax is paid solely by employers.[22] The UI tax payment *(T)* that an employer must make for each employee is given by

$$T = tW \quad \text{if } W \leq W_B \tag{15.3}$$

and

$$T = tW_B \quad \text{if } W > W_B,$$

where t is the employer's UI tax rate, W is an employee's earnings during the calendar year, and W_B is the *taxable wage base,* the level of earnings after which no UI tax payments are required. In 1984 the taxable wage base was $7,000 in most states; employers had to pay UI taxes on the first $7,000 of earnings for each employee.

The employer's UI tax rate is determined by general economic conditions in a state, the industry the employer is operating in, and the employer's *layoff experience.* The last term is defined differently in different states; the underlying notion is that since the UI system is an insurance system, employers who lay off lots of workers and make heavy demands on the system's resources should be assigned a higher UI tax rate. This practice is referred to as *experience rating.*

Experience rating is typically *imperfect* in the sense that the marginal cost to an employer of laying off an additional worker (in terms of a higher UI tax rate) is often less than the added UI benefits the system must pay out to that worker. Imperfect experience rating is illustrated in Figure 15.5, which plots the relationship between an employer's UI tax rate and that firm's layoff experience. (We shall interpret *layoff experience* to mean the probability that employees in the firm will be on layoff. Clearly, this probability depends both on the frequency with which the firm lays off workers and the average duration of time until they are recalled to their positions.)

Each state has a minimum UI tax rate, and below this rate—t_{min} in Figure 15.5—the firm's UI tax rate cannot fall. After a firm's layoff experience reaches

---

[22]Recall from our discussion in Chapter 3 that this fact tells us nothing about who really bears the burden of the tax.

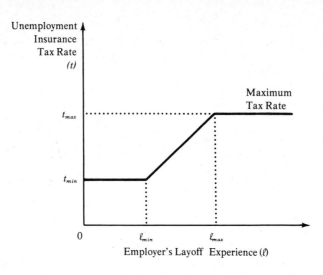

FIGURE 15.5 **Imperfectly Experience-Rated Unemployment Insurance Tax Rate**

some critical value, l_{min}, the firm's UI tax rate rises with increased layoff experience over some range. In each state there is also a ceiling on the UI tax rate, t_{max}, and after this tax rate is reached additional layoffs will not alter the firm's tax rate.[23] The system is *imperfectly* experience rated because for firms below l_{min} or above l_{max}, variations in their layoff rate have no effect on their UI tax rate.[24] Further, over the range that the tax rate is increasing with layoff experience, the increase is not large enough in most states to make the employer's marginal cost of a layoff (in terms of the increased UI taxes the firm must pay) equal to the marginal UI benefits the laid-off employees receive.

The key characteristics of the UI system that influence the desirability of temporary layoffs are the *imperfect experience rating* of the UI payroll tax and the *federal tax treatment* of UI benefits that workers receive. To understand the influence of these characteristics, suppose first that the UI system were constructed in such a way that its tax rates were perfectly experience rated and the benefits it paid out (for example, half of previous earnings) were completely taxable. A firm laying off a worker would have to pay added UI taxes equal to the full UI benefit received by the worker, so it saves just half of the worker's wages by the layoff; the *worker's* spendable income would be cut in half if he or she were laid off.

Now suppose instead that the UI tax rate employers must pay is totally independent of their layoff experience (no experience rating) and that UI benefits are not subject to any personal income taxes. A *firm* saves a laid-off worker's *entire*

---

[23]In actuality the UI tax rate changes discretely (as a step function) over the range l_{min} to l_{max}, not continuously as we have drawn in Figure 15.5. For expository convenience, we ignore this complication.

[24]Such a system of UI financing leads to interindustry subsidies, in which industries (such as banking) with virtually no layoffs still must pay the minimum tax, and these industries subsidize those industries (such as construction) that have very high layoffs but pay only the maximum rate.

wages because its UI taxes do not rise as a result of the layoff. The worker still gets a benefit equal to half of prior earnings, but since these benefits are not taxable, his or her spendable income drops by *less* than half. Thus, compared to a UI system with perfect experience rating and completely taxable benefits, it is easy to see that the current system, which has imperfect experience rating and does not tax all benefits, enhances the attractiveness of layoffs to both employer and employee.[25] Put differently, these characteristics of the UI system tend to increase the level of demand-deficient unemployment over what it would be if experience rating were perfect and benefits were completely taxable.

Seasonal Unemployment

Seasonal unemployment is similar to demand-deficient unemployment in that it is induced by fluctuations in the demand for labor. Here, however, the fluctuations can be regularly anticipated and follow a systematic pattern over the course of a year. For example, the demand for agricultural employees declines after the planting season and remains low until the harvest season. Similarly, the demand for construction workers in Snowbelt states falls during winter months. Finally, the demand for production workers falls in certain industries during the season of the year when plants are retooling to handle annual model changes; examples here include both the Detroit automotive industry (new car models) and the New York City apparel industry (new fashion designs).

The issue remains, why do employers respond to seasonal patterns of demand by laying off workers rather than reducing wage rates or hours of work? All the answers cited for why cyclical unemployment and temporary layoffs for cyclical reasons exist also pertain here. Indeed, one study has shown that the expansion (in the early 1970s) of the unemployment insurance system that led to the coverage of most agricultural employees was associated with a substantial increase in seasonal unemployment in agriculture.[26]

One may question, however, why workers would accept jobs in industries in which they knew in advance they would be unemployed for a portion of the year. For some workers, the existence of UI benefits along with the knowledge that they will be rehired as a matter of course at the end of the slack demand season may allow them to treat such periods as paid vacations. However, since UI benefits typically replace less than half of an unemployed worker's previous gross earnings and even smaller fractions for high-wage workers (see Figure 15.4), most workers will not find such a situation desirable. To attract workers to such seasonal industries, firms will have to pay workers higher wages to compensate them for being periodically unemployed. In fact, casual observation suggests that the hourly wages of construction workers are substantially higher than the hourly wages of comparably skilled manufacturing workers who work more hours each year. More

---

[25]This statement is not always true since employed workers often lose fringe benefits and the ability to take advantage of on-the-job training options.

[26]Barry Chiswick, ''The Effect of Unemployment Compensation on a Seasonal Industry: Agriculture,'' *Journal of Political Economy* 84(June 1976):591–602.

formally, recent econometric studies confirm that, other things held constant (including workers' skill levels), wages are higher in industries in which workers' expected annual durations of unemployment are longer.[27] (For a more complete analysis of this issue, see Appendix 8A.)

The existence of wage differentials that compensate workers in high-unemployment industries for the risk of unemployment makes it difficult to evaluate whether this type of unemployment is voluntary or involuntary in nature. On the one hand, in an *ex ante* (or "before the fact") sense, workers have voluntarily agreed to be employed in industries that offer higher wages *and* higher probabilities of unemployment than offered elsewhere. On the other hand, once on the job (*ex post*, or "after the fact") employees prefer to remain employed rather than becoming unemployed. Such unemployment may be considered either voluntary or involuntary, then, depending upon the perspective one is taking.

THE DEMOGRAPHIC STRUCTURE OF UNEMPLOYMENT RATES

The Full-Employment Unemployment Rate

Table 15.3 presents data on unemployment rates for various age/race/sex groups in 1980. The patterns indicated in Table 15.3 for 1980 are similar to the patterns for other years: high unemployment rates for teens and young adults of each race/sex group relative to older adults in these groups; nonwhite unemployment rates roughly double white unemployment rates for most age/sex groups; and female unemployment rates higher than male rates for whites. The high unemployment rates of nonwhite teenagers, which ranged between 33.0 and 40.4 percent in 1980, have been of particular concern to policymakers and have led to numerous programs to reduce nonwhite teenage unemployment during the late 1970s and early 1980s.

Over recent decades, the age/race/sex composition of the labor force has changed dramatically due to the growing labor force participation rates of females and to increases in the relative sizes of the teenage and nonwhite populations. Between 1960 and 1980 the proportion of the labor force that was female grew from 33.4 to 42.6 percent, the proportion that was nonwhite grew from 11.1 to 12.0 percent, and the proportion that was teenaged grew from 7.0 to 8.8 percent.[28] The increase in the relative labor force shares of those groups that have relatively higher unemployment rates has led to an increase in the overall unemployment rate that is associated with any given level of labor market tightness. Indeed, one investigator

---

[27]John Abowd and Orley Ashenfelter, "Anticipated Unemployment, Temporary Layoffs, and Compensating Wage Differentials," in Sherwin Rosen, ed., *Studies in Labor Markets* (Chicago, Ill., University of Chicago Press, 1981), pp. 141–70. Robert H. Topel, "Equilibrium Earnings, Turnover, and Unemployment: New Evidence," *Journal of Labor Economics* 2(October 1984):500–22. Topel also shows that, other things equal, high UI benefits *reduce* the compensating wage differential paid for the risk of unemployment.

[28]U.S. Department of Labor, *1981 Employment and Training Report of the President* (Washington, D.C.: U.S. Government Printing Office, 1981), Table A4.

**TABLE 15.3　Unemployment Rates in 1980
by Demographic Groups**

Age	White Male	White Female	Nonwhite Male	Nonwhite Female	All
16–17	18.5	17.3	37.0	40.4	
18–19	14.6	13.0	33.0	34.9	
20–24	11.1	8.5	22.3	21.8	
25–34	6.0	6.3	12.5	12.3	
35–44	3.6	4.9	7.8	7.8	
45–54	3.3	4.3	6.6	6.3	
55–64	3.1	3.1	6.0	4.7	
65+	2.5	2.9	8.8	4.7	
Total	6.1	6.5	13.3	13.1	7.1

SOURCE: U.S. Department of Labor, *1981 Employment and Training Report of the President* (Washington, D.C.: U.S. Government Printing Office, 1981), Table A30.

has concluded that demographic shifts in the composition of the labor force alone probably are responsible for the fact that the overall unemployment rate was at least 1 percentage point higher in the late 1970s and early 1980s than it was in the mid-1960s for any given level of overall labor market tightness.[29] The demographic changes have also led to an increase in the *full employment* (or *natural*) *rate* of unemployment—the unemployment rate that is consistent with a zero excess demand for labor. While an aggregate unemployment rate of 4 percent was considered a reasonable unemployment goal for policymakers in the mid-1960s, policymakers and academic economists rarely referred to targets below 5.5 percent by the late 1970s.

Why Do Unemployment Rates Vary Across Groups?

Calculations such as those just referred to take the age/race/sex structure of unemployment rates as fixed, and hence it is natural to ask why this structure exists.[30] As equation (15.2) and equation (15A.7) in the appendix indicate, a group's unemployment rate might be high because its members have difficulty finding jobs once unemployed, because they have difficulty (for voluntary or involuntary reasons) remaining employed once a job is found, or because they frequently enter and exit the labor force. The appropriate policy prescriptions will depend on the relative size of these monthly flows from one labor market state to another and on which of the flows is most responsible for the high rate.

　　One data source that is helpful in making such a determination is the monthly *Current Population Survey (CPS)*. Since three quarters of the individuals in the CPS sample one month are also included in the sample the next month, it is possible to

---

[29]James Tobin, "Stabilization Policy Ten Years After," *Brookings Papers on Economic Activity,* 1980–1, pp. 19–72.

[30]This section draws heavily on Ronald G. Ehrenberg, "The Demographic Structure of Unemployment Rates and Labor Market Transition Probabilities," *Research in Labor Economics* 3(1980):241–93.

compute the number of individuals in a particular age/race/sex group who move between various labor market states in a month. Since 1967, when definitional changes in the CPS occurred, these monthly *gross-flow data* have been tabulated by the Bureau of Labor Statistics (BLS), although they have not been published. Dividing these gross flows by the size of the appropriate group in the previous month yields estimates of the probability that an individual of a given age, race, and sex will go from one labor market state to another; these probabilities are called *transition probabilities*.

Table 15.4 presents estimates of the *average monthly transition probabilities* (the proportion of individuals in each labor market state who leave that state for each other state by the next month) for 16 age/race/sex cohorts during July 1967–September 1977. Equation (15A.7) in the appendix and the data in this table allow us to estimate the extent to which a relatively high unemployment rate for a group is

TABLE 15.4   Average Monthly Transition Probabilities (July 1967–September 1977)

	P_{en}	P_{ne}	P_{un}	P_{nu}	P_{eu}	P_{ue}
(A) White males						
16–19	0.114	0.150	0.308	0.072	0.041	0.301
20–24	0.036	0.192	0.153	0.069	0.026	0.322
25–59	0.003	0.072	0.100	0.032	0.010	0.321
60+	0.047	0.027	0.162	0.004	0.006	0.227
(B) White females						
16–19	0.138	0.101	0.327	0.058	0.029	0.280
20–24	0.051	0.058	0.148	0.036	0.018	0.355
25–59	0.045	0.045	0.265	0.012	0.010	0.213
60+	0.072	0.013	0.198	0.002	0.003	0.099
(C) Black males						
16–19	0.151	0.095	0.344	0.096	0.062	0.197
20–24	0.034	0.132	0.121	0.083	0.036	0.219
25–59	0.011	0.092	0.131	0.044	0.018	0.310
60+	0.045	0.025	0.336	0.008	0.009	0.167
(D) Black females						
16–19	0.185	0.049	0.371	0.085	0.040	0.180
20–24	0.062	0.068	0.287	0.066	0.022	0.118
25–59	0.039	0.049	0.324	0.036	0.012	0.205
60+	0.098	0.020	0.160	0.003	0.002	0.309

Note: Each probability represents the mean proportion in each labor market state in a month who move to each other labor market state in the next month. The proportions are based upon gross flow data that have been adjusted by researchers at the Urban Institute to correct for errors in the data.

P_{en} = fraction of employed who leave the labor force.

P_{ne} = fraction of those not in the labor force who enter the labor force and find employment.

P_{un} = fraction of unemployed who leave the labor force.

P_{nu} = fraction of those not in the labor force who enter the labor force and become unemployed.

P_{eu} = fraction of employed who become unemployed.

P_{ue} = fraction of unemployed who become employed.

caused by the values of each of its transition probabilities. Put another way, this information can be used to determine by how much a group's relative unemployment rate would change if we replaced any one of its transition probabilities with the comparable probability for a reference group (such as white adult males) that has a relatively low unemployment rate. Since different governmental policies will likely affect different transition probabilities, this determination may suggest the types of policies to stress in seeking to alter the demographic structure of unemployment rates.

The first two columns in Table 15.5 present data for each demographic group on the *actual* average unemployment rate of the group over the 1967–77 period (u_m) and the *estimated* average group unemployment rate (u_e) obtained when one substitutes the mean values of the group's transition probabilities from Table 15.4 into equation (15A.7). Since equation (15A.7) is formally correct only in periods of labor market balance (when the labor market flows into each of the states roughly equal the flows out of the states), it is reassuring to note the correspondence between the two unemployment series, especially the close matches in the 25–59 and 60+ age groups.

TABLE 15.5 **Variations in Transition Probabilities and Simulated Relative Unemployment Rates**

	u_m	u_e	R	R_{en}	R_{ne}	R_{un}	R_{nu}	R_{eu}	R_{ue}
(A) White males									
16–19	13.9	13.3	4.7	2.7	6.3	6.2	3.5	3.0	4.5
20–24	8.1	7.6	2.7	2.1	3.5	3.0	2.3	1.6	2.7
25–59	2.9	2.8	1.0	1.0	1.0	1.0	1.0	1.0	1.0
60+	3.2	3.2	1.1	0.6	0.8	1.3	3.4	1.5	0.9
(B) White females									
16–19	14.1	14.1	5.0	2.1	5.9	6.7	3.8	4.0	4.7
20–24	8.0	7.6	2.7	1.4	2.5	2.9	2.6	2.2	2.9
25–59	4.5	4.5	1.6	0.9	1.3	2.3	2.6	1.6	1.3
60+	3.3	3.6	1.3	0.4	0.5	1.8	9.2	2.1	0.7
(C) Black males									
16–19	28.8	27.3	9.8	5.3	10.8	12.8	6.5	6.8	7.8
20–24	14.8	14.3	5.1	4.0	5.8	5.3	4.2	2.6	3.9
25–59	5.5	5.2	1.9	1.7	1.9	2.0	1.8	1.2	1.8
60+	4.9	4.6	1.6	0.8	1.0	2.8	3.6	1.7	1.2
(D) Black females									
16–19	34.3	33.2	11.9	4.2	10.2	15.0	7.8	10.2	9.1
20–24	17.3	16.6	5.9	3.0	5.8	8.5	4.2	4.7	3.6
25–59	7.0	6.9	2.5	1.2	2.0	3.5	2.3	2.3	1.9
60+	3.2	3.0	1.1	0.2	0.4	1.2	5.1	1.7	1.0

Note: White males age 25–29 are used as the reference group.

u_m = average unemployment rate during the period.

u_e = estimated average unemployment rate using equation (15A.7) and mean value of transition probabilities for that group.

R = estimated average unemployment rate of the group relative to the estimated average unemployment rate of white males 25–59.

R_{ij} = estimated value of R if P_{ij} for the group is replaced by P_{ij} for white males 25–59.

SOURCE: Based on adjusted gross flow data.

The third column in the table presents the ratio *(R)* of the estimated average unemployment rate of each group during the period relative to the estimated average unemployment rate of the *reference* group (white males 25–59). For example, this ratio for white male teenagers (4.7) is computed by dividing their u_e (13.3) by the u_e for 25–59-year-old white males (2.8). The next six columns contain calculations of the estimated values of this ratio when the values of each transition probability are replaced, one at a time, by the equivalent probability for white males 25–59. That is, data in the last six columns indicate what the group's relative unemployment rate would be if we changed, one at a time, each transition probability to the reference group's level. Comparisons of columns (4) through (9) to column (3) indicate which transition probabilities are the major sources of difference between the unemployment rate of a particular group and that of white males age 25–59. If *R* decreases significantly when a given transition probability is replaced by its reference group counterpart, there is room for government policies to try to alter that probability.

High teenage unemployment rates (relative to adult male unemployment rates) stem primarily from the high probability that teenagers will leave employment to move out of the labor force *(P_en)* and that teenagers will move into unemployment from either employment *(P_eu)* or out-of-labor-force *(P_nu)* status.[31] Teens, then, move into and out of the labor force frequently and frequently lose or voluntarily leave their jobs. For nonwhite teens, low probabilities of moving from unemployment to employment *(P_ue)*—that is, of finding a job—also play a role.

The primary source of high relative unemployment for white female adults is the large flow from employment to out-of-labor-force status *(P_en)*; they frequently leave the labor force directly from employment status. Lower probabilities of moving into employment *(P_ne* and *P_ue)* also increase adult female unemployment. The major cause of high nonwhite adult male (25–59) unemployment is the group's high probability of voluntarily or involuntarily leaving employment to become unemployed *(P_eu)*; nonwhite adult males have difficulty holding jobs. In contrast, the relatively high nonwhite adult female unemployment rate is due primarily to the group's high probability of leaving the labor force from employment status *(P_en)* and to the low probability of unemployed group members finding employment *(P_ue)*, results that are very similar to those for adult white females.

A similar simulation exercise can be performed to see why nonwhite teenage unemployment rates tend to be double those of white teenagers. (These comparisons use white teens as the reference group.) Save for *P_un*, differences in all the transition probabilities appear to be factors, at least to a degree. For both males and females, however, lower probabilities of finding employment *(P_ne* and *P_ue)* have the largest influence on the relative teenage unemployment rates. A key question for policymakers to answer then is, Why do nonwhite teens have greater difficulty finding employment than white teens?

A number of potential explanations have been offered. Some revolve around the methods of job search used. For example, it has been argued that nonwhites rely

---

[31] For a discussion of how government policies in another country (Sweden) affected these parameters, and hence the teenage/adult unemployment ratio, see Linda Leighton and Siv Gustafsson, "Differential Patterns of Unemployment in Sweden," in *Research in Labor Economics,* vol. 6, 1984.

on institutions such as the Employment Service to find jobs, while white teens tend to find jobs through friends and neighbors.[32] Others focus on the growing concentration of nonwhite youths in the central cities, while employment opportunities have been moving to the suburbs and nonmetropolitan areas. However, the data indicate that nonwhite teenage unemployment rates are higher than white teenage unemployment rates in all types of geographic areas (central city, suburban, and nonmetropolitan).[33] Moreoever, if nonwhite youths had been reallocated across areas so that, in each, their proportionate representation relative to white youths was the same, the data suggest that the overall black/white teenage unemployment rate differential would have fallen by less than 10 percent.

Other explanations revolve around more traditional supply and demand factors, including the relative growth in the nonwhite teenage population coupled with increases in the minimum wage, the possible reduced willingness of nonwhite teens to accept low-wage jobs, the reduction in the size of the armed forces, employer prejudice against nonwhite teens, and the possibly lower-quality education that nonwhite teens receive, especially in inner-city areas, that may reduce their perceived attractiveness to employers.[34] It is clear, however, that no single explanation is sufficient to account for the much higher rates of nonwhite teenage unemployment.

SEARCH UNEMPLOYMENT AND THE ROLE OF UNEMPLOYMENT INSURANCE BENEFITS

As noted earlier in the chapter, because information about job opportunities and workers' characteristics is imperfect, it will take time for job matches to be made between unemployed workers and potential employers. Other things equal, the lower the probability that unemployed workers will become employed in a period (the lower is P_{ue}), the higher will be their expected duration of unemployment and the higher will be the unemployment rate.

Critics of the unemployment insurance system often point out that the existence of UI benefits reduces the costs of being unemployed and may prolong unemployed workers' job search.[35] Supporters of the UI system respond that an explicit purpose of the UI system when it was founded in the late 1930s was to provide unemployed

---

[32]Paul Osterman, ''Racial Differentials in Male Youth Unemployment,'' in U.S. Department of Labor, *Conference Report on Youth Unemployment: Its Measurement and Meaning* (Washington, D.C.: U.S. Government Printing Office, 1978).

[33]U.S. Department of Labor, *1978 Employment and Training Report of the President* (Washington, D.C.: U.S. Government Printing Office, 1978), p.73; and David Elwood, ''Mismatch Between Inner City Residences and Suburban Jobs'' (paper presented at the National Bureau of Economic Research Conference on Inner City Black Youth Unemployment, Cambridge, Mass., August 1983).

[34]Evidence on minimum wage effects was discussed in Chapter 3. For evidence that black teens may have higher wage aspirations than white teens of comparable characteristics, see Harry Holzer, ''Duration of Unemployment and Job Search'' (paper presented at the National Bureau of Economic Research Conference on Inner City Black Youth Unemployment, Cambridge, Mass., August 1983).

[35]Martin Feldstein, ''The Economics of the New Unemployment,'' *Public Interest* 33(Fall 1973):3–42.

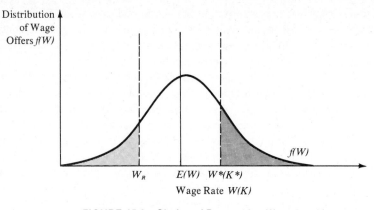

FIGURE 15.6   Choice of Reservation Wage in a Model
of Job Search

workers with temporary resources to enable them to turn down low-wage jobs that
were not commensurate with their skill levels and to keep searching for better
jobs.[36] That is, many believe that while the existence of UI benefits might prolong
spells of unemployment, such benefits also might lead to higher postunemployment
wages and better job matches, and better job matches might reduce subsequent job
turnover, thus providing a further benefit to society.

Before we turn to the empirical evidence on these points, analyzing a formal
model of job search will yield implications about a variety of labor market phenomena in addition to the role of UI benefits in job search.[37] This model will make the
key assumption that wages are associated with the characteristics of jobs, not with
the specific individuals who fill them.[38]

Suppose that employers differ in the set of minimum hiring standards that they
have. Hiring standards may include educational requirements, job training, work
experience, performance on test scores, etc. For expositional convenience, suppose
this set of attributes can be summarized in a single variable, K, which will denote
the minimum skill level a job requires. Associated with each job is a wage, $W(K)$—
a wage that is a function of the required skill level and not of the particular
characteristics of the people hired. We assume that the wage rate is an increasing
function of the minimum required skill level and that two employers that have the
same hiring standard will offer the same wage.

Because different employers have different hiring standards, there will be a
distribution of wage offers associated with job vacancies in the labor market. This
distribution of wage offers is denoted by $f(W)$ in Figure 15.6. As one moves to the
right in the figure, the minimum required skill level and offered wage on a job
increase. Since $f(W)$ represents a *probability distribution* of wage offers, the area

[36]William Haber and Merrill Murray, *Unemployment Insurance in the American Economy* (Homewood,
Ill.: Irwin, 1966), pp.26–35.

[37]Our discussion here draws heavily on Dale T. Mortensen, "Job Search, the Duration of Unemployment, and the Phillips Curve," *American Economic Review* 60(December 1970):847–62.

[38]Such an assumption has been made in another context by Lester Thurow, *Generating Inequality* (New
York: Basic Books, 1975).

under the curve sums to one (that is, the distribution contains 100 percent of all wage offers in the market). Each wage offer (on the horizontal axis) is shown in relation to that offer's share in the distribution (on the vertical axis).

Now suppose a given unemployed individual has skill level K^*. Since no firm will hire a worker who does not meet its hiring standards, the maximum wage that this individual could hope to receive is $W^*(K^*)$. If he or she knew which firms had a hiring standard of K^*, he or she would apply to them and, since the individual meets their hiring standards, would be hired at a wage of W^*, assuming a vacancy existed.

Suppose, instead, that job market information is imperfect in the sense that, while the individual knows the shape of the distribution of wage offers, $f(W)$, he or she does *not* know what each individual firm's wage offer or hiring standard will be. One can conceptualize job search as a process in which the person randomly knocks on the doors of personnel departments of firms. If the firm's hiring standard exceeds K^*, the person is rejected for the job. However, if the hiring standard is K^* or less, the person is offered the job. While the individual might find it advantageous to accumulate a number of jobs offers and then accept the best, job seekers— especially at the lower-skilled end of the skill ladder—are not always allowed such a luxury. Rather, they must make instantaneous decisions about whether or not to accept a job offer because otherwise the offer will be extended to a different applicant.

How does an unemployed worker know whether to accept a particular job offer? One strategy is to decide on a *minimum acceptance* (or *reservation*) *wage* and then to accept (reject) any offer above (below) this level. The critical question then is, How is this reservation wage determined?

To answer this question, suppose W_R is the reservation wage that is chosen (in Figure 15.6) by a person who has skill level K^*. Now observe that this individual's job application will be rejected by any firm that offers a wage higher than $W^*(K^*)$; the person will not meet its minimum hiring standards. Similarly, the person will reject any job offers that call for a wage less than W_R. Hence, the probability that he or she will find an acceptable job in any period is simply the unshaded area under the curve between W_R and W^*. The higher this probability, the lower the expected duration of unemployment. Given that the person finds a job, his or her expected wage is simply the weighted average of the job offers in the W_R to W^* range. This average or expected wage is denoted by $E(W)$ in Figure 15.6.

If the individual were to choose a slightly higher reservation wage, his or her choice would have two effects. On the one hand, since the person would now reject more low-wage jobs, his or her expected or average wage (once employed) would increase. On the other hand, by rejecting more job offers, he or she also decreases the probability of finding an acceptable job in any given period, thus increasing the expected duration of unemployment. Put another way, higher reservation wages lead to the costs of longer expected spells of unemployment, but also to the benefits of higher expected wages once a job is found. Each unemployed individual will choose his or her reservation wage so that, at the margin, the expected costs of longer spells of unemployment just equal the expected benefits of higher postunemployment wages. That is, the reservation wage should be chosen so that the marginal benefit from a higher reservation wage just equals its marginal cost.

This simple model and associated decision rule lead to a number of implications. First, as long as the reservation wage is not set equal to the minimum wage offered in the market, the probability of finding a job will be less than one and hence some *search unemployment* will result. *Search unemployment* occurs when an individual does not necessarily accept the first job that is offered to him or her and is a rational strategy in a world of imperfect information.[39]

Second, since the reservation wage will always be chosen to be less than the wage commensurate with the individual's skill level, $W^*(K^*)$, virtually all individuals will be *underemployed* once they find a job (in the sense that their expected earnings will be less than W^*). This underemployment is a cost of imperfect information; better labor market information would improve the job-matching process.

Third, due to random luck, otherwise identical individuals will wind up receiving different wages. Two identical individuals who have the same skill level should choose the same reservation wage and should have the same *expected* post-unemployment wage. However, the wages they actually wind up with would depend upon pure luck—the wage offer between W_R and W^* they happened to find. In a world of imperfect information, then, no economic model can explain all the variation in wages across individuals.

Fourth, anything that reduces the cost of an individual's being unemployed should lead the person to increase his or her reservation wage, and should thus lead to longer durations of unemployment and higher expected postunemployment wages. Since higher UI benefits reduce individuals' costs of unemployment, increasing such benefits should be associated with longer spells of unemployment and higher postunemployment wages.

In recent years, numerous studies have sought to estimate the effects of UI benefits on durations of unemployment and postunemployment wages.[40] In the main, these studies use data on individuals and exploit the fact that the replacement rate (the fraction of previous earnings that UI benefits replace) varies (*within* states) with individuals' previous earnings levels (see Figure 15.4) and also *across* states. Evidence from these studies suggests quite strongly that higher UI replacement rates are associated with longer durations of unemployment; raising the replacement rate from 0.4 to 0.5 of previous weekly earnings may increase the average spell of

---

[39]Voluntary search unemployment is but one form of frictional unemployment and frictional unemployment is but one form of overall unemployment; thus, only a portion of unemployment is of the voluntary search nature. Indeed, the data suggest that many unemployed workers never reject any job offer; see, for example, U.S. Bureau of Labor Statistics, Bulletin 1886, *Job Seeking Methods Used by American Workers* (Washington, D.C.: U.S. Government Printing Office, 1975).

[40]See, for example, Ronald G. Ehrenberg and Ronald L. Oaxaca, "Unemployment Insurance, Duration of Unemployment and Subsequent Wage Gain," *American Economic Review* 66(December 1976): 754–66. Many of the studies are summarized in Daniel S. Hamermesh, *Jobless Pay and the Economy* (Baltimore: Johns Hopkins University Press, 1977) and are critiqued in Finis Welch, "What Have We Learned From Empirical Studies of Unemployment Insurance," *Industrial and Labor Relations Review* 30(July 1977):451–61. A more recent study that also tests to see if reservation wages decline as workers' spells of unemployment lengthen is Nicholas Kiefer and George Neumann, "An Empirical Job Search Model with a Test of the Constant Reservation Wage Hypothesis," *Journal of Political Economy* 87(February 1979):89–107.

Example 15.2

Unemployment Insurance Benefits in Great Britain

Evidence that more generous unemployment insurance benefits lead to higher levels of unemployment is not confined to the United States. For example, Daniel Benjamin and Levis Kochin have found three pieces of information that seem to confirm the relationship for Great Britain during the period between World Wars I and II:

1. Increases in the aggregate British unemployment rate, even after controlling for the level of aggregate demand, were associated with increases in the British UI replacement rate over the 1920–38 period.
2. Teenagers, many of whom were either not eligible for UI benefits during this period or who received very low benefits relative to their wages, had unemployment rates that were only a fraction of the adult unemployment rate. Further, the unemployment rate jumped markedly at ages 18 and 21, when UI benefits increased.
3. In 1932, the year a change in the British UI regulations reduced the possibility that unemployed married women could receive UI benefits, the unemployment rate for married women dropped sharply relative to the rate for males.

SOURCE: See Daniel Benjamin and Levis Kochin, "Searching for an Explanation of Unemployment in Interwar Britain,"*Journal of Political Economy* 87(June 1979):441–78. Several comments, which challenge some of their findings, appear in the April 1982 issue of the journal.

---

unemployment by one half to one week. In contrast, the evidence on the effects of postunemployment wages is much more mixed. For example, one study found that higher replacement rates were associated with higher postunemployment wage rates for adults but not for teenagers.[41]

Fifth, anything that increases individuals' discount rates, or their need for current income relative to future income, should lead to lower reservation wages and hence to shorter expected durations of unemployment and lower postunemployment wages. Thus, unemployed individuals from poor families may well settle for lower-paying jobs than equally skilled unemployed individuals from higher-income families.

Sixth, the shorter the length of time that an individual expects to be employed, the smaller will be the payoff to job search activities and hence the lower will be the reservation wage. This lower reservation wage will lead to shorter durations of unemployment and lower postunemployment wages for individuals with short expected job tenure.

---

[41]Ehrenberg and Oaxaca, "Unemployment Insurance." The results for teens may imply that (a) unemployed teens do not search actively for work, (b) unemployed teens' job search is not productive, perhaps because of the narrow range of job opportunities they face, or (c) unemployed teens may search for jobs that offer greater training options and possible higher future wages, although not higher current wages. The available data do not permit one to determine which of these alternatives is correct.

Finally, increases in skill level—say, by means of participation in a government job-training program—will have two effects on unemployed workers. On the
one hand, their W^* will increase, which, other things equal, will increase the
proportion of jobs they are qualified for, decrease their expected duration of
unemployment, and increase their expected postunemployment wage. On the other
hand, an increase in skill level will induce them to raise their reservation wage,
which will increase the proportion of low-wage job offers they turn down and tend
to increase both their expected duration of unemployment and their expected
postunemployment wage. Thus, while unambiguously increasing expected postunemployment wages, an increase in skill levels has an ambiguous effect on the
duration of unemployment. This final implication has direct bearing on how one
should evaluate the effectiveness of government-sponsored training programs. One
should *not* evaluate them on the basis of the initial post-program employment
experience of program graduates; these individuals may rationally remain unemployed for a while, searching for jobs commensurate with their new skill levels.
Rather, evaluations should be based on the longer-run experiences of program
graduates.[42]

NORMATIVE ISSUES IN UNEMPLOYMENT

Is unemployment a serious problem? Certainly some level of frictional unemployment is unavoidable in a dynamic world fraught with imperfect information.
Moreover, as we have seen, the parameters of the UI system encourage both
additional search unemployment and temporary layoff (cyclical and seasonal)
unemployment. Nonetheless, when unemployment rises above its full-employment
or natural level, resources are being wasted. More than 25 years ago Arthur Okun
pointed out that every 1-percentage-point decline in the aggregate unemployment
rate was associated with a 3-percentage-point increase in the output our society
produces. That relationship appears to have held up through 1975, although since
1975 it is more in the range of a 2-percentage-point increase in output. Even this last
number, however, suggests the great costs our society pays for excessively high
rates of unemployment.[43] Thus, while it is unlikely that zero unemployment would
be an optimal rate, policies to reduce cyclical unemployment (in a noninflationary
manner) are clearly desirable. Improving the functioning of labor markets would
also reduce frictional and structural unemployment; however, the benefits of

---

[42] An additional reason for doing this is that program effects may depreciate over time. For example, after
completion of a training program, unemployed workers may be able to find a job. However, if they
lose that job, the program may have no further positive effect on them. In this case, the short-run
effects of a program might exceed its long-run effects. Knowledge of how long program effects last is
clearly important.

[43] Arthur Okun, "Potential GNP: Its Measurement and Significance," reprinted in Arthur Okun, ed., *The
Political Economy of Prosperity* (Washington, D.C.: Brookings Institute, 1970). Recent evidence
suggests that the relationship is more in the range of 2.2 to 1. See Robert J. Gordon and Robert E.
Hall, "Arthur M. Okun 1928–1980," *Brookings Papers on Economic Activity*, 1980–1, pp. 1–5.

reduced unemployment must be weighed against the costs generated by the policies designed to accomplish this objective in each case.[44]

In addition to concern over the cost of unemployment, society should also be concerned about the distribution of unemployment across age/race/sex groups. As Table 15.3 indicated, the incidence of unemployment is higher among females than males, among nonwhites than whites, and among teens than nonteens. We have traced the labor market flows that are associated with these differentials. White female adult unemployment rates are high because of proportionately large flows of women from employment to out-of-labor-force status, which suggests that some of their higher labor turnover (and unemployment) may be voluntary. In contrast, the major cause of high nonwhite adult male unemployment rates is the high probability of members of that group leaving or losing their jobs to become unemployed; the fact that they remain attached to the labor force suggests that their unemployment problem is serious and that the case for government intervention is strong.

What about the high teenage unemployment rates, especially those of nonwhite teens? Is the high unemployment rate for teens a serious problem that policymakers should address? Some doubt the seriousness of the problem, pointing out that unemployment rates decline rapidly as youths reach their early twenties (see Table 15.3). To these doubters, high teenage unemployment rates are symptomatic of the process of job turnover and search that occurs when new entrants to the labor force seek to aquire information about labor markets and their own productive ability. Moreover, proponents of this view could note that approximately 50 percent of unemployed 16–19-year-olds and 90 percent of unemployed 16–17-year-olds are enrolled in school.[45] Of in-school unemployed youths, 50 percent were searching only for temporary jobs in 1976 and only 10 percent had become unemployed by losing their previous job.[46] Finally, they could cite evidence that teenage unemployment is not always associated with low family incomes. For example, data from the *1976 Survey of Income and Education,* a large national survey conducted by the Census Bureau, indicate that less than 26 percent of unemployed youths age 16 to 24 came from families whose family income fell below the poverty line.[47]

Of course, these arguments neglect a number of important points. First, a substantial body of evidence indicates that youth unemployment is highly correlated with youth criminal activity; thus, there are costs to society, as well as to the youths,

---

[44]An additional cost of unemployment is that it is often associated with increased incidence of physical and mental ailments. For a summary of some of the evidence on this point, see Frank Trippet, "The Anguish of the Jobless," *Time,* January 18, 1982, p.90.

[45]See Arvil Adams and Garth Mangum, *The Lingering Crisis of Youth Unemployment* (Kalamazoo, Mich.: W.E. Upjohn Institute, 1978), Chap. 3.

[46]Adams and Mangum, *The Lingering Crisis of Youth Unemployment.*

[47]*U.S. Congressional Budget Office, Youth Unemployment: The Outlook and Some Policy Strategies* (Washington, D.C.: U.S. Government Printing Office, April 1978), Appendix Table A–5. It is worth noting, however, that this table also indicates that youth unemployment rates decline with family income and that more than 45 percent of unemployed *nonwhite* youths come from families with family incomes below the poverty line. Put another way, youth unemployment is much more highly correlated with poverty for nonwhites than it is for whites.

of youth unemployment. Second, much youth unemployment is concentrated among nonwhite youths, and the distributional implications of this fact may be unacceptable to society, especially given the higher correlation between youth unemployment and poverty that exists for nonwhites. Finally, the effects of youth unemployment may be long lasting and unemployed teenagers may face reduced long-run earnings and employment prospects compared to teenagers who do not suffer unemployment. Although unemployment rates decline rapidly with age for younger adults, individuals who suffered unemployment as teenagers might be "scarred" in the sense of having relatively higher probabilities of adult unemployment or commanding relatively lower adult wage rates.

Somewhat surprisingly, until recently there was no evidence on the long-run effects of teenage unemployment. Indeed, as late as 1976 Richard Freeman asserted that

> there is no evidence that having considerable unemployment and related poor work experience at a young age "scars" a person for life. Teenage unemployment *may* have deleterious effects on work attitudes, investment in job skills, lifetime income, and related labor market experiences, but this has *not* been documented. Teenage unemployment may be purely a transitional problem without long-term consequences.[48]

Since 1976, however, four studies using data on younger males and standard statistical methods have addressed this issue.[49] These studies do *not* all use data from a common time period, use the same sample restrictions (out-of-school youths or all youths), focus on the same outcome variable (earnings or unemployment), or use the same research methodology (simple correlation or multiple regression analysis). Nonetheless, the evidence does suggest that unemployment of *nonwhite* male teens is associated, on average, with long-run adverse labor market effects. However, the evidence on persistence effects of white male teenage unemployment is less clear. Thus, these studies at first glance appear to support public concern, at least for nonwhites, about the long-run effects of teenage unemployment.

Unfortunately, these studies did *not* identify whether it is the experience of unemployment *per se* or some unobserved characteristics of the teenage unemployed that lead to subsequent adverse labor market outcomes. If the experience of unemployment is responsible, then policies to reduce teenage unemployment may have long-run positive effects. However, if unobservable characteristics are responsible—for example, if teens who become unemployed are less motivated or able, other things equal, than those who find employment—then it is less clear that

---

[48]Richard Freeman, "Teenage Unemployment: Can Reallocating Resources Help?" in U.S. Congressional Budget Office, *The Teenage Unemployment Problem: What Are the Options?* (Washington, D.C.: U.S. Government Printing Office,1976).

[49]See Wayne Stevenson, "The Relationship Between Early Work Experience and Future Employability," in Adams and Mangum, eds., *The Lingering Crisis of Youth Unemployment*, pp. 93–124; Paul Osterman, "Race Differentials in Male Youth Unemployment," in U.S. Department of Labor, *Conference Report on Youth Unemployment: Its Measurement and Meaning* (Washington, D.C.: U.S. Government Printing Office, 1978); Joseph Antos and Wesley Mellow, *The Youth Labor Market: A Dynamic Overview* (Washington, D.C.: U.S. Government Printing Office, 1979); and Brian Becker and Stephen Hills, "Teenage Unemployment: Some Evidence on the Long-Run Effects on Wages," *Journal of Human Resources* 15(Summer 1980):354–72.

policies to reduce teenage unemployment will have long-lasting effects. Other studies that have attempted to identify whether the experience of unemployment *per se* matters in the long run have yielded ambiguous results, some finding that an early employment experience has a positive effect on later employment for teens but others finding very little effect.[50] Thus, our knowledge about whether teenage unemployment has long-run scarring effects is still quite imprecise.

REVIEW QUESTIONS

1. A presidential hopeful is campaigning to raise unemployment compensation benefits and lower the full-employment target from 6 percent to 5.5 percent. Comment on the compatibility of these goals.
2. Government officials find it useful to measure the nation's "economic health." The unemployment rate is currently used as major indicator of the relative strength of labor supply and demand. Do you think the unemployment rate is becoming more or less useful as an indicator of labor market tightness? What other measures might serve this purpose better?
3. The unemployment rate is a stock concept (something like the amount of water in a lake at a given time). The level of unemployment goes up or down as the *flows* into unemployment exceed or are slower than the flows out of unemployment. Is it important for policy purposes to accurately measure the *flows* into and out of unemployment, or is knowing the *level* of unemployment enough for most purposes? Justify your answer.
4. Is the following question true, false, or uncertain? "Increasing the level of unemployment insurance benefits will prolong the average length of spells of unemployment. Hence, a policy of raising UI benefit levels is not socially desirable." Explain your answer.
5. Recent empirical evidence cited in the chapter suggests that unemployed workers' reservation wages decline as their spells of unemployment lengthen. That is, the longer they have been unemployed, the lower are their reservation wages. Why might this be true?

SELECTED READINGS

Baily, Martin. "Wages and Employment Under Uncertain Demand." *Review of Economic Studies* 41(January 1974):37–50.

Clark, Kim B., and Summers, Lawrence. "Labor Market Dynamics and Unemployment: A Reconsideration." *Brookings Papers on Economic Activity*, 1979–1, pp. 13–60.

Feldstein, Martin. "The Economics of the New Unemployment." *Public Interest* 33(Fall 1973):3–42.

Feldstein, Martin. "The Importance of Temporary Layoffs: An Empirical Analysis." *Brookings Papers on Economic Activity*, 1975–3, pp. 725–44.

Freeman, Richard, and Wise, David. *The Youth Labor Market Problem: Its Nature, Causes, and Consequences*. Chicago, Ill.: University of Chicago Press, 1982.

National Commission on Employment and Unemployment Statistics. *Counting the Labor Force*. Washington, D.C.: U.S. Government Printing Office, 1979.

---

[50]David Ellwood, "Teenage Unemployment: Permanent Scars or Temporary Blemishes"; Mary Corcoran, "The Employment, Wage, and Fertility Consequences of Teenage Women's Nonemployment"; and Robert Meyer and David Wise, "High School Preparation and Early Labor Force Experience"; all in Richard B. Freeman and David A. Wise, eds., *The Youth Labor Market Problem: Its Nature, Causes, and Consequences* (Chicago, Ill.: University of Chicago Press, 1982), pp. 349–85, 391–423, and 277–344.

APPENDIX 15A

The Relationship Between the Unemployment Rate and Labor Market Flows

The objective of this appendix is to formally derive the exact equation whose implications equation (15.2) in the text summarizes. This equation relates a group's unemployment rate (**u**) to the proportions of its members that move between employment, unemployment, and not-in-the-labor-force status each month. As in equation (15.2), let P_{ij} denote the proportion of individuals in a group in labor market state i that move to labor market state j during the period, where the different states are employed *(e)*, unemployed *(u)*, and not in the labor force *(n)*. The numbers of people in each of these states at the start of a period are denoted by E, U, and N, respectively.

Labor market equilibrium is defined as a situation in which the number of employed individuals and the number of unemployed individuals both remain constant over time. In this case, the number of unemployed people at the start of a period who obtain jobs plus the number of people out of the labor force at the start of a period who obtain jobs is just equal to the number of people employed at the start of the period who become unemployed or drop out of the labor force during the period. That is,

$$P_{ue}U + P_{ne}N = (P_{eu} + P_{en})E$$
$$\underset{\text{who become employed}}{\text{the number}} = \underset{\text{who leave employment}}{\text{the number}}$$

(15A.1)

Similarly, in equilibrium the number of people who become unemployed during the period (because of losing or leaving their previous jobs or unsuccessfully entering the labor force) just equals the number who leave unemployment (either because they found a job or because they left the labor force):

$$P_{eu}E + P_{nu}N = (P_{ue} + P_{un})U$$
$$\underset{\text{who become unemployed}}{\text{the number}} = \underset{\text{who leave unemployment}}{\text{the number}}$$

(15A.2)

Multiplying (15A.1) by P_{nu} and (15A.2) by P_{ne} and then subtracting (15A.2) from (15A.1), one obtains:

$$P_{ue}P_{nu}U - P_{eu}P_{ne}E = (P_{eu} + P_{en})P_{nu}E - (P_{ue} + P_{un})P_{ne}U \quad (15A.3)$$

or

$$[P_{ue}P_{nu} + P_{ne}(P_{ue} + P_{un})]U = [P_{eu}P_{ne} + P_{nu}(P_{eu} + P_{en})]E \quad (15A.4)$$

Hence, in equilibrium the numbers of unemployed and employed individuals, solving from equation (15A.4), are related by

$$E = U\frac{[P_{ue}P_{nu} + P_{ne}(P_{ue} + P_{un})]}{[P_{eu}P_{ne} + P_{nu}(P_{eu} + P_{en})]} \quad (15A.5)$$

$$= U\frac{[(P_{ne} + P_{nu})P_{ue} + P_{ne}P_{un}]}{[(P_{ne} + P_{nu})P_{eu} + P_{nu}P_{en}]}$$

The unemployment rate is now defined as the number of unemployed individuals divided by the sum of the unemployed and the employed:

$$\mathbf{u} = \frac{U}{(U + E)} \quad (15A.6)$$

Substituting (15A.5) into (15A.6) and simplifying yields:

$$\mathbf{u} = \frac{1}{1 + \left[\dfrac{(P_{ne} + P_{nu})P_{ue} + (P_{ne})(P_{un})}{(P_{ne} + P_{nu})P_{eu} + (P_{nu})(P_{en})}\right]} \quad (15A.7)$$

Thus, a group's unemployment rate depends upon the flow of its members between all three labor market states. Moreover, one can show that this equation implies that increases in P_{eu}, P_{en}, and P_{nu} all lead to increases in the unemployment rate, while increases in P_{ue}, P_{un}, and P_{ne} all lead to decreases in the unemployment rate.

This appendix is based on Steven T. Marston, "Employment Instability and High Unemployment Rates," *Brookings Papers on Economic Activity,* 1976–1, pp. 169–203.

16

Inflation and Unemployment

INTRODUCTION

Throughout most of the 1970s and early 1980s the United States was faced with relatively high rates of wage and price *inflation* (that is, with relatively rapid and generally pervasive increases in wages and prices). Further, these increases were taking place in the context of high unemployment rates, so the country seemed to suffer the consequences of both inflation *and* unemployment at the same time. Simultaneously high rates of inflation and unemployment challenged the long-held belief that inflation would diminish if unemployment rose—a belief that seemed to have held out hope that government fiscal or monetary policies could be skillfully used to maneuver the economy to tolerable levels of both inflation and unemployment.

The causes and consequences of inflation, and the fiscal and monetary policies to remedy it, are beyond the scope of labor economics. Our intent in this chapter is to analyze the relationship between inflation and unemployment so that the connections between what happens in the labor market and what happens to prices in general are more clearly understood. Moreover, because our focus is on the labor market, we shall emphasize the price of labor—the wage rate—when discussing the issue of inflation.

Measuring Wage Inflation

The overall rate of *wage inflation* in the economy is the annual percentage rate of increase in some composite measure of hourly earnings in the economy. The construction of such an index is a considerable task because *average* hourly earnings can change, even if the wage scales for every individual *job* remain constant. For example, if there is a shift in the distribution of employment towards high-wage industries (such as construction) and away from low-wage industries (such as retail trade), average hourly earnings will increase. Similarly, if there is a shift towards increased usage of highly paid skilled workers and away from lower-paid unskilled workers, average hourly earnings will increase. To take another example, if the age distribution of the work force shifts towards relatively fewer lower-paid new entrants, average hourly earnings will increase. Finally, if more overtime hours for which premium pay is received are worked relative to straight time hours, average hourly earnings will again increase, other things equal.[1]

The problem involved in all these examples is that average hourly earnings in the economy $(\overline{W})$ is a weighted average of the earnings of individuals in each industry/occupation/experience group (W_i). The weight assigned to each group's earnings (f_i) depends upon the fraction of all hours worked in the economy by individuals in the group and the fraction of hours worked by the group for which premium pay is received. Changes in average hourly earnings may therefore reflect changes in the weights as well as changes in the wage scales of each group. Focusing simply on the growth of average hourly earnings, then, may give one a misleading impression of what is happening to wage scales for particular jobs.[2]

To partially take the above problem into account, government statisticians have constructed an index of adjusted average hourly earnings for nonsupervisory workers in the private nonagricultural sector. This index, which controls for changes in the industrial composition of employment and changes in overtime hours in manufacturing, is one of the most comprehensive measures of wage changes available.[3]

---

[1] The regulated industry example first discussed in Chapter 9 illustrated the importance of these factors. As part of the regulatory case, the rate of wage inflation had to be computed for a utility's employees over the August 1973 to August 1976 period. The cumulative percentage wage increase in union wage scales called for in the company's union contracts was 32.1 percent; however, the increase in average hourly earnings was 42.1 percent. The difference in this example was primarily due to the changing skill mix and age distributions of the utility's employees. For details, see Ronald Ehrenberg, *The Regulatory Process and Labor Earnings* (New York: Academic Press, 1979), Chap. 2.

[2] To see this point more clearly, suppose that there are n different industry/occupation/experience groups in the economy. Then average hourly earnings of all workers are given by

$$\overline{W} = \sum_{i=1}^{n} W_i f_i$$

and the percentage change in average hourly earnings is *approximately* equal to

$$\dot{\overline{W}} \approx \sum_{i=1}^{n} \dot{W}_i f_i + \sum_{i=1}^{n} W_i \dot{f}_i + \sum_{i=1}^{n} \dot{W}_i \dot{f}_i \, ,$$

where percentage change is indicated by a dot over a variable. Even if all wage rates were constant ($\dot{W}_i$ equal to zero for all i), average hourly earnings could still change if the weights changed, for in this case

$$\dot{\overline{W}} = \sum_{i=1}^{n} W_i \dot{f}_i$$

[3] The index only partially controls for the problem of distinguishing between changes in wage scales and changes in the composition of employment because it makes no adjustment for changes in the *occupational* or *age* distributions of the work force.

TABLE 16.1   Unemployment Rate and Percentage Change in Earnings and Prices in the United States

Year	Percent Change in Adjusted Hourly Earnings of Nonsupervisory Workers in the Private Nonagricultural Sector	Unemployment Rate	Percent Change in the GNP Deflator
1963	2.8	5.7	1.5
1964	2.8	5.2	1.5
1965	3.6	4.5	2.2
1966	4.3	3.8	3.2
1967	5.0	3.8	3.0
1968	6.1	3.6	4.4
1969	6.7	3.5	5.1
1970	6.6	4.9	5.4
1971	7.2	5.9	5.0
1972	6.2	5.6	4.2
1973	6.2	4.9	5.8
1974	8.0	5.6	8.8
1975	8.4	8.5	9.3
1976	7.2	7.7	5.2
1977	7.6	7.1	5.8
1978	8.1	6.1	7.4
1979	8.0	5.8	8.6
1980	9.0	7.0	9.3
1981	9.1	7.5	9.4
1982	6.8	9.5	6.0
1983	4.6	9.5	4.2

SOURCE: *1983 Economic Report of the President* (Washington, D.C.: U.S. Government Printing Offiice, 1984), Tables B3, B29, and B38.

As Table 16.1 indicates, between 1963 and 1983, this index increased at annual percentage rates of roughly 3 to 9 percent, with the annual percentage increase apparently increasing over time.

The Inflation/Unemployment Trade-off

For many years economists believed that stable negative relationships, or *trade-off curves,* existed between the rates of wage (and price) inflation, on the one hand, and the overall unemployment rate in the economy, on the other. That is, higher levels of unemployment were thought to be associated with lower rates of wage and price inflation, and vice versa. The relationship between unemployment and wage inflation was dubbed the *Phillips curve,* after the noted economist who was an early observer of its existence.[4] The Phillips curve was thought to provide a range of feasible options for policymakers; through the appropriate use of monetary or fiscal

---

[4]See A. W. Phillips, "The Relation Between Unemployment and the Rates of Change of Money Wage Rates in the United Kingdom, 1862–1957," *Economica* 25(November 1958):283–99.

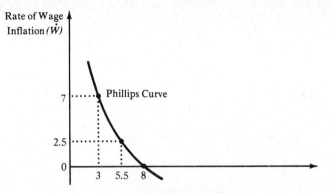

FIGURE 16.1 Phillips Curve Showing the Trade-off Between Wage Inflation and Unemployment for 1960

SOURCE: Adapted from Paul A. Samuelson and Robert M. Solow, "Our Menu of Policy Choices," *The Battle Against Inflation,* ed. Arthur M. Okun (New York: W. W. Norton, 1965), p. 74.

policy, they could choose any unemployment/inflation combination along the curve. For example, a paper in 1959 by two well-known economists claimed that in 1960 the country could choose among the following alternatives (illustrated in Figure 16.1): 8 percent unemployment and zero wage inflation, 5–6 percent unemployment and 2–3 percent wage inflation, and 3 percent unemployment and 7 percent wage inflation.[5]

Unfortunately, the well-defined, stable set of choices once thought to exist appears to have vanished. Table 16.1 contains data on both the unemployment rate and wage inflation from 1963 to 1982. These data indicate that during the 1960s a negative association did appear to exist between the unemployment rate and the rate of wage inflation. Indeed, the steady tightening of labor markets and decreasing unemployment rates of the late 1960s were associated with increasing rates of wage inflation. However, during the 1970s the relationship appears, at first glance, to have broken down; one often observes simultaneous increases in the rate of unemployment and the rate of wage inflation during that decade. The result is that, while an unemployment rate of 5.7 percent was associated with a wage-inflation rate of 2.8 percent in 1963, an almost identical unemployment rate of 5.6 percent was associated with wage-inflation rates of 6.2 to 8.0 percent during the 1970s. These data tend to suggest that the belief in a stable negative trade-off between inflation and unemployment is unwarranted.

An alternative interpretation of these data, however, is that, while a trade-off between the rates of inflation and unemployment exists at a *point in time,* the *position* of the trade-off curve is determined by a number of other factors that can change over time. The net effect of these other factors in recent years, it can be argued, has been to shift the trade-off curve shown in Figure 16.1 *upward and to the*

---

[5]Paul A. Samuelson and Robert M. Solow, "Our Menu of Policy Choices," in *The Battle Against Unemployment,* ed. Arthur M. Okun (New York: W. W. Norton, 1965), pp. 71–76.

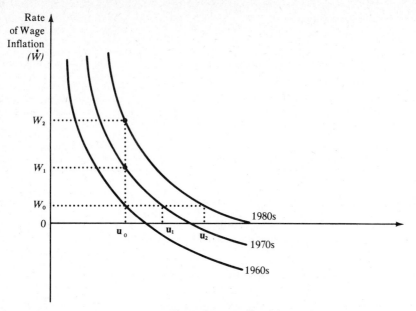

FIGURE 16.2   The Changing Trade-off Between the Rate of Wage Inflation and the Level of the Unemployment Rate

right. Thus, the trade-off society faces in the early 1980s may lie everywhere above the one that prevailed during the 1970s, which in turn was itself higher than the curve that prevailed during the 1960s (see Figure 16.2). Put another way, the argument underlying Figure 16.2 is that progressively higher rates of wage inflation ($\dot{W}_0$, $\dot{W}_1$, and $\dot{W}_2$) have become associated over time with any given level of unemployment (u_0 in Figure 16.2). Conversely, progressively higher unemployment rates (u_0, u_1, u_2) have become associated with any given level of wage inflation ($\dot{W}_0$). Indeed, some economists suggest that between 1960 and 1980, the trade-off may have shifted to the right by as much as 3 percentage points.[6] It is also possible that the Phillips curve has become much flatter over recent years, so that the decrease in wage inflation accompanying a 1-percentage-point increase in the unemployment rate is now smaller than it once was. This growing downward rigidity of wages has caused a loss of effectiveness in the traditional macroeconomic policies to combat inflation, and has increased the importance of alternative labor market policies.

The next section presents a simple conceptual model that examines why the trade-off between wage inflation and unemployment may exist and discusses the forces that may have caused the trade-off to shift over time. This model provides a framework that can be used to discuss the various labor market policies that might

---

[6]See, for example, James Tobin, "Stabilization Policy Ten Years After," *Brookings Papers on Economic Activity*, 1980–1, pp. 19–72.

enable policymakers to shift the trade-off curve in a more favorable direction.

This chapter will also discuss the relationship between wage and price behavior and consider the conditions under which a stable, long-run trade-off between *price* inflation and unemployment will occur. Although *at a point in time* a trade-off may exist between the rate of *wage* inflation and the unemployment rate, it does not necessarily follow that *in the long run* a stable trade-off exists between the rate of *price* inflation and the unemployment rate. Indeed, one school of thought argues that this long-run trade-off curve is vertical and that attempts to keep the unemployment rate artificially low will lead to ever accelerating rates of inflation.[7]

This chapter then considers the role of unions and the collective bargaining process. It explores why changing institutional arrangements, in particular the spread of *multiyear agreements* with *cost-of-living escalator clauses,* may have been partially responsible for the growing insensitivity of inflation to the unemployment rate.

The final section of the chapter returns to the central issue of how government policies might reduce the rate of inflation associated with any given level of unemployment. This section focuses on the various *incomes policies* that have been pursued in the United States since 1960—policies in which the government has tried directly to influence wages and prices by specifying "desired wage and price behavior," sometimes with enforcement mechanisms tied to the program (these include the wage-price guideposts of the Kennedy-Johnson years, the wage-price freeze and "Phase II" economic policies under the Nixon Administration, and the Carter voluntary anti-inflation guidelines). After discussing the available evidence on the effectiveness of these programs, we shall analyze the proposals for new innovative types of *tax-based incomes policies* that were proposed during the 1970s.[8]

THE WAGE INFLATION/UNEMPLOYMENT TRADE-OFF

The Basic Model

Figure 16.3 represents wage determination in a competitive labor market.[9] For simplicity we shall *initially* take product prices as fixed so that the demand and supply curves can be drawn in terms of the money wage *(W)* rather than the real wage. In this labor market, the equilibrium wage is W_0 and the equilibrium

---

[7]See, for example, Milton Friedman, "The Role of Monetary Policy," *American Economic Review* 58(March 1968):1–17, and *Rational Expectations—Fresh Ideas That Challenge Some Established Views of Policy Making* (Minneapolis, Minn.: Federal Reserve Bank of Minneapolis, 1977). An appendix to this chapter details these arguments.

[8]See, for example, Henry Wallich and Sidney Weintraub, "A Tax-Based Incomes Policy," *Journal of Economic Issues* 5(June 1971):1–19, and Arthur Okun, "The Great Stagflation Swamp," *Challenge* 20(November/December 1977):6–13.

[9]This section initially draws heavily on Richard Lipsey, "The Relation Between Unemployment and the Rate of Change in Money Wage Rates in the United Kingdom, 1862–1957: A Further Analysis," *Economica* 27(February 1960):1–31.

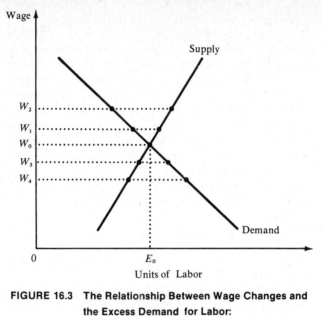

FIGURE 16.3   The Relationship Between Wage Changes and the Excess Demand for Labor: Prices Held Constant

employment level is E_0. We know from earlier chapters that whenever the wage is above W_0 it will fall, and that whenever it is below W_0 it will rise, to restore equilibrium.

How rapidly will the wage rate change when it is away from its equilibrium value? It seems reasonable to assume that the speed at which the wage rate changes is related to the extent to which the labor market is in disequilibrium, as measured by the excess demand for labor. Thus, although the wage rate will be increasing whenever it is below W_0 and a positive excess demand for labor exists, it is likely to be increasing more rapidly when it is at W_4 in Figure 16.3 than when it is at W_3. Similarly, while the wage rate will be falling whenever it is above W_0 and an excess supply (or negative excess demand) for labor exists, it is likely to be falling more rapidly when it is at W_2 than when it is at W_1.

The simplest possible way to formalize this idea is to assume that the percentage rate of change of wages $(\dot{W})$ is proportional to the excess demand for labor (X). Because a given *absolute* difference between quantity demanded and quantity supplied of labor $(D - S = 1,000$, say$)$ would indicate a greater degree of disequilibrium if 10,000 people were seeking work than if 100,000 were in the market, we will measure excess demand as $(D - S)/S$, so that

$$\dot{W} = \alpha X = \alpha[(D - S)/S]. \tag{16.1}$$

This relationship is depicted in panel (a) of Figure 16.4; the larger α is, the faster wages adjust to disequilibrium. Note that when supply exceeds demand, X— and hence W—will be negative. (One could, of course, allow the responses to be nonsymmetric to excess demands and escess supplies. For example, if wages are *sticky* in a downward direction. α would be smaller and the curve flatter in the region

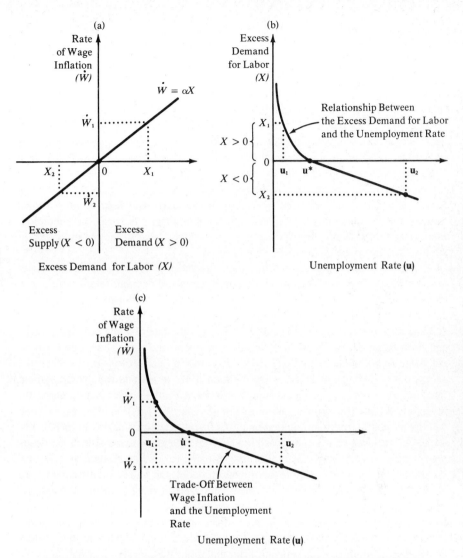

FIGURE 16.4   Derivation of the Trade-off Between the Rate of Wage Inflation and the Unemployment Rate

of excess supply that lies to the left of the vertical axis. However, for expository convenience we shall ignore this complication here.)

Unfortunately, because the excess demand for labor is usually not observable, it is necessary to replace it with an observable variable, such as the unemployment rate, when empirically analyzing wage changes. What is the relationship between the excess demand for labor and the unemployment rate (**u**)? We know from Chapter 15 that some unemployment exists even when labor markets are in balance with the overall quantity of labor demanded just equal to the overall quantity supplied ($X = 0$). This frictional unemployment occurs because normal job turnover and movements of people into and out of the labor market take place in circumstances where information is imperfect and job matching takes time. In panel (b) of

Figure 16.4, **u** is the unemployment rate that exists when the excess demand for labor is zero; this is often referred to in the economics literature as the *natural* or *full-employment rate* of unemployment (see Chapter 15).

As the excess demand for labor increases and labor markets become tighter, the unemployment rate will fall. Although the time it takes to make job matches can be reduced, it will probably take some time to fill job vacancies. As a result, the unemployment rate is not likely to fall below some positive level, and as that level is approached, any increases in excess demand will call forth progressively smaller reductions in the unemployment rate. The result is a nonlinear relationship between the unemployment rate and the excess demand for labor, as drawn in the $X > 0$ region of panel (b). In contrast, in the region of excess supply (below the horizontal axis, where $X < 0$), increases in excess supply may well lead to proportional increases in the unemployment rate. Thus, the relationship between the unemployment rate and the excess demand for labor is perhaps linear in the region of excess supply, as illustrated in panel (b) of Figure 16.4.

The two relationships shown in panels (a) and (b), the wage inflation/excess demand relationship and the unemployment rate/excess demand relationship, contain all the information required to derive the wage inflation/unemployment trade-off curve shown in panel (c). Refer in Figure 16.4 to the point where the excess demand for labor is zero. From panel (a) we know the rate of wage inflation is zero, and from panel (b) we know that the unemployment rate is **u**. Thus, one point on our wage inflation/unemployment trade-off curve in panel (c) is $(0, \mathbf{u})$. When the excess demand for labor is X_1, wage inflation is $\dot{W}_1$ in (a) and the unemployment rate is $\mathbf{u}_1$ in (b). When the excess supply of labor is X_2, the wage inflation rate is $\dot{W}_2$ in (a) and the unemployment rate is $\mathbf{u}_2$ in (b). Thus, $(\dot{W}_1, \mathbf{u}_1)$ and $(\dot{W}_2, \mathbf{u}_2)$ are two additional points on the inflation/unemployment trade-off curve in panel (c). Repeating the argument for all possible values of the excess demand for labor leads one to trace out the entire trade-off curve in panel (c) of Figure 16.4.

In the context of this simple labor market model, the trade-off between the rate of wage inflation and the unemployment rate arises from the postulated responsiveness of wages to the excess demand for labor. However, there are numerous forces that affect the *position* of the curve that traces out the aggregate relationship between the unemployment rate and the rate of wage inflation. Four of these forces are the current and expected rates of price inflation, the age/sex distribution of the labor force, the growth rate of employment and the labor force, and the dispersion of unemployment rates across markets.

Forces Affecting the Wage Inflation/Unemployment Trade-off

Price inflation.   So far we have assumed the price level to be fixed. However, current and expected future rates of price inflation clearly influence the rate of *money* wage inflation associated with any given level of excess demand for labor. Since both the demand and supply curves of labor are functions of the *real* wage rate, an increase in the *price* level requires a proportional increase in the *money* wage rate simply to keep the real wage and the excess demand for labor constant. The relationship between wage changes and the excess demand for labor described in Figures 16.3 and 16.4 actually refers to changes in the real wage (prices were assumed fixed while wages changed). Hence, the effect of price inflation is to *increase* the rate of money-wage inflation associated with any given level of the excess demand for labor.

Our discussion so far has assumed that labor markets are competitive and that all real wages are renegotiated continuously as labor market conditions change. Later in the chapter we shall introduce several institutional features of the collective bargaining process in the United States in our discussion. Here we shall consider how the introduction of one such feature, contracts that are negotiated only periodically, affects the analysis. From employees' perspectives, past price changes may influence wage demands during contract negotiations because they signify that real wages are below the level employees expected *if* such price changes were not fully anticipated at the time of the previous contract negotiations. Expected future price changes may also matter because they translate money-wage changes into expected real-wage changes. Similarly, from employers' perspectives, past and expected future price changes may affect their willingness to increase wages, as increases in output prices, *ceteris paribus,* reduce real wages and hence employers' costs of doing business.

Unambiguously, then, higher expected price changes should lead to higher wage changes in a world where wages are adjusted only periodically. It is unclear, however, whether an extra 1 percent increase in expected price inflation will lead to an extra 1 percent increase in money wages; this depends, among other things, on the relative bargaining power of employees and employers. Let us assume that a 1 percent increase in the expected rate of price inflation $(\dot{P}^e)$ shifts the rate of money-wage inflation associated with a given excess demand for labor up by γ percent, where γ may be less than or equal to one.[10] That is,

$$\dot{W} = \alpha X + \gamma \dot{P}^e \qquad 0 \le \gamma \le 1. \tag{16.2}$$

Equation (16.2) is illustrated by Figure 16.5. If the upward shift in the relationship between $\dot{W}$ and X in Figure 16.5 is translated back to panel (a) of Figure 16.4 and its implications for panel (c) are traced through panel (b), it should become clear that increases in the expected rate of price inflation cause the whole wage inflation/unemployment trade-off curve in panel (c) to shift up.[11]

Age/sex composition of the labor force.   Chapter 15 noted that women tend to have higher unemployment rates than men and that teenagers tend to have higher unemployment rates than adults. The aggregate unemployment rate associated with any given degree of labor market *tightness,* or excess demand for labor, is simply the weighted average of the unemployment rates for the various age/sex groups, with the weights being the share of the group in the overall labor force. During the

---

[10]For simplicity, we have focused only on expected price inflation and ignored past price inflation *per se* here. We also have restricted γ to be no greater than one; this need not always be the case.

[11]Of course, since wages are a substantial fraction of production costs, increases in the rate of wage inflation should lead, other things equal, to increases in the rate of price inflation. This interdependency will be discussed later in the chapter.

**FIGURE 16.5   Price Inflation Shifts Up the Wage-Inflation/
Excess-Demand-for-Labor Relationship**

1960s and 1970s the shares of teenagers and women in the labor force increased because of the growing share of teenagers in the population and increasing female labor force participation rate. Since these groups tend to have higher than average unemployment rates, the overall unemployment rate associated with any level of the excess demand for labor also increased, as illustrated in Figure 16.6.[12]

An increase in the level of unemployment associated with each level of the excess demand for labor implies, other things equal, that a higher unemployment rate will be associated with each rate of wage inflation. Put another way, the changing age/sex composition of the labor force has also caused the wage inflation/unemployment trade-off curve to shift up. At any level of the aggregate unemployment rate, the rate of wage inflation is higher than before. Furthermore, as indicated in Figure 16.6 (and in Chapter 15), the full-employment unemployment rate also has increased (from u_0 to u_1 in Figure 16.6).

The growth of employment and the labor force.   Another factor that might cause the excess-demand-for-labor/unemployment-rate relationship to shift up is the growth rate of employment and the labor force. Other things equal, the more rapidly aggregate employment is growing, the greater the number of job vacancies employers will have to fill. Even if the labor force is growing to keep pace with employment opportunities, rapid expansion may make it more difficult to match workers and jobs and, since voluntary and involuntary job turnover is highest among new employees, rapid expansion also increases the need to hire replacements, compounding employers' problems. Because of this, one might expect to observe a

---

[12]An early exposition of the importance of this factor is found in George Perry, '' Changing Labor Markets and Inflation,'' *Brookings Papers on Economic Activity*, 1970–3, pp. 411–41.

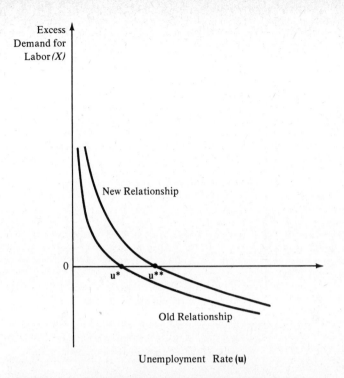

**FIGURE 16.6   Changing Age/Sex Composition of the Labor Force
Shifts Up the Excess-Demand-for-Labor/
Unemployment-Rate Relationship**

larger excess demand for labor associated with any given unemployment rate when employment is growing rapidly than when it is growing slowly.

In fact, both the civilian labor force and employment grew considerably faster during the 1970s than during the 1960s. There is evidence that the job vacancy rates (measured often by indices of help-wanted advertisements) associated with any given unemployment rate were also higher in the 1970s.[13]

The dispersion of unemployment rates.   The model of the wage inflation/unemployment trade-off that we have presented applies to a *single* labor market.[14] To obtain the wage inflation/unemployment trade-off for the *economy,* one must aggregate all the individual labor market relationships. If the unemployment rate differs across labor markets, the aggregate rate of wage inflation associated with any

---

[13]James L. Medoff, "U.S. Labor Markets: Imbalance, Wage Growth, and Productivity in the 1970's," *Brookings Papers on Economic Activity,* 1983–1, pp. 87–120, and Katharine Abraham, "Structural/Frictional vs. Demand Deficient Unemployment," *American Economic Review* 73(September 1983):708–24.

[14]The role of geographic dispersion in unemployment rates was emphasized early by Lipsey and G. C. Archibald, "The Phillips Curve and the Distribution of Unemployment," *American Economic Review* 59(May 1969):124–34. The importance of dispersion of unemployment across age/sex groups was emphasized in George Perry, "Changing Labor Markets and Inflation," *Brookings Papers on Economic Activity,* 1970–3.

FIGURE 16.7   Dispersion of Unemployment Rate Increases the Rate of Wage Inflation Associated with a Given Aggregate Unemployment Rate

given level of aggregate unemployment may be higher than it would be if the unemployment rate were the same in all markets.

To see why this is true, suppose there were only two labor markets in the whole economy, that they were identical in size, and that the same wage inflation/ unemployment trade-off curve (represented by T_0 in Figure 16.7) existed in both. Given any overall level of unemployment, the aggregate rate of wage inflation is approximately equal to the average of the rates of wage inflation in the two markets.[15] If initially the unemployment rate were **u** in *each* market, the rate of wage inflation in each would be zero, as would the overall rate of wage inflation.

Suppose now that the unemployment rate increases to $\mathbf{u} + \varepsilon$ in the first market and falls to $\mathbf{u} - \varepsilon$ in the second market, where ε is any positive number. Since the two markets are equal in size, the overall unemployment rate will remain at **u**. However, wages will fall at the rate of $\dot{W}_H$ in the high-unemployment market and rise at the rate of $\dot{W}_L$ in the low-unemployment market. As Figure 16.7 indicates, $\dot{W}_L$ is larger than $\dot{W}_H$ in absolute value; hence, the average rate of wage inflation in the economy, $[(\dot{W}_H + \dot{W}_L)/2]$, is positive. The dispersion in unemployment rates has led to a higher overall rate of wage inflation. Indeed, increasing the dispersion in the unemployment rates (increasing ε) would lead to an even higher overall rate of wage inflation.

Why does this result occur? In our simple example it occurs because the relationship between the excess demand for labor and the unemployment rate is

---

[15]We say "approximate" because once the unemployment rate differs between the two markets, a slightly higher weight should be assigned to the low unemployment market that will have relatively more *employed* workers.

nonlinear to the left of the full-employment unemployment rate (as explained earlier in relation to Figure 16.4).[16] As a result, there is more upward pressure put on wages in the tight labor market by an ε-percentage-point *decline* in unemployment than there is downward pressure put on wages in the loose labor market by an ε-percentage-point *rise*. Thus, the average rate of wage inflation increases.

Figure 16.7 shows that an increase in the dispersion of unemployment rates will increase the aggregate rate of wage inflation (in this model) for any aggregate unemployment rate less than the full-employment rate (**u** in Figure 16.7). Since the unemployment/excess demand for labor relationship was assumed to be linear to the right of **u,** small increases in the dispersion of unemployment rates around an aggregate unemployment rate like u_1 in Figure 16.7 will not necessarily lead to increases in the aggregate rate of wage inflation. However, if the dispersion is large enough that the nonlinear segment of T_0 is reached by the lower-unemployment market, then the aggregate rate of wage inflation will increase.

In sum, over a wide range of values of the unemployment rate, increases in the dispersion of unemployment rates across labor markets will increase the aggregate rate of wage inflation associated with the aggregate unemployment rate. Put another way, increases in the dispersion of unemployment rates can cause the aggregate wage inflation/unemployment trade-off curve to shift up. (While we have not yet defined precisely a *labor market* here, it is natural to think in terms of geographic markets. However, one could similarly analyze labor markets segmented by skill, age, sex, or race.)

Reasons for Shifts in the Trade-off Curve Over Time

Have the four major factors discussed above been responsible for the upward shift of the short-run wage inflation/unemployment tradeoff throughout the 1960s and 1970s? First, as Table 16.1 indicates, the percentage rate of change in the Gross National Product (GNP) *implicit price deflator,* a broad measure of the prices of all goods produced in the economy, trended upwards over the period.[17] To the extent that past price changes affect expectations of *future* price changes, this trend should have shifted the trade-off curve out (as employees incorporated these expected price changes into their wage demands).

Second, as noted earlier in this chapter and in Chapter 15, during the 1960s and 1970s there was an increase in the fraction of the labor force subject to higher than average unemployment rates. As Table 16.2 indicates, between 1960 and 1980 the share of teens in the labor force rose from 7.0 to 8.8 percent, and the share of

---

[16]This nonlinearity is not necessary to derive the general result, nor is it necessary to have identical wage inflation/unemployment trade-off curves in the two markets. (On this see Archibald, "The Phillips Curve and the Distribution of Unemployment.") For example, if both curves are linear, as long as the wage inflation/excess demand for labor relationship is flatter in the market that has the higher unemployment rate, the same result will occur.

[17]Another widely publicized price index is the Consumer Price Index (CPI), a measure of the cost of living for urban households that is published monthly by the Bureau of Labor Statistics. This index is the one that is typically used to calculate cost-of-living increases due under union contracts with cost-of-living escalator clauses. Because the GNP deflator and CPI measure different things, year-to-year percentage changes in the two indices often differ. However, over longer periods of time they yield roughly the same picture about the upward trend in the inflation rate.

TABLE 16.2   **Female and Teenage Shares of the Labor Force**

Year	Female Share	Teenage Share
1960	33.4	7.0
1965	35.2	7.9
1970	38.1	8.8
1975	39.9	9.5
1980	42.6	8.8

SOURCE: Based on *1981 Employment and Training Report of the President* (Washington, D.C.: U.S. Government Printing Office, 1981), Table A4.

women rose from 33.4 to 42.6 percent. Such demographic shifts alone have increased the overall rate of unemployment associated with any given level of wage inflation, perhaps by as much as 1 percentage point during the 1965–1980 period.[18]

Third, as noted above, there is evidence that the rapid growth of employment and the labor force during the 1970s has caused the job vacancy rate associated with any given rate of unemployment to increase. One study suggests that these changes may have caused the wage inflation/unemployment trade-off to shift up by as much as one-half to one percentage point.[19]

Finally, there is substantial evidence that the dispersion in the demographic distribution of unemployment rates has risen over the period. In particular, the unemployment rates of teenagers and white females have risen relative to the adult white male unemployment rate, and those for nonwhite teenagers have risen relative to those for white teenagers.[20] However, this increase in dispersion apparently has not had a substantial impact on the aggregate wage inflation/unemployment trade-off curve.[21]

Improving the Trade-off

The analyses above suggest ways government policies can reduce the rate of wage inflation associated with any given unemployment rate:

1. They can attempt to reduce the rate of wage inflation associated with any level of excess demand for labor, or shift the curve in panel (a) of Figure 16.4 or in Figure 16.5 down.
2. They can attempt to reduce the unemployment rate associated with any given level of the excess demand for labor, or shift the curve in panel (b) of Figure 16.4 down.
3. Finally, they can attempt to reduce the geographic or demographic dispersion of unemployment rates.

---

[18]James Tobin, "Stabilization Policy Ten Years After," *Brookings Papers on Economic Activity*, 1980–1, pp.19–72.

[19]James Medoff, "U.S. Labor Markets," pp. 110–11.

[20]Ronald Ehrenberg, "The Demographic Structure of Unemployment Rates and Labor Market Transition Probabilities," *Research in Labor Economics* 3(1980):241–93.

[21]For econometric evidence on this point, see Robert J. Gordon, "Can the Inflation of the 1970s Be Explained?" *Brookings Papers on Economic Activity*, 1977–1, pp. 353–74.

Example 16.1

Wage Inflation and Unemployment Around the World

The existence of a short-run trade-off between the rate of wage inflation and the unemployment rate is not unique to the United States. George Perry sought to estimate the magnitude of this trade-off for nine industrialized nations from the early 1960s to the mid-1970s; some of his results are summarized in the table below. This table presents his estimates of the percentage-point reduction in the rate of wage inflation that would have occurred in each country in the first year after the country's unemployment rate was allowed to increase by 25 percent (*not* percentage points). That is, if the unemployment rate in each country were increased from its mean value during the period to a level that was 25 percent higher, the table estimates how much lower the rate of wage inflation would have been in the first year following the change.

While this table indicates that a short-run trade-off exists between the rate of wage inflation and the level of the unemployment rate in all nine countries, the marginal effects on wage inflation are strikingly different in size. In the United States the marginal effect of unemployment on wage inflation, both in percentage-point terms and in relationship to the average level of wage inflation, is among the smallest listed. Determining why this effect in the United States is so small relative to that in other countries is beyond the scope of this text, but these data reemphasize the fact that aggregate demand policy alone will not be sufficient to eliminate wage inflation in the United States; alternative labor market policies will also be required.

Country	Percentage-Point Change in the Rate of Wage Inflation in the First Year	Average Annual Rate of Wage Inflation 1961–1974 (percent)
Belgium	−1.7	11.9
Canada	−1.5	6.6
Germany	−1.0	10.6
Italy	−6.2	13.0
Japan	−0.6	16.6
Netherlands	−0.8	13.1
Sweden	−0.3	10.3
United Kingdom	−0.5	9.3
United States	−0.3	5.0

SOURCE: George L. Perry, "Determinants of Wage Inflation Around the World," *Brookings Papers on Economic Activity* (1975–2), Tables 1 and 7.

SOURCE: George L. Perry, "Determinants of Wage Inflation Around the World," *Brookings Papers on Economic Activity* 5(1975–2), pp.403–35.

A number of policy tools are potentially available to achieve each goal.

Turning to the wage-inflation/excess-demand-for-labor relationship first, one obvious objective here is to reduce the expected rate of growth of prices. Over long periods of time this goal is accomplished primarily by restrictive monetary or fiscal policy. In the short run, *incomes policies*—policies by which the government tries directly to control or influence wage and price levels by the specification of standards governing when prices or wages can be changed—may also have an effect. Examples here include wage-price guidelines, temporary wage-price freezes, and tax-based incomes policies. (The concluding section of this chapter will discuss incomes policies in some detail.)

The wage-inflation/excess-demand-for-labor relationship may also be shifted down through government policies that increase the competitiveness of labor markets and remove institutional barriers that reduce the downward flexibility of wages. Examples of such policies include eliminating or relaxing the Davis-Bacon Act (discussed in Chapter 12) and deregulating industries, such as airlines and trucking, that have been regulated in ways that tended to reduce competition. While such policies would undoubtedly reduce the rate of wage inflation, we must caution that these programs have other objectives, and the cost of giving up these objectives would have to be balanced against the gains from reduced wage inflation.

With respect to reducing the rate of unemployment associated with any given level of excess demand for labor, the goal here would be to improve the efficiency of labor markets.[22] Many policies related to this goal were discussed in Chapter 15; they include improving job market information, improving the "job-matching services" offered by the U.S. Employment Service and private employment agencies, and increasing government-sponsored training programs to help reduce skill bottlenecks. One caution here, however, is that policies designed to reduce the unemployment rate may actually serve to increase it. For example, if potential job leavers—workers with some dissatisfaction with their jobs—knew that the government was actively pursuing a policy to reduce the length of time unemployed workers spent out of work, this knowledge might increase the probability that these workers would quit their jobs. One would have to balance the benefits from shorter durations of unemployment against the costs of a higher incidence of unemployment before deciding if such policies were worthwhile to implement.

The government can seek to reduce the geographic dispersion of unemployment rates by providing information about jobs in other areas to unemployed workers, by providing relocation allowances and subsidies for job search in different areas, and by administering public employment and training-program budgets in a way that increases allocations to areas with above-average unemployment rates.[23] The government can also seek to reduce the dispersion of unemployment rates across occupational or demographic groups by targeting employment and training programs, wage subsidies, tax credits, and relocation allowances on the groups with high unemployment rates.

---

[22]A long-time advocate of such policies is Charles Holt. See, for example, Charles Holt et al., "Manpower Proposals for Phase III," *Brookings Papers on Economic Activity,* 1971–3, pp. 703–22. For a more critical evaluation of these policies, see Robert Hall, "Prospects for Shifting the Phillips Curve Through Manpower Policy," *Brookings Papers on Economic Activity,* 1971–3, pp. 659–701.

[23]Employment and training program funds are often administered in this way.

Finally, independent of government policies, three demographic forces will be operating during the 1980s that will tend to reduce the unemployment rate associated with any level of excess demand for labor. First, the proportion of teenagers in the labor force will be declining (compare the 1975 and 1980 teenage shares of the labor force in Table 16.2). As a result of the decline in the birth rate in the 1960s and 1970s, less weight will be given to this relatively high unemployment rate group in computing the aggregate unemployment rate.

Second, while the proportion of females in the labor force will continue to increase, it is likely that the relative unemployment rate of females will decline. As discussed in Chapter 15, part of the reason for the relatively high unemployment rate of women is that many of them are fairly new entrants or reentrants to the labor force whose job turnover is high while they shop for desirable positions. As these women gain labor market experience and as the perception increases that women's attachment to the labor force is as permanent as men's, women's relative unemployment rates will likely fall.

Third, the aggregate growth of the labor force and employment is likely to slow down because fewer teens will be entering the labor market. As discussed above, slower employment growth may facilitate the job-matching process and reduce the unemployment rate associated with any given level of excess demand for labor.

WAGE INFLATION, PRICE INFLATION, PRODUCTIVITY, AND THE LONG-RUN TRADE-OFF

To move from the relationship between *wage* inflation and unemployment to an understanding of the relationship between *price* inflation and unemployment requires a model of how producers determine their product prices. The simple model presented here highlights the role of labor productivity growth in the inflationary process and shows how increases in the growth of labor productivity can help reduce price inflation.

Suppose producers determine their product prices by using a *constant percentage markup* over unit labor cost rule. That is,

$$P = k \cdot ULC \qquad (16.3)$$

where P represents product price, ULC represents unit labor cost—the labor cost of producing one unit of output—and k, which is a constant that is greater than one, represents the markup. Presumably k varies across firms as the share of labor cost in total costs of production varies (with smaller labor cost shares leading to larger values of k). It is also likely that k varies with the price elasticity of demand for the firms' products.[24] Although typically the size of markups does vary over the course of a business cycle, for expositional convenience we shall ignore this fact here.[25]

---

[24]Although we do not do so here, one can formally show that these statements are true for a profit-maximizing monopolist who faces a constant average-cost curve. In this case, the less elastic the price elasticity of demand for output, the greater k will be.

[25]For evidence on the cyclical variability of markups, see Robert J. Gordon, "The Impact of Aggregate Demand on Prices," *Brookings Papers on Economic Activity*, 1975–3, pp. 613–63.

FIGURE 16.8 The Relationships Between the Rates of Wage
and Price Inflation and (1) the Expected Rate
of Price Inflation and (2) the Rate
of Productivity Growth

Unit labor costs are equal to the costs per labor hour divided by output per labor hour (q), or labor productivity. Suppose, for simplicity, that we ignore all labor costs other than straight-time wages. Then labor costs per labor hour are equal to the wage rate (W) and

$$ULC = W/q. \qquad (16.4)$$

Substituting equation (16.4) into equation (16.3) and making use of the facts that the percentage change in the *product* of two variables equals the sum of the percentage changes of the two variables and the percentage change in the *ratio* of two variables equals the percentage change in the numerator minus the percentage change in the denominator, one obtains

$$\dot{P} = \dot{k} + \dot{W} - \dot{q}. \qquad (16.5)$$

Here a dot over a variable represents a percentage change, and thus $\dot{q}$ is the rate of growth of output per labor hour (or the rate of labor productivity growth).

Over time, the size of markups may change; for example, the drastic increase in the relative prices of energy since 1973 surely has led to increases in k. However, since this is a text in labor economics, not macroeconomics, we shall ignore this complication and assume that k remains constant (the constancy of k implies that labor's share of output also remains constant). Under this assumption,

$$\dot{P} = \dot{W} - \dot{q}. \qquad (16.6)$$

TABLE 16.3 Average Annual Rate of
Labor Productivity
Growth in the U.S.
Private Nonfarm Business
Sector (percent change
per year)

1948–54	1955–64	1965–74	1975–82
2.8	2.6	1.8	0.9

SOURCE: *1983 Economic Report of the President* (Washington, D.C.: U.S. Government Printing Office, 1983), Table B40.

Equation (16.6) asserts that the rate of price inflation equals the rate of wage inflation minus the rate of labor productivity growth. Thus, if wages increase at the rate of productivity growth *and* if markups do not change, prices will remain constant. Put another way, given any rate of wage inflation, an increase in the rate of growth of productivity will lead to a reduction in the rate of growth of prices if markups are constant.

Moreover, if one characterizes the trade-off between wage inflation and unemployment as $\dot{W} = f(\mathbf{u}) + \gamma\dot{P}^e$, then one can substitute $f(\mathbf{u}) + \gamma\dot{P}^e$ for $\dot{W}$ in equation (16.6) to obtain

$$\dot{P} = f(\mathbf{u}) + \gamma\dot{P}^e - \dot{q}. \qquad (16.7)$$

That is, as Figure 16.8 indicates, as long as productivity growth is positive, the price-inflation/unemployment trade-off that exists at any time lies everywhere below the wage-inflation/unemployment trade-off, with the vertical difference between the two curves being equal to the rate of labor productivity growth.

The Slowdown in Productivity Growth and Stagflation

During the late 1970s and early 1980s, one often read in the popular press that the slowdown in the rate of growth of labor productivity in the United States was at least partially responsible for high rates of price inflation that were associated with high rates of unemployment—a phenomenon commonly referred to as *stagflation*. Table 16.3 presents data on labor productivity growth in the United States that support this claim. For the private nonfarm business sector, productivity grew at about 2.7 percent per year over the 1948–1964 period. However, from 1965 to 1974 productivity growth fell to 1.8 percent a year, and during 1975–1982 it fell further to 0.9 percent a year. Indeed, the rate of productivity growth was essentially zero during the last five years of the last period. These shifts alone would cause the short-run aggregate price inflation/unemployment trade-off curve to be almost 2 percentage points higher during the late 1970s and early 1980s than it was during the 1950s and early 1960s [see equation (16.7)]. This figure should, however, be contrasted with the 5 to 10 percent annual rates of increase in the GNP deflator that occurred during the late 1970s and early 1980s. Thus, while the slowdown in productivity growth contributed to the worsening inflation/unemployment trade-off, it was not the entire cause; the other factors we have mentioned clearly were important.[26]

The Long-Run Trade-Off

Although *at a point in time* a trade-off exists between the rate of price inflation and the unemployment rate, it does not necessarily follow that *in the long run* a stable trade-off exists. Indeed, one school of thought argues that attempts to keep the unemployment rate artificially low—below the rate that is consistent with zero price inflation (when the expected rate of price inflation is zero)—will lead to ever-accelerating rates of inflation.[27] The reason for this acceleration is that attempts to reduce the unemployment rate through monetary or fiscal policy will lead to higher rates of wage and price inflation in the short run [see panel (c) of Figure 16.4 and Figure 16.8]. To the extent that *expectations* of inflation are conditioned by *actual* rates of inflation, such policies will increase the expected rate of price inflation, and the rates of wage and price inflation will continue to spiral upwards.

Whether this process will lead to ever-accelerating rates of wage and price inflation or ultimately to constant rates of wage and price inflation depends crucially on the responsiveness of money-wage increases to the expected rate of price inflation. In terms of our model, if all expected price increases are fully reflected in higher wages [$\gamma = 1$ in equation (16.2)], no long-run trade-off exists; attempts to force unemployment below its natural rate will cause ever-accelerating rates of inflation. To stabilize the inflation rate would require returning the unemployment rate to its natural rate. Hence, in this case, society can temporarily reduce the unemployment rate only at the cost of permanently higher rates of price inflation. To bring these higher rates of inflation down requires a further temporary increase in the unemployment rate.

In contrast, if expected price increases are *not* fully reflected in higher wage increases ($\gamma < 1$), a stable long-run trade-off between price inflation and unemployment will exist. That is, a constant rate of inflation will eventually become associated with any level of unemployment. (These propositions are formally derived in the appendix to this chapter.)

A key question for policymakers, then, is the extent to which expected increases in prices do lead to increases in wages. Empirical evidence on this question is ambiguous, and some economists assert that it is nearly impossible to answer the question from statistical estimates of γ in equations such as (16.7).[28] The consensus

---

[26]A note of caution: One must be careful not to confuse cyclical changes in productivity growth (see Chapter 5) with changes in the underlying trend; however, the downward trend does tend to persist even after one controls for cyclical factors. Why this has occurred is not completely understood, although some explanations have been offered (see Chapter 4).

[27]See Friedman, "The Role of Monetary Policy," and Edmund Phelps, "Phillips Curves, Expectations of Inflation, and Optimal Unemployment Over Time," *Economica* 34(August 1967):254–81, for early expositions of this view.

[28]See, for example, Robert Lucas, "Econometric Testing of the Natural Rate Hypothesis," in *The Econometrics of Price Determination,* ed. Otto Eckstein (Washington, D.C.: Board of Governors of the Federal Reserve System, 1972), pp. 5–15.

appears to be, however, that γ is less than one and that a stable long-run trade-off does exist. However, over time γ appears to have grown in size, leading to a less favorable short-run trade-off (in the sense that, given any level of expected price inflation, the short-run trade-off curve is higher in the mid- 1980s than it was in the 1960s and early 1970s). The evidence also appears to indicate that the short-run curve is flatter; thus, the marginal effect of a change in the unemployment rate on inflation appears to be smaller than it once was.[29]

UNIONS AND INFLATION

Less than 25 percent of the labor force is made up of union members (see Chapter 12). In spite of this fact, unions and the collective bargaining process in the United States are thought to exert a considerable influence on the position and shape of the wage inflation/unemployment trade-off curve for a number of reasons.

First, in several industries—such as steel, automobile, mining, trucking, and telephone—collective bargaining negotiations are conducted at the national level and are well publicized in the media. The resulting settlements are often thought to set a pattern for wage settlements in less heavily unionized industries and in the nonunion sector because of either imitative behavior in the former or attempts to compete for labor and keep unions out in the latter.[30] Our model suggests that if the economic conditions facing firms and unions in only a few key industries heavily influence the rate of wage inflation in other sectors, the effect of the *aggregate* unemployment rate on inflation will be reduced.

Evidence to support this view is quite limited, however. For example, during the 1970s wages in the above-mentioned highly unionized industries grew substantially relative to wages in the rest of the economy, suggesting that the settlements reached in these industries do not automatically spill over to other industries.[31] Wage patterns did appear to exist among firms *within* certain industries, such as automobiles, during much of the postwar period, but even these patterns broke down in the concession bargaining of the early 1980s, when firms in these industries faced different economic circumstances. For example, the United Automobile Workers granted larger concessions to the Chrysler Corporation, which was on the verge of bankruptcy, than to the General Motors Corporation and the Ford Motor Company, which were not. (When Chrysler turned a profit in 1983 and began to pay off loans ahead of schedule, however, workers at Chrysler were able to win back some of their earlier concessions.) More generally, attempts to formally test

---

[29]See, for example, George Perry, "Inflation in Theory and Practice," *Brookings Papers on Economic Activity,* 1980–1, pp. 207–42.

[30]For an early exposition of this view, see Otto Eckstein and Thomas Wilson, "The Determination of Money Wages in American Industry," *Quarterly Journal of Economics* 76(August 1962):379–414.

[31]See Daniel Mitchell, *Unions, Wages, and Inflation* (Washington, D.C.: Brookings Institution, 1980); and Marvin Kosters, "Wage and Price Behavior: Prospects and Policies," in *Contemporary Economic Problems, 1977,* ed. William Fellner (Washington, D.C.: American Enterprise Institute for Public Policy Research, 1977), pp. 159–203.

whether key wage bargains, or union wage gains in general, set a pattern for the rest of the economy have not reached definitive conclusions.[32]

Second, union contracts have increasingly become multiyear in nature and call for wage increases not only at the time the contract is signed, but also in subsequent years. While these increases may well be sensitive to the unemployment rate at the time the contract is signed—or, more precisely, to unions' and employers' *expectations* of the unemployment rate over the term of the contract—the contractual increases are not directly affected by the *actual* unemployment rate during the duration of the contract.

Formal econometric analyses indicate that wage increases specified in the *first* year of multiyear union contracts appear to be about as sensitive to the unemployment rate as wage increases in the nonunion sector. However, *deferred* wage increases specified in union contracts—those that occur in the second or third year of multiyear contracts—do not appear to be related to the actual unemployment rates during those years.[33] Hence, the increasing frequency of long-term union contracts in the economy *does* reduce the sensitivity of the overall rates of wage and price inflation to the unemployment rate, making the trade-off curves flatter.

Third, accompanying the growth of multiyear contracts has been the growth of *cost-of-living escalator clauses* in union contracts: clauses that call for wages to be automatically adjusted periodically as the price level changes. Approximately 20 percent of workers covered by major collective bargaining agreements (those that cover 1000 or more workers) had such provisions in their contracts in 1966. However, by the early 1980s this proportion had grown to over 60 percent.[34]

Escalator clauses typically give workers less than 100 percent protection against price inflation. Such contracts usually call for wages to increase by less than 1 percent for each 1 percent increase in prices, and sometimes *caps*—or maximum allowable cost-of-living increases—are also specified. Nevertheless, their existence should increase the sensitivity of wage inflation to price inflation and the evidence bears this out; union wage changes, especially those in contracts that call for cost-of-living escalators, appear to be more sensitive to price changes than do nonunion wage changes.[35] As noted earlier, larger values of γ in equation (16.2) lead to a higher short-run price inflation/unemployment trade-off curve. Hence, the growing prevalence of cost-of-living escalator clauses in union contracts may well have contributed to the upward shift in the short-run trade-off curves.

---

[32]See Daniel Mitchell, "Union Wage Determination: Policy Implications and Outlook," *Brookings Papers on Economic Activity*, 1978–3, pp. 537–82; Robert Flanagan, "Wage Interdependence in Unionized Labor Markets," *Brookings Papers on Economic Activity*, 1976–3, pp. 635–73; and Susan Vroman, "Direction of Wage Spillovers in Manufacturing," *Industrial and Labor Relations Review* 36(October 1982):102–12.

[33]Mitchell, "Union Wage Determination."

[34]See Ronald G. Ehrenberg, Leif Danziger, and Gee San, "Cost of Living Adjustment Clauses in Union Contracts: A Summary of Results," *Journal of Labor Economics* 1(July 1983):215–45; and Wallace Hendricks and Lawrence Kahn, "Determinants and Effects of Cost-of-Living Coverage in U.S. Collective Bargaining Agreements," *Industrial and Labor Relations Review* 36(April 1983):447–60, for discussions of the forces that caused this growth over time.

[35]Mitchell, "Union Wage Determination," and Hendricks and Kahn, "Determinants and Effects of Cost-of-Living Adjustment Clauses in Union Contracts."

A final reason why unions are thought to influence the position and shape of the trade-off curve is that union members are clearly concerned about maintaining their wage position relative to what they perceive are the wages of their *peer groups*. For example, at the national level automobile workers look at the wage gains won in the steel industry and vice versa. Whichever union settles first may set a pattern for the other union to follow in its negotiations, regardless of economic conditions in the latter industry. If this occurs, the responsiveness of wage and price inflation to unemployment would again be reduced.

Wage gains in several large national industries, such as automobile, steel, and rubber, clearly are highly correlated. However, it is difficult to disentangle the above *wage imitation* hypothesis from the hypothesis that wages in these industries are affected by a common set of variables. After all, steel is a major component of automobiles, as is rubber for the tires. It would, therefore, not be surprising to find that wage changes for workers in the three industries are highly correlated. Attempts to formally test whether wage imitation occurs among unions in these and other industries have not met with success.[36]

Our discussion suggests, then, that the collective bargaining process *per se* may well have contributed to the flattening and shifting up of the short-run inflation/unemployment trade-off curves. The increased prevalence of multiyear contracts is partially responsible for the flattening, and the increase in cost-of-living escalator clauses for the upward shift.[37] The effects of key settlements or other imitative behavior are uncertain.

INCOMES POLICIES

The inflation/unemployment trade-offs for both wages and prices that we face today are distinctly unfavorable and appear to indicate that persistent high rates of unemployment will be required to keep inflation at relatively low levels. How, then, can we hope to return the economy to a situation of both low unemployment and low inflation?

Clearly, the answer is to resort to structural policies that will improve the inflation/unemployment trade-off *per se*. Many of these policies were discussed earlier in the chapter. In the remainder of the chapter we shall focus in more detail on one of these—*incomes policies*. Incomes policies are policies in which the government tries to directly influence wage and price behavior by specifying

---

[36]See, for example, Robert Flanagan, "Wage Interdependencies in Unionized Labor Markets," *Brookings Papers on Economic Activity*, 1976–3; and Y. P. Mehra, "Spillovers in Wage Determination in U.S. Manufacturing Industries," *Review of Economics and Statistics* 58(August 1976):300–12.

[37]Another reason for the flattening of the trade-off curve in the nonunion sector relates to the growth of structured internal labor markets in which fluctuations in demand are met by temporary layoffs rather than money wage reductions, as discussed in Chapter 15. The "quantity adjustments" (layoffs) rather than "wage adjustments" at the individual firm level contribute to the growing insensitivity of wage changes to unemployment at the aggregate level. For an extensive discussion of this point, see Arthur Okun, "Inflation: Its Mechanics and Welfare Costs," *Brookings Papers on Economic Activity*, 1975–2, pp. 351–90; and Arthur Okun, *Prices and Quantities* (Washington, D.C.: Brookings Institution, 1981), pp. 351–90.

desired behavior. Sometimes the policies are completely voluntary, and sometimes enforcement mechanisms are built in to increase or guarantee compliance.

Incomes Policies in the United States

During the 1960–1980 period, a period over which the inflation/unemployment trade-off curve steadily shifted out, the United States tried several different types of incomes policies. In the early Kennedy-Johnson years (1962–1966), the Council of Economic Advisors tried to educate the public on the relationship between the rate of wage inflation, the rate of price inflation, and the rate of productivity growth— see equation (16.6). The council observed that if money-wage growth was held on average to the rate of labor productivity growth in the economy and if markups did not change, then prices would remain stable. The council suggested in 1964 that the trend rate of growth of productivity was roughly 3.2 percent per year (but compare this to the estimates in Table 16.3) and urged that employers and unions voluntarily limit their wage settlements to this level. This limitation would cause unit labor costs to rise in firms in which productivity growth was below average, leading to increases in prices there. However, unit labor costs would fall in firms with above-average rates of productivity growth, leading to price declines there (if profit margins remained constant). On average, then, prices would remain stable, and both nominal and real wages would increase 3.2 percent per year.

The guideposts worked reasonably well from 1962 to 1965 in the sense that the average rate of increase in wages was in fact below 3.2 percent during the period.[38] However, as labor markets tightened in the mid-1960s and the price inflation rate rose above 2 percent, the guideposts broke down and in 1967 the program was abandoned.

The next experience with incomes policies occurred during the Nixon Administration in August 1971. In response to increasing rates of price inflation (which averaged all of 5.3 percent in 1970), increasing unemployment, and a deteriorating trade balance, a comprehensive economic policy was announced. "Phase I," which lasted 90 days, called for a freeze—i.e., a zero rate of increase—on virtually all wages and prices. Phase I was followed in November 1971 by Phase II, which set standards for wage increases of 5.5 percent a year. If productivity grew at 3 to 3.5 percent a year and if profit margins were maintained, prices would then grow at 2 to 2.5 percent a year—see equation (16.6). Compliance was required by law under the program. However, a sufficient number of exemptions were granted that average hourly earnings growth was well above 5.5 percent a year (see Table 16.1). The program was terminated in January 1973 and replaced with a voluntary program of controls with no enforcement mechanism.

Finally, in October 1978 the Carter Administration announced a voluntary system of wage standards to help reduce inflation. Average hourly earnings and fringes per company were to increase at a rate of no more than 7 percent a year; for contracts with cost-of-living escalator clauses, compliance was evaluated at an

---

[38]This does not imply that the guideposts *caused* wage increases to average less than 3.2 percent. Evidence on their effect on the wage-inflation rate will be discussed below.

assumed 6 percent price inflation rate over the life of the contract.[39] Several groups of workers were exempted from having to satisfy the standards, including low-wage workers.

Contract settlements under the Carter program were monitored by the Council on Wage and Price Stability. However, its enforcement power was limited to calling violations of the voluntary standards to public attention. Other arms of government—Congress and the President—contributed to enforcement of the standards, however, through implicit or explicit threats that firms violating the standards would lose government contracts. Threats of other government action were made to particular industries; these included relaxation of import quotas (steel), deregulation (trucking), and sale of government stockpiles (copper) if wage settlements in these industries were not in compliance. As inflation continued to accelerate in 1979, the levels of permissible wage increases were raised for 1980. After the defeat of President Carter in the 1980 election, the program was terminated.

Did U.S. Incomes Policies Work?

Numerous attempts have been made to determine whether the Kennedy-Johnson wage/price guideposts and the Nixon Phase II economic program actually did hold the rates of wage and price inflation below the levels that would have existed in the *absence* of the programs. It is worth emphasizing that the comparisons these studies make are *not* of actual levels of wage and price inflation during the periods that the incomes policies were in effect with levels of inflation during the *previous* periods. Since the forces that affect inflation, such as unemployment rates and expected rates of inflation, change over time, such comparisons would be meaningless. Put another way, such comparisons could not disentangle the change in inflation rates caused by the incomes policies from the change in inflation rates caused by changes in other variables.

Rather, the methodology used in these studies is to use historical data to estimate generalizations of the inflation/unemployment trade-off curves specified earlier in this chapter and then to ask if these estimated relationships systematically changed during the periods that the incomes policies were in effect. That is, the researchers tried to determine whether the rates of inflation that were *predicted* using the historical relationship between unemployment and inflation (after controlling for the age/sex distribution of the labor force, the dispersion of unemployment rates, and expected inflation rates) really did exceed the *actual* inflation rates that occurred. If *predicted* rates of inflation exceeded *actual* rates, one could argue that the incomes policies were effective in bringing down inflation.

The answers these studies yielded are somewhat ambiguous. For example, George Perry found that the rate of wage inflation was some 0.6 to 1.2 points lower during the Kennedy-Johnson guidepost period than his model would otherwise have predicted, but Robert J. Gordon found that the guideposts had no effect on the rate

---

[39]The Carter policy did *not* apply on a *company* basis but on an *employee-group* basis within each company. The three types of employee groups considered were supervisors, nonunion-nonsupervisory employees, and workers covered by each collective bargaining agreement.

of wage inflation.[40] In contrast, Gordon found that the rate of wage inflation was held down during the Nixon Phase II incomes policy period—a result other researchers have also found.[41]

In evaluating these studies, however, one must remember that the fact that the rate of wage inflation appeared to be lower than a model predicted during the period the policy was in effect does not imply that the policy *caused* the reduction in the rate of inflation. Factors not included in the model that reduce the rate of wage inflation might have occurred at the same time. For example, the period during which the Kennedy-Johnson wage/price guideposts were in effect (1962–1966) was one of increased import competition for American steel manufacturers and one of rapid expansion of government-sponsored employee training programs to remove skill bottlenecks. Both these forces should have reduced the rate of wage inflation, the former by increasing the resistance of U.S. steel manufacturers to union wage demands and the latter by reducing the excess demand for labor. It is thus not an easy task to ascertain what the effects of incomes policies really are.

Why Are Incomes Policies Unpopular Among Economists?

Independent of the evidence on the effectiveness of incomes policies in moderating the rates of wage and price inflation, many economists are opposed to their use because the policies create inequities and efficiency losses in the economy.[42] The scope of this text does not permit our cataloging the case against incomes policies, but a few arguments can be mentioned.

First, rigid guidelines or standards implicitly freeze the distribution of income and create inequities. For example, individuals who have recently received large increases gain relative to those whose increases will be constrained by the policies. Unless most individuals are happy with their relative income positions at the time the policy is imposed and there is a social consensus on the need for the policy, the policy will invariably break down.

Second, such policies may create efficiency losses because rapidly expanding sectors of the economy that face personnel shortages are prevented from bidding up wages to attract labor. Once exceptions are systematically granted for the above reason, as was done in Phase II of the Nixon economic policy, the process of controlling wage increases becomes highly politicized, and the exceptions may be used to justify wage increases that exceed the standard in cases when waiving the

---

[40]Perry's initial study was George Perry, "Wages and the Guideposts," *American Economic Review* 57(September 1967):897–904. Additional results are found in George Perry, "Inflation in Theory and Practice," *Brookings Papers on Economic Activity,* 1980–1, pp. 207–42. Gordon's results are in his "Comment," *Brookings Papers on Economic Activity,* 1980–1, pp. 249–57.

[41]See Robert Gordon, "Wage Price Controls and the Shifting Phillips Curve," *Brookings Papers on Economic Activity,* 1972–2, pp. 385–421, and his "Comment." See also Bradley Askin and John Kraft, *Econometric Wage and Price Models: Assessing the Impact of the Economic Stabilization Program* (Lexington, Mass.: D. C. Heath, 1974).

[42]A now classic article that presents the case against incomes policies more completely is Milton Friedman, "What Price Guideposts?" in *Guidelines, Informal Controls, and the Market Place,* ed. George Shultz and Robert Alibers (Chicago: University of Chicago Press, 1966), pp. 17–40.

standard is not justified by economic conditions. More generally, incomes policies tend to be unevenly applied to different groups; those with political power gain relative to those without.

Finally, the administrative costs of incomes policies that contain enforcement procedures may be enormous. Simply costing out tens of thousands of labor contracts to ascertain compliance is no trivial task, especially when numerous fringe benefits are involved—many of whose costs can only be actuarially estimated or guessed at, as is true with pensions. The resources devoted both by government agencies to monitor the programs and by private employers to assure that they are in compliance may represent a substantial cost to society.

Tax-Based Incomes Policies

In recent years proposals have been set forth to establish a new form of incomes policy that would work through the federal personal and corporate income tax systems.[43] These *tax-based incomes policy (TIP)* proposals are based upon the notion that the tax system can be used to provide incentives for employees or employers to moderate wage and price increases.

One form of TIP uses the "carrot" of lower personal income tax rates, or tax credits. These would be granted to employees who work for firms whose average wage settlements do not exceed a specified critical value, if the rate of price inflation exceeds another specified value.[44] Panel (a) of Figure 16.9 shows the tax rate (t) on labor income for a representative individual whose wage settlement $(\dot{W})$ is less than the specified standard $(\dot{W}^C)$. If the actual rate of price increase exceeds V percent, the individual's normal tax rate (t_0) will be lowered by the fraction ϕ times the difference between the actual and critical value of the price inflation rate. That is,

$$
\begin{aligned}
t &= t_0 - \phi(\dot{P} - V) \quad &\text{if } \dot{W} \leq \dot{W}^C; \\
t &= t_0 \quad &\text{if } \dot{W} > \dot{W}^C.
\end{aligned}
\tag{16.8}
$$

By way of example, the Carter Administration's Real Wage Insurance Proposal called for wage and price standards of 7 percent $(V = \dot{W}^C = 7)$ and called for each one-percentage-point increase in the price inflation rate to lead to a one-percentage-point decrease in the tax rate $(\phi = 1)$.[45]

The idea behind such a scheme is that if the actual rate of price inflation were less than 7 percent, workers' real wages would not have declined if they confined their wage settlements to 7 percent. If, however, prices wound up increasing by

[43]See, for example, Henry Wallich and Sidney Weintraub, "A Tax-Based Incomes Policy," *Journal of Economic Issues* 5(June 1971):1–19; and Arthur Okun, "The Great Stagflation Swamp," *Challenge* 20(November/December 1977):6–13.

[44]See Okun, "The Great Stagflation Swamp." A variant of this emerged as the Carter Administration's "Real Wage Insurance" Proposal in January 1979. For a discussion of this proposal, see Robert J. Flanagan, "Real Wage Insurance as a Compliance Incentive," *Eastern Economic Journal* 5(October 1979):367–78.

[45]The proposal was also subject to certain "caps" or limits on the tax rebates, one of which is discussed below. See Flanagan, "Real Wage Insurance as a Compliance Incentive," for details.

**(a) Real Wage Insurance for Employees Whose
Wage Increases Are Less Than the Guidelines**

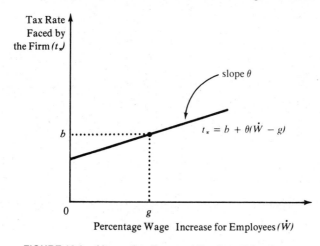

(b) Corporate Tax Rate Varies With Wage Increases

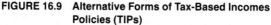

**FIGURE 16.9   Alternative Forms of Tax-Based Incomes
Policies (TIPs)**

more than 7 percent, workers would receive a tax credit or rebate to help protect
their real earnings. However, the tax credit (and hence real earnings protection)
would be granted *only* for the given year, and at the start of the next year their real
after-tax earnings (assuming $\dot{W} = 7$) would have declined by $\dot{P} - 7$ percent. If $\dot{P}$
were substantially greater than 7 percent, the decline would be sizeable. As such, it
is not surprising that this form of TIP was opposed by organized labor and failed to
win support in Congress.[46]

---

[46]The Carter proposal also "capped" the rebate, or decrease in the tax rate, at 3 percentage points—a
  move that was necessary to protect against an explosion in the size of the federal deficit. Not
  suprisingly, this limit further reduced labor support for the proposal.

Example 16.2
Incomes Policies During the Roman Empire

The use of incomes policies to combat inflation is not a recent innovation—and neither is the inflexbility in resource allocation caused by policies that fix prices. In the year 301 AD, after years of severe inflation, the Emperor Diocletian issued an edict fixing maximum prices and wages for the whole Roman Empire. Maximum wages were specified for more than 130 different categories of labor, and severe punishment was promised to anyone who violated the standards.

One would expect that the establishment of a rigid occupational wage structure with a maximum wage specified for each occupation would have had two effects. First, workers would have sought to leave occupations where compensation levels were fixed at relatively low levels (considering the work involved) and would have sought employment where wages happened to be fixed at relatively higher levels. These occupational flows could not be accompanied by wage changes (because wages were fixed), so one would expect that permanent surpluses and shortages would have developed. Second, some workers might have decided that the prevailing maximum wage scales did not offer sufficiently high rewards for their labor force participation and would have chosen not to participate. Either effect would have led to a reduction in the overall level of output.

Diocletian was apparently well aware of these potential difficulties and tried to head them off by restricting both occupational mobility and labor force participation decisions. Each worker was effectively tied to his job, and it was required that his children be brought up to succeed him. Not surprisingly, however, the removal of individuals' freedom of choice coupled with the wage ceilings effectively killed any incentives workers had to work hard or exhibit initiative. According to R. H. Barrow, "Production fell, and with it the standard of living; the rigid uniformity of a lifeless and static mediocrity prevailed."

SOURCES: H. Mitchell, "The Edict of Diocletian: A Study of Price Fixing in the Roman Empire," *Canadian Journal of Economics and Political Science* 13(February 1947):1–12; R. H. Barrow, *The Romans* (Baltimore, Md.: Penguin Books, 1949), p. 177.

A TIP proposal that works through the corporate profits tax rate and seeks to increase employers' incentives to bargain tough with their work forces seems to have more promise.[47] A representative scheme is plotted in panel (b) of Figure 16.9, where the tax rate on corporate profits faced by the firm, t_π, is assumed to vary

---

[47]See Wallich and Weintraub, "A Tax-Based Incomes Policy." A more recent advocate of a corporate-profit-based TIP is Laurence Seidman, "Tax-Based Incomes Policies," *Brookings Papers on Economic Activity*, 1978–2, pp. 301–48.

directly with the actual average percentage wage increase *(Ẇ)* granted by the firm. Specifically,

$$t_\pi = b + \theta(\dot{W} - g), \tag{16.9}$$

where *b* is the normal corporate profits tax rate, *g* is the specified wage standard, and θ is the marginal effect of a one-percentage-point increase in the wage settlement on the tax rate that the firm would pay.

If the actual wage settlement is equal to the standard *(W = g)*, the corporate tax rate remains at its normal level. However, larger increases would lead to higher tax rates and smaller increases would lead to lower tax rates. This proposal thus combines both a "carrot" (lower taxes) and a "stick" (higher taxes) approach; unlike the employee tax-based proposal, it also provides an incentive for the firm to depress wage increases *below* the standard. Presumably, by tying the firm's share of after-tax profits to its wage settlement, the scheme gives employers an extra incentive to stiffen their resistance to union wage demands and hold down wage increases. If price markups over costs remain unchanged, this policy would help reduce the rate of price inflation.

While such schemes hold out the promise of being able to shift inflation/ unemployment trade-off curves down, they are not without potential drawbacks and weaknesses. First, they raise all sorts of administrative problems.[48] For example, how does one handle numerous small firms, firms with no corporate tax liabilities, private nonprofit firms, and government agencies?[49] Or how does one collect the data necessary to include nonwage forms of compensation in the calculations? In this respect, these policies suffer from the same type of problems that any incomes policy with an enforcement mechanism built in would face.

Second, these policies focus on wages rather than prices, even though public concern is ultimately with the latter. The focus on wages is due to the difficulties involved in monitoring and measuring prices for millions of different products that are heterogeneous and whose quality can be easily varied. Employees are not likely to be receptive, though, to government intervention in labor markets if no attention is explicitly paid to product prices. Furthermore, a firm might agree to a large wage increase, resulting in an increased corporate tax rate, and then seek to negate this effect by passing the increased wage *and* tax costs on to consumers in the form of higher prices. Even supporters of such a scheme are aware of this potential problem, although they discount its importance.[50]

Finally, union leaders and members are not likely to be sympathetic to the policy.[51] On the one hand, even if the policy works and union members' real wages do not fall, the government—not union leaders—will get "credit" for the improvement. Thus, union leaders are not likely to be enthusiastic about the policy (see

---

[48]For a discussion of these problems, see Larry L. Dildine and Emil M. Sunley, "Administrative Problems of Tax-Based Incomes Policies," *Brookings Papers on Economic Activity,* 1978–2, pp. 363–89.

[49]One could, of course, restrict the scheme to employees of large, profitable, private firms; however, this creates obvious equity problems.

[50]Seidman, "Tax-Based Incomes Policies."

[51]Albert Rees, "New Policies to Fight Inflation: Sources of Skepticism," *Brookings Papers on Economic Activity,* 1978–2, pp. 453–77.

Chapter 12 for a discussion of the difference between the goals of union members and leaders). On the other hand, union members and leaders are both likely to resent a policy that provides direct financial incentives to management to resist union wage demands (tax cuts) but provides nothing for them. Indeed, because of this, stiffened management resistance may well lead to increases in the frequency and duration of strikes, especially immediately after the initial adoption of the policy.

In spite of these problems, the corporate profits variant of TIP does provide certain advantages over more traditional forms of incomes policies. Unlike direct controls or standards, it does not prohibit anything. Industries in which there is an excess demand for labor can agree to relatively high wage settlements, thereby avoiding shortages, as long as they are willing to pay the price of a higher corporate profits tax rate. Furthermore, it provides a means by which policymakers can short-circuit the inflationary process generated in the late 1960s and 1970s in which inflationary shocks, like oil price increases, fed into wage increases—which were then passed on to price increases, leading to a further wage-price spiral even after the initial shock was long past. The hope is that a decrease in the rate of wage inflation induced by a TIP would cause a decrease in the rate of price inflation, leading to further moderation in future wage and price increases and a winding down of inflation.

Of course, this line of reasoning suggests that any action the government takes that causes a one-time decline in the price level or decreases the rate of growth of prices will lead to lower wage increases and subsequent lower price increases, and thus also help short-circuit the wage-price spiral. As a result, a number of such proposals have been advocated.[52] These proposals include reducing the federal payroll tax that finances social security (which enters into employers' costs and hence their product price decisions), eliminating federal excise taxes on alcohol and tobacco, and reducing minimum wage rates and substituting a wage subsidy program for low-income workers. Each of these proposals would directly reduce employers' costs or product prices. None alone would solve the inflation problem, but a combination of these and other proposals might cause a significant one-time reduction in the price level (compared to what it would otherwise be). To the extent that this would feed back into lower rates of wage and price inflation, such proposals would serve to improve the inflation/unemployment trade-offs that the United States faces.

A Regulated Industry TIP

We conclude by returning to the regulated-industry example that has been discussed throughout this book, which illustrates both the complexity of policy analysis and the variety of analytic tools that must often be applied to analyze a single policy issue. In the battle against inflation, what policies can state public utility commissions pursue to moderate the rate of wage increases of utility employees and hence utility price increases?

---

[52]See, for example, Robert W. Crandall, ''Federal Government Initiatives to Reduce the Price,'' *Brookings Papers on Economic Activity*, 1978–2, pp. 401–40.

One possibility is for commissions to institute a variant of a tax-based incomes policy in the industries they regulate.[53] Under such a policy the fraction of negotiated increase in wage scales that a utility could pass on to consumers in the form of higher prices would be specified to be a function of the level of the increase, with greater increases corresponding to smaller fractional pass-throughs. Such a scheme would allow a utility to increase its revenues by *less* than its actual increase in wage costs if the increase in wages exceeded a specific amount, but by perhaps *more* than its actual increase if a smaller settlement were reached. In effect, this makes the utility's allowable rate of return a negative function of the size of the negotiated wage settlement, providing the utility with an extra incentive to resist union wage demands.

Examples of such schemes are shown in Figure 16.10, where the percent wage increase "allowed" for rate-setting purposes is plotted on the vertical axis ($\dot{W}_A$) and actual percent wage increase granted is plotted on the horizontal axis. The curve C in panel (a) of Figure 16.10 shows the percent wage increase that the commission will allow to be passed on to consumers in the form of higher prices for each level of the actual wage settlement. If the actual wage increase is h percent, the utility will be allowed to pass the entire settlement on to consumers. If it is more than h percent, the utility will recover less than the full increase; if it is less than h percent, it will recover more than the full increase. In the last case, however, the increase faced by consumers will still be less than h percent (for example, if the actual settlement is h_1, the commission will act as if it is h_2), so consumers will have gained by the utility's holding its labor costs below h percent.

If the commission is uncertain what rate of increase in wages should be passed on to consumers fully, it can specify a range of full cost recovery.[54] For example, in panel (b) of Figure 16.10, the curve D now shows the rate of wage increase the commission will allow to be passed on to consumers in the form of higher prices as a function of the actual settlement. Here wage settlements in the range h_3 to h_4 can be fully passed on.

Would such a scheme be an effective way of moderating inflation of utility prices? Many of the objections raised earlier to nationwide TIPs fail to hold here. Administrative problems would be minimal as commissions regularly set prices for a well-defined number of utilities (all who seek to earn profits), based upon detailed information about the utilities' costs. Since commissions set prices directly, one also does not have to worry about increased corporate profits tax liabilities being passed on to consumers in the form of higher prices (as one would with a nationwide TIP that worked through the corporate profits tax).

While these factors tend to increase the viability of the regulated-industry variant of a TIP, such a proposal would not win employee support. Indeed, workers in regulated industries might find an economy-wide TIP easier to swallow, since under the regulated-industry TIP only *their* relative earnings would suffer. As such,

---

[53]The discussion that follows draws heavily on Ehrenberg, *The Regulatory Process and Labor Earnings*, pp. 167–173.

[54]See Ehrenberg, *The Regulatory Process and Labor Earnings*, for a discussion of how this level of full recovery might be specified.

(a)

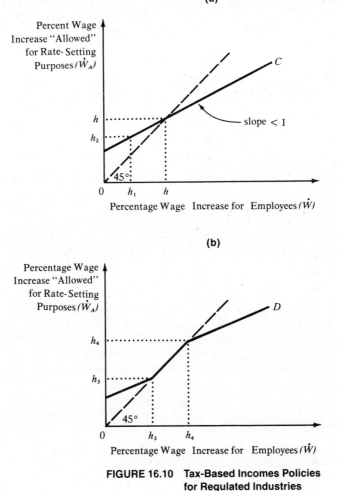

FIGURE 16.10   Tax-Based Incomes Policies
for Regulated Industries

one might expect increases in the frequency and duration of strikes in regulated industries, especially during the first few years of operation of the schemes (before unions and management fully adjusted to the change in the bargaining environment).

Presumably such service disruptions could be minimized if the regulated-industry TIP focused on unit-labor-cost increases rather than wage-scale increases. This focus would allow unions in regulated industries to engage in explicit or implicit productivity bargaining; larger productivity gains permit larger wage increases without any price changes—see equation (16.6). Union support might also be increased if the focus were on all input costs, not just labor costs. Ultimately, however, society may have to decide if the potential reduction in inflation from having a nationwide or regulated-industry TIP more than offsets the costs of short-run increases in strike activity. If it does, a strong case for these policies can be made.

REVIEW QUESTIONS

1. Why are the size of wage increases and the unemployment rate thought to be negatively related? How (and why) is this negative relationship affected by price inflation and the rising labor force participation of women? What can the government do to reduce the wage inflation associated with any level of unemployment?
2. Some years ago Great Britain instituted three related policies. First, it increased unemployment compensation benefits. Second, the government agreed to pay lump-sum benefits owed to anyone permanently fired by his or her employer. (Assume that previously the *employers* paid these benefits.) Third, the government placed a tax, to be paid by employers, on wages in *service* industries (wages in manufacturing were not taxed).
   a. Analyze the effects of these three policies on the labor market.
   b. Judging from the effects of these programs, what is (are) the *goal*(s) implicit in these policies?
3. Suppose the government were to adopt an incomes policy that allows workers to receive wage increases each January equal to the increase in the cost of living during the previous 12 months but *no* other increases. Would such a scheme help reduce the rate of inflation?
4. Some members of Congress have supported legislation requiring the federal government to undertake massive employment programs as long as the overall unemployment rate is above 4 percent. Evaluate such a program with respect to its effects on inflation.
5. "Incomes policies that specify that workers should receive percentage wage increases equal to their rate of productivity growth are doomed to failure because they will cause management's share of output to continually fall." Is this statement true, false, or uncertain? Explain your answer.
6. Evaluate the statement, "The slowdown of the rate of productivity growth in the United States is the primary factor responsible for simultaneous high rates of unemployment and inflation."

SELECTED READINGS

Flanagan, Robert. "Wage Interdependencies in Unionized Labor Markets." *Brookings Papers on Economic Activity,* 1976–3, pp. 635–73.

Friedman, Milton. "The Role of Monetary Policy." *American Economic Review* 58(March 1968):1–17.

Lipsey, Richard. "The Relation Between Unemployment and the Rate of Change in Money Wage Rates in the United Kingdom, 1862–1957: A Further Analysis." *Economica* 27(February 1960):1–31.

Medoff, James. "U.S. Labor Markets: Imbalance, Wage Growth, and Productivity in the 1970s." *Brookings Papers on Economic Activity,* 1983–1, pp. 87–120.

Mitchell, Daniel. *Unions, Wages and Inflation.* Washington, D.C.: Brookings Institution, 1980.

Okun, Arthur, and Perry, George, eds. "Innovative Policies to Slow Inflation." *Brookings Papers on Economic Activity,* 1978–2.

Tobin, James. "Stabilization Policy Ten Years After." *Brookings Papers on Economic Activity,* 1980–1, pp. 19–72.

APPENDIX 16A

Does a Long-Run Trade-off Exist Between the Rate of Price Inflation and the Unemployment Rate?

We have assumed that the short-run trade-off curve is given by

$$\dot{P} = f(\mathbf{u}) - \dot{q} + \gamma \dot{P}^e \qquad \gamma \leq 1 \qquad (16A.1)$$

Whether a long-run trade-off exists between the rate of price inflation and the unemployment rate depends crucially on how responsive money wage changes are to expectations of price inflation (which is captured by the parameter γ in our model) and on how expectations of price inflation are formed. To see the role of the responsiveness of wage changes to inflationary expectations, suppose for the sake of simplicity that the expected rate of price inflation in a period is equal to the actual rate of price inflation that occurred in the previous period. That is, suppose

$$\dot{P}^e = \dot{P}_{-1}. \qquad (16A.2)$$

Consider first the case when expected price increases are *not* fully reflected in wage increases, and to take a specific example suppose that γ is equal to $\frac{1}{2}$. In this case, the short-run price-inflation/unemployment trade-off is given by

$$\dot{P} = f(\mathbf{u}) - \dot{q} + \frac{1}{2}\dot{P}_{-1}. \qquad (16A.3)$$

If initially there were no price inflation in the economy, the trade-off curve would then be

$$\dot{P} = f(\mathbf{u}) - \dot{q}. \qquad (16A.4)$$

Figure 16A.1 provides a graphic representation of equation (16A.4), where T_0 is drawn as a straight line for expositional convenience. Note that if the unemployment rate were kept at $\mathbf{u}_0$, there would be no price inflation in the economy. (Note also that if labor productivity growth is positive, the price inflation/unemployment trade-off will lie below the wage inflation/unemployment trade-off, and hence $\mathbf{u}_0$ will typically be *less than* the full-employment unemployment rate, $\mathbf{u}$. This statement ignores complications caused by the dispersion in unemployment rates.)

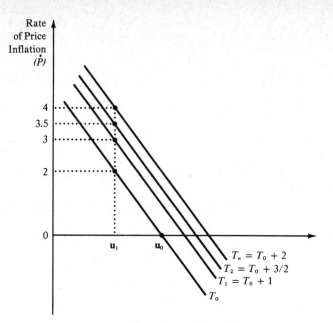

FIGURE 16A.1 **A Stable Long-Run Trade-off Between Price Inflation and the Unemployment Rate:**

$$\dot{P} = f(\mathbf{u}) - \dot{q} + \tfrac{1}{2}\dot{P}_{-1}$$

Now suppose that the government pursues a stimulative aggregate demand policy and reduces the unemployment rate to $\mathbf{u}_1$. As drawn in Figure 16A.1, this policy would yield a 2 percent rate of price inflation—which, from equation (16A.3), would shift the short-run trade-off in the next period up by 1 percentage point ($2 \times \tfrac{1}{2}$). This new curve is represented by T_1 in Figure 16A.1, and if the government sought to keep the unemployment rate at $\mathbf{u}_1$, the inflation rate would rise to 3 percent. However, this inflation rate would shift the trade-off in the next period up to T_2, which is $\tfrac{3}{2}$ ($3 \times \tfrac{1}{2}$) of a percentage point above the original trade-off, T_0. If the government again tried to keep the unemployment rate at $\mathbf{u}_1$, the rate of price inflation in the following period would rise to 3.5 percent.

This process of upward-shifting short-run trade-off curves would continue as long as the unemployment rate was kept at $\mathbf{u}_1$. Note, however, that because less than the expected price inflation rate is passed on in the form of higher wages ($\gamma < 1$), the magnitude of the shift becomes progressively smaller. Indeed, the inflation rate will eventually reach 4 percent, at which point the trade-off curve will have shifted to T_n, which is 2 percentage points above T_0. If the government then kept unemployment at $\mathbf{u}_1$, inflation in the next period would again be 4 percent and the upward spiral would stop. Hence, the inflation/unemployment combination ($4,\mathbf{u}_1$) is a point on the long-run trade-off curve. One could repeat this line of reasoning for other unemployment rates and trace out the entire long-run trade-off curve.

More succinctly, the long-run trade-off will be the locus of inflation/unemployment combinations for which the *actual* rate of price inflation ($\dot{P}$) equals the

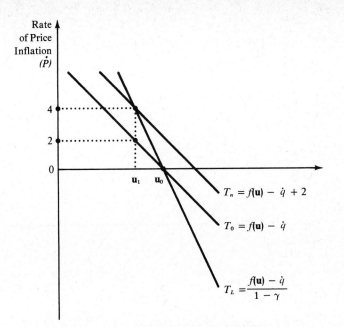

Rate of Price Inflation $(\dot{P})$

$T_n = f(\mathbf{u}) - \dot{q} + 2$

$T_0 = f(\mathbf{u}) - \dot{q}$

$T_L = \dfrac{f(\mathbf{u}) - \dot{q}}{1 - \gamma}$

Unemployment Rate **(u)**

FIGURE 16A.2   The Relationship of the Short-Run and Long-Run Trade-off Curves ($\gamma = 1/2$)

expected rate of inflation $(\dot{P}^e)$. In terms of equation (16.7) in the text, one can replace the expected inflation rate by the actual rate to obtain

$$\dot{P} = f(\mathbf{u}) + \gamma\dot{P} - \dot{q}. \qquad (16A.5)$$

Solving for the actual rate of inflation, one obtains:

$$\dot{P} = \frac{f(\mathbf{u})}{1 - \gamma} - \frac{\dot{q}}{1 - \gamma}. \qquad (16A.6)$$

Equation (16A.6) is the long-run price inflation/unemployment trade-off curve in our model. If wages respond at all to expected rates of price inflation (that is, if $\gamma >$ 0), the long-run trade-off curve (T_L) will be steeper than the short-run trade-off curves, as indicated in Figure 16A.2. Note in Figure 16A.2 that the inflation/ unemployment combinations of $(4,\mathbf{u}_1)$ and $(0,\mathbf{u}_0)$—each representing points where $\dot{P} = \dot{P}_e$—are both on T_L.

Put another way, increasing the unemployment rate by 1 percentage point will "buy" a larger reduction in inflation in the long run than it will in the short run if $\gamma > 0$. This difference in slope between the long-run and short-run trade-offs increases as γ becomes larger. Furthermore, the larger is γ, the greater will be the effect of a change in the rate of productivity growth on the long-run inflation rate, with decreases in productivity growth causing the long-run trade-off curve to shift up by more than would be the case if γ were smaller. Moreover, if $\gamma < 1$, a stable long-run relationship between $\dot{P}$ *and* **u** would exist.

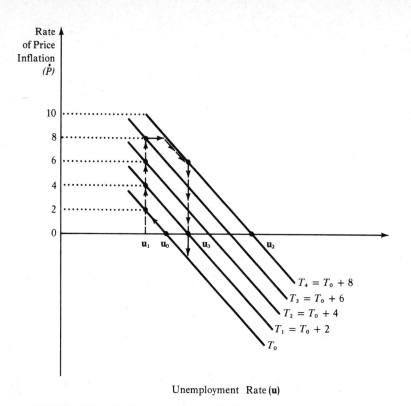

FIGURE 16A.3   No Stable Long-Run Trade-off Between Price Inflation and the Unemployment Rate: $\dot{P} = f(\mathbf{u}) - \dot{q} + \dot{P}_{-1}$

If γ equals 1, however, there is no stable long-run trade-off between the rate of price inflation and the rate of unemployment. Attempts to reduce the unemployment rate below $\mathbf{u}_0$ will lead to ever-accelerating rates of price inflation. To see this, we shall now assume that all the expected increase in prices is transmitted into higher wages ($\gamma = 1$). As a result, the short-run trade-off curve is given by

$$\dot{P} = f(\mathbf{u}) - \dot{q} + \dot{P}_{-1}. \tag{16A.7}$$

The curve T_0 in Figure 16A.3 represents the relationship in equation (16A.7) when the economy is initially at $\mathbf{u}_0$ and the past inflation rate is zero. Suppose again that aggregate demand policy is pursued to reduce the unemployment rate to $\mathbf{u}_1$, and an inflation rate of 2 percent initially results. In this case, the short-run trade-off in the next period *(T_1)* shifts up by 2 percentage points, and if $\mathbf{u}_1$ is maintained, the inflation rate would be 4 percent in the next period.

It should be obvious that, because of the one-for-one feedback from current price inflation to next period's wage inflation, the short-run trade-off curve will shift up vertically—*and the actual rate of price inflation will increase*—by 2 percentage points *every* period as long as the government keeps the unemployment rate at $\mathbf{u}_1$. The attempt to keep the unemployment rate below $\mathbf{u}_0$ thus leads to ever-increasing rates of price inflation; no stable rate of inflation can be maintained. (In terms of equation (16A.6), the long-run trade-off is infinite when $\gamma = 1$ because the denominator is zero.) For this reason $\mathbf{u}_0$ is often referred to in such models as the *nonaccelerating inflation rate of unemployment*, or the *NAIRU*.

To get the process of accelerating inflation to stop in this model, the government must return the unemployment rate to the NAIRU. In Figure 16A.3, if the unemployment rate is maintained at $\mathbf{u}_1$ for periods 0, 1, 2, and 3, the inflation rate will be 8 percent in period 3 and the trade-off curve will shift up to T_4 in period 4. *If the government then allows the unemployment rate to rise to $\mathbf{u}_0$ in period 4, the inflation rate will remain at 8 percent.* The trade-off curve in period 5 will be the same as the one in period 4, and as long as the unemployment rate stays at $\mathbf{u}_0$, the inflation rate will remain at 8 percent. To reduce the inflation rate back to zero, the government could tolerate a massive increase in the unemployment rate (to $\mathbf{u}_2$) for one period, at which point $\dot{P} = 0$, and unemployment could be returned to $\mathbf{u}_0$. Alternatively, the government could let unemployment increase to $\mathbf{u}_3$ for 4 periods, after which the economy would be back on T_0 and unemployment could be returned to $\mathbf{u}_0$ (note the downward arrows in Figure 16A.3).

If this model is correct, a short-run trade-off exists between the rate of price inflation and the level of the unemployment rate, but no such trade-off exists in the long run. Society can *temporarily* reduce the unemployment rate at the cost of *permanently* higher rates of price inflation. To bring these higher rates of inflation down requires a temporary increase in the unemployment rate.

Of course, both these models assume that individuals *naively* base their expectations of inflation only on the actual rate of inflation that occurred in the previous period. Another school of thought argues that individuals' expectations are formed *rationally* in the sense that they take account of all available information that is relevant, *including* the directions that government policy is moving. Such *rational expectations* theorists argue that, when formed rationally, people's expectations may frustrate the attempt by government to use aggregate demand policies.[1] While a full discussion of the rational expectations view would take us far into the domain of macroeconomics, we can illustrate its implications for the existence of the long-run trade-off curve quite simply.

Suppose initially that expectations of inflation are zero and the government takes action to stimulate the economy with the goal of reducing the unemployment rate. If individuals are aware of this action and the nature of the short-run trade-off curve (16A.1), they will realize that lower unemployment would imply a higher inflation rate. Hence, their expectations of inflation would increase and the short-run trade-off curve would shift up, possibly even before any effect on unemployment was felt. But with a higher short-run trade-off curve, individuals would realize that achieving the desired reduction in unemployment that the government is aiming for would require a still higher inflation rate. As a result, expectations of inflation would again increase, the short-run trade-off curve would again shift up, and the process would repeat itself.

---

[1] For a clear exposition of the rational expectations approach, see *Rational Expectations—Fresh Ideas That Challenge Some Established Views of Policy Making* (Minneapolis, Minnesota: Federal Reserve Bank of Minneapolis, 1977).

Obviously γ remains a key parameter in the model. If γ is less than 1, a stable long-run trade-off remains, although it should be clear that the stable higher inflation rate associated with a lower unemployment rate may be reached much more quickly in such a world than it would if the short-run trade-off curve did not shift up until after the government succeeded in reducing unemployment. If γ equals 1, once again no stable long-run trade-off exists. It should be stressed that the rational expectations viewpoint does *not* necessarily imply that γ equals 1. It is conceivable that, in a world in which collective bargaining takes place and contracts are negotiated periodically, workers may have rational expectations about inflation but do not have the bargaining power to win contracts that fully compensate them for anticipated inflation.

Name Index

Aaron, Benjamin, 413n, 415n, 425n
Abegglen, James, 139, 140n
Abowd, John M., 248n, 508n
Abraham, Katherine, 499n, 535n
Abrams, Elliott, 323n, 324n
Abrams, Franklin S., 324n
Ackerloff, George, 355n
Adams, Arvil, 519n, 520n
Adams, Charles, 433n
Addison, John, 401n
Aigner, Dennis J., 461n
Alchian, Armen, 63n, 340n
Alibers, Robert, 550n
Allen, Steven G., 159n, 340n, 380n, 401n,
    402n
Alpert, William, 398n
Anderson, C. A., 260n, 278n
Anderson, John, 156–57
Antos, Joseph, 520n
Archibald, G. C., 535n, 537n
Aronson, Robert, 498n
Arrow, Kenneth, 46n, 47n, 443n
Ashenfelter, Orley, 79n, 97n, 99n, 100n,
    106n, 248n, 260n, 284n, 305n, 371n,
    384, 395, 396n, 410n, 418n, 421n,
    422n, 440n, 443n, 445n, 459n, 481n,
    499n, 508n
Ashford, Nicholas, 45n
Askin, Bradley, 550n
Atherton, Wallace, 376n
Azariadis, Costas, 501n

Bailey, Martin, 501n
Bakke, E. Wight, 142n
Bally, Martin N., 107n
Barrett, Nancy, 470n
Barringer, R., 466n
Barrow, R. H., 553n
Bartel, Ann P., 306n
Bassi, Lauri J., 284n, 431n, 499n
Becker, Brian, 520n
Becker, Gary, 4n, 50n, 131n, 136, 193n,
    275n, 455n, 458n
Beer, S., 466n
Beller, Andrea H., 453n, 464n, 483n
Belous, Richard, 78n
Berg, Ivar, 280n, 302n
Bergmann, Barbara, 454n, 465n
Benjamin, Daniel, 517n
Bentham, Jeremy, 226n
Berndt, Ernst, 107n
Bickford, Lawrence C., 354n
Bishop, John, 106n
Blau, Francine, 317n, 328n
Blinder, A. S., 445n

Bloch, Farrell E., 318n, 396n
Bloom, David, 440n
Blum, James, 97n, 100n
Borjas, George, 101n, 102n, 175n, 189n,
    311n, 323, 448n, 460n
Borus, Michael, 443n
Boulding, Kenneth, 454n
Bowen, William G., 175n
Bowles, Samuel, 279n
Bowman, M. J., 260n, 278n
Briggs, Vernon, 380n
Brown, Charles, 78n, 233n, 402n, 482n
Brown, James, 410n
Bunting, Robert L., 66n
Burkhauser, Richard, 360n
Burtless, Gary, 213n
Burton, John F., Jr., 412n, 413n
Butler, Richard, 482n

Cain, Glen G., 461n, 464n, 490n
Caliner, Geoffrey, 448n
Capron, William, 46n, 47n
Carliner, Geoffrey, 311n
Chang, Hui, 421n
Chiswick, Barry R., 280n, 311n, 449n, 461n,
    481n, 507n
Chiswick, Carmel Ullman, 209n
Clark, Kim, 402n, 495n
Clark, M. Gardner, 284n
Colberg, Marshall R., 214n
Commons, John R., 370n
Connerton, Marie, 401n, 402n
Conyers, John, 127n
Cook, Alice, 476n
Corcoran, Mary, 445n, 452n, 521n
Corson, Walter, 499n
Cotterill, Philip, 100n
Courant, Paul, 421n, 431n
Cox, James, 379n
Crandall, Robert W., 555n
Crawford, Vincent, 440n

Dalton, James, 64n
Danziger, Leif, 546n
Darby, Michael R., 16n
DeFina, Robert H., 399n
Denison, Edward F., 107n
Dertouzos, J. N., 376n
Dildine, Larry L., 554n
Dillingham, Alan, 235n
Doeringer, Peter, 12n, 13n, 142n, 143n, 400n
Dorsey, Stuart, 235
Downs, Anthony, 416n
Duncan, Greg, 276n, 396n, 398n, 445n, 452n
Dunlop, John, 340n, 376n
Durden, Garey, 379n

Subject Index

TABLE 6.1   Labor Force Participation Rates of Females over 16 Years of Age, by Marital Status, 1900–1980 (percent)

Year	All Females	Single	Widowed, Divorced	Married
1900	20.6 (100)	45.9 (100)	32.5 (100)	5.6 (100)
1910	25.5 (124)	54.0 (118)	34.1 (105)	10.7 (191)
1920	24.0 (117)			9.0 (161)
1930	25.3 (123)	55.2 (120)	34.4 (106)	11.7 (209)
1940	26.7 (130)	53.1 (116)	33.7 (104)	13.8 (246)
1950	29.7 (144)	53.6 (117)	35.5 (109)	21.6 (386)
1960	35.7 (173)	42.9 (94)	38.7 (119)	30.6 (546)
1970	41.6 (202)	50.9 (111)	39.5 (122)	39.5 (705)
1980	51.7 (250)	61.2 (133)	44.1 (136)	50.2 (896)

Note: Index numbers, with 1900 = 100, are shown in parentheses.

SOURCES: 1900–1950: Clarence D. Long, *The Labor Force Under Changing Income and Employment* (Princeton: Princeton University Press), 1958, Table A-6.

1960: U.S. Department of Commerce, Bureau of the Census, *Census of Population, 1960: Employment Status* (Subject Reports PC(2)-6A), Table 4.

1970: U.S. Department of Commerce, Bureau of the Census, *Census of Population, 1970: Employment Status and Work Experience* (Subject Reports PC(2)-6A), Table 3.

1980: U.S. President, *Employment and Training Report of the President, 1980* (Washington, D.C.: U.S. Government Printing Office, 1981), Tables A2, B1. (The data for 1980 are not strictly comparable because they are derived from a monthly survey, not the decennial census.)

TABLE 6.2   Labor Force Participation Rates For Males, by Age, 1900–1980 (percent)

Year	14–19	20–24	25–44	45–64	Over 65
1900	61.1 (100)	91.7 (100)	96.3 (100)	93.3 (100)	68.3 (100)
1910	56.2 (92)	91.1 (99)	96.6 (100)	93.6 (100)	58.1 (85)
1920	52.6 (86)	90.9 (99)	97.1 (101)	93.8 (101)	60.1 (88)
1930	41.1 (67)	89.9 (98)	97.5 (101)	94.1 (101)	58.3 (85)
1940	34.4 (56)	88.0 (96)	95.0 (99)	88.7 (95)	41.5 (61)
1950	39.9 (65)	82.8 (90)	92.8 (96)	87.9 (94)	41.6 (61)
1960	38.1 (62)	86.1 (94)	95.2 (99)	89.0 (95)	30.6 (45)
1970	35.8 (59)	80.9 (88)	94.4 (98)	87.3 (94)	25.0 (37)
1980			95.4 (99)	82.2 (88)	19.1 (28)

Note: Index numbers, with 1900 = 100, are shown in parentheses.

SOURCES: 1900–1950: Clarence D. Long, *The Labor Force Under Changing Income and Employment* (Princeton: Princeton University Press), 1958, Table A-2.

1960: U.S. Department of Commerce, Bureau of the Census, *Census of Population, 1960: Employment Status* (Subject Reports PC(2)-6A), Table 1.

1970: U.S. Department of Commerce, Bureau of the Census, *Census of Population, 1970: Employment Status and Work Experience* (Subject Reports PC(2)-6A), Table 1.

1980: U.S. President, *Employment and Training Report of the President, 1981* (Washington, D.C.: U.S. Government Printing Office, 1981), Table A2. (The data for 1980 are not strictly comparable because they are derived from a monthly survey, not the decennial census. Reliable data for males under 25 are unavailable.)